THE

Golden Voyage

BY ROBERT C. ALBERTS

The Most Extraordinary Adventures
of Major Robert Stobo

The Golden Voyage: The Life and Times
of William Bingham 1752–1804

WILLIAM BINGHAM

Gilbert Stuart

Detail

THE
Golden Voyage

———————☆———————

The Life and Times

of

William Bingham

1752–1804

BY

ROBERT C. ALBERTS

Illustrated

Houghton Mifflin Company, Boston

1969

First printing w

Library of Congress Catalog Card Number: 69–15005
Printed in the United States of America

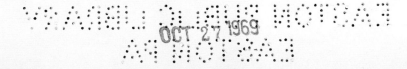

AGAIN, TO ZITA

☆

. . . you will make a Golden Voyage

Robert Morris to
William Bingham
October 20, 1776

Preface

IT IS DIFFICULT to understand why biographers for more than a century and a half have neglected a figure of such stature and importance as William Bingham. Economic historians have treated him with respect and admiration, but only two scholars have produced substantial works on Bingham, and no biographer has written his life. If the neglect was not simple oversight, I suspect that the reason, at least in later years, must have been a kind of prejudgment built on what Mark DeWolfe Howe calls "Jeffersonian bias" and "the prevailing dogma of liberalism." Bingham became wealthy during the American Revolution — therefore he must have been one of the numerous tribe of international war profiteers. He was a merchant and banker — therefore he must have been a dull fellow. He was a powerful figure among Federalist leaders — therefore he must have been an opponent of American democracy. He became the country's richest man — therefore he must have been an early Robber Baron and not worth serious attention.

If such prejudice was the reason, the joke is on those who ignored or rejected Bingham, for he was a good deal more than what they supposed him to be. In his youth he served as secretary of the Revolutionary Committee of Secret Correspondence and as agent of the Continental Congress in French Martinique, where he had outstanding success in procuring arms, outfitting privateers, organizing espionage activities, and generally stirring up trouble between France and England to the advantage of the United States. He owned a fleet of merchant ships, bought and attempted to develop four million acres of land, served on the boards of three colleges, and built bridges, canals, and the nation's first long turnpike. Though a conservative, he formed intimate friendships with some of the liberal and radical leaders of his time. As a Federalist senator and Philadelphia political power, he courageously broke with his party on two crucial issues: to save the country from a war with France and to avoid an internal revolution over the choice of a President.

Bingham was the prototype of the enlightened business leader of a later day, with a quite "modern" sense of his obligation to society and a vigorous confidence in the capacity of his country to grow through public improvements, industrial development, and practical application of the scientific discoveries of his age. He was Hamilton's economic advisor and the country's ablest banker in a time of violent social and ideological conflict, when the republic was shaping its policies and institutions and was struggling with the problems of precedent, procedure and growth. He was one of the first national planners. The economic structure he helped to create determined for all time the direction the nation was to follow, and it was the forerunner of the strong centralized government supported by liberals throughout the twentieth century.

It is sometimes possible for the biographer, in telling his subject's life story, also to tell the story of the period in which he lived — and in so doing to bring new light to the period through the play of personality, the narrative flow of connected events, and the impingement of those events on the subject. I have attempted to do this in *The Golden Voyage*. Whether or not I have succeeded, William Bingham is an almost perfect subject for this purpose. Though relatively unknown today, he was a major figure of his time; he knew everyone of prominence; and he was present and at the center of great events, from the organizing of the Revolution in 1775 to the purchase of the Louisiana Territory in 1803. The details of his life, moreover, can be largely recovered from a mass of documentation.

It is of added consequence that Bingham married Anne Willing — a bride at sixteen, a sensational social success in Europe at twenty, and the celebrated beauty who ruled for a decade over the famous "Republican Court," when Philadelphia was the nation's capital. Anne Bingham has not been ignored by history, but she has been often misjudged, and it is a pleasure to add to the record in telling the story of William Bingham and the enchanting woman who was his wife.

Except for the Appendices, the chapter headings and a few other places where a special flavor seemed desirable, I have modernized the orthography and punctuation of all quoted material. My reasons are borrowed from Wilmarth S. Lewis, editor of the letters of Horace Walpole: "What is amusing and 'flavoursome' in small doses becomes wearisome in large, and it imparts an air of quaintness to a text which was not apparent to the correspondents themselves." My notes are keyed on pages 479–529 by page number and identifying phrase. This has the double advantage of avoiding interruptions in the body of the text and of making the notes self-sufficient and understandable in themselves, without constant checking back and forth. My acknowledgments to manuscript and printed sources, and to the good people who have aided me in this work, appear on pages 445–448.

ROBERT C. ALBERTS

May 1, 1969
Duck Pond Hill
Somerset County, Pennsylvania

Contents

BOOK THREE: THE REPUBLICAN COURT

BOOK FOUR: IN A TIME OF CRISIS

Illustrations

(*frontispiece*)

WILLIAM BINGHAM by Gilbert Stuart. Detail.

(*following page 174*)

WILLIAM BINGHAM by Gilbert Stuart, 1795.
Balch Estate, Philadelphia, Pennsylvania

ROBERT MORRIS by Charles Willson Peale, c. 1782.
Independence National Historical Park Collection

THOMAS WILLING by Charles Willson Peale. *Library of Congress*

WHARF AT ARCH STREET by William Russell Birch, 1800.

WILLIAM BINGHAM by Gilbert Stuart, 1784.
Robert Malezicux-Dehon, Paris, France

ANNE WILLING BINGHAM WITH HER DAUGHTER MARIA MATILDA
by Gilbert Stuart, 1784. *Robert Malezieux-Dehon, Paris, France*

COLONEL WILLIAM STEPHENS SMITH by Mather Brown, 1786.
George C. Homans, Cambridge, Massachusetts

MRS. WILLIAM STEPHENS SMITH (Abigail — "Nabby" — Adams)
by Mather Brown, 1786. *George C. Homans, Cambridge, Massachusetts*

MRS. JOHN (Abigail) ADAMS by Mather Brown, 1785.
New York State Museum, Cooperstown

JOHN ADAMS by Charles Willson Peale, c. 1791–94.
Independence National Historical Park Collection

THE MARQUIS DE CHASTELLUX by Charles Willson Peale, 1782.
Independence National Historical Park Collection

LORD SHELBURNE, MARQUESS OF LANSDOWNE.
National Portrait Gallery, London

VIEW IN THIRD STREET, FROM SPRUCE STREET by William Russell Birch.
Independence National Historical Park Collection

LANSDOWN HOUSE by William Russell Birch.

MAJOR WILLIAM JACKSON from a miniature by an unknown artist.
Historical Society of Pennsylvania

MRS. WILLIAM JACKSON (Elizabeth Willing) by Gilbert Stuart.
The Pennsylvania Academy of the Fine Arts

ALEXANDER HAMILTON by Charles Willson Peale, c. 1791.
Independence National Historical Park Collection

THOMAS JEFFERSON by Charles Willson Peale, 1791.
Independence National Historical Park Collection

JOHN JAY by an unknown artist after John Trumbull.
Independence National Historical Park Collection

ROBERT GILMOR, SR., by Gilbert Stuart.
The Baltimore Museum of Art

DR. BENJAMIN RUSH from a pastel attributed to James Sharples, Sr.
Independence National Historical Park Collection

(following page 366)

ANNE BINGHAM from a sketch by Gilbert Stuart.
Francis F. Hart, M.D., Ambler, Pennsylvania. Frick Art Reference Library

LADY WASHINGTON'S RECEPTION by Daniel P. Huntington.
The Brooklyn Museum

BENJAMIN FRANKLIN by François Lazzarini.
The Library Company

GEORGE WASHINGTON: THE "LANSDOWNE" PORTRAIT by Gilbert Stuart.
The Pennsylvania Academy of the Fine Arts

HIGH STREET FROM THE COUNTRY MARKET PLACE
by William Russell Birch. *Independence National Historical Park Collection*

M A P

page 233

BOOK ONE

Machiavelli
in Paradise

☆

CHAPTER 1

A Certain Action at Delaware Bay

Resolved, That . . . the Committee of Secret Correspondence . . . be directed to apply to the Marine Committee for the use of one or more of the Continental Fleet; and that they send the same to the French West-India Islands, in order to procure, if possible, a number of Muskets, not exceeding ten thousand; and, further, that said Committee be directed to endeavour to discover the designs of the French in assembling so large a Fleet with so great a number of Troops in the West Indies, and whether they mean to act for or against America.

The Continental Congress
Saturday, May 18, 1776

HE WAS A YOUNG MAN in his early twenties, stocky, well dressed, wearing clothes of a Philadelphia cut. He sat upright in a boat from the Continental sloop *Wasp,* a dispatch case on his lap, his baggage piled around him. His eyes were alert, observing every movement in the bay. The sailors, sweating in the June heat, pulled toward a vessel some little distance down Cape May Road, near the mouth of Delaware Bay.

He saw a ship with clean, low lines, hull painted black, a keel of 100 feet, a beam of about 30 feet. The rigging was full, with three long mastheads for sky sails over royal sails rising high above her topgallant yards. She was ported for eighteen guns. As his boat drew nearer, he saw a blending of yellow at the ship's stern, a white molding running around her quarters, the figurehead of a woman at the prow. She was an unusual ship in having no quarter galleries to break the line of her hull. She flew the red and white striped flag of the Grand Union — the flag that General Washington had raised on New Year's Day of this year 1776 at Cambridge. This was the Continental sloop-of-war *Reprisal.* The young man's experienced eye may have recognized her as the former *Molly,* the three-masted merchantman bought in March by the Congress, converted into a war vessel, and now, under Captain Lambert Wickes, one of seven ships in the new Navy of the United Colonies.

He boarded the *Reprisal* and introduced himself: William Bingham of Philadelphia, in the service of the Continental Congress, bearing letters for Captain Wickes from the Secret Committee and the Committee of Secret Correspondence. He carried orders for the Captain to take him on board as a passenger and carry him to Martinique.

Captain Wickes read his letters, ordered Mr. Bingham's baggage to be taken on, and gave him a berth in officers' quarters. The Captain undoubtedly felt satisfaction at receiving an order to sail. Some weeks earlier he and several other captains had escorted down the Delaware a fleet of merchantmen loaded with goods to be exchanged for war supplies in friendly foreign ports. Now, with John Barry commanding the *Lexington* and Charles Alexander the *Wasp,* Wickes was performing sentry duty behind the shelter of Cape May, waiting for an opportunity to convoy the merchantmen out through the British blockade. Barry and Alexander earlier had seen some action and each had just been named to command one of the thirteen new frigates the Congress was building.* There was only one way Wickes might hope for one of the remaining ships and an advance in rank among the Continental captains. That was to free himself of convoy duty, the service every captain disliked, and get into the open sea where he could cruise against the enemy. This young man, Bingham, a government agent on a secret mission to the French island of Martinique, had brought him the opportunity he was hoping for.

Bingham found that the *Reprisal* was manned by a complement of 130, including officers and a company of some two dozen marines. Captain Wickes, thirty-four years old, a native of Kent County on the Eastern Shore of Maryland, was an unassuming and friendly master formerly in the employ of Willing, Morris and Company. He had his younger brother Richard aboard as third officer. The vessel was armed with eighteen iron carriage guns, nine on each side, double fortified, for six-pound shot. She had twenty light swivel guns mounted in her quarters and forecastle, and eight iron coehorns, or small mortars, in her tops.

In the hours that followed, Bingham imparted to Wickes and his officers the recent news of the war.

* A frigate was the equivalent of a cruiser in today's navy.

The British had evacuated Boston on March 17. No one knew their destination, but General Washington had set up his headquarters in New York and moved his troops to defend that city. The General and his lady had arrived in Philadelphia near the end of May for a short visit. With General Gates and General Mifflin, he reviewed nearly 2500 troops on the Commons. The Congress, members of the Pennsylvania Assembly, a group of clergymen, and thirty visiting Indians from the Six Nations occupied honored positions amid the vast concourse of observers.

A headquarters had been set up at Market and Ninth, where the women were to bring scraped lint and old linen and work on bandages. Citizens were requested to bring in all the lead they had, for which they would receive sixpence a pound; a committee was going from house to house to look for lead in rainspouts and in clock and window weights.

Philadelphia was buzzing with rumors. One of them had it that the British were sending over 45,000 troops to subdue the Colonies. On May 8, when the city had heard the sound of heavy cannon firing in the battle of the Delaware Capes, the flag was hoisted, the drum beat to arms, the militia fell out, a number of families fled, and the Library Company called a meeting to determine what to do with its books if the British came.

One rumor had been officially verified — that the British would send in German troops. They had signed agreements with the Landgrave of Hesse and the Margrave of Anspach to use mercenaries. There had been a burst of indignation throughout the city when this news was published on May 15, and many of those who had insisted that His Majesty would step in and correct the errors of his ministers now conceded that no accommodation was to be expected and all hopes for a reconciliation were dead.

On May 28, as Bingham was making his first preparations to leave the city, the *Pennsylvania Evening Post* had printed a resolution passed by the Virginia Convention: "To declare the united colonies free and independent States, absolved from all allegiance to, or dependence upon, the crown or parliament of Great Britain."

*

Several days after Bingham's arrival at Delaware Bay, more British vessels arrived at the mouth of the Bay. Captain Wickes repaired to his cabin to write a report to Congress.

On board the Reprisal
June 16, 1776

To the Honourable Committee of
Secret Correspondence, Philadelphia

GENTLEMEN:

I received your orders and instructions by Mr. Bingham, the 13th instant, but the shallop with the provisions did not arrive till this day. We have now got all the provisions on board, both from the Wasp and the shallop. You may depend on my best endeavours in your service to prosecute this voyage with the most expedition and advantage in my power. My people, all but two, are in good health, and the officers are well satisfied with this cruise, hoping thereby to render their country an essential service, as well as themselves. There is now one two-decker, two frigates, one twenty-gun ship, and a sloop of war lying in Old Kiln Road, and we are waiting an opportunity to get out by them with impatience; so you may depend upon our embracing the first favourable opportunity of getting out and proceeding on our intended cruise.

From, gentlemen, your most obliged humble servant,

LAMBERT WICKES

The wait was a long one. The hope for making a break lay in a spell of stormy weather and overcast days, but for almost two weeks the sun rose clear, and always revealed one or more of His Majesty's ships in the Bay or on the horizon.

About noon on Friday, June 28, came the first change in the weather — rain, light breezes, and a haze on the water. There was an expectant stir on the *Reprisal,* an exchange of signals with the other vessels in the bay. At five o'clock, a lookout on the Cape sighted a ship standing in from seaward with all sail crowded. This was identified as the brigantine *Nancy,* commanded by James Montgomery, anxiously expected about this time with a cargo picked up in St. Croix and St. Thomas for the Pennsylvania Committee of Safety. Montgomery was obviously going to make a run for the Cape and he as obviously was going to be headed off, for the British ships had sighted him and two frigates were already in pursuit.

Just before twilight, Montgomery, realizing he would be intercepted, veered north. The American captains must have known what he planned: to make a run for shallow water along the coast, perhaps at Turtle Gut Inlet, seven miles north, and send off his cargo in his boats before his ship was taken. If there was an intention to slip past the British that night, or any desire to benefit by the diversion provided by the *Nancy*'s arrival, it was ignored. Montgomery needed help, and help was at once dispatched. Captain Wickes lowered his barge and filled it with marines, his brother, Lieutenant Richard Wickes, in command. As senior captain present, John Barry, seated in his own ship's boat, had command of the operation. Another incipient naval hero, Joshua Barney, seventeen years old, was at the tiller of the craft from the *Wasp*. With the crews bending hard to their oars, the boats rounded the Cape and headed north to assist Captain Montgomery and the *Nancy*.

Montgomery had a crew of eleven men, six three-pound guns, and a cargo of 101 hogsheads of rum, sixty-two hogsheads of sugar, 386 half-barrels of gunpowder, and fifty firelocks. He had just begun to unload these into his boats for carrying across the narrow stretch of water to Turtle Gut Inlet when he saw the silhouettes of two British tenders and a manned armed boat. The British frigates, having lost their quarry, had anchored and sent these into shoal waters on a search. Montgomery (as he told and retold the story years later) declaimed, "These public stores must be protected to aid our destitute country in the dark hour of need, in the noble cause of liberty," and opened up with a broadside from his three-pounders. A fire fight followed between the *Nancy* and the British tenders, while the armed boat rowed off to bring the British warships.

About midnight, guided by the firing, the first of the American boats reached the *Nancy*. It was the barge from the *Reprisal,* and Lieutenant Wickes was first to board. He put his men to unloading the kegs of powder for transshipment. Captain Barry, when he arrived, knew that daylight would reveal British warships close enough to blow the *Nancy* out of the water. After conferring with Captain Montgomery, he ordered the ship run aground at the inlet and all hands to continue taking off the cargo. A detail under Lieutenant Wickes received it on shore and carried it back into the dunes under guard. By this time, a crowd of country people, wakened by the firing, had gathered. Some of these fetched wagons and hauled the kegs and arms to the inland shore, where they that day were loaded on the schooner *Wasp* and taken up the Delaware. One group arrived with a cannon, aimed it in the general direction of the British tenders, and began firing.

At dawn, Captains Barry and Montgomery sighted the two British frigates. By eight-thirty both of the vessels were within range. Their heavy guns fired bracketing shots and then found their target. One shot smashed the *Nancy*'s caboose; another carried away her mainmast a few feet above the deck. Five boats loaded with the British bluejackets and marines put out from the frigates. It was time to quit the ship in a hurry.

The firelocks and 286 kegs of powder were safely ashore; 100 kegs of powder remained in the hold. Barry ordered the men to smash in the heads of some of the kegs while Montgomery ran a train of powder from the hold to the cabin. He then wrapped fifty pounds of powder in the mainsail, dragged it across the open hatchway, and ordered the men into the boats. He laid a billet of burning wood on the mainsail, scrambled over the side, and pushed off.

The British in the advancing boats took this for a panic-stricken retreat and let out a lusty cheer. A longboat with six marines commanded by a mate won the race to the *Nancy*, and the men clambered aboard. At that moment the brand burned through the mainsail, ignited the powder, and fell onto the open kegs in the hold. There was a flash of flame, a roar that was heard forty miles north of Philadelphia, and there rose a great fiery cloud. Some 150 feet into the air went fragments of the *Nancy*, 163 hogsheads of vaporized rum and sugar, and seven British seamen.

When the debris stopped falling and the smoke cleared away, the water was littered with pieces of timber, a shattered longboat, parts of barrels, a gold-laced hat, a leg with a garter. The four British boats, their oars broken, some of their men injured, were seen struggling slowly back to their frigates. When they arrived there was a pause; then the British directed a furious cannonade at the single gun on the beach. After a time they weighed anchor and sailed away.

William Bingham, as an emissary of the Continental Congress, had been confined to the safety of the *Reprisal* during the action. That forenoon he watched the barge return, and he saw the sailors lift from it the dead body of Richard Wickes, the only American killed in the action. Standing on the shore after the destruction of the *Nancy* and just before his brother came marching up at the head of reinforcements, Lieutenant Wickes had been struck by a cannonball. Two days later, on Sunday, he was buried with "a very deceant sermon" in the meetinghouse yard at Cape May. His brother wrote, "We have this consolation, that he fought like a brave Man & was fore most in every Transaction of that Day, this is confessed by Captn. Barry whome was present all the Time."

Background for a Mission

*Mr. Bingham now goes out to Martinico in order to procure some arms
for the Government and with another view that I need not mention as
he will write to you. You can send advices under cover to him, but you'l
remember he is a young man, tho' a worthy young man.*

Robert Morris to Silas Deane
June 5, 1776

WILLIAM BINGHAM was twenty-four years old when he was appointed
a special agent of the Continental Congress and sent on a mission to
Martinique "to discover the designs of the French" and procure, "if
possible," ten thousand muskets for General Washington's army. He
came of good English stock and a solid, prosperous, middle-class Philadelphia family. His great-great-grandfather, John Bingham, was a
respected citizen and goldsmith of London who emigrated to Eve-
sham in Burlington County, New Jersey, sometime before 1680 and
died sometime before 1687.

John Bingham's son James, a blacksmith, removed to Philadelphia,
where he died in 1714, in his forty-sixth year, possessed of considerable landed property. He was a vestryman of Christ Church and he
and his wife Ann lie buried there. A tablet over the grave has the
following epitaph, surmounted by a face of a cherub and surrounded
by floriated edging:

*— Y reader ſtand
and sPend a tear
uPon the dust that
slumbers here,
And whilst thou readſt
the state of me,
Think on the glaſs
that runs for thee.*

His only son, James Bingham, became a saddler. He married Ann Budd, daughter of William and Ann Clapgut Budd of New Jersey, members of one of the principal families of that colony. Her grandfather, an early convert to Quakerism, had died a martyr for his faith in an English jail. James Bingham inherited substantial properties from his father and from his wife's family.

William, his only surviving son, was also a saddler. His friends called him Billy; he was an ensign in the Third Company of the Associated Regiment of Foot of Philadelphia; he saw service in the wars of 1748–60 against the French and Indians; and on September 19, 1745, he made an excellent marriage. His bride was Mary (Molly) Stamper, one of two daughters of John Stamper, a prosperous English merchant who, having moved to Philadelphia, had become an alderman and member of the Common Council and would soon become mayor of the city. A year before Molly's marriage to William Bingham, an admirer wrote in his diary:

> She was of the middle size — very well shap'd — her eyes were black, full of fire — they had something in them remarkably languishing and seem'd to speak the softness of a soul replete with goodness — her eyebrows black and finely arched. . . . Her neck, her arms and hands seem to have been — fitted for her face which was of a complection made up of the lilly and the rose. Such was her person and I assure you the charms of her mind and conversation was not less amiable.

William and Molly Stamper Bingham became the parents of three sons and two daughters. The fourth child and youngest son, born April 8, 1752, was named William for his father.

Young William was born into what had become one of the rising families of the province. His father had long since extended his business affairs beyond saddlery to become a merchant and in partnership with John Stamper had developed an extensive rum trade with the islands of the West Indies. Now he was a member of the Common Council, a vestryman of St. Peter's Protestant (Anglican) Church, and a charter member of the exclusive Dancing Assembly, founded in 1748. ("No Citizen to be admissible unless he is a Subscriber. No gentleman admissible in boots, coloured stocking, or undress.")

In 1761, young William's grandfather, Mayor Stamper, bought

from the Penn family the whole front on Pine Street from Second to Third for £1100 sterling. On this land he made various improvements and erected several fine houses, including a three-story house for himself of red- and blue-glazed brick. Mayor Stamper, with Judge Thomas Willing at Spruce and Third, was one of the few Philadelphians before the Revolution to have a carriage.

William was registered for the College of Philadelphia when he was six years old; he matriculated seven years later, in 1765, after undergoing an examination in Greek and Latin. The curriculum included geography, mathematics, logick, rhetorick, natural and moral philosophy, and heavy emphasis on study of the Greek and Latin authors. Roll was called every morning at eight o'clock, and those who were absent had a cross put to their names and were fined two coppers, though the younger boys were allowed to choose whether they would pay the fine or be ferruled. Organized athletics were unknown, but running "was all the rage" among the students in the 1760s, and every young man routinely used the Delaware for swimming, boating, and ice skating. Complaints about misbehavior among the students were common; they played practical jokes, failed to show the respect of former days for their teachers, missed classes, and did not always attend public worship on Sundays.

William was graduated with honors, one of a class of nine, on November 29, 1768. The day-long commencement exercises included seven exercises by the students, among them a Syllogistic Dispute in Latin on the question *Utrum mens humana sit immortalis* (whether the human mind is immortal), Mr. Bingham taking the negative; a Forensic Dispute on whether keeping slaves was lawful; an English oration on Liberty; and the Valedictory Oration by Mr. Bingham. The *Pennsylvania Gazette* reported, "The young gentlemen discovered much ingenuity in defending their several arguments, and in the composition of their several orations; which were delivered with proper grace and elocution; and the whole was received with the usual satisfaction and approbation of a genteel and candid audience."

The sequence of events over the next seven years is not clear. In 1769, when William was seventeen, his father died at age forty-six, lamented in the *Pennsylvania Gazette* as "a gentleman whose disinterested good-nature and kindness endeared him to all his acquaint-

ance. His death was that of a Christian, resigned, serene, and happy."
Young William continued or resumed his education around this
time, for he was graduated with a master of arts degree on June 28,
1771, at age nineteen. And at some point his mother, perhaps accompanied by John Stamper, called on the Quaker Thomas Wharton and
persuaded him to take her son into his business and teach him the arts
of the merchant. William seems to have learned rapidly and to have
made good use of some capital resources. A friend of later years wrote
in his memoirs:

> Mr. Bingham was a young Philadelphian of fortune, placed by his
> mother in Mr. Wharton's Compting House. He told me that while
> a clerk there he had two brigs at sea of his own. He was well edu-
> cated, shrewd & intelligent; very speculative in political events. . . .

His vessels were the twenty-ton brig *Sally,* built in Pennsylvania; and
the forty-ton brig *Elizabeth,* built in Delaware, which he owned in
partnership with the merchant master Robert Montgomery.

He may have named the *Elizabeth* for a young lady he was courting
about this time: Betsy Galloway, a great belle in Philadelphia. Betsy
was the only daughter of the Tory lawyer Joseph Galloway, who did
not approve of any of the suitors who came calling at his fine house
at Sixth and Market. He drove William Bingham away, and he shot
and wounded another suitor with whom Betsy was about to elope.

Among Americans in the period before the Revolution, Philadelphians almost alone followed the custom of spending a *Wanderjahr*
in Europe. Sons of wealthy Quaker and Anglican families made the
Grand Tour before settling down into a career as a merchant or in
one of the professions. William Bingham started out on such a tour
early in 1773. His itinerary is unknown, but he made valuable mercantile connections in Europe, he carried letters of introduction from
Dr. John Morgan, founder of the Medical School of the College of
Philadelphia, and he visited Leghorn. If he followed the customary
course, he spent seven to nine weeks in Italy; there visited Hercu-
laneum and the Tomb of Vergil; studied the old masters in the Italian galleries; followed the traditional route across France to England;
bought great quantities of bric-a-brac, objets d'art, garden statuary
and third-rate paintings; and returned home with a cosmopolitan

ease of behavior and continental savoir faire that distinguished Philadelphia society and impressed visitors from the other Colonial capitals.

Bingham returned from Europe to a city seething with resentment at British treatment of the Colonies — a resentment expressed chiefly through the business community. In 1766, some 400 Philadelphia merchants had met and resolved to import no more English goods until the Stamp Act was repealed. (Two of the leaders of that movement were Thomas Willing and Robert Morris, partners in the city's leading mercantile firm, both of whom were to have a profound influence on the life of William Bingham.) Two years later, the merchants met to record and publish their grievances. Though England was importing most of her steel from Germany, she forbade the Colonies to make steel. She prohibited plating and slitting mills, iron manufacture, and the making of hats and woolen goods. She excluded American traders and vessels from foreign markets. She imposed the English duty on all American products carried to other nations, even though the products were not landed in England. She charged a duty on Madeira wines. She shipped convicts and paupers to the Colonies.

In December, 1773, when Britain undertook forcibly to introduce tea into the Colonies through the East India Company, Philadelphia had its own kind of tea party: effective but decorous and open to the general public. Eight thousand persons attended an assembly in the State House yard to decide what to do about a shipment of tea just arrived in the East Indiaman *Polly*. Several previously prepared resolutions were passed without dissent. The captain of the ship was present; he agreed to comply with the wishes of the assembly and sailed away the next day, his cargo unbroken, carrying with him a "charriot" that had been built for Thomas Wharton and a set of bells cast for a community church.

In May, 1774, the silversmith Paul Revere rode into the city with news that Parliament was closing the port of Boston on June 1 and was moving its custom house to Salem; would the citizens of Pennsylvania send an expression of their feelings on this development, that the citizens of Massachusetts might be guided? A meeting of leaders of the community was held in the new City Tavern on Second Street.

They advised the citizens of Massachusetts to practice "prudence and moderation" but assured them that Pennsylvania would continue to stand firm "for the cause of American liberty." On June 1, despite Quaker opposition, most of the city's shops and stores were closed as an expression of sympathy for Boston. Flags were lowered to half staff, several churches held special services, and some patriots opened up Christ Church and rang its bells for hours in a muffled peal.

Two weeks later John Dickinson and Thomas Willing presided over a general meeting of citizens held in the State House yard. Eight resolutions were approved. The Boston Port Bill was declared to be illegal. It was agreed that the Colonies should convoke a Continental Congress, and a committee of forty-three was named to sound out the opinion of Pennsylvanians on the appointment of delegates to such a congress. A month later, under the call of this committee, a conference of delegates met in Carpenters' Hall, Judge Willing in the chair. The convention issued a declaration of colonial rights, condemned Parliament, pledged Pennsylvania's cooperation in united action with the other Colonies, and requested the Provincial Assembly to appoint delegates to a Continental Congress.

The First Continental Congress met in Carpenters' Hall on September 4, 1774, with delegates present from eleven Colonies. Among these were Patrick Henry, George Washington, and Richard Henry Lee of Virginia; John and Samuel Adams of Massachusetts; John Jay of New York; Silas Deane of Connecticut; Joseph Galloway, Thomas Mifflin, and John Dickinson of Pennsylvania. The Congress sat for six weeks, made a last appeal to Great Britain before resorting to arms, took a positive stand against imports from and exports to England, adopted a solemn declaration of rights, and adjourned to meet again the following May.

Late on the afternoon of April 24, 1775, an express rider from Trenton galloped into the city, went straight to the City Tavern and asked to see members of the Committee of Correspondence. He carried dispatches addressed "To all friends of American liberty," disclosing that on the previous Wednesday a brigade of British regulars, "without any provocation," had fired on and killed six New England militiamen at Lexington, and that a battle had followed with many killed on both sides. The news raced through Philadelphia that night. When it reached a hall where Robert Morris was presiding over a dinner of the Society of St. George, the guests were so greatly excited that they upset the table.

The Second Continental Congress convened two weeks later, this time in the Assembly Chamber of the State House. Thomas Willing and James Wilson had been added to the delegates from Pennsylvania, along with Dr. Benjamin Franklin, who four days earlier had been welcomed by the city on his return from England. The Congress (two days before the Battle of Bunker Hill) unanimously named Colonel Washington to the post of commander-in-chief of the Continental armies, fixing his pay and expenses at 500 dollars a month. He very shortly set out, with Major Generals Charles Lee and Philip Schuyler, to take command at Cambridge.

Throughout the summer and fall, the city worked to prepare itself for war. There was a stampede of volunteers, and these were put to drilling. Firearms were collected from the inhabitants. The earth in old cellars was dug up and treated for nitre for gunpowder. Tories were watched, threatened and sometimes manhandled; a certain Thomas Loosley was "exalted as a spectacle" at the London Coffee House and made to beg pardon for "illiberally and wickedly vilifying the measures of Congress." A newly appointed Committee of Public Safety headed by Dr. Franklin labored diligently and effectively, meeting every day but Sunday at six in the morning so as not to interfere with the work of Congress. It sought out arms and ammunition, erected barriers in the Delaware, established military hospitals and prisons, fixed prices of commodities, set up manufactures of firearms and gunpowder, and dealt with those who were suspected of being dangerous to the public interest.

The part William Bingham played in these events is not known, though as an enthusiastic young supporter of the patriot cause he must have stood in the crowds at the mass meetings, drilled with the volunteer home guard or the militia on the Commons, and joined the gentlemen on horseback who rode out to welcome and escort the delegates to Congress. In November, 1775, his actions became a matter of record. He took a post that placed him at the heart of the body where momentous decisions were being made.

On the 29th of that month, Congress created a standing Committee of Secret Correspondence "for the sole purpose of corresponding with

our friends in Great Britain, Ireland, and other parts of the world."
The Committee was authorized to act on its own initiative and to
employ agents as it found need. Benjamin Franklin was chairman;
the other members were John Dickinson, John Jay, Benjamin Harrison of Virginia, Thomas Johnson of Maryland, and (two months
later) Robert Morris. The Committee named William Bingham as
its secretary.*

The main intent of the Committee of Secret Correspondence was
to probe sentiment abroad and to determine the disposition of foreign governments — especially that of France — toward the American rebellion. Their attitude would influence basic decisions that
had to be made. Should the Colonies send diplomatic and commercial agents abroad? Should they open American ports to trade with
nations other than Great Britain, and on what terms? Should they
form alliances with friendly powers? Should they declare for independence?

Sailors and travelers returning from France reported that the
French were friendly to the American cause. Indeed, widespread sentiment in favor of American independence came from surprising persons and places. People joked that on this matter even Rousseau and
Voltaire held the same view — the only thing they had ever agreed
on. But there could be a vast gap between French popular opinion
and government policy. What reason had a Catholic Bourbon monarch, Louis XVI, to support a rebellion against a fellow monarch,
even if Protestant and English?

In December, 1775, there came to Philadelphia a mysterious stranger, a Frenchman named Archard de Bonvouloir. Secrecy and intrigue were common in the early months of the Revolution, for every
patriot knew the fear of feeling a halter around his neck; but Bonvou-

---

* The Committee of Secret Correspondence became the Committee of Foreign Affairs
on April 17, 1777, and was the forerunner of what is now the Department of State. It
is not to be confused with the Committees of Correspondence created in the different
Colonies under the urging of Samuel Adams.

It is also not to be confused with the Secret Committee, which Congress had created
on November 8, 1775, to procure arms and to handle exports and imports. That committee, renamed the Committee of Commerce on July 5, 1777, was the forerunner of
the Department of Commerce. Thomas Willing was the first chairman of the Secret
Committee. He asked in mid-December to be excused and was replaced by his partner,
Robert Morris, who thus served on the two most important committees created by
Congress. John Adams was indignant that he was appointed to neither committee; John
Jay spent a whole evening trying to mollify him.

loir's secrecy was extreme and odd. He wished to meet with the Committee of Secret Correspondence, but its members and its secretary — even Dr. Franklin, who was seventy and ailing from the gout — must go stealthily to the assigned rendezvous on the outskirts of the city, each one alone and by a different route in the dead of the night.

Bonvouloir told the Committee he was simply a Flemish merchant acting as a private citizen, but he hinted that he had been sent by the French government. Still, he was vague and would show no papers. He was asked if France would help the American Colonies. "That," the Frenchman replied, "seems to be a precipitous and even a hazardous question. Everything that takes place either in London or in France gets to be known in both places. Therefore, *Messieurs,* this is slippery business in the face of the English."

In case the Colonies should make proposals for a commercial accord, he was further asked, would France be content with exclusive rights to their trade for a certain period as repayment for shipment of war supplies? Bonvouloir would promise nothing.

The Committee suggested that with exclusive rights to American trade, France could immediately become the most powerful nation in Europe. "In return for even a little help," a member said, "the Colonies would promise an inviolable attachment in which they would never fail."

Finally the Frenchman put it clearly. "As long as you are subjects of Great Britain, we can not, and must not, do anything for you. The only means that you have of obtaining our support is by declaring yourselves independent."

The Committee members were impressed by Bonvouloir, and Dr. Franklin, who had his own ways of knowing what important people were thinking in the capitals of Europe, seemed to trust him.* They proposed that the Congress send an agent to negotiate a commercial accord with France, perhaps leading to a treaty of alliance. Congress so resolved. In March, 1776, it delegated Silas Deane to represent the

---

* Bonvouloir, a distinguished soldier, had indeed been sent by the French government to sound out the Colonies in an unofficial status. He reported back to his government that the ardor and determination of the Americans was "incredible"; that the Committee of Secret Correspondence worked efficiently; that the members wanted the French government to know that American affairs were going well; and that, in his opinion, the Americans would soon declare their independence. His remarks quoted above are taken verbatim from his report to Vergennes, the French foreign minister.

United Colonies in Paris. Deane was to act with the utmost secrecy and discretion; he was to go to Paris in the guise of a private merchant in search of trade.

The Secret Committee (of Commerce), charged with the enormous problem of procuring arms and supplies in a land that had almost no industry, turned to the merchant-shippers. It put Willing and Morris in complete charge of its commission contracts. The company had almost twenty years of experience; it had capital; and it had an international trading network. Morris appointed agents in the various Colonies to buy and ship out commodities and to receive and forward incoming shipments, all in the name of the Secret Committee. He set out to appoint agents to perform the same services in the key centers abroad — in France, at Cap François in Santo Domingo (French Haiti), at the Dutch island of St. Eustatius, at Curaçao, at Guadeloupe.

In this network, French Martinique was to be the entrepôt, the pivotal point. Morris wanted a man there who knew trade and could procure arms. Franklin wanted a man who would ably represent the Colonies and act as an intelligence agent at a critical place. Together they chose William Bingham, the young secretary of the Committee of Secret Correspondence. Thomas Paine would take Bingham's place as secretary of the Committee.

Bingham had a long conference with Robert Morris shortly before he left Philadelphia. Morris explained that Bingham, like Silas Deane, was to appear in Martinique as a private merchant interested only in moving goods to and from the West Indies. In this character Bingham would carry on a private business "in the mercantile line" with Willing and Morris for their mutual advantage. The Congress, of course, was aware that he, Morris, was continuing his private operations while serving the government.

First, Mr. Bingham was to watch for a private shipload of gunpowder that would be brought from Europe into Martinique or St. Eustatius by Captain Beall. Since Bingham had already invested £500 sterling in the undertaking, he would be eager to speed the shipment so that "this adventure may be brought to a happy conclusion for us all."

Second, Bingham was to make connections with some good French or Dutch house that would ship West Indies produce to Willing and

Morris. He would receive one-half the customary 5 per cent commission on the sale of such parcels sent in.

Third, he was to buy West Indies goods on credit up to £1000 or £1500* until Willing and Morris could send in private produce from the mainland as payment. Willing and Morris would be one-half concerned with Bingham in such adventures. Bingham would consign the West Indies goods to Willing and Morris to be sold "to the best advantage free of commission, you charging no commission on the purchase nor on the sale of the returns which we shall ship you. . . . In this way we will keep up a constant intercourse with you." Bingham was first to buy some linens or other European manufactures and send these back on the government vessel that conveyed him to Martinique.

Morris put the terms of this arrangement in a letter from Willing and Morris to William Bingham dated Saturday, June 3, 1776. "We shall be ready to transact rich business," he wrote cheerfully.

On the same day Bingham received a letter from the Committee of Secret Correspondence — three and a half pages of detailed instructions written by Dr. Franklin and signed by him and three other members of the Committee. The young man must have studied and weighed and pondered the contents of these orders.

> SIR,
> You are immediately to repair on board the Sloop Hornet Wm Hallock Esqr Comr. bound to Martinico; — On your arrival deliver the letter you are entrusted with to the General there and show him your credentials.
> You are earnestly to endeavour to procure from him 10,000 good musquets, well fitted with bayonets; if he cannot or will not supply them, you are to request his favor and influence in procuring them in that or any other island, if to be had.

Muskets and bayonets were needed, to be sure, but they were only a part of what was lacking. Thomas Willing, as head of "The Committee Appointed to Consider What Articles are Necessary for the Army," had turned in a report in December. The army needed everything. It needed 60,000 blankets, 130,000 yards of broadcloth for uniforms, 160,000 sewing needles, cloth for tenting, 300 tons of

---

* The value of the pound sterling was about $4.45 (gold or silver).

lead, 1,000,000 flints, 1500 tin boxes, iron wire, medicines, surgeons'
instruments, lint bandages — these, with other articles, costing
£116,467 sterling.

We propose to pay for them by remitting the produce of this country with all possible dispatch to any island that may be agreed on.

One thing was certain: trade was absolutely necessary if the Colonies were to survive. Their funds had been seized and their credit
stopped in England. They must establish new lines of credit elsewhere — in Holland, Spain, France, Germany, Russia. One way to
do this — about the only way — was to ship out commodities. Congress could send rice, tobacco, indigo, skins, furs, flour, lumber, and
ships' masts in payment for military stores. The question was, would
Congress, without any real authority to tax or to sequester, be able to
supply what it promised?

You are to take especial care, that the musquets you send are good.
We direct you to send 2,500 of them by the Hornet on her return &
the remainder in parcels not exceeding 1,000 in swift sailing well
escorted vessels, with directions to the masters to put into the first
port within the United Colonies, where they can safely land.
We desire you to obtain from the General if possible a French man
of war or frigate to convoy these vessels so far that they may be out
of the course of the British ships that are cruizing in the West Indies.

This was an old story to American merchants. For decades they
had been circumventing British restrictions on their trade with the
West Indies by a flourishing business in smuggled goods, with not a
little cooperation from British merchants and officials. The American masters knew the coves and bays along the coast, the bars and
reefs, the channels and shallows, in ways that left the British patrol
vessels helpless.

You are carefully to publish all the papers delivered to you by us
for that purpose & disperse them as much as you can throughout the
Dutch, English and French West Indies, having first obtained the
General's permission to do so in the latter.

That would be the second of his assigned duties: to promote the

American cause by the printed and spoken word. Dr. Franklin, a master of the art of propaganda, was acutely conscious of the importance of finding supporters and making friends abroad.

> You must with the greatest prudence endeavor to discern either by conversation with the General or others the designs of the French in assembling so large a fleet with a great number of troops in the West Indies & whether they mean to act for or against America.
> You are to convey to us the speediest intelligence of any discoveries you may make on this head.

For or against America? It was the crucial question. Something unusual was certainly developing in the French islands. Who could fathom the mysteries of French policy? They hated England. They were smarting under the humiliating terms of a lost war. Yet only fifteen years earlier they had been burning and plundering and murdering on the American frontier at the head of terrible bands of savages. Who knew for certain that the French and English had not, as some suspected, agreed to subjugate the American Colonies together and then divide them into spheres of control?

> You are to continue at Martinico untill we recall you and are to cultivate an intimate and friendly correspondence with the General and other persons of distinction there, that you may be enabled to procure all the usefull intelligence you can.

When he obtained intelligence of special importance, and if no other opportunity offered itself, he was to charter a fast sailing vessel and send her to an American port.

> You are to observe the strictest secrecy & not to discover any part of the business you are sent upon to any persons, but those to whom you are under an absolute necessity of communicating it in the transactions thereof. It will readily occur to you that an appearance of commercial views will effectually cover the political; therefore you will make frequent enquiries amongst their merchants what articles of this country's produce are most wanted in the Islands.

The Committee would send intelligence of events in the American Colonies, and Bingham was to make good use of this information in the West Indies. At the same time, he was to forward advices to Silas Deane in Paris, marking the source of each piece of information "and always distinguishing between what you think can be depended on and what is doubtful. In short, Sir, you are to be constantly on the watch, and give to Mr. Deane and us every information that you think connected with the interest or that can be improved to the advantage of the United Colonies."

He might find it useful to visit Guadeloupe, St. Eustatius, or other foreign islands, but in such cases he was to protect himself by always taking passage in foreign vessels, and he was not to be absent from Martinique for more than two weeks at a time. If he had any opportunity to contract on reasonable terms for arms, ammunition, or other articles wanted at home, he was to send word to the Committee and he would receive instructions.

The third of his major assigned duties followed:

> In the mean time you will encourage as many private adventurers as you can, by holding up the high prices we give, the low price of our produce, and as we have cruizers on this coast to watch the enemy's tenders, cutters etc. small vessels have a good chance of getting safe in & out of the bays, rivers & inlets on our coast.

"Private adventurers" also meant armed privateers, for Dr. Franklin and Mr. Morris had given him blank Letters of Marque and Reprisal. These, when filled out and registered with the Court of Admiralty, would license a captain "to fit out and set forth" the named vessel "in a warlike manner and by force of arms to attack, subdue, seize and take all ships and other vessels, goods, wares and merchandizes belonging to the Crown of Great-Britain."

The Committee had left the most difficult assignment until last. Bingham, acting as a private citizen, was to persuade the French to cease being a neutral nation and give active assistance to American naval vessels and privateers that captured English ships and cargoes.

> As we have already many cruizers & are daily adding to the number, you will take proper opportunities of sounding the Gen'l, & learn from him whether he could admit prizes made by our cruizers to be sent in & protected there untill proper opportunities offered for bringing them to the continent. But this being a matter of great

delicacy you must introduce it as a thing of your own & not as any part of your instructions.

Dated at Philadelphia, this 3 Day of June 1776

B. FRANKLIN
BENJ. HARRISON
JOHN DICKINSON
ROBT. MORRIS

*

Bingham took these instructions and his other papers, packed his bags, made his farewells to his friends and family, and boarded a light vessel that took him down the Delaware to where the *Hornet* lay at anchor. He found her with a sickly crew, her stern shattered from a recent engagement with the enemy, the hold making nine or ten inches of water every hour and increasing daily. He sent word of her unseaworthy condition back to Philadelphia.

After an idle wasted week with Captain Hallock aboard this ship, he received further orders from the Committee of Secret Correspondence, dated June 10:

> SIR:
>
> We are sorry for your disappointment of the sloop *Hornet;* but in consequence thereof we have procured an order to despatch the ship *Reprisal,* Captain Lambert Wickes. . . . You will consequently take your passage for Martinico on board the *Reprisal,* Captain Wickes; and hoping for a speedy and safe passage, and for a successful issue to the business you are charged with, we remain, sir, your humble servants,
>
>
>
> BENJAMIN HARRISON
> JOHN DICKINSON
> ROBERT MORRIS
>
>

With his letter were orders from the Secret Committee (of Commerce) for Captain Wickes to accept and act on the orders previously issued to Captain Hallock, signed with seven names and hoping for the captain that "this voyage will afford you an opportunity of rendering essential service to your country, and that you will bring us back a parcel of fine seamen, and a number of good prizes."

William Bingham again took up his baggage and his papers and boarded the small boat that would carry him to the *Reprisal*.

CHAPTER 3

First Days in Martinique

At Curracoa M. Isaac Gouverneur will receive & forward Goods for us;
. . . at Martinico William Bingham Esq, *who has already written you*
some letters, and with whom I expect you will support a constant Corres-
pondence both political & Commercial; he is a young Gent of good Edu-*
cation, Family & Fortune; his Correspondence has yet a good deal of the
fanciful young man in it, but Experience will cure him of this, and upon
the whole, I think he has abilities & merit, both in the Political and
Commercial Line.

Robert Morris to Silas Deane
September 12, 1776

ON WEDNESDAY MORNING, July 3, 1776, in clear weather and with a
good wind behind her, the *Reprisal* sailed out of Delaware Bay with
thirteen merchantmen. The coast was clear, the British warships having been recalled to take part in Howe's attack on New York. At
dusk, well out to sea, the merchant vessels scattered. (Three were
later captured.) Captain Wickes headed southeast for Martinique.

The weather stayed fair and the wind strong. Four months later,
when it carried him to France, Dr. Franklin would call the *Reprisal*
"a miserable vessel" and complain that he was badly fed, living
"chiefly on salt beef, the fowls being too hard for my teeth," so that
on arrival at Nantes he "had scarce strength to stand." But Franklin
was seventy years old, he was suffering from boils, and he sailed in
October through rough northern seas; and there is nothing to indicate that young Mr. Bingham found his Caribbean journey anything
but pleasant. It is known that he and Wickes became warm friends.

For all his anguish at the toughness of the fowls, Dr. Franklin
found the discipline and training on the *Reprisal* of superior quality,
calling it "equal to anything of the kind in the best ships of the
King's fleet." It was on this first cruise in command of the *Reprisal,*
with Bingham aboard, that Captain Wickes whipped his crew into
shape. Many of his men were inexperienced, recruited from the

towns and farms along the coast and from as far away as Baltimore, signed on for one year at $6.67 per month, a half-pint of rum per day, and prize money. Wickes drilled them hard at working the ship, at handling the guns, and at ship's housekeeping. He may have used a device learned from Captain Barry. When he found some of his men reluctant to climb the tall masts, Barry placed a keg of drinking water and a tin cup at the head of the mainmast. Anyone who wanted a drink had to climb to get it.

On Thursday, July 11, southeast of Bermuda, the *Reprisal* sighted and overtook a merchant ship flying the Union Jack. Captain Wickes ordered her to lie to and sent a party on board. She was the 240-ton *Friendship,* Captain Charles Mackay, inbound from Grenada to London with a cargo of rum, cocoa, coffee, and 500 hogsheads of sugar, worth an estimated £35,000.

Wickes permitted the British captain to bring his personal property and private papers with him to the *Reprisal* and generously promised him his freedom when they reached Martinique. He appointed Warrant Officer John Parks as the *Friendship*'s prize master, assigned him a prize crew of perhaps twenty men, and ordered him to sail for Philadelphia, or, if endangered, to any other American port. He gave Mr. Parks a letter to the Committee of Secret Correspondence ("We this day fell in with Captain Mackay in the ship Friendship . . . which ship I have taken. . . . Mr. Bingham is well, and desires his compliments to you. . . .")

Captain Wickes then addressed himself to the British crew. He told them of the attractions of life aboard an American naval vessel, working in the cause of freedom, sharing in the prize money for all captured vessels — 8.5 out of 20 equal parts for the seamen, share and share alike, with a double portion for the man who first sighted a ship later taken prize and a treble share for the first man to board her. The entire British crew and all the officers save Captain Mackay found the offer irresistibly attractive and volunteered to enter American service on the *Reprisal.*

In the next week, Wickes took two more prizes, enlisting most of their crews, and sent still another vessel on her way for lack of hands to man her.

The *Reprisal* sailed to the southeast, past the Virgin Islands, past

Guadeloupe. On July 27, Bingham saw Martinique, a gray shape, then a green land mass in a deep blue sea. The ship sailed west to curve around the northern coast to the island, past Pointe de Prêcheur, then down the western shore to round Pointe à la Mare.

It was five-thirty on a clear Saturday afternoon. To the north loomed the wrinkled, scarred flanks of magnificent Mont Pelée, its summit veiled in mist, its lower slopes green with foliage. The mountains became hills, and the hills sloped gently down to form a perfect amphitheater at the shore. There lay the lovely town of St. Pierre, the heart of the French West Indies, with its enormous cocoa palms and stone hillside terraces, its red-tiled roofs on white stone and yellow brick buildings, its twin white cathedral towers.

Captain Wickes took his glass and trained it on the harbor. There riding at anchor, as if in command, lay a British warship. It was a sloop-of-war named *Shark* and it showed sixteen nine-pound guns.

Captain Wickes was in a difficult situation. He had only eighty-seven of his original 130 American seamen aboard, having transferred the others to his three captured prizes. His men were inexperienced and untested in battle. He had thirty-six crew members on board who a few days earlier had been serving in English merchant ships; their loyalty, or at least their ardor, was questionable. The English ship, a vessel of the regular British navy with a trained crew, mounted heavier guns than his, and its presence in the harbor conceivably could mean that France had become England's ally. Nevertheless, Captain Wickes decided to engage the enemy. It would be the first battle fought by an American ship in foreign waters.

The shrill pipe of the boatswain ordered the men to their stations. The guns were loaded and run out, the decks sprinkled with sand.* John Maffit, the ship's surgeon, laid out his instruments, his bandages, and his medicines.

Wickes was conscious of the main purpose of his voyage: to deliver an agent of the Continental Congress safe and unharmed in Martinique. He lowered one of his boats. William Bingham, on the captain's orders, climbed down the ladder and with his baggage and papers was rowed to a wharf in the harbor. Standing beside his baggage, he watched HMS *Shark* slip her cables and stand out to sea

* To keep the crew from slipping on spilled blood.

to challenge the stranger. It was seven o'clock of a clear tropical evening. The entire population of St. Pierre was pouring out of homes and barracks, taverns and shops, to watch the fight.

The *Reprisal* crossed the mouth of the harbor. The *Shark* followed, closing the gap to within hailing distance: "This is His Majesty's Ship *Shark*. Heave to." Wickes, standing on his course, called back, "This is the ship *Reprisal* from Philadelphia, belonging to the Honorable, the Continental Congress." The Englishman hailed a second and a third time in French and English and then fired a shot across the bow of the *Reprisal*. Wickes turned his ship's head away from the wind to take a tack that bore him down on the enemy. His port guns discharged a broadside. The *Shark* returned the fire at once.

For twenty to thirty minutes the two vessels exchanged fire. One of the *Reprisal*'s guns burst, wounding a man in the arm. The *Shark* was hit three or four times and two of her men were wounded or killed. Then suddenly and unexpectedly, while the ships were maneuvering for position, there came the sound of firing from another quarter. One of the giant guns of the French fort fired a shot across the bow of the English ship. A second gun fired, the shot going through the main topmast stay sail. At this challenge, the *Shark* had no choice but to sheer off and stand out to sea.

The separate accounts of the engagement — French, British, and American — varied widely in the matter of who was winning at the time of this astonishing development. Indeed, one observer said the battle was being fought "without much damage to either that I can find." Young Bingham had no doubts as to the victor. "I was a spectator of the whole of it from the shore," he wrote in his official account. "And to the honor of America, the *Reprisal* damaged the *Shark* so much that she was forced to sheer off in order to refit, when the fort fired upon her and put an end to the engagement." This he called "a disgraceful and precipitate flight."

Bingham was present to greet Captain Wickes when he stepped ashore an hour later. The crowd gave him a wild and tumultuous welcome. Wickes, Bingham said, was "complimented and caressed beyond measure. . . . Never did I feel the sensation of joy in a more lively degree."

Bingham waited at once on the Governor at his residence. He introduced himself as an agent of the American Continental Congress and presented his credentials. Governor de Courcey was cordial. He first cleared up the mysterious presence of the British warship in French waters. Captain John Chapman had sailed the *Shark* into St. Pierre earlier that afternoon from Antigua. He had come to present a letter from the admiral in command of British naval forces in the West Indies to General le Comte d'Argout, military commander at Martinique — another complaint about what the English considered some French irregularity. General d'Argout was absent in Fort Royal (now Fort-de-France) thirty miles down the coast, and Captain Chapman had delivered his letter to Governor de Courcey. The French, Governor de Courcey said, had fired on the *Shark* for committing a hostile act in their territorial waters.*

Bingham then took up the subject of his mission. Governor de Courcey was encouraging and arranged for a conference when General d'Argout returned from Fort Royal. About midnight, the Governor received Captain Wickes. (It was the first formal call paid by an American naval officer on an official of a foreign state.) Wickes asked protection for his ship while in port and permission to careen and clean his hull for the return voyage. Both requests were granted.

Early next morning the *Shark* boldly sailed back into the harbor and anchored near the *Reprisal*. Captain Chapman had prepared a mild remonstrance at French conduct, a defense of his own, and a request that "your Excellency will be pleased to give me redress for this insult offer'd to his Brittanick Majesty's ship by permitting me to take possession of [the *Reprisal*]." But when he stepped ashore, he was surrounded by such a jeering and hooting crowd of Martinicos that, as Bingham reported with elation, he was "under the necessity of procuring a guard of six men to protect him from the insults of the mob." When the Englishman got General d'Argout's answer after a two-day wait in the harbor, he was ordered never again "to engage battle in our roads or under our forts . . . an act of hostility which I shall never tolerate. . . . I again assure you, Sir, of my entire neutrality in this affair."

---

* Chapman wrote in his log that on leaving the Governor's residence he had seen "a sail in the offing with colours which I was unacquainted with (being red and white striped with a union next the staff). . . . I had reason to believe [him] to be the property of his Brittanick Majesty's rebellious subjects in North America, upon which I thought it my duty to slip my cables and stand out to sea after him."

At some time in the next several days, Bingham was received in a formal conference by General d'Argout. The General was frank as well as cordial. He said that a frigate had come into port the previous Sunday with dispatches from the French court. These ordered the governors and commanders of all the French islands to put themselves in the best posture of defense and (in Bingham's words to the Congress) "to favor the Americans throughout all their ports and protect their commerce at sea, whenever and wherever they should find an opportunity." Mr. Bingham was free to report to his government that the French officials had been so ordered and were themselves friendly to the American cause.

The General agreed to provide convoys for American vessels partway to their home ports. He expressed regret that he was in no position to offer help in procuring the arms and powder that were needed. He suggested that a steady flow of communication be set up between Philadelphia and St. Pierre by means of a number of "fast sailing, well appointed vessels which are intended for the purpose of commerce, as well as to convey dispatches to and from this place." He would keep Mr. Bingham supplied with copies of all newspapers and public prints received from Europe.

Bingham then asked the crucial question: Might American vessels bring the prizes they captured into French ports for protection?

"If the American cruisers should bring any prizes into our ports," General d'Argout replied, "we will not prevent their selling or disposing of them as they should think proper." Indeed, it might be a good idea for Mr. Bingham to get some blank commissions from the American Congress and outfit American privateers at St. Pierre and Fort Royal.

Bingham hastened to tell Captain Wickes this splendid news. The cordiality of the French was pleasing and important, but the permission given to use French ports was of prodigious significance. It meant that the American captains sailing the Caribbean could have the ships they captured condemned by the Admiralty Court in Martinique and sold in the islands. That would save taking them to an American port, it would dispense with the assignment of men to the captured vessels as prize crews, and it would avoid the risk of recapture on the way to the mainland.

A few days later a British vessel sailed into port carrying a strong protest from the commanding British admiral and a demand that the American pirates and their ship be turned over to him for trial. Argout's reply was firm. He would not deliver up the American ship he had taken under his protection. The admiral was misinformed in this affair, and if he had been well acquainted with the character of the man he was addressing, no such demand would ever have been made. Argout gave Bingham copies of the correspondence with permission to send them to his government. Because of the British protest, he said, he would for the present withdraw his offer of convoys for American vessels.

Bingham was extraordinarily busy in the days that followed. He worked hard against the lethargy characteristic of a hot, tropical seaport town, where things were done, if done at all, with the utmost slowness, and were done best with bribery, or exertion of pressure from high places, or both. He worked in Martinique's notoriously cruel climate, under an August sun that blinded with its unrelenting glare, on into heat-oppressed nights that left a white inhabitant dizzy, weak and sleepless.

He called on Richard Harrison, a young American who had recently come to the island as a private trader and commercial agent representing Virginia. He presented letters from the Committee of Secret Correspondence instructing Harrison to turn over to him the cargoes, or the net proceeds of the cargoes if already sold, of the American sloops *Fanny* and *Peggy* "to do with it what he may desire." These were to pay for the arms and powder Bingham was to procure, and for his personal expenses. He found, probably with Harrison's help, a place to live, servants, and a *negociant* who would serve as a cover in receiving and sending his letters. He procured 500 muskets and a small quantity of powder — all that could be got — and held them ready to load on the *Reprisal* when she completed her refitting at Fort Royal. He had better luck with the linens and other dry goods he was to buy on his joint account with Willing and Morris, though the prices he paid were high. When offered a number of cavalry sabers, complete with scabbard chains, he bought these on the same private account.

He wrote and dispatched three letters to the Committee of Secret Correspondence (August 4, 15 and 26) reporting in detail and at length the events of the voyage to Martinique, his high opinion of

Captain Wickes, the battle off St. Pierre, the "flattering reception" given him, and the offers and proposals made by the French officials. With his second letter he enclosed "in confidence" the correspondence exchanged between the British admiral and General d'Argout.

The General had offered conveyance in his own pouch for a message to Silas Deane in Paris, and Bingham, assuming that what he sent would be opened and reported to higher French officials, wrote a letter that was (as he later told Deane) "rather guarded and reserved in the stile of it." He told the late news of the war (all good); of the strength of American arms; of the great advantages the French would derive from a commercial intercourse with America if she avowed herself the defender of American liberty; and of the determination of America's people "not to survive its liberties, but rather die the last of freemen than bear to live the first of slaves."

He wrote Deane again the following day by a conveyance in which he had more confidence, and poured out the story of the past several days. He closed with some exciting news from America.

> A Vessel arrived here yesterday from Baltimore; the captain assured me that whilst he was waiting in the Bay of Chesapeak for an opportunity to take his departure, he had spoke with a privateer, the commander of which informed him that Independence was absolutely declared by Congress, & that he went on board & saw the printed Declaration.
>
> May this then be the blessed aera from which America dates her freedom, happiness & glory. It is indeed our own fault if it is not; we must now set about laying the foundations of a free government.

Bingham next sent a report to Willing, Morris and Company on their private affairs. He lectured Mr. Morris on the different modes of conducting commerce between Europe and the American continent, with Martinique as the main way station in the transshipment of goods. He had learned that several ships were for sale or charter in St. Lucia — should he take them over? There were real advantages to be realized in chartering French vessels and French sailors to carry goods to the mainland. What goods were most wanted? He could buy a large store of French wines at a favorable price — would Willing and Morris want a half interest in such an adventure? Bingham then proposed a plan in which he would "seek intensive connections" with merchants in Europe and America. Did Mr. Morris think there would be any impropriety in his undertaking such a commercial matter while also conducting public business?

Near the end of August, Captain Wickes prepared to sail from Fort Royal with a graved and painted ship. While the muskets and powder, the swords and linens and dry goods were being taken aboard, a somewhat embarrassed William Bingham arrived with four young men in tow. He introduced these to Captain Wickes as French officers who were eager to fight as volunteers for the sacred cause of American freedom — as high-ranking officers, of course. None of the men had any money and none could speak a word of English. If Bingham told Wickes what he later wrote to Congress, he said that he had tried to discourage the men, but that General d'Argout had recommended them highly as men of merit, and he, Bingham, was in no position to embarrass the General by rejecting their proffered services. He knew the objections to hiring penniless Frenchmen who spoke no English; he would not make this a common practice. Captain Wickes made room for the men in the officers' quarters.

On August 26, just short of a month from his arrival in Martinique, Bingham gave Captain Wickes a packet of public and private letters and wished him good winds and a safe voyage. Nineteen days later, "without having taken any more prizes or met with any remarkable occurrence," Captain Wickes sailed up the Delaware, anchored at the Philadelphia wharf, and found that he was a hero. Bingham's letters from Martinique had preceded him and been published in virtually every newspaper in the Thirteen Independent States of North America, and he was now the famous victor in the sea battle with the *Shark*. He learned, too, that his three prizes taken on the voyage to Martinique had arrived safely and were in the hands of the Court of Admiralty for condemnation proceedings.*

Captain Wickes reported his vessel to Robert Morris and turned over to him his muskets, his powder, and his Frenchmen. He then turned over his private goods to Robert Morris in his role as a partner in Willing, Morris and Company. Morris sold these to the Philadelphia merchants Mease and Caldwell "at 100 per cent advance on the

---

* Neither Captain Wickes, nor any of his crew, nor their heirs, ever received the prize money due them for these captures. The Marine Committee had little money and kept bad records.

invoice," Bingham's one-half share of the net proceeds totaling £742.13.8. James Mease threw out 86 of the sabers as "very ordinary and unsaleable."

The most important information in Bingham's letters Morris kept to himself, since, as he explained in a formal statement written for the Committee of Secret Correspondence, "the Congress consists of too many members to keep secrets." Besides, he added, "Mr. Morris belongs to all the committees that can properly be employed in receiving and importing the expected supplies from Martinico." He showed the letters to a few friends (who reported them to other friends) and went over the entire correspondence with Franklin when he returned from New York, where he had been engaged with General Howe in fruitless discussions of a peace proposal.

*

In St. Pierre, Bingham busied himself with procuring military supplies and private merchandise. He contracted with at least three French merchant-masters to carry goods to the States of North America. He sent Morris a complete set of papers for a French sloop, with the suggestion that they be used for a vessel fitted out in Philadelphia. He cultivated General d'Argout, Governor de Courcey, and the Intendant, a Monsieur Tascher. A few ships came in from America carrying rice, indigo, tobacco, and flour, and these he sent back laden with the only things he could buy — salt, molasses, sugar, coffee, limes, and rum. Some of this he shipped on his private account with Willing and Morris, some of it for the Secret Committee (of Commerce). The Committee sold the goods at a high price but "we would have preferred more powder, muskets, etc." (So, presumably, would William Bingham.) He succeeded in loading the *Independence* with blankets, coarse cloth, and almost 1000 muskets. The ship was chased into Chincoteague Bay in Virginia, where it delivered its cargo safely. With the American vessels came answers to the first letters Bingham had sent from Martinique. "Your several letters . . . with the several enclosures . . . had been laid before Congress," Benjamin Franklin wrote for the Committee of Secret Correspondence. "We can therefore communicate that satisfaction which we dare say it must afford you to know, that you have so far obtained the approbation of that august body." Mr. Bingham was to convey to his Excellency, the General, "the warmest sentiments of esteem and respect for his person and character, and of gratitude for his favorable attention to the concerns of our much-injured country." Specifically, he was to thank the General "for the information he authorized you to give us . . . and particularly for his disposition to favor our commerce in port." The Committee had received the arms and powder by the *Reprisal*. "They come seasonably, and we wish there had been more. . . ."

With the ship *Betsy* came the first of what was to be a long series of letters from Willing, Morris and Company, written by Robert Morris in his freer, more outspoken character as private trader. The *Betsy* carried 1000 barrels of flour on the public account and forty-four hogsheads of tobacco on their private account. Mr. Morris hoped the tobacco would "get safe to market in which case we shall make a pleasing expedition all around."

On Bingham's question about the propriety of mixing public and private business, the answer was clear. "We (say R. M. the writer hereof) does not see any impropriety in your attending to commercial matters as that will not prevent your attending carefully and assiduously to the more important matters committed to your charge."

Morris was happy to render "a pleasing account sales" of the goods shipped in by Captain Wickes, sold outright to Mease and Caldwell. James Mease, he said, had told him that John Stamper, Esq. (Bingham's maternal grandfather) had "offered to pay him some money for your use but not having your orders nor any present opportunity of remitting it to you he thought it best not to receive it for the present." Morris had sold a shipment of molasses for Bingham and 100 barrels of limes sent jointly by Bingham and Richard Harrison "at vendue on the wharf" for a net profit of £214. This he would invest, as directed, in superfine flour which he would return with 400 additional barrels on the joint Bingham-Morris account.

Virginia and Ocracoke Inlet, North Carolina, were recommended as the safest places for running in merchandise. "Nails, glass (window glass) as well as glass ware is wanted, some coarse hats, coarse stockings and soldiers shoes would sell well. . . . Therefore we think you cannot be at a loss. . . . Nothing can come amiss."

Mr. Morris then favored his young colleague with some further advice:

We think if you could hire a small fast sailing French vessel and dispatch her immediately for Carolina . . . with a cargo of powder, some linens [several words illegible] etc. and you will make a Golden Voyage. You may interest us half or two thirds.

There is some British cruizers on that coast but if the vessel is small she may easily escape by lying hull too every morning at day break until she can see all round her. She will see the enemy when they cannot see her and by setting their course avoid em. She should not pass the Gulf Stream untill the latitude of Charles Town and then run right in. Don't loose a moment in executing this scheme. . . .

and some choice mercantile philosophy:

In short, when cargoes arrive either one way or tother the proffits are ever so great. It is well worth risquing largely for one arrival will pay for two, three or four losses. Therefore its best to keep doing something constantly.

CHAPTER 4

Some Events of a Publick Nature and of Great Importance

The Spirit of Enterprize has seized most people and they are making or trying to make Fortunes. Their attempts will probably have the happy affect of procuring us many Supplys that we stand much in need of.

Robert Morris to William Bingham
October 20, 1776

ST. PIERRE, the loveliest and gayest city in the West Indies, enchanted the stranger with its sounds, its colors, and its people.

Everywhere he heard the sounds of water. In the market square and in the hidden gardens there was the splashing of fountains. In the streets, water from the hills flowed with a ceaseless undertone down the deep, open runnels. Almost every day there were showers, torrents of rain falling in enormous drops. The creole street vendors cried their wares in a French patois pleasant to the ear — clothing, pottery, baskets, herbs, food — above all, food: snails and ducks, mangoes and alligator pears, limes and breadfruit, tiny fish (1000 in a single teacup), pastries, loaves shaped like cucumbers, small maize cakes wrapped in a piece of banana leaf, sweet rice cakes, cakes made of pounded codfish and beans. All day long he heard bare feet patting on the stone-flagged pavement. Three times — at six and twelve and six — the bells of the cathedral tower boomed, marking the rhythm of the day. From the hills at night came the pulsing murmur of crickets and lizards.

Everywhere in the city he saw brilliant, clear color. The steep, narrow streets climbing up the hillside in terraces of steps glowed in the sunlight. The tile roofs of the houses were red, the wooden shutters and verandas green, the cut-stone walls, for the most part, painted lemon-yellow. In the window boxes, on the stalls in the market square, in the gardens were azaleas, jasmine, violets, hibiscus, gardenias, plumbagoes, dahlias, lantanas. Before the city the sea was a deep but translucent blue, with a beach of pebbles and black volcanic sand. Behind the city the mountains were verdant with giant ferns, bamboo trees, and cocoa palms.

A drifting, aimless flow of people constantly filled the Grande Rue — officers and men of the newly reinforced French army, sailors from the fleet, merchant seamen of various nationalities from the ships anchored in the bay. The French *habitants* — 15,000 of them in all Martinique — went about their business of keeping house, running the city, shipping and receiving merchandise, managing the plantations and distilleries.

The pure-blooded Carib Indians, the remarkable race that had originally peopled this island, were gone. After almost a century and a half of French colonization, they had disappeared — they had intermarried, had been killed by overwork, strange diseases, and revolt and insurrection, or had fled to Barbados, St. Vincent, or Dominica. Their characteristics, however, survived them as dominant strains in the new natives of the island. These, a mixture of Carib Indian, African Negro and European white, were the handsomest mixed races of the West Indies. The men, dressed only in *lantchos,* breech-clouts, working in the snake-infested cane fields, in the fishing boats, in the slaughter houses and distilleries, were superbly muscled and proportioned. The *Martiniquaise* was famous for her beauty, grace and physical endurance. Her features were regular, her profile straight, her eyes large and melancholy, her hair rich, long and silky. She wore the turban peculiar to Martinique — a twisted Madras handkerchief, always with a stripe of yellow, fastened with gold brooches, a single end protruding straight up in front like a donkey ear.

Over all this scene loomed the massive, ominous bald mountain — Montagne Pelée, its scarred summit, four-fifths of a mile high, often veiled in white clouds.*

William Bingham fitted smoothly into this life, in the manner of

---

* On May 8, 1902, Mont Pelée erupted with two gigantic explosions, throwing out an all-enveloping cloud of gas and fire. In less than a minute, St. Pierre, then still the gayest, most beautiful and most important city in the French West Indies, was an inferno. All but one of the 28,000 people in the city were suffocated or burned to death in the greatest tragedy in the recorded history of the Western Hemisphere. The city is still in ruins.

an unattached young man in a strange land. He learned to go to sleep at noon; to change to fresh, dry clothes three times a day; to dine at seven; to retire after dinner, because activity ceased at sundown. When he walked in the streets, his mulatto boy walked behind him holding an umbrella over his head. If he walked beyond the edges of the city, he carried a cutlass to protect himself against the venomous fer-de-lance.

There was a French theater he could visit. There was a dancing school that met two or three times a week, where the French creole misses and their brothers learned their minuet and their pavanne. There were cockfights every Sunday morning, or a fight between a fer-de-lance and a mongoose. Social life among the French revolved around the residence and court of the Captain General of the French Caribbees, M. d'Argout. There were a few other Americans besides Bingham in St. Pierre — private merchants and agents of state governments drawn to a trade that had been illegal and was now subject only to the risks of war. They met in the American Coffee House. Bingham generally entertained officers of the visiting American ships in his home.

From time to time that fall American ships arrived in St. Pierre with merchandise and word from home. They brought news of the war, and the news was all bad. General Washington had suffered defeats at Brooklyn Heights and White Plains. Fort Washington on the Hudson fell, almost 3000 men laying down their arms and surrendering an enormous amount of equipment. Retreating through New Jersey, Washington called upon the farmers and villagers to scorch the earth before the invaders; instead, they welcomed the British troops as liberators. He retreated to the Pennsylvania side of the Delaware River with the remnant of a broken army and there swore he would retire beyond the Alleghenies if necessary to wage warfare from behind the mountain barrier.

General Charles Lee, second-ranking Continental officer, was taken in New Jersey, and the peculiar circumstances of his capture gave rise to ugly rumors. "Some are so hardy as to say that he was brought over by the liberal offers of the British general," Bingham wrote to Silas Deane, "but this must certainly be a falsehood. I would not stain the character of so brave a man, an enthusiast for liberty, with so foul a suspicion; neither could I decry human nature so much, as to believe such a proceeding possible. If it could be, how weak are the ties of moral and social duty!"

With one reversal following hard on another, the fine patriotic fervor that had brought a rush of volunteers to the colors a year earlier diminished, and Washington now had an army of fewer than 6000 poorly armed and provisioned men. The State of Maryland, according to rumor, was ready to renounce the Declaration of Independence and ask for terms with the British. John Dickinson was urging negotiations for peace "before we suffer indescribable calamities."

Philadelphia was in turmoil. Civil government ceased to exist. The military took over and removed the public stores from the city. The newspapers stopped publishing. Congress fled to Baltimore, leaving Robert Morris to run the government.* The lawmakers had only recently voted down Washington's plea for a standing army with three-year enlistments; now they overcame their fear of professional military men, their preference for one-year enlistments and their devotion to the state militia. They gave Washington virtually dictatorial powers for the next six months.

"To say that the affairs of America are in a desperate situation, whilst we keep united, is an absurdity," Bingham wrote to Silas Deane, one eye cocked on others who would intercept and read his letter. "Like the hydra headed monster it will push forth new armies in proportion to the numbers defeated. For my part, I have so much of the vertuous courage of an old Roman, as 'never to despair of the Commonwealth'; but indeed at present there is not the least shadow of reason, for I think matters are very favorable for America."

In November Bingham received an urgent, pleading letter from the Secret Committee (of Commerce) signed by Robert Morris and other members. It was delivered by Captain James Robinson, master of the Continental armed sloop *Sachem*, "dispatched for the sole purpose of bringing back such a supply of blankets, coarse cloth, coatings, flannels and other woolen goods suitable for winter wear as you can procure in Martinico. They are already much wanted and will be more so. Therefore we earnestly entreat you to exert your utmost interest to procure . . . a large supply of the above articles. . . . We

* Benjamin Harrison, fat, gross, and profane, wrote to Morris from Baltimore, "If you wish to please your friends, come soon to us, but if you desire to keep out of the damnedest hole in the world come not here. . . . In this infernal sink . . . there is not even a tavern that one can ride to for exercise and amusement."

must not be disappointed of these goods, therefore you must pledge the credit of the United States pretty freely."

Bingham, however, had tried to pledge that credit and failed. He had learned that neither the French merchants nor the governor of the island had confidence in the financial soundness of the United States. They would lend money and supply goods only on the personal guarantee of the young merchant and agent himself. In the first four months of his mission, Bingham risked his personal credit to the total of 250,000 livres Martinique* to buy arms, ammunition, clothing, and food on the public account.

From Robert Morris came what was, for a merchant, very nearly ultimate in despair:

> Our American affairs have not at this time so pleasing an aspect as we could wish, and should they grow much worse, it may not be a desirable thing to bring property hither. . . . It is possible our affairs may go so wrong that the property will be safer with you than with us. . . . If such event is likely to happen we will contrive you the earliest notice of it to prevent you shipping goods either on your or our account at any time when they might be likely to come into the jaws of the enemy.

In November there arrived in the Continental sloop *Independence* a load of tobacco and bar iron sent on the public account, and a young man, William Hodge of Philadelphia, bearing a whole sheaf of carefully sealed letters and documents. These, the Committee of Secret Correspondence said in one of several official letters that Hodge delivered to Bingham, were "of a publick nature and of great importance." Bingham would please to show Mr. Hodge (a young man "of good character, family and alertness in the public service") proper attention, assist him in procuring an immediate passage to France in a good ship, and supply him with any money he needed. "You will serve your country by forwarding Mr. Hodge without

* The approximate comparative value of the livre (replaced by the franc around 1794) was as follows:

1 livre of Paris equaled	19.1 cents
1 livre tournois equaled	15.3 cents
1 livre Martinique equaled	12.6 cents

Thus Bingham was in debt for the Congress for $31,500.

The livre of Paris was very roughly the equivalent of today's dollar in purchasing power.

delay; but you need not mention to the General how urgent we are on this point, unless you find it will promote his dispatch." Bingham was to let the Committee know the name of the vessel on which Hodge sailed and its master.

Young Mr. Hodge indeed carried with him the materials of an important international event. Congress, acting on intelligence coming in from its agents in London and Paris and from Bingham in St. Pierre, was now convinced that France, the ancient enemy and rival of Great Britain, was disposed to help the insurgent colonies. Four days after Captain Wickes had arrived in Philadelphia in mid-September with Bingham's letters, Congress approved a draft of a proposed treaty of amity and commerce between France and the revolting colonies. Silas Deane was raised in rank from Agent to Commissioner, and he was to be joined in Paris by two other Commissioners, Benjamin Franklin and Thomas Jefferson.* They were directed to hire or buy eight line-of-battle ships in Europe for the American service and to "live in such stile and manner at the court of France, as they may find suitable and necessary to support the dignity of their public character."

Franklin collected all his available cash — £4000 — and lent it to the Continental government. He gathered his two grandsons, one of them the natural son of his natural son ("a double-distilled bastard," Franklin's enemies called him) and on October 29, from Chester, he sailed in Captain Wickes' *Reprisal*. Wickes carried his charge and a £3000 cargo of indigo to Nantes in one month, capturing on the way two English brigs laden with cargoes of wine, alcohol, wood, and flaxseed. He then disguised his vessel as a merchantman and went on to become the terror of English shipping in European waters, a full year before John Paul Jones sailed into those waters in the *Ranger*.† Dr. Franklin went on to Paris to join a delighted Commissioner Deane and to receive an almost hysterical welcome by the French, who fancied that in this shrewd, sophisticated savant they saw a backwoods

---

* This was news requiring the deepest secrecy, but a few days later, as Robert Morris was on his way to the Senate House, an acquaintance stopped him to ask, "Are Dr. Franklin and Mr. Jefferson really going ambassador to Paris?"

† Captain Wickes and all but one of his crew of 130 men were lost in a storm off the Newfoundland Banks in November, 1777. The cook alone was rescued, apparently by a fishing vessel.

philosopher and patriot, the pure, simple, natural new man of the New World.

Mr. Jefferson, unfortunately, declined the appointment as Commissioner to France, and in his stead Congress chose Dr. Arthur Lee of Virginia, who was acting secretly as its agent in London. It was an unhappy choice, for Dr. Lee, a malevolent and sinister man, caused trouble and discord wherever he went. He went to France on receiving his appointment and within weeks was accusing Franklin and Deane of plundering the public and of conspiring against American independence.

Young William Hodge carried with him the advance documents of these great developments: a copy of the proposed treaty of amity and commerce, instructions to the Commissioners, and their "letters of credence." Duplicate and triplicate sets of these documents were delivered to Bingham by way of St. Eustatia and Cap François, both to be forwarded to Deane. Hodge sailed from St. Pierre in a good conveyance, carrying a friendly letter of introduction from Bingham. He arrived safely, and during his sojourn in France worked so openly and assiduously against Great Britain that he embarrassed the French government and so achieved the distinction of being the first American ever sentenced to a term in the Bastille.

In one of the several letters Hodge delivered to Bingham came some cryptic but pressing orders. Following instructions, he called on General d'Argout. Had the General received any arms or ammunition from a Monsieur Hortalez in France, with directions to deliver them to any persons properly authorized by Congress to receive them? The answer was no. Had the General had any advices of such shipments? Again, no. He was authorized by Congress to receive the shipments, Bingham said cautiously, giving his receipt on behalf of the United States. Would the General notify him when they did arrive? The General so promised.

Bingham followed the same procedure with Governor de Courcey, being careful, as instructed, to "open no more of this business than circumstances shall make absolutely necessary." The Governor knew nothing of Monsieur Hortalez or his shipments. Bingham then sailed in a French vessel to St. Eustatia, carrying his letters of authorization. There he addressed himself to Johannes de Graaf, the Dutch

Governor, a stanch friend of the American Colonies, asking the same questions and receiving the same answers. And then he sailed back to St. Pierre and waited for advices of M. Hortalez' shipments.

He was unwittingly involved in one of the most bizarre developments of the American Revolution. "Hortalez" was a cover name for Pierre Augustin Caron de Beaumarchais, forty-four, ex-watchmaker, ex-music teacher, playwright (*The Barber of Seville*), adventurer, courtier, and confidential agent of Louis XV and of his successor, Louis XVI.

Beaumarchais in 1775 went several times on the King's business to London. There, in contact with various political radicals, he developed a passionate enthusiasm for all things American, and especially for her armed resistance to Great Britain. Back in Paris, he read Bonvouloir's favorable report based on his secret meetings with the Committee of Secret Correspondence. Such a nation, he advised the King in a famous "Peace or War" memorandum, was invincible. If Britain won the war, she would defray her costs by seizing the French West Indian islands. If America won without French help, the Americans, enraged at France, would join the British in the attack. "What to do? We can preserve peace only by giving aid to the Americans. Two or three million [livres] may save us our sugar islands, worth three hundred."

Louis was persuaded by this specious reasoning and a plan was concocted that would furnish aid under the thin guise of a commercial venture headed by Beaumarchais. France and Spain each secretly gave him a subsidy of one million livres. He used this to found a commercial establishment, Roderique Hortalez and Co., and undertook to deliver to the Americans munitions selected for him from the arsenals of France. Beaumarchais paid for these arms out of his subsidy, and he was to demand payment from the Americans in American products. It was important, Foreign Minister Vergennes said, to make both the English and the Americans believe this was an individual enterprise in no way supported by the French government.

Beaumarchais revealed his plans to Arthur Lee in London in the summer of 1776. He promised to send £200,000 sterling in military supplies to America by way of Martinique, St. Eustatia and Cap François; American agents should make application to the governors of those islands. But with the arrival in Paris of Silas Deane, the commissioned agent of the American Congress, Beaumarchais naturally ceased to communicate with Lee and dealt only with Deane. Lee was furious. When Deane told Congress that it must pay for the French arms, Lee wrote that the arms were an outright gift from the King, that no payment was expected, and that Deane, as Robert Morris' partner, was an "adventurer" attempting to line his own pockets by charging for goods he had got for nothing — all this despite the fact that letters exchanged between Lee and Beaumarchais had specifically discussed what American products would be sent in payment.

Congress, confused at receiving two such conflicting reports from its agents, interspersed with occasional letters from Beaumarchais proclaiming in extravagant language his "indefatigable zeal" in the noble cause of American liberty, split into two factions. One, anti-Deane and anti-French, was led by the Lee brothers of Virginia (Arthur, Richard Henry, and Francis Lightfoot), Thomas Paine, and John and Samuel Adams of Boston. The other, pro-Deane and pro-French, was led by Robert Morris, James Madison, and John Jay. The two factions would in time become so embroiled that for six months, in the middle of a war of independence, all other work of the Congress virtually stopped.

"I shall send you in October," Deane wrote to Robert Morris from Bordeaux on September 17, "clothing for twenty thousand men, thirty thousand fusils, one hundred tons of powder, two hundred brass cannon, twenty-four brass mortars, with shells, shot, lead, etc., in proportion." For these and other goods, for chartering and equipping ships, and for advancing pay of officers and seamen, Beaumarchais spent not only the two million livres advanced him and an additional subsidy of one million livres, but went into debt to the French government for 2,600,000 livres more. (Like most others who lent money to the Americans during the Revolution, he was never repaid.) These were the arms and ammunition that William Bingham was to receive for the Congress in the West Indies and transship to the mainland.

Weeks passed, and some arms and supplies came in, but in nothing like the quantities described by Deane. The largest shipments were 200 tons of powder — 4000 barrels — sent from Nantes and Bordeaux. There were misfires in France; the French government blew hot and cold and recalled several vessels; and shipments were delayed because of a dispute over the route they should take. Franklin and some of the French thought the ships should proceed directly across the Atlantic to American ports to avoid the many British cruisers and privateers in the West Indies. Deane and some French felt the goods should be sent as French property as far as the West India islands and from there run into the mainland in American vessels. If these were overtaken, France would not be implicated. And as Bingham explained earnestly to the Commissioners in Paris, "Very few French masters of vessels are acquainted with the coast of America, and admitting they were, large ships cannot take the advantage of running into small inlets and harbors as lesser vessels may. Besides all the Continental [U.S.] vessels sail with skillful pilots, which greatly lessens the risk."

In the meantime, American vessels sailed into St. Pierre to carry back the Deane-Hortalez supplies. Bingham loaded their half-empty holds with such West India goods as he could buy for his government on credit: rum and molasses. Congress complained again that it was not getting the expected arms and ammunition but suggested that he charter another vessel and send more rum and molasses, to be paid for by return cargoes. The return cargoes, unfortunately, came seldom and never in quantity sufficient to pay for the produce Bingham had bought. He began to be dunned by French merchants and the island government.

He wrote on January 17, 1777, to acknowledge arrival of the brig *Cornelia and Molly* with a cargo of flour and tobacco, in which the Committee of Correspondence had one-third interest for the government, Willing and Morris held one-third, and other private investors owned the rest. Bingham itemized the total amount owed him by the government, Livres 211,948, "which I am now beginning to be pressed for, and which I hope from your speedy remittance I shall soon be enabled to discharge; otherwise my credit in a commercial capacity will be entirely ruined, for this place is noted for its punctuality in dealing." It was the first of many such pleas Bingham was to write.

Morris, writing for the committees of Congress, was apologetic.

I am very sensible how necessary it is that you should be well supported with remittances and as desirous of sending as you are of receiving them, indeed I fear you may have been distressed but at the same time it has not been in our power to do what we wished. You must be sensible that with a river full of ice, our bay full of men of war, and Gen. Howe at our gates would not admit of the usuall attention to business or the same facility in doing it, but I now hope to make you a little easier on this subject, after a while at least.

When he wrote these words, Morris was virtually running the affairs of the United States; he had sent General Washington $50,000 raised on his own signature, and he was engaged in a strenuous and successful effort to find other funds and supplies for the army.

Despite his disappointment, Bingham did not lessen his efforts to procure goods. "I went on as cheerfully in contracting new engagements for the service," he said later, "as if I had received the most ample remittances for the old ones."

About this time, the Committee of Secret Correspondence wrote to Franklin, Deane and Lee in Paris, "We observe that Mr. Deane sent his despatches for this Committee open to Mr. Bingham; but though we have a good opinion of that gentleman, yet we think him rather too young to be made acquainted with the business passing between you and us; and therefore wish this may not be done in cases of much importance."

Bingham's expanding private business gave him the means to forestall his creditors and to preserve the credit of his government. Morris now called for shipment of more private goods, having concluded that "our publick affairs wear a better aspect than when we wrote you last." With Messrs. Samuel and J. H. Delapp of Bordeaux he arranged a £2000 credit for Bingham to draw on. "The *Cornelia and Molly* shall go back to you," he wrote, "but not on Publick Account as we want to throw funds into your hands. Indeed we shall make you as many consignments as possible." Bingham somehow found goods for the Willing and Morris ships and for the new commercial contacts established by Morris. The deposits credited to his name in Philadelphia with John Benezet, his attorney and husband to his sister Hannah, mounted up.

The news of the surprise victory over the Hessians at Trenton on Christmas day, followed by the success at Princeton, indicated that American affairs indeed wore a better aspect. "Our countrymen, who had become rather too remiss and negligent," Bingham wrote triumphantly to Deane, "have now rouzed at the approach of danger, and have encountered it with spirit & intrepidity. . . . In consequence of this recent success, there is the greatest prospect of our opening the ensuing campaign, with singular & distinguished advantages."

Beaumarchais's ships began to arrive early in 1777, in time to have a profound effect on the campaign. They were handsome vessels and heavily laden — the *Amphitrite, Mercure, Flammand, Mère Bobie, Seine, Thérèse, Amélia,* and *Marie Catherine.* Most were sent direct from France to Portsmouth, New Hampshire, where they were received with great public acclamation. A lesser number sailed by way of the West Indies. All arrived safe in American ports except the frigate *Seine.*

Bingham removed two-thirds of the *Seine*'s enormous cargo (muskets, mortars, bombs, cloth, and camp equipage) for reshipment to American ports in smaller vessels. He then persuaded General d'Argout to try a stratagem on the British. The *Seine* was cleared out with papers as for a storeship dispatched to the French island of Miquelon, just south of Newfoundland, with the understanding that it would turn and make a run for Boston. The British captured the vessel, found a letter of instructions to the pilot signed by Bingham, and condemned ship and cargo as property of the rebellious Americans.

The French angrily protested the taking of their ship; the English replied with angrier charges of French duplicity; and the incident became a celebrated one and very nearly a casus belli. In his report to Congress, Bingham wrote:

> That part of her cargo which was taken out was consequently saved to the United States, & the capture of the remainder was so happily disposed to occasion a subject of reciprocal complaint & altercation betwixt the two courts, that everyone believed I had fixed the matter accordingly, & gave me credit for my plan, as a deep scheme of Machiavellian policy.

CHAPTER 5

The Fire Is Lighted at
the Extremities

*There is one Bingham an Agent from the Rebels who resides at Mar-
tinico, and who gives Commissions to Ships fitted out there, which are
manned by French Men and have at most one American on board; if
these Ships meet with any trading Vessel of ours, they take her, and
carry her into Some one of your Islands, where the Ship and Cargo
are sold: if on the contrary they are boarded by any of our Cruizers,
the Men all speak French and show French papers.*

Lord Stormont, British Minister at Versailles,
to the Comte de Vergennes, French Foreign Minister
Versailles, June 11, 1777

MILITARY SUPPLIES from France would help, but the great hope for
independence lay in drawing France into the war against England.
Every American official knew it, and bringing it about was the principal object of American policy in 1777.

William Carmichael of Maryland had a plan of action for making
France fight England. He was a wild and well-to-do young man, a
widower, who was enjoying life in England when the American Revolution broke out. He intended to go to St. Petersburg, for he had
heard that the Empress Catherine liked handsome young men and he
thought she might find "curiosity in an American." When he got to
Paris, however, patriotism overcame desire and he volunteered to
serve as secretary to Silas Deane. On June 25, 1777, in Paris, Carmichael unburdened himself in a long letter to William Bingham. He
made his point bluntly : "I think your situation [is] of singular consequence to bring on a war so necessary to assure our independence."
Unfortunately, the weak French court followed the "miserable policy" of avoiding war and shunning every action in Europe that might
appear to violate its treaties with England. Therefore, "it is our business to force a war on the two countries in spite of their inclinations

to the contrary." This might best be done by fitting out privateers in Martinique, manned with Frenchmen, and Bingham was the man to do it. This would excite the passions of the two nations and provoke them "to such atrocious acts of reprisal and mutual violence as will occasion clamors . . . altercations . . . and breach of treaty."

Bingham was six months or more ahead of Carmichael in this proposed course. According to a report he later made to the Congress, he "took an early and active part in the arming of privateers out of this port . . . generally manned with the subjects of France," and by the time Carmichael wrote he had a small fleet in action. He was under the orders of Congress to "encourage as many private adventurers as you can." He wanted capital, profit and supplies, and in 1777 the best way to get all three was to arm a merchant ship and engage in licensed buccaneering.

With Richard Harrison, the commercial agent for Virginia, as his first partner, and then with Robert Morris, Thomas Willing and others, Bingham would buy or engage a ship and sign up a captain. He would post a bond of between $10,000 and $20,000, depending on the size of the ship, as a guaranty of good conduct, and fill out one of his blank letters of Marque and Reprisal commissioning the captain to attack and seize British shipping. Shares were frequently sold in such vessels and were widely distributed and exchanged.

Bingham customarily engaged a crew for one voyage at a time. He advanced a bounty to the men, to be deducted from their prize money when their captured ships were brought into port, condemned by an Admiralty Court, and sold. Generally the meeting between privateer and merchantman was brief and bloodless. Bingham's ships, like most others, carried various sets of appropriate papers. Lord Stormont, British minister at Versailles, complained persistently to the French court that Bingham's privateers pretended to be French if boarded by British cruisers, but were belligerently American at the sight of a British merchant vessel.

The hunting was good in the West Indies. Up to February, 1777, Americans captured about 250 British vessels engaged in the rich West India trade, carrying cargoes worth an estimated $10 million. Of one fleet of sixty vessels bound from Ireland for the Indies, thirty-five were captured by American privateers. In the course of a single week, fourteen prize vessels were brought into Martinique. Insurance rates in England rose above the highest levels of the Seven Years War; British merchants began to ship their goods on French vessels; many of the British West India houses were ruined; the price of tobacco trebled; the revenues of England declined appreciably; and Parliament appointed a committee to conduct an inquiry. Prize goods were so plentiful in St. Pierre and Fort Royal that French sailors were going from door to door offering Irish linens for two dollars a piece and silk stockings for one dollar.

As a merchant with old friends and trading connections in England and its possessions, Robert Morris at first opposed privateering; but as time and the war progressed, and as America suffered desperately for want of a navy, his opposition softened. Early in 1777 there arrived as a passenger in St. Pierre Captain George Ord, a hero of a raid made two years earlier on the powder arsenal of Bermuda, for whom Morris had obtained a privateer's commission from the Congress. "You may depend on his good conduct and bravery," Morris wrote to Bingham, "and I hope you will procure a good vessel well manned and fitted for him. I think you should call her the *Retaliation*." Then, two months later: "I dare say Captain Ord and you have done something clever together by this time."

Bingham procured a ship for Captain Ord, a brig of eight guns with a crew of twenty-five, and called her the *Retaliation*. Morris wished his participation to be kept quiet, but on April 25, 1777, he informed Bingham, "My scruples about privateering are all done away. I have seen [so] much rapine, plunder and distruction denounced against and executed on the Americans that I join you in thinking it a duty to oppose and distress so merciless an enemy in every shape we can. Therefore it matters not who knows my concern with Ord as I am now ready to encrease the number of my engagements in that way."

And he added, "I have lately had the pleasure to hear that Ord in company with the *Rattlesnake* had taken and sent into Martinico nine sail of transport ships [and] two Guinea men [slavers] and two sail of transports into St. Eustatia. If this be true, and it seems well authenticated, we shall make a fine hand of it." The rumor was true, and Bingham found himself the fortunate part owner, by right of capture, of two armed Guinea ships carrying ivory and 498 African slaves.

The profits of such prizes were enormous. The net proceeds from the sale of one captured British cargo of coffee, rum, sugar, and molasses shipped out of Hispaniola (Haiti) amounted to £13,780, of which Bingham's share was £4593. Not all "adventures," of course, were so successful, and some ended in substantial loss with capture of ship, cargo, crew, and captain.

Bingham's most ambitious single privateering venture ended up as a costly failure, though it appears to have answered his main purpose of goading France and England into acts that would lead to war. It involved Coctiny de Prejent, an Acadian-born sea captain whom Bingham had sent with a cargo and a warm letter of recommendation to Robert Morris.

Prejent sold his small ship in Philadelphia and with Morris' help bought a brig, the *Esperance*, and loaded her with flour and lumber for Gaudeloupe. "Mr. Prejent has behaved much like a gentleman and a man of honor here," Morris wrote to Bingham. "Your recommendation induced us to join him in this concern." Willing and Morris invested £2609 in half ownership of Prejent's ship and cargo. "He had a very narrow escape at our cape," Morris said after Prejent sailed in February. "I hope Mons. Payint [sic] will send back the ship *Esperance* here loaden with molasses, if he does and she gets in the voyage will make a ministerial fortune. . . . We shall do great things indeed." A hundred hogsheads of molasses, he said, would bring £10,000.

Something went wrong, for in April Morris was "sorry to hear that Mr. Prejent's voyage from hence to Guadeloupe will end indifferently." Prejent sold the *Esperance* and cargo in Basseterre ("a fine ship sold under her value . . . shamefully given away," Morris wrote) and put the whole sum, including Morris' half share, into outfitting privateers. Bingham informed Morris that he had been "extremely importunate" with Prejent to obtain a settlement, but that "he has entered into the rage of privateering which employs all the funds he can lay his hands on, but I shall now insist upon his laying before me a state of that account." Bingham, however, invested "a considerable part" of 87,054 livres of government money (never recovered) in Prejent's privateers.

Prejent made an outstanding success of his privateering ventures. Indeed, he became a scourge of British shipping in the West Indies, and Lord Stormont three times made his depredations the occasion for protests to the French court. In July, Comte de Vergennes admitted that General d'Argout's conduct had been irregular in Martinique, but he insisted that it had been so without the approbation or knowledge of the French court. The French government had discovered, Vergennes said with a straight face, that Argout suffered himself to be governed entirely by a M. de Prejent, the very man Lord Stormont had complained about earlier. Consequently, Argout had been recalled and replaced by a new governor of Martinique, the Marquis de Bouillé. The new governor had found great abuses and had immediately proceeded to correct them. He had disarmed several vessels that cruised under American colors and punished the offenders.

Lord Stormont was not impressed.

> I interrupted M. de Vergennes to say that I was glad to hear that M. de Bouillé had taken a different line of conduct from his predecessor, but added that I knew he had had long conferences with Bingham, which I thought was *de très mauvais augure* [a very bad omen].

M. de Bouillé's character and instructions, Vergennes replied suavely, were such that he would act properly.

Six months later, Stormont was again in Vergennes' office. He complained first of certain improprieties in Europe.

> I told M. de Vergennes that serious as these grievances were, they were far short of what passed at Martinico. I then took my papers out of my pocket — and when I gave it to M. de Vergennes said that it would show him M. de Bouillé's conduct, as it really was, and begged him to peruse it with attention, and then tell me whether all this resembles Peace or War. I said this decently, but sharply. He seemed struck, took the paper, read it with great attention, and when he saw the number of Privateers fitted out by Prejean [sic], he exclaimed, Why, this is a fleet!

Vergennes swore that these developments were contrary to French policy and unknown to the French court. Stormont replied:

It is facts, Sir, we look to. It is by them alone that nations are to be judged. Your Governor suffers these privateers to be fitted out against us; he authorizes this Prejean to make war against the subjects of Great Britain. . . . In my apprehension of things, Martinico is making war against Great Britain.

I observed to his Excellency . . . You hate long reasoning, Sir, and I will be very short; I will say but this, if these acts of hostility, carried on against us at Martinico are suffered to continue, your Excellency and I are giving ourselves a great deal of unnecessary trouble in endeavoring to keep matters quiet here. *Vous Savez aussi bien que moi, M. le Comte, que si le Feu s'allume aux extrémités il gagnera bientôt le centre.** He did not dispute this, but assured me that the matter should be inquired into, and ended with saying, that the fellow Prejean must be removed.

Despite Prejent's power and success, he did not settle with Willing and Morris for the half-share he owed on the *Esperance* and its cargo. His action caused a quarrel, and very nearly a rupture, between Morris and Bingham.

Morris had always scolded his young partner for actions that displeased him, in the manner of an older man to an apprentice; and though the rebukes were interspersed with friendly praise, Bingham must have felt an accumulating resentment from his first weeks in Martinique. For example, Morris wrote as early as October 20, 1776:

Captain Lockhart says the business of his vessel was not well attended to or he might have been here some weeks ago. This should not happen. Vessels now sail at a monstrous expence and the dispatch ought to be quick. If you cannot attend closely you had better get Mr. Harrison or some other to do the business or hire an excellent clerk to assist you.

And on a shipment of blankets that Morris had expected:

I have in the meantime received [several letters] which I consider the least satisfactory of any I ever did receive from you because I think some of the bales of blankets would have come in the same

---

* You know as well as I do, Monsieur le Comte, that if the fire is lighted at the extremities it will soon arrive at the center.

vessels that brought these letters. Why they were not shipped I am at a loss to tell as I know that Captn Feariss took in freight not so advantageous to him as these blankets would have been and I am informed others did the same. If these goods are detained in order to force me to send vessels on purpose for them and by that means to force from me the remittances you write so pressingly for, it is very well. I shall only wish I had sooner known the ground we stand on.

With Morris' anger at the sins of Captain Prejent, the rebukes multiplied, and for a time Morris signed himself "Dear Sir, Your Obdt HbleSvt" instead of "Your Affectionate Friend."

Willing and Morris was heavily indebted to Bingham — 77,596 livres in January, 1778. The debt, Morris wrote, "sits heavy on me," and when Bingham asked Morris to "extinguish" it, there was further cause for rancor:

> I cannot help thinking you have been somewhat to blame in suffering W&M to be so basely treated by that Gent [Prejent]. You knew he had half of our ship, her cargo and freight in his hand. You knew he was ordered to pay you the whole and I really think it was your duty to have insisted on the payment whilst he had the money instead of suffering him to fit out privateers with it. . . . If you had done this you would have little reason to write me in so pressing a stile for remittances. I mention this affair that you may recollect the reason of our being in your debt, that it is in some degree unexpected and entirely your own fault. . . . You may gather that it is not necessary to be so pressing with me about remittances, indeed if I had been master of my time I should long since have had money in your hands instead of being indebted. . . .

And, finally, with dry irony:

> I shall be glad to hear that Mr. Prejent was so successful in Hispaniola as to have secured sufficient property there to pay his debts. As to himself, I fear he was lately killed in an engagement off the east end of Jamaica.

Bingham's letters to Morris and to Willing and Morris are lost. His responses to these rebukes can only be conjectured, and, in small part, recreated from Morris' side of the correspondence. The quarrel came to a head, eventually, and was resolved by a manly expression of regret from Morris:

> I attend particularly to that of the 14th whereby I observe mine of the 21st November has wounded your feelings. I am sorry for it. My own disappointment worked on my mind at the time and probably occasioned my expressions on the subject of our debt and detention of the blankets to be more pointed than they should have been. Be assured, my dear Sir, that my regard and friendship for you never altered or abated and this being the case I should not take notice of some expressions in your present letters that might afford room for animadversion if I were so disposed. Perhaps we have both said rather too much. Therefore let us stop.

Bingham was not a man to hold a grudge, and his next letter was accompanied by a present of sweetmeats and oranges for Mrs. Morris.

The last reference to the Prejent affair appears in a letter of January 27, 1779, from Bingham to the Committee of Commerce (formerly the Secret Committee). In this letter he itemized the sale of several prizes credited to the account of Congress, and he told of shipping fifty cases of arms. He once again rendered a statement of the sums Congress owed him on the public account and again begged for payment. And he explained his inability to collect the money owed by Captain Prejent:

> I was induced to give credit to Mr. Prejent for so large a sum as appears in the sales against him, from the consideration of the employments that he made of the articles he stands indebted for, which was fitting out privateers to cruize against the enemies of the United States.

Throughout their dispute, Bingham and Morris conducted their business and personal affairs as usual. They went to considerable pains together to rescue Charles Willing, Thomas Willing's brother, from "a most disagreeable situation" he had involved himself in as a merchant in Barbados, resulting from a draft for £7000 written without funds to cover it. Morris dispatched Captain Nicholas Biddle and the *Randolph* to the West Indies with detailed orders to call at once on William Bingham for military stores. ("As you command the first American frigate that has got to sea, it is expected that you contend warmly on all necessary occasions for the honor of the American flag.") The medicines sent in by Bingham on their private account sold in Virginia "at the highest prices ever given." And Morris reported, "Mr. John Benezet hinted to me that your mother might possibly want some money. I sent her word she could command from me whatever she wanted and I shall supply her on your account whenever she chooses." Bingham sent her $1600 through Morris.

In July (1777), Bingham waited on the new governor of Martinique, the Marquis de Bouillé, and offered the congratulations of the Committee on his appointment to the post. François Claude Amour, the Marquis de Bouillé, member of an ancient family of France, was a career officer who had joined the army at fourteen and become a colonel at twenty-two. Now, at thirty-eight, he had been made governor general of Les Iles du Vent — the Windward Islands — to pacify mounting English resentment at the war being waged from Martinique. Bingham's relations with General d'Argout had been friendly and effective, and now Argout had been sacrificed to further French policy. What would his relations be with a new governor sent to introduce a new policy?

At the time of Bouillé's appointment, the English were seizing and condemning American goods found on French ships, even though the goods had been bought and were being delivered by French merchants. Bingham was forced to send a number of ships to Europe in order to dispose of produce he could not sell in the West Indies. To the Commissioners in Paris he wrote on May 19:

> French merchants at present absolutely refuse to purchase for the European market; as many of their vessels have been already visited, and American produce . . . taken out and confiscated. This is a matter of a very alarming nature, strikes deep at the root of our commerce with the West Indies, and indeed will effectually put a stop to it. . . . Surely the French nation will not put up with such a wanton exertion of authority which the English assume to themselves. Surely they will not permit so gross an insult to be offered to their flag without resenting it.*

* Franklin gave this letter to M. Grand, leading banker-merchant in France, for distribution in influential French circles.

Governor d'Argout and the West Indian French merchants vehemently protested the English seizures, but they continued.

On Bouillé's arrival in Martinique, he announced a stunning reversal of French policy. France would now permit England to stop her ships without protest, search them, and remove any American goods found. This ruling was followed by others as drastic. The French issued orders to stop the vessels loading for American ports in France, ordered American privateers out of French harbors, prohibited the sale of prizes in French ports, and returned some captured British ships in French ports to their owners. The French had lighted the fire at the extremities; now they were alarmed at what they had done. Vergennes was not yet ready for war with England; a strong faction in France was opposed to war; and so French policy veered.

From Bingham's letters it is apparent that he believed the French moves were temporary and imposed solely for the sake of appearances. Several long private conferences with the new governor — the meetings Stormont felt were such a bad omen — strengthened him in this belief. Bouillé was no weakling; but in 1777 he was considerate, cooperative and friendly to William Bingham to such a degree that he seems almost to have been manipulated by that determined young man.*

"My situation at this time was critical," Bingham later reported to Congress.

> [France] seemed determined to adhere to the principles of political prudence, in avoiding every step that might lead to a declaration of war. The expostulations of the British Governor against my conduct became every day more and more importunate, but a political maneuvre which I had recourse to, and which would not be prudent to commit to paper, inclined the General not to regard them, although I am confident he thus acted in violation of positive orders received from his court. . . .

Many of the trading cities of England, he said, had sent petitions to Parliament complaining of the active part the people of Martinique

---

* Fifteen years later, early in the French Revolution, Bouillé ruthlessly suppressed a mutiny of his soldiers at Metz and put down an uprising of the garrison at Nancy with what was considered "cruel energy."

were taking in the American war and of the depredations committed on their property. The French court frequently issued "ordonnances" requiring the governor of Martinique to remedy and redress the grievances complained of.

> But I always found some plausible pretext to prevent their taking effect; — sometimes, by acting in such a manner as to save appearances; — sometimes by convincing the General that it was naturally to be expected that the reins of government would be relaxed, at a distance from the seat of empire, and that these ordonnances were only political strokes, intended to appease the minds of the English, untill France was prepared to assume a higher and more imposing tone. Indeed, I . . . have often been complained of to the General as a very dangerous person.

By August 1, Bingham was so deep in the new governor's confidence that he was able to report to Congress the movement of a French sloop of war to the American coast on a secret mission. Paul Wentworth, an American who was chief of British spies in Paris, reported the news to the British head of intelligence: "W. Bingham writes that the Governor of Martinique was dispatching a frigate or sloop of war to New York, pretendedly to demand some French subjects detained by Admiral and General Howe, but in truth to the Colonies on a secret service which he does not mention."

Little important news of this kind, no matter how secret, escaped British intelligence. Wentworth, in the fall of 1776, had recruited into his service Dr. Edward Bancroft of Massachusetts, thirty-two, writer, inventor, authority on tropical plants, member of the Royal College of Physicians, member of the Royal Society under the sponsorship of his friend and confidant, Benjamin Franklin. Dr. Bancroft became Dr. Franklin's secretary, lived in his household in Paris through the first year of his service, and conveyed detailed information to London on everything of interest concerning the Commissioners. He wrote his reports in invisible ink, signed them "Edward Edwards," placed them in bottles, sealed the bottles, and deposited them in a hole in a tree on the south terrace of the Tuileries. A messenger picked these up at nine-thirty every Tuesday evening and left behind in other bottles any communications to Bancroft from Lord Stormont. Bancroft lived in daily terror of being detected and disgraced; but he would live out his long life in America after the war, honored as a patriot and intimate of the great Dr. Franklin. Dr. Arthur Lee suspected that Dr. Bancroft was an English spy — but Dr. Arthur Lee was inclined to think everyone was an English spy. He did not, however, suspect his own secretary, a Mr. Holker, who was also one of Paul Wentworth's agents.

Bancroft, of course, was the source of the embarrassingly detailed information Stormont reported to the Comte de Vergennes on the activities of Bingham, Beaumarchais, Deane, Argout, and Bouillé. Bingham never knew it, but on one occasion Dr. Bancroft directed at him the most insulting comment a spy can make on a victim. On May 27, 1777, he wrote in his invisible ink, "The agent at Martinico, Mr. Bingham, writes us often, but his letters are not of great importance, though perhaps some extracts from them may not be altogether useless."

CHAPTER 6

☆

The Fire Reaches the Center

We are highly pleased with your assiduity in business, for the facility of which we wish you in future to put only one letter on each sheet and to number them progressively beginning your next with Number One at the top. . . . We will like in future your omission of philosophical and rhetorical compositions — matter and politeness being all that is necessary in letters of business. We keep no copy of this letter.

Secret Committee to William Bingham
September (?) 1777

FRENCH POLICY became still more cautious in the autumn of 1777, for clearly the Americans seemed about to lose the war. Washington had not been able to conduct a spring or summer campaign. Burgoyne was moving down from Canada in command of a large army; he had taken Ticonderoga and was heading for Albany. Howe was marching to take Philadelphia.

On Sunday, August 24, the main body of the American army, about 10,000 men, marched through Philadelphia with Washington and Lafayette riding at their head. The column crossed the floating bridge at High (Market) Street and took up positions south of the city. In order to impress the populace, a pathetic effort was made to dress the troops smartly. Each man wore a sprig of green in his cap as a symbol of the uniform he did not have, and on that day he was relieved of carrying his mess kettle. "Strollers" were kept out of the line. The drums and fifes of each brigade were ordered to play a quick step, "but with such moderation that the men may step to it without dancing along or totally disregarding the music, which has been too often the case."

These men were disastrously defeated a few weeks later at Brandywine in Chester County, and again at Paoli and at Germantown. Congress and the state government fled the city once again, this time inland to Lancaster. The State House bell was taken to Allentown, the public money of Pennsylvania was sent to Easton, and the High Street bridge was removed.

General Howe sent word to the townspeople through Thomas Willing that they should stay quietly in their homes when the city was occupied; no person or property would be molested. The city waited. On the morning of September 26, Lord Cornwallis led some 3000 men down the Second Street Road, past Christ Church, past the Old Court House, through Market Square. He rode at the head of two squadrons of smartly uniformed light dragoons, followed by a train of artillery and splendidly equipped companies of red-coated, white-wigged grenadiers. The Hessian grenadiers followed: green-clad with yellow leggings, their helmets fronted with brass, their faces somber and fierce with huge mustachios, their drums seeming to beat out the words *plunder, plunder, plunder.* Except for some cheering Tories, the inhabitants were quiet.

Cornwallis set up a temporary camp in the area at the south edge of town, known as "Society Hill" (because it was land that had been given to the Free Society of Traders), and arrayed his artillery in the State House yard. General Howe took for his quarters the fine Market Street house of the departed Richard Penn. He appointed Joseph Galloway as civilian head of the city.

Thomas Willing remained in Philadelphia throughout the occupation, doing so, he later explained, to keep his business and property from being confiscated by the British and so lost to the republic. He and his family — a wife and ten children, the oldest of them a girl of thirteen — remained socially aloof from the British. When Lord Howe sent Galloway to the house with an oath of allegiance, Willing refused to sign it. Morris disapproved of Willing's decision to remain in the occupied city and because of it dissolved the partnership between them. "I shall henceforth do business in my own name and on my own account," he wrote to Bingham.

By the rules of warfare of that day, the fall of an enemy's capital city meant his capitulation and the end of the war. Many Englishmen felt that nothing now remained but to clean up isolated pockets of rebel resistance. Certainly the loss was a blow to patriot hopes. Philadelphia was the largest city on the American continent, the busiest seaport, the shipbuilder, the center of finance, commerce, government, and manufacturing.

Bingham was deeply shocked. In sending the news to the Commissioners at Paris he wrote, "I think [Washington's] army could not have behaved with that bravery, which should distinguish troops, to whom the defence of a city that was the seat of Congress and the pride of America, was committed — neither do I think they have acted with that vigor and effect, which might be expected in a band of freemen, voluntarily engaging in the noblest of causes, and contending for all that is dear and valuable." But he felt that the advantages the enemy would derive from the conquest were "rather specious than real, rather splendid that substantial." The war, he knew, would continue and the Americans would win.

Two weeks later he had news of a "glorious success" to forward to Paris — a success to which he had contributed by his own procurement of arms and supplies. General Burgoyne had surrendered his entire army of 5700 men at Saratoga, including six generals, 300 other officers, and large quantities of stores. "I sincerely congratulate you and all the friends of America," Bingham wrote to Franklin. "What effect this important intelligence may have on the policies of Europe is impossible to foretell; I hope at least that the Court of France may be influenced by it to take a more decisive part in our favour."

On December 28, 1777, he was writing triumphantly that General Bouillé had reversed himself and lifted all the curbs on American activities. "Our prizes have not only been publicly received, but privateers have been armed in the ports, and no restrictions have been laid upon shipping arms or ammunition on board my American vessels. . . . I have not only shipped arms . . . but have procured a frigate to convoy them clear of the British cruizers amongst the island. Twelve sail of merchant vessels destined for the Continent took the benefit of this convoy." The hiding place in the hollow tree in the Tuileries began to receive longer and longer lists of military goods shipped to America by way of the West Indies: the *Amelia* with nineteen brass field cannon, 6561 cannon balls, 288 bombs, 200 barrels of powder, 120 bars of lead and a quantity of entrenching tools; the *Maria and Catherine* with thirty-four brass four-pounders, 16,-072 cannon balls, 2700 hand grenades . . .

France, Bingham concluded, had "only wanted time to garrison her islands, and put her navy on a respectable footing. . . . It was a sacrifice of pride to interest, intended to amuse her enemy, and thereby answer the purposes of the day." When the French threw out a hint that the Americans should begin to pay the regular 1 per cent import duty on captured English goods brought into the French island ports, Bingham readily agreed. He did so, he explained, for political advantage: "This will make our prizes have the appearance of a regular entry in the Custom House and will quicken the resentment of the English." He predicted that war must break out between France and England by spring.

In December (1777), the French, fearful that the Americans might come to terms with the British (a fear subtly furthered by Dr. Franklin), told the Commissioners that they had decided to recognize the independence of the American states and would give them an annual subsidy of two million francs. A month later they were ready to enter into an alliance. Vergennes, the French secretary of foreign affairs, invited Dr. Franklin to draw up its terms.

Two French-American treaties were initialed in Paris. One was a treaty of friendship and commerce, the other a defensive alliance to become effective if war broke out between France and England. Neither nation was to conclude a peace or truce until American independence had been recognized, and neither was to deal with Britain without the consent and full knowledge of the other.

"We are at the height of our joy here," Morris wrote to Bingham. "You may set it down as a certainty that Great Britain has lost America and that these states are free and independent. I take it for granted that an European war must immediately ensue, and that you will form your plans and take your measures accordingly." Bingham had scarcely digested this news when word came that the enemy had evacuated Philadelphia. The occupation was a failure: it had not crushed American resistance, and it divided the British army into two costly installations almost one hundred miles apart. The British fleet sailed out of Philadelphia in June (1778) with 3000 unhappy American Loyalists aboard. The British troops marched north to join their main force at New York.

Washington broke camp at Valley Forge, where he had spent a desperate, desolate winter, receiving little help or support from a country that was generally well-fed, prosperous and busy. He pursued the

British into New Jersey and engaged them at Monmouth, but he was denied a victory because of the misconduct of General Charles Lee.*

On June 17, French and British ships exchanged fire and the two countries were at war.

John Adams arrived in Paris in July to replace Silas Deane, who had been recalled to face charges of profiteering and fraud, and immediately became embroiled in the quarrel between Drs. Franklin and Lee, the other two Commissioners. Mr. Adams, a man of some vanity, was overshadowed by Dr. Franklin. He disapproved of Dr. Franklin.† He disapproved of the French and of Franklin's dependence on their aid. And so he sided with Dr. Lee; and, though he was not diplomatically accredited to France, he peremptorily instructed Vergennes to deal with him "without the intervention of any third person" (i.e., Franklin). Vergennes replied that he would not see Adams again nor answer his letters; he instructed his minister in Philadelphia to inform Congress that Adams had shown "a rigidity, a pedantry, an arrogance and a self-love that render him incapable of dealing with political subjects."

Deane brought back presents and letters from the French court and was conspicuously honored in being accompanied by the Chevalier Gérard, first French minister to the United States. He returned to find himself attacked with the utmost ferocity. Denied permission by Congress to meet his accusers or to testify in person, he took his defense to the public press and was there pilloried by a master of invective, Thomas Paine.

In attacking Deane, the radicals were really striking at Deane's sponsor, Robert Morris, the most powerful merchant in America. The "furious Whigs" of Pennsylvania hated Morris for his refusal to swear allegiance to the radical constitution they had forced on Pennsylvania in 1776 and for leading the movement to repeal it. The dominant bloc in Congress distrusted Morris for his conservative economic principles and for his insistence that no government could work effectively without a strong executive arm. When the public

---

* Lee had been exchanged and restored to his command. During his captivity, he had given Sir William Howe a detailed plan on how best to defeat the Americans.
† In one letter to his friend James Warren, Adams described Franklin as selfish, vain and ambitious, jealous and envious, false and deceitful, and added, "I wish with all my soul he was out of public service."

ignored their orders setting the price of commodities and their decrees that paper bills were worth what they were not, the Whigs blamed the "profiteers," which meant Robert Morris.

*

Throughout these months, William Bingham flourished as a private trader and went deeper into debt and closer to ruin as a public official.

His commercial network had grown to include agents in Virginia, North and South Carolina, Massachusetts, Connecticut, Rhode Island, Curaçao, several ports in France, and, in Philadelphia, John Holker, the French consul. Invoices of Jenifer and Hooe, an Alexandria firm, show that he was now shipping such articles as hardware and cutlery, nails, shoes, stockings, sacking, ink, mirrors, cotton and wool cards, soap, medicines, Bohea tea, sugar, coffee, and broadcloth.

Young Benjamin Harrison, Jr., deputy paymaster for the Southern army and son of a member of the Committee of Foreign Affairs, heard of Bingham's success in trade and wrote "to renew our old acquaintance and friendship." Mr. Harrison had something on his mind:

> Be assured that I have a lively remembrance of our former intimacy & with pleasure reflect on the many agreeable moments that we have spent together. . . . I am about to enter into a little trade and am in hopes to have two or three little vessels at sea before long. Perhaps we may do something to our mutual advantage in them. In the meantime, I shall think myself under the greatest obligation to you if you will hand my name to your correspondents in Europe and the West Indies for their consignments to here. . . . I am married much to my satisfaction. May have any French lady taken you into that happy state?

The desire to share in the fortunes then being made in trade and privateering was widespread. Richard Peters, secretary to the Board of War, expressed a common sentiment in August, 1780, when he wrote plaintively to his friend Robert Morris: "I am conscious of deserving some share of the advantages of this diabolical war. I have earned it by my labor, and by my losses I have gained a right to demand something from Fortune. . . . I shall pay my court to her through you, and by that if it be *possible and proper* I may have a small share in the Privateer Circle."

Bingham apparently continued to carry on most of his business with Morris. For one shipment of rum, sugar, and "sundry merchandize" brought into Philadelphia by the *Retaliation,* Morris received £43,994, Bingham £29,329, and Captain Ord £14,664. But with France in the war, this profitable private trade began to languish and then to stagnate. Bingham's work became more and more that of a consular officer, with responsibilities for finding emergency supplies for naval ships, getting American seamen out of jail, and protecting the interests of his government in the Admiralty Court and with the General, the Governor, and the Intendant. He set up with the British admiral, Sir John Byron,* a system for exchange of American prisoners, paying to feed, clothe, and transport these men back to the mainland. The prisoners were a heavy drain on his resources, but his sole concern seems to have been to exchange as many as possible. Andrew Nihell, a typical case, was charged with piracy on the high seas under the American flag. Bingham paid for his lawyer, an English and German interpreter, jail fees, a pair of irons, and hire of a canoe to put him on a vessel bound for St. Eustatius, total 648 livres, including his own 5 per cent commission as agent.

Late in 1778, Bingham played host to the most successful of the American privateers, Gustavus Conyngham, the fierce Irish master of the eighteen-gun cutter *Revenge.* Conyngham sailed into St. Pierre following eighteen months of forays off the coast of Great Britain and in the Mediterranean, during which he took twenty-seven English prizes and sank or burned thirty-three other vessels. Bingham contracted with Conyngham to continue such forays in the West Indies. He procured supplies for his ship, engaged his crew and gave them an advance against their prize money, supplied him with intelligence on the sailings of French and English vessels, and wrote out his sailing orders. ("Another grand object that must attract your attention is the endeavouring to capture some of the transports that have sailed from Newport bound for the English West India Islands. It appears that they have suffered by a gale of wind & have lost their convoy, so

* Grandfather of the poet.

that perhaps they will fall an easy prey. No recompense could requite the services you would render your country by capturing some of those that have troops on board, as it might perhaps hinder the success of their operations in these seas. . . .") Conyngham captured several prizes of little value and took two British privateers before sailing for Philadelphia early in 1779, carrying fifty chests of arms Bingham had bought for the Committee of Commerce.

In August, 1778, on learning of the outbreak of hostilities between France and England, Bingham had asked permission of Congress to resign his post and return home. There was now no longer any need for "neutral" ports in the West Indies as entrepôts for shipments to and from America; nor were those ports any longer a protection to American vessels or prizes against British attack. He had supplied the Martinique *Gazette* with news until, in Bingham's words, it had "obtained the character in Europe of being the most authentic portrait of military operations in America"; but this propaganda service no longer carried its old importance. Bingham felt that he had completed his mission in Martinique and could be replaced by a commercial agent living on the island.

There were other more personal reasons that caused him to request a recall. He was finding his continued residence in Martinique unbearable.

There was, for one thing, the state of his health. Prolonged residence in the debilitating climate of Martinique sapped the vitality of Caucasians and, in the words of a talented visitor of a century later, "induced a lethargy that mastered habit and purpose.

> It is a sense of vital exhaustion painful as the misery of convalescence; the least effort provokes a perspiration profuse enough to saturate clothing, and the limbs ache as from muscular overstrain. . . . With the loss of bodily energy ensues a more than corresponding loss of mental activity and strength. . . . You will ask yourself how much longer can you endure the prodigious light, and the furnace heat of blinding blue days, and the void misery of sleepless nights, and the curse of insects, and the sound of the mandibles of enormous roaches devouring the few books in your possession. . . .*

It is not known to what degree Bingham suffered this malaise, but

* Lafcadio Hearn, *Two Years in the French West Indies*, 1890, 389, 412–17.

twice, in asking to be recalled, he said that the state of his health made his return absolutely necessary. There were indignities in his situation, moreover, that made it intolerable.

Five months passed before any spokesman for Congress referred to his request to come home, and nineteen months before a second reference gave him permission. For one year, from April, 1777, to March, 1778, he received no word, no letters, from any of the three committees of Congress he served, though vessels came into St. Pierre frequently from the American mainland. He first learned of the French-American treaty by reading of it in a Dominican gazette and was reduced to asking its terms and content of General Bouillé — who naturally raised his eyebrows at the American agent's lack of information.* In letter after letter Bingham pleaded for news, information and answers to his queries, but "my letters have been treated with a peculiar inattention by not being thought worthy of an answer." Congress, shaken by feuds, constantly on the verge of total insolvency, unwilling to delegate the least authority outside its ranks despite Robert Morris' plea for an executive arm, its committees sitting in judgment on the payment of $16.39 for ferriage and of $22 for supplies to two sick men in a hospital — Congress was a year or more behind in its paper work and had more serious worries than keeping its foreign agents apprised of developments.

The Commissioners in Paris were no better correspondents. Bingham received no letters from Dr. Franklin or his colleagues in the twelve months following April, 1777. "I am very unhappy to find myself so neglected in a correspondence," he wrote to Franklin on March 5, 1778, "which various motives prompt me most assiduously to cultivate.

> Congress had reason to expect a variety of intelligence from this quarter. I have faithfully and diligently furnished them with all that I could procure; but I am afraid that I have not answered their expectations in this point; however, I have this connotation, *Quod potui, feci; facient meliora potentes.*†

* The Committee of Foreign Affairs wrote to Bingham from York on May 14, 1778, informing him of the signing of the treaty. Bingham never received the letter.
   The letter to Bingham quoted at the head of this chapter, written sometime in the summer of 1777, apparently was never sent. See Notes and Sources, page 479.
† I've done my best — let abler men do better.

He had, he said, another reason that urged him to be, and perhaps justified him in being, so importunate.

> The General [Bouillé], regarding the interests of France and America as altogether inseparable, has thrown off all reserve, and constantly communicates to me the nature and purport of such of his dispatches as have any regard to the situation of our affairs. He expects an equal return of political information on my side, which, from my limited and confined knowledge of what passes in Europe, I am unhappily deprived of an opportunity of giving him.

To the Commissioners he wrote again on June 16:

> It is a long time since I have had the honor of receiving any of your commands, and am the more surprised at it, as a packet boat has arrived with dispatches for the General, informing him of a treaty of alliance and commerce being concluded betwixt the Court of Versailles and the United States of America. . . .
>
> I humbly think that I should be made acquainted with its contents, that I might act in conformity thereto, and as far as my small influence will reach, cooperate accordingly. . . .
>
> As Agent for the United States of America in the West Indies, every circumstance that regards the country that I represent, and that forms a subject of controversy, immediately falls under my notice and attention; but how shall I govern myself with any degree of prudence or precision, or according to the terms that Treaty prescribes, when I am entirely ignorant of what it contains?

Finally, there was the weight of the huge debt he had incurred in buying supplies and services for the Congress, for which he was held personally responsible and for which he was constantly being dunned. "I have daily expected remittances from the [American] continent," he wrote to the Congress in January, 1778, "and have been daily disappointed. My sinking credit and embarrassed situation have been a subject of mirth in all the W. India gazettes and are circumstances which in this place tend greatly to derogate from the respect due to the appointment with which you have been pleased to honor me." He was reluctant to draw on the Commissioners in Paris without authorization. He was in "a state of perplexity, uneasiness and suspense" and told of being "racked with persecution" from those to whom he owed money. Judgments had been recovered against him several times in court, he said, but General Bouillé had suspended their execution. "The impropriety of having recourse to his authority for such a purpose, must appear strikingly obvious; it will tend to sink me into disgrace and to lessen the esteem I might otherwise be held in."

Since Congress seemed unable or unwilling to ship him enough public goods to balance his account, Bingham proposed a solution. A number of persons in America had considerable funds in the West Indies from the sale of prizes brought into French ports. They could not easily get possession of these moneys in America. Perhaps Congress could buy these funds, transfer a credit against them to the West Indies, and in this way deliver money out of the continent. This eminently practical proposal was ignored, and when Bingham suggested it again a year later, the Navy Board replied in the eternal language of bureaucracy: it had referred the letter to Congress and "whatever orders this Board may receive from Congress on that subject, shall be executed with all the alacrity in their power."

In the meantime, James Lovell, forty, Congressman from Massachusetts, had undertaken to bring some order to the muddled affairs of Congress. A graduate of Harvard, Lovell in 1771 had delivered the first oration at the site of the Boston Massacre, and he had spent the first year of the Revolution in a Halifax prison, charged with espionage. As chairman of the Committee of Foreign Affairs, he was a tireless worker and was for months on end its only active member. (He did not see his wife and children for five years.) Lovell believed strongly that Congress should retain all executive power in its own hands through its committees, and in striving to make that unworkable system work, he was a diligent public servant.*

Although he was a part of the political faction that was attacking Robert Morris and Silas Deane, Lovell went out of his way to be friendly and generous to William Bingham. He broke his committee's year-long silence with four letters in three months, beginning on

---

* For amusement he wrote letters to John Adams' wife Abigail that were naughty with double entendres and protestations of his ardor. Abigail scolded him, but she continued the correspondence, and she saved the letters.

March 2, 1778, with thanks "for many letters, both of interesting advice and ingenious political speculation." These, he said, had been particularly acceptable to Congress because no word had been received from the Commissioners for ten months. The long silence and neglect by the Committee, he confessed frankly, was unaccountable and beyond apology. "Your situation must have been very disagreeable, indeed, in consequence of the failure of remittances from hence." On April 16, he sent Bingham a most welcome letter authorizing him to draw bills of exchange on the Honorable Commissioners at Paris to the amount of 100,000 livres tournois ($15,300).

This payment of hard cash gave Bingham something of a breathing spell, but it came at a time when he was being presented with enormous new charges that he could neither refuse nor control. These were for Continental Navy vessels that began to sail into St. Pierre and Fort Royal to careen and refit, with instructions in writing to give the bills to the agent there, Mr. Bingham. The Navy Board, without funds or the prospect of getting any, simply told their captains that William Bingham would take care of everything. Bingham wrote directly to James Lovell requesting permission to charge these expenses to the Commissioners at Paris. To do so, Lovell replied, would be improper, and permission was denied.

Early in February, 1779, the brig *General Gates* and the frigate *Deane* arrived in St. Pierre, each wanting "very considerable outfits." The *Deane* carried a number of English prisoners, "the maintenance of whom at this time of scarcity and distress," Bingham said, "amounts to extravagant sums." Captain Nicholson of the *Deane*, moreover, demanded 20,000 livres with which to pay his officers. When Bingham demurred, Captain Nicholson became angry. "A perseverance in not complying with my request," he said, "will be attended with very prejudicial consequences, as your refusal has already created the greatest discontent in my Corps of Officers, which I am afraid will ripen into disgust for the service." Bingham raised the required sum — 90,910 livres Martinique — by borrowing it from the government of Martinique.

On April 13, 1779, he advised the Committee for Foreign Affairs that he had presumed to draw again on Dr. Franklin for 100,000 livres tournois to pay these and other charges, and he included a two-page lecture to the members on how to reform "the fatal and amazing depreciation of our Continental currency." To Dr. Franklin he explained that, having weighed the "cruel alternatives," he had thought it proper and advisable to pass his draft on for payment in Paris; he could do nothing else.

CHAPTER 7

Last Days in Martinique

Our agent here is in high estimation. I really believe, from everything I hear, that he has done his duty faithfully, and that he well deserves the notice and approbation of Congress.

John Jay to the President of Congress
St. Pierre, Martinique, December 26, 1779

JOHN JAY resigned his post as president of Congress, his membership on six Congressional committees, and his position as chief justice of the State of New York, to undertake a mission that was virtually hopeless: to persuade Spain to form an alliance with the United States and to lend them some millions of dollars.

He sailed on October 26, 1779. His vessel was the Continental frigate *Confederacy*, Captain Seth Harding, launched in November of the previous year. She had a 125-foot keel, thirty-six guns, and a crew and marine fighting force of about 300 men.*

Jay was a descendant of French Huguenots and son of one of New York's wealthiest and most influential families. At thirty-four, he was just under six feet in height, rather thin but well formed, with a colorless complexion, penetrating black eyes, aquiline nose, and a pointed chin. He commonly dressed in black. He was conservative by nature and by political inclination, but as a delegate to the first and second Continental Congresses he had unreservedly supported economic sanctions against Great Britain and had worked for the Declaration of Independence. He was the author of the open letter Congress had addressed to the "oppressed inhabitants of Canada" in 1775 vainly inviting them to throw off their "unmerited degradation" and join the Colonies in the uprising against Britain.

With him now were his wife Sarah, daughter of the patriot gover-

---

* For comparison: the frigate *Constitution* ("Old Ironsides"), launched in 1797 and now in Boston Harbor, had forty-four guns, 400 men, and an overall length of 204 feet.

nor of New Jersey; her brother, Colonel H. Brockholst Livingston, who was to serve as Jay's personal secretary; and William Carmichael, the former secretary to the Commissioners at Paris, returning to Europe with Jay to serve as his secretary of the legation. Also on the vessel was the Chevalier Gérard, who had been replaced as French minister for reasons of health, though it was rumored that the anti-French faction in Congress had driven him from his post in revenge for having supported Silas Deane and causing the recall of Arthur Lee. Mrs. Jay, a famous young beauty, carried a lock of General Washington's hair, sent her by the General himself with a gracious farewell letter. M. Gérard carried letters addressed to himself and to Louis XVI, "Great, Faithful and Beloved Friend and Ally," written by John Jay as president of Congress, praising Gérard's prudence, integrity, ability, and diligence as minister.

All went well for ten days. The passengers were (in Livingston's words) "very commodiously settled" on board. Mrs. Jay took French lessons daily from the Chevalier Gérard, who had formed "a very strong attachment" to her. The larder was well stocked and there was a large flock of poultry that in one form or another supplied fresh food. Then, some eleven hundred miles out of Delaware Bay, south of the Newfoundland Banks, the *Confederacy* ran into trouble. The frigate was sailing before a brisk wind in cross seas at about nine knots when, suddenly and unaccountably, between four and five o'clock in the morning, the mainmast splintered and fell, bringing down with it the other two masts, cracking the bowsprit, and injuring two crewmen, one of them fatally.* The situation was made doubly disastrous that night when a gale came up and the rudder shaft of the helpless, wallowing vessel was wrenched and split.

The ship drifted aimlessly for two weeks while Captain Harding worked his crew to rig jury masts, repair sails and patch up the rudder. He then turned to Gérard and Jay for orders, since they were responsible for naming his port of destination. Gérard, eager to get to France, insisted obdurately that they sail some nine hundred miles east to the Azores, though those islands had no harbor or repair facilities. He was supported by William Carmichael, who had begun to

---

* Apparently the ropes, tightly rigged in a colder climate, slackened in the warm air of the Gulf Stream. Captain Harding was later questioned and cleared by a naval board of inquiry.

reveal a talent for making mischief that would trouble Jay throughout his mission. Jay, who had been seasick most of the time, agreed with Harding and a council of officers that the safer course was to sail south to Martinique and there take another ship to Europe. Over Gérard's angry protests the course was set for that island.

On the morning of Saturday, December 18, after seven weeks at sea, Mrs. Jay was delighted to discover that "we were sailing close along the most verdant, romantic country I ever beheld." The *Confederacy,* her holds now awash with six feet of water, put into St. Pierre that day.

They were met by William Bingham, the Continental Agent. As their official host, Bingham was so gallant that Sally Jay confessed she had never been more charmed by anything of the kind. The Jays stayed as guests in his house during their wait for a passage to Spain. Bingham, of course, had known Jay (seven years his senior) in their work together on the Committee of Secret Correspondence in 1775–76. In Martinique or later they became firm friends; Bingham was apparently the only person who addressed Jay as "Jack." Mrs. Jay, married in 1774, seems always, even in their intimate moments, to have called her husband "My dear Mr. Jay."

General Bouillé and the admiral of the French fleet were all obliging courtesy. The *Confederacy* should be convoyed at once to the naval base at Fort Royal, where no effort would be spared to refit her. The Jay and Gérard parties would be carried to Toulon in the French frigate *Aurore,* scheduled to sail on the 28th.

The stranded voyagers made the best of their remaining days before sailing. The post commander held a regimental review in their honor. Mrs. Jay shopped, visited sugar mills in the surrounding country, observed the island's bee culture, and saw a wild native dance, presumably with Bingham as an escort. Mr. Jay bought a box of liqueurs as a present for General Washington, and Bingham matched it with another. (The General reported ruefully that "they both suffered much by the roughness of the transportation.")* Mr. Jay also bought "a very fine Negro boy of fifteen years old," and he wrote five letters to Congress setting forth in minute detail every as-

---

* Bingham earlier had sent General and Mrs. Washington a more carefully packed present of a set of Nanking china. It had belonged to Lady Belle Hamilton, wife of the solicitor general of the British West Indies, and had been captured and sold at an auction of prize goods in St. Pierre.

pect of his troubles with Mr. Gérard. William Carmichael, gifted as a raconteur, told and retold to St. Pierre society and officialdom his amusing version of the quarrel between Mr. Jay and Mr. Gérard.

The officers of the *Confederacy* attended the playhouse to see an English farce, *The Deserter,* but found it "much altered" and "ruined with a multiplicity of singing." One officer visited a brothel and there had a difference of opinion with an acting lieutenant from one of the French frigates in the harbor. This led to a quarrel and a challenge. At six o'clock the next morning, the two parties and their proper attendants were conducted in the *Confederacy*'s barge to an isolated spot northward of the town, where they landed; each fired two shots at the other without injury, and departed the best of friends.

Jay was disturbed to find that the officers of the *Confederacy* were without money or the means of getting any, and he did "what perhaps I shall be blamed for, but my pride as an American and my feelings as a man were not on this occasion to be resisted." He drew a bill on Dr. Franklin for 100 guineas as an advance on his salary and ordered it distributed among the officers. To Congress he wrote:

> The idea of our officers being obliged to sneak, as they phrase it, from the company of French officers, for fear of running in debt with them for a bottle of wine or a bowl of punch, because not able to pay for their share of the reckoning, was too humiliating to be tolerable, and too destructive to that pride and opinion of independent equality which I wish to see influence all our officers. Besides, some of them wanted necessaries too much to be comfortable, or, in this country, decent. . . . Indeed, it would have given me pleasure to have done something towards covering the nakedness of the crew; but the expense I have been put to by coming here and the preparations for another voyage would not admit of it.

On learning of Jay's intended gift from his salary, Bingham offered to advance 100 guineas to the officers himself and add that sum to the mountain of charges against Congress. Jay gratefully accepted.

In his meetings with Bingham, Jay discussed the cost of repairing the ship, and Bingham expressed the hope that government funds could be procured to pay for the work, for he could not manage it himself. In his letter of December 22, Jay wrote to Congress, "The agent here tells me he is without cash and in debt on the public account. I fear he has been neglected. I shall, however, defer saying anything further on this subject till I shall be better informed."

In further conversations with Bingham and with General Bouillé, Jay soon became better informed. He was shocked and distressed at what he learned — at the enormous debt Congress owed to Bingham, which he in turn owed to his creditors on the island; the long silences in Philadelphia and Paris; the judgments obtained against him; the open mockery at his plight printed in the island newspapers. Now, Jay learned, Bingham was under an additional strain, for Dr. Franklin had refused to honor his draft covering the expenses incurred in refitting the *General Gates* and the *Deane*. Dr. Franklin was having problems of his own, trying to borrow money to meet the drafts that Congress was constantly drawing on him — on what had come to be known as "The Bank of Hope." In rejecting Bingham's draft he wrote, not unreasonably, "If every agent of Congress in different parts of the world is permitted to run into debt and draw upon me at pleasure to support his credit, under the idea of its being necessary to do so for the honor of Congress, the difficulty upon me would be too great."

Bingham had first learned of his dishonored drafts on October 9, when M. de Vaivre, the Intendant, had summoned him to his office. He must have gone with apprehension, for this man was at odds politically and socially with Bingham's friend and protector, General Bouillé.

The drafts were on the Intendant's desk. He demanded from Bingham his personal promissory note of hand for 150,000 livres, subject to "faithful and punctual discharge" within six months, and an interest payment of 10 per cent. Bingham signed, since he "could not with propriety refuse his request."

Jay also learned that Bingham was deeply troubled by a lawsuit that had placed a lien against his property at home, brought as the result of a step Bingham had taken in his capacity as agent of the Congress. On January 29, 1779, the Massachusetts privateer *Pilgrim* had brought a ship into St. Pierre, the *Hope,* claiming her as an English prize of war. Both ship and cargo, however, had Danish papers, and the crew spoke only Danish; this clearly appeared to be neutral property illegally seized. The prize master had already gone aboard the *Hope* when Bingham intervened, took over the vessel, and placed her again under the command of her captain. The cargo, 983 barrels of flour, was perishable, and so Bingham, acting on Bouillé's written order, sold it at a good price, gave the captain money with which to make some necessary repairs to his vessel, and held the balance in escrow until Congress should decide who was the lawful owner of the vessel. Now Bingham had learned that the American owners of the privateer *Pilgrim* were suing him for his action in depriving them of a lawful prize and had attached property in the hands of his agents in Massachusetts and Pennsylvania. Congress seemed indifferent to his problem, and William Tudor, his attorney in Boston, wrote that the *Hope* had had two sets of papers and almost certainly was British property. The case of the *Pilgrim* hung heavily on Bingham.

On Sunday, the day after Christmas, John Jay wrote to Samuel Huntington, his successor as president of Congress. He praised Bingham's performance as agent, his services in getting the *Confederacy* berthed, and the high regard in which French officials held him.

> This leads me to take the liberty of remarking that it would probably be much for the public interest if Congress were to pay off all private debts due from them to subjects of France, and have none but national engagements with that kingdom. The debts unavoidably contracted here for the outfit of the *Deane*, etc., ought certainly to be paid. Our credit and reputation suffer from such delay.

Jay resumed his journey on December 28 and on January 22, after an uneventful voyage, arrived in Spain, where he was to endure two years of rebuffs and frustration, ending in failure. While he was on the high seas, Congress coolly spent £100,000 of the money it was hoped he might borrow in Spain and sent the drafts to the Spanish court for payment.

Bingham applied himself cheerfully to the problems of repairing the *Confederacy*, for he had decided that this would be his last major piece of business on the island. He would sail for home on this ship and assume that Congress, by its silence, had assented to his sixteen-month-old plea to be recalled.

His first task was to persuade the French officials, including the unfriendly Intendant, to extend him credit once again, this time for the fittings, supplies and provisions necessary to make the *Confeder-*

acy seaworthy. Masts were the greatest difficulty. He obtained a promise of these from French stores on his return promise that the American Congress would replace them with a shipment from the mainland. Bingham wrote the Board of Admiralty (successor to the Marine Committee) on December 28; it acknowledged his letter two months later and ordered the masts to be sent.*

On Sunday morning, March 12, 1779, the *Confederacy* took a pilot on board, warped out of her dock at Fort Royal, and sailed to St. Pierre. Within two weeks, she would be ready to sail for the United States.

Bingham had already prepared for Congress an eight-page recapitulation of his work, "a clear and succinct account of my Agency during my Residence in this Place.

> Whether my agency has been interesting to America, by promoting the glorious cause she is engaged in, is left to your august body to determine; — for my own part, I claim no merit but from the purity & rectitude of my intentions, my activity, & my zeal for your service; — The public interest alone has always been my guide — but if I have undertaken a task beyond my abilities to accomplish I cannot expect to be honoured with the public approbation, which invariable in its decisions, never consults any thing but its own advantage; — in that case, I shall be more afflicted, than surprized.

He ended his letter with the same Latin quotation he had written to Dr. Franklin, this time providing a translation.

> If my services had been more conspicuous, I might perhaps have had much to fear from the voice of calumny — their mediocrity thus may have protected me from the pursuits of the envious, which however could never have deprived me of the consolation to think, — that for the good of my Country
> Quod Potui, feci; — faciant meliora potentes!
> I've done my best — let abler men do more.

He signed his name with his usual exuberant flourish.†

---

* A private journal kept by Captain Joseph Hardy, in command of the marines on the *Confederacy*, gives a picture of activities on the island and of the problems that Bingham and Captain Seth Harding faced over the next several months. Extracts appear in Appendix 1, page 451.
† The report appears in full as Appendix 2, page 454.

His other main duty was to name an agent to serve in his place, and for this he chose two gentlemen "of known integrity and ability," merchants of the firm Parson, Alston and Company. In instructions to his successors, he laid down, four days before sailing, a series of rules and admonitions. They give an excellent picture of how William Bingham saw his responsibilities.

Should any Continental vessels arrive in need of assistance for repairs and supplies, Parson and Alston were to apply to the General and the Intendant.

They were immediately to inform the Commercial Committee of any prizes brought in by Continental cruisers and of any remittances in produce received.

When English prisoners arrived on board American vessels, these were to be delivered to the General to be exchanged for American seamen in the enemy's possession. The Americans were to be forwarded to the mainland at the speediest opportunity.

When any American trading vessel arrived, they were to assist the captain in the sale of his cargo. If he was imposed on by the purchasers, they were to apply to the General or the Governor, "whom you will always find happily disposed to protect the rights of Americans."

If any material alteration took place in the currency of the markets, or any favorable opportunity offered itself for speculation in American produce, they were to inform the Commercial Committee.

"Should any important Intelligence arrive from Europe or any material events take place in the West Indies, that may affect the Interests of or be conducive to the advantage of the United States, lose no time in transmitting the same to Congress, with suitable reflections on the subject."

On Tuesday, March 28, Captain Hardy's diary recorded that the *Confederacy* "received on board a large quantity of cocoa ship'd by Mr. Bingham." On Wednesday evening, "Mr. Bingham sent on board the greatest part of his baggage." It was accompanied by a servant, a mulatto boy he was taking with him to America.

Bingham boarded the ship next morning. With him he carried the warm good wishes of General the Marquis de Bouillé and a letter from him to the president of the American Congress attesting to the distinguished manner with which M. Bingham had compared himself:

I have the pleasure to assure your Excellency that no one could have taken more interest than he in the subjects of the United States. I [words illegible] more intelligence, more fairness, wisdom and moderation. . . . The position that he leaves could not be filled more worthily. . . . I refer you to the accounts that he has given your Excellency of our actual forces, their position, and their effects, which we have shown him.

At 10 A.M. the *Confederacy* ran up its flag for sailing and got under weigh. It had under its convoy five merchant ships, two American and three French. At the mouth of the harbor, Captain Harding saluted the town of St. Pierre and the warships in the road with thirteen guns. He received a farewell salute of eleven guns in response.

BOOK TWO

The Prince
of Merchants
and the Queen
of Beauty

CHAPTER 8

Enter Anne Willing

The sentiments of the people in this country I found surprisingly altered since I left it; they were no longer governed by that pure, disinterested patriotism, which distinguished the Infancy of the contest; private Interest seemed to predominate over every other Consideration that regarded the public weal. It was necessary that they should experience some signal misfortune to rouse them into activity.

William Bingham to John Jay
July 1, 1780

HE FOUND Philadelphia drab and shabby, worn from four years of war and still showing the ravages of the British occupation. Trees had been cut down and fences torn up to feed British bonfires and cookstoves. Gardens had been trampled, and the gutted houses were not yet repaired. The potter's field beside the Walnut Street Prison showed some hundreds of rough unsodded mounds, the graves of men who had suffered maltreatment and died as prisoners of the British.

The city was still recovering from the coldest winter in living memory. In January, Bingham was told, the temperature rose to the freezing point on only one day. The snow was up to four feet deep that month, the ice sixteen to eighteen inches thick, the frost four to five feet in the ground. Trees had exploded, squirrels perished in their holes, many partridges were found dead, the feet and ears of cattle were frostbitten, and fire engines were rendered useless by the intense cold. In early March the Delaware was still frozen and closed to navigation. The hardships and privations of the army encamped at Morristown were worse than those endured at Valley Forge the year before. In January, when conditions were no longer to be endured, General Washington took matters into his own hands: he sent out armed detachments with orders to bring back forced levies of cattle and grain.

William Bingham greeted his family and friends and settled down, presumably with his mother in the Pine Street house. He immediately presented General Bouillé's letter of commendation to Congress. It was read aloud on Monday, May 1, the day after his arrival in the city; President Samuel Huntington wrote in return of the great pleasure he felt in finding that Mr. Bingham's conduct was "agreeable to the French nation and more especially that it meets with your approbation."

He drew up a memorial on the lawsuit brought against him in the affair of the privateer ship *Pilgrim,* asking for an appearance before an appropriate committee so that he could set forth "a true and impartial state of this matter." He filed a claim with Congress for salary, expenses and debts due him from his four years of service in Martinique. And he enlisted as a private in the militia — in the Second Company of the Fourth Battalion of the Philadelphia Association, under the command of Colonel Paul Cox.

As Bingham made his rounds in the city, his mulatto boy dutifully followed him about, bearing his umbrella, holding it open and aloft when the sun shone or the rain fell. The townsfolk tittered; it seemed that umbrellas, though introduced into Philadelphia eight or nine years earlier, were considered effeminate. Bingham told his boy to desist.

He was pleased to learn that Congress, early in March, had given him formal permission to return home and had directed the Board of Treasury to pay him or his agent, John Benezet, £5000 sterling "to discharge in part the debt due him." John Jay's letter from Martinique had produced action, though, ironically, the money was raised by drawing against the sums Jay was expected to borrow in Spain.

Congress appointed James Lovell and George Clymer as a special committee to review and pass on Bingham's claim. Since no one could remember and there were no written records of the terms under which Congress had sent him to Martinique, Lovell wrote to Robert Morris: "I must therefore beg you to be at the trouble of recollecting & minuting down for our use the nature and extent of the encouragement given to him by the Committee of Secret Correspondence of which you was at that time the most laborious member." Finding that Bingham had to pay immediately certain obligations he had contracted on behalf of the United States, the Committee recommended that £7000 more be paid him on account.

Congress so acted, again drawing on Mr. Jay's nonexistent funds in Spain. The balance of Bingham's claim still to be considered totaled 507,641 livres Martinique currency for commercial transactions made for the United States, plus 110,324 livres for salary and expenses.

In drawing rooms and counting houses, on the streets and in the taverns, in conferences with his fellow merchants, Bingham found the conversation turning repeatedly to three topics: inflation, the struggle for power in Pennsylvania, and the gloomy progress of the war.

Congress, he had discovered on arriving in Philadelphia, had just devalued the Continental currency at the rate of forty paper dollars for one of specie. By this virtual declaration of bankruptcy it reduced to $5 million the $200 million of internal debt it had incurred by its "prodigious emissions" of paper currency. The merchants had agreed to the repudiation as a last resort, but the currency was not so easily stabilized. Rather than accept almost worthless paper in payment, citizens concealed themselves from those who owed them money; storekeepers hid their wares; farmers still refused to sell their produce for anything but hard money or other merchandise. Gold and silver actually were in plentiful supply, but in obedience to Gresham's unwritten law, those who had specie kept it out of circulation. Congress called a convention early in 1780 to regulate prices. The Radicals, Dr. Benjamin Rush said, "expect to see all the miracles of transubstantiation, and all the mysteries of alchemy performed in an instant upon the currency. . . . The folly & madness of mankind used to distress me — But I have learned to hear & talk of errors in Government with composure." Only six states attended the convention and the delegates adjourned without taking up the subject for which they had been called together.

As a merchant and a man of property, Bingham found himself drawn inevitably into the bearpit of Pennsylvania politics. He joined the conservative group led by John Dickinson and Robert Morris in what was essentially a counterrevolution: an attempt to recover the state assembly and the city government from the Radicals who had taken control of both.

The Radicals, under the leadership of George Bryan, port officer of Philadelphia, and Charles Willson Peale, naturalist and painter, had reached their apogee in the November just past (1779) with seizure of what they considered a symbol and citadel of conservative power. The College of Philadelphia, they said, was dominated by trustees, including Robert Morris, Thomas Willing and James Wilson, who opposed the liberal state constitution, fought price controls, defended suspected Loyalists in the courts, and were Episcopalians. (The Radicals were of the Presbyterian spirit.) It was necessary "to keep public education in patriotic hands," because "seminaries of learning . . . when in the hands of dangerous and disaffected men . . . have troubled the peace of society, shaken the government, and often caused tumult, sedition and bloodshed." And so the assembly, without a judicial hearing, repealed the college charter, dismissed the faculty and trustees, confiscated the college estates, including its endowments, and turned everything over to a new college — a state institution controlled by the political party that ruled the state.*

In seizing the college, the Radicals overreached themselves. They were being criticized for the failure of their economic and fiscal policies. Now, with the destruction of an institution of which the whole city had always been proud, a strong conservative reaction set in. Bingham wrote of these events to John Jay in Madrid on July 1. "Gentlemen of known abilities and integrity," he said, were coming to the fore. The public "will soon discover the immense difference that will arise in their favor" with affairs managed by men of this caliber.†

If political events were encouraging, the war news was unrelievedly calamitous. People were tired of the war, or indifferent, or filled with despair because they could see no hope of victory. Their political leaders seemed unable to do anything but quarrel among themselves and propose unrealistic diplomatic deals with other nations. Of the country's 435,000 adult males of military age, fewer than 30,000 were in service, and only 13,000 of those were Continental troops, the others serving in the state militias. With the collapse of the govern-

* "The disruption of the College destroyed for the time being one of the two most democratic and liberal-spirited schools in America, and the damage it wrought was not fully repaired until after the Civil War." — Allan Nevins, *The American States During and After the Revolution*, 1924. The College became the University of Pennsylvania in 1791.
† He added news of an "unlucky accident" that had happened in Philadelphia to their friend Gouverneur Morris. "In attempting to drive a pair of wild horses in a phaeton, he was thrown out and in the fall his left leg caught in the wheel and was greatly shattered. He was under the necessity of having it amputated below the knee and is now in a fair way of recovery."

ment's credit, the Continental supply system ceased to function. The farmers were refusing to plant beyond their family needs, for fear their crops would be confiscated. The states were prosperous, but Washington's army was neglected, lacking food, clothing and pay; it had been idle for almost two years and was stirring with mutiny. The French were deeply discouraged at the lack of American self-reliance. French Minister Luzerne was ordered to tell the Americans to stop begging for money and that "it is time for them to relieve His Majesty from the heavy burdens of a war which he had undertaken and carries on for their sake." George III declared that, unless some disaster hit Britain, the Americans would be forced to sue for peace that summer. General Washington wrote to Congress, "We seem to be verging so fast to destruction that I am filled with sensations to which I have been a stranger till within these three months."

Catastrophe came in May with the fall of Charleston in South Carolina. The nation lost 5466 men captured, great quantities of guns, muskets, ammunition and other military stores, and four of the precious Continental frigates. It was the worst defeat of the war — a heavier loss than Burgoyne had suffered at Saratoga — but more was to follow. The British and their Indian allies began a series of attacks on the western frontier. General Gates, whose abilities as a commander were considered in some quarters superior to Washington's, blundered into an overwhelming defeat at Camden, South Carolina, losing about 1000 men — nearly a third of his army. In September, Major General Benedict Arnold, only recently transferred from his military command of Philadelphia to the fort at West Point on the Hudson, was discovered in treasonable negotiations with the enemy. His Philadelphia estate was confiscated; his wife Margaret, of the Philadelphia Shippens, was ordered to leave the city; his two-faced effigy was dragged through the streets, hanged and burned.

The loss of Charleston and its garrison, Bingham told Jay, was the "signal misfortune" necessary to rouse the people into activity. There were signs of a new spirit, he said, on the discovery of the danger that faced the nation. The nation's merchants and men of property took full-scale concerted action to help the government. Their purpose was undoubtedly patriotic, but they were not unhappy that the course of "correct principles" they followed embarrassed the Radicals and furthered their own programs. Early in June a small group of Philadelphia merchants and lawyers met privately and agreed to use the weight of their influence and fortunes to relieve the national distress. Among them were Robert Morris, Thomas Willing, James Wilson, and William Bingham.

These men called a general meeting of moneyed people at the City Tavern. "The greatest and most vigorous exertions are necessary," Wilson said, reading from his prospectus, "for the successful management of the just and necessary war in which we are engaged with Great Britain." They should pool their resources and raise £300,-000 with which to buy provisions and rum for the army. Each subscriber would bond himself to pay the amount of his pledge in gold or silver, one-tenth at once and the balance in installments as demanded. A purchasing agency would be created, known as the Bank of Pennsylvania and capitalized at £300,000, to buy and transport the supplies. The working personnel of the bank would receive "reasonable compensations," but none of the subscribers, directors or inspectors should "derive the least pecuniary advantage to themselves or families from this exertion." The directors would be authorized to borrow money on the credit of the bank for periods up to six months and to issue special bank notes bearing interest at 6 per cent.

The assemblage in the City Tavern accepted and approved the plan. It elected Tench Francis, Jr. (husband of Thomas Willing's sister), as factor, and Robert Morris as chairman of the board of inspectors. Those present pledged £270,000, and within a few days that sum was further increased to £315,000, with ninety-two persons subscribing in all. Three men — one of them Robert Morris — subscribed £10,000 each. Twenty-seven — including Bingham, Wilson, and John Benezet (married to Bingham's sister Hannah) — gave £5000. Dr. Rush gave £2000. Bingham reported to John Jay:

> At an alarming moment when the treasury was exhausted and the army suffering and threatening to disband for the want of provisions, the virtue of individuals was roused, which warded off the impending blow. A bank was established on private credit under the auspices of gentlemen of the first fortune in this city. . . . The subscription was filled up in a few days and much larger sums might have been procured. . . . If the same public-spirited establishments take place in every State, we shall derive the greatest and most essential advantages from them.

On June 21, a committee officially advised Congress that a bank had been organized, it was prepared to supply and transport 3 million rations and 300 hogsheads of rum to the army, and it now needed only the recognition and cooperation of the government. Congress unanimously resolved that it entertained a high sense of the liberal offer made and accepted the same "as a distinguished proof of the patriotism of the subscribers."

James Madison wrote to Thomas Jefferson that the greatest hopes of feeding the soldiers were now founded on this "patriotic scheme of opulent merchants" of Philadelphia. The *Pennsylvania Packet* ran on its front page what surely must be the only poem ever printed to a bank, or certainly the worst:

> *Has not the loss of Charlestown prov'd once more*
> *That where the soul's engaged*
> *Danger becomes a stimulus to action?*
> *Look at those large and honorable aids*
> *By voluntary contributions rais'd*
> *Which this fair city gives — her splendid Bank*
> *And liberal subscriptions; whence are they*
> *But from the arduous feeling of the soul*
> *Rous'd by some new and unforeseen misfortune?*

The bank opened for business on July 17, and on that day Morris sent 500 barrels of flour, with appropriate publicity, on their way to General Nathanael Greene's army in the South. Tench Francis proceeded to buy up and store large supplies of provisions. Within a few weeks the idea and organization of the Bank of Pennsylvania spread to Boston, New York, and Baltimore.

*

How, or when, or where it happened is not known; but on one of those summer days, between drilling with the militia, and tending to his affairs as a merchant, and helping to found the bank, and settling his account with Congress, and defending himself in the *Pilgrim* lawsuit, William Bingham discovered Anne Willing. She had been twelve — not yet twelve — when he sailed for Martinique; now she was, or would shortly be, sixteen, and she was the most beautiful young woman in Philadelphia.

Anne, called Nancy, was the daughter of Thomas Willing — the oldest daughter and so, in the manner of that day, entitled to be known simply as *Miss Willing*. There were, besides her, Charles, fourteen; Thomas Mayne, thirteen; Elizabeth, twelve; Mary, ten; Dorothy, eight; George, six; Richard, five; Abigail, three; and William Shippen, one.

The meeting between Anne and William may have come about by chance; they could have met on the street, in a shop, or on a Sunday morning at Christ Church. Perhaps Thomas Willing brought his young business associate home to dinner after a meeting in his office. There was no reason for either family to disapprove of any friendship between the two. Indeed, the light of speculation must have flickered in the eyes of Mrs. Thomas Willing and her friend and neighbor, Molly Stamper Bingham. Here were a son of twenty-eight who was eligible, rich and still unmarried and a daughter of sixteen whose grace and beauty were being noticed in the city.

Anne's grandfather, Charles Willing, the founder of the American branch of the family, had come to Philadelphia in 1728, at eighteen, to take charge of the Willings' American business. His father was a prosperous and influential shipping merchant of Bristol, England. Two years after his arrival, Charles Willing married Anne Shippen, and over the next two decades he fathered eleven children, ten of whom lived to maturity. The oldest of these, born in 1731, was Thomas Willing, Anne's father. Thomas was sent at nine years of age to England, where, under the care of his grandmother and his uncle, he received his education. Before returning to America, he studied law for a time in the Inner Temple.

When Charles Willing died in 1754 of "nervous or gaol fever" contracted while visiting one of his ships in the harbor, Thomas Willing took over the family house and grounds on Third Street and the business on Front Street, complete with ships, wharves, inventory, and connections throughout much of Europe and the West Indies. As one of his first acts he named a junior partner, Robert Morris, whom his father had taken into his office as a clerk at the age of sixteen, when Robert Morris senior, a tobacco merchant, was killed in an accident. Thomas Willing was then twenty-three; Robert Morris was twenty.

Willing left most of the operation of Willing, Morris and Company in his partner's hands, for he devoted much of his time to public affairs. He had been elected mayor of the city in 1763, an associate justice of the Supreme Court of the Province four years later, a trustee of the College in 1760, a member of the American Philosophical Society in 1768. As an organizer and leader of the merchants' opposition to Great Britain's economic policies, he had signed his name first among those who declared against the importation of British goods. He was president of the Provincial Congress held in 1774, a delegate in the two following years to the Continental Congress, and a member of the Pennsylvania Committee of Public Safety.

At thirty-two, Thomas Willing married Ann McCall, who was fourteen years his junior. Mrs. Willing's amiable features are preserved in portraits by Robert Feke and Charles Peale; her good manners are immortalized in an episode that occurred at one of the first Assembly dances. As told in a letter of that day:

> There happened a little mistake at the beginning, which at some other times might have produced disturbances. The Governor would have opened the Assembly with Mrs. —— but she refused him, I suppose because he had not been to visit her. After Mrs. —— refusal, two or three ladies out of modesty & from no manner of ill design excused themselves so that the Governor was put a little to his shifts, when Mrs. Willing now Mrs. Mayoress in a most genteel manner put herself into his way and on the Governor seeing this instance of her good nature he jumped at the occasion & they danced the first minuet.

In this summer of 1780, Thomas Willing was under something of a cloud in Philadelphia. He had remained in the city, even though aloof, during the British occupation; and as a delegate to the Second Congress he had refused to support or vote for the Declaration of Independence, "not only because I thought America at that time unequal to such a conflict as must ensue — having neither Army, ammunity, or military experience — but chiefly because the delegates of Pennsylvania were not then authorized by their injunctions from the Assembly, or the voice of the people at large, to join in such a vote." Only his work in financing and supplying the revolutionary armies had restored some of the luster to Judge Willing's reputation.

The relations between Willing and Robert Morris had been cordial, even affectionate, and they remained friendly even after Morris dissolved the partnership in 1778. (It was reestablished in 1783.) Morris, in these years, was being revealed as the dominant partner. The dependence of Willing on the younger man is indicated by a letter he wrote at a time of crisis. Willing had heard in the fall of 1777 that the integrity of his company was being attacked in Europe by rumor and innuendo, and that his bills were being protested to the amount of £36,000. To Morris he wrote:

> This is a shock I was not prepared for, by you, or any the least suspicion of my own & you must know how horrid & distressing my feelings must be on the occasion, to have such a demand come upon me, unprepared as I am to satisfy it, is terrible indeed. Ruin & gaol stare me in the face. If the news is true, I fear I shall sink under it. You alone can calm my fears, if it is false, or put me in a way to extricate myself if you believe it is true.

Morris protected Willing by instructing his agents to give him credit.

The house in which Anne Willing grew up, built by her grandfather Charles Willing, was one of the finest and most spacious in the city. With its large grounds, its gardens and giant oak trees, it occupied part of the block encompassed by Third, Fourth, Spruce and Willing's Alley. The quality of the Willing household was briefly suggested by John Adams, who dined there on October 11, 1774 (when Anne was ten):

> Dined at Mr. Willings, who is a Judge of the Supreme Court here, with the gentlemen from Virginia, Maryland and New York. A most splendid feast again — turtle and every thing else. . . . Mr. Willing is the most sociable, agreeable man of all.

Anne was given the careful education characteristic of the Philadelphia of that day, where the advanced and liberal theories of the Quakers on the education of young women had taken root. Girls were taught to read, write, and speak their own language correctly; to speak a second and even a third language; to play the harpsichord, sing ballads, dance, draw, paint on glass, and embroider. Particular emphasis was placed on the ability to write a good letter — a requisite for any girl who considered herself fit for polite society. The Library Company, the Loganian Collection, the law books in the State House, and the books in the College — all these were closed to Anne by reason of her sex; but the city had many circulating libraries she could use. (Henry Fielding and Samuel Richardson were the most popular authors.) One European visitor reported that the ladies of Philadelphia possessed great beauty, natural ease and charm, but that "they are still anxiously attentive to the more important embellishments of the mind."

Anne had also the advantages conferred by five doting and attentive aunts, sisters of her father. The oldest of these at forty-seven, Aunt Anne, described in the family Bible entry as "beautiful, amiable and accomplished," was the wife of Tench Francis, Jr. Colonel Henry Bouquet, the Swiss soldier, savior of the western frontier with a brilliant victory over the Indians in the French and Indian War, had courted Aunt Anne, and though rejected, he had willed her his only possessions: five tracts of land.

Aunt Mary (Molly), forty, known for her wit, was the second wife of William Byrd III of the great Westover estate in Virginia. His first wife had died mysteriously in a fall from a window, and Molly Willing had married the widower so soon thereafter that some cruel jesters had called her "Willing Molly." Colonel Byrd was a fine gentleman and a brave soldier; he was also a wastrel and a rake. He mortgaged his silver plate, his 159 slaves, and Westover, and he was in danger of losing all of these when on New Year's Day in 1777, he killed himself. Molly, left with a large family to raise, by good management rescued Westover, the silver, and the slaves. She now lived infrequently in Philadelphia. General Washington used the Byrds' former Philadelphia house as his headquarters and residence through many months of the war. It was separated from the Willing house by an open garden; and in these years, first as a child and then as a young woman, Anne Willing was a frequent and welcome visitor in the Washington household.

Aunt Abigail, thirty-three, had never married and lived with her widowed mother. Aunt Margaret (Peggy), twenty-seven, was married to the prominent brewer Robert Hare. The Hares had fled the city during the British occupation to take refuge with Aunt Mary in Westover.

Aunt Elizabeth (Betsy), thirty-eight, lived two houses down. Her husband was Samuel Powel, son and heir of "the rich carpenter" who had built more than ninety houses in Philadelphia. Powel had graduated in one of the first classes of the College of Philadelphia; he had traveled widely in Europe and there had met Voltaire at Ferney; he was helping to subsidize the painter Benjamin West; he had been the last mayor of the city under the Provincial government and was now speaker of the Pennsylvania Assembly. His great-nephew, Joshua Francis Fisher, considered him conceited and priggish as a man and precise and peremptory as a husband. Betsy Willing had earlier set her cap for John Dickinson, unsuccessfully; had had "a rather serious flirtation in Virginia" with Richard Henry Lee; had turned down a Mr. Beverly of Virginia, reportedly worth £80,000; and had accepted Mr. Powel as a last resort.

The young Anne was, for that day, somewhat above middle size. Her portraits show a face with a Fragonard beauty; all who described her spoke of her grace. A social historian of the time said of Anne Willing, "Her manners were a gift."

William Bingham fell in love with this girl who was just turning woman, twelve years younger than he. He asked Thomas Willing for his daughter's hand in marriage. The application was favorably received, and a marriage contract was drawn up.

The wedding was held late in the afternoon on Thursday, October 26, 1780. Christ Church was thronged with relatives of the bride and her bridegroom: Willings, Benezets, Powels, Stampers, Byrds, Hares, Francises, Coxes, McCalls, Shippens. Mrs. Willing, seven months big with her thirteenth child, rejoiced and wept at the marriage of her first. The Right Reverend Dr. William White, later the first Protestant Episcopal bishop of Pennsylvania, handsome in his white linen sleeves and rich vestments, performed the service. The two-line notice in the *Pennsylvania Gazette* was simple: "Married Thursday evening, William Bingham Esq. to Miss Willing."

Miss Anna Rawle, daughter of a Loyalist family, wrote to her mother:

> Speaking of handsome women brings Nancy Willing to my mind. She might set for the Queen of Beauty, and is lately married to

Bingham, who returned from the West Indies with an immense fortune. They have set out in highest style; nobody here will be able to make the figure they do; equipage, house, cloathes, are all the newest taste, — and yet some people wonder at the match. She but sixteen and such a perfect form. His appearance is less amiable.

CHAPTER 9

Of Death, a Bank, and Marching Armies

I am exceedingly attached to that institution [the Bank of North America], and most fervently wish it the most brilliant success.

William Bingham to Thomas Willing
July 30, 1783

IN THAT AUTUMN of 1780, the one cheerful aspect of an otherwise gloomy military situation was the presence of some 6000 French troops encamped at Newport in Rhode Island, waiting for the proper time and opportunity to strike their ancient enemy. These were France's best, splendidly equipped and uniformed, superbly trained and officered. With them they brought not only hope, but also considerable quantities of money, all gold and silver, that flowed like an infusion into the bankrupt American economy.

The commander of the French expeditionary force, Lieutenant General the Comte de Rochambeau, like his fellow officers, was astonished at an army in which even merchants, in an emergency, served as privates and whose soldiers were ragged, untrained and undisciplined. "Send us ships, troops and money," he wrote to Vergennes, "but do not depend upon these people, nor upon their means."

Third in command of this army was Major General the Marquis de Chastellux, forty-six, author, liberal philosopher, friend of Voltaire, member of the French Academy, intimate of the house of Orleans, and (because he spoke English) confidant of General Washington. Chastellux had a devouring curiosity about all things American. Late that fall, accompanied by three servants and an extra horse, he made a three-week tour that ended in Philadelphia. There he stayed with the Chevalier de la Luzerne, the French minister. Luzerne sent him to call on Mr. and Mrs. Bingham; and so it was that one of the first views of the Binghams, husband and wife, comes through the eyes of a man who, the following year, would put everything he saw into one of the most widely read travel books of the age.

On Monday morning, December 4, General Chastellux inspected, with several delegates to Congress, the Pennsylvania State House. That afternoon he received a visit from Mr. James Wilson, "a celebrated lawyer and author of several pamphlets on current affairs." He dined privately with Luzerne and then

> [I] went to see Mrs. Bingham, a young and handsome woman, only seventeen [sixteen]; her husband, who was there according to the American custom, is only twenty-five [twenty-eight]. He was agent of Congress at Martinique, whence he has returned with a tolerable knowledge of French, and with much attachment to the Marquis de Bouillé.

On Wednesday, Chastellux toured the Brandywine battlefield with six other French officers, all of them handsome, rich and noble, including the Marquis de Lafayette, the Vicomte de Noailles (Lafayette's brother-in-law), and the Comte de Damas (one of Rochambeau's aides-de-camp). On Friday he dined with the president of Congress, called on Samuel Adams to hold a long political colloquy, and made his leisurely way back home to dress for a ball Luzerne was giving "for a select society, on the occasion of a marriage."

> There were about twenty women, a dozen or fifteen of whom were dancers; each of the latter had her "partner," as is the custom in America . . . with whom she must dance the whole evening, without being allowed to take another. . . . Strangers generally have the privilege of being "complimented with the handsomest ladies." The Comte de Damas thus had Mrs. Bingham for his partner, and the Vicomte de Noailles, Miss [Nancy] Shippen. Both of them, like true philosophers, testified a great respect for the custom of the country, by not leaving their handsome partners during the whole evening; they furthermore compelled the admiration of the whole assembly by the grace and nobility with which they danced. . . . The ball was interrupted towards midnight by a supper, served café-style, at several different tables.

Sarah Jay, writing to Mrs. Robert Morris from Madrid, supposed that the Morrises were pleased with the Bingham marriage, "as it promises happiness to the parties interested." John Jay sent his congratulations

> on the happiness you derive from the most delicate of all connections with one of the most lovely of her sex. As I am always pleased to find those happy who I think deserve to be so, it gave me very sensible satisfaction to hear that you had both made so judicious a choice, notwithstanding the veil which that sweet fascinating passion often draws over our eyes and understanding. . . . Mrs. Jay . . . never speaks of Martinico without expressing how much we are indebted to you for the agreeable manner in which we passed the time we stayed there.

Jay asked Bingham "to give me advices of . . . the state of the parties, the views of leading individuals, and . . . intelligence respecting our friends and others." He supplied a cipher Bingham was to use, based on Entick's *New Spelling Dictionary*.

> Add twenty to the number of the page, and ten to that of the word you use. Distinguish the first column by a dot over the first figure, and the second column by a dot over the second figure. For instance, the word duration is the first word in the first column for the 139th page, and must be thus written, i̇59 11.

Gouverneur Morris seems to have been a frequent guest at the Binghams' following his recovery from the loss of his leg, for on November 25, Robert R. Livingston, John Jay's former law partner and a member of the Congress from New York, wrote Morris, "I congratulate you in your restoration to the beau monde. . . . I am told you are Master of the Ceremonies to La Belle Madame Bingham. I consider you as enlisted for the season as I am persuaded she will claim all the attention you can possibly spare."

Social gaiety was suddenly cut short for the Binghams in December, when Anne's mother lay in with her thirteenth child. She never recovered from the birth, and on February 29, 1781, she died. She was carried to the Christ Church grounds, followed by nine motherless children from the ages of fourteen to less than two years. She died, according to her obituary, "greatly and deservedly regretted" and possessing "every virtue that can adorn the female character." It is probable that Abigail Willing, unmarried at thirty-three, moved into the large Third Street house and undertook to rear her brother's children. The thirteenth child, christened Henry, died that summer.

The family suffered still another loss when John Benezet, Bingham's commercial agent, husband of his sister Hannah, made his will, called in his debts with an advertisement in the *Gazette*, and sailed away on a business trip to Europe. His ship was lost and he was never heard of again. A few months later, John Stamper, Bingham's maternal grandfather, died at an advanced age.

*

The year 1781 opened with a mutiny in the army and the first halting attempts to bring administrative reform and efficiency into the national government. Some 1300 men of the Pennsylvania division revolted at Morristown on New Year's Day, incensed at what they considered extensions of their enlistments and at a $25 bounty being paid to recruits while they had been unpaid for months. They killed an officer, wounded several others, and marched behind their sergeants, with six pieces of cannon, toward Philadelphia. The Radical leader Joseph Reed, Robert Morris' political enemy, met the men at Trenton and pacified them. They paraded and returned to camp, where they handed over to the authorities several spies the British had sent among them to encourage the revolt. Concessions were made under which more than half the men left the service. There were no reprisals, and the only executions were of the British spies, who were hanged. When the New Jersey Line mutinied three weeks later, General Washington sent a force that surprised the men, forced them to parade unarmed, and had two of the leaders executed.

Mutiny had the effect of strengthening the growing movement in the country toward administrative and fiscal reform and stronger centralized authority in the national government. Conservative delegates dominated the new Congress when it opened its session in November.

The leaders of this political revolt — men of the propertied, mercantile class — were determined to remove economic restraints, restore the public credit, and introduce more efficient management in Congress. At the same time, they saw in a strong central government some protection against what they called "the democratical spirit" in the states, as exemplified by the radical government in Pennsylvania. With the failure of old methods, conservative ideas had now won popular support. Even Thomas Paine reexamined his postulates. "While the war was carried on by emissions [of currency]," he wrote to Joseph Reed, "the poor were of equal use in government with the rich. But when the means must be drawn from the country . . . unless the wealthier part throw in their aid, public measures must go heavily on."

Congress reluctantly abandoned its attempt to run the country through committees and boards made up of its own members. It adopted a bold new concept: separate administrative departments for war, foreign affairs, naval affairs, and finance, each run by an individual executive responsible to Congress and with authority to act.

William Bingham sought appointment to the new post of Minister for Foreign Affairs. He proposed himself cautiously in a letter to Thomas Burke, veteran member of Congress from North Carolina, who replied:

> As in my judgement you are the most proper person I can think of for that department, you may rely on my best endeavours to impress on other gentlemen sentiments similar to my own. Your conduct in the departments you have hitherto filled gives every reason for relying on you in future, and has proved your abilities to be equal to the most arduous and delicate affairs. If you are appointed to this new office I shall consider it an acquis[it]ion to the public service.

James Madison, Arthur Lee, Robert R. Livingston, and Richard Law of Connecticut were the others considered for the post. Bingham was eliminated at once, though not, as Burke explained, for personal reasons.

> Every one to whom I have spoken of you have expressed themselves handsomely, but objected to the chusing so many officers in one state of the Union. This is the only objection, and in a new jealous republic it is impossible to surmount such objections.

Livingston of New York was appointed to the post. He rented a small office on Philadelphia's Sixth Street, hired two clerks, and served without distinction and under constantly frustrating conditions for eighteen months. On one occasion, having made arrangements at a tavern for a dinner to be given in honor of the Minister of France, he had difficulty convincing Congress that he himself should be invited. On another, Robert Morris had to explain with some emphasis that the Minister for Foreign Affairs was not entitled to collect a 5 per cent commission on the salaries of the department's employees.

Only one man was considered for the post of Superintendent of Finance. Congress offered Robert Morris the appointment in February, 1781, without a dissenting voice, though his old and implacable enemy Sam Adams withheld his vote. Morris did not immediately accept, and then accepted only on two conditions. Congress must record in its minutes, "that no doubt may arise or reflections be cast on this score hereafter," its understanding that Morris would continue his private mercantile connections and engagements. And he was to have the absolute power of dismissing from office or employment all persons concerned in the official expenditure of public moneys. Congress objected to these stipulations, but when Morris refused to accept the post without them, it conceded on both. During the weeks the delegates were deliberating these points, Maryland ratified the Articles of Confederation, and amid much public acclamation the states became in name, if not in fact, a working confederacy.

Morris named Gouverneur Morris as his assistant. He then proceeded with characteristic energy to lay the foundations of a national state that would have "power, consequence, grandeur." He reorganized the treasury department in order to introduce "regularity" into its affairs. He substituted his own personal credit, in the form of "Morris Notes," for the credit lost by the government he was serving — $20, $50, and $80 denominations drawn against himself and used as currency. He appointed commissioners to settle the great accumulated pile of claims on the government. He abolished the high-salaried and inefficient purchasing commissaries and began to supply the army in the European manner by "contracts with private men of substance and talents." He repealed the regulations setting a compulsory value on paper currency as legal tender. To achieve free trade, he removed the embargoes on export of goods, guaranteeing to Congress that the change would cause no shortage of supplies for the army. "It is inconsistent with the principles of liberty," he said, "to prevent a man from the free disposal of his property as he may think fit."

As the capstone of his restructuring program, Morris undertook to create a commercial bank. The Bank of Pennsylvania had performed the function for which it had been created, and now, its capital depleted, was inactive.* What was needed was a full-fledged bank of deposit, discount, and issue — a permanent, federally chartered banking institution that could borrow money, float loans abroad, print notes redeemable in specie on demand, provide the convenience of deposit banking, and serve as an instrument of exchange and an organ for the regulation of finance. Three days after he took office, Morris submitted to Congress "a plan for establishing a national bank for the United States of North America." In this project he drew heavily on the services of his friend William Bingham.

Bingham had been spending some time with Morris in settling his 617,641-livre account as agent in the West Indies. Morris had never satisfied the request for information from James Lovell and the special committee of Congress, and in August, 1781, a year later, Bingham patiently asked him "to make a few remarks on this business," adding, "I should think myself inexcusable in troubling you on the subject, if you was not the only person who is thoroughly acquainted with it." Morris met with Bingham to discuss the matter, and on September 7 he wrote to Lovell, "It is very certain that the emoluments arising to Mr. Bingham from the commercial business of Congress fell short of what was expected, and it is equally certain that the inconvenience arising from his constant advances and consequent distresses must far outbalance the commissions he drew."

The Committee continued to delay. Bingham thereupon sent a one-page memorial to Congress pleading for an immediate advance on the balance due him. He owed £34,000 ($150,960), he said, which he had obtained by pledging the credit of the United States and by procuring "the collateral security of several gentlemen resident in Martinique, who from the failure of these expected remittances will be involved in the greatest distress." He requested one-third of the

---

* It was, Morris said, "in fact nothing more than a patriotic subscription of continental money . . . for the purpose of purchasing provisions for a starving army."

amount due, "the remainder not demanding so immediate an attention."

Morris arranged with Franklin to give Bingham a credit of 100,000 livres in Europe, since he was "greatly in advance for the United States and justice requires that [his] situation be alleviated." A few days later, Congress accepted the recommendation of its committee and resolved that his expense account of 110,324 livres be paid with interest at 6 per cent dating back to June, 1781. The largest and final part of his account he finally received in the spring of 1783, three years after his return from Martinique.

Morris was then and later charged with partiality in thus settling the account of his friend and former business partner from a depleted treasury and at a time when his waiting room was thronged with other creditors. Having a contempt for those who did not understand the workings of finance and the ways of merchants, Morris never bothered to defend such payments, other than to say it was his policy to pay all debts owing to persons who had contracted them abroad. The greatest part of Bingham's debt was owed, in turn, to the French government. It is reasonable to suppose that Morris took this into account in recommending payment.

Dr. Arthur Lee made no protest in Congress when the payment was voted, because he recognized that the money was actually owed to foreign creditors, but he disapproved of it nonetheless. A six-page handwritten document among his papers entitled "Observations on Mr. Bingham's Accts" reads, in part:

> We have seen Mr. Bingham receive from the Treasury of the U.S. a full payment for all his demands arising from his transactions in the W. Indies & the Treasury books shew, that he was paid in specie. This was done by the absolute authority of Mr. Morris . . . nor is there a single instance in which his partners or his favorites were not paid in specie, while the Army was almost mutinying for want of pay, & clothing.

Dr. Lee presumed that Bingham would pay his foreign creditors with government loan certificates "when he had received hard money for what was in fact due to them, tho he represented it as due to himself." In this he underestimated both the intelligence and power of the French.

Through the summer of 1781, while these negotiations were proceeding, Bingham worked closely with the three men most active in the affairs of the proposed Bank of North America. Robert Morris was the guiding spirit, though as the nation's Superintendent of Finance he of course could hold no post as officer or director. James Wilson undertook to advise on legal matters and to counter the strong political opposition that was certain to arise. Thomas Willing, it was understood, would be put forth for president of the institution. To William Bingham fell the responsibility of drawing up the by-laws of the nation's first bank.*

A subscription of $400,000 was to be raised in shares of $400 each, payable in gold or silver. The incorporation was to become effective when the entire $400,000 had been subscribed. Twelve directors were to be chosen annually by the stockholders to regulate the affairs of the bank. None of them was to receive compensation except by consent of the stockholders. They would meet every Thursday morning. The directors were to elect one of their number each year as president and two of their number each quarter as inspectors. The inspectors were to deliver to the United States Superintendent of Finance, every evening except Sunday, an accurate account of the day's business, including a statement of the note obligations and cash on hand. The Superintendent had the right at all times to examine the bank's books and papers.

The shares were to be freely transferable, and the directors were to be at liberty to open new subscriptions to the capital stock as often and upon such terms as they should see proper. The bank's notes, payable on demand, were by law to be made receivable for taxes, duties and debts in every state of the union, and were to be counted as specie in the settlement of accounts between the states and the United States. Congress would be asked to recommend to the states that no other bank be established, or bankers permitted, within the states for the duration of the war, and that counterfeiting the bank's notes be made a felony.

Congress approved the plan for the Bank of North America on

---

* The late James Wettereau, specialist in American banking history, in 1937 called William Bingham "perhaps the ablest banker of the period." He rendered this judgment largely on the basis of the minutes of the Bank of the United States (founded in 1791) which he had discovered. He was not aware that Bingham wrote the bylaws of the Bank of North America.

May 26, 1781, by a bare majority of one state. (Pennsylvania, because its vote was split, did not approve the resolution.) Robert Morris published the document, with a statement of purpose, two days later. In a prospectus to investors he said, " . . . We shall only have to appeal to the interest of mankind which in most cases will do more than their Patriotism." To John Jay he wrote of his hope to "unite the several States more closely together in one general money connexion, and indisolubly to attach many powerful individuals to the cause of our country by the strong principle of self-love and the immediate sense of private interest."

A shop with a forty-foot front, belonging to Tench Francis, Jr., was leased and remodeled for the banking offices. It was situated on the north (or Market Street) side of Chestnut Street, a short distance west of Third. Dr. Franklin's house stood on a small street to the rear. On a small court nearly opposite was the trade union club where Thomas Willing, sixteen years earlier, had headed the movement to force repeal of the Stamp Act by refusing to import British goods.

Bingham invested $42,800 in the bank — ninety-five shares for himself, five for his wife, and seven for his mother. Benjamin Franklin bought one share to show his good will. Subscriptions were alarmingly slow, however, and by October, only $70,000 had been collected. Investors were not interested, especially those from the South: they feared an unfavorable outcome to the war; the prospect of profit was remote; or they were simply afraid to trust their savings to a new, untried, and uncertain venture.

Morris placed great hopes on a ship, the *Trumbull,* which he dispatched to Havana loaded with flour and carrying bills of exchange on Madrid and promises of more flour. He hoped to realize $400,000 on the voyage, most of which he would invest for the government in the bank; but the *Trumbull* was captured and the hopes dashed. "We have learnt to bear losses and endure disappointments," Morris said, "and what is still better we have courage always to try again"; but the prospects for the Bank of North America looked bleak in the fall of 1781.

One reason the bank's affairs did not prosper was that Robert Morris was working around the clock to supply Washington's army. The commander in chief had come to depend on Morris as someone who could almost magically procure provisions, transportation and money.

His requests were becoming more frequent, harder to fulfill, and sometimes peremptory in tone. Washington was embarking on a great gamble, a master stroke, that could win the war and save the Revolution.

General Lord Cornwallis, harried by attacks from American forces in the South, had drawn his army, totaling some 7200 men, into the peninsula formed by the James and York rivers in Virginia. There, at Yorktown, he was building a military and naval base. He was in a secure and defensible position — so long as Britain controlled the sea approaches. The French, however, had decided to commit a navy as well as an army to the American war. From Rear Admiral the Count de Grasse came word that he had arrived in the West Indies with his fleet, and that he would sail for the Chesapeake on August 13 carrying 3000 soldiers from the Santo Domingo garrison. Washington and Rochambeau accordingly drew up plans to converge the French fleet and the American and French armies on Yorktown.

The allied armies started to move late in July, Washington leaving an elaborately contrived deception on the New Jersey shore opposite Staten Island to make the English think he meant to attack New York.

On the afternoon of August 30, the First Troop of Philadelphia City Cavalry, the militia and a number of citizens on horseback paraded to the outskirts of the city to greet and escort his excellency, the commander in chief of the American armies, and the Generals Rochambeau and Chastellux, accompanied by their various suites. Washington called on the principal citizens gathered at the City Tavern, took his noon meal with the other generals at the home of Robert Morris, where he was to stay while in town, and then, followed by a pressing concourse of admirers, paid his respects to Congress in the Assembly Chamber at the State House. That evening the city was illuminated, the streets so thronged with people that windows were broken in the crush.

For several days the troops poured into the city. The Americans arrived first, on Sunday, September 2 — 5600 ragged and tattered Continentals in a dusty column two miles long. The French, having marched 548 miles in thirty-seven days, began to arrive the following morning. The French generals rode out to meet the first division of their army and halted it one mile from the edge of town. The men brushed and chalked their uniforms, put on their decorations, dressed their ranks, and resumed the march into Philadelphia with General Rochambeau at their head, the regimental bands playing field music.

Ships in the Delaware saluted the troops with cannonades. Great crowds, cheering and waving, gathered along the streets. The division marched down Front Street, up Chestnut past the State House, and encamped on a plain along the Schuylkill. There was much admiring comment on their appearance and manner — their good spirits, their disciplined precision in marching, their clean and elegant uniforms. The regiment of Soissonnais, pride of the French army, made the deepest impression in its uniforms of white broadcloth with rose-colored lapel facings, its polished metal accoutrements, its grenadier hats surmounted by white and rose-colored plumes. The regimental chaplain, the Abbé Robin, wrote back to France:

> The arrival of the French army at Philadelphia was more like a triumph, than simply a passing through the place. . . . They marched through the town, with the military music playing before them, which is always particularly pleasing to the Americans; the streets were crowded with people, and the ladies appeared at the windows in their most brilliant attire. All Philadelphia was astonished to see people, who had endured the fatigues of a long journey, so ruddy and handsome, and even wondered that there could possibly be *Frenchmen* of so genteel an appearance.

On Tuesday, the French troops marched past the State House, there to be reviewed by the generals with their staffs, the French minister, the honorable Members of Congress, and other dignitaries. Chief Justice Thomas McKean, President of Congress, appeared on the steps attired in a rich black velvet suit, a sword at his side. He and thirteen of the delegates to Congress, one from each state, were to take a royal salute ordinarily given to crowned heads of state.

President McKean whispered to General Rochambeau, "Should I salute or not?"

"When the troops pass before the King," Rochambeau replied, "his Majesty kindly condescends to salute them."

But McKean was worried. Would not a salute seem to say that he was assuming the trappings of royalty? He and the thirteen Congressmen compromised the issue. Every time the colors dipped and the officers of the line saluted, they removed their hats and bowed.

Bingham attended a banquet that evening held by the Chevalier de la Luzerne for 180 officers and gentlemen guests. During one of the early courses, according to the Abbé Robin,

> an express arrived: a disquieting silence immediately seized every guest — our eyes were fixed upon the Chevalier de la Luzerne, every one endeavouring to guess what the message would turn out to be. "Thirty-six ships of the line," said he, "commanded by Monsieur le Comte de Grasse, are arrived in Chesapeak-Bay, and three thousand men have landed and opened a communication with the Marquis de la Fayette." Joy and good humour, immediately resumed their place on every countenance.

During these momentous events a complication arose. The American troops were of the New England and middle states, and they refused to march any farther south unless given one month's back pay in hard money. Washington turned to Robert Morris, who borrowed $40,000 on his personal credit, half of it from Rochambeau's war chest and half from his fellow merchants in Philadelphia. Washington received the money with an expression of gratitude and asked Morris to get boats to convey the troops from the Head of Elk (Elkton) down Chesapeake Bay to Yorktown.

The troops marched south and the city was quiet again. A long period of waiting followed. News came at intervals from the field throughout September and into October, generally six to seven days behind the event. Cornwallis was besieged; heavy guns had been emplaced; parallel trenches were being dug toward the enemy defenses.

At three o'clock on the morning of October 22, a Monday, an express rider galloped into town and asked an old German watchman to show him the way to Justice McKean's house. The watchman took him there. The rider banged on the door, wakened the household and the neighbors, and delivered his message.

The watchman continued his rounds of the city, candles in the houses lighting up behind him, inhabitants pouring into the streets, as he called out, "Basht dree o'-glock, und Gornvul-lis isht da-ken."

CHAPTER 10

A Victory and a Voyage

I was much disappointed and indeed mortified to find that you are not in the Delegation to Congress: I lose a particular Pleasure which I should have enjoyed in serving with you. However, you must still direct your Attention to public life. Your Country will soon call for you; and you must, as others have done, obey the Call, notwithstanding previous unhandsome Treatment.

James Wilson to William Bingham
November 25, 1782

FOR TWO DAYS the city waited, cautiously hoping the report of victory at Yorktown was true. On October 24 (1781), an aide-de-camp arrived with dispatches from General Washington, having been delayed ten hours when his open boat ran onto shoals in Chesapeake Bay. Yorktown had fallen; General Cornwallis had surrendered.

Officials of the state and the nation gathered to congratulate one another. Congress met at eleven that morning and resolved that it would "at two o'clock this day go in procession to the Dutch Lutheran Church, and return thanks to Almighty God, for crowning the allied arms of the United States and France, with success." Flags were raised on the State House. At noon, troops of the city fired an artillery salute in the State House yard that was answered by the ships in the harbor. A *Te Deum* was sung in "the Romish Church." The city government announced that "those citizens who chuse to ILLU-MINATE on the glorious occasion" might do so that evening between six and nine o'clock, and it added, "Decorum and harmony are recommended to every citizen, and general discountenance to the least appearance of riot." Decorum and harmony were lacking, however, as a mob roamed the streets breaking windows and threatening the inhabitants — pacifist Quakers and suspected Loyalists — of houses that did not have lighted candles on their windowsills.

Saturday afternoon, November 3, the First City Troop cantered out to meet a detachment from Yorktown bearing twenty-four flags and banners taken from the British and German regiments. These were escorted the length of Market Street, past hushed and awestruck crowds, to the Delaware River, then along Front to Chestnut Street, and so back to the State House, where they were "laid down" before Congress.

At the end of the month, General and Mrs. Washington arrived amid wild public acclamation and prepared for a long stay in Philadelphia. They took the Byrd-Chew house, next door to the Powels, one house down from the Willings.

Robert Morris called an organization meeting of Bank of North America stockholders at the City Tavern on November 1. Twenty-five men were present. Subscriptions were still lagging, Morris reported, but means had come to hand that should make it possible to start up the institution. Some 2,500,000 livres ($477,500) in gold and silver coin had arrived in Boston, part loan and part gift from France. Morris had sent Tench Francis and a detachment of armed soldiers to fetch this money.* Francis built fourteen wagons in Boston according to Morris' detailed instructions, hired twenty-eight teams of oxen, loaded the coin into boxes lashed on the axles, and successfully brought men, wagons, and money on a two-month journey, some of it through British-infested territory. He arrived in Philadelphia just after the celebration of the victory at Yorktown. Morris promptly invested $253,200 of the money for the government in 633 shares of Bank of North America stock, thus raising the bank's subscribed capital to some $325,000.

The stockholders elected Thomas Willing president of the bank and chose twelve directors, one of whom was William Bingham. Tench Francis, his firm attachment to the cause of America demonstrated, was named cashier.

Though the subscription was still 200 shares short of the 1000-share goal, the directors resolved to apply to Congress for the charter of incorporation. The measure was introduced in December, 1781. There was considerable opposition, chiefly from those who (presaging a more monumental struggle on the same issue a decade later)

---

* Because of his family's long service to the Penns as land agents, Francis had from time to time been accused of Loyalist sympathies. This dangerous expedition, Morris thought, would give him "an opportunity to shew his firm attachment to the cause of America."

insisted that the Congress of the Confederation had no explicit power to incorporate a bank of the nation. The preceding Congress, however, had pledged its support of the bank, and so, on the last day of the year, the charter was approved.

There was a rush of last-minute preparations. Remodeling was completed on Tench Francis' converted shop. Banking hours were to be from ten to one and from three to five. There were six regular employees; Cashier Francis at $1000 a year, a teller, a sub-teller, an accomptant, a clerk, and a porter ($160).

The Bank of North America opened its doors with appropriate ceremonies on Monday, January 7, 1782. General Washington himself dignified the occasion with his presence. William Bingham was presumably there; if he was not present, it was because Anne Bingham, the day before, had been safely delivered of a child, a girl to be named Ann Louisa.

Several years later, when a group of Boston merchants obtained a charter incorporating the Massachusetts Bank, they sought information and advice from Thomas Willing. He replied:

> . . . The business was as much a novelty to us . . . as it can possibly be to you. It was a pathless wilderness, ground but little known to this side of the Atlantick. No book then spoke of the interior arrangements or rules observed in Europe — accident alone threw in our way even the form of an English bank bill. All was to us a mystery.
>
> In this situation, we adopted the only safe method to avoid confusion. Educated as merchants, we resolved to pursue the road we were best acquainted with. We established our books on a simple mercantile plan. . . . You may proceed without fear.

Robert Morris borrowed $400,000 from the bank for the government at 6 per cent per annum, the bank paying out the loans in its own engraved banknotes. Morris paid these for the government to army contractors, who, unfortunately, instead of circulating the notes, turned them in for specie. In Philadelphia, the notes were accepted at par, but in New England and parts of the South they were discounted as much as 15 per cent.

The amount of specie in the bank's vaults dwindled alarmingly. Willing and Francis contrived to make a great display of silver coins on the tables and counters. The porter wheeled around boxes marked "Silver" that may or may not have contained more coins. Silver was carried from the bank with casual ostentation, as though it had been lent out at interest, and was then returned quietly to the vault to be reused in the same manner.

By spring, conditions improved and the bank righted itself. Connecticut passed an act declaring the bank's notes receivable in payment of taxes, Rhode Island passed a law for punishment of those who counterfeited its notes or embezzled its funds, and Massachusetts gave the bank a charter as a corporation of the state. Morris sold $50,000 worth of bank stock to financial interests in Holland. The bank notes began to circulate everywhere at par and the value of the stock rose. The new institution was proving useful to the government as a fiscal agency and as a source of short-term loans, and it was acting as a stimulant to the economy. In November, 1782, President Willing happily reported on "the progress the Bank has made in regard to the number of its customers and the extensive circulation of its notes," and spoke of the "present flourishing situation and flattering prospects." The dividend for the first year's operations was almost 9 per cent, of which the government, as owner of five-eighths of the stock, got the major share. The strongest objection now voiced in the Assembly was that "the punctuality required (by) the bank (in repayment of loans) throws honest men into hands of usurers."

*

The months that followed were busy and prosperous ones for Bingham, the bank, and the new nation. The British still had two large armies on American soil, but there was little fighting save on the western frontier and on the seas. The British House of Commons voted in March (1782) against continuing the war, the Lord North ministry fell, and an emissary began informal peace talks in Paris with Franklin. The United States of North America, lately the United Colonies, took on the air and the spirit of a country that had survived and won a long, hard war.

In October, 1782, Bingham and two partners founded the mercantile house of Bingham, Inglis and Gilmor. Samuel Inglis, one of the directors of the bank, headed the firm of Samuel Inglis and Company, in which Morris and Willing had an interest. Robert Gilmor, a strikingly handsome Baltimore merchant, thirty-four years of age, had met and favorably impressed Bingham and his associates in business dealings on trips to Philadelphia.

According to Gilmor, his two partners, expecting a treaty to be signed with England, were eager to form a trading establishment at Amsterdam. They offered its management to Gilmor "as being from their experience of his manner of transacting business the fittest person for their purpose." Bingham and Inglis furnished four-fifths of the capital, Gilmor one-fifth, and the Willing and Morris firm its blessing. Gilmor embarked for Europe in November with his wife, four children, a white nurse and a colored maid. Morris gave him letters of recommendation he would find useful, even in wartime, if captured by the British.

Bingham also formed a land partnership about this time with James Wilson. Wilson had been buying up choice tracts while making his rounds as a lawyer. His limited resources soon exhausted, he applied to certain Dutch merchants for capital to complete "a very extensive system of works" on the Delaware River, consisting of iron-rolling and -slitting mills, gristmills, sawmills, and a forge. When the merchants turned him down, Wilson asked Bingham to find him other capitalists in Europe.

Bingham promised to do what he could and then came back with a counterproposal that Wilson supervise the formation of a company to buy land through New York's newly opened land office. Wilson laid down his conditions for accepting. For his trouble he wanted one-fourth of the lands purchased, capital of between £60,000 and £100,-000 sterling, and not more than three partners. The product of these negotiations was the Canaan Company, formed by four partners with the intent of buying 100,000 acres on the Susquehanna River in south-central New York. The company began by acquiring a tract of 30,600 acres on both sides of the river, including the site of what was to become the town of Binghamton.

Bingham, however, seems to have improved his fortune most rapidly while acting alone as a speculator in the money market. He had an understanding of economics and financial matters that was uncommonly acute for that day. He had intelligence sources that sent him information hours or days before it was received by those with whom he was dealing. He had an intuitive sense of where money was to be made and the cool self-assurance required to gamble and win. "We had in Pennsylvania," Charles Biddle wrote in his *Autobiography,* "State inland money, so called because the inland was to be sold to redeem it.

> This however soon depreciated to eight for one specie dollar. At this time Mr. William Bingham was in Reading. Speaking to him of the money he advised me to buy up some of it; but I expected it would go as the Continental money did and therefore did not do it. I believe Mr. Bingham purchased a large amount of it. Soon after you could not get a dollar of it for a specie dollar, for it carried interest, and there was not enough of it issued to pay for the inland, which was sold in lots and purchasers were obliged to pay in those bills or in specie, so that the holders received principal and interest.

Bingham was, in the considered judgment of Robert Gilmor's son, "very speculative in political events, by which he made a great deal of money, as see a particular account of him in the Marquis de Chastellux's 'Travels in America.' " Gilmor had read the first English edition (unauthorized) of the *Travels,* translated, edited and copiously annotated by a George Grieve. Bingham, according to Grieve, "gained a very considerable sum" by wagering on the outcome of a naval battle (the Battle of the Saints, largest naval engagement of the American Revolution) between Count de Grasse and Admiral George Rodney. The English decisively defeated the French, capturing Admiral de Grasse and six of his vessels. The Radicals refused to believe that the English were capable of such a victory, and the betting became frenetic. There was little doubt, according to Grieve, that Bingham had "secret and sure intelligence from his connection with the islands." He and his friends in the secret indulged the Radicals "to the utmost of their enthusiasm." Eventually news came of the French defeat and the capture of Grasse. "If the policies were all paid," Grieve said, Bingham and his friends "must have gained prodigious sums, for no less than from £80,000 to £100,000 sterling were calculated to be written."

During these months, Bingham contributed a considerable amount of time and effort to public causes. Philadelphia was an enlightened city in an enlightened age, but his proclivity for public service, much of it unpaid, seems unusual even for that place and time.

He served, in the summer of 1781, as chairman of a committee appointed by the State of Pennsylvania to take care of a large number of southerners, principally from Charleston, who had been taken prisoner by the British the previous year. Some hundreds had died in captivity, and now the British were bringing the ragged survivors up the Delaware under flags of truce and turning them back to American hands. Bingham and four committeemen raised a loan of $30,000, to be repaid by Congress, obtained charitable donations for the further relief of the refugees, and billeted them in the homes of Philadelphians. An appeal for help was made to the Quaker community, with the explanation that such aid to distressed fellow Americans could not conflict with the Quaker scruples against war. Robert Morris further pledged that their contributions would not "on any pretence" be diverted to other use. The Friends declined to help. They pleaded poverty, complained about the oppressive laws of the state, and said they needed all their resources for their "own needy brethren." *

In 1782, Bingham served as one of three commissioners for Pennsylvania appointed to negotiate a treaty with commissioners from New Jersey. They effected "a peaceable and equitable division" of the islands of the Delaware River between the two states.

During this period, Bingham was caught up and swept along by an irresistible force that went under the name Benjamin Rush. Dr. Rush, a man of passionate, varied, and inexhaustible enthusiasms and dislikes, had convinced himself that Pennsylvania needed a second college and that it should be established in the remote frontier town of Carlisle.

Carlisle lay in the Cumberland Valley 120 hard miles west of Philadelphia and eighteen miles west of the Susquehanna. It had only 300 houses; the Scotch-Irish inhabitants were mostly rough, illiterate, heavy-drinking farmers much given to brawling. Rush was making a thoroughly impractical proposal, and one destined for endless difficulties. Wiser heads told him so, but contradiction always stimulated Rush to even greater efforts. He drew Bingham into his plans.

The idea of the college was first discussed and plans laid among a small group of friends meeting at Bingham's house — specifically, on

---

* In October, 1777, a committee of "weighty friends" had waited upon General Washington to express the Society's utter condemnation of warfare and to offer a protest against all hostilities, past or present, including the American fight for independence.

his porch. Whether the meeting was called to consider the founding of a new college, or whether the subject came up spontaneously, is not known; but Rush forever after gave the phrase *Bingham's porch* a mystical, symbolic quality and, through the difficult and discouraging years that followed, sometimes used it as a cryptic rallying cry: "All will end well. *Bingham's porch!*"

Bingham agreed to subscribe £400 in loan office certificates — $1775 — and to serve as a trustee. Rush used his friend's name, his contribution and his promised support as a weapon both to beat down opposition and to impress potential donors. He chose the name John and Mary's College (for John Dickinson, president of the state, and his wife Mary) and drew up a prospectus in the form of a letter. In Carlisle, he said, the students could live more economically than in Philadelphia and would not be subjected to the city's low moral tone. There would be no student dormitories because "the custom of crowding boys together under one roof is the remains of monkish ignorance. It exposes them to many vices and unfits them for future commerce and connections in the world. Men are made to live in families. They cannot therefore be too early and too constantly preserved in a close connection with them."

Rush applied for a charter from the Assembly, meeting formidable opposition from the Presbyterian Church and the Radical Whigs. He worked tirelessly to raise money and to persuade some outstanding European scholar to come and live in the demi-paradise of the Cumberland Valley, there to head the new college, which now was to be named Dickinson College.

*

The summer of 1782 was the happiest Philadelphia had known in a decade. The war was now clearly over and won. The British evacuated Savannah in July; General Sir Guy Carleton, the new British commander, publicly conceded American independence in August; and in Paris in September four American Commissioners — Franklin, Adams, Jay, and Henry Laurens — began formal negotiations for peace. They violated the solemn pledge of their country in dealing with the British apart from the French, and they incurred sharp criticism in Congress for doing so; but Vergennes forgave the breach of faith. Almost everywhere in America the French were popular, ad-

mired and courted. The French were themselves happy in this brave
new world where they had at once served the cause of mankind and
humbled the perfidious English. During one expedition of officers
touring a battlefield, there was such a flow of exuberance that the
country people at the inn could not understand how they "could be
so hilarious without being drunk, and thought they had gone crazy."

In April, the Chevalier de la Luzerne announced the birth of a
French Dauphin, and Philadelphia was filled with joy. Congress ordered a display of transparencies by Charles Willson Peale in the
State House yard, with Queen Marie Antoinette as the main figure.
Luzerne responded with a splendid party at his residence at Sixth
and Chestnut. For a fortnight the town talked of nothing else, and
on the great day the hairdressers were so busy that some women had
to have their hair done between four and six in the morning. More
than 1100 guests, including General and Lady Washington, started to
arrive at 7:30 P.M. amid enormous crowds of onlookers. They heard
a concert, watched fireworks "of superior and unrivalled excellence,"
walked through illuminated gardens, danced in a hall built by the
architect L'Enfant, ate a supper at midnight, and went home at three
in the morning.

The winter season was brilliant. The Southwark Theater, closed
since the British occupation, reopened as the "Academy of Polite Science" (so named as not to offend the godly). The first performance
was held in Washington's honor; the play was Beaumarchais' *Eugénie,*
and a grand transparency symbolizing the union of the states, undoubtedly by Mr. Peale, was shown on the stage. The Dancing Assembly was reopened, still rigidly aristocratic but with the Tories
specifically excluded. The first dolls since the war, dressed in the latest styles, arrived from England, and the modes were immediately
copied. For the men, hair in a cue, powdered; a light-colored coat
with a narrow cape, very long in the back, with monogrammed silver
buttons; striped stockings; pointed shoes. For the women, high
wooden heels fancifully cut; rich brocades and taffetas; hoops flat-
tened before and after standing out a full two feet on each side; high,
built-up "Gainsborough" hats adorned with tall feathers.

The Bingham house was a favorite of society, and especially of the
titled French officers. Monsieur Bingham was amiable; he spoke a
"tolerable" French; he was rich, for he had just lent Robert Morris

$20,000 to pay government bills; he was important, for he had been mentioned as a possible candidate for the American Congress. His only fault was that he was, in the American manner, overly attentive to Madame Bingham. Madame Bingham was *ravissante et charmante;* she spoke a delightful French; she served excellent food; she was happy that her Uncle James had returned alive, if not healthy, from a terrible British prison ship in New York harbor.

Dr. Arthur Lee, a bachelor, observing the gaiety of the season with a jaundiced eye, disapproved. To Boston's James Warren, he wrote of the new manners.

> They are as little worthy of panygeric as an awkward imitation of the French can make them. . . . Mr. Morris, Mr. Bingham, Mr. [James] Ross, and others, who have made large fortunes during this war, employ their wealth in a manner not very consistent with that unostentatious virtue which ought to animate our infant republic. Extravagance, ostentation and dissipation distinguish what are called the ladies of the first rank.

In May, 1783, with the war over, the Binghams, their sixteen-month-old daughter Nan and several servants embarked for England. Bingham planned to combine business and pleasure in a long stay in Europe. He had been rejected for a seat in Congress in favor of a more experienced first-line candidate, and so he was free to travel. He would attempt to obtain gifts of money, books, and scientific instruments for the new college at Carlisle. He would try to straighten out an inheritance that was being withheld from Thomas Willing. He would show Europe to Anne — and Anne to Europe.

CHAPTER 11

Mr. and Mrs. Bingham
of Cavendish Square

The United States at present offer three millions of inhabitants, rapidly increasing in numbers, all of whom consume more or less of British manufactures, — the productions of art and industry, — in return for which, they give the raw materials — the produce of agriculture, in their native state.

How infatuated must the councils of your country be, which could tend but for a moment, to disturb so beneficial an intercourse; or suspend the sweets of so lucrative a commerce!

Letter from an American
Now Resident in London
to a Member of Parliament
by William Bingham, Esquire
London, 1783

IT WAS Anne Bingham's first ocean crossing. She managed to overcome her fear of the five-week voyage, but was successively seasick, homesick, and morning-sick (she was two months pregnant). For some unclear reason, and in what her husband called an act of "extreme complaisance," she gave up her stateroom to accept a temporary berth made up in a drafty cabin and caught a cold that lasted well into the summer. She was fortunate in having the companionship of her Aunt Margaret, Mrs. Robert Hare, who was traveling with her husband (the brewer) and their young son for an extended visit to England.

The voyage began in Philadelphia in one of the Willing and Morris ships, the *Commerce,* Captain Thomas Truxtun,* and ended at Gravesend in early July. It was an uneventful and calm crossing on an Atlantic free for the first time in almost eight years from the dep-

---

* Captain Truxtun, twenty-eight, had been a successful privateersman during the Revolution. In 1786, he sailed the first Philadelphia ship to China, Robert Morris' *Canton,* and in 1798 he became a naval hero in the half-war with France.

redations of British warships and privateers. Bingham took a house in Bloomsbury Square, which he described to his father-in-law as one of the most agreeable situations in London, with the country so close that a carriage could be off the pavements in five minutes. This, he wrote, was a desirable circumstance, for Anne's constitution was delicate, and she needed to ride out in the fresh country air.

He found that they were received with particular marks of attention and civility, and expressed the conventional surprise "that there can be so sudden a transition in the mind, from the extremes of war and violence, to the cultivation of affection and friendly intercourse." The United States, he said, and especially Pennsylvania were regarded in Europe as an asylum for the poor and oppressed. He found many American Loyalists in London who were eager to return home, but the few who had already done so had come back to England disappointed and embittered. There was some resentment in London at the treatment they had received.

Bingham tried to obtain a large loan for James Wilson ("You know it to be of much importance to me to be supplied with money," Wilson wrote) but without success. He bought a silver teapot for Thomas Willing and some copper saucepans lined with silver, as he had been commissioned to do. He began inquiries into the annuities left from the estate of Willing's uncle in Gloucestershire, and sent back three pipes of wine — one as a present for Willing, two to be stored for his own use. He reported to Willing that the Bank of North America bore a high repute in Europe. Would it be possible for him to buy fifty more shares of its stock in an unlisted name?

The family of John Penn, last Provincial governor of Pennsylvania and grandson of its founder, was especially agreeable and attentive. William and Anne made several excursions during the summer to the Penns' country seat at Richmond, with Anne expressing raptures at the high cultivation of the countryside. "We leave London for Brighthelmstone in a few days," Bingham wrote to Willing. "Mr. Penn's family is to be one of the party. We expect to remain there about a month, from whence we shall make a tour to some of the most improved country seats. Nancy is convinced already that it is impossible to be satiated with the pleasures of this country."

In August, Bingham made a two-week trip to Amsterdam, leaving Anne and the child Nan with the Penns at Brighthelmstone. He went to consult with Robert Gilmor, his partner, about the new establishment and to discuss a family matter with him. Willing's first son, Charles, Anne's oldest brother, was a wild young man of seventeen who had developed some bad habits and found some disreputable companions. Bingham reported from Amsterdam that Gilmor, a man of severe manner, would take Charles into his compting house and into his own home and would "pay every attention to his morals, education and other improvements, that he would to his own son." Would it be possible to buy one hundred shares of bank stock instead of fifty?

"Our success increases daily," Willing wrote to Bingham in September. "Our circulation is widely extended, customers are above 700 — our weekly receipts and payments one million at least." And in a note of exultation, "We are beyond the reach of envy or jealousy, and our stock has risen to 15 per cent above the first cost. . . . The confinement is great, but I have the best of all rewards, the general voice of approbation." The hours had been extended from nine to one and three to six. He was able to get only seventeen shares for Bingham.

John Jay arrived in London on October 15. He was triumphant from peace negotiations in Paris that gave the United States remarkably favorable terms — all the territory up to the Mississippi River, the province of Maine, and the right to fish off the Newfoundland Banks. Jay was suffering from acute insomnia and a pain in the chest, and on his doctor's orders was to relax and take the waters at Bath. During the weeks he stayed in London (Mrs. Jay had remained in Paris), he lived with the Binghams. They had moved that fall to 30 Harley Street, Cavendish Square, and until the end of November the house was busy with crowds of American friends calling on Jay. One of these was John Adams, plump, florid and nearing fifty, who had followed across the Channel to make his first visit to London.

Jay came down with a violent attack of dysentery and an acute inflammation of the throat, but on his recovery he visited the Royal Society to spend an evening at a club of "honest Whigs." Bingham introduced him there to the presiding officer, the great Dr. Richard Price, celebrated liberal theologian, philosopher, and defender of American rights throughout the Revolution ("With whom," Bingham wrote to Dr. Rush, "I am on terms of friendly intercourse").

Jay made up a party to visit the Drury Lane Theater to see Mrs. Sarah Siddons display her talents as Belvidera, heroine of Thomas Otway's *Venice Preserved*.

Among those who called at 30 Harley Street to see Jay was one of the unhappiest men in London: Silas Deane, former American Commissioner in Paris, now an exiled apostate, embittered, ill, and (despite Arthur Lee's charges of plundering his government) impoverished. In May, 1781, Deane had written friends in America declaring that the struggle for independence was hopeless and advising them to push for a reconciliation with England; the British, by prearrangement with Deane, intercepted the letters and printed them as propaganda.

Jay had valiantly defended Deane in Philadelphia five years earlier; now he refused to see him. Deane left his card at the Binghams' and wrote two letters. In a pained and painful reply, Jay wrote of the cruel necessity he felt himself under to reject his former friend's advances.

> You are either exceedingly injured, or you are no friend to America; and while doubts remain on that point, all connexion between us must be suspended. . . . I was told by more than one, on whose information I thought I could rely, that you received visits from, and was on terms of familiarity with General Arnold. Every American who gives his hand to that man, in my opinion, pollutes it.
>
> I think it my duty to deal thus candidly with you, and I assure you, with equal sincerity, that it would give me cordial satisfaction to find you able to acquit yourself in the judgment of the dispassionate and impartial. . . . That you may perform it successfully, whenever you undertake it, is the sincere wish and desire of, sir,
>
> Your most obedient humble servant,
>
> JOHN JAY

As a merchant and a representative of other American merchants, Bingham hoped for a commercial treaty with Britain, and part of his reason for being in London was to make such "commercial arrangements" as he could and to sound out and report on English trading intentions. He became deeply involved in a way he had not expected or intended.

With the end of the war, the United States was discovering, to its surprise, that it must trade with Britain to survive. It had most-favored-nation status with France, but France did not need America's raw materials, and America did not need France's luxury goods. America's natural trading partner was Britain.

In this exchange, however, the United States was now no longer a part of Britain's closed trading system. She was a foreign nation subject to British Navigation Laws. America might ship raw materials and produce to England, but her manufactured goods were barred. Her ships were prohibited by a Restraining Proclamation from trading directly with the British West Indies, either in buying, selling or the carrying trade, despite the anguished cries of the British West Indies merchants; all goods must be carried to and from the islands in British ships.

There was a move in England in 1783 to liberalize Britain's trade policy with America. Lord Shelburne, the prime minister, called for such a change, and his protégé, young William Pitt, Chancellor of the Exchequer, guided by the free-trade principles of his friend Adam Smith, entered a bill for that purpose in Parliament. After all, the United States was by far England's best customer; 90 per cent of U.S. imports of manufactured goods in the burst of postwar prosperity were English-made. But the Shelburne ministry fell, the bill languished, and British opinion and policy suddenly hardened against making trade concessions to the United States.

The major influence in causing this shift in attitudes was a pamphlet produced in July, 1783, by John Baker Holroyd, Lord Sheffield, reputedly written for him by Silas Deane. Its title was *"Observations on the Commerce of the United States,"* and within a year's time it had run into six printings. Sheffield (or Deane) argued brilliantly that the United States had no choice but to trade with England; that in return for concessions she had nothing to offer that England did not already have; and that therefore England had no need to grant special favors to a captive customer. Americans could not get goods elsewhere of comparable quality, or at so low a price, or with such credit terms. The states were in such a condition of ruin and confusion under the Confederacy that they would never act in concert to impose a duty on imports from Britain. Indeed, New England might very well break away from the union and beg to return to the empire.

Outraged by these sentiments, William Bingham sat down and "in a hurry" composed a fourteen-page pamphlet entitled *Letter from an American Now Resident in London to a Member of Parliament on the Subject of the Restraining Proclamation, and Containing Strictures on Lord Sheffield's Pamphlet on the Commerce of the United States.*

England, he said, had already brought her affairs to the brink of ruin, from continuing too long a slave to imposture and delusion. It was time for her to recover from her lethargy, but that would be difficult if ignorant and interested writers imposed their ill-digested and pernicious systems on the public mind and subverted a commercial connection between Great Britain and the United States.

It was an insult to common sense to suppose that a proud American people would submit to English restrictions and still open their ports to British vessels and freely indulge them with the liberty of carrying off their produce. The states, on the contrary, would, from a sense of common interest, unite more closely and form one general system of a commercial retaliation. They would restrict the import of British manufactures as they had done under the Non-Importation agreements on the eve of the Revolution. They would industrialize, build up their shipping, and train seamen.

What then would become of all those useful British artisans who were employed in supplying the American demand? They would flee to America,

> a country where civil and religious liberty are upheld in all their purity, — where, by the exertion of a few years of honest industry, an imigrant is morally sure of being furnished with the means of becoming an independent freeholder, — a country, that has laid no impolitic restraints on naturalization; — whose yoke is easy, and whose burthen's light; and which indulgently holds out its arms for the reception of the weary and heavy laden of all nations; and which, notwithstanding the attempts of Great Britain to enslave it, would generously offer an asylum for her persecuted sons.

The pamphlet was eloquent in its phrasing and cogent in its reasoning, and it went to three printings, but it did not change British minds. There was no commercial treaty. The trading policy laid down in 1783 would dominate stormy Anglo-American relationships for three decades to come.

Bingham distributed his pamphlet to people of influence in both countries. (It was published in Philadelphia over his name in March, 1784.) To Willing he wrote:

I expected that this pamphlet that was circulating with such mischievous effects, would have been answered by some of those who are officially concerned in forming our commercial arrangements. But not finding this to be the case. . . . I hastily committed to the press, the enclosed sheets, and it has given me heartfelt satisfaction to observe the good effects it has met with.

At this point, Bingham brought up for the first time the possibility of his taking a government post in Europe. Colonel Alexander Hamilton, he told Willing, was "very much bent" on having him serve on a commission to work out a commercial treaty with Great Britain. "I am confident," he wrote, "that from the *practical* knowledge I have of the trade of America, that I could render some services in the negotiations of this business." In writing to Dr. Rush on November 6, he included the exhortation, "Tell Congress of the need to immediately appoint a minister, or a resident, to this Court. Some person cloathed with a delegated authority of the United States, is absolutely necessary here, to watch over our political interest, and to improve every favorable circumstance to proper advantage."

Three weeks later, he decided that he would be willing to fill that post himself. He sent his pamphlet to his friend Thomas Fitzsimmons,* with whom he had corresponded on the matter, with a long letter reporting on the commercial situation.

If . . . Congress would think proper to appoint me as their minister here, for the purpose of forming any necessary arrangements, as the basis of future intercourse betwixt the two countries, I will make my time of residence here, subservient to my views of rendering them services, and that on the most disinterested principles.

It would look too much like parade to have it made known that I have made such offers. I assure you they proceed from a conviction

---

* Thomas Fitzsimmons (1741–1811) was an Irish-born merchant, Revolutionary soldier, Congressman from Philadelphia and fellow director of the Bank of North America. He was one of the few Roman Catholics of the time active in public positions of prominence. He was a founder of the Insurance Company of North America. Variant spellings are Fitzsimons and FitzSimons.

that it is in my power to serve my country from having some practical knowledge of its commercial interests, which you must be sensible is essentially necessary in forming arrangements for its commercial connections. I therefore trust to your discretion and delicacy, the use you will make of my offer.

William Bingham began to "feel most sensibly" for Anne as her time drew near. "Her sweet and amiable disposition," he wrote to Willing, "can accommodate itself to her situation, wherever she may be placed," but it was difficult at such a time to be without "the endearing attention of a few sincere friends." Mrs. Hare offered to come up from the country to attend her niece, but Bingham was reluctant to leave Anne long enough to fetch her.

Life was complicated at this difficult hour by the arrival of a scolding letter from her Aunt Anne, Mrs. Tench Francis. Bingham replied in a letter to Willing:

> You must not wonder that her letters are expressing of a fondness for this country — the novelty of so many agreeable objects must naturally make a pleasing impression, and to a young mind, a very forcible one.
>
> Indeed, she possesses virtues, which were but little known in America, or she might have escaped the ill directed censure of some of her relations, which have often given her the most exquisite and poignant distress.
>
> A letter recently received from her Aunt Francis (though originating from the most affectionate views) has caused the tears of sensibility most plentifully to flow from her. It seems intended in a pointed manner to address advice to her, as if she stood in very urgent need of it.
>
> For my part, I do not believe that in thought, word, or deed, she was ever imprudent.
>
> I am not blinded by prejudice — but I wish those who take the liberty of censuring her would follow the advice of the Scriptures — and "go and do likewise" — for if the world was universally as good as her, there would be no occasion for a Heaven hereafter, to reward the virtuous. I sincerely wish, that you may be equally blessed in all your children, and I am confident that you will be the happiest father in the Universe.

Three pages later, his anger somewhat subsided, he closed his letter discreetly with, "Perhaps Mrs. Francis's feelings might be hurt by communicating to her my opinion of her letter. I therefore would not have it mentioned. I know the goodness of her heart and give her credit for her intentions."

On December 9, 1783, Anne was "safely delivered . . . of a fine girl and is now perfectly recovered. . . . Nan has become extremely jealous of the little stranger and cannot bear to see it command so great a portion of her Mama's attention." The child was named Maria Matilda.

That fall, Bingham received flattering letters from Dr. Rush and the trustees of Dickinson College notifying him formally that he had been elected a trustee and begging him to obtain not only contributions in *cash*, but in such books and philosophical apparatus as would be necessary and useful in a college. ("Your access we know will be *easy* to the wealthy and great, and your companions will be chosen from among the liberal and public spirited.") Bingham was sanguine at first on his prospects:

> There may probably be found many who would wish to encourage our undertaking — men of pure and liberal principles — citizens of the world, who carry their ideas beyond the contracted limits of their own society, and look on all mankind as their brothers.
>
> Such persons will contribute from a benevolence of heart — from a view of dignifying the human species, by expanding the light of knowledge amongst them.

A few months later he had bad news for Dr. Rush and the trustees:

> It gives me pain to inform you that my disappointment has been as great as it was unexpected. . . .
>
> I sought those characters whose reputation stood the highest for liberality and sentiment, and who, from the purest principle, had befriended the Revolution of America.
>
> I informed them of the benevolent views of the founders of this establishment, and of the beneficial effects that would result to humanity from planting the seeds of knowledge in that western country, at present remote from all access to the improvement of the human mind.

They have invariably informed me that no success could now be expected in this undertaking.

His letter was read aloud at the fourth meeting of the trustees of the college, held at Carlisle on April 6, 1784, presided over by John Dickinson.

Bingham consoled Dr. Rush with a copy of his trade pamphlet, a copperplate of an air balloon that had been "constructed for the purpose of accommodating a person who intended to take a long voyage through the regions of the air," and his considered analysis of the significance of this new scientific development:

> Great expectations are formed of the improvements that will be made of the discovery, and of the useful purposes to which they may be converted.
>
> By the assistance of small air balloons attached to different parts of the human body that will be exactly sufficient to keep it suspended in air, in equilibrium, and with the help of a pair of wings, what can prevent its making a progress through the air with great facility? Will not this be a cheap and easy method of travelling?

Bingham conducted brisk but troubled trading ventures during his stay in London. He became "concerned in three speculations which will demand near sixteen thousand pounds sterling, cash — one of which is four hundred chests of Bohea tea and one hundred of Hyson." With Thomas Fitzsimmons he engaged in some unnamed trading enterprise in the East Indies. He received £4651 for tobacco delivered to Nantes; on 1373 hogsheads that had been taken to Philadelphia for shipment Bingham had been, in Willing's words, grossly abused in Maryland and ill used by "those men on James River." The tobacco was three years old; it had stood on the bare ground and contained so many rotten leaves that "no person would even touch it at the warehouse." Of the tobacco received in Nantes, twenty-three hogsheads had to be hand-picked by Bingham's agent.

Bingham then received two shocking setbacks. Samuel Inglis, his new partner, died quite unexpectedly; and Willing and Robert Morris (their firm was now Willing, Morris and Swanwick) withdrew their support of Bingham, Inglis and Gilmor Company. Bingham wrote to Willing on December 29:

I am sincerely sorry that it will not suit the new establishment of W. M & S. to continue a concern with Gilmor. . . . Mr. Gilmor has never received since Mr. Inglis's death a single line from W. M. & S. which I think extremely inattentive. . . . This man left a very excellent business in Maryland, encountered the dangers of the sea and of the enemy at a very boisterous season of the year — after his arrival in France met with very great difficulties in his progress to Holland in the midst of winter, where a few days after his journey, his wife lay in of twins, who both died in consequence of the many sufferings she had been exposed to. He had just begun to see brighter prospects when Mr. Inglis's death blasted all his hopes.

However, in order to prevent his suffering by these disappointments, I have made him two offers, one of which I expect he will make choice of, and either will put him in as eligible a situation as he before was.

Bingham learned to his astonishment that Willing and Morris were not aware of the articles of co-partnership Inglis had signed "on behalf of your House, of which he was acting partner, having reason at the time of executing them to believe that they were done with your privity and consent." But worse was to follow. On February 19, 1784, he wrote to Willing:

I should always have been ready to have dissolved (the partnership). But our consent in this case was not even solicited; but circular letters were dispatched to all the correspondents of the House, notifying this event, whilst the partner at Amsterdam was entirely ignorant of the circumstances and was continually corresponding with the connections of the House.

These hurt sentiments and hard words were interspersed on both sides with affectionate family news, political gossip, developments at the bank, and travel plans.

From Willing to Bingham:

Tench Francis was suffering from the gout . . . Bingham's mother visited the bank to sign some papers and persuaded the management to sell her six shares of stock . . . Aunt Abigail sent Anne a cask of apples from the country place. ("Capt. Truxtun insisted that he would have the pleasure to carry them — Nancy is his very great favorite — he speaks of her to every one in raptures.") . . . He would not send his son Charles to Mr. Gilmor after all, because Charles was not fit to be trusted in Amsterdam. He would be sent instead to sea "to break the neck of a set of bad company and other ill consequences of his stay here." . . . A regiment of mutinous Pennsylvania troops had marched on Philadelphia, threatened to loot the bank, surrounded the State House, and demanded that Congress give them their back pay; the outraged lawmakers moved the national capital to Princeton. ("We shall laugh at it hereafter over a glass of wine. They must finally sit down *here* and here *only*.") . . . The bank's transactions were averaging 280 entries per day. The directors intended to enlarge the outstanding stock by 1000 shares at $500 each. Hannah Benezet, Bingham's sister, widow of two years, had married the Reverend Robert Blackwell, D.D., of St. Peter's Church,

> to the surprise and dissatisfaction too of very many. She begs her love to you. . . . She has reserved all her estate, real and personal too by an act of settlement by which she can by will, dispose of both as she pleases, not only what she now has, but any reversion after her mother's death also. I'm sorry for this event 'twas foolish & somewhat indelicate too — I don't think her health was in a state to justify such an engagement — she can't live long.

From Bingham to Willing:

He was not surprised at the convulsions of the army, for until public justice was done to the creditors of the United States, the country could never enjoy a state of peace and tranquility . . . The government should watch with a vigilant and attentive eye the large remittances lately made in specie to England, for if they were continued the country would be drained of gold . . . Nan was cutting her teeth and would be inoculated against smallpox . . . Enclosed was a print of an air balloon constructed to make a first crossing of the English Channel betwixt Dover and Calais . . . David Hartley, M.P. from Hull, had conferred with him for two hours before leaving for Paris to make certain trade proposals to the American commissioners there . . . Mr. Pitt was the idol of the people in as great a degree as ever his father was . . . Confidentially, some of Mr. Morris' connections were causing very material injury to his name and credit . . . It would be an injustice to diminish the value of the present bank stock by increasing the number of shares. If someone desired to buy stock, he could get it by offering the holders what would induce them to part with it.

> Those who invested their money in this fund, encountered all the chances that it was exposed to. If, by any fortuitous circumstances it had miscarried, who would have contributed towards making a reparation to the stockholders? It has fortunately succeeded; who then has a right to diminish the profits of success?
>
> Should such a measure be adopted, it would remove all encouragement for establishing new institutions, the prospects of which are generally doubtful at the first outset. And in a young country that enterprizing spirit should not be repressed. . . .
>
> Whilst I was employed in forming the Bye Laws of the Bank, I had an idea of proposing one, which I now think would have been very proper to have inserted as a fundamental regulation, which was — that when ever the stock rose to a certain advance, the directors should summon the proprietors together, and propose an increase of Capital.

Bingham asked his father-in-law to be so obliging as to inform him if the amount of stock was increased. If that was done, he would immediately dispose of his own shares.

One of the influential Englishmen with whom Bingham formed a friendship at this time was the pro-American political and intellectual radical, Benjamin Vaughan. Two years earlier, Lord Shelburne, then prime minister, had sent Vaughan to Paris to discuss possible peace terms with Franklin, and Vaughan had served as Shelburne's observer throughout the formal negotiations. It is probable that John Jay, one of the Peace Commissioners, had brought Vaughan to the Bingham house in Cavendish Square during his stay in London. In any case, this man introduced the Binghams into very high company indeed: that of Lord and Lady Shelburne.

William Petty Fitzmaurice, descendant of the lords of Kerry (patented in the year 1181), Baron Wycombe, Earl of Shelburne, soon to be Marquess of Lansdowne, loved intellectual company and treasured his friendships. Joseph Priestley had been his librarian and resident philosopher for eight years, until he retired in 1780 on a pension of

£150 a year. Jeremy Bentham, political theorist and exponent of Utilitarianism, had been raised (in his own words) "from the bottomless pit of humiliation" to live and work at Shelburne's country estate. Bentham called him "one of the pleasantest men to live with that ever God put breath into."

Shelburne had enlightened political views far in advance of his time. He favored Parliamentary reform, Catholic emancipation, and a foreign trade policy that the English would not adopt for another three generations. He held that popular liberty was essential to vigorous government, and he was, Bentham said, "the only minister I ever heard of who did not fear the people." Shelburne was, above all, a friend of the Americans — "a better friend," John Adams was to testify, "than either Fox or Burke." He had freed Henry Laurens from the Tower of London and sent him to join his fellow Commissioners in Paris; it was through his contacts with Franklin in 1782 that peace negotiations had been started. He had resigned as prime minister in February, 1783, after eight months in office, over the charge that he was offering greater concessions to the Americans than they were entitled to.

Shelburne's driving purpose was to draw the United States from her French allies and to win back and hold American trade "by justice, liberality and attention." His views on trade were very close to those expressed by William Bingham in his pamphlet. For this, among other reasons, he became interested in Bingham and asked his help in forming a "Committee of Gentlemen who might sketch out the leading features of a commercial system betwixt the two countries which might serve as the basis for the treaty whenever the negociation opened." He extended to the Binghams what they later acknowledged as "civilities" and "polite attention," and he began a friendship with William Bingham that continued until the day when one of them sat at the deathbed of the other.

As Lord Shelburne's guests, the Binghams dined at Shelburne House on Berkeley Square and spent some days at Bowood Park, near Calne, in Wiltshire. Shelburne House, designed for Lord Bute by the master architect Robert Adam, had been bought and completed by Shelburne in 1765–68. It was especially celebrated for its typical Adam white-on-gray dining room in the south pavilion. The room had a Joseph Rose plaster ceiling personally supervised in the construction by Adam; wood carving by John Gilbert; a magnificent marble chimney piece; a huge Palladian window; and nine niches containing larger-than-life-size statues of Marcus Aurelius, Mercury, and other classic figures recently excavated at Rome.* The house was the gathering place of Whig society, and the Binghams met there an impressive group of intellectuals, scholars, bluestockings and political leaders. One of these was Francis Baring, the merchant-banker. A director of the East India Company, just elected to Parliament as a Whig, Baring was a particular friend of Lord Shelburne and a frequent guest in his home.

Bowood Park, one of England's fine country houses, offered hospitality that was at once munificent, friendly and easygoing. Guests dined with the family or alone in their own apartment as they chose. They could wander through the park, sit by the lake Lord Shelburne had created, play billiards or chess, browse in the library, stroll through the picture gallery, discourse with Mr. Bentham, and pay due respects to Lady Louisa, the earl's second wife, a gentle hostess who spoke fluent French and understood Latin.†

The Binghams spent the month of March (1784) in Bath, then the center of English fashion. There they drank the waters and took the baths (good for rheumatism, gout, neuralgia, sciatica, diseases of the liver, and scrofulous infections). They viewed the Crescent, visited the elegant shops, the public buildings and the card rooms, listened to concerts in the Assembly Room, danced in the "dancing rooms," took the air in rides into the countryside, and called on friends. Bingham's old friend, the Marquis de Bouillé, had been in Bath for some time and had received there, Bingham said, "very flattering marks of attention." Bingham to Willing:

> The West India Merchants and Planters gave him a public dinner, as a testimony of the very high opinion they entertain of his generous and humane conduct towards the inhabitants of the conquered islands. This is a rare example of a vanquished enemy treating their conqueror with disinterested and unsolicited marks of respect and

* Shelburne House proper still stands; it was converted to a club in 1930. The south pavilion was torn down early in this century. The dining room has been installed intact, but with changed proportions, in the Metropolitan Museum in New York. Eight of the nine statues there are replicas.
† Bowood Park, occupied by the eighth Marquess of Lansdowne, still has one wing of the house, the chapel and clock tower, its terraces, the artificial lake and a gatehouse.

attention. Such traits of character seem rather to appertain to the days of chivalry.

In April, Bingham and his family traveled with Bouillé and some other French gentlemen to Bristol, where they found "a perpetual scene of debauchery, riot and confusion" because of the month-long election campaign. They spent a day there with the Hares and made their way circuitously back to London, visiting Woodstock, Blenheim, Stowe, Oxford, "and many other equally attractive places and country seats." They planned to leave in a few weeks for a tour of the Continent.

In June, Bingham wrote to Willing that to please Nancy he had decided to stay in Europe another year, "which is a circumstance not altogether agreeable to my inclinations, as I had not prepared myself for so long an absence." Both children had whooping cough, but they made excellent travelers, with Nan now becoming very amusing. Nancy had grown fatter, which was "no detriment to her appearance."

Her sensibilities are all alive on the subject of the family. She desires me to say everything that is tender and affectionate to you. 'Tis to you alone, that I can with propriety confess, that she grows every day more amiable and engaging.

CHAPTER 12

The Grand Tour: 1784–86

Mrs. Bingham . . . taken altogether, is the finest woman I ever saw.

Mrs. John (Abigail) Adams
to her sister
London, September 30, 1785

THE BINGHAMS crossed the channel from Harwich to Hellevoetsluis, Holland, continued their route to Rotterdam, where they remained some days, and proceeded through Delft to The Hague. There they called on their countryman John Adams, whom they had last seen at their Cavendish Square house on his visit to London six months earlier. They brought him the news from a late-dated letter from Philadelphia that Thomas Jefferson had been appointed to succeed John Jay as one of the three ministers plenipotentiary to France.

Adams held the post of minister to the court at The Hague in addition to being one of the ministers at Paris. During his visit to London he had received word that "an immense flock of new bills" had arrived, drawn by Robert Morris on the Barings; that there were insufficient funds in Europe to honor them; and that the credit of the United States would be ruined. With his son and secretary, John Quincy, seventeen, he had made a desperate and dangerously stormy return trip across the North Sea to Holland. There he pleaded with the Dutch bankers for an American loan and got 2,000,000 guilders, repayable by 1807, at the "enormously avaricious" rate of around 6 per cent. (With this money Morris was able to pay off the notes he had written to provide demobilization pay for the army. Harassed by Congressional investigations, he quit his office on November 1, 1784, leaving a Treasury surplus of $21,000.)

At the time the Binghams met him, John Adams was a troubled man. He wanted to confound his enemies in Congress, resign and sail for home without waiting to be recalled, but he expected his wife and daughter to join him shortly, and he passionately desired to become minister to the Court of St. James's. He had written a letter to Secretary Livingston explaining how he was better qualified to serve in that post than was Dr. Franklin.

"Last night at Court," he wrote in his diary on Tuesday, June 22, 1784, "one of the Ladies of Honour, told me, that the supper was given, in a great measure, for Mrs. Bingham. *Cette super a été donne, en grand partie, pour elle.** There was great enquiry after her, and much admiration expressed by all who had seen her, of her beauty. As the Princess of Orange was enquiring of me concerning her, and her journey to Spa, Paris, Italy, the Spanish minister said 'She would form herself at Paris.' I replied very quick but smiling '*J'espere qu'elle ne se formera [pas] a Paris, qu'elle est deja formée.'** This produced as hearty a laugh as is permitted at Court both from the Princess and the Comte."

The Binghams stayed ten days at The Hague, thanked Adams for his "polite attentions," and set off by way of Leyden and Haarlem to Amsterdam, where they were entertained by Henry Hope, senior partner and dominant member of the great Dutch banking firm Hope and Company. There Bingham completed arrangements to form a partnership, Robert Gilmor and Company, with Gilmor returning to the United States to work out of Baltimore. After a stay of some weeks they traveled on to Paris. They took a suite of rooms at the Hotel Muscovy, hired a corps of servants, bought a carriage and four horses, and settled down for a long stay.

Bingham was pleased with his tour. "To spend a portion of the younger part of life in such various scenes of pleasure and improvement," he wrote to Willing, "is laying up a fund of usefull knowledge and agreeable reflection for our riper years, which in all circumstances and situations, will become a permanent source of enjoyment. . . .

> Should you discover any change in your daughter, I can assure you, it will be for the better. Her amiable disposition and endearing behaviour admitted of no improvement, nor her attachment to you and her brothers and sisters, of any addition. Her constant intercourse with the fashionable world may have polished her manners, and a continual variety of new scenes may have furnished reflections,

* "This supper was given, in great measure, for her. . . . I hope that she is not formed in Paris, because she is already formed."

which would other wise have lain dormant, for want of opportunities to call them forth. Her judgment is consequently riper, and her knowledge of mankind, more correct and extensive. She has seen the best of company, which it was my pride and pleasure to have her introduced into.

Anne Bingham liked Holland and hoped William might get a diplomatic post there. (He was considered but passed over because he was believed to be too much under the influence of the British.) Paris she found enchanting in its excitement and variety. She came upon the city in its last full-blown brilliance at the end of an era, shortly before a period of chaos and terror. A city of some 700,000, Paris was thronged with foreign visitors and with young officers who had come back from a victorious war in America, wearing the decoration of a republican army, their pockets filled with I.O.U.'s for back pay from the American Congress, their minds filled with ideas from the new world. This was a time of scholarly revelation, of new theories, experiments and advances in all the sciences, of the utmost confidence in the power of education to improve human nature. Reform and progress were the subject of general discussion in the world's most skeptical and articulate society. The countryside was destitute and the peasants' bread was made of pounded roots and herbs; but the philosophers believed that the golden age was close at hand. No one who had not lived in Paris before the Revolution, Prince Talleyrand later said, had any idea how pleasant life could be.

The women's coiffures were towering and the young men's hats enormous. People were talking of Beaumarchais' new play, *The Marriage of Figaro,* at the Comédie Française; of the Italian alchemist Cagliostro; of the Austrian physician Mesmer with his cures through "animal magnetism"; of the music of Gluck, Mozart and Grétry; of the beauty of their queen from Austria, Marie Antoinette; of the rage for Freemasonry; and of the latest balloon ascension.

There was an inordinate curiosity about Americans in Europe after the Revolution; and entry into this society was easy for a rich, educated American with friends in high places and a wife whose beauty and amiable manners everyone had read about in Chastellux's *Travels.* Bingham first visited Dr. Franklin at Passy. He had last seen Franklin in Philadelphia eight years earlier, when he received his instructions for his mission to Martinique; now, calling to deliver a letter from Mr. Adams, he found him suffering from the stone and the gout. The Binghams became sometime members of the concourse of Franklin's friends and admirers at Passy.

They called on General Chastellux in his elegant apartment on the Quai des Théatins. He had just become a marquis, had published another book, *Considerations on Animal Magnetism,* and was working on an extended, revised and "public" edition of his *Travels* in which he softened several of the "personal strictures" that had given offense to some of his American friends. (He deleted, no doubt to the Binghams' amusement, a reference to Aunt Elizabeth Powel: ". . . she talks a great deal; she honored me with her friendship and found me very meritorious because I meritoriously listened to her.")

Jefferson arrived early in August, very tall, thin, loose-jointed, with blue-gray eyes, a freckled complexion and red hair. He was forty-one. He would represent southern interests in working with Adams and Franklin to negotiate commercial treaties with twenty-three powers in Europe and Africa. Bingham had corresponded with Jefferson on matters of trade, and now he called to pay his respects. Jefferson did not like Bingham, but he admired Anne Bingham, and with her over the next year and a half he carried on a harmless flirtation. It was the gallantry of a widower twice the woman's age who knew that he was perfectly safe from involvement.

Anne adapted herself readily to the customs and conditions of this strange new land. "The state of society in different countries," she said philosophically, "requires corresponding manners and qualifications." In this society the newcomer to the city made the first call; there were no introductions at large parties; the men and women alternated beside each other at the table instead of sitting separately, the men down one side, the women down the other, as in America; the gentleman smelled the serving of meat before it was put on his partner's plate to make sure it was not spoiled; the men wore swords and kissed each other in greetings and leavetakings. In this society the husbands took mistresses; the wives took lovers; the servants performed one household function only and refused to perform any other. In this city the streets were putrid with filth; one-half the children were reputedly illegitimate; and some 52,000 women were registered prostitutes; but the Parisians of all classes had grace and style, an animation and spirit, that was to be found nowhere else on earth.

The women, Anne found, seemed frivolous to American eyes, but they were "more accomplished, and understand the intercourse of society better than in any other country." To Mr. Jefferson, with whom she was debating the nature of the French character, Anne later wrote:

> We are irresistibly pleased with them, because they possess the happy art of making us pleased with ourselves. Their education is of a higher cast, and by great cultivation they procure a happy variety of genius, which forms their conversation, to please either the fop, or the philosopher. . . .
> The agreeable resources of Paris must certainly please and instruct every class of characters. The Arts of Elegance are there considered essential, and are carried to a state of perfection; the mind is continually gratified with the admiration of works of taste.

"I have the pleasure of knowing you too well," she said slyly, "to doubt of your subscribing to this opinion." *

The Adams family arrived in the second week of August and moved into an enormous, ill-furnished mansion leased from the Comte de Rouault in the suburb of Auteuil, four miles out of Paris near the Bois de Boulogne. Mrs. Adams was an alert, sprightly woman of forty years, with black eyes and sharp features. She had a forthright manner, sometimes an edged tongue, and always a strong character. Her Puritan New England background and her training as a parson's daughter were ameliorated by intellectual curiosity, a taste for reading, and an admirable ability to observe and describe. She read and understood but did not speak French. Her daughter Abigail, known as "Nabby," was nineteen and in love with a moody Boston lawyer, Royall Tyler, eight years her senior, who was proving to be a most difficult and undependable fiancé. She had a good figure, reddish hair, her father's blue eyes, an admirable complexion, and a tendency to blush. History owes a debt to Nabby, for she kept a diary of what she saw, felt and thought during her stay in Europe.

In their first weeks in Paris, the Adamses attended the Comédie Française. ("I am not fond of comedy in general," said Nabby; "I had rather be improved than amused.") They visited Notre Dame and St. Sulpice. ("These were very beautiful. I have not knowledge

* Anne Bingham's letter to Jefferson appears as Appendix 3, page 464.

sufficient to describe them.") They went to the garden of the Tuileries and paid a crown each, with some 10,000 others, to see the ascension of a hydrogen balloon. On September 1, the Adamses dined "by invitation" at Dr. Franklin's with a number of gentlemen and the famous Madame Helvétius — rich, high-born, sixty-year-old widow of the famous philosopher. Dr. Franklin, Nabby observed, was the man on whom "the world had passed such high encomiums, perhaps justly." On Madame Helvétius: "Odious indeed do our sex appear when divested of those ornaments, with which modesty and delicacy adorn them."

William and Anne Bingham dined with the Adamses at Auteuil on Saturday, September 25, in a company of twenty persons, all but four of them Americans. Mrs. Adams, meeting Anne for the first time, was charmed — but with reservations. To her friend Mercy Warren in Boston she described her as "a very young lady, not more than twenty, very agreeable, and very handsome; rather too much given to the foibles of the country for the mother of two children, which she already is." And to her niece:

> He is said to be rich and to have an income of four thousand a year. . . . 'tis said he wishes for an appointment here as foreign minister; he lives at a much greater expense than any American Minister can afford to do. Mrs. Bingham is a fine figure and a beautiful person; her manners are easy and affable, but she was too young to come abroad without a pilot, gives too much into the follies of this country, has money enough and knows how to lavish it with an unsparing hand. Less money and more years may make her wiser, but she is so handsome she must be pardoned.

Nabby, on the other hand, was all open, unreserved admiration:

> Mr. B. is possessed of a large fortune — both very young. Mrs. B. is only 20; she was married at 16; she is pretty, a good figure, but rather still. She has not been long enough in this country to have gained that ease of air and manner which is peculiar to the women here; and when it does not exceed the bounds of delicacy, is very pleasing. Mrs. B. has been in Europe two years. I admire her that she is not in the smallest degree tinctured by indelicacy. She has, from the little acquaintance I have had with her, genuine principles; she is very sprightly and very pleasing.

Five days later the Binghams dined with Jefferson. The Adamses were there, and Nabby, the child of innocence, storing up impressions for her diary. Mr. Jefferson was "an agreeable man." Colonel David Humphreys, secretary to the commercial treaty commissioners, was not an agreeable man but was a worthy character nevertheless. Mrs. Bingham, she found again, "has a most pleasing address and a very happy turn of expression, with a good deal of politeness — she will not fail to please. Mr. B. is an agreeable man — he is delicately attentive, and his behavior to Madame is very pleasing."

Three weeks later, on October 19, Nabby permitted herself an acid observation — an echo, one imagines, of some comment by her parents.

Mr. Bingham came flourishing out in the morning to accompany Pappa to Versailles to be presented to his most Christian majesty, the King of France, with his four horses and three servants, in all the pomp of an American merchant. About twelve they returned, as there was no Court.

By this time, Nabby was a friend of Anne Bingham — the only American woman she knew of her own age and the only one in whom she could confide. Three days after the misfire at Versailles, the Adamses breakfasted with the Binghams and went with them to see the Duke de Chartres' gardens, which, Nabby felt, demonstrated how very inadequate were the French compared to the British. They were accompanied by a French gentleman, "a very agreeable man who has been in America, and was perhaps improved." Four days later:

We all dined with Mr. and Mrs. Bingham at their hotel. . . . There was much company: Mrs. B. gains my love and admiration, more and more every time I see her; she is possessed of more ease and politeness in her behaviour, than any person I have seen. She joins in every conversation in company; and when engaged herself in conversing with you, she will, by joining directly in another chit chat with another party, convince you, that she was all attention to every one. She has a taste for show, but not above her circumstances. Mr. B. is an agreeable man, but seems to feel the superiority of fortune more than Mrs. B.

On Tuesday, October 30th, the presentation at Court was brought off:

> Papa went to Versailles by himself last Tuesday: he introduced Mr. J. [Jackson], Mr. T. [?], and Mr. B., the first gentlemen in private characters, that have been introduced at this court. Mr. B.'s ambition promoted it; what it will promote him to I know not; if to what he wishes, it is easily determined [i.e., a diplomatic post].

A few days later, another dinner, and this time Nabby felt her first disillusionment with her friend Anne Bingham. The cause was the Mr. Jackson who had been presented at court.

Major William Jackson (who was destined to play an important role in Bingham's life) had been born in England and reared a gentleman in South Carolina. He had served during the war as an aide to General Benjamin Lincoln and in 1781 accompanied young Colonel John Laurens and Thomas Paine to France in a swaggering mission ordered by Congress to "support" Franklin's appeal for French aid. Paine and Laurens returned to America with two and a half million livres in silver, a gift that Franklin had wrung out of Vergennes by the most astute diplomacy, and presented it to the Congress as the product of their own efforts alone. Major Jackson remained in Europe to demand possession of another one and a half million livres Franklin had borrowed and was holding for unpaid bills. Jackson charged that Laurens had raised the money, hinted that Franklin meant to steal it, and threatened to file suit if he did not get it. Franklin, his patience exhausted, ridiculed the "young gentleman" for his superior airs and reminded him that the "special department and employ in public affairs, of which you are so vain, is but of yesterday, and would never have existed but by my concurrence." Two months later Jackson discovered that the captain on whose ship he would have sailed with the money was in the pay of the English. He wrote Franklin a contrite letter of apology, declaring that America was indebted to Franklin's prudence for the preservation of the money.

In November, 1783, Major Jackson had set out for Europe again; he called on Bingham in London with a credit, a letter and a proposal from Robert Morris for "a line of business" among the three of them that "promises success equal to the most sanguine wishes." According

to Morris, Jackson was "inclined to believe that you can be useful to
him and I have encouraged him . . . in that belief."

Major Jackson was twenty-five, he was single, and he made a most
pleasing impression on Nabby Adams. "My papa calls him the Sir
Charles Grandison* of this age," she wrote in her diary. "I was never
acquainted with him until I came to France; I consider it an acquisition." And at a party a few days later Major Jackson was "my favour-
ite."

The evening began splendidly with a compliment from the Baron
de Staël, Swedish ambassador to France, not yet married to Mlle.
Necker —

> . . . a man of five and thirty, but appears no more than twenty-
> seven at most; he is tall, graceful in his person, a fine complexion,
> good color, good features, in short a very handsome man. . . . He
> told my brother that a French lady of my age would appear ten
> years older than I did, their complexions being so very dark, add-
> ing that one could not find in France so good a complexion as
> mine; I could with justice have returned the compliment, if it was
> one.

And then:

> I sat next to Mr. Jackson at table, and next to him was seated
> Madame Bingham who by an exuberance of sprightliness and wit,
> slips from the path of being perfectly agreeable; a little judgment
> would amend whatever defects may appear.

The agreeable Major Jackson was apparently more interested in the
charming Madame Bingham, with her useful husband, than in Miss
Abigail.

Sometime in the next month or so the Binghams moved to the
Palais Royal. Mrs. Adams and her daughter visited there for the first
time on January 20, 1785. Nabby remembered but forgave the excess
of exuberance and the lack of judgment.

> I was quite as much pleased with her as ever, and must confess
> that she has excellencies that overbalance every want of judgment,

* An ideal eighteenth-century gentleman, hero of the novel of that name (1753) by
Samuel Richardson.

or that love of gay life, which is very conspicuous in her, but which I do not wonder at at all. It is united with so many agreeable and amiable qualities, that it is impossible not to admire her. They are really domestic, and the principles of affection and domestic happiness are so very apparent, that I never see them that I do not gain a higher opinion of that state.

But at the next meeting, Nabby's struggles with her Puritan heritage and her Braintree background produced some moralizing:

> February 7th. To-day we dined with Mr. Jefferson. He invited us to come and see all Paris . . . it being the last day but one of the Carnival, and to go to the mask ball in the evening, which we did not attend. . . . Mrs. B. says it is the only amusement that is not superior here, to what they have in London. She is so delighted with Paris, that she says she shall never go to America with her own consent; she expects to be carried in the spring. I confess I cannot form an idea of this disposition. She has, I believe, by this time laid the foundation of a future life of unhappiness.

The following week the Binghams dined at Dr. Franklin's in a large company. The Adams family was there; Lord Mount Morris, an Irish volunteer in the American army; another Irish gentleman whom Nabby found "passable"; the Marquis de Lafayette, only recently returned from America, and the Marquise; and John Jeffries, physician and scientist. A month earlier, Dr. Jeffries and the French aeronaut Jean Pierre Blanchard had crossed the English channel in a balloon, from Dover to Calais, Jeffries making the first scientific observations of the free air, observing the temperatures, pressures and humidity to a height of 9309 feet. Nabby sat next to Dr. Jeffries at dinner.

> I made some inquiries respecting his late voyage aeriel; he did not seem fond of speaking of it; he said he felt no difference from his height in the air, but that the air was finer and obliged them to breathe oftener, and that it was very cold.
> Lord Mount Morris attracted my attention. He is a very handsome man. . . . He looked inquiring, but Madame Bingham, who is well acquainted with his lordship, engrossed all his attention.

Two weeks later, on February 21:

> Dined at the Marquis de la Fayette's with a circle of Americans.
> . . . I was seated at table between Mr. B. and the Irish gentleman
> whose name I have forgotten; he was very civil, but nothing very
> remarkable in him. Mr. B. was insupportably disagreeable. I can-
> not but dislike his manners in general; to his wife they are better
> than any man I have known.
>
> Mrs. B. was as ever, engaging. The elegance of her dress de-
> mands a description; a black velvet dress with pink satin sleeves
> and stomacher, a pink satin petticoat, and over it a skirt of white
> crape, spotted all over with gray fur; the sides of the gown open in
> front, and bottom of the coat trimmed with paste; it was superb,
> and the gracefulness of the person made it appear to peculiar ad-
> vantage. To avoid singularity, and the observation of the company
> she goes into, she wears more rouge than is advantageous to her;
> I was pleased with a little upon her, but she has become quite a
> French woman in this respect.*

Early in March, Anne Bingham rode out to Auteuil to have tea
with Mrs. and Miss Adams. Nabby's worst forebodings about her
friend were unfortunately coming to pass:

> The bloom of the rose is fading — dissipation will blast the fair-
> est flower that ever bloomed; in her it is verified; 'tis a pity so
> much delicacy and beauty should be sacrificed to a few weeks of
> pleasure.

Anne's health and beauty seem to have made a remarkable recovery,
for in the middle of the month:

> We had a large company to dine, the Marquis de la Fayette and
> lady, the Chevalier de la Luzerne, Mr. Brandson the Dutch Ambas-
> sador Extraordinary, Mr. and Mrs. B. The latter has a great share
> of grace, united with a vivacity that is enchanting, but without
> much dignity; grace depends upon the person, actions, and man-

* Mrs. Bingham's dressmaker was the famous Mlle. Bertin, milliner to the Queen of
France and the courts of Spain and Portugal, whose fashions were copied throughout
Europe and in America. Nabby visited her workshop, a large room where twenty girls
were working. Mlle. Bertin went bankrupt the following year.

ners; dignity is placed in the mind; the latter she has not; she is nevertheless, a charming woman. . . .

The Binghams left Paris in April, 1785, to spend some months in London before making another visit to Holland and a tour of Switzerland and Italy. Nabby bade farewell to Mrs. Bingham:

> I could not but regret her leaving Paris, although I have seen but little of her, yet I never see her without feeling a degree of regard for her. She is most sweetly amiable, possessed of a great share of sensibility: had she married a man of sense and judgment, who would have endeavoured to turn her attention to something more important than dress and show, and recommended them only as ornaments to adorn good sense, and an improved mind, she would have shown with distinguished lustre, in every point of view; for even now, she is possessed of many qualifications to make her beloved and respected. I have not formed such an opinion of Mr. Bingham. I am mistaken if he does not lack some essential qualifications to make him either respected or admired.

The Adamses followed the Binghams to London the following month. After an acrimonious debate in Congress and much discussion on the extent of his vanity, Adams had been appointed the first minister to the Court of St. James's. They left Paris with a copy of Mr. Jefferson's newly published *Notes on Virginia* as a going-away present. Jefferson, said Mrs. Adams, was "one of the choice ones of the earth."

Bingham apologetically informed Willing from London of his intention to stay in Europe one more year, despite pressing business at home, in order to indulge "Nancy's strong inclination to visit Switzerland and Italy." Willing responded: "It was very natural for Nancy to wish to gratify her curiosity fully, by staying another year. She had crossed the Ocean already, and had an indulgent friend in you, ready and able to gratify her. I am contented; and the more so as my state of health is good and I've as fair a chance as ever of living to see her, should your return be delayed till next year." A few months later: "Your account of my dearest Nancy and the little ones affords me great joy. I thank her much for her frequent letters to me. They are sprightly and judicious and would have entertained even a stranger; to me they were as a feast, on which paternal pride and affection had ample room to be gratified. God bless her, you, and those endearing pledges of affection which are with you. I long to embrace you all."

During the second visit to London, Bingham called on Gilbert Stuart, one of the five American painters busy in England. (The others were Benjamin West, John Singleton Copley, John Trumbull, and young Mather Brown.) Stuart had come penniless to England in 1775, had served for some years as a pupil of Benjamin West, living in his household, and in 1782 had struck out on his own. His "Portrait of a Gentleman Skating," exhibited at the Royal Academy that year, had created a stir in London; its transparent color and its lifelike effect had made Stuart famous overnight. Now he shared honors with Reynolds, Romney, and Gainsborough as a master of portraiture. He was earning some £1500 a year painting the great figures of the day, and he was spending far beyond that amount in lavish living. He was a big man who dressed in a disorderly manner, used a half-pound of snuff a day, and cared nothing whatsoever about business details.

Bingham called at Stuart's splendid house on New Burlington Street, off Regent Street, and asked him to paint a family portrait as a present for his wife. The proposal was all wrong for Stuart. He disliked painting children, he especially disliked painting them with their mothers, and he almost never painted family groups. Nevertheless, perhaps because of a fee larger than his usual thirty guineas per head, he accepted the commission.

The Binghams went to Mr. Stuart's painting room* in his residence. This would be a large canvas, an outdoor scene with trees. The artist placed Mrs. Bingham as the central figure, dressed in a flowing white dress gathered in at the waist, her dark auburn hair hanging down in long curls onto her left shoulder. She stood by her husband's horse, on which she held Maria Matilda, dressed in a tight-fitting bonnet and a white dress, while looking down at her older daughter, Ann Louisa. Stuart had the older girl pulling at her mother's dress, demanding recognition, showing plainly that she was jealous of the attention being paid to Maria. William Bingham wore a scarlet hunting coat and white neckcloth; his lightly powdered hair was tied with a black bow. The artist placed him at the

* The term *studio* had not yet been brought from Italy to England.

left side of the canvas, turning to look at the scene with amusement.

Stuart painted the head and shoulders of Anne and the full figure of Maria with great skill and care; he painted William Bingham and Ann Louisa more roughly and barely blocked in the outline of the horse. Then, for some unknown reason, he stopped. He may have been dissatisfied with his subjects or with his own performance. He may have reverted to his strong prejudice against painting children and groups. Legend has it that Stuart resented some directions Mrs. Bingham wished him to follow in the arrangement of the picture. Even a mild request would have been enough to cause Stuart to throw down his brushes, for he was quick to take offense at any criticism, real, implied or fancied. The painting was never finished.*

The Binghams spent some weeks in the spring of 1785 making a 500-mile tour of those parts of England they had not seen, inspecting the great houses, gardens and architectural masterpieces of the country — "a species of pleasurable pursuit," Bingham said, "of which I have grown exceedingly fond."

On their return to London they saw something of the Adamses. John Quincy had sailed for America to begin his law studies at Harvard. Nabby had broken off her engagement to the unreliable Royall Tyler in Boston and was about to make the mistake of her life by falling in love with the tall, handsome, genteel secretary to the American legation, William Stephens Smith.† Lieutenant Colonel Smith, thirty, a graduate of Princeton, son of a prominent New York merchant, had served through the war on the staffs of four generals, concluding with General Washington, who had assigned him to supervise the evacuation of New York City by the British. In courting Nabby, he laid before John Adams a most impressive collection of testimonials as to his character and abilities.

As the American minister's wife, Mrs. Adams took occasion to compare the qualities of American and English women. To her sister she wrote:

* Mrs. Bingham took it to America and, not caring for the work, eventually gave it to Henry Clymer, husband to her sister Mary. Clymer consulted the artist Thomas Sully, and on his advice and under his direction the canvas was divided into three pictures. Two of these are reproduced in this volume.

† Mrs. Cranch, Mrs. Adams' sister, wrote that Tyler was "dismally mortified" at losing Nabby. There is reason to believe that he may have been the victim of malicious gossip circulated by Mrs. Cranch in her jealousy that he did not court one of her own daughters.

Notwithstanding the English boast so much of their beauties . . . I have not seen a lady in England who can bear a comparison with Mrs. Bingham, Mrs. Platt, and a Miss Hamilton, who is a Philadelphia young lady. Amongst the most celebrated of their beauties stands the Dutchess of Devonshire, who is masculine in her appearance. Lady Salisbury is small and genteel, but her complexion is bad; and Lady Talbot is not a Mrs. Bingham, who taken altogether is the finest woman I ever saw. The intelligence of her countenance, or rather I ought to say animation, the elegance of her form, and the affability of her manners, converts you into admiration, and one has only to lament too much dissipation and frivolity of amusement, which has weand her from her native country; and given her a passion and thirst after all the luxuries of Europe.

On July 30, the Binghams were again on the Continent, again in The Hague. From that city Bingham wrote to Jefferson (who had just succeeded Dr. Franklin as the sole United States minister to France) requesting a letter of introduction to the French minister at the court of Beuvelles. "Mr. Jay writes me," he said, "that federal ideas were daily gaining ground, which would probably influence the states to extend the powers of Congress." The news could hardly have been pleasing to Jefferson, who opposed strengthening the federal government at the expense of the states. Jay had succeeded Livingston as minister for foreign affairs. This news, Bingham wrote cryptically to Jay, was not welcome in France, for he was known as pro-British and anti-French. "You may well imagine, then, that your appointment was *not regarded with satisfaction.* Nor will the congratulations you will receive on it from certain persons [i.e., Jefferson] be sincere." "Your observations," Jay replied, "coincide exactly with what I expected on that subject."

In August the Binghams were in Paris, where they visited Jefferson. On August 28 they left Paris to return to The Hague. Some weeks later they were again in Paris and with Jefferson, on their way to tour Switzerland and Italy with the Marquis de Bouillé. At the end of December they were back in Paris, prepared to leave for a few weeks in London and then for America.

Jefferson gave them various packages to carry: letters and diplomatic papers for Mr. Adams; a letter to John Jay; a set of crayons for Francis Hopkinson in London; a copy of Linnaeus's *Systema Vege-*

tabilium for John Bartram in Philadelphia. In making her farewell to Jefferson, Anne Bingham promised to write him, within one year of her return to America, a letter "of respectable length" telling him "truly and honestly" whether she did not find "the tranquil pleasures of America preferable to the empty bustle of Paris."*

Jefferson did not feel any regret at parting from William Bingham. A year later he would write out for James Madison (partly in code) his opinions of various figures in public life, expressed with the commingled generosity, waspishness and suspicion of motives for which Jefferson became famous and which would lead him to quarrel with Adams, Hamilton, Washington, John Marshall and virtually every other public figure of the Federalist period whose views did not reflect his own:

> Tho' Bingham is not in diplomatic office yet as he wishes to be so I will mention such circumstances of him as you might otherwise be deceived in. He will make you believe he was on the most intimate footing with the first characters in Europe and versed in the secrets of every cabinet. Not a word of this is true. He had a rage for being presented to great men and had no modesty in the methods by which he could effect it. If he obtained access afterwards, it was with such as who were susceptible of impression from the beauty of his wife. I must except the Marquis de Bouilli, who had been an old acquaintance.

Near the close of his thirty-month stay in Europe, Bingham was pleased with what he had seen and done. To Dr. Rush from Paris:

> I have made a delightful tour through some of the northern parts of Europe, through Holland, part of Germany, and Flanders.
>
> My situation here is perfectly agreeable [word indecipherable] *utili dulci* in all my pursuits; for no country surpasses this in all the improvements of the arts and sciences; nor has any people carried the enjoyment of social pleasure to so high a state of perfection.
>
> I am peculiarly fortunate in my acquaintances, which lay amongst the first class of characters in the country.
>
> Many persons are surprized, that with an ample fortune, sufficient to supply the full extent of my desires in Europe, I should

* See Appendix 3, page 464.

still incline to return to America — but these people are but little acquainted with that *Amor Patria* that distinguishes the American character.

Besides, my life has hitherto been so much engaged in the tumultuous scenes of business and pleasure, that I have not had an opportunity of indulging my favorite enjoyment, which is retirement and books. I anticipate the moments with heartfelt satisfaction, that I shall devote to such pursuits, and I find no prospect of doing it untill my return to America.

Anne Bingham was now something of a public figure in London; a picture of her had been engraved and was being sold in the shops. Mrs. Adams wrote to her son John on February 16, 1786:

> Mr. and Mrs. Bingham arrived here about three weeks ago with a full determination to go out to America in March, but having as usual spared no pains to get introduced to the families of Lord Landsdown and my Lady Lucans, they are so *supremely blest* that poor America looks like a bugbear to them. "O! I know, Mrs. Bingham, you wont go out this spring. Give me but ten years and take all the rest of my life." Who can withstand [such] flattery and admiration? What female mind, young, beautiful, rich — must she not be more than woman if vanity was not the predominant passion?

Writing to her brother about the same time, Miss Abigail echoed her mother's sharp comment:

> Mrs. Bingham called upon us early to request Mamma to present her at Court on Thursday where I suppose she will make a fine figure. . . .
> Mr. Barthelemy and Mr. and Mrs. Bingham called in the evening. They had dined with Lord Lansdowne, and called to let us know it, I suppose. . . .
> Mrs. B—— is coming quite into fashion here, and she is very much admired. The hairdresser, who dresses us upon court days, inquired of Mamma whether she knew the lady so much talked of from America — Mrs. Bingham. He had heard of her from a lady who saw her at Lord Lucan's, where she was much admired. At last, speaking of Miss [Ann] Hamilton, he said, with a twirl of his

comb, "Well, it does not signify but the American ladies do beat the English all to nothing."

The presentation at Court was a splendid success and a fitting climax to the three-year stay in Europe. The occasion was the celebration of Queen Charlotte's birthday — that "haughty, proud, imperious dame," as Mrs. Adams called her, small, wide-mouthed and pug-nosed, who had been as short with the American minister's women as George III had been courteous. The presentation was made in the afternoon at St. James's Palace. Nabby reported on the event for John Quincy:

> Mamma says, if admiration could make this lady happy, she must be so, for she never saw one so much stared at. "There she goes," cried one. "What an elegant woman," another said as he passed. . . . [Word illegible] say she is not void of vanity, and if not, must have been gratified — she is indeed a fine woman.

There was a crush in the drawing room; they moved with the line to the King, being careful not to violate etiquette by speaking to him before being spoken to. He was a stout, middle-aged man with a florid complexion and blond eyebrows and would have looked very well, Mrs. Adams thought, "if he had not sacrificed so much to Bacchus." He addressed a polite question to each person as presented — generally, "Have you taken a walk today?" or, "Do you get out much in this weather?" After a two-hour wait in line, they were spoken to by the Queen and, at five o'clock, left the Palace.

They dined hastily and hurried back to the Palace to get good seats for the ball. Sir Clement Cottrell, the master of ceremonies, met them at the door of the ballroom and escorted them to the box reserved for foreign ministers. The Prince of Wales (later to become George IV) entered with the two elder princesses a little before nine, conducting himself, Nabby observed, with "a careless, lounging air which I suppose is called ease and politeness. . . . He is very fat and looks stuffd."

A bugle blew at nine and everyone rose. The King and Queen entered and circled the room, each in opposite directions, speaking to the ladies who had been selected to take part in the dancing. Mrs. Adams described the event for John Quincy:

I accompanied [Mrs. Bingham] last Thursday to Court . . . and I own I felt not a little proud of her. St. James's did not, and could not produce another so fine woman. Yet it was the most crowded drawing room I ever attended. . . . You know this ladies [word illegible] in dress is truly elegant. She had prepared herself in France for this occasion, and being more fleshy than I have seen her before, she is consequently handsomer than ever. "She shown a goddess and she moved a queen." *

The various whispers which I heard around me, and the pressing of the ladies to get a sight of her, was really curious and must have added an *attom* to the old *score,* for she [the Queen] could not but see how attractive she was. "Is she an American, is she an American?" I heard frequently repeated, and even the *ladies* were *obliged to confess* that she was truly an elegant woman. "You have," said an English lord to me, but whose name I know not, "one of the finest ladies to present that I ever saw." The Emperor's Ambassador whispered your Pappa, "Sir, your country produces exceeding fine women!"

The Prince of Wales opened the ball by dancing a minuet with the Princess Royal and then with the younger princess. Six couples then danced a set of country dances, the Prince and Princess Royal at the head. At eleven the Prince asked the Queen's permission to continue but she dissented, the royal family retired, and the ball ended. Declared Miss Abigail, "I have seen quite as good in the Assembly at Boston, but it would argue a great want of taste to say so."

Ten days later, Miss Abigail wrote to her brother:

Mr. Bingham called this morn — there baggage is all on board and they are only waiting for a fair wind. He made a declaration this morning that if he got safely to America, there was nothing in the world that should induce him to come again to Europe — he was heartily sick and tired of a wandering life and longed to get home and settled in his business — but after all I guess there was a mental reservation in all this. What think you!

The Binghams sailed on a Monday in March in a severe snowstorm. With them they had a prodigious quantity of personal posses-

* "She moves a goddess, and she looks a queen." Alexander Pope, *The Iliad,* Book III, line 208.

sions, including a large number of trunks filled with Paris finery for Anne. The Algerian pirates were active at the time, and a fellow Philadelphian visiting England, William Hamilton of Woodlands on the Schuylkill, expressed some mock concern. After witnessing their departure, he wrote to a friend:

Mr. Bingham and his family are to be passengers with Willet. He takes two carriages and 8 servants, etc., and imagine means to make a great show. What a terrible thing it would be if the lady was to get into the Dey's seraglio.

CHAPTER 13

"Rest for the Sole of My Foot"

Having now spent the greatest portion of my latter years in an un-settled situation in foreign countries, and having fully indulged the spirit of curiosity, I am determined to "find rest for the sole of my foot" * and to confine my future residence to my native place.

William Bingham to Thomas Willing
December 10, 1784

DURING HIS STAY in Europe, Bingham conceived the idea of building a house on his return to Philadelphia — one suitable for entertaining on a large scale and for receiving out-of-town guests. He would build in the Society Hill section of town, in the southern half of the long block bounded east and west by Third and Fourth streets, north by Willings Alley, and south by Spruce Street. This was land the British had used during the occupation as a parade ground; boys were using it now to fly their kites.

He cast about in England for a model to copy, for he found that the architecture there exhibited "a remarkable show of simplicity united with elegance, and is exceedingly well calculated for the meridian of our country." He chose a house where he and Anne were frequent guests — the town residence of George Montagu, the fourth Duke of Manchester, in Manchester Square, London.† He sketched a plan of this mansion, enlarging it somewhat, and employed an architect "to execute it properly" with the precise dimensions of every room.

This he sent to Willing with the request ("I do not know in what manner to apologize for the trouble this will give you") that he draw up "a Bill of Scantling" for cutting the lumber. He begged Willing to show the plan only to those who needed to see it, "as it would only expose it to criticism. I wish it may meet your approbation. The

---

* Genesis VIII, 9: "But the dove found no rest for the sole of her foot."
† Manchester House, built in 1776, became known as Hertford House. It is now a museum, housing the Wallace Collection.

best rooms will be in the first story" (i.e., on the second floor). At the Manufactory of Coade, London, he bought marble jambs and head-pieces for chimneys, marble slabs, and composition stone ornaments consisting of fascia, medallions, entablatures, moldings, and keystones.

Willing ordered 100,000 feet of cedar and pine boards to be sawed "at the best mill" at the current price less 5 per cent. He "piled up abt. 50,000 feet of as fine boards as I ever saw" and then stopped buying "because the price was so high." He advised Bingham to ship certain building materials from England.

> Bring out with you sash glass, sash cords, and *brass cogs or pulleys* — they are best [there] and very dear here — locks for out doors, parlour and closet — hinges of all sorts — sprig [pointed] nails long and short, 8″ 10″ 20″ and brass nails — sheet lead, and window lead heavy cast. The charge here for the work is as high as the lead. Colours all ready ground in oil — bolts, padlocks, and one or two dozen good stock locks. Don't forget six dozen or more of the brass cogs or pulleys, for the sashes to run upon, the wooden ones are ever out of order. . . . Do get good brass locks for the parlour doors, those which are fixed in the woodwork and hid by it, called mortise locks — are often out of order, and then the door is injured and split to get at them.

Bingham also requested Willing to sell all his silver plate, his set of Nankin tea china, and his looking glasses, "for the most they will bring," for he and Anne planned to buy most of their household furnishings in Europe. They spent a great deal of their time in making these purchases. In Italy they bought paintings, busts, and mantel ornaments; in France, carpets, textiles, and china; in England, furniture, china, and nearly 2000 ounces of silver in tureens, vases, bowls, urns, dishes, trays, candlesticks, ladles and knives, forks and spoons. They bought the first silver-pronged forks seen in America.*

Among their purchases were eighteen large mirrors; six large arm chairs and a matching sofa covered with Gobelin tapestry; twenty rush-bottom chairs; twelve mahogany arm chairs; twenty-four mahogany chairs with morocco bottoms; a set of twelve rosewood chairs from Seddons in London, the backs in the form of a lyre, with

---

* American silver forks had steel tines and silver handles. Knives had blades with rounded blunt ends so that they could be safely put into the mouth.

festoons of pink and yellow silk; a harpsichord; a pianoforte; two japanned dove cages; seven urn mahogany knife cases; fourteen patent brass lamps; china dinner and tea sets, most of it French, some of it Sèvres, one a 350-piece set of blue china with gilt edges; marble busts of Voltaire, Rousseau and Franklin; a full-length portrait of Mrs. Siddons in "The Grecian Daughter"; and (for Anne's bedroom) a mahogany bedstead seven feet square with canopy and curtains.*

When Anne's uncle, Robert Hare, returned to America in the summer of 1785, Bingham gave him the house plan and arranged with him to lay the foundation and build the "shell." It is probable, then, that this much had been done when the Binghams arrived in Philadelphia around the middle of May, 1786. The house was completed or nearing completion that September, for Ann Warder, an English Quaker girl who had recently arrived in the city, wrote in her diary on September 26: "Looked at Bingham's new house which causes much talk here being upon a new plan, but not very genteel, I think, as it much resembles some of our heavy public buildings — bow windows back and front, with figures of stucco work."

During the months of construction, the Binghams rented William Logan's three-story brick town house on Second Street between Chestnut and Walnut. There they took up life as they had left it three years earlier. It was a good life, if quieter than the one they had found in the foreign capitals and spas.

Philadelphia had grown to a city of 4600 houses and 32,000 inhabitants. It was a progressive community. The streets were well lighted and policed, paved with stones to the edge of town at Ninth Street, with no signs allowed to extend over the sidewalks save those of inns and taverns. There was now a daily newspaper — the first successful daily in the United States — John Dunlap and David Claypoole's *Pennsylvania Packet and Daily Advertiser*. Passenger ships sailed twice a week for New York, where the Congress met, and two stage coaches departed for New York every day except Sunday. Under the city's enlightened penal reform, those imprisoned for debt were housed separately from the criminals. As many as 2000 emigrants were coming off the ships each week, some of them Germans, many of them Irish, most of them redemptioners to be sold at auction

* See Appendix 4, page 467, for an inventory of the Binghams' household effects.

as indentured servants to pay their passage. All were absorbed in the city or by the inland towns and farms. There was work for everyone; a rough carpenter could make 80 cents a day. Every trade had its meeting place, its rules and its apprentices.*

Each Tuesday and Friday night the "butter bells" rang to remind the citizenry that tomorrow was market day. Well before daybreak the market carts and lumbering Conestoga wagons began to line the curbs. Farmers displayed their produce in stalls under the colonnaded arched roof that ran for several blocks down the middle of High Street. The market was clean, orderly and quiet, and the prices were low. There were sections for meat, fish, and poultry (fowl were bought live), for butter and cheese, for fruits, vegetables and roots, for baked goods, for wood, coal, hay and flowers. Housewives rose at five-thirty on these days and, to the astonishment of foreign visitors, were at market by six-thirty or seven o'clock, each followed by a servant carrying a basket.

Philadelphia's harbor was generally filled with ships coming, going or at anchor at the merchants' wharves. The arrival of goods from England was always the occasion for bustle and excitement. The boxes and bales were unpacked on Front Street in good weather and the goods sold to the retail merchants on the spot. The arrival of a vessel from the East Indies, China or India at the end of a two-year voyage was a very special matter. William Bingham had set up a silent partnership with Mordecai Lewis, a rich Quaker merchant who in 1784 had succeeded him as director at the Bank of North America. Through Mordecai Lewis and Company, Bingham was part owner of seven ships engaged in the China trade, and with Robert Gilmor and Company he owned several others. He would have personally greeted each of these as it sailed up the Delaware laden with the treasures of the East.

For entertainment there were the theater, the Dancing Assembly held every fortnight during the season in Oeller's Hotel, and an occasional traveling circus or riding company. Charles Willson Peale had just opened a museum in his house at Third and Lombard Streets — one shilling per visit, one dollar for an annual ticket. There he

---

* The Frenchman Moreau de St. Méry wrote, "The workmen are proud and unbearably haughty. They never have all the tools they need, and they pretend to do everything without a ladder which they should have brought."

showed his portraits of the leaders of the American Revolution and "a Repository of Natural Curiosities": the teeth (later the bones) of the mammoth discovered in Kentucky, stuffed exotic birds, animals and reptiles in habitat groups, a rattlesnake's fangs mounted under a magnifying glass, curious petrifactions, several lifelike wax figures, Esquimaux costumes, Indian scalps, wampum and dress, and a pair of shoes, four inches long, made in China for bound feet.

An amusement of which Anne Bingham was especially fond was the sleighing party. It was a pleasure she shared with much of the city. An English visitor, a musician named William Priest, described it:

> Every moment that will admit of sleighing is seized on with avidity. The tavern and innkeepers are up all night; and the whole country is in motion. . . . Our planters daughters provide hot sand, which they place in bags at the bottom of the sleigh. Their sweethearts attend with a couple of horses and away they glide with astonishing velocity; visiting their friends for many miles round the country. But in large towns, in order to have a sleighing frolic in *style,* it is necessary to provide a *fiddler,* who is placed at the head of the sleigh and plays all the way. At every inn they meet with on the road, the company alight and have a dance.

But the social life revolved mainly around entertainment in the home. To pay a call and drink tea was a regular custom. There were many out-of-town visitors, and so always a reason to give a dinner party. During the first winter after their return, Anne appeared in her Paris creations. Molly Tilghman, a Maryland girl visiting the city, described one of these to her friend Polly Pearse:

> One piece of intelligence respecting Mrs. Byngham's elegance, I may venture to give you as news. . . . Aunt Lawrence is my informant. After speaking in high terms of Mrs. B's beauty, she says that a few nights before she had blaz'd upon a large party at Mr. [Robert] Morris's in a dress which eclips'd any that has yet been seen. A Robe a la Turke of black velvet, rich white sattin petticoat, body and sleeves, the whole trim'd with ermine. A large bouquet of natural flowers supported by a knot of diamonds, large buckles, necklace and earrings of diamonds, her head ornamented with diamond sprigs interspers'd with artificial flowers, above all, wav'd a

towering plume of snow white feathers. Can you imagine a dress more strikingly beautiful. How happy is it for the world in general, my dear Polly, that splendor is not necessary to real happiness. If it was, what wou'd become of such little people as you and I?

Sometime late in 1786 or early in 1787, the Spruce Street house — already known as the "Mansion House" — was completed, and the Binghams took up residence there.

Bingham had set out to build the finest and best-furnished house in America, and there is evidence that his contemporaries felt he had succeeded. The whole area, including extensive gardens, was surrounded by a high painted board fence, which caused some critical comment, though high fences were not uncommon in the city. A circular driveway led to the entrance set back from Third Street and raised only one step. The floor of the wide hall was of marble in a mosaic pattern — the first of its kind seen in America. The center staircase, built of white marble, was broad enough to hold flowers on both sides on special occasions.

It was a three-story house with spacious rooms. The study, the library and the banqueting room opened to the right on the ground floor, with the ballroom and several parlors on the left, one of them leading into an extensive conservatory. The drawing room, dining room, card room and bedchambers were on the second floor. (Anne had a state bedroom, holding the curtained seven-foot bed, and a boudoir.) The walls of the house were hung with the paintings chosen so lovingly in Europe, the elegant carpets were laid, the mantels adorned with their ornaments, the pedestals topped with their busts and bronze figures, the japanned dove cages filled with birds.

The windows overlooked almost three acres of gardens "rich with curious and rare clumps and shades of trees," including orange, lemon and citron trees set out in tubs, and rows of Lombardy poplars, new to America. An alley called Bingham's Court led into the grounds and to spacious stables, with a greenhouse and various "domestic offices" nearby. Two fawns, a gift of the Jacob Reads of South Carolina, grazed on the lawn. "They sport and frolic," Bingham wrote to Read in thanks, "and are a perpetual fund of amusement to my children." The imported servants, many of them dressed in livery, included coachmen, footmen, a butler, a head housekeeper, a confectioner, a French cook, a gardener, and the lesser servants usual in other households.*

The Boston architect Charles Bulfinch wrote in 1789:

> . . . The house of Mr. Bingham . . . is in a stile which would be esteemed splendid even in the most luxurious part of Europe. Elegance of construction, white marble staircase, valuable paintings, the richest furniture and the utmost magnificence of decoration makes it a palace in my opinion far too rich for any man in this country. We are told that his mode of living is fully equal to this appearance of his house. Of this we shall be better able to judge in a few hours as we are to dine there today.

Henry Wansey, an English traveler, a textile merchant, dined at the Mansion House and in his inevitable book on life among the Americans wrote, "I found a magnificent house and gardens in the best English style, with elegant and even superb furniture." The dining room, he said in a passage that puzzles the imagination, "was papered in the French taste, after the style of the Vatican at Rome." Said a cousin of Mrs. Bingham many years later, "I have never seen any private house more admirably adapted for the reception of company."

The Binghams began at once to receive company and did so in a style somewhat too brilliant for a Quaker city in a new republic. But certainly a large number of people enjoyed the Binghams' hospitality with the gay life that accompanied it, and the many out-of-town visitors who were put up there instead of at the flea-infested hotels were appreciative and grateful.

The closest look at the style of the Bingham household was provided by Samuel Breck, a young friend and neighbor who had moved from Boston. Years later, as one of the last survivors of a bygone era, he wrote:

> William Bingham, a millionaire . . . lived in the most showy style of any American. The forms at his house were not suited to our manners. I was often at his parties, at which each guest was

---

* The butler, Wickham, and the housekeeper afterwards married, Bingham giving them money to establish a business; they founded a respectable merchant family. Brown, a coachman, became a thriving grocer.

announced; first, at the entrance-door his name was called aloud, and taken up by a servant on the stairs, who passed it on to the man in waiting at the drawing-room door. In this drawing-room the furniture was superb Gobelin, and the folding doors were covered with mirrors, which reflected the figures of the company, so as to deceive an untravelled countryman, who, having been paraded up the marble stairway amid the echoes of his name — ofttimes made very ridiculous by the queer manner in which the servants pronounced it — would enter the brilliant apartment and salute the looking-glasses instead of the master and mistress of the house and their guests.

This silly fashion of announcing by name did not last long, and was put a stop to by the following ridiculous occurence: On a gala-evening an eminent physician, Dr. Kuhn, and his step-daughter, drove up to the door. A servant asked who was in the carriage. "The doctor and Miss Peggy," was the reply. "The doctor and Miss Peggy!" cried out the man stationed at the door. "The doctor and Miss Peggy!" bawled out he of the stairs, which was taken up by the liveried footman at the door of the drawing-room, into which Miss Peggy and her papa entered amid the laugh and jokes of the company. This and several preceding blunders caused the custom, albeit a short-lived one, to be suppressed.*

*

In the time left over from running his business, building his house and indulging Anne in her efforts to bring European elegance to Philadelphia, William Bingham was busy in an extraordinary variety of social, civic, political and speculative activities in the years 1786–1788.

Within a month of his return to the city, he, James Wilson and R. L. Hooper — the Canaan Company — completed the purchase of the 32,620 acres of land in New York State for which they had been negotiating. New York, needing to raise money, charged the going price for remote and unoccupied lands: 12.25 cents an acre.

Bingham was made an honorary member of the Pennsylvania Society of the Cincinnati — the state chapter of the fraternal, patriotic,

---

* Senator James Monroe, on hearing his name called by a uniformed Bingham footman, replied, "Coming"; and on hearing it announced a second time, called back, "Coming as soon as I can get my greatcoat off!"

and professedly non-political society formed by officers of the Continental army, with Washington as its president-general. He was further honored by election to The American Philosophical Society Held at Philadelphia for Promoting Useful Knowledge. The Society, founded in 1743 at the suggestion of Franklin as an outgrowth of his Junto club, had been meeting in Carpenters' Hall, at the University, and sometimes in Franklin's home. It had recently been given a plot of ground behind the State House on which to build a Philosophical Hall, but subscriptions lagged and the Society was in financial trouble. Bingham's contribution of £20, made before his election as a member, seems modest enough, but it was the sixth largest on a long list of early subscribers.

Franklin had returned to the city in the fall of 1785 to a tumultuous welcome. Hundreds of friends, dignitaries and delegations called during the early weeks. As soon as he was free to do so, he turned his attention to the Philosophical Society building program. He contributed a second £100, made a loan of £500, and brought his considerable influence to bear on members and prospective members to subscribe, to increase their earlier subscriptions, and to pay the amounts promised. Philosophical Hall was completed in the fall of 1789 and a first quiet meeting was held on Friday, November 20, of that year. Dr. Franklin, confined to his home by what was to be his last illness, was not present.

Franklin hoped to create a society that would do for political science what the American Philosophical Society was doing for the natural sciences, and so on February 9, 1787, he formed the Society for Political Enquiries, for Mutual Improvement in the Knowledge of Government, and for the Advancement of Political Science. William Bingham and George Clymer were elected vice presidents under Franklin's presidency. The membership was limited to fifty residents, with meetings held fortnightly in the large room of Dr. Franklin's house. The discussions were limited to "general politics" only, the object stated as "the elucidation of the science of government and the furtherance of human happiness." Among the other charter members were James Wilson, Robert Morris, Gouverneur Morris, Thomas Paine, and Benjamin Rush, who was planning someday to write and publish a volume on Dr. Franklin's conversations.

As an owner of real property, Bingham joined the Hand-in-Hand Company — a combination fire brigade, social club, and fire insurance company (the oldest in America, founded 1752, Benjamin Franklin, director), whose formal name was the Philadelphia Contributionship for the Insurance of Houses from Loss by Fire. The membership was distinguished; the fire mark displayed on their houses was four leaden hands crossed and clasped at the wrists. The members met at irregular intervals for the purpose, Franklin said with a straight face, of "discoursing and communicating such ideas as occurred to us upon the subject of fires as might be useful in our conduct on such occasions."

Early in 1788, Bingham organized and headed a military unit: the Second Troop of Philadelphia Light Horse, an unpaid volunteer company of fifty men. The dashing Major William Jackson, who was now studying law in Philadelphia, transferred from the First Troop to become Captain Bingham's lieutenant. Bingham's corps of dragoons attracted the sons of many prominent families — men who liked companionship and a splendid uniform, or who felt (in the words of a historian of the First Philadelphia Troop) that "in time of stress it is well for the State to have a class to call on who will die as gayly as they dance, and will pour out their blood, as they were wont to do with their fortunes, for faith and honor, for sentiment and ideals." The troop met on the first and third Monday of each month, paraded on any and all state occasions, and mixed good food and drink, fellowship and military drill in agreeable proportions.

In these years, Bingham was involved, as a donor and as a trustee, with three institutions of higher learning. Following a conservative victory in the state elections of 1786, the new Assembly passed a bill restoring the College of Philadelphia to its original status. The seizure of 1779 was called "repugnant to justice, a violation of the Constitution of this Commonwealth, and dangerous in its precedents to all incorporated bodies, and to the rights and franchises thereof." The first meeting of the trustees was held in Dr. Franklin's house, the fourteen surviving trustees of the earlier board all being present. Bingham was elected a trustee at this meeting and was named treasurer of the board.

On August 23, 1786, Dr. Rush dined at the Binghams', finding the dinner "plentiful and elegant, and the company very agreeable." It was possibly on this occasion that he drew Bingham to participate in his newest enthusiasm: the founding of a German College and Charity School in Lancaster, to be known as Franklin (later Franklin and Marshall) College. Bingham contributed £150 and accompanied Rush to Lancaster the following June on a twofold mission: to attend the dedication ceremonies of the college and, in Rush's words, to attempt "to introduce knowledge and civilization" among the Germans, "who at present unfortunately exhibit the most melancholy proofs of ignorance." Bingham took with him one of his closest friends, Francis Corbin, member of the Virginia House of Delegates.

The party left Philadelphia on Monday and arrived at 2 P.M. the following day. Trustee William Hamilton of Bush Hill and Woodlands (he who had jokingly prayed that Mrs. Bingham might not be captured by the Dey of Algiers) was already there, as was William Rawle, a brilliant young lawyer. The meeting of some thirty of the trustees was opened with a speech by Dr. Rush. ("In the course of a few years by means of this College the names of German, Irishman and Englishman will be lost in the general name of Pennsylvanian.")

The next day the faculty, the trustees, the clergy, and certain respectable citizens of the town, sweating in their heavy coats and woolen stockings, proceeded from the courthouse to the Lutheran Church, where they heard sermons preached in German and English and listened to hymns and to odes composed for the occasion. Some eighty gentlemen dined at the public house of the town. "The design of this dinner was to make us better acquainted with each other," said Dr. Rush in an upwelling of liberal goodwill toward all nationalities, races, and creeds.

> I improved it for this purpose by setting near and talking alternately with a Lutheran, a Calvanist, a Roman Catholic, and a Moravian minister — all of whom I found to be sensible, agreeable men. My companions from the city enjoyed this instance of my attention to our new acquaintances. Nor were they deficient in similar acts of familiar intercourse with them. Mr. Hamilton charmed everybody with his easy behavior. Mr. Bingham interested the gravest of our German company in national politics, while Mr. Rawle forced his way into their hearts at once by conversing with them upon the subject of their College in *their own language.*

Dr. Rush's chief educational activities, however, were still directed to Dickinson College in Carlisle. He had persuaded Dr. Charles Nisbet, a noted Presbyterian clergyman and scholar, to leave Scotland, sacrificing a life pension of £120, to bring his family to America and take over a flourishing and prosperous new college. Nisbet was outraged, then morose, then ill, at what he found. The college was "a tomb." The one building for classes was inadequate and the addition to it a "hogpen." The faculty was too small and was overworked. There were no funds and no books. The sun was too hot, the climate bad, and Mrs. Nisbet's meat would not keep overnight without spoiling. The roof of his bedrooms leaked. The town officials were "a mean set of rogues," and it cost him twice as much to live in Carlisle as it had cost him in Montrose.

Drs. Nisbet and Rush conceived a cordial hatred for one another and exchanged acrimonious letters. Nisbet recovered from his illness, resigned, and set out to return to Scotland. The only passage he could get, however, was in a ship commanded by an Irish captain, and rather than suffer that indignity and danger, he went back to Carlisle, there to live "like a pelican in the wilderness . . . without friends or society." When he sent back word of his hardships, unhappiness and homesickness to his friends in Scotland, Rush thoughtfully wrote to inform them that the letters "were written under a deranged state of mind, occasioned by a fever which fixed itself upon his brain."

*

In November, 1784, writing from Paris, Bingham had expressed to Rush his disappointment at the instability and lack of progress of the Confederation of States. "I am convinced," he wrote, "that our country will never be great or respectable, without some important changes in our Constitution." And the following September, from The Hague:

Our miserable pitifull system has occasioned the United States to become a "byword amongst nations" and as a member of this great Republic, I have my feelings daily tortured with the consideration and contrast of *what we are, and what we ought to be.*

Now, in the fall of 1786, he was given the chance to improve conditions at the source. He was elected a member of the Continental Congress. In November, he traveled with Anne to New York, there to serve as one of the representatives of the sovereign State of Pennsylvania in a Congress that was dying, in a federal union that was dissolving in disorder.

CHAPTER 14

In the Service
of State and Country

There must be a Power lodged Somewhere, to form Commercial Regula-
tions, whose Effects must be general & pervade every part of the Union.
. . . (America) wants nothing now but a strong efficient Government,
which will command Respect & Confidence abroad, & act with Vigor &
Energy at home. . . . I am convinced that all our political Misfortunes
flow from the Weakness of our federal Government.

William Bingham to Lord Lansdowne
March 4, 1787

BINGHAM presented his credentials to Charles Thomson, zealous and
faithful secretary of the Continental Congress, on Monday, November 20, 1786.* He was two weeks late, since the Congress was to meet
each year on the first Monday in November; but he could well have
stayed longer in Philadelphia. Several months passed before a quorum of seven states could be formed. While waiting, William and
Anne Bingham spent some time with the Jays; apparently they took a
house in New York for the winter.

The failure to convene as scheduled was normal for a Congress that
had become, in this eleventh year of independence, little more than
an occasional meeting place of men who considered themselves am-
bassadors from the various states. The government had no general
executive, no general judiciary, no army, no navy, no money, no
credit, no power to tax. John Hancock of Massachusetts, elected president of the Congress in 1785, never bothered to attend.

The approval of nine states was required to enact any significant
legislation, which meant that any combination of five states could
shackle the federal power. In 1786, not one state complied with the
assessment laid on it, and not enough money was collected to pay the
interest on the national debt. Virginia had its own secretary for for-

* Congress met in New York City Hall, Wall Street.

eign affairs. Georgia signed its own treaties with the Indians. The New England states looked on the Continental Congress almost as a foreign government.

John Jay, whose portrait hung in Mr. Peale's museum with the other fathers of the Revolution, was perhaps the only widely known figure in the Congress of 1786–87. There were a few brilliant young members, such as Rufus King of Massachusetts and James Madison of Virginia, but the Congress did not often attract the ablest and most experienced men, for the real interest, money and power lay in the state legislatures. Young Abigail Adams, now back in America and beginning an uneasy life as Mrs. William Stephens Smith, wrote to her mother from New York after dining with the president and some members of Congress, "Had you been present you would have trembled for your country, to have *seen*, and *heard*, and *observed* the men who compose its rulers."

One wonders why Bingham, a leading merchant and one of the richest men of the country, took a post in a body that had little honor and no power. If he had been ambitious, he could have done better in the Pennsylvania legislature. Perhaps he felt the need for training in the Congress as a prelude to higher things. He may have been chosen by the Philadelphia merchants to watch after "the commercial interests." Or he may simply have longed to write, as he did, to his friends in Europe that he had been honored by appointment to the Congress.

It is possible, on the other hand, that Bingham genuinely felt the anguish his letters show at the weaknesses of the Congress and that he went to serve in the one place where he could best work for the "strong efficient Government" he desired. If this was so, fate has played an unkind trick on William Bingham. History has given him little attention, but one statement is commonly associated with his name, and generally with obloquy: that he was the first public figure to declare openly in Congress for a dissolution of the Union.

The source for the statement seems of the highest order. "The members from the Southern and Middle States," James Madison wrote in his private "Notes of Debates" on February 21, 1787, "seemed generally anxious for some republican organization of the system which would preserve the Union and give due energy to the Government of it. Mr. Bingham alone avowed his wishes that the

Confederacy might be divided into several distinct confederacies, its great extent and various interests being incompatible with a single Government."

It seems certain that Madison was mistaken.* Bingham was under clearly contrary instructions from his state, prepared by a committee headed by Robert Morris: "Perusal of federal measures and federal interest will be the principal object of your attention." Bingham's letters, his actions in Congress and his votes all bespoke unreserved support for (in his words) "A firm, vigorous and energetic government, such as so extensive a country demands" — a government that could preserve order at home and negotiate trade treaties abroad. With his closest friends and political associates, James Wilson, Robert Morris, Gouverneur Morris, Jay, and Hamilton, he was an earnest advocate of a closer union of the states and a strong central power. He was a nationalist — a Federalist.

While waiting for the Congress to round up enough members to convene, Bingham wrote a long letter to Dr. Richard Price in London:

> I must confess that I did not find the United States in as flourishing a situation as I had reason to expect. . . . The specie of the country, which after the war constituted its only circulating medium, has been almost wholly exported; and many of the states have had recourse to the dangerous expedient of paper money, which by not being in general well funded, has in many instances, greatly depreciated.

Bingham might have mentioned that the very severe shortage of specie, combined with bad business conditions, was causing property foreclosures, imprisonment for debt, and widespread unrest. In Massachusetts, a body of armed men led by one Captain Daniel Shays had captured courthouses, besieged the legislature and marched on the state arsenal to demand (among other things) an end to the requirement that taxes be paid in hard money. Bingham continued:

---

* Madison would not have been seeking to discredit Bingham for political reasons, for his journal was not printed until many years later. Curiously, Madison was himself accused in 1808 of having held an extremist position in the Constitutional Convention. Notes made by Convention Delegate Robert Yates were distorted by a political opponent to charge that Madison had favored abolition of state powers in a totally consolidated union.

The Confederation is likewise an evil of an alarming nature. It does not possess sufficient power. . . . The individual states, from the sufferings they are exposed to from the weakness and inefficiency of the Confederacy, seem disposed to vest Congress with such authorities as are necessary to pursue and preserve the general interests of the Union. This will make their administration respectable abroad, and vigorous at home.

This was a most sanguine account of a move that few others regarded so hopefully. A convention of five states had met in Annapolis in September, 1786, and under the skillful manipulation of Hamilton and Madison had asked the state legislatures to send commissioners to a convention in Philadelphia the following May. The expressed purpose was to authorize such federal legislation "as the situation of public affairs may be found to require." This was meant to convey, and was so understood, that the Articles of Confederation were to be reviewed and perhaps revised.

Bingham was not unduly discouraged or alarmed by the bad business conditions, the tariff walls that were being set up between the states, the threats of dissolution of the Union, the whispers of the need for a military dictatorship or a monarchy, or by Shays' Rebellion, which, even as he was writing to Dr. Price, was spreading to Vermont, New Hampshire and Connecticut.

Our resources are great, the industry and intelligence of our people are not to be surpassed, and I do not believe there exists a greater fund of public and private virtue than in this country. Nothing is wanting but a good Government to direct their advantages to public good and private benefit.

We have daily accessions of inhabitants, from emigrations from different parts of Europe, particularly Germany. It is a pleasing circumstance to a benevolent mind to contemplate the advantageous situation this class of people is placed in, on their arrival here.

From being in a state of vassalage in their own country, mere hewers of wood and drawers of water, they find themselves entitled to all the rights of citizenship in a free country, and with a small pittance enabled to purchase a freehold for themselves and family.

It is really fortunate for human nature, that there is a country, where the oppressed of all nations may find a secure asylum.

Congress managed to produce a quorum of seven states on January 17, 1787; it lasted only one day, for the sole representative of one of the states wandered away on January 18. Recovering its quorum for a few days on February 2, it attempted to elect a president, but no nominee had the support of more than two states. General Arthur St. Clair of Pennsylvania was finally elected as a compromise choice. Congress then took up the 1783 peace treaty for discussion. Britain still held a dozen frontier forts in violation of the treaty; she refused to give them up until the United States, under the terms of the treaty, paid their prewar debts. Since Congress had no money and no influence with the states, the discussion died.

Bingham served on a special committee with Madison, Rufus King and Charles Pinckney to recommend on the suspension of enlistments in the Continental army. He was appointed to the Committee on Indian Treaties, of which Dr. Arthur Lee was the leading specialist. He called with Mr. Madison on Don Diego de Guardoqui, the Spanish ambassador, and had a long talk about Spain's intention of closing the Mississippi River to American commerce. Bingham said that the western people were "exceedingly alarmed" at the idea and were forming committees to protect their interest. Señor Guardoqui replied that he was sorry for it, that the westerners mistook their interest, that the two nations should live in harmony, and that Spain owned both banks of the river and would never admit the United States right to navigation.

A copy of the Annapolis resolution had been sent to Congress out of "motives of respect" and was brought to the floor for debate. Shays' Rebellion had worked a sudden change in many minds in favor of a stronger national government, but Congress was in a sad dilemma on the issue of calling a constitutional convention. The members, Madison wrote to Washington, "have been much divided and embarrassed on the question whether their taking an interest in the measure would impede or promote it."

Massachusetts came forward with a motion: that a convention of delegates assemble at Philadelphia in May "for the sole and express purpose of revising the Articles of Confederation." The motion was carried. Many felt that the Convention would be severely limited by this specific restriction. Bingham had no such feeling. To Lord Lansdowne he wrote on March 4:

WILLIAM BINGHAM
Gilbert Stuart

William Bingham, at age forty-three the richest man and the
largest land owner in America, had Gilbert Stuart paint this portrait in 1795, the year he was elected United States Senator from
Pennsylvania. The portrait appeared on the front page of the
New York Times 169 years later (see pages 430, 432).

ROBERT MORRIS AND
THOMAS WILLING

Charles Willson Peale

The two partners in the powerful firm
of Willing, Morris and Company, Philadelphia merchants, played decisive roles
in William Bingham's career. Morris
sent him to Martinique during the Revolution to act as his business partner
and as agent of the Continental Congress. Willing served with him on the
board of the nation's first bank and
gave him his daughter Anne's hand in
marriage.

WHARF AT ARCH STREET, 1800
William Russell Birch

From these wharves on the Delaware River, Bingham's ships plied
the oceans as far east as India and China and opened up trade with
the South American La Plata region. The world's first boat pro-
pelled by steam, built by John Fitch, departed from the Arch
Street Wharf under its own power on July 20, 1786.

WILLIAM BINGHAM
Gilbert Stuart

Stuart began a group portrait of the Bingham family in London
in 1784 but, for some unknown reason, never finished the work
(see pages 149–50). The artist Thomas Sully later divided the
canvas into three parts, two of which are shown here and at right.

Anne Willing Bingham with her Daughter
Maria Matilda
Gilbert Stuart

COLONEL WILLIAM STEPHENS
SMITH, 1786

Mather Brown

MRS. WILLIAM STEPHENS SMITH
(ABIGAIL — "NABBY" — ADAMS), 1786

Mather Brown

MRS. JOHN (ABIGAIL) ADAMS, 1785

Mather Brown

JOHN ADAMS, ca. 1791–94

Charles Willson Peale

THE MARQUIS
DE CHASTELLUX, 1782
Charles Willson Peale

General François Jean Chastellux, third in line of command of the French army aiding the Americans, called on the Binghams shortly after their marriage and described them in one of the most widely read travel books of the time.

LORD SHELBURNE,
MARQUESS OF LANSDOWNE

*Unknown artist, after
Sir Joshua Reynolds*

Shelburne, England's pro-American prime minister near the close of the Revolution, was Bingham's closest friend in England.

LANSDOWN HOUSE
William Russell Birch

VIEW IN THIRD STREET, FROM SPRUCE STREET
William Russell Birch

Bingham's two Philadelphia residences: the Mansion House
at Third and Spruce, built by Bingham in 1786 and considered the finest house in America; and Lansdown House, a
landed estate on the Schuylkill River built by a member of
the Penn family. Neither is now standing.

MAJOR WILLIAM JACKSON
Miniature by an unknown artist

Major Jackson, Secretary of
the Constitutional Convention and
President Washington's "writing aide,"
spent two years in Europe trying to
sell Bingham's Maine lands. On his
return to Philadelphia he married
Anne Bingham's sister Elizabeth.

MRS. WILLIAM
(ELIZABETH WILLING)
JACKSON
Gilbert Stuart

ALEXANDER HAMILTON, ca. 1791
Charles Willson Peale

THOMAS JEFFERSON, 1791
Charles Willson Peale

Bingham was close to Hamilton
and Jay, his political allies.
Jefferson admired and corresponded
with Anne Bingham.

JOHN JAY
Unknown artist,
after John Trumbull

ROBERT GILMOR, SENIOR
Gilbert Stuart

Two of Bingham's closest associates were Robert Gilmor of Baltimore, merchant, his business partner for fifteen years; and Dr. Rush, who used Bingham's money and influence in founding Dickinson and Franklin and Marshall colleges.

DR. BENJAMIN RUSH
*Pastel attributed to
James Sharples, Sr.*

The defects of the confederated systems are so glaring and the necessity of a speedy and affectual revision and amendment so generally acknowledged, that Congress have recommended to the states to appoint, and many of the states have accordingly (and all will), come to the resolution of appointing deligates to a general convention . . . for the purpose of forming and making a report to Congress of such a federal constitution as may be suited to the exigencies of the Union.

Having the honor of a seat in Congress, as representative of the state of Pennsylvania, I was very active in promoting this measure.*

Bingham returned home in March, 1787, though Congress held its quorum and managed to function until May 12, when a number of its members left to attend the Constitutional Convention in Philadelphia. (Ten members of Congress, including Rufus King and James Madison, were delegates to the Convention.) On Sunday, May 13, the Philadelphia dragoons and a concourse of "mounted citizens" rode out to Gray's Ferry across the Schuylkill to welcome General Washington. The great man was escorted in his carriage, amid cheering crowds, chiming bells, and saluting artillery, to Mrs. Mary House's boardinghouse, much favored by the Virginians. Robert Morris, however, pressed the General to lodge with him throughout the Convention, and he had his baggage moved to the Morris house at Market near Sixth. Mrs. House presumably had no trouble filling her canceled reservation, for the city was crowded at the time with meetings of the Society of the Cincinnati, the Presbyterian Synod, the Baptists, and the Pennsylvania Society for the Abolition of Slavery (Benjamin Franklin, president).

Washington called at once on Dr. Franklin, who, as president of the state, was host to the Convention. On Friday, Mrs. Morris and "some other ladies" took him to College Hall to hear an impoverished Irish lady give readings and a dissertation on the Powers of Eloquence. (He found her "tolerable.") On Sunday he drank tea at Samuel Powel's, and the following day, as recorded in his diary, "Dined and drank tea at Mr. Bingham's, splendor shown."

The Convention, delayed eleven days for late delegates to arrive, convened on Friday, May 25. Twelve state legislatures had ap-

* This was written eleven days after Madison charged in his journal entry that Bingham favored a division of the Union into confederacies.

pointed sixty-two delegates. (Rhode Island, controlled by radical anti-federalists, refused to participate.) Of these, fifty-five delegates went to the Convention, though there were seldom more than thirty in attendance at one time. They received no pay and no expense money for their services. The average age of the delegates was just above forty. Five were under thirty; four were sixty or older; Franklin was the oldest at eighty-one, Jonathan Dayton of New Jersey the youngest at twenty-six. Nine were foreign-born; thirty were college graduates; eight had signed the Declaration of Independence; twenty-eight had served or were serving in the Congress.

The Pennsylvania delegation of eight was the largest, the most unified and probably the strongest in experience and prestige. A caucus of "Philadelphia Nationalists" had met on December 9 in the Half Moon Tavern across from the State House to name men who reflected their views: George Clymer, Jared Ingersoll (the city's leading lawyer), Thomas Mifflin, James Wilson, Gouverneur Morris, Robert Morris, and Thomas Fitzsimmons (one of two Roman Catholics at the Convention). Dr. Franklin's name had been added later.

The delegates met in the large first-floor hall at the east, or Delaware River end of the State House, in which the Second Continental Congress had held its meetings. To deaden the sounds of the wagons and carriages, earth was spread over the cobblestones of the surrounding streets. The delegates resolved to conduct their sessions in strictest secrecy; they would publish no minutes and reveal nothing in their conversation or letters until the results were known. They placed sentinels at the doors, kept the windows closed on all but the hottest days, and individually obeyed the resolution with remarkable fidelity.

Some developments, however, were generally known, and a man in Bingham's position would have known others. General Washington was the presiding officer, chosen unanimously for that post on the nomination of Robert Morris. Major William Jackson had requested Washington to recommend him as official secretary of the Convention, and on Colonel Hamilton's nomination he was chosen over William Temple Franklin. In a caucus held just before the Convention opened, the Virginia and Pennsylvania delegates had decided to ignore the directive of the Congress, scrap rather than amend the Articles of Confederation, and build an entirely new framework for a national government. Several of the delegates returned home when it became clear that the Convention would follow this course.

The delegates sat from 11 A.M. to 4 P.M., six days a week, and frequently continued their committee sessions into the evening. Despite the hard work and the increasing heat of the summer, there was still a great deal of social activity, with Washington as the prize catch at any gathering. Robert Morris entertained lavishly and often, though he was embarrassed at one large party when word spread that some of his drafts had been dishonored. ("A little mal apropos," Washington called it.) Washington went to a wedding, two benefit concerts, twice to the theater, twice to John Bartram's botanical gardens, and to a high mass at St. Joseph's Roman Catholic Chapel in Willings Alley. He sat for Charles Peale to have his sixth portrait painted by that artist. He inspected at Dr. Franklin's a mangle for pressing clothes but did not go down to the wharves with the crowds on August 22 to see an odd character named John Fitch successfully operate the first steamboat. During a ten-day recess of the Convention he went fishing with Gouverneur and Robert Morris and rode on to spend some reflective hours at the campsite at Valley Forge.

He dined, or drank tea, or both, in a score of homes, including those of Thomas Willing, Tench Francis, George Clymer, Dr. Rush, and (most often — eight times) Samuel Powel. He dined again with the Binghams, drank tea with them on three other occasions, and on June 13 "spent the evening at Mr. Bingham's."

*

Secretary Charles Thomson wrote a dignified plea to Bingham on June 25 to return to New York "to form a house." ("I think it of great importance to the honor and safety of the Confederacy that Congress should be in session and the form at least of government kept up in the present situation of affairs.") He wrote again on July 8 urging him to come or at least to "hasten on some of your colleagues," signing it, "With much esteem and affection, etc." The secretary was more than a little embarrassed at the unaccountable absence of President Arthur St. Clair. "It has I assure you given a good deal of offense. If I knew where to direct a letter to him I would take the liberty to write and urge him to come as speedily as possible."

Bingham tore himself away from the excitement of Philadelphia to return to New York and duty, but he arrived too late to vote on the one outstanding piece of legislation passed by the Congress of the Confederation — an act that has been called "one of the greatest and most original of the contributions of America to the modern world of political thought." The dying Congress had revitalized itself long enough to pass the Great Northwest Ordinance, last of several laws that provided the means for bringing the lands north of the Ohio River into the Union.

The merchants, shipowners, and planters in the seaboard cities feared the demands of the uncouth, uncontrollable west, and there was a strong desire to treat the western territories as provinces. Instead, in a series of enlightened ordinances originally outlined by Jefferson, the lands were divided into a gridiron township pattern; territorial representation was allowed in Congress for every 5000 free male inhabitants; territories were admitted into the Union as states "on an equal footing with the original states in all respects whatever" when they had 60,000 free inhabitants; public education was provided for with grants of one section of land in each township; and slavery was prohibited. The Ordinance was passed on July 13, 1787, with a declared quorum of only eight states present — less than the required number — and only eighteen Congressmen voting, one of whom declared against. Pennsylvania was not represented.*

Bingham did arrive in New York in time to become a target in the first large lobbying campaign launched in the United States. The Ohio Company of Associates had been formed to buy, resell, and settle some millions of acres of the Northwest Territory. Each participant was permitted to subscribe up to $5000 in the company, payable in the certificates of indebtedness that Congress had issued to soldiers in lieu of pay. It was hoped that Congress would accept these veterans' certificates at face value in payment for the land. The proposition was made more attractive with the formation of a subsidiary, the Scioto Company, which secretly admitted a number of Congressmen, their friends and their relatives. The Ohio Company presented a memorial to Congress in the spring of 1787 requesting a charter for both companies.

* The Northwest Territory became the states of Ohio, Illinois, Indiana, Michigan, and Wisconsin. Jefferson had divided the territory into ten states to be named Sylvania, Michigania, Chersonesus, Assenisipia, Metropotamia, Illinoia, Saratoga, Polypotamia, Pelispia, and Washington.

The Ohio Company employed a Reverend Manasseh Cutler, forty-five, an ordained Congregational minister of Ipswich, Massachusetts, as its agent, made him a director, and sent him off to win over the Congress. Cutler was a versatile man. He was a graduate of Yale, a student of law and divinity, a medical practitioner, and a "scientific botanist," and he had served four years in Congress. His greatest talent, however, was that of political persuasion. A contemporary described him perfectly as to type: "He was much given to relating anecdotes, and making himself agreeable."

Dr. Cutler visited Philadelphia during the Constitutional Convention, obtained letters of introduction to various members of the Congress, and descended on New York on July 18 with drafts for $143,-000 and an offer to buy "six or seven million acres" of the public lands. Congress, starved for money, was receptive. Five members, however, were opposed. The boundaries of the land requested were uncertain, the terms of payment vague, the price low. The Ohio Company offered $1 million for a million and a half acres (66.67 cents an acre) and demanded an option for the Scioto Company to buy an additional three and a half million acres at the same rate for speculation. Veterans' certificates were considered of little value, and while some speculators, including Bingham, felt they were a good investment risk, they were currently worth only twelve cents on the dollar. Thus the real offer for the land was about eight cents an acre.

Dr. Cutler called on Colonel William Duer, a rich and influential Congressman from New York who was secretary of the Treasury Board that had been formed to succeed Robert Morris. Duer promised to assist him. In Dr. Cutler's diary:

> As there are a number in Congress decidedly opposed to my terms of negotiation, and some to any contract, I wish now to ascertain the number for and against, and who they are, and must then, if possible, bring the opponents over.

Duer revealed who they were. Cutler wrote:

> Clarke, Bingham, Yates, Kearney and Few are the troublesome fellows. They must be attacked by my friends at their lodgings.

When Congress offered terms that were not acceptable, Dr. Cutler announced sadly that he would withdraw his offer, leave New York, and buy the lands on better terms from some of the states or even from the Indians. His worried supporters in Congress begged him to stay and promised to "make every exertion" in his behalf. Cutler regretfully but firmly declared that he saw no prospect of a contract and would leave. The lobbying effort was intensified. The southern members were held by a promise to make their favorite, Arthur St. Clair, governor of the new territory. Duer emphasized and broadened the opportunities of the members to invest quietly in the Scioto Company. Dr. Cutler:

> We now entered into the true spirit of negotiations with great bodies; every machine in the city that it was possible to set to work we now put in motion. Few, Bingham, and Kearney are our principal opposers. Of Few and Bingham there is hope, but to bring over that stubborn mule of a Kearney I think is beyond our power.

The recalcitrants were besieged on all sides. They met with remonstrances on the streets, argument in their lodgings, persuasion in the coffee houses, appeals to their cupidity in the corridors, and calls to patriotism on the floor of Congress. They still did not give in.

On July 26, Dr. Cutler again announced his imminent departure and showed up on Wall Street with his packed bags around him. Yates and Bingham gave way under the pressure, and Few followed a day later. Kearney alone remained stubborn to the last. On the afternoon of the 27th, Congress passed the bill as Cutler wanted it, and the Ohio Company was given immediate possession of five million acres. The Reverend Dr. Cutler returned to Boston and proceeded to write a pamphlet on the glories of the western territory.

The Ohio Company began settlement of the Northwest Territory in the following spring of 1788, when forty-seven colonists from New England, under General Rufus Putnam, floated down the Ohio from Pittsburgh and founded the town of Marietta (named for Marie Antoinette) at the mouth of the Muskingum River. The Scioto Company settled a few hundred unhappy French colonists downriver at Gallipolis (by error in the wrong place), but it never took up any of its option on the three and a half million acres. Neither company made money. Hamilton, St. Clair, Duer and Richard Henry Lee, among other Congressmen, owned Scioto shares. There is no evidence that Bingham took any part in this speculation.

CHAPTER 15

Last Chance for Union

Moved: That Congress do agree thereto and that it [the Federal Constitution] be recommended to the legislatures of the several states to cause conventions to be held as speedily as may be to the end that the same may be adopted ratified and confirmed.

Motion of William Bingham of Pennsylvania
and Edward Carrington of Virginia in
the Congress, September 24, 1787

BINGHAM ATTENDED the sessions of Congress throughout July. He was appointed to the Finance Committee and participated in the fruitless annual exercise of estimating the fiscal requirements of the government and sending out requisitions to the states, which the states ignored. His committee on Indian Affairs drew up a general treaty to be offered to the Indians "northward of Ohio and about Lake Erie." The Indians looked to the British for protection and had no interest in a treaty, general or otherwise.

The real interest of Congress in these days lay in what was happening in Philadelphia. The people, in Madison's words, were "big with expectation." There were criticism, surprise, and admiration at the profound secrecy that was being maintained, and there were rumors and counter-rumors. To set the record straight on one point, the delegates let it be known on August 18 that "We never once thought of a king."

Bingham returned to Philadelphia in August and met with his party colleagues to discuss means of getting the constitution ratified in Pennsylvania.

The Convention expected to conclude its work and send the new constitution to New York during the third week in September. It would request the Congress to forward the document to the states to be voted on by popularly elected constitutional conventions in each state. The Pennsylvania anti-Federalists, knowing that Pennsylvania was a pivotal state and that opposition there would strengthen the forces of anti-Federal opposition everywhere, intended to do everything in their power to avoid calling a state convention, or to delay the call if that was impossible. They were determined that the Federalist-dominated Assembly should not be permitted to decide this issue before the November elections. After the election, the new Assembly should decide when, where and whether to call the convention. The anti-Federalists would wage a vigorous campaign to win the Assembly, control any constitutional convention that had to be held, and so defeat the proposed constitution in Pennsylvania.

The Pennsylvania Federalists decided that they might be able to thwart these tactics if they moved swiftly and decisively. They drew up a plan. As soon as Congress acted on the constitution, Bingham was to speed the news to the Federalist leaders in Philadelphia. They would take the anti-Federalists by surprise with an unexpected motion in the Assembly to convene a state constitutional convention. The motion might possibly pass before the opposition had time to rally and organize.

The proposed Constitution of the United States of America, edited and polished by Gouverneur Morris, was approved at the last session of the Convention on Monday, September 17. Thirty-nine delegates put their names to the document, General Washington signing first. Three of the delegates present, and two who had absented themselves, refused their signatures. George Mason of Virginia declared that he would cut off his right hand before he would sign; he wanted a Bill of Rights. All eight Pennsylvania delegates signed.

Major William Jackson turned over his sparse records of the Convention, collected $866.60 for four months of work performed with singular lack of distinction, and set out for New York with the engrossed and signed Constitution in his luggage. With it was a resolution of the Convention suggesting that the Congress submit the document to the states for their assent and ratification. In a letter to Secretary Thomson, General Washington said, "In all our deliberations on this subject we kept steadily in our view, that which appears to us the greatest interest of every true American, the consolidation of our Union, in which is involved our prosperity, felicity, safety, perhaps our national existence." Major Jackson's packet was opened in New York three days later, on Thursday, September 20, and the seven articles and 4000 words of the proposed Constitution were read to an astonished Congress.

This was an utter and absolute rejection of the Articles of Confederation and Perpetual Union. It would create a national government with powers far greater than any exercised by George III or his Parliament. The authority of the states was curbed. State officials were expressly bound to enforce the acts of the central legislative body, the Congress. States could not issue legal-tender paper money; they were denied the right to impair the obligation of contract; they could not tax imports and they could not make treaties.

The Constitution proposed a single strong executive to be known as a President, independent of the legislative power and possessing concentrated authority to administer the government. He was to be commander in chief of the army and navy and of the state militia when called into the national service. He had power to disapprove an act of the Congress, but the Congress could re-pass the act with a two-thirds majority, and the Senate could remove the President from office by impeachment. The President was to be appointed to a four-year term by electors in the states. These were to be chosen as the state legislatures might decide, their number equaling the number of members the state had in the Congress.

The Congress, holding all legislative power, consisted of two bodies. One, called the Senate, was made up of two members from each state, regardless of its size. They were to be elected to a six-year term by the state legislatures, with one-third of the Senators to be chosen every second year. The other body was a House of Representatives made up of one member for every 30,000 free persons, with every five "other persons" (slaves) equaling three free persons in the computation. House members were to be chosen by the people every two years.

The Congress had the power to tax, impose duties on foreign imports, maintain an army and navy, call forth the militia, coin and borrow money, regulate commerce between the states and with foreign governments, sell public lands, protect the states from invasion and domestic violence, define and punish piracy on the high seas, declare war, and pay the debts contracted by the earlier congresses and by the states. Votes were to be recorded and issues decided, not by the states, but by individual members.

The Congress could not impose any tax or duty on exports. It could not interfere with the slave trade for twenty years. It had no power to negative laws passed by the states; that right was reserved to a body to be called the Supreme Court, which held the judicial power of the country. Its justices were to be nominated for life terms by the President, subject to ratification by the Senate.

There was no property requirement for holding federal office, not even in the United States Senate or for the Presidency, nor was there any article protecting property rights. There was provision for amending the Constitution with a single exception: the right of each state to have an equal number of Senators was not subject to amendment. The states were not broken up and redivided; their boundaries remained the same. New states could be admitted to the Union.

Much of the Congress was lukewarm, and a strong minority was decidedly chilly, toward this revolutionary document. Richard Henry Lee of Virginia immediately drew up formal propositions for "essential alterations" and spoke of the need for another constitutional convention.

The full document was published in the *Pennsylvania Packet* two days after the Convention adjourned and in other papers throughout the country a few days later. In Pennsylvania, 1500 copies were printed in pamphlet form, 500 of them in German. The national debate began. The Federalists considered this the last chance for union. The anti-Federalists, speaking "in the cause of liberty and mankind," felt that the new form of government "would surely result in a monarchy or a tyrannical aristocracy" and might lead to civil war. The proposed constitution would cost too much; it would ruin the state governments or reduce them to corporations; liberty of the press was not assured; the federal judiciary would destroy the judiciary of the states; and there was no provision against a standing army. As for George Washington and Benjamin Franklin, the two once-great Americans who supported this document, the anti-Federalists concluded that the one was incompetent and the other senile.

Bingham was not present at the reading in Congress on September 20, for reasons that apparently were known to Thomas Fitzsimmons in Philadelphia, to whom he reported the following day:

It was yesterday received and read in Congress, and Wednesday next fixed as the day for its consideration. If I had been present,

I should certainly have [opposed] its postponement to so distant a day. As from enquiry I find that every state on the floor of Congress is disposed to adopt it, I will endeavor to bring on the question immediately. I shall urge as an argument the favorable disposition of our [Pennsylvania] assembly, which is now in sessions. I will inform you of the result as soon as possible.

Congress began its debate and discussion. Richard Henry Lee and a colleague moved that the Constitution be submitted to the states, but that it be sent with the warning that the Convention had acted unconstitutionally under the Articles of the Confederation. The motion was not carried. Another member moved that the Constitution be sent to the states with a reprimand to the Convention for exceeding its authority. That too was voted down. Bingham and Edward Carrington of Virginia went to the opposite extreme and entered a motion that the Congress not only send the Constitution to the states, but that they do so with the clear recommendation that they act speedily to adopt, ratify and confirm it. Their motion was not passed.

On Friday, September 28, after skirmishes and consultations lasting eight days, the members reached a compromise. They would send the Constitution to the states with a bland, brief and utterly noncommittal resolution. Bingham and the other zealous advocates came to support this measure so that the precious words "Resolved Unanimously" might accompany the Constitution on its journey to the state capitals. Bingham apparently determined on Wednesday or Thursday that an agreement was reached and that approval would shortly be voted. He sent off one of his express riders with this news to his colleagues in Philadelphia.

On Friday morning, with every Federalist member in his seat, George Clymer rose to speak in the Pennsylvania Assembly. He opened the question of providing for a convention of delegates to consider the forthcoming federal constitution. The unsuspecting anti-Federalists, all of them from the interior and western counties, were galvanized into action, and a very long debate ensued. Robert Whitehill of Carlisle protested that Mr. Clymer was out of order. Congress had not even sent them the Constitution, he said, nor any request to consider it. No such motion could be made without notice given beforehand. The motion could not even be voted on until it had passed three readings. The matter should be postponed until the

Assembly could have time to consider such an important subject. In all of this he was quite correct, but Thomas Fitzsimmons rose to declare blandly that the measure was too important to delay. Whitehill replied that its importance was the very reason it should be treated with deliberation.

Daniel Clymer, cousin of George, declaimed: "As this subject is before us, let us not hesitate, but eagerly embrace the glorious opportunity of being foremost in its adoption. Let us not hesitate, because it is damping the ardor with which it should be pursued. Sir, it is throwing cold water on the flame that warms the breast of every friend of liberty."

The anti-Federalists were shouted down with cries of "Question! Question!" The question was put and carried by a vote of 43 to 19. On Whitehill's motion, the session was adjourned until four o'clock that afternoon, at which time, he said, the date, place and method of choosing the delegates to consider the Constitution would be voted on. There was much laughter and self-congratulation at the Federalist luncheon tables on how smoothly and cleverly everything had been carried off.

When the session resumed at four o'clock, not one minority member was in the chamber, which meant that the Assembly was two votes short of the forty-six required for a quorum, and that no business could be conducted. The Federalists, indignant at this breach of trust, sent the sergeant at arms to round up at least two of the absent members. He returned with the information that he had found them at Major Adam Boyd's boardinghouse on Sixth Street, but "I told the gentlemen that the Speaker and the House had sent for them, and says they, 'There is no House.'"

Mr. Speaker: "Did you let them know they were desired to attend?"

Sergeant: "Yes, Sir, but they told me they could not attend this afternoon, for they had not made up their minds, yet."

The Federalists, outwitted, baffled and angry, debated on what to do next. They searched the books and found no law that compelled an absent member to attend, the only penalty being loss of one-third of a day's pay if he was absent. The Assembly recessed until nine-thirty the following morning, which was the day set for adjournment.

The affair was discussed in the taverns until midnight, with liberal abuse for the nineteen recalcitrant members and much conjecture on what the minority would do when the Assembly reconvened.

Sometime during the early morning, Bingham's messenger came spurring into town with the news that Congress had acted on the Constitution. By riding all night and changing horses at prearranged intervals along the way, he had managed to reach Philadelphia just twelve hours after the signing of the resolution in New York.

When the Speaker took the chair next morning and called the roll, no minority members were present and again no quorum could be declared. George Clymer rose and presented to the chair a packet of documents he had received that morning from New York. It was, he said, a resolution of the Congress, passed unanimously, requesting the legislature of each state to put the proposed Constitution to a vote of a popularly elected convention. It had been signed yesterday, and Mr. Bingham had forwarded it to him by express rider, "having chosen this mode in preference to the ordinary conveyance by post."

Fortified with this new evidence of regularity, the Speaker again sent the sergeant, accompanied by the assistant clerk, to find the members and request their attendance. They returned to report that they had seen some of the members on the streets, but that these had "mended their pace" and escaped. They had confronted James Mc-Calmont of Franklin County and Jacob Miley of Dauphin County at Major Boyd's and shown them the resolution of Congress, but both refused to come to the chamber. The anti-Federalist leaders were behind locked doors, preparing an address to their constituents in which they set forth their objections to the proposed Constitution.

In the meantime, word had spread around the city that the anti-Federalist members had "absconded" from their duties. A crowd of men gathered, and as time passed they grew impatient. They marched off in search of any two absent members. At Major Boyd's, they broke down the doors, pulled McCalmont and Miley from the house, and dragged them, protesting and struggling, through the streets to the State House. There the two men, their clothes dirtied and torn, were thrust into the Assembly chamber and pinioned in their seats. The clerk wrote in his minutes, in what must be considered something of an understatement: "The Speaker left the chair, and in a few minutes Mr. James McCalmont and Mr. Jacob Miley entered the House. The Speaker resumed the chair, and the roll was called."

McCalmont said, "I was brought into the assembly room by force, contrary to my wishes. I beg to be dismissed the house."

Thomas Fitzsimmons: "I would be glad to know if any member of the house was guilty of forcing the gentleman from the determination of absenting himself; if there is, I think it necessary that the house mark such conduct with their disapprobation. But we are to consider, Sir, that the member is now here, and that the business of the State cannot be accomplished, if any one is suffered to withdraw: from which consideration I conclude, it will be extremely improper for any member to leave this house."

McCalmont: "I desire that the rules may be read, and I will agree to stand by the decision of the house."

The rules were read. Every member who did not answer on calling the roll should pay two shillings and sixpence, or if there was no quorum without him, five shillings.

McCalmont rose in his place, took some loose silver from his pocket, held it out and said, "Well, Sir, here is your five shillings to let me go."

The crowd ringing the chamber roared with laughter.

Speaker: "The person appointed to receive fines is not in his place. If he was, the member should not pay a fine. He has not broken the rule. He has appeared and answered to his name and therefore may retain his money."

Fitzsimmons: "I am a friend to good order and decorum, but I believe the gentleman's complaint is not to be redressed by the house. The member himself has trespassed. . . . He has perhaps offered the greatest indignity to the legislature of Pennsylvania, which could be offered. He has, Sir, tendered you a fine of five shillings in order to be permitted to destroy the business, if not the good government of the State. On this, Sir, I will make no reflection; the member is here now, and we may determine that he shall stay, not only on constitutional ground, but from the law of nature, that will not suffer any body to destroy its own existence prematurely."

As the time for a vote neared, McCalmont leaped from his seat and ran for the door. The crowd yelled "Stop him!" He was collared and led back to his seat. A question was put: Shall Mr. McCalmont have leave of absence? It was passed "almost unanimously in the negative."

A motion was then made that the delegates to the state convention be elected on the first Tuesday in November. McCalmont objected that this was much too early and moved the last Tuesday in December. His motion failed. He moved the third Tuesday in December, then the second Tuesday, with the same result.

The motion was made that the convention should sit in Philadelphia. McCalmont moved to alter this to Carlisle, but he was not upheld. He then moved that the city be Lancaster, and he was enthusiastically seconded by the member from Lancaster. His motion was put to the vote and defeated 30 to 15.

The formal resolution that the election of delegates be held on November 6, 1787, and that the Convention be held in Philadelphia on November 20, was passed by a vote of 44 to 2. The assembly adjourned and Mr. McCalmont and Mr. Miley were released.

The five weeks that followed saw a stormy and sometimes violent campaign for control of the delegates to be elected to the state convention. The anti-Federalists attacked the new plan of government for containing "the seeds of aristocracy and centralization"; and as "a scheme of the wealthy and ambitious, who in every community think they have the right to lord it over their fellow creatures." They declared that the high-handed and outrageous treatment their assemblymen had received on September 29 was exactly what might be expected under the new government.

Philadelphia elected delegates overwhelmingly in favor of ratification, and they heavily outnumbered the delegates from the inland country, most of whom were opposed. The state convention opened on November 20 and sat for three weeks, five days of that time being taken up by an anti-Federalist filibuster. James Wilson brilliantly led the forces for ratification, for which he was later mobbed and severely beaten in Carlisle. Ratification was voted on December 12 by a margin of 46 to 23, and Pennsylvania became the first large state, a few days after Delaware, to approve the federal Constitution. On December 13, businesses were closed in Philadelphia and the citizens celebrated the ratification by ringing church bells, firing off cannon and parading in the streets. When the celebration was over, the state's Federalists prepared to open an attack on Pennsylvania's radical constitution.

The following June, 1788, the Constitution became the law of the land when it was ratified by the last of the required nine states. For his work in getting the Constitution through Congress and the Pennsylvania Assembly, and for his later attempts in Congress to have the new federal capital placed in Philadelphia, William Bingham was mentioned favorably as a prospect for the new Congress, or the State Assembly, or even as the first governor of Pennsylvania.

BOOK THREE

The Republican
Court

CHAPTER 16

The Master Builders

The present Period is very favorable for carrying into Effect a System of Taxation, as the Affections of the People are so rivetted to the New Government, that their minds will be easily conciliated to all its operations.

William Bingham to Alexander Hamilton
November 25, 1789

DR. WILLIAM SHIPPEN, the well-known surgeon and medical educator, had a wife from Virginia. It was no doubt for this reason that he gave a dinner for the delegation of Virginia Congressmen when they stopped in Philadelphia in March, 1789, en route to New York to attend the first session of the Congress under the new government. John Page was there, the planter patriot, an old and warm friend of Thomas Jefferson. James Madison came. So did Richard Henry Lee, traveling north to serve the government he had opposed so vigorously both in the Old Congress and in the Virginia ratifying convention. He carried with him a Bill of Rights that he and Madison intended to push through the new Congress. Dr. Shippen also invited some guests from the city: Dr. Ashbel Green, young pastor of the Second Presbyterian Church; Thomas McKean, Chief Justice of Pennsylvania; and William Bingham, merchant and second-term member of the Old Congress, which had not met since October and was now about to expire and turn over its records to the new national body.*

In the course of the dinner, Justice McKean turned to Mr. Madison and asked, "Sir, have you thought of a title for the President?" Mr. Madison replied, "No, sir, I have not. In my opinion, no title other than that of President is necessary or proper." McKean countered: "Yes, sir, he must have a title. I have been examining the titles

---

* John Page later became governor of Virginia; Dr. Green became president of the College of New Jersey at Princeton.

of the princes of Europe to discover one that has not been appropriated. 'Most Serene Highness' is used, but Serene Highness without the 'Most' is not. I think it is proper that our chief magistrate should be known as 'His Serene Highness the President of the United States.' " An amicable controversy followed, Justice McKean maintaining his position, the Virginians holding that "President of the United States" was proper and sufficient. William Bingham remained silent or expressed a view that has been lost to history.

The controversy was continued less amicably in the new United States Senate. That body was closed to the public until 1794, but its daily proceedings through its first two years were recorded in the diary of a striking character from the frontier country of Pennsylvania. He was William Maclay, fifty-one years of age, 6 feet, 3 inches tall, lawyer, judge, Pennsylvania assemblyman, deputy surveyor, founder of the town of Sunbury. Maclay had been elected in January, 1789, with Robert Morris, to the Senate of the United States. He and Morris pulled straws; he drew the two-year term, Morris the six-year term. Maclay was dour, caustic, suspicious of the motives of others, distrustful of aristocrats, merchants and New Englanders, a Diogenes forever searching and forever failing to find an honest man. He spent much of his two years in the Senate striving to have the nation's capital placed in Harrisburg. One may charitably assume that he was in no way influenced by the fact that he owned the ground on which he proposed that the capitol building be erected.

For one week before the President's inauguration on April 30, and for two weeks thereafter, the Senate did little but discuss the thorny problems of language and titles, protocol and procedures. "We are in a wilderness, without a single footstep to guide us," James Madison, leader of the House of Representatives, wrote to Thomas Jefferson in Paris.

John Adams, the Vice President, newly returned from the Court of St. James's and presiding over the Senate wearing his sword, was in a quandary on how to conduct himself. He wanted to call the sergeant at arms "The Usher of the Black Rod" and was rebuked by Senator Maclay. A Committee on Titles was appointed at Mr. Adams' urging. It deliberated for some days and recommended that the chief executive be addressed, "His Highness, the President of the United States of America, and Protector of the Liberties of the Same." Senator Maclay and some other members of the leveling, democratic spirit objected, citing the language of the Constitution itself. Said Mr. Adams, "What will the common people of foreign countries, what will the sailors and soldiers say? George Washington, President of the United States? They will despise him *to all eternity!*"

Mr. Adams (his colleagues had begun to call him "His Rotundity") was perplexed on other points as well:

> Gentlemen, I feel great difficulty how to act. . . . I am Vice-President. In this I am nothing, but I may be everything. But I am president also of the Senate. When the President comes into the Senate, what shall I be? I can not be [president] then. No, gentlemen, I can not, I can not. I wish the gentlemen to think what I shall be.

Again:

> Gentlemen, I wish for the direction of the Senate. The President will, I suppose, address the Congress. How shall I behave? How shall we receive it? Shall it be standing or sitting?

*

On April 20, Captain Bingham put on his black buckskin breeches, long boots with flaring tops, buff waistcoat with four rows of buttons, blue and buff coat, and leather cap with bearskin crest. With his sword at his side and his pair of horseman's pistols in his saddle holster, he led his Troop of Horse to the southern border of the state, there, with a multitude of dignitaries, to meet and escort President-Elect Washington into the city. Washington had left Mount Vernon oppressed with anxious and painful thoughts, but he submitted to the ceaseless adulation with stoic dignity, considering it a necessary though personally distasteful part of his new office. His journey to New York was a continuous progress of cheering crowds, pealing bells, saluting cannon, parading militia, receptions, dinners, and entertainments.

On meeting the large delegation from Philadelphia, Washington left his post chaise and mounted a white charger. The pontoon bridge across the Schuylkill was decked with cedar branches, flags and two triumphal arches. From the second of the arches, a child in a white dress trimmed with foliage (C.W. Peale's thirteen-year-old daughter Angelica), "assisted by certain machinery," let drop a crown of laurel to hang above Washington's unsuspecting brow, to the approving roar of the multitude. The President sat down to a dinner for 250 at the City Tavern and stayed the night with Robert Morris. Bingham and his troop escorted him next morning to the New Jersey state line, and at the Assumpink Bridge relinquished him in a pouring rain to a party of matrons and maidens, the latter dressed all in white and singing an ode composed for the occasion. Overhead was a huge banner, THE DEFENDER OF THE MOTHERS WILL BE THE PROTECTOR OF THE DAUGHTERS.

General Washington was conveyed across the Hudson River to Manhattan Island in a barge rowed by thirteen ships' captains, all in white. John Jay, General Henry Knox, and other dignitaries accompanied him in a second barge. The reporter for the *Gazette of the United States* was so overcome that he began his story, "It is impossible to do justice to an attempt to describe the scene exhibited in his Excellency's approach to the city."

Washington took the oath of office on April 30 in Federal Hall, on a balcony overlooking Wall Street.* The United States had a government — the first in history with a written constitution, the first planned and designed as a republic of self-governing free men.

In France one week later, the three Estates General — clergy, nobility, and commons — met at Versailles as a parliamentary body for the first time since 1614. The harvest had been bad in France; food was short; the treasury was depleted; the economy had never recovered from the money and supplies given to the Americans in the war; the country was stifled by an upper stratum of nobles and clergymen who, as a class, owned two-fifths of the land and produced almost nothing. The following month, Mirabeau and the commoners declared themselves a National Assembly, and there was a surge of hope for reform of the medieval political and social structure of the country. In July, a mob in search of ammunition stormed the Bastille, the fortress and state prison that had become a symbol of absolutism. It

* He wore a suit of American homespun provided by General Knox, manufactured at his mill in Hartford.

killed the governor, freed the inmates (seven in number), and turned reform into revolution.

*

Bingham had spent the spring and summer of 1788 in New York during his second term in the Old Congress, devoting much of his time to the ratification fight in states other than his own, working at the changeover of government, and striving to persuade the Congressmen to name Philadelphia as the new capital. Willing, in his letters to Bingham, had described the magnificent day-long "Grand Federal Procession" on July 4, held in joint celebration of Independence Day and of ratification of the Constitution. Lieutenant Jackson had led Bingham's Troop of Horse in the parade; Willing himself had marched at the head of the city's merchants. Willing wrote in July and August:

> I am truly sorry for your very long detention from us — but remember that an absence now may cost you and others many long year's of the like inconvenience hereafter.

> Nancy and the children are perfectly well — nothing could have pacified her under your long absence, but the universal approbation which she daily hears of your spirited exertions in favor of the great point.

> Your exertions are very pleasing to most folks here, and your constant attention in giving such regular information, will not be forgot soon. Where so much is at stake, it's natural to feel great anxiety; and though we may not be finally gratified in the extent of our wishes, yet we read with pleasure an account of the daily proceedings and steps taken by our friends to bring it about.
>
> Your reasons are well founded, and your sentiments are conveyed in language clear and intelligible; and some handsome things frequently drop from those I communicate your letters to. Nancy and the little girls are all quite well. The former is so nearly crazy at your long absence, that, although she has not yet *walked* in her sleep, yet she started up in her bed last night, dreaming of you, I suppose, and knocked her head violently against the wall. She complains of her head yet, and we all laugh heartily at her complaints — so you may believe she is not very bad.

The southern states had opposed Philadelphia as the new capital because it was too Federalist and because the Quakers harried their delegates with proposals for emancipating the slaves. They voted down Baltimore because it was too close to Philadelphia; and with the help of anti-Federalist Rhode Island, which had openly expressed its determination not to join the Union, they committed the new Congress to New York. ("The indecency of such conduct on the part of Rhode Island," Bingham wrote to Willing, "struck even their own partisans with astonishment.")

Bingham had returned to Philadelphia in the fall of 1788, but now, a year later, he and Anne were spending much of their time in New York. He had not run for reelection and was not a member of the new government, but he was constantly in touch with the men who were. The Philadelphia delegation was made up of Senator Morris and Congressmen George Clymer and Thomas Fitzsimmons. James Wilson was one of five associate justices of the Supreme Court under Chief Justice John Jay. General Knox of Massachusetts, President Washington's Secretary of War, was the only man from the old government to retain his office. Young Alexander Hamilton as Secretary of the Treasury, Edmund Randolph as Attorney General, and Thomas Jefferson, Secretary of State, composed the rest of the cabinet. Mr. Jefferson, on the way home from France, was not expected for some weeks.

Bingham was concerned with both commercial and Pennsylvania affairs in New York. The year before, he had represented his state government, with a colleague, in buying Northwest Pennsylvania and the Erie Triangle from the Congress (for $625,000, or seventy-five cents an acre) and from the Delaware and Wyandotte Indians. Now the new Congress was debating the surveys of the land and the propriety of the treaties with the Indians. Bingham apparently was present to testify or lobby for his state. In his spare time he was involved in a corporation set up to administer relief for clergymen's widows, and he was attempting to persuade the state Assembly to make a cash grant to Dickinson College.

The President and the Congress turned to Secretary Hamilton more than to any other single person to transform the Constitution from a plan to a working program. It was a very considerable undertaking. As the French were learning, writing a constitution was one thing; making it work was quite another.

Four days after he took office, Hamilton was asked by his chief clerk how the books of the United States should be kept. Six days later, the Congress asked him to prepare a report on the ways and means of supporting the credit of the government. With characteristic zest and confidence, he set out to have a report ready for Congress when it reconvened for its second session in February, 1790.

The picture was bleak enough. The country was just emerging from a depression. The Congress of the Confederation had transferred to its successor nothing but obligations; the treasury was empty. The total debt of the nation was staggering — more than $20 for each person in the country. The foreign debt was almost $12 million, of which $1.5 million was in past-due interest owing the French government. The national internal debt was about $42.5 million, payable in interest-bearing treasury certificates issued during the war to buy supplies and to pay the troops. About one-third of this debt represented unpaid interest. Fewer than one-fourth of the certificates of indebtedness were in the hands of the original owners; the others had long since been sold at far less than their face value. The certificates had dropped as low as twenty-one cents on the dollar; they were now selling at about fifty cents. There was strong pressure on the Congress from some quarters to call in and pay off the certificates at their reduced market price.* The states had an internal debt of about $21 million, payable in state certificates, which brought the total public debt of the nation to some $75 million.

National and state certificates were traded like any other securities and were bought up by those who wanted to speculate and those who wanted to invest. (Harvard College owned $102,922 in Massachusetts certificates.) Owners in the southern states were not inclined to believe that either type of certificate would ever be made good. As a result, the prices of both were low there and they had naturally gravitated to the northern states.

The amount of Bingham's holdings in national and state certifi-

* Veterans' certificates had risen from a low of ten cents on the dollar to about thirty cents. Veterans', treasury, and state certificates should not be confused with the Continental paper currency, totaling some $80 million, some of which was eventually redeemed at 1 cent on the dollar.

cates is not known, but it must have been very large, for he began to buy early and made no secret of his conviction that they were a good speculative investment. In 1778, while in Martinique, he had asked Robert Morris and Joseph Warren of Boston, among others, to buy treasury certificates for him whenever they were available; Morris on one occasion had tried to get $40,000 worth but could find only $8000. In the fall of 1789, Bingham borrowed £60,000 sterling from Dutch bankers on ninety-day credit and used the money to buy treasury certificates, paying a premium purchase price of nine shillings to the pound when the current price was below eight shillings. Seeing such persistence, Bingham's enemies called him "a bloodhound certificate man."

On October 10, 1789, Alexander Hamilton wrote to Bingham (in a letter marked *private*) to ask his advice on tax and tariff laws.

> Knowing as I do your zeal for whatever concerns the public good and relying upon your care and intelligence I take the liberty to request your aid . . . for which purpose I have enclosed a number of queries, to which I shall be obliged by as full particular and accurate answers as possible.
>
> May I also take the liberty [to request of] you that you will from time to time favor me with communications with regard to . . . any thoughts that may occur to you concerning the financing and debts of the United States.

Bingham had known Colonel Hamilton well in Philadelphia in 1781 –83; corresponded with him during the stay in Europe; entertained him often at the Mansion House on Third Street; and worked with him in New York in the Old Congress in 1788. He knew Hamilton's economic philosophy and principles. To a remarkable degree they were identical with his own.

Both men had absorbed the practical, pragmatic ideas of Robert Morris; even allowing for the greater reach and brilliance of Hamilton's mind, the language and sentiments of the three were now virtually interchangeable and indistinguishable. Morris had written of his desire for a national state with "power, consequence, grandeur." He spoke of the need "to attach many powerful individuals to the cause of our country by the strong principles of self-love and the immediate sense of private interest," and of the need to make wealth flow "into those hands which could render it most productive." The words and philosophy were reflected and echoed by his two younger apostles. Hamilton and Bingham spoke for the business community, but both had a larger vision of the prosperity and strength possible for the United States in an industrial economy. They agreed, in Hamilton's words, that "the spirit of manufacturing must become the general spirit of the nation, and be incorporated, as it were, into their very essence." They were persistent in their predictions of a bright American future, especially when writing to England, whence they hoped to draw skilled labor, machinery and that "precious acquisition," investment capital.

Like Hamilton, Bingham understood the complexities of banking and finance. He perceived the financial and industrial revolution that was taking place in England and admired the young William Pitt who was helping to bring it about. He knew that currency and credit were the lifeblood of an economy, that the United States was anemic from lack of both, and that they could be supplied only by a national commercial banking system. As one of a merchant class trained in the code that contracts involved honor, Bingham believed that the basis of national credit and effective government lay in meeting national obligations, both foreign and domestic, at their full value.

Bingham grasped perfectly one bold basic principle that was to become the cornerstone of the nation's fiscal program. The public debt of $75 million was not a burden but a blessing. It provided the means to achieve the political centralization that Hamilton, Bingham and the other Federalists wanted. Since men were ruled by self-love and self-interest, the heart of a creditor would always lie where his treasure was. A federal debt would cause holders of public securities to look to the federal government rather than to the states for payment. It would justify federal taxation and enlarged federal powers, and would bring the government and men of property and substance together in a close working partnership. The resources of the country would be drawn forth to produce an industrial momentum and growth that would strengthen and benefit the entire national economy.

With this background and philosophy, Bingham wrote a 5000-word reply to Hamilton. ("A disposition to comply with your desires has induced me to convey my opinions freely.") He sent it off on November 25. The letter was not made public, and its existence, or at least its significance, remained unknown for 141 years.*

Bingham, of course, strongly urged that the new government make a particular effort to satisfy the public creditors by offering them a payment "consistent with the principles of justice and equity." These constituted the moneyed interests of the country, to whom the government would often have recourse. He recognized the criticism this course would arouse. People would claim that many of the creditors had bought the public securities on very low terms and could afford to submit to a reduction in their value, but such reasoning had no foundation. The public securities, like other property, had always brought their market price. The scarcity of money had reduced even real property to 40 per cent below its prewar value. The securities had dropped even lower, simply because the public had little confidence in the power of the government to make them good. The purchaser, therefore

> may be resembled to a dealer in a lottery, where there are many blanks to a prize. Would it be just to contest the payment due to the fortunate ticket, because it had comparatively cost a trifle?

Bingham proposed that the public debt be consolidated and funded — that is, that it be paid off by creating another debt. Creditors would exchange their outstanding certificates, with the interest due, for capital stock or annuities in the United States Government bearing 6 per cent interest. There was every reason to believe that

* In 1931, the late James O. Wettereau, professor of economics at New York University and specialist in the history of banking, discovered the letter in the archives of the Connecticut Historical Society. It was among the papers of Hamilton's successor in the Treasury Department, Oliver Wolcott, Jr., to whom Hamilton, on his retirement, had given certain treasured "Confidential Letters." Bingham's letter, Professor Wettereau found, recommended "virtually all of the essential measures subsequently proposed by the Secretary of the Treasury for restoring public credit." Two modern biographers of Hamilton have accepted this judgment. Broadus Mitchell, professor of economics and author of a two-volume biography (1957, 1962), concludes, "Correspondence between the advice offered and what Hamilton urged in his first reports [to the Congress] is so close as to justify the presumption of strong specific influence." John C. Miller, professor of history at Stanford University, in *Alexander Hamilton: Portrait in Paradox* (1959), says, "All the ingredients of what came to be known as Hamiltonian finance were contained in this letter." Harold C. Syrett, editor of the definitive edition of Hamilton's papers now in progress, finds "many similarities of expression between [Hamilton's] Report [on Public Credit] and the letter which Hamilton received from William Bingham."

they would forego their demand for their capital and fit into this arrangement for the sake of the interest.

He recommended that a sinking fund system be created for gradually reducing the national debt, partly because of its propaganda value: "The impression which it gives to the world, from the disposition and powers which it manifests, is very favorable to credit.

> Besides, this country is happily circumstanced to support such a system, when it is considered, that an increase of population and consequently of industry, of internal consumption and external commerce, will naturally swell the produce of the taxes beyond the estimates of a moderate calculation. . . . It is inconceivable what a progress, a respectable appropriation of revenue would make in the diminution of the debt in a few years, by the operation of compound interest.*

He recommended that a comprehensive revenue system be developed sufficient to pay the interest on the debt. Other nations mortgaged their revenues to their creditors; if the United States did less, the value of its funds would depreciate and the confidence of the creditors would be impaired, with pernicious effects that would be felt in all future dealings. The taxes should be so varied as to include every class of citizens, each of whom should support the federal treasury "proportionately with their circumstances." Some taxes were less objectionable than others. He listed eight such categories: a tax on legal documents, on transfer of property, on bonds and mortgages, on transfer of stock ("paid without murmur and collected with facility"), on tavern licenses, on insurance policies, on estates at death (a half year's income of the public stock a person owned at time of death), and on articles of consumption, including spiritous liquors, sugar, coffee, tea, salt, and pepper. But

> to propose taxes is at any rate an arduous and invidious task; as it is impossible to select those, that are free from solid and manifest objection, considering the various interests of the different states.
>
> However, a zeal for the national credit will necessarily impel the Government, to bring the revenue to such a state, as will enable it, after all the demands of the public service are satisfied, to afford

---

* The foreign debt of the United States was extinguished in 1835.

a surplus, which if applied to the gradual diminution of the National Debt, will hold out a hope of future relaxation from taxes, and will place the country in a situation to support that rank of power and grandeur which she is entitled to enjoy.

Conscious of the recent rebellions in New England caused, in part, by the lack of circulating money, he emphasized the need "to endeavor, by all possible means, to increase the quality of circulating medium." This could be effected by gradually and imperceptibly withdrawing the country's gold and silver from circulation and supplying the full demand by substituting paper money. This, however, was not to be legal tender in the form of bills of credit issued by the states, as had been done heretofore. It was, rather, to be the circulating bank notes of a commercial national bank. The capital of the bank should be as large as necessary for the purposes of circulation. Indeed, it was the government's duty to see that such funds should be sufficient to answer all the bank's engagements and thereby secure the fullest public confidence —

> especially as the government will give a sanction to the circulating notes of the bank by receiving them in taxes, duties, etc. . . . A close and intimate connection will naturally take place betwixt the government and this institution, cemented by the strongest ties that can bind them together — viz — a common interest.

The government might issue treasury notes, and the bank would receive and pay them under prescribed conditions; but the government should not have the right to issue a larger sum than the president and directors of the bank thought proper and prudent.

"I know of no subject," Bingham wrote at the close of an analysis that was at once brilliant and prophetic, "that is so little understood or has been less profoundly examined by the legislative characters of America, than that of Finance — and yet there is no one that so deeply involves the essential interests of the country." He ended his letter with a statement intended to gratify Hamilton.

> Much dependence is placed on your exertions, and I am happy to find that there is a general disposition, to give you credit by anticipation, for the soundness of your systems, and the honesty of your views.

He could not resist a bid to find out the Secretary's intentions:

> P.S. I shall be very happy at a leisure moment to be informed, how far any of my sentiments coincide with yours.

Hamilton submitted four Reports to Congress, the first in January, 1790, setting forth a fiscal program for the nation. The government would fund the national debt, paying it off in full and at face value to the latest holders of the certificates of indebtedness. It would assume the war debts of the states and pay them off in the same way. It would create a sinking fund system and set up a Bank of the United States. It would raise tariffs on imports and place excise taxes on various articles of use, including distilled liquors.

Hamilton's Report on Public Credit was almost the sole subject of debate throughout the second session of the first Congress, extending through the first eight months of 1790. James Madison had worked with Hamilton to restore the public credit and create a strong federal government, but now, worried by lack of support among the people who had sent him to Congress, he joined Thomas Jefferson in leading a campaign to defeat Hamilton's entire program. The split in Congress and in the President's cabinet produced a development no one had planned for: two political parties with different principles and programs battling each other for power.

Jefferson and Madison opposed Hamilton's funding program because it would reduce the powers of the states and throw a windfall of millions of dollars into the hands of the secondary holders of treasury certificates, most of whom were in the North. They insisted that the original owners of the certificates should share in the profit resulting from their redemption at face value, with the secondary holders receiving only the market price. There was no record of original ownership, the plan would have been an administrative nightmare, and Madison and Jefferson knew it; but the opportunity thus presented to attack the rich northern merchants and financiers and to champion the cause of veterans, patriots, widows, orphans and the common man was too attractive to be passed by.

The two men opposed federal assumption of the states' debts because the North stood to gain about four times as much as the South and, again, because it would reduce the states' powers and perhaps lead to an interference with the right to own slaves. They opposed creation of a national bank on the ground that the Constitution did not say a national bank could be created. They opposed increased tariffs because these benefited northern manufacturers and raised the price of goods imported into the southern states.

Hamilton's program passed the Senate without difficulty and the House by a narrow margin. Assumption of the states' debts was actually defeated in the House, but as the result of a deal between Hamilton and Jefferson the bill was recommitted and approved by a margin of three votes. The southerners permitted its passage in return for removing the national capital from New York to Philadelphia and thence permanently, after ten years, to a new Federal City on an enclave on the Potomac between Maryland and Virginia. Jefferson later declared that Hamilton had deceived and tricked him in a matter he did not fully comprehend.

President Washington deliberated for some weeks on whether to sign the bill creating a national bank. He asked his cabinet members for their written opinions. Jefferson declared that the bank was not needed, that Congress had no authority to create it, and that the enacted bill was therefore unconstitutional. Hamilton defended the right of Congress to act under the principle of implied powers: "Every power vested in a government is in its nature sovereign, and includes . . . a right to employ all the means requisite and fairly applicable to the attainment of the ends of such power." * The President signed the bill and it became law. Richard Henry Lee talked of "an insolent northern majority" and the possibility of a southern secession.

The Funding Act became law on August 4, 1790, and at one stroke William Bingham and the other holders of some $60 million in treasury and state securities saw their investment double in value.† The Act had logic on its side, and for the new government to have acted otherwise would have been a violation of contract and a subversion of the public credit. Dead national and state obligations, moreover, were transformed into a flow of working capital, with the most stimu-

---

* "The Opinion on the Constitutionality of the Bank . . . was perhaps the most brilliant and influential one-man effort in the long history of American constitutional law." — Clinton Rossiter, *Alexander Hamilton and the Constitution,* 1964.
† On the other hand, such upgrading of certificates meant great financial loss and in some cases ruin to land speculators, of whom Bingham could have been one, who had contracted to pay for public lands with depreciated certificates.

lating and productive results. But popular indignation ran high at the thought of a speculator — probably a Loyalist at heart — receiving $5000, plus ten years' back interest, for a security he had bought from a veteran of the Revolution for $750. Benjamin Rush called it highway robbery, and because of it he changed his political convictions once again and became an anti-Federalist and a democrat. "Your funding system," he wrote to his friend and Congressman, Thomas Fitzsimmons,

> is to me a monster, calculated to sow the seeds of every vice and calamity in our country. . . . The whole profits of the war will soon center in the hands of American Tories, Amsterdam Jews, and London brokers, while the brave men who deserved them will end their lives in jails and hospitals or beg their bread from door to door. . . . I never think of it without lamenting that I am an American. . . . Our vitals are unsound, and we must finally perish under the weight of Mr. Hamilton's "public blessing" which you have imposed upon our country.

*

In March, 1789, Benjamin Rush, James Wilson, William Bingham and three others had signed a petition to the Pennsylvania Assembly asking for a convention to reform the state constitution. The convention met in the spring of 1790 and drew up a form of state government modeled on that of the federal government, with a governor as chief executive, an independent judiciary, and a legislature with two houses.

While the convention was meeting in the State House, the author of the first state constitution, Dr. Franklin, died. He was eighty-four, and he had spent his last year in his bedroom, suffering intense pain from the stone except when relieved by opium.

The city put aside its political differences long enough to give him the most elaborate funeral America had ever seen. Twenty thousand people, nearly half the city, lined the streets on April 21 along the route of the procession from the State House. The ships in the harbor lowered their flags to half-mast; cannon sounded every minute; the church bells rang a muffled peal. All the clergy of the city led the procession to the Christ Church burying ground at the corner of Fifth and Arch streets. The coffin followed directly behind, carried by six bearers: General Thomas Mifflin, president of the state; Thomas McKean, chief justice; Thomas Willing, president of the Bank of North America; Samuel Powel, mayor of the city; David Rittenhouse, professor of astronomy at the College of Philadelphia; and William Bingham, vice president of the Society of Political Enquiries. They were followed by the family and closest friends, members of the state Assembly, judges of the Supreme Court, the gentlemen of the bar, the printers with their journeymen and apprentices, the Philosophical Society, and "sundry other societies, together with a numerous and respectable body of citizens." A battery of cannon fired as the coffin was being lowered into the grave.

Dr. Rush divided a lock of Franklin's hair and sent it to Dr. Richard Price in London and the Marquis de Lafayette in Paris. The United States House of Representatives wore mourning for thirteen days. (The Senate refused to do so.) The French National Assembly heard a eulogy of "the sage of two worlds" by Mirabeau and sent a flowery letter of sympathy to the American government. John Adams read it aloud to the Senate with ill-concealed distaste for both sender and subject.

Franklin had been somewhat "out of fashion" in his last years in Philadelphia and had incurred the distrust of the merchants for his liberal views, but Bingham's admiration never diminished. He had expressed a desire to give a full-length, life-size marble statue of Franklin to the Library Company, and discussed the costume with Franklin, who elected to appear in a Roman toga and "with a Roman head." Bingham sent a Franklin bust, a sketch of the full figure and 500 guineas to the famous sculptor François Lazzarini, who carved a figure in Italy from Carrara marble. It arrived after the Doctor's death. To the directors of the Library Company Bingham wrote:

> The respect I bore to the memory of that deceased patriot, philosopher and statesman, Dr. Franklin, induced me to engage to carry your intentions, of erecting a marble statue to perpetuate, in the minds of his fellow-citizens, the recollections of his public and private virtues, in full effect.
>
> The statue is, at length, arrived, and I have the honor of enclosing you the bill of lading. If I may credit the communications of my correspondents, it is fashioned out of a beautiful block of marble and is executed in a very masterly stile, and is, in every

respect, worthy of the distinguished personage whom it is intended to represent. As such I request your acceptance of it, and to believe me a sincere friend to your Institution.

The directors accepted the work with "the warmest acknowledgements" as "not only the first ornament of their building, but as the most finished specimen of sculpture America can exhibit." They placed it in a niche at the front of the building with a suitable inscription.*

The Congress recessed at the end of August (1790) and left New York forever, reconvening in December in the city from which it had been driven seven years earlier by the threats of mutinous soldiers. It met each day from ten to four in the new Congress Hall a few feet west of the State House, the Representatives holding forth for all to see on the first floor, the Senators behind closed and guarded doors on the second.

Bingham was considered a likely candidate for governor under the new state constitution, but he lacked any widespread public support and Thomas Mifflin was nominated and elected to the office. In the new bicameral state Assembly, the house of representatives, elected annually, was to represent the common people; the senate, elected every four years, was to represent the propertied class and restrain the demagoguery of the representatives. Bingham, though now probably the richest man in America, was elected a state representative. When the Assembly convened for the first time in the State House that December, the sixty-nine members of the house — including a number of fire-eating anti-Federalist frontiersmen — unanimously elected Bingham their speaker. The post was an important one, for the speaker appointed the committees of the house, and the house would have the main voice in Pennsylvania's share in building a viable national government.

On January 6, 1791, Senator William Maclay, even more truculent and suspicious in Philadelphia than he had been in New York, spent the evening at the Mansion House on Third Street. He returned home to write in his diary:

* The legend grew up through the years that after the Library Company closed at the end of each working day, the statue descended and headed for the nearest saloon. After some wanderings, the original now stands in the entry hall of the new Library Company building at 1314 Locust Street. The hands have been lost through erosion of the soft marble.

Dined this day with Mr. Bingham. I can not say that he affects to entertain in a style beyond everything in this place, or perhaps in America. He really does so. There is a propriety, a neatness, a cleanliness that adds to the splendor of his costly furniture and elegant apartments. I am told that he is my enemy. I believe it. But let not malice harbor with me. It is not as William Maclay that he opposes me, but as the object that stands in the way of his wishes and the dictates of his ambitions, and on this principle he would oppose perfection itself.

CHAPTER 17

The Eagle Rising from a Rock

[Your son] will observe a Country, that in the Space of a few Years, under the Impulse and Operation of a Government wisely constituted, and universally approved of, has multiplied its Resources in an astonishing Degree, and has attained a Political Splendor, beyond the most Sanguine Predictions of its best Friends. He will view a People, active, enterprizing, and intelligent, worthy of their origin, who in their private Well being, and public Happiness, approach the golden Age of Man, as nearly as the Inhabitants of any Part of the Globe.

William Bingham to
The Marquis of Lansdowne
October 22, 1791

ABIGAIL ADAMS was reluctant to move with the government from New York in the fall of 1791. Philadelphia was expensive, its climate was bad for her rheumatism, and she hated to part from her daughter Nabby, now Mrs. William Smith, mother of one and expecting, whose husband was frequently and unaccountably absent from New York. Within a few weeks, however, she was reconciled.

"The ladies here are well-educated, well-bred, and well-dressed," she wrote to her sister. "There is much more society here than in New York, and I am much better pleased and satisfied than I expected to be." She met with "one continued scene of parties upon parties, balls and entertainments equal to any European city. . . . Friendliness [is] kept up with all the principal families, who appear to live in great harmony, and we meet at all the parties nearly the same company." To her daughter she wrote, "Mrs. Bingham has been twice to see me. I think she is more amiable and beautiful than ever. . . . [She] made many kind inquiries after you."

President and Mrs. Washington took over Robert Morris' residence at Sixth and High streets, the Morrises moving to one of their other houses. The President had not entertained in New York, because his mother was fatally ill; but now, every other Tuesday afternoon, from three to four, he held a stiff and grimly formal reception for gentlemen in the state dining room. Mrs. Washington received every other Friday evening in an upstairs drawing room. The President attended in a more relaxed and informal manner, since he was not then acting as the chief executive. He paid gallant attention to the ladies, and often devoted himself to the prettiest in the room. The President was almost genial, for Mr. Hamilton's financial program was producing an economic miracle and the condition of the country was good. Philadelphia alone was shipping close to $7 million a year in exports, one-fourth the country's total.

Abigail Adams made her first public appearance at Mrs. Washington's reception on the night before Christmas, 1791. Two days later she reported to Nabby:

> The room became full before I left it, and the circle very brilliant. How could it be otherwise, when the dazzling Mrs. Bingham and her beautiful sisters were there;* the Misses Allen, and Misses Chew; in short, a constellation of beauties? I am serious when I say so, for I really think them what I describe them. Mrs. Bingham has certainly given laws to the ladies here, in fashion and elegance; their manners and appearance are superior to what I have seen.

Philadelphia was the national capital again after a lapse of seven years, and though few people believed the government would really move to the Potomac site in ten years, everyone seemed determined to make the city too attractive to leave. "You have never seen anything like the frenzy which has seized upon the inhabitants here," a visitor wrote. "They have been half mad ever since this city became the seat of government; and there is no limit to their prodigality."

The pendulum had swung back from the austere democratic spirit of the Revolutionary period. The city was host to many uniformed diplomats from the European courts, each with his ideas of the etiquette expected of a new government, even if republican in form, and their ideas inevitably had some influence on the Federalist leaders of the so-called Republican Court. The Duc de la Rochefoucauld-Liancourt called Philadelphia "perhaps the most agreeable [city]

---

* Anne's beautiful sisters, all single, were Elizabeth, twenty-three, Mary, twenty-one, and Dorothy, nineteen. Abigail, fourteen, would not have been present.

of the United States for a foreigner," and admitted that he had seen balls "where the splendor of the room, and the richness of the dresses, did not suffer by comparison with Europe." William Bingham, writing to John Penn in January, 1792, remarked that Philadelphia "has become a much more pleasing residence than when you left it. There is a greater resource in the numbers as well as choice of society, and I have no doubt you will be gratified on your return."

The Binghams were the acknowledged leaders of this society. The Mansion House was thronged with relatives and friends; with visitors in the city to see Bingham on business; with members of Congress and officials of the government; with visiting Europeans, house guests, who had arrived carrying letters of introduction from friends, including one or the other of three marquises in Europe: Lansdowne, Lafayette, or Bouillé.

Anne Bingham was the uncrowned queen of the Republican Court. With the transfer of the national government to Philadelphia, her pleasant parties took on a new significance. She was conducting her country's first (and last) salon in the European manner, a drawing room of the style of Lady Holland in London or of the earlier Madame du Deffand in Paris. Her parties attracted women who were beautiful and accomplished, men who were handsome, or rich, or powerful in government or business. President and Mrs. Washington could often be found at the Mansion House or at the Bingham summer home on the Schuylkill.

But the main attraction at Anne Bingham's parties was light-hearted Anne herself. She was twenty-seven in 1791 and at the height of her grace, vivacity and vitality. A contemporary, Samuel Breck, observed:

> Mrs. Bingham's conversational cleverness in French and English, graceful manners, and polite tact in doing the honors of her splendid establishment, rendered it exceedingly attractive.

Joshua Francis Fisher, her cousin, wrote of her:

> . . . [Bingham's] beautiful wife and her sisters, some of whom were as handsome as herself, attracted to her drawing room all that was distinguished and accomplished in the country. . . . Certainly there never was in our country a series of such distinguished *réunions*.

Brilliant balls, sumptuous dinners and constant receptions. . . .
She was not regularly beautiful, but had a combination of expression, grace and figure, which made her the most attractive
woman of her day. She was not witty, but bright, always at her ease,
and extremely kind and courteous to all.

Two incidents illustrate Anne Bingham's quality as a hostess and a
woman. John Adams, dining at the Binghams', was seated beside his
hostess and was pleased to find that he was able to carry on "something of a political conversation with her." He went away bemused,
convinced that Mrs. Bingham, if not brilliant, nonetheless had "more
ideas on the subject" than he had suspected, "and a correcter judge-
ment."

On another occasion, the churlish Samuel Chase, chief judge of the
Baltimore criminal court, later to become a Supreme Court tyrant in
the execution of the Alien and Sedition laws, dined at the Mansion
House and sat at Anne Bingham's right hand. He adjusted his spec-
tacles and looked with distaste at the food placed before him. Turning to his hostess, he remarked, "A very pretty dinner, Madam, but
there is not a thing on your table I can eat."

Was there any other dish she could get him that he would like,
Anne Bingham asked. "Yes, Madam," he replied, "a beefsteak or a
piece of roast beef, will please me better than anything else." A servant was summoned and given a whispered order. In a remarkably
short time he returned bearing a dish of roast beef and several bottles
of stout. Judge Chase devoured the food, washing it down with the
stout, and then turned to his hostess with a satisfied air. "There,
Madam, I have made a sensible and excellent dinner, but no thanks
to your French cook." And Anne Bingham, who had learned the art
of the French women "in making us pleased with ourselves," no
doubt gave him a smile worthy of a fine compliment.

William Bingham continued to buy much of his furnishings for the
Mansion House, and Anne Bingham many of her clothes, through
agents in Europe, the company's ships carrying the goods to Philadelphia. It was a tedious, slow and often unsatisfactory way to shop.
Bingham, for example, ordered some table linen in the summer of
1791; it arrived in March, 1793, but was "too small for the purposes I
intended." In the spring of 1792, he ordered from Liverpool "a

handsome set of Queen's ware edged with chocolate or some other dark color. . . . I wish my crest to be placed on each piece, which is an Eagle Rising from a Rock — such as you will see designated on the seal of this letter." He added, "I wish a handsome desert set, of a proportionate size, at the same time. I shall thank you to recommend this order to be executed with taste, and to be shipped in good order and well packed."

To his friend Benjamin Vaughan in London he sent £500 with the request that he would

> be so good as to send me a barometer and thermometer of an excellent quality, and invest the balance in some of Argand's lamps of the most approved form for lighting dining rooms. . . . If you have any book of much celebrity on the subject of naval architecture, I will be obliged to you to send it to me.

Bingham also ordered china from France, one such order calling for "24 small coffee cups, with a design similar to those used by the Queen and the Duke d'Angouléme," and some pretty porcelain figures and groups to decorate a large table. He imported such table delicacies as French wines, mocha coffee, mustard, dried sweetmeats and fruits, olives, olive oil, and vinegar (twenty gallons "of the best quality for table usage"). In June, 1791, he wrote to France (in excellent French) for thirty-six pots of face cream for Anne and thirty-six "rouleaux of pommade" of six different varieties, including *fleur d'orange* and *jasmin d'Espagne;* six pounds of powder of three varieties, and laces, artificial flowers and feathers for dress and hair ornaments. Four months later, when her husband sent for "eleven dozen white silk stockings for a man" and "twelve collars for winter, of a pretty taste and simple," she ordered "two dozen white gloves (very fine)" and twenty-four more pots of face cream and pommade and four more pounds of powder — presumably buying for her female relatives as well as herself.

There was at this time such a change in the style of dress as comes only once or twice in a century. Women began to abandon their high-heeled shoes for low-heeled slippers; their towering powdered head-dresses for natural hair flowing in ringlets on the shoulders; their elaborate hats for small bonnets; their brocaded silk gowns for simple robes of dimity and muslin flowing in the manner of ancient Greece and Rome, with short sleeves, low-cut bodices, and waists raised almost to the armpits.

The change in male attire was equally marked. Men began to wear their hair short and unpowdered, with no tied-up queues. They wore round hats instead of cocked tricornes, and white cambric stocks wound around the throat and buckled in the back instead of the usual broad black ribbon. They replaced their velvet, silk, and satin suits of rich colors and embroidery with cloth of dark colors. Their long coats became short, with high collars and without stiffeners in the tails; waistcoats, which had touched the knees, now scarcely reached the hips. They discontinued wearing swords, discarded wrist ruffles, and used shoe laces instead of shoe buckles. Stockings of striped yarn, like those being worn in Paris, replaced black or white silk stockings, except on formal occasions. Then pantaloons began to take the place of knee breeches, and long stockings were seen less and less.

These changes in dress, male and female, were a reflection of the fashions *à la républicaine,* a part of the leveling process of the new France. They were welcomed in the United States, where there was general enthusiasm for all things French — spirit, ideas, fashions. France, emulating America, with Lafayette at the head of its National Guard, was carrying forward its reform and revolution at a far faster pace than had been hoped for. A few skeptical Federalists, however, had grave doubts as to the ability of the French to digest their revolution. John Adams, Alexander Hamilton, and Gouverneur Morris declared almost from the first, with remarkable prescience, that the French were incapable of self-government and that their revolution would produce an unlimited monarchy or would turn into civil war and anarchy and end up in the hands of a single powerful tyrant. But the great body of opinion rejoiced that America had served as a model for a republican France and that the voice of liberty was being answered in other countries in Europe. On April 9, 1791, acting for the Pennsylvania House of Representatives, William Bingham, Speaker, sent congratulations and ardent good wishes to the French National Assembly in "the cause in which your nation is so warmly engaged."

One of the French republican leaders, Jean-Pierre Brissot, an author who used the pen name Brissot de Warville, had visited the United States in 1788 "to examine the effects of liberty on the character of man, of society, and of government." Entertained by the Binghams, he was offended by the splendor of their manner of living and commented on it with moralistic reproof in his *New Travels in the United States of America,* published in Paris in three volumes in 1792:

> A very ingenious woman in this town is reproached with having contributed more than all others to introduce this taste for luxury. I really regret to see her husband, who appears to be well informed, and of an amiable character, affect, in his buildings and furniture, a pomp which ought for ever to have been a stranger to Philadelphia; and why? to draw around him the gaudy prigs and parasites of Europe. And what does he gain by it? jealousy; the reproach of his fellow-citizens, and the ridicule of strangers. When a man enjoys pecuniary advantages, and at the same time possesses genius, knowledge, reflection, and the love of doing good, how easy it is to make himself beloved and esteemed, by employing his fortune, and perhaps increasing it, in enterprises useful to the public!

Brissot was not discouraged by this evidence of aristocracy in a country which otherwise "will, perhaps, give us a glance at the highest perfection of human life that we are permitted to hope for," since in the next paragraph he found that

> Notwithstanding the fatal effects that might be expected here from luxury, we may say with truth, that there is no town where morals are more respected. Adultery is not known here; there is no instance of a wife, of any sect, who has failed in her duty.

When he learned that the Estates-General were assembling, Brissot returned to France, in Quaker garb, to hasten the Revolution and assume a position of power as leader of the Girondists, sometimes called the "Brissotins."

Bingham was a wealthy and prominent citizen, a powerful Federalist leader, and an exponent of certain controversial causes, living at a time when the press was beginning a decade of unbridled personal invective and abuse. As such, he was inevitably open to "jealousy, the reproach of his fellow-citizens and the ridicule of strangers." James

T. Callender, one of the several character assassins encouraged and supported by Thomas Jefferson, struck mildly at Bingham in an attack directed primarily at John Adams. He heartily despised both Mr. Adams' person and his merit, he said, and would sooner pass an evening with a Poughkeepsie farmer than with Adams and all his bought or borrowed luster. "In the same estimation, do I hold Mr. Bingham, the breeches-maker's son, at Philadelphia. The trade, I hope, will not take offence at my classing him amongst them."

Congressman Sedgwick spoke sardonically of dining with Mrs. Robert Blackwell, sister of "Mr. usually styled Count Bingham." Joshua Francis Fisher wrote:

> . . . [Mr. Bingham] was . . . one of the wealthiest of our citizens and a very gentlemanly person too, I believe, though born of very humble stock. [He] was lavish of his wealth, acquired, some thought, in a discreditable way, partly in privateering and speculating in Government Warrants; for in those days many thought fair and intelligent enterprise and honourable industry the only proper foundations to fortune.

The source of Bingham's wealth was the theme of an open attack, made by a leading poet-satirist of the day. Peter Markoe, born in the Virgin Islands about 1732, was the author of a tragedy for the stage and a volume of miscellaneous poems. In 1788, he produced a book-length satire, *The Times, A Poem,* in which, in limping iambic pentameter couplets, he chastised those he disliked and distrusted. He fell upon Bingham as Rapax.

> *What tho' the pomp of wealth, the pride of power,*
> *Swell thy mean heart and gild thy present hour. . . .*
> *Tho' to thy mansion wits and fops repair,*
> *To game, to feast, to saunter, and to stare, —*
> *Thine eyes amid the crowd, who fawn and bend,*
> *View many a parasite, but not one friend,*
> *Virtue and sense indignant stand aloof,*
> *Whilst each knave's friendship is a keen reproof.*
> *But say from what bright deeds dost thou derive*
> *That wealth which bids thee rival British Clive?*
> *Wrung from the hardy sons of toil and war*
> *By arts which petty scoundrels would abhor,*

> *Thy villainy has raised those vast supplies*
> *Which lift thy* Pandemonium *to the skies!* . . .
> *Thy life those useful lessons shall bestow,*
> *That* pride *is meanness, and that* guilt *is woe.*

There is only one instance in which Bingham was accused of dishonest conduct. The charge was recorded in the diary kept by Senator William Maclay:

> February 27, Sunday [1791] — This day made inquiries of George Remsen, one of the clerks of Hamilton's office, respecting a story which is circulating with respect to Bingham having got thirty-six thousand dollars of counterfeit certificates registered and a new certificate for them. He declares the fact is so. These certificates have been copied from genuine certificates, the counterfeits handed to the Auditor (Milligan), passed by him to the Register (Nourse), and a new certificate given for the amount. Thus the counterfeits being disposed of, there could be no danger of detection, as the genuine and counterfeit ones could never meet. Now, the genuine ones coming forward to be loaned, the fraud is found out.

Maclay heard later in the day the rumor that John Swanwick, of Willing, Morris and Swanwick Company, was involved in the same way to the amount of $20,000. "Hell surely must have emptied her rascals upon us," Maclay exclaimed, "or we never could have been served thus!" The next day, he mentioned Bingham's $36,000 to Robert Morris.

> It seems it is the same which Swanwick had. A Charles Young owed Swanwick, and was arrested in New York for the debt on his return from Boston; paid these certificates to Swanwick; was discharged; they were registered. Swanwick sold to Bingham for twelve hundred pounds, knowing the state of the registered certificates. This cast an air of innocence over the transaction. Perhaps we shall hear more of it.

No more than this was ever reported on the rumor of the fraudulent certificates, though Remsen promised to give Maclay more information on the subject.

It is hard to believe that a man of Bingham's stature and good sense, with all his other means for making money, would endanger his social and financial position for the relatively small sum of $31,700. His correspondence shows that he was meticulously careful to refer questionable matters to his attorney, William Lewis.* Presuming that he did so in this case, Lewis must have told him that the registration of the certificates was correct and legal.

Perhaps Bingham's best defense lies in the fact that Maclay was a notoriously untrustworthy witness. He was Bingham's political enemy, and his diary makes it clear that he thought all his enemies, and not a few of his friends, dishonest and dishonorable. He found, as he said, "the basest selfishness in almost every public transaction." President Washington wished to tread on the neck of the Senate, and the creatures that surrounded him wished to place a crown on his head, "that they may have the handling of its jewels." There was no honor in any Senator east of the Hudson. New Yorkers "are the vilest of people; their vices have not the palliation of being manly." Robert Morris was "certainly the greatest blackguard . . . I ever heard open a mouth." Alexander Hamilton was a "damnable Villain."

*

Late in 1791, Bingham was considering whether he should not retire from his commercial enterprises to leave himself free for other activities. To Robert Montgomery, a friend who asked his help in obtaining a consular office, he wrote in October:

> I have for some time past confined my pursuits of business within very narrow bounds, as preparatory to retiring from it altogether. I know that if I was to carry it on with spirit and avidity, I should greatly increase my fortune; but I think . . . that amongst the most important lessons that experience teaches us, is that of moderation in our desires as connected with our happiness.

Bingham was busier than he had ever been, and in a wider variety of activities.

As Speaker of the Pennsylvania House, he was attempting to help James Wilson in a plan to write a digest of the laws of the state, and

---

* For example, Clement Biddle to Robert Gilchrist, June 20, 1790: "I also waited on Mr. Bingham with [a] receipt which he desired to show his lawyer. . . . If he approves it he will pay the money."

Charles Willson Peale in an effort to have the State take over and support his museum of natural history. He was co-owner, with his sister Hannah's husband, the Reverend Dr. Robert Blackwell, of the "Bunch of Grapes" inn on Third Street. He was carrying on a heavy correspondence relating to the rents on his properties* and with associates who wanted to borrow money or were unable to pay back the money they had already borrowed.

At the solicitation of his friends, he allowed his name to be entered as a candidate for the United States Congress in the fall of 1792. "I have permitted it rather reluctantly," he told Robert Gilmor, "as it is not desireable to be brought forward when party spirit and cabal are at such a height as in Pennsylvania." Washington and Adams were reelected to second terms, though the Federalists lost control of the lower house of Congress to the Jeffersonian Republicans. Bingham was defeated but was not disappointed, "as it renders me an entire master of the employment of my time, which before was very considerably devoted to public business."

There was, he told Gilmor, "a great deal of intrigue and maneuvering . . . to obtain a seat at the Board [of the Bank of the United States]. For my part I shall give myself no trouble about it, as I would view my being left out with indifference, if not pleasure, although my name is introduced into all the lists." He was elected one of twenty-five directors and thanked Gilmor for his "friendly compliments," allowing that his election "was flattering, because it was unanimous." He then became "actively employed . . . in forwarding the movements of the Bank" and, in fact, soon became one of its dominant directors. On July 4, 1791, the bank had placed 25,000 shares of stock on sale at $400 each; within two hours these had been oversubscribed by 4600 shares; and within a month the $25 scrip of deposit entitling the holder to buy one share was selling for $325. Bingham, wishing "to subscribe pretty largely with the bank," had withdrawn £5000 for that purpose from his share of the accumulated profits of Robert Gilmor and Company. The bank opened its doors in Carpenters' Hall on December 12, 1791. Thomas Willing had left the presidency of the Bank of North America to head the new institution.

---

* He asked Captain John Barry to vacate a small tenement let to him in order to relieve "the distress of a poor Irish family who have nothing but the exertions of their friends on which they can rely."

Bingham was beginning to buy large tracts of land in north-central Pennsylvania. He was on the board of managers of the new Pennsylvania Society for Promoting the Improvement of Roads and Inland Navigation, and he had agreed to serve as president of a private company formed to build a turnpike from Philadelphia to Lancaster. He was active in the Pennsylvania Society for the Encouragement of Manufactures and Useful Arts, which installed a busy textile factory in a building he owned on Market Street and set out to manufacture better "jeans" than those imported from England. He was investigating the possibility of starting an iron manufactory near Wilkes-Barre with the "stone coal" (anthracite) that had been discovered there, and he would soon study a proposition by which he offered to invest £30,000* in a hand-cranked machine to comb the seeds out of cotton, invented jointly by William Pearce and Thomas Marshall. He was building up a definitive collection of all the pamphlets printed during the Revolutionary period. He was seriously interested in creating an outstanding "town garden" at the Mansion House, after a plan drawn up for him by Lord Lansdowne. And he was now spending a considerable amount of his time at two country estates.

In 1789, he had leased from John Penn, who was in England, a house and 142 acres of land on a hill on the west bank of the Schuylkill. It was named, by sheer coincidence, Lansdown House, and it was the largest and most elaborate of all the summer estates along the river. "The buildings are excellent," he wrote to his friend General Knox, "the land good, and the local situation of the place, very agreeable and commanding." †

The other country seat he bought in the summer of 1791. On the coast of northern New Jersey, on a promontory known as Black Point

* At the beginning of 1791, the Bank of North America abandoned pounds, shillings and pence and adopted dollars and cents. The English system was often used, however, for some years thereafter. The American dollar sign ($) did not make its appearance until after 1800.

† On June 23, 1795, Vice President John Adams wrote to Abigail, "Went to Lansdowne on Sunday, about a half a mile on this side of Judge Peter's, where you once dined. The place is very retired, but very beautiful — a splendid house, gravel walks, shrubberies, and clumps of trees in the English style — on the banks of the Schuylkill."

John Penn had built Lansdown around 1773, giving it that name long before the Earl of Shelburne became the Marquess of Lansdowne.

overlooking the sea near the mouth of the Shrewsbury River, he took over some two hundred acres and a large, architecturally undistinguished old farmhouse called "Bellevue." He was the first to set the fashion for having summer houses in that region; and in the age-old manner of city folk who buy country houses and are carried away by a passion for alterations and improvements, he proceeded to rebuild Bellevue as a summer residence for his family. He engaged a William Lloyd to oversee the work and to live on the farm as manager the year round. He ordered "a number of young locust trees and some poplars" to be planted. He added two wings to the house, modernized the interior, and built a greenhouse, a barn, a milk house, and an ice house. He found rather soon that the work cost him "considerably more than it was at first calculated."

For a new barn, Bingham sent ten thousand shingles to Black Point by a vessel that was to drop them off on her way to New York. In May, 1792, he wrote to Lloyd:

> In building the barn, you will doubtless pay attention to some necessary appendages, that relate to the care of poultry, pigs, etc., for as I wish, when my family are on the farm, to be as independent as possible, with respecte to these supplies, it becomes expedient to make provision for raising them. At the same time, I wish you to pay particular attention to having a good milk house, so circumstanced as to preserve milk at least 48 hours.

He had a strong inclination, he said, to visit the Point in June or July, at which time he hoped to find the ice house completed.

He sent a shipment of furniture by a boat that sailed down the Delaware from Philadelphia and up the coast to New York. There it was loaded on another boat for Black Point. He bought other pieces from his agent in New York, on one occasion ordering "four dozen handsome Windsor chairs. . . . If they were painted straw color and picked out with green I should prefer it." On the roof of the house there was a "sky parlor" with an excellent view, and for this he ordered certain equipment from Vaughan in London:

> Will you permit me to take the liberty of requesting you to procure for me a land telescope, to carry with me into the country,

for the purpose of viewing objects from a situation which commands a very extensive sea and land prospect? I wish it to be very excellent in its kind, though not very expensive.

I have seen concave mirrors, which reflect the surrounding country, and where there is much diversity of appearance, have a happy effect in exhibiting prospects, concentred into a small compass. I wish likewise one of them, as well as a spy glass of a good quality.

In order to free himself to spend his summers at Black Point, Bingham resigned his command of the Troop of Light Horse, explaining that his absence from the city would be "incompatible with that attention of training and maneuvering the Troop, its new establishment will demand." He arranged to have the Philadelphia newspapers sent to his agent in New York, "which you will please send to me by conveyances that may from time to time offer."

Bingham's intention to retire from business was fortified by some minor losses in the trade of Robert Gilmor and Company with the Far East. Was there any point, he asked Gilmor, in tying up money in a two-year voyage halfway around the world? Such a voyage was bound to be a gamble, since the United States had to compete with the British, whose interest rates were only one-third as much as those in America, and with the Portuguese, who did not have to pay "any ship money for their vessels in the ports of China." Capital, he thought, "could be better employed in watching the ebbs and flows of internal business, than in foreign speculations."

He changed his mind about retiring, however, when several of his ships came into port with exceptionally profitable cargoes. The *Harmony,* which he owned with Robert Gilmor and Mordecai Lewis, returned from China and India with a cargo that was expected to earn £17,000 sterling. The *Louisa* was dispatched to Marseilles in the fall of 1791 with a cargo of tobacco, risking capture in the Mediterranean by the pirates of Algiers. Bingham felt that the Algerines would not be abroad so late in the season and that French houses in Philadelphia were exaggerating the danger of attack that trade with the Mediterranean ports "may be altogether confined to one or two French houses." The *Louisa* was the first tobacco ship to reach France that fall. She sold her cargo at a top price and returned safely to port with a cargo of vinegar, olives, olive oil, brandies, silk umbrellas, and fans ("which Marseilles furnishes cheaper than any other part of the world"), netting $20,000 for the voyage. "This is certainly a very handsome speculation," Bingham wrote to Gilmor, and he decided to continue his trading activities.

Early in 1792, the speculation that had come with Hamilton's program and economic prosperity was getting out of hand. Securities, and especially the stocks of the state banks, were selling at inflated prices. Bingham had been speculating heavily in bank stock, but now he scented trouble. The directors of some of the banks, he wrote to Gilmor in December, 1791, had placed their institutions in a dangerous position "by giving credits of too great an extent, by excessive discounts." In January, 1792, he advised Gilmor to dispose of certain bank stock, as it "has certainly reached a price that probably it will not support." Six weeks later, he reported to Gilmor that New York was seeing

> some great convulsions amongst the monied men and dealers in the funds. They are so pushed that they cannot take up their notes at the bank, which will not only be very injurious to them but distressing to an extensive circle of their connections.

Most prominent of the moneyed men was the opulent, flamboyant and reckless Colonel William Duer of New York who, six years earlier as a member of the Continental Congress, had helped the Reverend Manasseh Cutler to buy the Ohio lands from the government. In March, Duer found himself overextended and unable to pay his enormous obligations, including a $250,000 debt to the government. He stopped payment on some of his notes (on which he was paying as much as 5 and 6 per cent interest a month) and fled to debtors' prison for physical protection. In the panic that followed, he was joined there by a number of his friends, colleagues and creditors.

The stock of the state banks plummeted; prices of other securities dropped 20 per cent in a few weeks. At the very beginning of the panic he had foreseen, Bingham wrote to Gilmor, "Great speculation might now successfully be made, by those who have the command of money." In order to raise cash, investors were selling securities at whatever prices they could get. If he followed the advice he strongly urged on Gilmor, Bingham bought up three-per-cent and six-per-cent government stocks at distressed prices.

Bingham's partner, Mordecai Lewis, faced with bankruptcy during the 1792 panic, was compelled to go to New York to straighten out his affairs. Bingham asked Gilmor, who was going to New York on other business, to see Lewis there and "together adopt the best method of extrication from the perplexing scenes that surround you." He would have accompanied Lewis himself, he said,

> had it not been for the surmises that would naturally have arisen in the public mind on finding us impelled at the same time to a journey to New York . . . and a conclusion would probably be drawn that we were deeply concerned in the unfavorable transactions of that city.

Lewis suffered no serious damage. By fall, the Panic of 1792 — the Duer Panic — was over.

As one of those who had "the command of money," Bingham made the most of the opportunities presented by desperate speculators selling their property for whatever it would bring. He was approached by a friend who had bought certain lands in the District of Maine which he now was unable to pay for. Bingham agreed to take over his interest in these lands. He pledged himself to buy some two million acres and optioned another one million — about one-ninth of Maine.

CHAPTER 18

The Lands in the East

The copy of the contract in your possession exhibits the price, terms of payment, and settlement etc. etc. of the two millions of acres agreed for on the 1st of July 1791. One of the said millions is admirably situated for navigation between the rivers Scoodic and Penobscot. The other million although more distant from the sea is also well situated. It commences twelve miles north of the lands of the Plymouth Company, above the flowing of the tide on the Kennebec River, and extends on both sides thereof. . . .

General Henry Knox to William Bingham
December 2, 1792

BINGHAM had always been interested in acquiring land. He had inherited a number of Bingham-Stamper parcels in and around Philadelphia and he had invested in others. He told Henry Wansey, an inquisitive Wiltshire textile merchant who presented a letter of introduction and was invited to dinner, that in 1783 he had bought for £850 a piece of land adjoining Philadelphia, that he had never laid out more than £20 developing it, and that it was yielding an income of £850 a year. Forty acres of his pasture land, he said, fatted forty-one oxen in one year for the Philadelphia market, without any corn whatever being given them. "This," opined Mr. Wansey, "must be very profitable indeed. But such beef is not equal to ours."

Bingham bought other property in Baltimore, placing its management under the care of Robert Gilmor. He was offered some lots in the new Federal City on the Potomac (where Robert Morris and his new land company associate, John Nicholson, comptroller of Pennsylvania, had bought 7234 lots), but he "was not disposed to purchase" for the curious reason that "property at such a distance is attended with considerable inconvenience in the management."

In the spring of 1792, when the Pennsylvania legislature placed on sale some 4,000,000 acres, largely in the central part of the state, Bingham promptly took out warrants to buy about 340,000 acres.

This, he told Gilmor, was a considerable quantity of land but not nearly so much as he had hoped to get. He later increased his purchases (which he called "ventures") to a total of 1,160,000 acres, investing the very substantial sum of £50,000 or more.* Bingham convinced himself that such property, however wild and remote, was a tremendous bargain. Though the buyer had to pay for surveying his own lands, the purchase price was only one shilling to one shilling sixpence per acre. The Indians had formally relinquished their titles, the lands were exempt from taxation for ten years, and they could be owned directly by aliens — a right not granted by any other state. Their value, Bingham felt, seemed certain to rise because of immigration and because the increase in the number of banks lending money at low interest would provide the necessary capital for large purchases. Practically every man of property in the country was engaged in buying and selling land, and tracts could always be sold as a commodity of trade.

Bingham engaged John Adlum, a surveyor of established reputation, to select his land and lay his warrants, choosing tracts with fertile soil and "easy access to water navigation." By the spring of 1793, Adlum had surveyed 430,000 acres of Bingham's land, lying in one area between the two branches of the Susquehanna, and he promised to survey 230,000 more that summer. For months to come, letters arrived at the elegant Mansion House bearing such datelines as "Camp at the Canoe Place on the heads of the Allegheny River" and "Camp on Toby's Creek near the Niccory Town Path." †

The largest land areas up for sale were in the District of Maine, owned by the Commonwealth of Massachusetts. Bingham became involved in these lands through Major General Henry Knox, onetime proprietor of Boston's London Book Shop, a hero of the Revolution as an artillery specialist, Washington's friend and "favorite general," now his Secretary of War. Knox had expensive tastes but moderate resources, and he was engaged in various optimistic speculations designed to improve his fortunes. The most ambitious

---

* His lands lay for the most part in what became the northern tier counties of Bradford, Tioga, Potter, and McKean. The rest was in Clarion, Clinton, Elk, Clearfield, Monroe, Armstrong, Jefferson, Venango, Lycoming, and Northampton counties.

† Surveying was a well-paid business, and Adlum eventually amassed a fortune that enabled him to devote all his time to his real interest — the study, cultivation and improvement of American grapes, with special attention to the Catawba variety.

of these was undertaken with the wealthy Colonel William Duer of New York. Together, in July, 1791, they bought at ten cents an acre two tracts of land in the District of Maine totaling a little over 2,000,-000 acres. The following spring they acquired another million at twenty and twenty-one cents an acre, including the eastern half of Mount Desert Island. They bought these properties from the Massachusetts Land Committee for a down payment of $10,000 and a promise to pay something between $400,000 and $500,000.

It was about the time the first payment of $25,000 was due to the Commonwealth of Massachusetts that Duer's affairs collapsed and he took refuge in New York's debtors' prison. There he struggled to realize something on his one unattached asset — his rights in more than 3,000,000 acres of land in Maine. As his associate, Knox went in search of someone with capital. The path led straight to William Bingham.

Henry Knox and his wife Lucy were an imposing couple; together they weighed almost 550 pounds. Samuel Breck described the general's "fine, lofty and well proportioned figure" and his "bland and dignified manners — sprightly, very playful, yet of sensible conversation. He was indeed a very distinguished as well as very amiable man." The Knoxes had been close friends of the Binghams for at least eight years; they had named their fourth son, born in 1784, William Bingham Knox. Lucy Flucker Knox, daughter of the prewar Royal Secretary of Massachusetts, had inherited much land in Maine, and she and the General intended to build a house at Thomaston on the St. George River. Anne Bingham was at this time persuading them to make it the most sumptuous house in America — a crescent-shaped villa in the European style with a cupola, twenty-four fireplaces, and numerous outbuildings. As a frequent guest at the Mansion House, Knox found ample opportunity to interest Bingham in taking over Duer's share of the Maine lands. Duer, writing from prison, allowed that "Mr. Bingham . . . is certainly solid," but said he was negotiating with other possible purchasers.

Bingham pored over maps and reports of surveyors, explorers and travelers. The land was remote, rugged, uncleared and, with its cold climate and short growing season, not well suited for farming. It had little development or organization, and money was so scarce in most of the communities that business, including that of the prostitutes, was done by barter, pins being the most common medium of exchange. Of the 96,000 inhabitants of the District, about 85,000 lived in three western counties and more than half lived west of Portland, all outside of the Duer-Knox tracts. The lands in question were inhabited by a few thousand fishermen and lumbermen; many were squatters with little respect for ownership of land or timber. The country was not favorably known; popular opinion held it to be a huge wasteland hardly fit for human habitation. Bingham nevertheless concluded that this region could be made to blossom, or at least that he could resell it at a profit, and he decided to push ahead with the most extensive and costly venture he had yet undertaken. He signed a preliminary agreement with General Knox and then sought an agent to go to New York and close the deal with Duer.

He chose Major William Jackson, whom he had first met in London in 1784 bearing a letter of recommendation from Robert Morris. After concluding his services as secretary for the Constitutional Convention, Jackson had completed his law studies and served until 1791 as one of Washington's "writing aides," usually traveling in full dress uniform with the President. Bingham had recommended him in March, 1789, unsuccessfully, for the post of secretary to the newly formed United States Senate. In December, 1792, Washington offered him the position of adjutant-general of the Army of the United States; Jackson refused because of "an engagement of the heart, involving the happiness of a most amiable woman, who is, as she ought to be, peculiarly dear to me." The amiable woman was Elizabeth (Betsy) Willing, twenty-four, Anne Bingham's oldest sister. The feeling was reciprocated, but Judge Willing was unalterably opposed to the match because of Jackson's dubious financial record. Anne and William Bingham had interceded with Judge Willing on Jackson's behalf, without success.

For his services as Bingham's agent in New York, Jackson was to receive the residuary profits on the sale of 100,000 acres of land. The extent and duration of the services were not specifically stated, and this was to lead to trouble several years later.

Bingham, Knox, Jackson, and Bingham's attorney, William Lewis, worked through most of the night of December 20–21 (1792) drawing up the papers for the proposed transaction with Duer. Jackson took the stage for New York that morning, armed with documents, letters, and means of payment. In New York he found that his client was indeed competing against another purchaser, a Dutch agent named Theophile Cazenove, and he spent several days in his lodgings drawing up additional papers so that the transaction might be concluded on his first call.

Accompanied by a witness, he went to the room where Duer was confined and explained Bingham's proposition. Duer objected to certain stipulations, and Jackson waived these on his own authority. Duer finally agreed to sign and told Jackson to come back in a fort-night when the documents had been prepared. "They are already prepared," Jackson said, and produced his papers. Duer filled in the blanks and signed. Jackson paid over $74,600 in notes from Bingham to Knox, endorsed over to Duer, as payment. "On my return to Phil-adelphia, a few days sooner than was expected," Jackson later re-ported, "I found Mr. Bingham greatly agitated, lest I had not been able to complete the business. . . . He applauded my conduct and said he was greatly obliged by what I had done."

Early in January, 1793, Bingham left for Boston to have the trans-fer of Duer's rights approved by the state, taking Major Jackson with him. He carried letters of introduction and a suggested agenda of procedure prepared by his friend Harry Knox. He was well received by the important people of the city. "The hospitalities of this place," he wrote to Knox, "are such that they encroach much on hours of business. I am charmed with the people and their manners." Gover-nor John Hancock "has been remarkably civil and full of atten-tions." Jackson became known as "The Laughing Major," and Bing-ham was fed great amounts of Boston fish and venison at a round of dinners. It had been learned that he and Anne were seeking to pro-duce a son and heir, and he was assured that these foods would so invigorate him that he would obtain his wish. A friend wrote to Knox that Mr. Bingham made a great impression on Boston and han-dled his affairs with "manner and address."

The Maine contracts were transferred to Bingham on January 28. All the lands were in William Bingham's name, with Knox to receive one-third of the profits on their sale and Bingham two-thirds. (Knox's lands were put in Bingham's name as security for money Knox had borrowed.) There were sixteen deeds for 2,000,000 acres and deeds for six townships and an option on a "back tract" of about

1,000,000 acres not yet surveyed. He made a first payment of $25,983 and gave fourteen bonds to the state to guarantee payment. Half of his deeds were to be held in escrow in Boston to insure performance of the contract. Bingham was committed to pay $311,250 in this new venture. He was to establish 2500 settlers on the land by 1803 and was to pay a penalty of $30 for each deficient settler on that date.

On his return to Philadelphia he launched a campaign to promote, publicize and sell a part of his eastern holdings. The best opportunities for quick and profitable sales of his large tracts lay in Europe, with "the best market and the most inviting offers" likely to be found in England. He hoped to sell half of his lands to foreign investors, thus reducing his heavy annual installment payments to Massachusetts, and to retain the other half against the expected rise in value. To do this successfully he would need a pamphlet extolling the virtues of the Maine lands and an agent to call on prospects in Europe.

He produced the pamphlet by a shrewd device. To General Benjamin Lincoln, living in Hingham, Massachusetts, he sent forty-four questions on the characteristics of the District. General Lincoln's name and war record were remembered in Europe and he was something of an authority on Maine lands. His answers to Bingham's questions had an appearance of judicious reserve and restrained enthusiasm. The population of the District was growing at a rate double that of the national average. The land lay in such a high, healthy latitude that "the inhabitants become strong and nervous and labour ceases to be a burthen"; many people there lived to an advanced age "because they inhale a salubrious atmosphere." The soil was friendly to grain and other crops and fish were to be taken from the ocean within a line's length of the shore. There was no coal or copper, but there was an abundance of "ginseng," * lime and timber and a superabundance of stone. The harbors were accessible and deep and water power was plentiful. Only two things were needed to make Maine a North American Eden: roads and development capital. Bingham used these questions and answers, with some testimonials from several

---

* Ginseng, a root, was much in demand, especially in the Orient, for its supposed medicinal power to restore sexual virility to the aged and impotent and to produce male children.

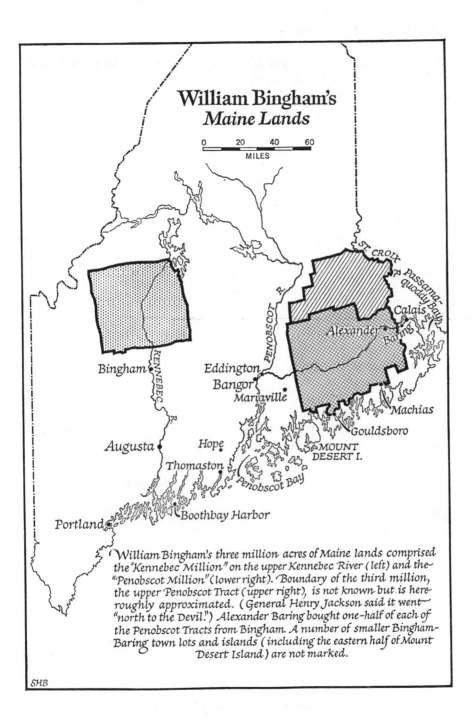

William Bingham's
Maine Lands

0   20   40   60
MILES

ST. CROIX

Passama-
quoddy Bay

PENOBSCOT R.

KENNEBEC

Calais

Alexander

Baring

Bingham

Eddington

Bangor

Mariaville

Machias

Augusta

Hope

Gouldsboro

Thomaston

MOUNT
DESERT I.

Penobscot Bay

Portland

Boothbay Harbor

William Bingham's three million acres of Maine lands comprised the "Kennebec Million" on the upper Kennebec River (left) and the "Penobscot Million" (lower right). Boundary of the third million, the upper Penobscot Tract (upper right), is not known but is here roughly approximated. (General Henry Jackson said it went "north to the Devil.") Alexander Baring bought one-half of each of the Penobscot Tracts from Bingham. A number of smaller Bingham-Baring town lots and islands (including the eastern half of Mount Desert Island) are not marked.

SHB

other citizens, as the basis for his pamphlet, printed in Philadelphia in the spring of 1793: "A Description of the Situation, Climate, Soil and Productions of Certain Tracts of Land in the District of Maine."

For his European agent, Bingham again chose William Jackson. He was familiar with England and the continent, and he would be received with respect as the President's former personal secretary. Jackson was reluctant to undertake the mission to Europe, though perhaps not so reluctant as he later claimed. He had resumed his professional pursuits "and had no more intention of going from this country than I had of passing to the moon." He still hoped to marry Betsy Willing, despite her father's objections, and did not want to be separated from her. On the other hand, he had no estate and was in debt. Bingham promised that he would be liberally rewarded, and on this ground Jackson accepted the mission. He was to have the residuary profit on the sale of 100,000 acres of Maine lands and would, Bingham wrote, "meet with a disposition very favorably inclined to a further gratification for your services."

> Ignorant of what will be the fate of this attempt at a sale of these lands, and not knowing what modification the business will assume before it is finally completed, there cannot precisely be determined at present what further compensation it will be proper to allow for your services and exertions.

It was not made clear in this casual agreement whether the acres referred to were the same as those promised for his earlier services in January or a second 100,000 added to the first for further services.

Bingham wrote to all the financial houses in England and Holland with which he had dealings. To connections in Ireland he proposed that a company of persecuted Irish Catholics might be formed to settle his lands. To his various correspondents he described "a fine fertile country, well watered, fit for grain or pasturage, abounding in lumber, and in a position to avail itself of the fisheries, and from all these resources to carry on a great external commerce." All the vacant lands in the United States would so soon be taken up by the rapidly expanding population, he explained, that any European capitalist who bought these acres at such a bargain would make an enormous profit. It was advantageous to buy lands already surveyed and in private hands rather than from a state, for it was difficult to handle such details from Europe.

Jackson was instructed to attempt to sell up to one half of the Maine lands at from five to seven shillings an acre. He carried maps, surveys, a power of attorney, a bundle of the Maine pamphlets, letters of introduction to Bingham's friends and business associates, and a bill of exchange for £200 sterling toward his expenses.

Three weeks before his departure, Jackson sent Bingham a long emotional outpouring of his troubles with Thomas Willing and an unreserved disclosure of the financial conduct for which Willing had criticized him. He wrote to Bingham, he said, as to one "whose friendship has so essentially contributed to my happiness, and whose favorable opinion I can never forfeit by an intentional wrong." Mr. Willing, he said, had told Elizabeth that he would never be reconciled to a marriage because of the state of his affairs, and that it would save everyone a great deal of pain if, previous to his departure for Europe, Major Jackson took measures to prevent disagreeable consequences from persons having claims against him when he arrived there.

> The observation was cruel in the extreme, and, in every view, unworthy of so good a man — it could only have proceeded from the vengeful calumny with which I have been traduced, and he abused. He has my forgiveness — and I hope, most sincerely, for his own peace, that he will for ever forget that he made the observation.

He had honorably discharged all his foreign obligations, he said, refusing to go into bankruptcy and preferring to mortgage his property and to part "with the hard earned reward of my military service (my commutation certificate) at a depreciation of four to one." All his other debts did not exceed £500.

> I should be sorry to pain Mr. Willing by asking him whether such conduct indicated dishonor, or formed a ground for the unkind thought he expressed to one who was but too much interested, and felt too keenly the severe insinuation. . . .
>
> My soul abhors a lie. If these declarations obtain your credence, I shall hope to preserve a friendship, which, without servility, I confess to be essential to my happiness.

Major Jackson sailed on June 16, 1793, and remained abroad for almost two years.

*

Despite the wild speculation in stock and land, an industrial base was being laid for the nation. Factories had been built in the towns and along the water courses of the middle and eastern states. Pennsylvania, Delaware, and New Jersey had fifty-three paper mills; these states were producing 350 tons of steel annually, and their production of iron rods for nails had soared to 600 tons. Newburyport, Massachusetts, had a machine for making nails. A woolen mill in Hartford, Connecticut, was turning out 5000 yards of cloth a year, and a cotton mill just started in Pawtucket, Rhode Island, had two water-powered carding machines built from designs smuggled out of England in the head of an apprentice. Steam power was being adapted to several manufacturing processes; the nation was startled to hear that a peck and a half of coal could do as much work as a horse in a whole day.

These industrial developments were accompanied by a wave of public improvements — bridges, dams, canals, roads. Since there was opposition to the use of public funds for such purposes, most were financed by lotteries or by the organization of private stock companies, operating with the blessing of the state legislatures. Governor Mifflin was authorized to incorporate a company to build a lock canal between the Schuylkill and the Susquehanna rivers. There was talk that someday the canal would be extended the entire length of the state, west to the Allegheny River at Pittsburgh, and that a good, solid road would be built all the way to the Susquehanna.

In June, 1791, a private turnpike company was formed "for making an artificial road from the City of Philadelphia to the Borough of Lancaster" — a distance of sixty-six miles. It was the first stone turnpike of substantial length in the country, and the most costly and ambitious public works project undertaken up to that time. One thousand shares of stock were offered for sale at $300 each and they were so heavily oversubscribed in an almost riotous contest that 2276 shares spoken for were placed in a wheel and reduced to 1000 by lot. The legislature authorized the incorporation in April, 1792, with the right to erect gates every seven miles, levy tolls, fix the width of wheels and the number of horses to a wagon, and take over property by eminent domain. In July the subscribers met to organize and to elect officers and a board of twelve managers. They named William Bingham as president and manager of the company.

Bingham had been pushing the turnpike in the state Assembly. American roads were notoriously bad,* and the old dirt road between Philadelphia and Lancaster was one of the worst. Coaches and wagons were overturned, their riders hurt or killed, their horses ruined by the strain. Most serious of all, the farm produce of the Susquehanna Valley was being shipped by water to Baltimore at the expense of Philadelphia.

Bingham devoted a great deal of his time over the next three years to the Lancaster Pike. On August 10, 1792, he set out for a tour of the entire road, having that same day returned "from a view of the projected route of the Canal." He first ordered a more detailed survey than the one already prepared. He divided the road into five sections, placing a superintendent with extensive powers in charge of each, with orders to use local materials wherever possible but to buy materials, provisions for the laborers and feed for the horses and oxen as cheaply as was consistent with good quality. He relied very heavily on the method that Robert Morris had turned to in supplying the armies in the Revolution: letting contracts to responsible persons capable of carrying them out. He recruited laborers from New England. Near the end of 1792 he reported for his board to the state legislature, through Governor Mifflin:

> The track of the road has been staked. The materials will now be collected. Measures have been taken to insure the requisite number of laborers and every exertion will be made to complete with oeconomy and dispatch the important work.

Construction began, as planned, in the spring of 1793. The roadbed was of impacted crushed stone, after the manner developed by the Scotsman John Macadam.

The road, though not completed, was opened for use in 1794.† A stagecoach carrying ten passengers and luggage was now able to leave Philadelphia at five o'clock in the evening and reach Lancaster at five

* A stagecoach that left Philadelphia on February 5, 1796, took five days to go to Baltimore. There were times in bad winter weather when no stagecoach set out for weeks.
† It had been built at a cost of $465,000, or an average of about $7000 a mile.

the following morning. Within a short time there were sixty-one inns and taverns along the road, bearing such names as Red Lion, Rising Sun, Cross Keys, and White Horse. (The charges were twenty-five cents per person for lodging, twenty-five cents for each meal, and fifty cents for each horse.) Francis Bailey, an eminent English scientist, traveling on the way to Cincinnati in 1796, called the road "a masterpiece of its kind" and Pennsylvania a "public-spirited state" for building it. Bingham's friend Jacob Hiltzheimer, who had helped push the turnpike bill through the Assembly, on his first trip to Lancaster frequently descended from his carriage to inspect the road. He was happy to record in his diary that it was in generally good condition and always measured exactly twenty-one feet in width.

Bingham resigned his managerial office in January, 1796, when the road was completed. Over the next quarter-century the investment paid its shareowners more than 10 per cent a year. For forty years the Lancaster Pike was one of the principal arteries of American commerce — and remained the best-built road in the country.

During the construction of the turnpike, Bingham had reason to be grateful to a fiery young radical from the western part of the state, a Swiss-born immigrant named Albert Gallatin. A well-educated, adventurous member of a good Geneva family, Gallatin had migrated to America in 1780, at nineteen. A French businessman for whom he was serving as interpreter persuaded him to take over the management of a large tract in Western Pennsylvania. There, a lonely, homely widower of twenty-nine who spoke English with a heavy French accent, he bought land, built a mansion he called "Friendship Hill," and organized, not very successfully, various frontier enterprises. When he distinguished himself as a delegate to the convention that revised the Pennsylvania Constitution, his career as political spokesman for frontier democracy was assured. Elected in 1790 to the Pennsylvania House of Representatives, he worked incessantly and showed a remarkable understanding of the intricacies of public finance.

Bingham, as Speaker of the House, conceived a wholesome respect for Gallatin's abilities. He appointed him to no fewer than forty committees, most of which relied on their new member to draw up their bills and prepare their reports. In September, 1791, when Gallatin delivered a cogent and logical argument against the Federalist position on a certain issue, Bingham announced that he was so impressed that he would not attempt an answer until he had carefully reexamined the question. Assemblyman Jacob Hiltzheimer, a stanch Federalist, confessed that Gallatin's speeches were "masterful" and "very forceful."

Unlike his frontier colleagues, Gallatin had no prejudices against banks, merchants, or capitalist development. He was a member, with Bingham, of the Society for Roads and Inland Navigation; he understood the function of a banking system; and he recognized the need for industrial growth in a predominantly agricultural economy. He gave Bingham welcome support against those who opposed construction of the Lancaster Turnpike.

Many of the farmers between Philadelphia and Lancaster, and especially the Pennsylvania Germans, fought the turnpike from the beginning. They protested the road's crossing their land, the payment of tolls, and the restrictions on their vehicles. When they could not stop the work, they demanded that the road be rerouted this way and that to suit their convenience. Gallatin upheld the turnpike board, and his voice, coming from the frontier rather than from the city, was powerful and persuasive. When the turnpike was put into use, the farmers reversed their position. They found that their vehicles could carry twice as much produce in less time, and that the restriction of eight horses to a wagon instead of the usual twelve to sixteen was reasonable. At the height of the summer season as many as a thousand giant, sway-backed, red-and-blue Conestoga wagons used the turnpike in a single day.

Though the Pennsylvania Assembly was dominated by Federalists, it surprisingly elected Gallatin over fourteen other nominees, of whom Bingham was one, to succeed the cantankerous William Maclay as United States Senator in the Third Congress. Hiltzheimer must have expressed Bingham's feelings as well as his own when he confided to his diary, "The next House will miss him very much."

With his unusual affinity for those who held political views far to the left of his own (Franklin, Benjamin Vaughan, Richard Price, Lansdowne), Bingham, in fact, had become friends with Albert Gallatin. The two were to remain friends through one of the most violently partisan decades the country was ever to know.

CHAPTER 19

In the Year of Plague and Terror

*There is nothing new here since Saturday but an account from Paris of
the trial, condemnation and execution of the Deputies Brissot, Ver-
gniaud, Duprat, Gensonnsé, Valasé, who stabbed himself to death when
his sentence was pronounced, Lehardi, Ducos, Boyer, Fonpedde, Boileau,
Gardier, Duchâtel, Sillery, Fauchet, Duperret, Lasource, Carra, Beauvau,
Mainvieille, Antiboul, Vigie and Lacaze, as authors of or accomplices
in a conspiracy against the unity and indivisibility of the Republic — or
more probably as the enemies of the prevailing Party — of whose passions and power this is a dreadful example.*

William Jackson to William Bingham
London, November 11, 1793

THE NATIONAL PARTIES were born in the contest over Hamilton's
financial program and began to take shape in the 1792 election. Now
they were polarizing on a single issue: the United States position on
the French Revolution.

Events in France were moving fast, and in the summer of 1792 they
took an ugly turn. An underworld of criminals from Marseilles,
Genoa, Sicily, and Greece was drifting to Paris to dominate the street
mobs. Leaders were emerging whose loathsome qualities were not to
be matched until the second third of the twentieth century: the
scrofulous, homicidal maniac Marat, president of the Jacobin Clubs;
Hébert, criminally insane leader of the Paris Commune; Robespierre, pallid, methodical, prudish, who would murder Frenchmen of
all classes and degrees to bring them to Reason and Virtue; his hench-
man Saint-Just, cold, and reptilian; his agent Carrier in Brittany, who
had a pathological hatred of children ("They . . . must be butch-
ered without mercy").

Late in August, 1792, some 4000 persons were arrested as "sus-
pects" in Paris, some of them aristocrats, many of them priests, most
of them ordinary citizens who had offended the neighborhood leaders
of the Paris Commune. About 1500 of these were massacred, not

methodically by mock trial and guillotine as in the later manner, but in one September week of mass butchery in which howling mobs pulled them from their prisons and cut and tore their bodies apart on the streets.

Louis XVI was beheaded in January. A month later, France declared war on England, to the encouragement of the passionate idealist Brissot de Warville, leader of the Girondists, who felt that "this people needs a war to consolidate them . . . to purge away the vice of despotism . . . to drive out the men who corrupt them."

As a Federalist, Bingham feared for the safety of England before the marauding armies of the French Revolution. As a merchant, he objectively saw that the war would shift the bulk of the shipping trade to the neutral nations. "It cannot but tend," he wrote to Gilmor, "to pour great riches into America, especially if our flag should be respected by the belligerent powers."

The Republicans supported France and its war against Britain. They formed Democratic Societies as American versions of the Jacobin Clubs, borrowing the ideas and jargon of the French originals. ("The seeds of luxury appear to have taken root in our domestic soil," one American Society resolved, "and the jealous eye of patriotism already regards the spirit of freedom and equality as eclipsed by the pride of wealth and the arrogance of power.") Those who questioned recent events in France were accused of wanting a monarchy in the United States. The Federalists had turned against the Revolution with the September massacre and the execution of Louis. They felt that France was now being ruled by madmen and that the Revolution no longer had the right to be identified with the cause of liberty. They regarded the Democratic Societies as instruments for importing French subversion.

French sympathies were especially strong in Philadelphia, the capital city. The Southwark Theater played the Marseillaise before each performance, the audience rising to sing in a chorus with the orchestra. Bands of high-spirited Republican patriots marched together to sing the anthem beneath the windows of the Mansion House, home of that symbol of Federalist power and opulent luxury, William Bingham. In the spring of 1793, with the arrival in the city of a new French minister, Edmond Genêt, enthusiasm for the French Revolution became intense, almost frenzied.

France had a fifteen-year-old alliance with the United States, and she had every confidence that it would be honored with material help in the war against the old common enemy, England. (England, too, thought that France would receive such help.) Brissot, of the new Girondist ministry, sent Genêt to organize American help. He was a handsome, engaging, arrogant young man, and when he landed in Charleston on April 8, 1793, he carried a request for certain accommodations. Interest payments on the $2,300,000 debt still owing to France should be advanced, the money to be spent in the United States for war supplies. U.S. ports were to be used to fit out warships and privateers and to receive prizes. American citizens would be commissioned to raise regiments and ships' complements for the war. Genêt's secret orders were to liberate Canada and bring it within "the American constellation"; to send agents to join other French agents already active in Kentucky, where they would encourage a mission to sail down the Mississippi and take New Orleans and Louisiana from Spain; to arouse the Indians on the frontier; and to force the United States into a war with England.

Genêt began to effect this program in Charleston some five weeks before presenting his credentials to the American government. He made the city a naval base for France, authorized French consuls to act as judges of admiralty in trial and condemnation of prizes, and swore a number of American citizens to oaths of allegiance to the French Republic. He then made his way in a leisurely manner to Philadelphia, moving from one ovation to another, acting, General Knox complained, as though the United States were one of the departments of France. Washington hurried to the capital from Mount Vernon and issued a proclamation that the United States would maintain absolute neutrality in the war between Britain and France.

In Philadelphia Genêt was welcomed by a cheering throng of 6000 persons and a delegation of seven distinguished Republicans headed by David Rittenhouse. The city had been alerted to the visitor's approach by the firing of three cannon on the French man-of-war *L'Ambuscade*. This vessel, a frigate, had anchored at the Market Street wharf several days earlier with a British prize, the brig *Little Sarah*, taken in Delaware Bay. On the same day, Bingham attended a mass meeting of some 300 of the city's principal merchants. They elected to send a delegation to the President with a resolution: they approved the proclamation of neutrality, would obey it strictly themselves, and would "discountenance in the most pointed manner any contrary disposition in others."

At the end of May, Citizen Bompard, captain of *L'Ambuscade*, gave a naval dinner aboard his vessel for a select few of Philadelphia's citizens in order that they might come to know Citizen Genêt better. William Bingham was one of the guests, along with Mr. Jefferson, Governor Mifflin, General Knox, and several others. *L'Ambuscade* was splendidly decorated. Her bow and stern figureheads wore liberty caps; there was another cap atop the fore-topgallant mast, and others on gilded anchors on her quarter galleries. High on her foremast floated a banner reading, "Enemies of equality, reform or tremble."

The diners drank toasts to French-American friendship and after the meal they joined in "patriotic hymns . . . sung with the liveliest sensibility." As the guests were about to leave, the boatswain, a Citizen Dupont, spoke for the crew about French-American friendship in an "artless and energetic" address "replete with feeling." Governor Mifflin responded by expressing his most sincere wishes for the happiness of the French nation and the success of *L'Ambuscade*. There is no record of what Bingham thought of this affair; but Genêt, in a report carried back to France by his aide, "a zealous friend of liberty who has followed me everywhere," railed at "the base idolatry of the English Constitution by the big capitalists, the big merchants." Power had changed hands again in France, however, and the bored revolutionists ignored the report and threw the friend of liberty who carried it into prison to await his turn for the guillotine.

Genêt overreached himself. He complained that "old Washington" had insulted his country by receiving him in a room that displayed a bust of Louis XVI, and when the President refused to allow the *Little Sarah* to sail as an armed French privateer, he ordered it to sail anyway and threatened to go over the President's head to the American people. The American people read Genêt's insulting correspondence (leaked to the press by Hamilton on Washington's instruction) and poured in resolutions of support for the President. A new French minister arrived with instructions to disavow his Girondist predecessor and to send him back to France under arrest. Citizen

Genêt wisely declined to return. He asked and got political asylum, became a gentleman farmer, married Governor Clinton's daughter, and devoted himself to inventing a new kind of lifeboat and a steam-powered balloon.

In France, in July, 1793, a gentle, convent-bred girl named Charlotte Corday stabbed Marat to death, and the raw anarchy of the Revolution became a cold, organized reign of terror. The twenty-one Girondist deputies, Brissot among them, were sentenced in a single trial and beheaded in one batch. The Queen, Marie Antoinette, went to the guillotine in October. Civil war broke out, with some twenty departments in rebellion against the revolutionary government. The Great Terror began in Paris in April, 1794, with Robespierre's consolidation of power and the execution of Danton. Victims were tried in groups in the morning, sentenced after lunch, and taken to the scaffold by the middle of the afternoon. On June 10, the government published a decree outlawing all defense of "conspirators"; accusation alone was enough to obtain conviction. In the next forty-seven days, 1366 victims were taken to the scaffold in batches of forty to fifty, beheaded at the rate of one every two minutes, and their headless bodies thrown into waiting straw-lined carts. The stones of the Place de la Revolution (now Place de la Concorde) were so soaked with blood that cattle refused to cross it and those living nearby were sickened by the terrible odor. On July 27, Robespierre was overthrown; he and his closest associates were guillotined, and the year-long Reign of Terror ended. Nearly 8000 persons, most of whom had been waiting for trial and immediate execution, were freed from the ten prisons of Paris.

Gouverneur Morris, the only minister from a foreign state in Paris during the Terror, witnessed these events and described them to the Secretary of State. Mr. Jefferson was not deeply disturbed. Mr. Morris, he said, was "a high-flying monarchy man, shutting his eyes and his faith to every fact against his wishes; and, believing everything he desires to be true, has kept the President's mind constantly poisoned with his forebodings." William Short, a young radical who had been Jefferson's private secretary in Paris, wrote of the horror he felt at what he saw in Paris as early as 1792. Jefferson rebuked his protégé with a classic statement of the ideologue who justifies massacre in what he feels is a noble cause.

The tone of your letters had for some time given me pain, on account of the extreme warmth with which they censured the proceedings of the Jacobins of France. . . . Many guilty persons fell without the forms of trial, and with them some innocent. . . . It was necessary to use the arm of the people, a machine not quite so blind as balls and bombs, but blind to a certain degree. . . .

The liberty of the whole earth was depending on the issue of the contest, and was ever such a prize won with so little innocent blood? My own affections have been deeply wounded by some of the martyrs to this cause, but rather than it should have failed, I would have seen half the earth desolated.

Were there but an Adam and Eve left in every country, and left free, it would be better than as it now is. . . . My sentiments . . . are really those of 99 in an hundred of our citizens.

He warned of the harm that Short might suffer in his career if he continued to express such views.

[Your] temper of mind . . . would be extremely disrelished if known to your countrymen. . . . There are in the U. S. some characters of opposite principles. . . . Excepting them, this country is entirely republican, friends to the constitution. . . . The little party above mentioned have espoused it only as a stepping stone to monarchy. . . . The successes of republicanism in France have given the coup de grace to their prospects, and I hope to their projects.

I have developed to you faithfully the sentiments of your country, that you may govern yourself accordingly.

On December 31, 1793, Jefferson resigned his office as Secretary of State and retired from public life to his estate at Monticello. He left with two firm convictions: There was a conspiracy under way, headed by John Adams and Alexander Hamilton, to put a king on an American throne. The liberty of the whole earth depended on what was happening in France.

*

The French Revolution had spread to the colony of Santo Domingo in the summer of 1791. In a preconcerted uprising throughout the island on the night of August 23, white inhabitants were attacked while sleeping. Many were massacred; a few escaped to the fortified cities; and a bloody war began that eventually drove the French from the island. Refugees began to land in Philadelphia in 1793, haggard, half-starved, penniless, separated from their families, some of them suffering from a pestilential fever. By the end of August, more than 2000 had arrived in Philadelphia. None of the ships that brought them was inspected or quarantined. The refugees were fed, clothed, sheltered, and absorbed into the community or sent on to France. Some $14,600 was collected for refugee aid. The theater company and John Bill Ricketts, celebrated equestrian of the Ricketts Circus, gave benefit performances.

It was the hottest, driest, dustiest summer in anyone's memory, and particular notice was taken of the unusual number of mosquitoes and other insects. Bingham, sometime in July, left with Anne, the children and various servants to spend several months on the Jersey shore at Bellevue. Word of disaster reached them there a few weeks later. Early in August, there appeared several cases of what Dr. Rush diagnosed as "bilious remitting yellow fever." The sickness increased, and spread, and mounted into an epidemic. Dr. Rush advised his friends to leave the city. Deaths averaged a dozen a day in August; in the first half of September, they averaged twenty-three; in the second half, nearly seventy. On October 11, there were 119 deaths.

No one knew what caused the sickness, where it came from, how to treat it, or whether it was contagious. Up to half of Philadephia's 55,000 inhabitants fled to distant towns and villages, until these refused to accept or even to pass through any more persons from the stricken area. Those who stayed purified the air with bonfires, sprinkled vinegar, tobacco, garlic, or camphor around their homes, held vinegar-soaked sponges to their noses when they went abroad, and tried to avoid contact with their fellowmen. Civil government and public administration began to break down. Mail delivery ceased. Four of the five daily papers stopped publication. No business was transacted at the banks; wages were unpaid; and ships could not sail for lack of crews. Stagecoaches were filled and would accept reservations only from those who paid the full fare to the end of the line. The church bells tolled incessantly until an order was given to stop.

President Washington and Mr. Jefferson departed around September 10, leaving General Knox in charge of the government. General Knox thought it advisable to leave for Boston a few days later and was quarantined for more than four weeks in Elizabethtown, New Jersey. William Lewis, Bingham's attorney, fled with his family and wrote back to his neighbor, Dr. Rush, "I never left Philadelphia with so much pleasure as yesterday nor never found such pleasure in the country as I do today." Samuel Breck had to return to the city to see to the clearance of one of his ships at the Walnut Street wharf. Starting back to the country, he passed William Bingham's house. From the buildings on the grounds where he was lodging, the Vicomte de Noailles leaned out of a window and cried, "Fly as soon as you can, for pestilence is all around us!"

Thomas Willing was stricken and recovered; Samuel Powel, his brother-in-law and neighbor, was stricken and died. Alexander Hamilton became ill on September 5, and for some days his condition was a matter of widespread concern. Thomas Jefferson felt the Secretary was shamming. "Knox takes flight," he wrote to Madison:

> Hamilton is ill of the fever, as is said. He had two physicians out at his house the night before last. His family think him in danger, and he puts himself so by his excessive alarm. He had been miserable several days before from a firm persuasion he should catch it. A man as timid as he is on the water, as timid on horseback, as timid in sickness, would be a phenomenon if his courage of which he has the reputation in military occasions were genuine.*

Dr. Rush distinguished, indeed immortalized himself by his medical services during the three months of the epidemic. He worked tirelessly, courageously and devotedly, and his presence brought the desperate populace hope and reassurance. He also brought them a treatment that would have killed many a patient in good health and must have killed or hastened the death of hundreds of unfortunates in Philadephia in 1793.

For several weeks, Dr. Rush tried the traditional remedy: wrapping the patient in vinegar-soaked blankets and drenching him at intervals with cold water. On August 29, he gave a patient who was apparently in terminal condition a massive emetic, an equally mas-

---

* Colonel Hamilton left King's College (Columbia) to march off at the head of an artillery company. He was with Washington at Valley Forge, crossed the Delaware in the Christmas Eve attack on Trenton, and stormed the English breastworks at Yorktown. Jefferson did not see military service during the Revolution, spending most of his time at Monticello.

sive purge, and a bloodletting, all to remove the "inflammatory humours" of the body. When the patient somehow survived this treatment and recovered from the fever, Dr. Rush was struck as by a divine revelation. He broadcast his discovery with jubilation and thanksgiving: the dreaded yellow fever, when treated by his new remedy, was "no more than a common cold." "Never before," he declared, "did I experience such sublime joy as I now felt in contemplating the success of my remedies. It repaid me for all the toils and studies of my life. . . . It was the triumph of a principle in medicine."

Thenceforth Dr. Rush attacked his weakened patients with a regimen that depleted what little strength they had left. As an emetic, he gave them three doses, one every six hours, of ten grains of calomel (mercurous oxide), and as a purgative, fifteen grains of jalap. At the same time, he removed a quart of blood, to be followed by two or three more quarts in the next three days and continued, if necessary, until "four-fifths of the blood contained in the body are drawn away." (Dr. Rush was under the impression that the body contained twice as much blood as it actually had.) His patients continued to die, as did three of his own apprentices, but Dr. Rush, with his enormous capacity for self-delusion, said simply that they had not begun his treatment soon enough or that his regimen had not been properly followed. Some of the other physicians opposed or questioned "Dr. Rush's Mercurial Sweating Purge," and these Dr. Rush accused of envy, wrongheadedness and conspiratorial plots against him.

The first light frost came on Monday, October 28; the mosquitoes died; the great epidemic ended. People returned to the cities and took up normal life again. An estimated 5000 inhabitants had died of the fever — one in every eleven. Two leaders of the Democratic Societies were gone. With their deaths, and Genêt's retirement, and a rebuke by President Washington, the Societies lost much of their impetus and power as instruments of Republican political policy. Vice President Adams, perhaps exaggerating to prove a point, claimed much later that the yellow fever in Philadelphia in the summer of 1793 saved the United States from an uprising by ten thousand Republicans and "a fatal revolution of government."

*

During these months, Major Jackson's reports from England were numerous, long, well-written, and informative. Arriving in London in July, 1793, he at once used Bingham's connections and letters to meet persons of influence and wealth. He became intimate with Thomas Pinckney, the American minister, spent six or seven days with Lord Lansdowne at Bowood, and dined with Benjamin Vaughan, M.P. He called on Dr. Joseph Priestley and gave his son a letter of introduction to Bingham for a trip he was making "to fix on a spot for the establishment of his father and family, who will remove to America." He presented himself to Sir Francis Baring of the famous Baring Brothers banking house and made several visits to Sir Francis' country seat, where he "received the most hospitable and friendly attentions." He found Sir Francis "a very amiable and intelligent man" and one sincerely disposed to help him in the sale of Bingham's lands. He met Sir Francis' oldest son, Alexander, who was in training as "the principal assistant in Mr. Hope's counting house," and impressed him with the advantages of speculating in choice Maine lands.

Between these visits, Jackson executed various errands and commissions. He bought a custom-built mangle for the Mansion House "made entirely of mahogany and on an improved principle." He shipped this on one of Bingham's vessels, putting inside a case containing seven ladies' hats with feathers. He had a medallion set in jewels for Mrs. Bingham, with a diamond knot, a laurel, and a cypher — a "rich and beautiful ornament" that cost £102 15s. He filled orders for a set of plated dishes, some garden seeds, and music books for the Misses Bingham. But he sold none of Bingham's lands.

In December, 1793, he left for France, armed with a "particular passport" issued by Minister Pinckney and letters of introduction from Thomas Jefferson and George Washington. He asked Bingham not to alarm Miss Elizabeth Willing by telling her of his trip to France, "although I do not think there is the smallest risque." On landing at Boulogne, he was imprisoned for eleven days because a gentleman from Boston traveling on the same ship was found to be carrying (innocently) some forged documents. Jackson blamed Gouverneur Morris for not obtaining his freedom sooner, and in Paris he and Morris exchanged strong words.

Jackson met with the Committee of Public Safety and through

them offered the French government 2,000,000 acres of land "lying on the Atlantic Ocean and abounding in the best masts and an inexhaustible quantity of naval and other timber, capable of furnishing immense supplies of lumber and provisions to the [French] colonies." The Committee declined to buy the land. To do so, they said, would seem to countenance the translation of property and the emigration of citizens from France at a time when both were needed for the Revolution. Jackson had trouble obtaining return passage to England. Having spent almost four months in France, he took particular pains to justify to Bingham so large an expenditure of time and money.

Jackson returned from France an extreme enthusiast for the French Revolution, with admiration for the efficiency of the total conscription of French manpower and justification for the Reign of Terror, some of the worst excesses of which he must have witnessed. "All that has been related of Grecian and Roman valour and patriotism," he wrote to Bingham, "is realized, at this moment, in the daring courage, and decisive conduct of this unrivalled nation." He concluded that Robespierre's execution of Danton and his deputies in the Convention "will give a stability to the power of this all-influential body . . . and will enable them to call forth the remaining resources of this inexhaustible people." The picture of France on the eve of the Great Terror he found "pleasing and splendid."

What William Bingham thought of these radical sentiments is not known, but at one point he felt obliged to rebuke his agent for using his name indiscreetly and improperly. Jackson's reply, written August 20, 1794, is an astonishing document. It is a scathing and savagely contemptuous personal attack on President Washington, the friend and patron who had made him secretary of the Constitutional Convention, employed him for two years as his private secretary (1789–91), and offered him a high post in the army.*

Jackson's is the only letter extant of an involved correspondence, but from it alone the events leading to the exchange can be clearly recreated. Following their meeting in Paris, Gouverneur Morris sent a harsh report of Jackson's conduct to America, charging that he had

---

* Jackson's letter first appeared in 1954 in Allis, *Maine Lands*, I, 354. Jackson did not use Washington's name, which is probably the reason that, as far as I can determine, no historian and no biographer of Washington has ever before referred to his letter.

expressed some views of Washington that were personally uncomplimentary. This information reached Bingham, and he questioned Jackson, apparently in a not-unfriendly manner, suggesting that Jackson had hurt himself with the President and advising him to guard his tongue more carefully. Jackson replied to Bingham:

> The remarks which may have been written from Paris, on my conversations while there, do not affect me in the smallest degree. They are but individual untruths added to the general falsehoods, which have proceeded from the pen of a wretch, whose conduct as a minister, can never be excused, and whose morals, as a man, can never be defended.

Jackson's "wretch," of course, was Gouverneur Morris. A bachelor, Morris was having a love affair with Madame Adelaide de Flauhaut, whom he was sharing, in the French manner, with her husband, with the son of Lord Lansdowne, and with Charles Maurice de Talleyrand, the former Bishop of Autun, father of one of her children.

> I regret exceedingly that you should find yourself implicated by any part of my conversations, and having never connected you, in any possible way, with my political opinions while in France, I cannot conceive how this has been.
>
> As to myself, I have a very short observation to make on the supposition that my conversations in Paris have been of serious injury to me. The attainment to any of my wishes will be utterly independent of *our marble fountain of honor and office.* His sentiments therefore on my subject, and the communications of his creatures are regarded by me with equal indifference and contempt.
>
> In common with those, who were desirous to make the reputation of this *automaton* useful to our country, I have assisted to uphold it, and, in *some hundred instances,* I have shielded this *man of stone* from the detection of his successful and bare faced imposture, by giving him a dress, which neither nature nor education ever intended he should wear. The return I have met is such as might have been expected from proud ignorance and base ingratitude. His heart and his head are in strict unison, the marble coldness of the one replies to the leaden dullness of the other and form together a perfect whole.
>
> Having, however, no inclination to attack the brazen wall of his

factitious fame, and being withheld by a regard to the consistency of former opinions, I shall adopt your counsel, and, from henceforth, consign him and his measures to silent contempt.

Should any part of this vindication carry an aspect of vanity, let the cause which has extorted it be considered, and I think I shall be forgiven.

Jackson concentrated one last assault on the House of Baring before returning to America. Since Hope and Company and its chief assistant, Alexander Baring, were indicating no interest in buying the lands in partnership with Baring Brothers, Jackson tried to persuade Sir Francis Baring to go it alone. He drew up a complicated financial proposal, assuring Sir Francis that "the speculation . . . is the most certain and the most profitable that ever was offered to the public." He reported Mr. Bingham's advice that the lands were "daily rising in value." Jackson presented these views in writing on a Friday night in April, 1795, when he was honored by an invitation to dine with the Barings *en famille* in Devonshire Square. Sir Francis would not commit himself. He observed that "a private circumstance" had just taken place which had "a very unfavorable influence on American credit and negotiation." Robert Morris and his associates had drawn and endorsed "bills to an immense amount" on European houses, "all of which must be protested and sent back, no funds being provided for their payment." Jackson then offered Sir Francis, on his own authority, a one-half interest in the Maine lands at the new, relatively low price of two shillings sterling — forty-four cents — an acre, subject to Bingham's approval.

Jackson sailed from Bristol on May 8, having spent two years in unsuccessful attempts to sell his principal's property. He did not feel that his efforts had been entirely fruitless, however, for he carried with him a letter from Sir Francis Baring to William Bingham, written two weeks before he sailed, expressing interest in the latest proposal and declaring that he would await word from Mr. Bingham before proceeding further. Jackson would have been gratified to know that the Hopes and the Barings had decided to send young Alexander Baring to America later in the year to look at the land in Maine, with a view to making Mr. Bingham an offer.

☆

CHAPTER 20

The Senator from Pennsylvania

*Old Blair [McClenachan] then threw the treaty [Jay's Treaty] to the
mob and advised them to "kick it to hell." The mob . . . put the
paper on a pole and proceeded to the French Minister's house, where
they performed some ceremony. The treaty was moreover burned before
Mr. Hammond's, Mr. Bond's, and Mr. Bingham's houses. Some of Mr.
Bingham's windows were broken and Viscount Noailles somewhat hurt
by attempting to ride over the mob.*

Oliver Wolcott to his wife
Philadelphia, July 26, 1795

"THE RUMOUR of war between America and England," William Jackson wrote to Bingham from London in August, 1793, "has been very
strong. . . . Twelve guineas have been given at Lloyds to ensure
peace with America for six months."

England, fighting not very successfully against France, firm in her
determination to cut off the trade of neutral nations with France and
its colonies, seemed arrogantly determined to drive the United States
to war. Bingham reflected the indignation of American merchants in
a letter to Lord Lansdowne:

There are bounds to prudence, when it becomes pusillanimity.
Our neutrality has been so outrageously violated, and the aggressions on the part of the British Government have been so flagrant,
that a spirit has been roused, which it requires all the calm and
temperate character of our sober thinking people to moderate.

Late in 1793, Britain ordered her privateers and fleet commanders
to stop, search, and bring in for adjudication any American vessel
carrying French or American goods meant as supplies for the French,
even if not contraband. Some 250 vessels were taken in the West
Indies, and almost half of these were condemned and confiscated.
The crews were maltreated and the officers insulted. Seamen born in

Britain, even if naturalized Americans, were impressed into the British service. The British moderated their actions in January, 1794, but American opinion was in a fury such as had not been seen since the days of the Stamp Act. The Republicans had argued in vain for an alliance with France in her war against England. They had violently opposed the neutrality proclamation. Now they demanded retaliation.

James Madison rose in the House in January to propose seven resolutions of economic retaliation that would have produced, at the very least, a commercial war with England. Lord Dorchester, governor-general of Canada, moved troops into American territory on the frontier and, addressing the Indian tribes, declared that there would be war with the United States within a year. The British consul in Baltimore fled to Philadelphia to avoid bodily harm. Even such moderate Republican leaders as Governor Mifflin, Justice McKean, and Congressman Frederick Muhlenberg, leader of the Pennsylvania Germans, were calling for war with England. In the spring of 1794, war seemed inevitable.

Federalist leaders decided on a course of action to avoid the conflict. They placed a one-month embargo on the export of goods in American ships, and passed bills in Congress for expanding the size of the militia, building frigates, and fortifying the seaport towns. At the same time, they took steps to mobilize the business community — the merchants — to support an accommodation with Britain and to protest against Madison's retaliatory resolutions. And they asked the President to send a special envoy to London in a final attempt at reconciliation. John Jay was named to the English mission after Robert Morris refused it. William Bingham and Thomas Fitzsimmons were chosen to mobilize the support of the merchants.

It was not an easy thing to manage. The merchants had just published a blistering protest against British seizures of their vessels and mistreatment of their crews. Even those Federalist merchants with closest ties to the British houses were indignant at British actions — and not all large merchants were pro-English Federalists. John Swanwick, of Willing and Swanwick, for example, and the wild Irishman Blair McClenachan, were pro-French Republicans.

On the other hand, the British had a case, and most merchants knew it. American merchant vessels were crowded with British seamen who had deserted. Most seizures were of cargoes carried for others; an American shipmaster would commonly pick up a cargo at a French West Indies port, enter it at an American customs house, and transship it to France as U.S. goods. American masters were noted for their ability to swear convincingly to their innocence "through a nine-inch plank." George Hammond, the British minister, promised to pay reparations for the vessels his government detained. The French, who refused to pay reparations, were plundering United States vessels almost as freely as the British — eighty of them in the winter of 1793–1794.

The United States was in no position to fight England. She had no navy, no real army, no armaments, no coastal defenses. Republican leaders, though they seemed eager to risk a war with England, regularly voted against measures to rearm the country. Federalist leaders felt that the country was weak and needed, above all else, time in which to rearm, grow and build up its internal productive capacity.

But the most pressing arguments against retaliation were economic. Britain supplied most of the country's capital — Hamilton's so-called "essential ingredient." She was twice as good a customer as France. Two-thirds of United States revenues came from trade with Britain, much of it from duties levied on imports, all of it needed to maintain the credit of the government. An American embargo on trade would convulse the American economy, whereas Britain would easily survive it. The United States was not powerful enough to change British policy through economic pressure or threats, as Mr. Madison was to learn in 1812.

Early in March, 1794, Bingham and Fitzsimmons called their meeting of merchants to denounce the proposed Republican resolutions against England. Something went wrong. A demonstration broke out on the floor in favor of the resolutions, and Bingham and Fitzsimmons were forced to give up any attempt to get their petition approved, though they collected as many individual signatures as they could. A few days later they presented the petition to the President carrying the names of some hundreds of merchants, the additional signatures obtained after the meeting. It was understood that for their work, Bingham or Fitzsimmons would be nominated to succeed Robert Morris in 1795 as United States Senator from Pennsylvania.

Measures calling for economic retaliation passed the House, and in a form that probably would have resulted in war. The Federalists managed to get a tie count in the Senate, where John Adams, voting from the chair, defeated the measures. Jay sailed for England on May 12. There were demonstrations against him even while he was on the high seas, conducted by Republicans who feared that he would surrender American rights and who perhaps hoped that the mission would fail. Bingham wrote to Lansdowne, urging him to use his influence to make Jay's mission a successful one: "The federal or moderate party, who urged this measure . . . have pledged themselves for the consequences." If the mission failed, he said, those who were most friendly to Britain would be induced to change their views and "their country will be thrown irresistibly into the arms of France." But he did not believe the British would allow the overture to fail.

> It is so much the interest of G. Britain as a manufacturing people, to cherish an unrestrained commerce with this country whilst it enjoys almost a monopoly of the supplies that furnish it, that I can scarcely suppose, that a want of disposition can exert on her part, to continue on good terms. She enjoys in our connection, most of the advantages of colonies, without the expense of protection. Our increasing population and increasing wealth create a corresponding demand for British manufactures, which shows how our well being advances her prosperity.

Jay spent the summer and fall in negotiations. Lord Grenville, the British foreign secretary, received him courteously, even cordially, but rejected each point as it was raised, and he regularly protested the rabidly pro-French speech and actions of the new United States minister to France, James Monroe. Jay's position was strengthened in August when General Anthony Wayne, at the head of 3000 troops, while the British looked on from the walls of Fort Miami, Ohio, decisively defeated the Indians at the Battle of Fallen Timbers. The victory weakened Indian faith in the British and ended once and for all the Indian threat to the Ohio country.

*

That same fall of 1794, the Western Pennsylvania counties broke into an armed insurrection against the government's excise tax on whiskey. When negotiations between the federal government and the Whiskey Rebels failed, Washington called out the militia of four states. Hamilton led an army of more than 13,000 men, including Bingham's former Troop of Horse, across the western mountains, and the insurrection faded away. Some dozen or so "characters fit for examples" (in Hamilton's phrase) were taken to Philadelphia, where they were paraded down High Street, each with the word *insurgent* on his hat. Two were convicted of treason; both were pardoned by Washington. An extraordinary number of western leaders, including Albert Gallatin, revealed that their real intent in consorting with the Rebels had been to urge them to act with moderation. The federal government established its right to enforce laws and collect taxes, but the Federalists reaped a harvest of hatred on the frontier.

On February 26, 1795, the Pennsylvania legislature met in joint session to choose a Senator to succeed Robert Morris. The House proposed Thomas Fitzsimmons and the Speaker, William Bingham, both Federalists, against Peter Muhlenberg and two other Republican nominees. Because of the Genêt affair and the Whiskey Rebellion, the tide of conservatism was running high. Bingham was elected over Muhlenberg by a vote of 58 to 35, and so became the fourth Senator from Pennsylvania, salary six dollars a day when Congress was in session.

The Fourth Congress was to be convened the following December, but President Washington called the Senate into extraordinary session on June 8, 1795, "to decide whether they will advise and consent that the treaty be made" which John Jay had sent back from London. Washington had kept this treaty under lock and key for four months before he could bring himself to submit it to a vote. It was a humiliating document, and Bingham, with the other Federalist Senators, was appalled when he read it.

Jay had obtained a promise from England to evacuate the western posts within eighteen months after the treaty was ratified; to pay for the American ships and cargoes it had illegally seized (some $10 million); to fix a northeast boundary between the United States and Canada; to permit goods to move freely across the United States-Canadian border; to admit U.S. ships under seventy tons burden to trade with the British West Indies; and to receive U.S. ships in the ports of British-controlled India.

In return for these concessions, the United States was to guarantee payment of the private debts contracted by colonials before the Revolution. American ships were not to carry any of the five staples produced in the West Indies (molasses, sugar, coffee, cocoa, cotton) to Europe or to any other ports outside the United States, "reasonable sea stores excepted." The United States would accept the British concept of maritime law and the rights of neutrals by permitting Britain to stop and search its vessels for contraband and to remove the contraband in return for compensation. It would give up for ten years the right to impose any tariff or tonnage discrimination on British ships or goods; permit free navigation and trading rights on the Mississippi; and allow British subjects to cross United States frontiers at will, trade on United States soil, and retain lands occupied in the United States without becoming United States citizens. There was no provision protecting American seamen from British press gangs. There was no recompense for slaves the British had taken with them after the peace of 1783.

For sixteen days the Senators debated the Jay Treaty behind locked doors. The Republicans charged that the treaty contained shameful terms that would make France an enemy and the United States an inferior ally of Britain. The Federalists replied that the United States needed peace with Britain; they were buying peace; and rejection of the treaty would mean war. The Republicans insisted that Britain was breathing its "last gasp" in its war with the French Republic and therefore was no threat to the United States. The Federalists replied that Britain would win its war and that French influence was becoming so strong that the United States was in danger of becoming a French satellite.

The Senate vote was 20 to 10 for approval of the treaty — the bare two-thirds required — William Bingham voting in favor. The galling article restricting the West India trade, however, was rejected and the treaty was sent to England for concurrence with the change. The contents of the treaty were to be withheld from the public until it had become law, but one of the Senators defiantly gave his copy to the Republican press, which printed it in full. A wave of fury, freely and eloquently expressed, swept the country. The cry, Washington said, "was like that against a mad dog." John Jay, returning from a prolonged stay in England, observed wryly that he could have found his way across the country by the light of his burning effigies. The Richmond *Gazette* threatened to petition for Virginia's secession from the Union "if the treaty entered into by that d—n arch traitor J—n J–y with the British tyrant should be ratified." Charles Pinckney of South Carolina moved in Congress to request the President to begin impeachment proceedings against Jay. John Dickinson was so enraged that he changed his party and became a Republican. On the wall of the house of a Massachusetts Senator who had voted for the treaty were chalked the words, "Damn John Jay! Damn everyone who won't damn John Jay! Damn everyone who won't put lights in his windows and sit up all night damning John Jay!"

In Philadelphia, Republicans held a protest meeting in the State House yard attended by 6000 persons (according to the Republicans) or 1500 persons (according to the Federalists). Secretary of the Treasury Oliver Wolcott was present and found that "the actors were an ignorant mob, of the class which is most disaffected and violent." But Dr. William Shippen was chairman, and on the platform were men of the caliber of John Swanwick, Peter Muhlenberg, merchant Stephen Girard, and Chief Justice Thomas McKean. The crowd listened twice to the reading of a memorial to the President against the treaty and then shouted their unanimous approval. A hero of the Irish uprising against England was introduced and cheered. Blair McClenachan leaped to the stage waving a fistful of papers and cried out, "What a damned treaty! I make a motion that every good citizen in this assembly kick this damned treaty to hell!"

Someone put the treaty on the end of a pole, and a crowd of 300 paraded to the residence of the French minister, whom they serenaded with rousing cheers. They then marched to the English minister's residence, ceremoniously burned the treaty, and hurled insults at the closed windows. They did the same before the house of Mr. Bond, the British consul, and from there proceeded to Senator Bingham's house at Third and Spruce. There another copy of the treaty was produced and burned. Someone threw a stone and broke a window. More stones were thrown and more windows broken. The Vicomte de Noailles, a guest of the Binghams, mounted one of the horses in the stables, cantered out the gate and charged into the mob.

He rode through a shower of stones and curses and withdrew, slightly injured. The crowd dispersed without causing further damage.

*

It was during the excitement of these days that Major William Jackson returned from his unsuccessful mission to Europe. The Binghams received him (in Jackson's words) with "the most flattering welcome" and invited him to stay at the Mansion House until he was settled. Bingham thanked him for his "most unwearied efforts" and agreed with the proposal that one million acres be sold to the Barings at a reduced price. "I think so well of the connection," he said, "that I would make great sacrifices to gain it."

Judge Willing had softened toward Jackson's suit for his daughter's hand, and on November 11, 1795, Elizabeth Willing, twenty-seven, was married to Major Jackson, thirty-six, in her father's house. It was one of the brilliant social functions of the Washington administration. The ceremony was performed by Bishop William White, who had married William Bingham and Anne Willing fifteen years earlier. He was assisted by Dr. Robert Blackwell. Anne Bingham stood beside her father in the receiving line to greet such honored guests as Alexander Hamilton, Mr. and Mrs. Robert Morris, General Knox, General Benjamin Lincoln, and the Vicomte de Noailles. President Washington, Jackson's man of marble coldness and leaden dullness, honored the wedding with his presence, accompanied by Mrs. Washington. He then gave Jackson a government post by which he might earn his living — that of Surveyor of Customs at the Port of Philadelphia.*

The Fourth Congress convened on Monday morning, December 7, 1795, in the new Congress Hall beside the State House. William Bingham and James Ross, a Federalist of imposing stature and commanding presence from Pittsburgh, reported themselves present for Pennsylvania. The Senators notified the House and the President that it had a quorum, and the two bodies met the following day in the House chamber to hear the President read his address.

* From Boston a few months later, Alexander Baring wrote cryptically to J. W. Hope, his employer, in London: "I understand Major Jackson is married to Miss Bingham, I mean Miss Willing. The Major in general did not please here. I hope this is not an anticipation of his profits, for I believe that [his ability to please] is his chief dependence. It is whispered in the Court of Scandal that family circumstances rendered the event necessary. I mean merely an unconquerable attachment."

The situation of public affairs, Mr. Washington said, afforded just cause for contentment, satisfaction and mutual congratulation. The war with the northwest Indians had been terminated. The country had stayed out of the war in Europe without violating any obligation to others. Agriculture, commerce, and manufactures were prospering beyond former example. United States trade was being molested, but the molestations were overbalanced by the benefits being derived from the country's neutral position. "Is it too much to say that our country exhibits a spectacle of national happiness never surpassed, if ever before equalled?" The gentlemen of the Senate and of the House of Representatives would have laid before them measures to protect the Indians from the lawless part of the frontier inhabitants, to improve the operations of the mint, and to revise the military establishment and strengthen the defenses of the country.

It was a painful occasion, for the President looked haggard and old, and he had grown choleric under the storm of Republican abuse that had been directed at him after he put his signature to the Jay Treaty. His second administration was drawing to a close in an outburst of party rancor. None of the giants of his original bi-partisan cabinet was now in the government, for Hamilton had retired to private law practice in New York one year after Jefferson's departure, and Knox had left to concentrate on his land speculations. Their successors — Wolcott in the Treasury, Timothy Pickering in State, and James McHenry in War — were undistinguished holders of offices that abler men had refused to accept. Washington was addressing legislators, some of whom had recently accused him of being incompetent, of assuming royal airs, and of completing the destruction of American freedom.

The House met on the first floor of Congress Hall—105 Representatives from fifteen states, Vermont and Kentucky having been admitted to the Union in 1791 and 1792. The sessions were open to the public, who sat or stood in a balcony ringing the back of the room. Proceedings were informal, loquacious, and often noisy.

Albert Gallatin was beginning to succeed James Madison as leader of the narrow Republican majority in the House, partly because of his mastery of the details of public finance, partly because of Madison's happy preoccupation with his bride of a few months, the twenty-seven-year-old widow Dolley Todd. Gallatin had served only briefly as a Senator, the Federalist members having expelled him on the technical ground that he had not been an American citizen the required nine years, but actually because he had been a gadfly to Secretary Hamilton and his party in the handling of the national finances. The Western Pennsylvania counties then sent him back in the fall of 1794 to serve as their Representative.

The thirty Senators met on the second floor in a chamber overlooking the State House garden. Their proceedings were conducted in a quite different manner. According to an observer, everything was marked by "the most delightful silence, the most beautiful order, gravity, and personal dignity of manner. The very atmosphere of the place seemed to inspire wisdom, mildness and condescension." Like the other Senators, Bingham dressed richly and conservatively, appearing each morning freshly shaven and with his hair full-powdered. He sat in a large red morocco chair at one of the twenty-eight desks arranged in a semicircle; he wore his hat throughout the sessions. Vice President Adams presided from a plain chair on a platform at the south end of the chamber, sitting behind a small mahogany table festooned with green silk. When any member talked to another while a Senator had the floor, Mr. Adams would tap gently three times on the table with his silver pencil case, whereupon order would be restored. On cold days, some or all of the Senators would occasionally leave their seats and stand around the fireplace while business was being transacted. "In the Senate," Abigail Adams wrote to her sister, "they have harmonized well, no unbecoming heats or animosity." The sessions of the Senate were not open to the public, though an exception had been made during the hearings on Mr. Gallatin's fitness for holding office. It was felt that the Senate gallery, filled chiefly with Philadelphians, would unduly influence the members; and that since few Senators could resist making oratorical speeches to display their eloquence, an audience would increase the cost of government.

Bingham attended the Senate sessions regularly and conscientiously. From the first he was given extraordinary committee responsibilities, many of them relating to financial and maritime matters. He reported to the President for the Senate on completion of the nation's three new frigates. He headed or served on committees to draw up passports for ships and vessels; to regulate exports of domestic distilled spirits; to determine what regulations should be prepared covering the resignation of a Senator; and to write an act authorizing the President to lay and revoke embargoes. There is no evidence that he spoke often or long in debate (such records were not kept in the early decades of the Congress), but, with his banking and mercantile connections and his training in the Pennsylvania Assembly, he obviously held considerable power behind the scenes. Federalist groups began to assemble in his house to discuss party policy, and these meetings grew into the first secret party caucuses. Within a few months after his election, Bingham was rumored to be the President's choice as minister to France, succeeding James Monroe, whose open and proselytizing partiality for France was offending the Federalists. Madison reported the rumor to Monroe early in 1796, adding, "I entirely disbelieve it; but the whisper marks the wishes of those who propagate it."

The Senate proceedings were uneventful. There were no outstanding political leaders among the members, and the issues taken up were relatively unimportant. When the French Republic presented the colors of the country to the United States, the Senators debated for two days on whether the phrase "magnanimous nation" should appear in the resolution of thanks. Bingham voted with the Federalist majority to expunge the phrase and to adopt a resolution of markedly restrained gratitude.

The real excitement of the session was found in the House. There Republicans and Federalists were engaged in the country's first great party battles, in which national policy and rules of precedent and procedure were being hammered out for all time. Under Gallatin's leadership, the small Republican majority set out to bring the Treasury Department and its expenditures under House control; and they moved to establish dominance over the executive branch in the making of treaties and the conduct of foreign affairs. This they did by demanding access to the President's correspondence relating to the Jay Treaty and by moving to deny appropriations of funds needed to implement the treaty. House Republicans and Federalists girded themselves for a fierce struggle on these issues.

Much of Bingham's attention during these months was diverted by personal affairs. He had seriously overextended himself in his land purchases, needed money to meet his commitments, and was in an embarrassing if not actually desperate financial situation.

With the failure of Major Jackson's mission in Europe, Bingham had begun a tedious and expensive campaign to develop his Maine lands for sale in smaller parcels to groups of settlers and American investors and speculators. For this he needed an agent and manager. He found one in General David Cobb, forty-seven, of Taunton, Massachusetts, who had served with distinction as one of Washington's aides-de-camp. Bingham had met and entertained Cobb when he came to Philadelphia as a member of the Third Congress.*

Cobb was a competent and faithful manager, but he sold no land and his bills for improvements and expenses added to his employer's financial difficulties. As early as February, 1793, Bingham had indicated to Robert Gilmor that his payments were going to be difficult to meet, but now they had mounted up to an even heavier obligation than he had expected. Money was scarce in Philadelphia in the winter of 1795–1796 — so scarce that Knox's notes, even with Bingham's endorsement, were "selling at a shameful discount." Bingham owed a discounted note for $10,000 in part payment of the year's installment to Massachusetts, due that fall, and he confessed to Knox that he did not know where to get the money. "It is quite a novel thing to me to be thrown into such difficulties," he said, "and I do not bear the situation with much equanimity."

He had "never expended so much thought" on anything, he told Knox, as he had on the Maine lands, and he added doubtfully, "I hope I shall be recompensed for my exertions." Knox, to whom debt was no novel circumstance (he had owed Bingham $17,000 since 1793), assured his friend that he would indeed be recompensed many times over if he would only hold on until the flood of settlers began to pour in. Bingham allowed that his descendants might profit, but in the meantime he was struggling to meet the various payments that were falling due. In this adversity he swore to take one corrective measure: he would endorse no more notes for his friends, though they were making "constant applications" to him.

Bingham's financial problems were heightened by the international situation. If war should break out between the United States

* Cobb wrote to a friend on January 19, 1794, "I dine at Morris, Bingham's, Breck's, Knox's, the best fellow of the whole . . . — any where — and I drink tea, form evening parties and frolic with the girls at all their houses. I bow to the President once a week at his levee, and once a week to Mrs. Washington and the ladies at her drawing room, but still it is not Boston."

and England, undeveloped, unproductive lands, with their taxes, would become an insupportable burden. On the other hand, if the Jay Treaty finally became operative and the western posts were placed in American hands, the lands north of the Ohio would draw off potential settlers and investors from the East. In either case, General Wayne's victory and the treaty he had signed with the Indians, Bingham observed, would be "followed by immense additional sales of lands in the Western Territory."

In the absence of any sales at home, Bingham looked once again across the seas. "Viewing the distressed situation in which I am placed for want of funds," he told Knox, "I am persuaded of the propriety of again attempting the European market." He suggested that Knox or Cobb go to Europe to do what Major Jackson had been unable to do. He would not hesitate a moment himself, he said, "in embarking for Europe on this business, if I was not prevented by the necessity of my attending the next session of Congress." And he wrote four letters in quick succession to Sir Francis Baring offering to sell 1,000,000 acres in an undivided tract at the price Major Jackson had proposed — two shillings an acre.

It was a sacrifice, he told Knox, but he made the proposal "as well to relieve my present necessities, as from a conviction that such a connection would most essentially benefit the future arrangements of this property." If the offer was not accepted, he said, "I shall be in a most cruel and embarassed situation." On the other hand, if the Barings bought, it would "set us at our ease and lay the foundation of a lasting fortune, and thereby recompense us fully for our trouble and time."

Sir Francis replied that the property was now being offered under terms that merited serious attention. He would state "in a most correct, unequivocal manner, my desire to make a considerable investment in American lands upon reasonable terms," and he preferred to form the investment in conjunction with Bingham and his associates. Still, he was not prepared to conclude the negotiations at such a distance.

> I have determined to put all the papers in the hands of my son, who will embark in a few days for America, with instructions for his proceedings; and as I have a perfect confidence in his prudence,

discretion, and judgment, he will also be authorized to conclude with you for the purchase, on such terms as he may think proper.

His son would also conduct some business on the voyage for Messrs. Hope, but he would have time to pay his respects to Bingham in Philadelphia during the winter, after landing at Boston.

Bingham had suggested that he might request a loan from the House of Baring, with stock as security. Sir Francis took this up at the end of his letter.

> There remains however a circumstance very material to yourself. I mean your personal convenience; and in order to provide for that, and to embrace the whole of the subject in the most effectual manner, you are welcome to draw on my House for a sum from five to eight thousand pounds sterling, to be reimbursed from the sale proposed if it shall take place. . . .

Bingham sprang into action on receiving this letter, and in the weeks that followed a stream of instructions flowed north to General Cobb in Gouldsborough, General Knox in New York, and Knox's agent, General Henry Jackson (no relation to William Jackson), in Boston.

Cobb was to hasten to Boston, there to meet young Mr. Baring, as if by accident rather than by design, and testify from firsthand experience to the value of the lands. He was to discover what society Baring was frequenting "and whether there is any reason to suppose he has had his mind poisoned or perverted" on the desirability of Maine lands. General Jackson was to "prepare the way for the arrival of this young gentleman" by alerting his friends and having them ready to testify in favor of the lands, using much "delicacy and discretion" in so doing. When Baring came to New York on the way to Philadelphia, General Knox was to take measures through the intervention of third persons to give him some conception of the great bargain he was being offered.

Generals Cobb, Jackson, and Knox were all to observe the utmost secrecy, that other land agents might not learn the purpose of Baring's visit. They were to do what they could to speed the visitor on his way to Philadelphia, so as to avoid "a long, perhaps fatal delay." And they were to give no indication whatsoever that Bingham needed to sell or felt any "importunity" to close the bargain. Bluff Harry Knox disapproved of these "delicate touches." To Cobb he said, "My conduct would be different. I would produce the facts."

By the time of Baring's expected arrival, all preparations had been made to give the young man — he was only twenty-one — "a just idea of the real value and rising importance of these Maine lands."

CHAPTER 21

The Barings Strike a Bargain

I think if Baring could be alarmed at an apparent indifference or indis-position to the bargain on my part, it would have a good effect.

William Bingham to General Cobb
January 7, 1796

His [Bingham's] anxiety that I should escape him increased visibly and was answered by additional indifference.

Alexander Baring to Hope and Company
May 26, 1796

ALEXANDER BARING arrived in Boston on November 29, 1795, after a rough sixty-seven-day voyage. Rejecting an offer by the Hopes to pay his expenses on the trip, he had declared that the salary they gave him was "abundantly liberal." He carried letters of introduction to his father's American correspondents and a letter of credit for £100,000, with permission to increase it to £125,000 "if any desirable end may thereby be attained." He was under an injunction from his father not to bring back an American wife. "A wife," said Sir Francis, "is best suited to the home in which she was raised, and cannot be formed or trained a second time."

The House of Baring, only thirty-three years old, was one of the outstanding merchant-banking establishments of Europe. The founder of the English family, Johann Baring, son of a Lutheran minister of Bremen, emigrated to England in 1717. He married the daughter of a wealthy grocer, thereby beginning the tradition that the Baring men always married women with money.

In 1763, two of his sons founded the export-import house of John and Francis Baring. The firm prospered. Francis Baring, the domi-nant partner, became a director of the East India Company in 1779 and was chairman in 1792–93. Serving almost continuously as a

Whig Member of Parliament, after 1784 he was an advisor to two prime ministers, Lord Shelburne (Lansdowne) and William Pitt the Younger. Pitt called him "the backbone and salvation of the country" and in 1793 made him a baronet. The Barings built their business on three main principles: integrity in their dealings; shrewd use of the mechanism of influence and control; and concentration on getting intelligence information faster than their competitors.

Sir Francis' oldest son, Thomas, was more interested in collecting art than in business, and it was soon determined that the second son, Alexander, would be groomed as the successor. He was sent to train in Amsterdam with the Dutch merchant-banking firm of Hope and Company. When the French revolutionary armies occupied Holland in the winter of 1794–95, the partners fled to London, taking their movable assets with them. Young Baring remained behind and showed much good sense and courage in getting another $2,000,000 of the Hope property safely to England. He was a favorite of Henry Hope, the senior partner;* and when the Hopes decided to join the Barings in an investment in American lands (Hopes three-fourths, Barings one-fourth), they chose him to inspect the prospective properties. Henry Baring, Alexander's younger brother, was already in Philadelphia, where he had been welcomed and entertained by the Binghams.

Alexander Baring stayed in Boston at the home of John Codman, a friend of General Knox, and was at once introduced to the best Boston families. He was, in the words of a contemporary, "rather a heavy-looking young man, with a hesitating manner, but seems very clear in his ideas and unassuming in his manners." He questioned knowledgeable people, read all the available literature, and decided within eight days that very few Americans knew anything about lands "and nobody so much as I do myself." He would, he said, "know every detail which interests us" before he left for New York.

Baring chanced to meet a General David Cobb at "a very social Christmas dinner and evening" in the home of a Boston merchant; always in search of "interesting and informed characters" from whom to collect information about the lands in Maine, he listened carefully to what the General had to say. Cobb reported to Bingham:

* Twenty years earlier, Adam Smith had dedicated *The Wealth of Nations* to Henry Hope.

I occasionally conversed with him on a variety of little subjects, with an intention to find him out and to make myself as agreeable to him as possible, always observing to keep the ultimate point in view.

Baring found Cobb so agreeable that, on learning of his intention to make a trip to Philadelphia, he invited him to accompany his party on the mail stage to New York. Cobb declared that nothing would give him greater pleasure, and if he could possibly finish up his business in Boston, he would certainly do so. To Bingham:

I have made dining and tea parties for him through the town. . . . [He] is a young fellow who has more of the manner of a counting house than a court — no art or cunning about him, a good heart, but I believe a Dutchman [i.e., stubborn] in negotiation.

Cobb delivered a letter in which Bingham welcomed Baring to America, urged Baring to talk freely with Cobb, extolled the virtues of the Maine lands, and explained ingeniously why those lands were not more popular. (The great profits of lumbering and fishing on the shore had attracted the lower classes of people. These had led lives of comparative indolence, accompanied by debauchery and dissipation, and so had injured the reputation of the country.)

Baring answered this letter suavely, apologizing for his delay in leaving for Philadelphia and promising to avail himself of Cobb's "usefull and authentic information." Privately, he decided that Bingham had sent Cobb to spy on him, but he somehow convinced himself that Cobb had no idea why he was in America. Cobb, in turn, assumed correctly that "he does not consider me as having any concern in influencing his opinion in favor of the Eastern Lands." Not surprisingly, Baring reported back to England that wherever he went he found the Maine lands "well thought of, collectively considered." On the last day of the year, Baring set out for New York in the stage, accompanied by John Codman and General Cobb. The journey took one week, with some delay when the coach overturned in the mud at Rye at three o'clock in the morning.

General Knox lost no time in calling on Baring, whom he found with Cobb and to whom he presented another letter from Bingham. He explained in confidence that Bingham was "exceedingly rich" and that the low price he was asking for his lands owed to his desire to make "so respectable a connection." His character and station in society, Knox said, forbade him from taking the steps others had taken to inflate the reputation of his lands. Knox wrote to Bingham:

> In appearance he seems the brother and a strong but large likeness of the young [Henry] Baring now in Philadelphia — less polish, a countenance rather buttoned up, but without the least particle of disingenuousness or want of candor. . . . He is intelligent, charmed with the climate and appearance of New England, says . . . that the people in Europe have no adequate idea of our happy situation.

In the six-day period from January 7 to 12, Cobb and Knox wrote eight letters to Bingham from New York. (Knox had advised his friend that Bingham "dearly loves long letters.") Cobb was impressed with the depth of Baring's knowledge of Bingham's land. "I have made myself so necessary to him," he wrote, "that the poor fellow would be exceedingly distressed at my seperation." Knox reported that Baring would buy no other than Maine lands, that the sole consideration was price, and that the Barings wished to make a respectable connection with an American house. Would Mr. Bingham have the kindness to lend him $5000 until the 10th of March? And would he please prevail on Mr. Baring to make him a loan? "The sum which would place me completely at my ease would be 50,000 dollars."

Bingham sent his agents advice, encouragement and exhortations to hurry Baring on to Philadelphia. Cobb was to hint at the disagreeable situation Bingham was placed in with such a long delay, being unable to accept other favorable offers for his land or to plan for its improvement. Could he find out the nature of the business Baring was transacting in New York for the Hopes? He must not forget "to mention the dislike to the [New York] Genesee country on account of its unhealthiness, which has turned the attention of the eastern states to the Maine lands." He would lend the General $5000 and make every friendly exertion to arrange the loan from Baring.

Baring and Cobb arrived in the city on Saturday afternoon, January 15. Cobb conducted Baring to his quarters and called on his employer to make a report and to receive his commendation. The next morning the two principals met for the first time.

Bingham felt that his offer had really been accepted in London, that Alexander Baring had authority only to bargain down the price, and that in the few weeks in America he could have formed no judgment on the lands; and he hoped that his carefully laid stratagems had pressured Baring into a quick decision. On all these points he was soon undeceived. Baring was quite calm, he was in no hurry, and he was noncommittal. One week after the arrival, Bingham wrote Knox that he "had made every effort (without appearing too importunate) to induce him to come forward and enter into a formal agreement." Baring promised to do so but did not act. Bingham found his conduct inexplicable. Was he assuming an air of indifference to force down the price? Was he trying to make up his mind? Or was he simply reluctant to appear too hasty? Did he know how desperately Bingham needed to sell? "It cannot be long, on the score of decency," Bingham said without much conviction, "before he makes his ultimate propositions."

Cobb was disgusted by the delay. He did not much like Pennsylvania, having found it on his earlier visits quite inferior to Massachusetts. "Quakerism," he said, "the avarice of trade, and the lordly, rascally manners of the great have here totally destroyed the social principles." He passed his time visiting his friends from his days in Congress, consuming vast quantities of oysters, and drinking "damn much wine." He undertook to "push" Baring to a decision, but Baring would not be pushed. "Bingham's anxieties will not let him rest," Cobb wrote to Knox, "when in fact I am the only poor devil that essentially suffers by this cursed delay."

Days dragged on, with the three men spending evening after evening in negotiations that got nowhere. To Bingham's distress, word leaked out about the purpose of Baring's visit; Bingham feared the young man would be "assailed with a variety of offers from all quarters." Two weeks after Baring's arrival, Bingham was striving hard to show "a perfect indifference on the subject" so as to create an apprehension in Baring's mind. The effort was complicated by a severe attack of gout that lasted two weeks and confined Bingham to his bed for two days. "I feel myself in a very disagreeable situation with respect to this gentleman," he wrote to Knox. "I lament more than ever my necessities which oblige me to submit to the whims and caprices of others."

Knox knew that if the sale was not completed, he was ruined. Bingham, for his part, would have $213,000 in debts fall due within the next few months and he had almost no "active funds" with which to pay them. He owed $100,000 to bankers in Holland on a loan secured by stock; $45,000 to Philadelphia banks for loans made to buy the Pennsylvania lands; $30,000 to the State of Massachusetts as the annual payment on the Kennebec tract; and $38,000 on his notes to William Duer. For reasons of policy, he would not accept Sir Francis Baring's proffered loan. He had an equity of more than half a million dollars in his partnership with Robert Gilmor, but this he could obtain only by dissolving the firm and shutting off his main source of income. He was so desperate that he took steps (later rescinded) to end the partnership. "I am determined," he said, "to make every sacrifice to free myself from the embarrassments I have lately been placed in, as it is extreme folly on any consideration of profit to continue in such a situation."

Bingham would have been reassured if he had known what was in his young visitor's mind. Baring had long ago decided that he would invest in the Maine lands. He was delaying simply to have his offer at a reduced price appear more attractive when he got around to making it. "I had constant conversations with Bingham from the time of my arrival," he reported back to London. "He is a very talkative man and I found no difficulty in learning of his character and ideas."

Baring marveled at the bustling activity he found in America:

> Every town or village you come to, houses are building in every corner, and in every part of the country you pass through, the woods are clearing from the grounds. It has really the appearance of a major creation of a new world. The same wonderfull increase in value of property strikes you every where.

He was favorably impressed with the Bingham-Knox-Cobb combination and felt that this was precisely the connection the Hopes and the Barings needed to become dominant American houses in England. "We have the first characters in the country," he said, "both as to property, influence and management."

On February 2, Baring drew up a twenty-nine-page memorial for Bingham (who complained privately of "prolix communications in writing") setting forth in the worst possible light all the disadvantages of the proposed Maine purchase. He sent this "depreciating memoir" to London with some pride. In his formal report on these events written several months later he said:

> I . . . mustered up all the arguments I could recollect against the speculation and in this light you must consider this paper, but not as my real ideas. Most of the objections are exagerated, many unfounded. . . .
>
> The memorial had completely the effect I expected. . . . He appeared to think the objections whether right or wrong strongly impressed in my mind and his anxiety that I should escape him increased visibly and was answered by additional indifference. We met constantly.

Baring's first formal offer, made in the memorial, was a shock. He would pay two shillings an acre for one-half of the million-acre Penobscot Lower Tract situated between the Penobscot and Schoodic (St. Croix) rivers. He had heard bad reports of the other million acres in the Kennebec Tract and had no interest whatsoever in that area.

Bingham declared that he would never separate the two tracts, and certainly not at the low price offered. He asked Baring to make an offer on one-half of the Kennebec Tract. Baring refused. The negotiations were stalemated for several days. During this time, Bingham was appalled to learn that Baring was talking with two of the country's largest land speculators, both of them known to be frantically eager to sell: Robert Morris and James Wilson.

A few evenings later, Baring called at the Mansion House and resumed negotiations. He outlined a map on the carpet. On it he showed the Penobscot Lower Tract, one-half of which he would buy, and the Kennebec Tract, which he did not want. Then he added the third million, on which Bingham held options — the Upper Tract adjoining the Penobscot lands. He was interested in these, and was willing to pay a shilling and a half for one million acres — half from the Penobscot Lower Tract, half from the optioned Upper Tract. Bingham refused.

The offer (in Baring's words) "was shifted and turned in many shapes." Baring observed that Bingham had bought some valuable townships, including that of Gouldsborough at the south end of the Lower Tract. He would pay one and a half shillings an acre for half of the Upper Tract and two shillings for half of the Lower Tract, provided the townships were included. Bingham protested that these lands were valuable and had cost him dearly.

He was sorely tried. Two shillings was too low for the Lower Tract. He hated to diminish the value of the Kennebec Tract by seeing it separated and rejected. And in order to exercise his options and produce a clear title on the Upper Tract, he would have to pay out $300,000. With his other obligations, this would bring his total payable debts to $560,400.

He would receive a total of $401,000 from Baring for the Lower and Upper Tracts. This would leave him with $159,400 to pay. Instead of clearing up his obligations and realizing a surplus, he would still be forced to pay out money he did not have. On the other hand, he would now own the other half of the Upper Million. He would realize a profit of seventeen and one-third cents an acre on the Lower Tract and seven and two-thirds cents on the Upper. And the Baring name and resources would enhance the value of the whole area.

Bingham spent all day Friday, February 4, in conference with General Cobb. He then dispatched a letter to Baring asking for another conference the following day. Baring agreed, stipulating that Cobb should not be present. Cobb spent the day in his quarters while Bingham and Baring conferred. Baring repeated his final offer and Bingham asked for clarification on certain points. The two men parted. Baring summarized his offer in an ultimatum delivered the same day.

> There, Sir, are the conditions of purchase I proposed and from which I can not recede in the slightest degree. . . . I have always positively refused making any additional allowance for Gouldboro or any other particular tract, and on that my decision is irrevocable, as it is on everything relative to the question of price, which I have offered to the full extent of my ability, and indeed stretched it beyond my original intention with much difficulty and hesitation.
>
> I shall have the honour of waiting on you in one hour and a half.

When Baring called to receive his answer, Bingham was ready to capitulate. "And so," Baring wrote proudly to London, "the bargain was closed."

When he heard that I conversed with Morris, Wilson, etc., he began to fear he should lose me, and I believe determined to make sure of me at my offer under the idea that I should not raise it, in which he was mistaken, for I had made up my intention of coming to two shillings for the whole and might perhaps have made some allowance for the additional purchases.

And he added:

His temper is very warm and he is strongly attached to property. He made the bargain with a good deal of agitation and difficulty.

On Friday, February 11, General Cobb wrote in his diary: "All this day with Bingham. . . . The contract between him and Baring adjusted and general directions given to me for my conduct." Bingham gave the General a present of 100 guineas for his good services.

To General Knox, Bingham sent the unhappy news that there would be no profit to be divided. He explained the terms of the sale in detail, doing his best to convince the General (and perhaps himself) that he had made a good bargain. "It is impossible to have a more agreeable and I believe profitable connection. . . . I have no doubt that the eventual advantage of this sale will be very great." The Barings wished to treat the whole Penobscot area as one common concern and, Bingham felt, "having planted the tree, they will water it." In the meantime, would the General see if Massachusetts might be willing to deliver up the optioned deeds on the Upper Tract for one-half the amount due in cash, the other half to be taken care of with secured notes?

Knox's pleas for financial help became more frequent, less restrained. "Unless you can in some shape or other obtain from Mr. Baring the sum of 50,000 dollars . . . I shall indeed be in great distress. . . . I give you carte blanche as to terms, only get me the money. If 60,000 dollars it would be complete." And then the inevitable self-justification of the mendicant: "The sum I want will be nothing comparatively to him or his concern, and it will be *everything to me*."

Bingham answered these tedious supplications with courtesy and patience; he explained his inability to help by laying forth with candor his own financial difficulties. When Baring refused to make the loan, Knox sent word that the news had left him prostrate and that he was desperate. Bingham lent him another $8000 and later endorsed a note on which Baring made him a loan of $17,800 (and which Bingham eventually had to pay).

Bingham's difficulties were heightened by endless delays in collecting the deeds and other documents needed to complete the contract. As a gentleman, Baring gave no written promise to buy and Bingham, of course, requested none. He had not the remotest doubt of Baring's integrity, he told Knox in pressing him to hurry up with the papers, but accidents could happen, and "a great deal of low intrigue and management" was being used "to disgust him with these lands that he may turn his attention to others differently situated." Baring was "delicate in his enquiries on the subject, but often asks me when the titles may be expected." He had employed an attorney to examine all the papers — a Mr. Wilcocks, whom Bingham called "a very scrutinizing character."

Baring, now relaxed and affable, was enjoying his long wait in Philadelphia. He was interested in American politics and spent days on end watching the operations of the Congress — sometimes in the Senate (now open every morning to the public), where his friend Bingham was one of the protagonists; more often in the House, where monumental battles were being fought between Federalists and Republicans. He reported his observations at length to his family and associates at home, recognizing their need to understand this fledgling nation with its radical new institutions and to assess its soundness for investment. Baring was optimistic, even enthusiastic about the nation's chances of survival, though he felt that the "discordance of politics" would someday cause a separation between the North and the South, and he congratulated his associates that the land they had bought was in a "safe" part of the country.

He saw Albert Gallatin win his fight to put the House in control of the expenditures of the Treasury Department, a committee of ways and means being formed to receive the reports of the Secretary and superintend the conduct of his office. He watched the Republicans attempt to achieve the same control over the executive branch in the conduct of foreign affairs.

The Jay Treaty — the nation's first — had been approved by the Senate and signed by the President. The English had returned it early in January with consent to drop the article limiting West Indies trade. It was now the law of the land, but the House had yet to appropriate the funds needed to put the treaty into effect. Madison and Gallatin proposed to repudiate the treaty by refusing to vote this appropriation, and thus establish the right of the House to control, or at least to share in, the treaty-making power of the President and the Senate.

The Republican assault began on March 2, 1796, with a resolution that the President turn over to the House his original instructions to John Jay and all other correspondence relating to the negotiations with England. Washington politely but firmly refused to submit the papers on the ground that the assent of the House was not necessary to the validity of a treaty. The President's reply, Bingham wrote to Knox, "is firm, sensible and dignified, and has made a great impression, being almost universally well received."

Alexander Baring, watching intently from the gallery, discussing the developments frequently with Bingham, interpreted the President's refusal as an evidence of national stability.

> Washington, whose character it is in vain to praise, has shown us that the powers given him are great and that the executive of this country is susceptible of vigorous exertions. He some time past called out 12,000 men to quell the western insurrection without any authority from or communication with Congress and lately you will have seen that he refused an application on the part of the House of Representatives for papers which he thought they had no right to claim. Both these were actions a King of England would not dare to have done, yet here it was considered the mere execution of a constitutional duty, caused no murmurs and was generally applauded.

The debate now turned to the main issue: that the House had the right to determine the expediency or inexpediency of carrying treaties into effect. Gallatin spoke brilliantly for the affirmative. He denounced Washington and Jay. Federalist threats that war with Britain would certainly follow a rejection of the treaty, he declared, were calculated to work on the timidity of the House. The Federalists were simply saying that the people had nothing to do with the law but to obey it. These sentiments, delivered with a French accent, were more than Uriah Tracy, Connecticut Federalist, could bear:

> The people where I am most acquainted, whatever might be the character of other parts of the Union . . . will not dance around a whiskey pole today and curse their government, and upon hearing of a military force sneak into a swamp. . . . I cannot be thankful to that gentleman for coming all the way from Geneva to give Americans a character for pusillanimity.

On being called to order, Mr. Tracy asked pardon of Mr. Gallatin and the House and apologized briefly for becoming too personal and speaking with too much heat.

Hamilton, who had been directing Federalist policy from New York, urged his party to mobilize public support and to use the great prestige of the President. Thomas Willing undertook to arouse the merchants. With a decline in trade with Britain, public opinion had become less hostile to the treaty, and petitions in its favor began to pour in to Congressmen and the President. Gallatin, with some embarrassment, entered such a petition from his own constituents in Western Pennsylvania; they held that British evacuation of the western posts was of overriding importance.

The issue turned in favor of the Federalists on April 28, when Fisher Ames of Dedham, Massachusetts, the greatest orator of the day, rose to speak. He stood pale and trembling, for he was afflicted with a pulmonary illness that had sapped his strength. Word had circulated that Ames would speak, and people dropped what they were doing to hurry to Congress Hall. The Senate recessed and Bingham joined the other members in the House gallery. John Adams was in the audience, seated beside Irish-born Supreme Court Justice James Iredell; Alexander Baring was there, and his countryman Joseph Priestley, and others who decades later would boast that they had heard Fisher Ames deliver his famous speech on the Jay Treaty.

Speaking without text or notes, he began in a low, faltering voice, with an artful reference to his illness:

> I entertain the hope, perhaps a rash one, that my strength will hold me out to speak a few minutes.

Step by step, he led his rapt audience through a virtuoso display of logic, sarcasm and emotional pleading.

The charge that the President and the Senate were stripping the House of its power and forcing the treaty down the members' throats by "a scheme of coercion and terror" was a false assertion impossible to reason away. The nation as a whole wanted the treaty; only one branch of the legislature, the victims of lingering hatreds toward Britain, wished to reject it. Britain had no influence in America and could have none. France, possessed of popular enthusiasm and party attachments, had too much influence on American politics.

> Any foreign influence is too much, and ought to be destroyed. I detest the man, and disdain the spirits, that can bend to a mean subserviency to the view of any nation. It is enough to be Americans; that character comprehends our duties, and ought to engross our attachments.

Rejection of the treaty would mean confusion and dishonor. If the peace continued despite the rejection, so would the British possession of the western forts. But rejection would surely mean war:

> On this theme, my emotions are unutterable. If I could find words for them, if my powers bore any proportion to my zeal, I would swell my voice to such a note of remonstrance, it should reach every log-house beyond the mountains. I would say to the inhabitants, wake from your false security; your cruel dangers, your more cruel apprehensions are soon to be renewed; the wounds, yet unhealed, are to be torn open again; in the daytime, your path through the woods will be ambushed; the darkness of midnight will glitter with the blaze of your dwellings. You are a father — the blood of your sons shall fatten your corn-field. You are a mother — the warwhoop shall wake the sleep of the cradle.

The reduced state of his health, he continued, had unfitted him for much exertion of body or mind, and he had intended to remain silent. Yet when he came to the moment of the deciding vote, he started back with dread from the edge of the pit into which the nation was plunging.

> I have thus been led by my feelings to speak more at length than I had intended. Yet I have perhaps as little personal interest in the

event as any one here. There is, I believe, no member, who will not think his chance to be a witness of the consequences greater than mine. If, however, the vote should pass to reject, and a spirit should rise, as it will, with the public disorders, to make "confusion worse confounded," even I, slender and almost broken as my hold upon life is, may outlive the government and constitution of my country.

Ames, exhausted, sank back into his chair before a hushed audience. He had spoken for ninety minutes.

"My God!" whispered James Iredell to John Adams during the speech, "how great he is!"

"He is delightful," Adams replied.

Iredell again: "Gracious God! how great he has been!"

"He has been noble," replied Adams.

"Bless my stars!" said Iredell. "I never heard anything so great since I was born!"

"It is divine," replied Adams.

"Our feelings beat in unison," Adams wrote in describing the scene to Abigail. "Tears enough were shed. Not a dry eye, I believe, in the house, except some of the jackasses who had occasioned the necessity of the oratory. These attempted to laugh, but their visages grinned horrible ghastly smiles." Baring sent the Ames speech to London, describing it as "very able" and "worth reading, though the delivery pleased me more." Priestley, who had heard the Parliamentary speeches of Pitt, Burke, and Fox, declared that he had never listened to such bewitching oratory. Albert Gallatin, listening from the other side of the aisle, called it "brilliant and eloquent," though it "treated but incidentally of the constitutional question" he and Madison had raised.

The following day, the House, sitting as a committee of the whole, voted on the measure. A number of Republicans had succumbed to Ames' oratory or to pressure from their districts and the vote was 49 to 49. Frederick Muhlenberg, Republican, occupying the chair, cast the deciding vote. He chose to support the treaty.* Several Republicans were missing from the floor when the vote was taken, including the fiery and fearless leader from the western country, William Find-

---

* The vote ruined his political career and almost cost him his life. Several days later, his demented Republican brother-in-law stabbed him in a rage.

ley, who found the moment opportune to step out and express a
trunk. The Pittsburgh *Gazette* voiced regret that the trunk was not
his casket.

The next day the House formally approved by three votes resolutions to appropriate $80,808 and pass the laws necessary to put the
Jay Treaty into effect. The great debate was over; the House had
created "a precedence of compliance." The western forts would be
evacuated, and federal income from trade with England would continue.

*

During these weeks, when not in the House gallery, Baring spent
much time with the Binghams at the Mansion House and at Lansdown on the Schuylkill. He and Bingham had plans to draw up for
their "common concern" in the Maine lands; the Bingham food was
good; the company was pleasant. The girls were lively and attractive
— Nan, who had been fourteen in January, and Maria, who would
be thirteen in December. They spoke Italian rather well and French
almost as a mother tongue, and on the testimony of one young visitor,
"conversed well on any subject."

In his reports to London during this period, Baring examined his
host and partner with an inquisitorial eye. It is unfortunate that the
only known extended contemporary character study of William Bingham is from these letters. Baring was flushed with triumph at bringing off what he mistakenly thought was a brilliant coup for his firm
and his family. He felt the natural arrogance of a younger man
toward an older, and perhaps of a young Englishman toward an older
American. Bingham's lasting friendships with others, testimony from
some who knew him, and a remarkable tribute from Sir Francis Baring himself (page 428) indicate that young Baring's portrait was
immature and overdrawn.

Baring was more and more satisfied, he said, with the investment
he had made and with the people with whom he was engaged. He
found Bingham "extremely candid and communicative" and he respected his "disposition to close enquiry" because it precluded "all
apprehensions of extravagance."

Upon knowing characters in this country better and being personally acquainted with all leading ones in the places I have been in, I am very much pleased with our selection of Bingham, and can even say that I know none, though many in other respects better, that would have been suited at all for the situation he is in with us. Large property, honour, abilities are seldom found together, but in him the former could not be wished better and the last two are very sufficient and above par as this world goes. . . .

I believe I understand pretty well both his disposition and his situation; we are on very good terms and always have been, so much so that I am always confidentially consulted on all important business that regards him and could I believe lead him to anything within tolerable bounds of reason. . . .

But Alexander Baring, in 1796, did not admire William Bingham as a person.

He is not generally liked, being rather too high and proud for this country, where but very little will do. I agree with him very well and think a good understanding likely to be maintained. He is undoubtedly the richest man in this country and his affairs are not embarrassed or likely to become so by any further speculations. He is a timid and cautious man. His property cannot be short of £4 or 500/M sterling, his expenses annually about £5,000 sterling. The house he lives in with ground round it is estimated worth near £50/M sterling. . . .

I don't dislike Bingham. His manners are a little too aristocratic for this country, but they will do for us. He has very great confidence in me. . . . He is not a dashing man nor inclined to new speculations at present. . . .

There is a littleness about the man in trifles that will make him for instance dispute all the tavern bills on the road, but when he thinks the world looks at him, his pride makes him make up that artificial character which he thinks a man of his fortune should have. He knows how to treat his equals but not his inferiors and is consequently unpopular or he would otherwise have been raised to the Vice President's chair. . . .

Great vanity and purse-pride are perceivable in all his actions; he is consequently not generally liked and attaches nobody, and from a narrowness of mind which naturally leads him to a want of confidence in everybody, I have some difficulty to prevail on him to give that latitude of action to his agent [Cobb] which is indispensable.

One of the plans worked out by Baring was to mount a combined pleasure and business expedition to the Maine lands, taking along the Bingham ladies and several guests, as soon as the Senate adjourned early in June.

He wrote to London:

I have encouraged Bingham to take his wife and family as the show will have effect on the country and the procession make a noise in the New England states from whence the population is expected. . . . People wonder how such a new country can accommodate such fine ladies in travelling and every lady's curiosity is raised to the highest. The ladies' company and presence on the lands will be of infinite benefit. . . . Small causes beget often great effects.

One wonders if Anne Bingham was not the guiding spirit of the great excursion to Maine. A three-month trip to Maine by way of New York, Boston and Portsmouth would be a gay adventure. The Vicomte de Noailles would be a charming traveling companion. The children would enjoy it, and Nan, now almost a grown woman, would have the companionship of young Mr. Baring, with whom she got along very well. Mr. Baring would also have for company Mrs. Bingham's youngest sister, Abigail Willing, soon to be twenty years of age. Mr. Baring — son of Sir Francis Baring, a partner in Hope and Company, twenty-one years of age, rich, unmarried and unspoken for.

CHAPTER 22

Mr. Bingham
Administers an Oath of Office

Mr. Bingham is so well versed in the Politics of this place, and South of it, and so well acquainted with the movements in both houses of Congress, that it would be a Work of Supererogation in me, to give you the details. To him I refer you for such relations as are interesting.

President Washington to
General Henry Knox
Philadelphia, June 9, 1796

THE EXPEDITION left for New York on June 13, spent a few days there, and proceeded by boat through Long Island Sound to Newport in Rhode Island. The intention was to sail on to Providence and Boston, but because the passage to Newport had been a rough one, the second leg of the journey was made by stagecoach. "The ladies suffered exceedingly by sea sickness," Bingham wrote to General Knox, "which has impressed on them a very serious dislike to water excursions." He hoped they would forget their troubles; if they did not, he feared he would never get them as far as Knox's house at Thomaston, Maine. There were eight principals in the party: the Binghams and their two daughters, Alexander Baring, Abigail Willing, John Richards, and Vicomte de Noailles. They were attended by a number of servants.

John Richards was an English traveler, the twenty-eight-year-old son of a respectable gentleman of Hampshire. Baring had fallen in with him on the trip from Boston to Philadelphia and soon thereafter retained him as the Baring-Hope land agent in America. Richards, by coincidence, was carrying a letter of warm recommendation to Bingham from John Jay in England. He had "a taste for drawing."

Louis-Marie de Noailles, forty, had known the Binghams in Paris thirteen years earlier. In 1789-91, he had played a leading part in the early French Revolution, moving the decrees that abolished feudal privileges, serving for a time as president of the Constituent Assembly, and unsuccessfully leading one of the armies of the Revolution. He left France with permission but was then proscribed; his wife was guillotined in July, 1794, with her mother and her grandmother.

Noailles had salvaged some fragment of his fortune, and in Philadelphia became an active trader and speculator. He spent his working hours at the coffee house where the merchants met, or at the stock exchange. Samuel Breck said that Noailles drove bargains as earnestly as any regular-bred son of a counting house. He and another Frenchman of means, Omer Talon, late in 1793 bought from Robert Morris 1600 acres on the great bend of the Susquehanna River in Bradford County, there founding a settlement, Azilum, for French refugees. Noailles was, in Baring's words, "a necessary family appendage" in the Bingham household. He had the use of the Bingham servants and kitchen when he entertained in his third-story room at the end of the garden. Angelica Schuyler Church once wrote to Alexander Hamilton, her sister's husband, "We dine tomorrow with Mrs. Bingham and Viscomte *Importance.*" His form, Breck said, "was perfect; a fine face; tall, graceful, the first amateur dancer of the age; and possessed of very pleasing manners." He was also an accomplished violinist. In 1781, to set an example for his regiment, Noailles had marched on foot from Newport to join Washington's army on the Hudson. Now, because of an accident, he walked with a limp. While teaching the Misses Bingham a step — perhaps one he had used as Marie Antoinette's favorite dancing partner — he sprang into the air, fell, sprained an ankle, and was lame ever after.

In writing to London about the trip, Baring had asked his associates if they would permit their names to be given to towns in Maine, since "we have a number to give. The ladies of our party are exercising their inventing geniuses and if you have any predilections or prejudices pray mention them. . . . We shall of course have a Hopetown, a Binghamville, etc. etc. etc." From his father came the suggestions *Adrianople, Williamston,* and *Philipsville* or *Philipsburg* for members of the Hope family. Sir Francis urged his son to be very careful when he went into the Maine woods, lest his health be undermined by the swamps and fogs. The complexion of Americans, Sir

Francis said, proved how unhealthy most of the country was. He further urged Alexander to keep close control over the property and not "admit the slightest shade of democracy" in the operations of the agents.

The expedition reached Boston on June 22 and there was greeted by General Knox and taken to boardinghouses he had reserved, the four men in one, the four women in another. (The town was crowded, the legislature being in session.) The President of the United States had presented his compliments to Bingham on June 9; wished him, Mrs. Bingham and the whole party a pleasant journey and a safe return; asked him to deliver a letter to General Knox; and sent along a report Bingham had inquired about "on the Subject of Manures." Washington sent his condolences on the death by diphtheria of two more of Knox's children. They were the seventh and eighth lost out of twelve, one of the two being William Bingham's ten-year-old namesake, William Bingham Knox.

The members of the expedition stayed in Boston for three weeks while Bingham and Baring worked on their common land matters. A three-day journey by stage brought the travelers to Portland, a town of about 3000 inhabitants, many of them, Baring found, "very respectable and rich."

There they were met by a packet, the *Mercury,* chartered for the next forty days at a cost of $533. The boat took them sixty miles to the wharf of General Knox's house, "Montpelier," at the town of Thomaston — "a neat village of near seventy houses and a church," ten miles up the St. George River from the coast. Baring found Knox's house "a very fine one and the whole of his stile rather bordering on magnificence." Montpelier attracted a great deal of attention, was talked of everywhere and brought many visitors to Maine, but it was, Baring thought, "an unnecessary expense." Knox operated a 200-acre model farm, where he bred "a vast number of horses," and ran a lime kiln, a brickyard, a shipyard, sawmills, gristmills, and a store for the sale of imported articles — all at a continuing loss. The guests and their hosts played cards and billiards, rode the saddle horses, drove in the carriages, and went picknicking along the banks of the St. George River.

Anne Bingham, her sister and her two daughters (whom Knox called "the young immortals") remained for the next three weeks at

Montpelier while the men sailed off with General Knox in the *Mercury*. The only glimpse of this interval in the Knox household is given by a visitor, a Reverend Paul Coffin, who on August 15 wrote in his diary:

> Dined at General Knox'. . . . His house draws air beyond all the ventilators which I had before seen. I was almost frozen for three hours before we took dinner and plenty of wine. The General being absent, gone East, in a Portland packet with Mr. Bingham, I dined with Mrs. Knox and her daughters, and Mrs. Bingham and her sister and daughter [sic]. We had a merry dinner, the little Misses talking French in a gay mood. Mrs. Bingham was sensible, had been in France, could talk of European politicks, and give the history of the late King of France, etc.

The *Mercury* sailed across Penobscot Bay and east among the islands off the coast, past Mount Desert Island, the eastern half of which Knox had bought for £100. ("Precious appendages to our property," Baring called them, "and I wish we owned more of them.") They sailed around Schoodic Point and up the bay to Gouldsborough, where Bingham and Baring first saw the land they had bought. Baring found only three comfortable houses there, one of them General Cobb's, and he was alarmed that this was the place where the settlers would land. "I could have wished," he said, "it had not looked so frightfully barren." Cobb joined the men when they resumed their journey eastward along the coast. They came to the eastern extremity of the purchase at Passamaquoddy, entering the Bay between Quoddy Head and Campobello Island. They proceeded up the Schoodic River (St. Croix) to St. Stephen and thence in Indian canoes as far as the falls (Calais, Maine), almost losing Noailles by a drowning accident.

For almost a week they were becalmed in Passamaquoddy Bay, all the time so tormented by mosquitoes that Baring complained he had not slept two hours in several nights. While waiting for the wind to rise, he wrote a long letter to his brother-in-law, Pierre César Labouchère. He complained of being becalmed, "which if you were much accustomed to the sea, you would know is a most tedious situation," and of "the immensity of musketoes; they plague us beyond anything you could conceive. . . ." He asked Labouchère to convey some advice to Henry Philip Hope, who was expected in America in the fall:

> Desire him to bring out a servant and a good groom that he can depend on, also three good horses — one or two light chairs for *me*, since I much regret I did not take them. They are not luxuries but indispensable, for you can not travel without them and every thing of the kind here is twice as dear and much worse, and good servants are not to be had. I am particularly fortunate in John, who is a real treasure. . . .
>
> Setting aside the gratification I receive from this excursion on the score of business, it has been an agreable thing on that of pleasure. Our ladies are everything we could wish and put up with the inconveniences very well.

At Machias the party divided into two parts. Knox and Richards returned with the vessel to Gouldsborough. Bingham, Baring, Noailles and Cobb made a two-day, fifty-mile journey on horseback, at first over a mere path through the forest, "terribly bad," then on a road passing through a number of small settlements. Boarding the *Mercury* again at Gouldsborough, they sailed to join the women at Montpelier, lingered a few days, and then continued on to Portland. There Bingham wrote his letter of thanks to General and Mrs. Knox. He had seen several of the most noted inhabitants of Portland, he said, and had corrected their ignorant and mistaken ideas about the Eastern Country. The expedition arrived in Philadelphia on September 22 after a journey of some 1500 miles and an absence of 100 days.

Baring told his experiences and views in a sixty-eight-page letter addressed to Hope and Company. He was favorably impressed with what he had seen. The inhabitants had a proper understanding of the meaning of private property.

> You find a newspaper in almost every farm house and seldom meet anybody who has not a tolerable idea of European politics and a very good one of his own. . . . Every person can read and write and the village of Warren has even a circulating library. . . . At all the chief points of settlement there are steady and respectable characters which give the tone to the others and so far from any irreligion prevailing, we found the country infested with a pack of fanatical

itinerant Methodist preachers that had disturbed the community and were rather obnoxious in the other extreme.

He returned from the trip convinced that the New England people, who were emigrating to the southwest in great numbers, would soon direct their attention more and more to Maine, and that the tide of population would turn to the north.

> Though my ideas of the thing were in many instances erroneous, yet considering all circumstances my expectations have been very much exceeded and my opinions of the speculation have never in any instance been shaken.

Still, he was somewhat sobered by his experiences, and he indicated that he never again would buy a million acres of land before he had seen it.

> Printed informations, though they may be correctly true, by telling only part of the truth and hiding what may be prejudicial, must always be deceptive and give an inadequate idea of the object.

*

Two months before the Maine expedition, William and Anne Bingham had persuaded President Washington to sit for a portrait by Gilbert Stuart. The work was to be a present from Mrs. Bingham to Lord Lansdowne.

Stuart had left Ireland in 1792 pursued by creditors, arriving in New York after an absence of seventeen years. Two years later he came to Philadelphia expressly to persuade the President to sit for him. It was natural for Bingham and Stuart to overlook their earlier differences in London. Stuart was the most noted portrait painter working in America; Bingham had become the country's leading patron of the arts. Bingham, moreover, was sensitive about the scarcity of artistic talent in America. In a letter to the Italian sculptor Ceracchi, he said, "From the rapid rise of this country, and its increasing resources, I have little doubt of a considerable change speedily taking place relative to the encouragement of works of genius and taste."

Stuart had painted one portrait of Washington — the head-and-shoulders "Vaughan Portrait," of which Bingham owned a Stuart-painted replica. Now he wished to paint a full-length figure. Washington disliked the tedium of sitting for his portrait, and he especially disliked sitting for Stuart, who had annoyed him with impudent talk during the first sessions. But William Bingham asked and Anne Bingham cajoled, and on April 11, 1796, Washington wrote:

> SIR: I am under promise to Mrs. Bingham to sit for you tomorrow, at nine o'clock, and wishing to know if it be convenient to you that I should do so, and whether it shall be at your own house (as she talked of the State House), I send this note to you to ask information.

Washington appeared at Stuart's house at Sixth and Chestnut in full dress, with lace at the wrists and throat, carrying his court sword. He was wearing a new set of badly fitting false teeth (soon discarded) that distorted the lower part of his face. Stuart placed him between an over-elaborate chair and an equally ornate table, his right hand extended majestically, palm up, standing against three Doric columns, a purple and gold curtain, and a sky with a rainbow. He painted on a canvas five feet by eight feet.

Stuart finished the portrait in November. Bingham, after ordering a replica for himself painted by Stuart, shipped the original to England. To his friend Rufus King, minister to the Court of St. James's, he wrote:

> I have sent by the present opportunity a full length portrait of the President. It is executed by Stewart (who is well known in London) with a great deal of enthusiasm, and in his best manner, and does great credit to the American artist. It is intended as a present on the part of Mrs. Bingham to Lord Lansdowne. As a warm friend of the United States and a great admirer of the President, it cannot have a better destination.
>
> The frame that accompanies it is manufactured in Philada. with much taste and elegance. It has been suggested that some difficulties may exist relative to its admission: in which case I must request your interference to obviate them.

Lansdowne, of course, was delighted. His letter to Mrs. Bingham is not extant, but he referred to the painting in a letter to Major William Jackson, with whom he had been corresponding:

I have received the picture, which is in every respect worthy of the original. I consider it as a very magnificent compliment, and the respect I have for both Mr. and Mrs. Bingham will always enhance the value of it to me and my family. . . . General Washington's conduct is above all praise. He has left a noble example to sovereigns and nations, present and to come.*

Stuart later claimed that he asked Bingham to reserve the engraving rights of the painting when he sent it to Lord Lansdowne, since, as he said, he hoped to "rescue myself from pecuniary embarrassment and to provide for a numerous family at the close of an anxious life" by having it engraved in England. Bingham's pride in American art would have induced him to make the reservation; but he either neglected to do so or was unaware that he was responsible for Lansdowne's actions. The following July he wrote to King:

I received your letter of April 26th, with several inclosures from the Marquis of Lansdown, who, I am pleased to find, is much gratified with the portrait of the President. Stewart has been much disappointed in his hopes relative to profits, which he expected to derive from this picture. He had wrote to his friend, Benjamin West, requesting him to engage an able artist to execute an engraving therefrom, which, from the general admiration the picture attracted, might have been disposed of to great advantage in this country. He has not heard from Mr. West, and he is fearful that Lord Lansdown's obliging character may induce him to permit some other artist to take off the impression.

It was too late. Benjamin West apparently had not acted on Stuart's letter, and Lansdowne had given the English engraver James Heath permission to reproduce the portrait. The engraving was an inferior one, the artist was called "Gabriel Stuart," and Gilbert Stuart received no payment. He wrote to Lansdowne for an explanation (there is no record of Lansdowne's reply) and he called on Bingham.

How, he asked, did Mr. Bingham propose to compensate him for the injury he had sustained by the publication of the print? Bingham

* The portrait sent to Lansdowne now belongs to Lady Rosebery of South Queensbury, West Lothian, Scotland. Bingham's replica hangs in the Pennsylvania Academy of the Fine Arts.

apparently denied his responsibility, and he certainly refused to pay compensation. The words grew heated, until Bingham finally demanded, "Do you have anything in writing?" Stuart had nothing in writing and he stormed out of the house. He sought in vain to obtain compensation under the law. Even in his old age he trembled with rage when he spoke of his confrontation with William Bingham; he had come to blame all his financial troubles on that one misfortune.

*

By the summer of 1796, it was widely known that President Washington would not run for a third term. His decision became official when, on September 17, he published a farewell message to the American people (written largely by Hamilton). He warned against the excessive party spirit that was dividing Americans and against "permanent, inveterate antipathies against particular nations [i.e., Britain] and passionate attachments to others [France]. . . . Against the insidious wiles of foreign influence the jealousy of a free people ought to be *constantly* awake, since history and experience prove that foreign influence is one of the most baneful foes of republican government."

The President's Farewell Address was, Fisher Ames said, "a signal, like dropping a hat, for the party racers to start." The majority of the Federalists supported John Adams and Thomas Pinckney; the Republicans supported Thomas Jefferson and Aaron Burr. There were newspaper articles, pamphlets, and political rallies, but little public campaigning as such, and none by the two principals. The election was held and the nation began to wait the long weeks until the electoral college could meet and determine the results. The shocking defeat of lesser Federalist candidates in Pennsylvania, Bingham attributed to "the most unwearied exertions, accompanied by some bribery, and not a little chicane . . . very essentially aided . . . by Mr. Adet's strokes of diplomatic finesse." *

The second session of the Fourth Congress opened on Monday, December 5. In his address to both houses assembled, President Washington called for creation of a national university devoted to the science of legislation, a military academy to nurture a military spirit, a naval force, and national industrial plants to produce armaments.

* Pierre Adet, French minister to the United States.

He asked for an increase in the pay of government officials. He deplored the extensive injuries the French Republic was inflicting on American ships in the West Indies. The country, he said, was experiencing a most rapid aggrandizement, both political and commercial.

> The situation in which I now stand, for the last time, in the midst of the representatives of the people of the United States, naturally recalls the period when the administration of the present form of government commenced; and I cannot omit the occasion to congratulate you and my country on the success of the experiment.

Bingham was named one of three Senators to draw up an affectionate response to the President's message. In the House, twelve Republicans voted against making any reply to the President, one of them a gaunt, raw-boned, thirty-year-old frontier lawyer named Andrew Jackson, representing the new state of Tennessee.

By the middle of December, it was understood that Adams would probably win the presidency by a narrow margin and that Jefferson, with the second highest number of electoral votes, would become Vice President. Abigail Adams lamented that, as a President's wife, she would have to "impose a silence upon myself, when I long to talk." "A woman *can* be silent," her husband reassured her, "when she will."

Congress continued to work until the inauguration. Bingham voted for acts for relief of persons imprisoned for debt; to provide for the widows and orphans of officers killed in the half-war with France (defeated); against a loan to the city of Washington for buildings (passed); to admit Tennessee as the sixteenth state; and to provide each Senator with five copies of three newspapers. On February 8, the Senators trooped to the chamber of the House to attend the opening of the sealed votes of the electors. As expected, Adams was to become President, Jefferson, his opponent, Vice President. Adams had won by three electoral votes.

One week later, Adams delivered his valedictory to his fellow Senators. The following day, William Bingham was elected president pro tempore of the Senate. His first duty was to sign a somewhat long and flowery response to Adams' address. ("For you we implore the best reward of virtuous deeds — the grateful approbation of your constituents and the smiles of Heaven.")

On the evening before the inauguration ceremonies, William and Anne Bingham were guests at a dinner given by President Washington for those with whom he had been most closely associated during his eight years in office. President-elect Adams was the guest of honor. (Mrs. Adams was in Braintree looking after his eighty-eight-year-old mother.) Alexander Hamilton and Thomas Jefferson were present. Save for the ceremonies on the morrow, it was the last time these four founding fathers were together.

Jefferson had arrived in Philadelphia the day before, traveling alone in the public stage, carrying the manuscript of a work in progress, *A Manual of Parliamentary Practice,* and the bones of a mastodon he had acquired, to be presented to the Philosophical Society, of which he was now president. He had intended to stay at home during the inauguration, but when he heard it rumored that he would decline the Vice Presidency as beneath his acceptance, he decided to appear "as a mark of respect for the public."

The dinner was merry. The President looked benign, relaxed and almost cheerful. When the cloth was removed, he rose to say, "Ladies and gentlemen, this is the last time I shall drink your health as a public man. I do it with sincerity, and wishing you all possible happiness." Bishop William White reported, "This put an end to all pleasantry and forced the tears into many eyes."

Next morning, Saturday, March 4, 1797, Bingham proceeded through the multitude crowding Chestnut Street to Congress Hall. At exactly eleven o'clock he called the United States Senate to order. Twenty-four of the thirty members answered to the roll call. Mr. Jefferson was present, dressed in a long blue single-breasted coat buttoned to the waist, his sandy hair lightly powdered and queued with a black ribbon hanging far down his back. When Bingham introduced him, Jefferson rose and delivered a brief address, his voice low and indistinct. He deplored his lack of practice in parliamentary procedure, but promised diligence and the most rigorous and inflexible impartiality. The union of the states was the first of blessings, the preservation of the Constitution the first of duties. He had no political ambitions. He revered the talents and integrity of the eminent character (John Adams) who had preceded him as Vice President, whose cordial and uninterrupted friendship he had enjoyed through a long course of years.

Jefferson then moved to the presiding officer's small mahogany table. Bingham administered the oath of office and relinquished his chair to the new Vice President. The clerk read the credentials of the eight new Senators and Jefferson administered their oaths. These brief ceremonies concluded, Jefferson and Bingham led the Senators in a column of twos down to the larger House chamber. The room and its gallery were filled, according to the press, with "a very crowded auditory of the principal inhabitants of the city," including the foreign ministers and consuls in uniform, the heads of the departments, and General James Wilkinson, commander in chief of the American army and bribed agent of the Spanish government. Many House members had given their seats to the ladies of the audience. The four Supreme Court Justices were seated at a table before the Speaker's chair. Mr. Washington, dressed in black, sat as a private citizen in a chair a little before the seats assigned to the Senators. Vice President Jefferson, amid the applause of the crowd, took the chair at the right of the Speaker's chair, now empty and waiting for the President. The assemblage sat in silence.

At high noon there was a bustle at the wide center door and a murmuring, "The President!" and "President Adams!" Mr. Adams entered, followed by the members of the cabinet and by the federal marshal of the district and his officers. He was wearing a suit of pearl-colored broadcloth, wrist ruffles, white silk stockings, one of the new large black hats shaped like a crescent, a cockade, and a sword. His hair was in a queue, fully powdered and bagged. He walked slowly down the main aisle to "loud and reiterated applause," bowing to right and left, until he ascended to the Speaker's chair and sat down. There was another silence.

After a time, Mr. Adams rose, bowed three times to different parts of the audience, and began to read his inaugural address. It was a moderate speech, aimed more at reassuring the Republicans (his critics said) than at pleasing the Federalists. Four times he declared his veneration for the Constitution and his devotion to "the amiable and interesting system of government . . . which the people of America have exhibited to the admiration and anxiety of the wise and virtuous of all nations." He emphatically denied that he wished the executive or the Senate to be "more permanent," or that he had "ever entertained a thought of promoting any alteration . . . but such as the people themselves, in the course of their experience, should see and feel to be necessary or expedient and . . . according to the constitution itself, adopt and ordain." He drew attention to the dangers of party government for party gains rather than for the national welfare. He warned against foreign influences in the country's elections and declared his determination to continue the system of neutrality and impartiality among the belligerent powers of Europe. He had a personal esteem for the French nation born of years of residence among its people. He ended with a statement of his personal creed, delivered in one astonishing sentence 726 words long, filling two printed pages.

When the applause subsided, the President descended to the table at the front of the chamber, and Chief Justice Ellsworth, almost as an afterthought, administered the oath of office. President Adams kissed the Bible, resumed his chair and sat awhile in silence. He then rose, bowed to the assemblage, and, preceded by the officers who had accompanied him, made his way up the main aisle and out of the chamber.

Of the inauguration, John Adams wrote to Abigail, "All agree that, taken together, it was the sublimist thing ever exhibited in America." Indeed, for the first time in history, a large republican government had successfully transferred the power of elective office.

That evening Bingham attended a mighty farewell dinner given for Washington by the merchants of Philadelphia, Thomas Willing and Thomas Fitzsimmons presiding. A company of some 240 assembled at Oeller's Tavern at Sixth and Chestnut and from there marched two by two across the street to the circular amphitheater of Rickett's Circus — the President, the Vice President, members of the Congress, cabinet members, officers of rank of the Revolution, foreign ministers, and other noted citizens and guests. As the procession entered, an orchestra struck up "Washington's March." The amphitheater had been converted to a banquet hall. Richardet, the leading French restaurateur, "master of the City Tavern," served "the most choice viands which money could purchase or art prepare." On the raising of a curtain, an "emblematic painting" — a colored transparency — was revealed, representing a life-size female, the Genius of America, in the act of crowning Washington with a laurel, her hand pointing to an altar on which were inscribed the words, *Public Grati-*

tude. The remains of the feast were given to the prisoners in the jail and the sick in the hospital.

The following Monday, in his first act as President, Adams called his cabinet together to discuss what action to take in the worsening crisis with France. In one of the greatest blunders of his administration, he had retained Washington's cabinet as his own. He chose to do this because he knew that his party wanted it; because he had seen the extreme difficulty with which Washington had obtained competent secretaries for ill-paid posts subject to abuse; and because, with no precedent established, it was perhaps proper to carry over cabinet members from one administration to the next.

Oliver Wolcott, thirty-seven, Secretary of the Treasury, a Yale graduate, a successful lawyer, and a member of a distinguished Connecticut family, was an able, hard-working and (by his own lights) conscientious public official.

James McHenry, forty-four, of Maryland, Secretary of War, was a man of some inherited wealth. He had come from Ireland at eighteen for his health, studied medicine under Benjamin Rush, and served as a staff physician during the Revolution. He had campaigned effectively for adoption of the federal Constitution in Maryland.

Timothy Pickering, fifty-two, of Connecticut, Secretary of State, was a career official with limited financial resources who had distinguished himself as an administrator during the Revolution. He had a profound distrust of anyone who deviated in the slightest degree from the tenets of Federalism as laid down by Alexander Hamilton and Timothy Pickering. Years later he described his concept of a department head as he had seen it in 1797: "To prevent, as far as practicable, the mischievous measures of a wrong-headed president." On December 17, 1795, in response to an invitation to dinner extended by Mrs. Bingham, he had written her husband the following revealing letter:

It is not easy for me, even in matters where fashion might countenance or authorize it, to offer an apology that has not truth for its basis. Let me, then, tell you that Mrs. Pickering and I are constrained to forego many pleasures of society, because we cannot persuade ourselves to enter on a career of expenses which, being far beyond our income, would lead to ruin. . . . Mrs. Bingham's good sense will be satisfied with this reason for Mrs. Pickering's declining to accept her invitation.

But Mrs. Pickering is aware that, while a public man, I cannot seclude myself from the world, and therefore often urges, on my part singly, an intercourse which is *useful,* as well as agreeable. I shall then, with pleasure, dine with you occasionally, but without promising to reciprocate all your civilities. You may expect me to indulge in the pleasure of your company on Tuesday.

These three cabinet officers looked to Alexander Hamilton for leadership and in all important policy matters followed his instructions. With this peculiar loyalty, and in the act of supplying Hamilton with information on administration matters without Adams' knowledge, they very soon became willing accomplices in constant, unseemly intrigues against the President.

In France, the Directory considered the election of John Adams an insult second only to the approval of the Jay Treaty. When Charles Cotesworth Pinckney landed in France to succeed James Monroe as minister, the Directors refused to receive him and brusquely ordered him to leave French soil. Adams told his cabinet that he felt he should send one more emissary to France in an earnest effort to avoid open war, and that he should be an outstanding Republican. It would be improper to send Mr. Jefferson, but perhaps Mr. Madison would undertake the mission.

The secretaries consulted Hamilton on the advisability of further negotiations with France; they then advised the President that a mission should be sent. They suggested that it would be necessary for them to resign in a body, however, if Mr. Adams sent Mr. Madison. The President accepted the ultimatum. Madison having already declined to serve, Adams named a trio of commissioners: Pinckney, Elbridge Gerry, and John Marshall.

In seeking peace with France, Adams also presented a program to Congress for defense of the nation if negotiations failed. The Republicans opposed these measures. England, they announced happily, was about to collapse. The Bank of England had stopped payment of specie. Ireland was in rebellion. There was mutiny in the navy. King George III had been stoned in his carriage on his way to Parliament, and Pitt was resorting to the most repressive measures to beat down dissent among the British people. The French revolutionary armies, by contrast, were everywhere successful on the Continent and would soon be occupying London and ruling England.

Vice President Jefferson, having admired a succession of French revolutionary leaders — the Girondists, Mirabeau, Danton, Marat, Robespierre, the Directors — now admired a new figure, "that wonderful man Bonaparte," and hailed his victories as "splendid . . . miraculous." This brilliant leader, he felt, was likely to restore peace to Europe. If the Federalists could be restrained from declaring war on France, Napoleon would at the same time preserve peace for the United States. "The best anchor of our hope," he said, "is an invasion of England. If they republicanize that country, all will be safe with us."

BOOK FOUR

In a Time
of Crisis

CHAPTER 23

The Doombah and Other Visitors

Mr. Bingham . . . not only gave me a general invitation to his house, but offered to take care of my great sheep during my stay in America. This fine animal had arrived in perfect health, as had my Santipore cow.

Thomas Twining, *Travels in America,*
April, 1796.

THROUGH THE last decade of the century, Philadelphia was filled with foreign visitors. There were travelers driven by curiosity or idealism to study and report on the great American political experiment; men of talent and wealth representing the governments of Europe, accompanied by their wives and daughters; men of science searching out the animal and plant life of the western world; representatives of Europe's commercial houses. The French were the dominant group, conspicuous for their speech, dress and manners. There were some 10,000 exiles and refugees: royalists fleeing the republicans, republicans fleeing the terrorists, colonials fleeing the uprisings in the West Indies, all sprinkled with political agents sent to gather information about the young republic or to influence its policies.

The French congregated in the area around Walnut Street between Third and Fourth; they had their own cafés and clubs and newspapers. The liberals used as their headquarters the bookshop at Front and Walnut streets run by Moreau de St. Méry, a lawyer, leader in the early Revolution, scholar in the laws and customs of the French West Indies, now a bookseller, printer, pamphleteer, and vendor, on the side, of the first contraceptives sold in America. The French played in the orchestras of the city, dressed hair, ran *pensions,* repaired watches, opened millinery shops, and taught dancing, music, fencing and languages. Their restaurants introduced new words, new tastes and new dishes into American life. The men discussed French politics endlessly, deplored the peculiar social propriety of the beautiful but cold American women, and read to each other from the books they were writing on life among the Americans (some seventy of which were actually published). The Binghams had known many of these people in Europe, and they were all received at the Mansion House with cordial hospitality.

One of the visitors was Charles Maurice, Prince de Talleyrand-Périgord, Bishop of Autun, forty-three years of age in 1797, crippled scion of two of the oldest and most powerful families of France, destined to become the best-known and most controversial statesman of Napoleonic times. Expelled from England under the alien act, he came to America as a secret agent of the French government, with letters of recommendation from Lord Lansdowne to President Washington and William Bingham. Washington refused to receive him, for fear of offending the French republican government, and because Gouverneur Morris had reported, "I consider this man polished, cold, tricky, ambitious and bad." Bingham read the letter Talleyrand carried and made him welcome.

Talleyrand spent thirty unhappy, restless months in America, traveling from state to state, conceiving a contempt for Americans as money-mad — all save Alexander Hamilton, whom he later rated with Napoleon and Charles Fox as one of the three great men of his era. In the summer of 1795 he was sailing the coast of Maine and found himself storm-bound in the small harbor town of Machias. He asked the man in whose house he lodged, Mr. Phineas Bruce, a lawyer and leading citizen, if he had ever been to Philadelphia. No, not yet, said Mr. Bruce. Did he know General Washington? No, he had never seen him. "If you should go to Philadelphia," said Talleyrand, "will you be pleased to see that great man?" "Why, yes, I shall," replied Mr. Bruce, "but I should very much like to see Mr. Bingham, who, they say, is so rich."

Talleyrand did not report this amusing episode to the Binghams when he returned to Philadelphia. He had taken a lady of color as his mistress, appearing arm-in-arm with her in public, shocking even the French residents of the city; and the doors of the Mansion House had been closed to him. He embarked for France that fall, one of the first to return after the Terror.

*

François Alexandre la Rochefoucauld, Duc de Liancourt, fifty, who had been Grand Master of the King's Wardrobe, arrived from England with letters of introduction from John Jay. (Unless it was solely on business matters, a letter of introduction required at least an invitation to dinner.) He traveled the length and breadth of the country, wrote a study of Philadelphia prison life, became a member of the American Philosophical Society, and returned to France to write an eight-volume account of his travels in America, considerable portions of which he took without acknowledgment from the journals of his friend Moreau de St. Méry.

Having traveled through parts of Maine, the duke deplored Bingham's ownership of so much of those lands.

> Those gentlemen [speculators] . . . expect from the unaided operation of time an increase in the value of their lands, which, however, will not by that slow process ever take place in those northern countries.
>
> Such is said to be the plan intended to be pursued by Mr. Bingham, who, after having sold to Mr. Baring for sixty thousand pounds sterling one-half of the twelve hundred thousand acres of land which he possesses at the head of the Penobscot River, continues to hold the entire tract in conjunction with him as partner on equal terms. He besides owns three [two] millions more of acres in other parts of the district of Maine. So much the worse for him. . . . He cannot long be certain of quietly keeping in his hands such extensive tracts of land: and Mr. Bingham's popularity will not screen him from the inconvenience which, in a country like this, may attend the possession of so large a portion of the soil kept idle and unproductive in the hope of an exorbitant gain.

In a "sketch of the temper of the people of Philadelphia," La Rochefoucauld allowed that the women were more beautiful than those in Europe, and that the city was "perhaps the most agreeable in the United States for a foreigner." He charged, nevertheless, that Philadelphians showed no discrimination in inviting people into their homes, rudely dropped all those who on further acquaintance were found to have no wealth, and paid incessant attention to the accumulation of money, "which passion is not diminished even by the possession of the greatest fortune. To mend his circumstances is the predominant idea of every man in this country."

Bingham, with a good many other Philadelphians, was indignant when he received reports from Paris on the duke's book. The resentment against America, he wrote to Rufus King, arose from disappointed hopes.

> When he first arrived in this country he sought it as an asylum, and was so highly gratified, that he was extravagant in its praises. But when he saw a prospect open for his return into France, and supposed that he could facilitate his views by his abuse of the United States and the people, he regarded every object with a jaundiced eye. This opinion of his conduct arose from my own observations and I have been told, is confirmed by the publication of his book. . . . I hope some answer will be made to it; for such sentiments, falling from so great a height, may make a considerable impression, and be injurious to the American character.

*

Constantine François Chasseboeuf, Comte de Volney, forty, was still a wealthy man despite imprisonment, a narrow escape from the guillotine, and exile. As an outstanding scholar, scientist and author, Volney was welcomed at the Mansion House, and he dined there often, though he seems to have been rather poor company. Samuel Breck called him a man "of proud spirit and sour temper, jealous of the least appearance of slight, presuming much on his ability as a writer. . . . He had the arrogance to assert that the talents of Washington would not have raised him above the rank of colonel in the French service."

Like Brissot de Warville before him, Volney expected to find a new breed of man in America and was unforgiving toward what he did find. Americans were bigoted, avaricious, and tiresome; their women never washed themselves;* their patriotism caused them to think their country had a good climate; their revolutionary courage had become enervated by their dependence on such European luxuries as fine-papered parlors, satin chairs, and carpets.

During his three years in America, Volney visited almost every state and traveled as far west as Detroit. "Compared with France," he wrote, "we may say that the entire country is one vast forest." Of his western journey: "I scarce traveled three miles together on open and

---

* Lafayette: "American women are very pretty, very simple, and of a charming cleanliness."

cleared land." There were whispers in Philadelphia that the French government had sent Volney to America to prepare for French re-occupation of the Louisiana territories being held by Spain.

*

Louis Philippe, Duc d' Orléans, twenty-three, oldest son of the guillotined "Citizen Philippe Egalité," now first in line of succession to the French throne, was teaching geometry in Switzerland under an assumed name when Gouverneur Morris induced him to go to America, placing at his disposal an unlimited letter of credit. Louis lived in Philadelphia lodgings above a barber shop until he was joined by his younger brothers, the Duc de Montpensier and the Comte de Beaujolais. All three were frequent guests at the Bingham house.

It was there that Louis met Anne Bingham's pretty younger sister, Abigail. On the trip to Maine, Alexander Baring had not become interested in Abigail; Louis lost no time falling seriously in love with her. He was fascinated, Samuel Breck observed, by her handsome person and polished and graceful deportment, and he drew, "in the artistic style, a beautiful portrait of her, which I saw on the mantel-piece in one of the parlors of the Bingham house, where it was exhibited to a large company of visitors." Louis Philippe was pretender to the French throne; Abigail was a commoner, a Protestant and an American. Louis, nonetheless, formally courted her.

The city watched the courtship with attention. There must have been a buzzing of conferences throughout the large family relationship. Mrs. John Redman Coxe, wife of a leading physician of the city, wrote to her relatives in South Carolina, "It is reported that Abby Willing is to be married to the Duke of Orleans who you know arrived some time before you left us — I do not know whether it is correct but it is the general report." Louis, indeed, had approached Judge Willing and asked for his youngest daughter's hand in marriage.

Thomas Willing had become something of a character in the city. Now sixty-six, he persisted in his old-fashioned dress and behind his back was called, mockingly but not unkindly, "Old Square Toes." *

* "The Binghams and Willings are civil and attentive. I dine with Old Square Toes on Tuesday evening — no common favor this." Harrison Gray Otis to his wife.

People along the route knew that it was noon when they saw him making his way home from the bank for lunch; strangers frequently mistook him for President Washington, to whom he bore a marked resemblance. Whatever the occasion and whoever the company, Judge Willing served cup custard and Madeira in his parlor at nine o'clock; and if his children stayed beyond ten o'clock he would send them away with the words, "There's a welcome to come and a welcome to go."

Following Louis' visit to Judge Willing, the courtship stopped.

Mrs. Coxe: "Miss Willing's match is broken off — the reason is *never* to be known. It was thought a very extraordinary thing at the beginning and this has not lessened the surprise of the native." Gradually a "reason" became known and caused merriment wherever the story was told. Willing was said to have heard the duke's proposal and then to have replied gravely, "If you have no claim to the throne of France, you are no match for my daughter; and if you ever become King, she will be no match for you." Perhaps the real reason was somewhat less amusing. Willing would not consent to the marriage unless it was sanctioned by Louis Philippe's mother, the Dowager Duchess, Louise Marie Adelaide de Bourbon, who of course sent back an emphatic *non*.

The disappointed duke toured the south and west with his two brothers, attended by one servant and supported by a letter of credit supplied by Robert Gilmor of Baltimore, "to make use of in case they should fall short of funds in their journey." They traveled to Mount Vernon and thence into Kentucky, Tennessee, Ohio, western Pennsylvania, western New York, and back to Philadelphia. In a forest after leaving Niagara Falls they met Alexander Baring and Henry Philip Hope on their way to the Falls. Abigail Willing, some years later, married Richard Peters, a nephew of Judge Peters. Louis married a Bourbon princess, Maria Amelia, daughter of Ferdinand IV, King of Naples and of the Two Sicilies. On the birth of the Peters' first child, he sent a gift of a porcelain cup to Abigail.*

*

William Russell Birch, friend and associate of Joshua Reynolds,

---

* It is in the possession of Miss Elizabeth Macfarlane of Pittsburgh, a descendant of Henry and Mary Willing Clymer.

known as a painter of portraits and landscapes and for his development of a unique method of enamel painting, came to America in 1794, at age thirty-nine, with his wife and children. He brought with him only one letter of introduction: from Benjamin West, president of the Royal Academy, to William Bingham. Birch wrote in his memoirs:

> Mr. Bingham was my first employer in America, to instruct his two daughters in drawing at his own house, attended with one of their friends — three scolars twice a week, at half a guinea per lesson each. I then built me a furnace. I painted a full-size picture in enamel of Mr. Bingham and a smaller one from it for Miss Bingham. . . . Finding orders for portraits came in fluently, I gave up my scolars.

Birch began a celebrated series of views and historic buildings of Philadelphia. He also painted the country seats of the region, including Bingham's Lansdown on the Schuylkill.*

*

In the summer of 1796, a young English gentleman, a Mr. Sherlock, toured the western part of Virginia, Maryland and Pennsylvania in company with Robert Gilmor, Jr., twenty-two, son of Bingham's business partner. The following year, Sherlock persuaded young Gilmor to accompany him on a tour of the eastern states. Accordingly, on July 24, 1797, they took the North Point stagecoach out of Baltimore, crossed the Bay to Chestertown, and proceeded on to Philadelphia. In writing of this tour, Gilmor gave the best and most detailed account of life in the Bingham household — an extraordinary picture of what appears to have been a most pleasant society.

They called first on the Vicomte de Noailles, who that evening drove them out to Lansdown, Mr. Bingham's delightful country residence.

> It is a most superb place, and supposed to be the best country house in America. It commands a noble view of the Schuylkill and

---

* Birch's son Thomas, born in 1779, became a pioneer American landscape and marine painter and continued his father's series of historic views and buildings. To laymen, their styles are indistinguishable.

the seats in the neighbourhood, and at a distance the steeples of some of the churches in Philadelphia.

The two Bingham girls, now fifteen and thirteen, had as their guests the two daughters of "the celebrated Count de Grasse."

> The Miss Binghams I found very much improved since I last saw them, both in their persons and accomplishments. They are certainly very fine girls. . . . These young ladies are mere children in point of years, and have only improved their natural talents and acquired information from the extensive and variety of acquaintance they are obliged to make from their peculiar situation in life, aided by the stimulus of example which the talents of conspicuous characters daily set before them.

Gilmor and Sherlock rode out to Germantown the next day to visit Gilbert Stuart at his home, presenting a letter of introduction from Noailles. They inspected Bingham's copy of the President's portrait and saw a number of other portraits of "distinguished characters," all unfinished. They returned to Philadelphia

> in time to dress for dinner and the carriage we hired for the day carried us out to Lansdown where we dined with Mr. Bingham's family, some of Mrs. B's relations and several Spaniards who went out with the Viscount de N[oailles]. The day was passed in a pleasant, agreable manner. The company got to exercises of strength and activity in which we were joined by the young ladies, who proved that though accomplishments of a masculine nature were commonly appropriated to the gentlemen, yet they were not incompatible with female delicacy and indulgence when conducted in a suitable manner.

Gilmor called next day on the Duc d'Orleans and his brothers, "who had just returned from their jaunt to the western and northern part of America . . . quite fatigued with the hardships they had endured." He spent the following morning visiting

> and went to dine at Lansdown. Mr. Clymer drove Mr. Bingham and myself out in his phaeton. The three princes [Orleans, Montpensier, Beaujolais] dined with us and in the evening the usual sports on the lawn were resumed, and the party was a very pleasant and agreable

one among people whom we should never have expected such perfect freedom and ease.

They left a few days later for New York, Newport, Providence, and Boston. Sherlock left to return to Baltimore; Gilmor attended a splendid dinner in Faneuil Hall for President Adams and (in one of the New England phrases that fascinated him) "made a tarry" of several weeks in that country.

Returning to Philadelphia early in September, Gilmor passed a number of people on the road who were fleeing another outbreak of yellow fever in the city. By prearrangement, Noailles met him at Frankford and took him through the outskirts of the city directly to Lansdown, where he "experienced the most welcome reception from Mr. Bingham's family I had met with since my absence.

A great deal of company came out to dinner today, among which were the three princes. We spent a charming afternoon and at night Mr. Bingham would not permit me to leave his house but insisted on my staying there all the time I meant to spend near Philadelphia.

I remained here about a week, passing my time in the most agreable manner. Company were continually visiting Lansdowne, and added to its own made a most sociable society. During the day I either amused myself with hunting or retired to the library where Stuart was engaged in painting the whole family. In the evening we played at the French game of the lottery, in which we were occasionally joined by the princes and viscount who staid after night. Our party was increased by the arrival of Mr. Alexander Baring (son of Sir Francis Baring) whom Mr. Bingham invited to stay in the family. He is an extraordinary young man, of great mercantile talents and possessed of much information. Though a young man of about 25, he is respected by all the old characters who know him. . . .

One day the family of the British minister, Mr. Liston, dined at Lansdowne; in his suite were Mr. Thornton, Mr. Brown, and Lord Henry Stuart, all secretaries and assistants. . . . The day passed as usual; very agreable and the company did not sit long at table, particularly the young people who assembled in the portico and on the lawn.

*

In April, 1796, there arrived in Philadelphia an Englishman who surely must rank as one of the most engaging and agreeable young men ever to visit these shores. He was Thomas Twining, son of the family of tea merchants, nephew of a leading classical scholar of the age, who had shipped out to India at sixteen and now, four years later, was returning to England for a visit between two terms of residence. He chose to travel by way of America. In India he had been received by the Great Mogul,* and now he dreamed of being received by President Washington.

For his journey back to the western world, Twining assembled an astonishing collection of curiosities, all described in an account of his travels he wrote a few years later. There were a number of oil paintings of Indian scenes; models of the principal machines and implements used in Indian agriculture and manufacturing; the bottom half of a huge oyster shell weighing more than 100 pounds; a great Kabul sheep; a small, thin, long-haired black Tibetan goat; a monkey from the north of India; a doombah;† ten fat sheep for eating ("the American captains having the reputation of keeping rather an indifferent table, living, it was said, principally on salt beef and sourcrout"); bales of hay for the sheep; and a small white Bengal or Santipore cow. Twining had obtained the cow on the promise that it would be an object of interest and care in the country to which he was going.

He signed up for passage for himself, servants, menagerie and baggage in an American ship, the *India,* 357 days out of Philadelphia on her second voyage to the Far East, owned by Robert Gilmor, Mordecai Lewis, and William Bingham. The captain was John Ashmead, a tall, mild-mannered man with thin, silvery hair falling to the collar of his old-fashioned coat, whom Twining took to be a Quaker perhaps sixty-five years old.‡

The *India,* laden with a cargo of spices and cloth, sailed down the Ganges on December 9, 1795, and entered Delaware Bay a little less

---

* The emperor of the Mogul, or Moslem empire in India, founded in 1526.

† I am indebted to Dr. J. Kenneth Doutt, Curator of Mammals at the Carnegie Museum in Pittsburgh, for the probable identification of Twining's doombah: "Assuming that 'doombah' may be a phonetic spelling, there are the following possibilities: Koh-i-dumba (mountain sheep) in Pushtu, which is the Shapo, or Urial (*Ovis vignei*). Less likely, Dabmo or Danmo of the Ladaki dialect, for the Sakin, or Asiatic Ibex (*Capra sibirica*)."

‡ He was fifty-seven and a Baptist.

than four months and a little more than 14,000 miles later. Twining described the scene:

> Having passed several ships, the *India* entered the line and took her station along one of the wharves, which extended nearly the whole length of the city, and in a few minutes I *stepped ashore* without even the aid of a plank, the ship's side touching the wharf.
>
> It being evening, when many people were about, the quay was crowded with persons curious to witness an arrival from Bengal.

He was setting off with his trunk to a tavern when he was pressed to go to Mordecai Lewis' house.

> This worthy citizen received me very kindly, saying, "How dost thou do, friend? I am glad to see thee." . . . I drank tea with these good people, in whom I found a kindness which the simplicity of their manners seemed to make the more cordial. The safe arrival of their ship at a favorable market put all the family in good spirits.

After tea, he was taken to call on the Binghams at the Mansion House.

> Mr. Bingham . . . was the principal person in Philadelphia, and the wealthiest, probably, in the Union. His house stood alone, and occupied, with the gardens attached to it, a spacious piece of ground. It was by far the handsomest residence in the city. I found here a large party. Besides Mr. and Mrs. Bingham and their two daughters, were Count de Noailles, Count [Alexandre de] Tilley, Mr. Alexander Baring, and others. . . .

Bingham gave Twining a standing invitation to visit him and arranged to pasture the animals on the lawn of the Mansion House. The young man took lodgings at the Francis Hotel and was pleased to find himself dining at a large table among members of Congress, with the head chair reserved for Vice President Adams. After his first breakfast on buckwheat cakes, about which he had heard so much on the voyage from India and which he obligingly found superior to English crumpets, he went again to the Mansion House

> where I found my doombah grazing upon the garden lawn at the back of the house. While I was looking at it with Mr. Bingham,

several inhabitants of the city came to gratify their curiosity, for Mr. Bingham, having observed this, had ordered that everybody should be admitted, and considerable numbers had already come to the garden in consequence. My Bengal cow, which I found in a stable not far off, also had numerous visitors.

Twining presented his large oyster shell to Peale's Museum, where it was "very graciously accepted," and called on the English minister to ask him to arrange an introduction to President Washington.

On Sunday, April 10, he went to hear the celebrated Dr. Priestley preach. The chapel was so crowded that he was obliged to stand near the door and could judge of the doctor's eloquence only by the pleasure it seemed to afford his hearers. Then he

> . . . dined and drank tea with Mr. Bingham, met the Count de Noailles, Count Tilley, the celebrated Monsr. Volney, the two Messrs. Barings, and several members of the Senate and House of Representatives — in all a very large party. Mr. Volney, next whom I sat at dinner, was very inquisitive about India. Mr. Alexander Baring, who sat nearly opposite to me, took a leading part in the general conversation.

Noailles introduced him to a Dr. Ross, who took him to call on Dr. Priestley.

> Dr. Ross, in his friendly zeal, introduced me somewhat in the style of a showman at a country fair: "Mr. Twining — just arrived from Bengal — a great traveller on the Ganges — has been received by the Great Moghol," etc. The Doctor, his simplicity unchanged by this recital, received me with hearty kindness. He placed me near the fire, and took a chair by my side. I soon found that he was as inquisitive as Dr. Ross had represented him to be. . . . Among other things, he spoke of the great sheep in Mr. Bingham's garden, expressing his intention of seeing it.

Twining took Dr. Priestley to the *India* to show him the skin of his Tibetan goat, to convince him that cashmere was a product of a goat, not of a sheep. The doctor was so impressed that Twining persuaded him to take it as a gift. He accepted with reluctance but with obvious pleasure, and a sailor carried the skin to the doctor's house.

12th April. — Breakfasted, as usual, with the Members of Congress, with whom I was now upon easy terms. As we stood round the fire, one of these gentlemen, Mr. Gallatin, examined the ends of my muslin neckcloth, and much surprise was expressed when I mentioned the cost at Santipore. Many questions were asked me respecting the qualities and prices of the fabrics of India, and it is not impossible that the lowness of the latter suggested the idea of a profitable speculation, the object of almost every American at this period. . . .

9th May. — . . . After dinner Monsieur Volney and I walked out together. He told me he should probably publish some account of America. He examined things as we went about very minutely, and in some of his surveys made me his assistant. Having taken the measure of my step, he requested me to walk from one side of the street to the other, while he with his pocket-book in his hand counted the number of my paces, and noted down their equivalent in feet. . . .

Sunday, [May] 16th. — In a sermon Dr. Priestley preached to-day, he referred to what I had said to him about the Hindoos. Dined with Mr. Bingham, Mr. Baring, Count de Noailles, and several members of the two Houses of Congress — in all a large party. After the company had retired, remained with the family and Mr. Baring.

[May] 25th. . . . As I was walking up Chestnut Street this afternoon a tall gentleman in a blue coat, on the opposite side, was pointed out to me as Monsieur Talleyrand. . . . I understood that the Bishop, for so he was called notwithstanding his blue coat, was not upon good terms with Mr. Bingham's family, or I should probably have met him amongst the other emigrants from France at Mrs. Bingham's parties.

Twining had received his invitation to attend President Washington's levee and, after much consideration on its propriety, dressed in the costume of an Indian court for the occasion. While surrounded by admiring members of Congress, he was disappointed to receive word from the English consul that important public business had made it impossible for the President to appear. A month later, after trips to Baltimore and the Federal City (Washington), he found occasion to visit the President privately at his home.

He lived in a small red brick house on the left side of High [Market] Street. . . . There was nothing in the exterior of the house that denoted the rank of its possessor. Next door was a hair-dresser. . . .

There was nobody in the room, but in a minute Mrs. Washington came in, when I repeated the object of my calling, and put into her hands the letter for General Washington, and the miniature [brought from Baltimore]. . . .

Mrs. Washington was a middle-sized lady, rather stout; her manner extremely kind and unaffected. She sat down on the sofa, and invited me to sit by her. . . . The door opened, and Mrs. Washington and myself rising, she said, "The President," and introduced me to him. Never did I feel more interest than at this moment, when I saw the tall, upright, venerable figure of this great man advancing towards me to take me by the hand. There was a seriousness in his manner which seemed to contribute to the impressive dignity of his person, without diminishing the confidence and ease which the benevolence of his countenance and the kindness of his address inspired. There are persons in whose appearance one looks in vain for the qualities they are known to possess, but the appearance of General Washington harmonized in a singular manner with the dignity and modesty of his public life. So completely did he *look* the great and good man he really was, that I felt rather respect than awe in his presence.

The President thanked him for the miniature and, sitting with him by the fire, questioned him about his arrival in America, his sea voyage, his trip to Baltimore and Washington, his opinion of the latter city, and trade between India and America.

In the course of the conversation I mentioned the particular regard and respect with which Lord Cornwallis always spoke of him. He received the communication in the most courteous manner, inquired about his lordship, and expressed for him much esteem.

When Twining rose to take his leave after about three-quarters of an hour, the President invited him to come to tea that evening. In an excess of delicacy, Twining declined because of another engagement, no doubt to Washington's surprise and possibly to his amusement. It was "a wrong and injudicious decision, for which I have since reproached myself. No engagement should have prevented my accepting such an invitation."

Twining sailed for Newcastle early in June and never visited

America again. He returned to India, served there until 1805, and retired before he was thirty. Back in England again, he married, lived for twenty years in France, and finished out his long life at Twickenham, dying in 1861 at eighty-five. In a lecture to his neighbors in England, he said that in his lifetime he "had been intrusted with the reform of an extensive department of the public administration [in India], had been appointed judge of a great district, had held the charge of a country containing more than ten thousand towns and villages, and more than two millions of people, and had been received by the Great Mogul on his throne in the old world and by General Washington in the new."

CHAPTER 24

Panic and Passion in Philadelphia

Bankruptcies are daily happening in our great towns. A stagnation is taking place in business of all kinds; the wages of labor are lowering; property of all kinds is much diminished in value; disappointment in their views, joined to a great scarcity of money, has put an end to the various extravagant speculations, which disgraced the country; many of those who engaged deeply are ruined and involved great numbers in their misfortunes.

William Bingham to Rufus King
Philadelphia, July 10, 1797

THE "DUER PANIC" of 1792 had been short and limited in its effects; the panic of 1796–97 was severe, widespread and prolonged. In a six-week period, 150 companies failed and sixty-four merchants and speculators, some of them distinguished men, were taken off to debtors' prison. James Wilson had been shored up by a £5013 loan from Bingham, but he sank deeper and deeper into debt. In 1797, while traveling on his rounds as a Supreme Court justice, easing his mental torment by drinking whiskey and reading novels, he was thrown into a New Jersey prison. He died the following year owing enormous sums. Blair McClenachan was jailed for debt after (according to Dr. Rush) selling his estate to his children to defraud his creditors. Thomas Fitzsimmons was ruined, partly because of a loan of $160,-000 he had made to Robert Morris.

The collapse of Morris and his partners, James Greenleaf and John Nicholson, sent a shudder through the economy. When Morris fell, he carried dozens of others down with him, and the normal sympathy felt for a patriot who had rendered great service to his country was modified by the knowledge that he had dragged some of the best families into poverty and misery. Alexander Hamilton, John Jay, Bishop White (Mrs. Morris' brother), and Thomas Willing lost money through Morris. Albert Gallatin, who had sold his western lands to

Morris, lost a much-needed $3000. George Harrison, who had married into the Francis-Willing families, lost a fortune, and as a result defaulted on a $40,000 debt he owed to William Bingham.

Friends had tried to dissuade Morris from reckless speculation and compulsive extravagance at a time when his drafts were being returned for lack of funds. Washington warned him against overextending himself on land purchases. Thomas Willing served for a time on the board of Morris' North American Land Company, which owned some six million acres in six states; but he withdrew when the Bank of the United States threatened to sue if Morris did not make good "the paper lying in the bank." Morris paid a large personal debt to Willing by transferring a fraudulent claim against a third party. Willing did not prosecute his old friend and former partner.

"My property is so extensive," Morris declared, "that it cannot fail to carry me through, and all I want is a little time. . . . I expect before long to come forth in triumph." But immigration to the United States had virtually stopped; the capital funds of Europe were being used to support or to fight the French armies that were overrunning the Continent; money in Philadelphia cost 2 per cent interest a month — when it could be found; and land sales were at a standstill.

In 1795, when already in desperate straits, Morris began to build the most magnificent house yet erected in America — a marble palace occupying the block bounded by Chestnut, Walnut, Seventh and Eighth streets. Architect Pierre L'Enfant, a master of alluring estimates, promised to build it for a total cost of $60,000. The cost had reached very nearly $1 million in 1797 when Morris stopped the work and covered one unfinished marble wing with a roof of sheet iron rolled in his mill at Morrisville. About this time, a ship sailed up the Delaware carrying 5000 guineas' worth of mirrors Morris had ordered in Europe.

His lands were being sold for taxes. The row of brick houses he had started in Washington City was being plundered or occupied by squatters. His debts were estimated at something between $10 million and $30 million; his notes were selling for 15 per cent of their face value, purely as speculation. "There is no bearing with things," he cried out. "I believe I shall go mad. Every day brings forward scenes and troubles almost unsupportable."

He locked himself in his house on the Schuylkill, with constables and bailiffs camping around bonfires on his lawn. Finally he was apprehended and taken to a whitewashed cell in the Walnut Street prison. He moved in his own furniture — a writing desk, a copying press, a bedstead and bedding, a settee, chairs and mirrors. He worked over his accounts and letter books in a vain attempt to bring some order into his affairs. His wife Molly lived in a small room across the street from the jail, visited him daily, and paid the charges levied against imprisoned debtors: cell rent and meals. General Washington dined with Morris in his cell when he visited Philadelphia. He and Mrs. Washington invited Mrs. Morris and her daughter to visit Mount Vernon and stay as long as they wished.

The marble palace and the whole block on which it stood were sold at auction in December, 1797, for $46,000; the building was dismantled, the marble salvaged, the deep foundation filled in. "The lot alone," Bingham observed wryly, "would have brought that much a few years earlier."

Bingham was the only large capitalist and speculator who was not ruined in these perilous times, though he was hard-pressed throughout 1796 and 1797. "There never was such a calamitous period," he wrote to Knox. "The disappointments that have arisen from the non payment of such immense sums as have been thrown into the market by our great speculators, have occasioned such a stagnation as was never before experienced."

As pressed for money as he was, Bingham took one step in April, 1797, that indicates he was sure of his ability to meet his obligations. James Greenleaf, through marriage, had become owner of the Lansdown estate, which he continued to rent to Bingham. When he went under with Morris with debts totaling $1,800,000, the property was put up for sale, and Bingham bought it as "an establishment" for his wife. He paid $31,050, of which $24,050 was raised by a mortgage. He confessed later that he had "foolishly given too large a sum . . . that he might gratify Mrs. Bingham."

Alexander Baring had criticized Bingham for "caution and diffidence" in not taking decisive action to develop the Maine lands. His character, Baring wrote, "is rather indolent; he has never set about working these lands actively but always been attempting to sell them in their rough state, which is a very wrong principle." But now, when he shared the responsibility, Baring spent almost the entire year of 1797 traveling about the country, making an economic study to determine whether further investment in the country was justified. He toured the southern states in the spring. With Henry Philip Hope,* a "sleeping partner" in Hope and Company, he visited Western New York to study land operations. The two men continued on into Canada, down the St. Lawrence to New Brunswick, and across into Maine for another look at their purchase. Baring returned to Philadelphia late in November, in time for a strategy meeting with Bingham and their Maine agents, Richards and Cobb. Knox, sinking into a quagmire of debt, apparently was not invited to attend.

At this meeting, Baring presented an ambitious, detailed, 7800-word program for developing the lands in Maine. To his associates in London he explained that he had wanted Bingham to draw up the program, so that he might have an added incentive in following it,

> but I could not bring him to it, and in fact his ideas were not organized. You will observe several corrections of no material consequence, and they were made chiefly to humour his opinions when he gave any. He is very much pleased with the whole and as you will observe, I have put it out of his power to clog our agents in details.

The partners apparently had expressed some alarm at Baring's descriptions of Bingham's deficiencies.

> From some expressions in your letters I rather apprehend that I have given a more unfavorable impression of Mr. B's character as an associate in this business than I intended. I pointed out the weak parts to shew the necessity of guarding them and the means taken to effect it. They are not dangerous and I believe you will find them secured by our plan.

Among other things, Cobb and Richards were to repair and paint the houses and other buildings in Gouldsborough, including Cobb's home, "to look neat, which would remove much of the horrors of the place." Young Baring, having analyzed the American character, felt it advisable to instruct General Cobb on how to behave among the

---

* A collector of art and precious stones, Hope acquired the famous $44\frac{1}{4}$-carat blue India diamond that still bears his name.

inhabitants of the region. The agents were to act without overfamiliarity. "People you will have to deal with," he observed, "are better managed by keeping them at a certain distance and creating without haughtiness a considerable portion of awe and respect." He devoted his final instructions to what he called "attention to puffing."

> Every stroke of the axe in your woods should be heard in Massachusetts and Connecticut, every hut should be called a village and every village a town. When you have fixed your Land Office, you should advertize in all the principal New England papers that the tract is ready for settlement, with a short account of the advantages of the country and progress of improvements. . . . You will find your reputation spread rapidly and visitors to the country will follow.

Baring was confident that his plan would succeed in a short time. "Nothing of the kind," he said, "has ever been attempted in America on a more susceptible object or under such promising agency." The venerable Henry Hope, though 3000 miles away, assessed the situation somewhat more astutely than his young partner. He had concluded that developing the Maine lands would require a lifetime of work and the resources of the Bank of England.

The two agents returned to Maine and proceeded, as best they could, to put the new program into effect. Beset by demands for money from all sides, Bingham quarreled with Cobb over these expenditures. The one asset that would have produced some income was timber, but the agents were bound by Baring's program to discourage lumbering and attempt to establish (on unsuitable soil) thriving farming communities.

With a program drawn up, an English agent working on the site with Cobb, and three trustees holding the lands for the Barings and Hopes, the time had come for Alexander Baring to return home. He seemed reluctant to do so. In May, 1797, he had written his father that he would resign himself "to any situation or spot on the globe where I thought my duties called me," but he felt he should stay in America and look after the interests of his English partners. The next day he wrote again to say that remaining in America would be *"a very great advantage to me. . . .* But I do not wish my personal benefit to weigh either with them [the Hopes] or you. Decide as you please and I am content. . . . But whatever *you do pray don't keep me hang in suspense."* In November, he announced that the time for his departure was imminent; but four months later, reporting to Bingham from Boston, he referred cryptically to his many reasons for wishing to hurry back to Philadelphia. One month later, however, he informed his company that he was quite willing to go on one day's notice to "any part of the world you please."

Miss Ann Bingham was the cause of this vacillation and change of plans. Baring had fallen in love with his partner's sixteen-year-old daughter.

It is not known whether Miss Ann (and perhaps her mother) set out to capture young Mr. Baring; or whether Mr. Baring wooed a young lady who was indifferent; or whether any other suitors were involved; or what William Bingham's role may have been in this obviously desirable match. One can only imagine the anxious suspense, quarrels, raptures, supplication and willful separation that must have attended the courtship. Presumably the young man was conscious that he was disobeying his father's order not to marry an American girl; he did not confide in his father in the early stages of his suit.

In any event, very soon after his offer to go anywhere in the world, Baring proposed to Ann Bingham. He was accepted and received her parents' blessing. The engagement was announced and the wedding set for October, 1798. On his son's letter of a year earlier, Sir Francis Baring wrote the perhaps sardonic, perhaps amused comment: "A. B. proposes to remain in America — his object must then have been a marriage with Miss Bingham."

*

The second session of the Fifth Congress (destined to be one of the most momentous in the country's early history) was delayed by bad weather, bad roads, and uncertainty caused by the summer's yellow fever epidemic. On Wednesday, November 22, 1797, after a delay of nine days, Senator Bingham led a joint delegation to inform President Adams that a quorum of the two houses had assembled; he reported back to the Senate that the President would address a joint session the following day at twelve o'clock.

The President turned almost at once to the matter that was on everyone's mind: the near-war with France. The two envoys extraordinary, Elbridge Gerry and John Marshall, he said, had joined their colleague, Charles Cotesworth Pinckney, in Holland and arrived in Paris around the 19th of September. He hoped for a settlement with France compatible with the safety, honor, and interests of the United States; but nothing had yet occurred to warrant a change in the defense measures he had recommended in the special session last spring. Indeed, increasing depredations by the French on American shipping strengthened the reason for their adoption. "Whatever may be the issue of the negotiation with France," he said, "and whether the war in Europe is or is not to continue, I hold it most certain that perfect tranquillity and order will not soon be obtained. . . . We should make every exertion to protect our commerce and to place our country in a suitable posture of defence, as the only sure means of preserving both."

The Federalists considered the address a wise and moderate statement of national policy; the Republicans called it a virtual declaration of war against the French Republic. Both parties waited tensely for news from the envoys in Paris. French attacks on American vessels continued. More than 340 ships worth an estimated $55 million were taken in an eighteen-month period because they carried goods declared to be contraband by France, or lacked special papers required under a new interpretation of French law. Bingham lamented that he was placed in "considerable difficulties" because of the detention in French ports of ships he owned or had an interest in.

Bingham doubted (in a letter to Rufus King) that the American envoys would be received, or, if received, that their negotiations would be successful. "If war should ensue," he said, "I dread the disorganization and extreme disorder which will arise out of it, especially in the southern parts of the union." *

Weeks passed and no word came from Pinckney, Marshall, and Gerry. Party feeling ran high, and debate in the House grew heated. Near the end of January, just before roll call, Roger Griswold, Connecticut Federalist, taunted Matthew Lyon, Vermont Republican, on his military record. Lyon spat in his face; Griswold struck him with a

* Bingham assumed that a French invasion, if attempted, would take place in the South. It lay nearest to Louisiana and the French islands, contained the most friends of the French Republic, was the weakest part of the country, and had a slave population that might be armed and encouraged to revolt.

large yellow hickory cane; Lyon retaliated with iron tongs taken from the House fireplace; and the two men grappled on the floor until pulled apart.

The press — newspapers and pamphlets — grew abusive beyond any previous (or later) experience in the republic. There were twelve newspapers in Philadelphia in 1798, and of these, Benjamin Franklin Bache's anti-Federalist *Aurora and General Advertiser* was the most vituperative. Bache had embittered Washington's last two years in office with a drumfire of scurrilous charges: he had been an utterly incompetent general who had robbed his starving troops for his own pecuniary gain; he was, with Hamilton's connivance, collecting money illegally as President; he had debauched his country's liberties. Now, joined by other Republican editors, Bache assaulted President Adams and his cabinet. Adams, "the blind, bald, crippled, toothless, querulous Adams," the "Duke of Braintree," was a mad despot, an enemy of the people and of the rights of man, a champion of aristocracy who was determined to subvert American freedom.

The Federalist press retaliated in kind — most effectively through the pages of *Porcupine's Gazette,* started in March, 1797, by William Cobbett ("Peter Porcupine"), expatriate English journalist. Bache, he said, was "the son of one of Dr. Franklin's bastards" and looked like "a fellow who has been about a week or ten days on a gibbet." Franklin himself was "his crafty and lecherous old hypocrite of a grandfather, whose very statue seems to gloat on the wenches as they walk the State House yard." Dr. Priestley was "a malignant old Tartuffe." David Rittenhouse had taken French gold to betray his country. Jacobins were "a sort of flesh-flies that naturally settle on the excremental and corrupted parts of the body politic." Abigail Adams observed, not without admiration, that Peter Porcupine "can write very handsomely, and he can descend and be as low and vulgar as a fish wife." Back in England some years later, Cobbett told the younger William Pitt: "Of the violence, the rage of the time, no man not upon the spot can form an adequate idea."

In February, 1798, with still no word from the Commissioners in Paris, Adams asked his cabinet members for their views on what action to take if the French rejected his offer of negotiations or demanded concessions the United States could not comply with. Wolcott, Pickering, and McHenry, having already consulted Alexander Hamilton on these points, advised that the American people were averse to war and would be particularly averse to a war with France. The best course would be to keep the avenues open for negotiation, conduct limited hostilities where necessary, and impress upon Congress the need to appropriate increased revenues for a vigorous defense. McHenry sent, as his own, Hamilton's advice on the tone the President's message should take if the mission failed. It should be "cautious, solemn, grave, and perfectly derobed of all asperity or insult."

At the time when he was thus formulating national policy from his New York law office, Hamilton was grievously tormented by a public scandal — a bedroom-and-blackmail scandal that weakened his leadership in his party and ruined any chances he had for a nomination for the presidency. In this tawdry affair, Bingham, as Hamilton's friend, played a curious and puzzling role.

The story had begun six years earlier, in the summer of 1791. To Hamilton's office on Chestnut Street one day came a young woman, a Maria Reynolds, who was pretty, appealing and in distress. She had been deserted by her husband, she said, and needed money to return to her friends in New York. Would Mr. Hamilton help her? Mr. Hamilton would, but he had no money with him. Could he bring it to her home that evening? He went to the address she gave, a rooming house on Market Street, with a bank note in his pocket. Mrs. Reynolds greeted him at the head of the stairs on the second floor and invited him into her bedroom. He followed her, gave her the money, and talked for a while. He quickly became aware that additional consolation would be acceptable. A few moments later he was in bed with her.

Hamilton was busy that summer running the Treasury Department, defending himself against Republican charges of corruption, and writing his Report on Manufactures, but he found time to meet frequently with Maria Reynolds. Generally she came to his house, his wife Betsy having taken the children to Albany to spend the summer with her father.

In due course, Mrs. Reynolds' husband made his appearance. He had discovered his wife's infidelity, he declared in an outraged letter. "I am determined to have satisfaction. . . . You took advantage of a poor broken harted woman. . . . You have acted the part of the most cruelest man in existance. . . . She ses there is no other man that she care for in this world. now Sir you have been the cause of cooling her affections for me." James Reynolds, however, was not an unreasonable man. For $1000 he would leave Philadelphia and Maria and never return. Having made one foolish mistake, Hamilton made another; he paid the money. The Republicans were accusing him of robbing the United States Treasury of enormous sums, but he had trouble raising $1000 and had to pay it in two installments. Reynolds gave him a receipt marked "in full of all demands."

The visits to Mrs. Reynolds continued through the winter and into the summer of 1792, and so did the demands for money. (Reynolds once asked for $300 with which to speculate in Lancaster Turnpike stock.) When Hamilton tried to end the liaison, Reynolds blusteringly accused him of disrespect for his wife. Maria sent appeals so moving that more than 175 years later they tempt one to regard her (mistakenly) as an innocent woman, or a driven one, in deep anguish.

> oh Col hamilton what have I done that you should thus Neglect me Is it because I am unhappy But stop I will not say you have for perhaps you have caled and have found no opportunity to Come In at least I hope you have I am now A lone and shall be for a few days. . . . oh my deer freend how shal I plede Enough what shall I say Let me beg of you to Come and if you never se me again oh if you think It best I will submit to It and take a long and last adieu.

Again:

> I have kept my Bed those tow dayes and now rise from my pilliow which your Neglect has filled with the shorpest Thorns. . . . I only do it to Ease a heart which is ready Burst with Greef. . . . for God sake be not so voed of all humanity as to deni me this Last request. . . . oh my head I can rite no more do something to Ease My heart.

In the summer of 1792, Reynolds was arrested and imprisoned for attempting to collect a fraudulent claim against the government, on a charge filed by Oliver Wolcott, Hamilton's comptroller of the Treasury. In jail, Reynolds bragged that he had information that would ruin Hamilton. The Secretary, he said, was deeply concerned in speculation and had frequently given him Treasury funds for that purpose. Word of this came to three of Hamilton's political enemies: Frederick Muhlenberg, former speaker of the House, Congressman Abraham Venable, and Senator James Monroe. These three visited Reynolds in jail and Mrs. Reynolds at home and came away with documents and a story that apparently confirmed what they had long believed. They considered going to President Washington to demand Hamilton's dismissal. Instead, they decided to give Hamilton an opportunity to explain himself.

He received the committee of three with Wolcott at his side. They produced the letters and documents supplied by Reynolds. Hamilton heard them out and then told the whole story of liaison and extortion, producing the letters he had received from the Reynoldses. Muhlenberg and Venable tried to stop him halfway through his tale; they were satisfied that there was clearly no evidence that reflected on his conduct as a public official. Monroe agreed with this declaration, and all three swore that as gentlemen they would seal up their papers and never divulge what they had learned. Shortly thereafter, Monroe told the story and sent copies of the documents to Thomas Jefferson.

The secret was kept until the summer of 1797. During the acrimonious political exchanges of those months, the Federalists managed to discharge one of their most annoying critics, John Beckley, from his post as clerk of the House of Representatives. Beckley's secretary had copied the Reynolds documents for Muhlenberg, Venable and Monroe; Beckley had thoughtfully kept copies for himself; and now he resolved to use them to take revenge. He had worked with James T. Callender, the thoroughly unscrupulous journalist who was operating with Jefferson's occasional support and encouragement. To this man he gave the whole Hamilton-Reynolds story as he had heard it, complete with documents.

As Callender told it in a continuing series of pamphlets, Maria Reynolds was an innocent victim of a hypocritical seducer, and James Reynolds had been one of Hamilton's numerous agents in his illicit personal speculations. The pamphlets caused a national sensation.

Hamilton printed a denial in a Republican newspaper, attributing the charges to party spirit, and he asked Muhlenberg, Venable and Monroe to reaffirm publicly their belief in his integrity. The first two responded to Hamilton's satisfaction, but Monroe, who had never fully believed Hamilton's story and was now embittered by his recent dismissal as minister to France, made no answer to this, nor to a second letter.

Hamilton called on Monroe, each with a friend present. Hamilton demanded to know if Monroe had given Callender the Reynolds documents. Monroe angrily replied that he had not. Heated words followed.

Hamilton: "Your representation is totally false."

Monroe, rising: "Do you say I represent falsely? You are a scoundrel!"

Hamilton, rising: "I will meet you like a gentleman."

Monroe: "I am ready. Get your pistols."

Their friends quieted the two men. After a more controlled discussion, everyone agreed to forget what had been said and Monroe consented to issue a joint statement with Muhlenberg and Venable.

Monroe, however, consulted with Jefferson and Madison and, perhaps on their advice, delayed sending the statement. In the meantime, another installment of Callender's story appeared, this one quoting Monroe in a manner prejudicial to Hamilton's honor as a Treasury official. Hamilton called in Major William Jackson, asked him to serve as his second, with authority to choose a time and place for a duel, and gave him a letter for Monroe that was virtually a challenge. ("You have been and are activated by motives toward me malignant and dishonorable.")

Monroe named Aaron Burr as his second, gave him an equally insulting letter (with permission to withhold it if he felt that course advisable) and instructed him to ask Hamilton if he meant to provoke a formal challenge.* Burr withheld Monroe's letter, pacified Hamilton, mollified Monroe, and persuaded the two to draw back from a duel. Each man, explaining that he felt he was responding to a challenge from the other, agreed to let the matter drop.

Hamilton now made his third blunder. Nothing was more important to him than his reputation as an incorruptible public servant, and in order to protect it he resolved to write and publish a full account of the Reynolds affair. His friends pleaded with him, insisting

---

* Monroe laid down one stipulation. Before fighting the duel, he would need three months in which to finish a book defending his conduct as minister to France.

that he would only harm himself, his family and his party. Major Jackson advised him that a controversy with Callender "would only furnish fresh *pabulum* for the virulent invective and abuse of faction to feed on. . . . Your friends and every impartial man are convinced of your purity as a public officer — and no one among them can suppose that you are called on to furnish the Presbyterian pulpits with subject matter of declamation, however irrelevant, against the best political interests of our country." But Hamilton was not to be deterred.

The pamphlet that appeared in August, 1797, was a unique and astonishing work: a frank, detailed and embarrassingly repentant confession of sexual misconduct by Washington's protégé, a hero of the Revolution, a former cabinet member, a present party leader. By quoting the full letters from James and Maria Reynolds, Hamilton proved conclusively that the charge of misuse of federal funds was baseless. "It is necessary," he said, "to suppose me not only unprincipled but a fool to imagine that I would not have found better means of gratifying a criminal avarice, and could have stooped to employ such vile instruments for such insignificant ends."

Major Jackson was right; the Republicans were delighted. They added scorn and ridicule as a new weapon and retreated not a step from their original charges. To some, Maria Reynolds was "an amiable and virtuous wife, seduced from the affections of her husband by artifice and intrigue"; to others she was a strumpet. In either case Hamilton was damned. One reviewer (possibly Beckley) said that Hamilton "holds himself out as trotting from one lodging in Philadelphia to another after . . . a prostitute." Another declared that a man who had made his own home "the rendezvous of his whoredom; taking advantage of the absence of his wife and children to introduce a prostitute to those sacred abodes of conjugal, and filial retirement, to gratify his wicked purposes" could lay claim to no merit except, possibly, that of virility.

"Myself and most of his other friends," General Knox wrote to General Cobb, "conceive this confession humiliating in the extreme, and such a text as will serve his enemies." General Cobb was more philosophic: "Hamilton is fallen for the present, but if he fornicates with every female in the cities of New York and Philadelphia, he will rise again, for purity of character, after a long period of political existence, is not necessary for public patronage." Most of the party leaders agreed with Knox.

Hamilton had grouped his letters, affidavits and other documents at the end of his pamphlet. Any gentleman who wished to see them, he wrote, might call on William Bingham, Esquire, "who is . . . so obliging as to permit me to deposit with him . . . for inspection all the original papers which are contained in the appendix of this narrative." His intentions were clear and understandable, but his actions were not. A mystery has arisen as to just what did happen to the papers that were supposedly deposited with Bingham.

Two years after the publication of the pamphlet, Hamilton wrote urgently to James McHenry in Philadelphia, asking him to get the original papers from Bingham and forward them at once to him in New York. Bingham was at Lansdown. McHenry immediately sent his servant there with a note. The servant returned with a letter which McHenry the same day sent on to Hamilton:

> It surely must have escaped Gen[l] Hamilton's recollection that the papers he alludes to were never deposited with me.
>
> After reading the publication in which he mentioned this deposit being thus made, I was surprised at the omission. . . .

He had not reminded Hamilton of the circumstance, Bingham said, because nobody had applied to him to inspect the papers and he thought "it would not have been delicate to have addressed him on the subject."

Broadus Mitchell, who discovered these letters, writes in his biography of Hamilton (1962):

> The episode is strange on several accounts. In the pamphlet Hamilton said he had Bingham's permission to be the keeper of the evidence, but Bingham knew nothing of this until he saw it in print. However, in the hurry of bringing out the distasteful pamphlet Hamilton likely took for granted Bingham's willingness. Why did Hamilton not immediately afterward put the papers with Bingham? If he sent them by a friend who failed to deliver them, it was not McHenry, for the latter took pains to say "I do not remember to have seen the papers alluded to." If Hamilton lodged the documents with another, it would have been someone in Philadelphia;

Wolcott comes to mind, but this impassioned archive is not among his effects. Where are these letters of entreaty, blackmail, and reproach? Why was Hamilton suddenly eager to have them in his hands again?

The mystery, Mitchell points out, is compounded by a still later development. In July, 1801, on the eve of a trip to Europe, Bingham wrote to Hamilton: "Having a packet of papers which by your desire were deposited with me, and which have long laid dormant in my possession . . . permit me to return them to you." Were these the Reynolds papers? If they were, why had Bingham forgotten, or refused to admit, that he had them?

Half-War with France

*Long since, in my opinion, a wise policy required a declaration of war
[against France]. . . . Should it pass the House, there is no doubt it will
prevail in the Senate. Indeed I know no man, except our friend Bingham, who can be called federal, who will not vote for it.*

Theodore Sedgwick to Rufus King
Philadelphia, July 1, 1798

ON MONDAY, MARCH 19, 1798, John Adams sent a message to Congress. Dispatches, he said, had been received from Paris, examined,
and maturely considered. Though everything possible had been
done, the American envoys were unable to complete their mission on
terms compatible with the nation's safety, honor and essential interests. The country should rearm and prepare to defend its commerce
and territory. By Presidential order, American merchant vessels
would now be permitted to sail under arms.

The Republicans were outraged. Vice President Jefferson privately called the message "insane." Gallatin demanded to know why
the Federalists did not ask Congress for a declaration of war, if they
were willing to go to war without a declaration. Others called the
Federalists "war hawks" and Adams "a hoary-headed incendiary"
whose first aim was a war with France "in order to yoke us into an
alliance with the British tyrant." The charge against her husband
hurt Abigail Adams. "What benifit can war be to him?" she asked.
"He has no ambition for military glory. He cannot add by war to his
peace, comfort or happiness. It must accumulate upon him an additional load of care, toil, trouble, malice, hatred, and I dare say revenge."

Adams, expecting a full-scale war,* withheld the contents of the

---

* Abigail acted on this belief; she bought fifty pounds of coffee and 150 pounds of
brown sugar for the larder of the Presidential mansion. To her sister she wrote on
June 25, "I expect Congress to declare war before they rise."

dispatches until his envoys could leave France in safety. Republicans in the House demanded that the documents be made available to Congress, though Gallatin warned them that they might be walking into a trap. The Federalist leaders, he felt — Senators Sedgwick, Tracy, and Bingham, Representatives Dayton, Bayard, Otis, and Harper — obviously knew the contents of the dispatches, and they were too bland, too quiet, and too willing to have them made public. But Jefferson had implanted the idea that Adams was holding back the papers because they contained information harmful to him or his party, and the Republican clamor could neither be stilled nor denied. To the amusement of the Federalists, the resolution to read the dispatches passed the Republican-controlled House on April 2 by a large majority. The next day, the House and Senate, in separate sessions, cleared their galleries, locked and put guards at the doors, and sat back to listen to the recounting of one of the strangest episodes in the history of diplomacy.

The American envoys — Marshall, Pinckney, and Gerry — had arrived in Paris at an unpropitious time. The Directory was at the height of its power. Napoleon had won an unbroken series of victories on the Continent and imposed peace treaties on several defeated nations. The extremist Directors, friends of Napoleon, had just arrested their moderate opponents and shipped them, with many of their followers, to the penal colony of Cayenne in French Guiana. The Directors refused to see the Americans, and Talleyrand, their new foreign minister, coldly, courteously refused to accept their credentials.

After days of waiting, they were visited by a Monsieur Bellarni, secret agent to Talleyrand, who introduced three shadowy figures named Hottinguer, Bellamy, and Hauteval. (In releasing the dispatches, Secretary of State Pickering prudently substituted the letters W, X, Y and Z for Bellarni and his companions.) Three things would be necessary, they said, before the Directors would consent to receive the Americans. The envoys would have to apologize in writing for certain statements President Adams had made in his inaugural address last May. They must promise to make a $12,800,000 loan to France. And they should produce a *douceur* — a "sweetener" — of some $250,000 for M. Talleyrand.*

* During his several years as foreign minister under the Directory, Talleyrand (who

Pinckney, Marshall, and Gerry were slow to understand the demands. Hottinguer (X) at last broke out impatiently, "Gentlemen, you do not speak to the point; it is money; it is expected that you will offer money. Nothing can be obtained here without money." Bellamy (Y): "You must pay money; you must pay a great deal of money." Hottinguer, Bellamy, or Hauteval: "Don't you know that everything is bought in Paris? Do you dream that you can get on with this Government without paying your way?" Pinckney stammered out an answer: "It is no, no, not a sixpence" — a declaration which, when it crossed the ocean, was somewhat improved to "Millions for defense, but not one cent for tribute!"

When the Americans continued to refuse the demands of Messieurs X, Y, and Z, Beaumarchais, as charming and witty as ever at sixty-seven, appeared on the scene. He greeted John Marshall warmly, for Marshall was his attorney in his suit to collect unpaid claims for money and goods he had advanced to the American government during the War of Independence. He would be happy, he said, to credit the $250,000 payment to M. Talleyrand against his own claim. Marshall refused. "France," Beaumarchais advised the Americans, "considers herself sufficiently powerful to give the law to the world." She was exacting money from all the countries around her to finish the war against England; all who did not help her must accept the consequences.

More direct threats were then conveyed. The Directors were ready "to take a decided course with America" if the envoys did not soften their stand. The Americans should remember the fate of Genoa and Venice. Nor should they expect help from England, for France would soon invade that country and break her. Where would America be then? The pro-French Republican party in America, moreover, "strongly in our interest," would thwart the measures of Mr. Adams and his Federalist friends.

In Philadelphia, the House and Senate listened to these revelations in shocked silence. The Republican majority in the House quickly voted to keep the dispatches from being made public, but Senate Federalists called for open publication. The complete text appeared

despised Americans because of their passion for acquiring money) extorted an estimated $625,000 in bribes from various defeated or threatened countries.

in the newspapers; the government distributed 10,000 copies in pamphlet form.* These hit the country with a violent blow.

"The Jacobins in the Senate and House were struck dumb," Abigail Adams wrote to her sister with satisfaction, "and opened not their mouths, not having their cue" from Talleyrand's agents in America. Republicans dropped from the party, Fisher Ames said, "like windfalls from an apple tree in September." Jefferson, his impressions "very disagreeable and confused," told his party that there must be some mistake; the dispatches contained the "most artful misrepresentations"; the Directors, high-minded and magnanimous men, were above suspicion, and X, Y, and Z were obviously swindlers acting without the knowledge or authority of the Directory or of Talleyrand. The best course now, he said, was to work for an adjournment on the plea that the members should consult their constituents in this grave crisis. For his part, he felt it his duty to remain silent. A number of his colleagues agreed; they simply fled from the session of Congress and went home, leaving Gallatin to defend the Republican position.

Addresses of support poured in to the government. The merchants of Philadelphia held a meeting and sent a letter of thanks to the President for "his firm and steady conduct." Some 1100 young men of Philadelphia marched in a column of twos to martial music, the Federalist black cockade in their hats, to stand before Adams' residence and there declare their support of his administration.† John Adams, never widely popular (Alexander Baring judged him "a man of rather dull genius and no popular talents"), was suddenly a public hero, warmly acclaimed when he appeared before the people. The new songs "Hail, Columbia!" and "Adams and Liberty!" were played over and over. The French cockade and the revolutionary marching song "Ça Ira" were seen and heard no more.

Early in June, John Marshall arrived in Boston, having put forth the American position in a strong memorial to Talleyrand before demanding his passport. Entering Philadelphia on his way to Richmond, he received a welcome second only to those given Washington. The Federalist members of Congress, William Bingham among

* It was the first printing of a U. S. public document.
† Their leader and spokesman was seventeen-year-old Robert Hare, Anne Bingham's nephew, who as a child in 1783 had sailed with the Binghams to England.

them, rode out to meet him at Frankford and held a formal dinner at Oeller's Tavern as a tribute of "affection, approbation and respect." Bingham wrote to Rufus King in London:

> The spirit of the people is roused, and the enthusiasm which prevails would astonish those persons who recently contemplated the apparent apathy of the American character. . . .
>
> By the addresses from all quarters of the Union you will observe that the people are ripe for the support of the most decisive measures of the government. There is more danger at present of overstepping the bounds of prudence than of falling short in the adoption of such a system as the occasion may call for.

In the spring of 1798, the seventeen Federalist members of the Senate met in William Bingham's house. It was proposed that the Federalists — with a majority of two in the Senate — should follow a new legislative procedure known as a "caucus." They would assemble at intervals in Bingham's house to vote in private on important measures, and all those present would then firmly support the majority position in the Senate. The decision to follow this course was carried by a vote of nine to eight; the minority members accepted it; and on most of the ensuing legislation the Federalist Senators voted as a bloc. Bingham stood with his party in support of "the most decisive measures" short of a declaration of war. He headed a three-man committee to draw up plans for creating a Department of the Navy, independent of the Army and with cabinet rank, and he voted for the bill (passed). He voted to authorize a militia force of 80,000 men; to raise a regular army of 10,000; to build twelve more warships; and to appropriate $250,000 to fortify ports and harbors and $800,000 for military supplies.* He voted to suspend commercial intercourse with France, to abrogate all treaties between the two countries, and to encourage the capture of armed French vessels on the high seas, either by American warships or by armed merchant ships sailing as privateers.†

In June, the Federalists did indeed, as Bingham had feared, over-

---

* A contract for 10,000 flintlock muskets was given to Eli Whitney of New Haven through his friend Oliver Wolcott. Whitney manufactured these under his new principle of mass production based on use of interchangeable parts.
† He also presented a memorial calling for printing a journal of the proceedings of Congress and again voted against an appropriation to complete the buildings in Washington (again passed).

step the bounds of prudence. They decided that the time had come to set the country right with a series of laws to curb aliens and punish sedition. They lengthened the required residence before naturalization from five to fourteen years for aliens arriving after 1795. They empowered the President to arrest, imprison and expel, by executive decree, those aliens he considered dangerous to the peace and safety of the country. They passed a Sedition Act to fine and imprison any person convicted in a jury trial of conspiring to oppose or interfere with the legal measures of government, or of publishing any false, scandalous or malicious writing against the President or the Congress.

The Federalists considered the Sedition Act — the most important of the new laws — as a measure necessary to protect the republic against treason, subversion, insurrection, and civil war. They also considered it a means of silencing and punishing their political enemies. Unfortunately, they believed the two aims to be synonymous. In Gallatin's words, they "altogether confounded evidences of dissatisfaction at certain measures of Administration with a decided hatred against government of their own choice."

Not one Federalist leader opposed these measures when they were enacted. Washington, Adams, and Hamilton supported them. So did John Jay, Gouverneur Morris, and a score of lesser men. Bingham voted to pass the Naturalization and the Alien Laws. His votes on the Sedition Act indicate doubts and perhaps moral or political perturbation. Senator James Lloyd of Maryland, author of the bill, wrote it to accord with his conviction (expressed to General Washington) that war with France was "necessary to enable us to lay our hands on traitors." Bingham voted against bringing in the Lloyd bill, against allowing it a second reading, and for sending it to committee for revision — thus ignoring the agreement reached in party caucus in his own home. He voted to allow the recast bill a third reading, but withheld his vote for final passage, as did several other Federalist members.*

---

* In what is sometimes called the "Federalist Reign of Terror," Adams used the Alien Act to expel two aliens, both Irish journalists. The possibility of trouble caused some thousands of Frenchmen to return to France, among them Count Volney, his faith in American republican virtues crushed. The Alien Enemies Act, a war measure, was not applied; it is still in force today. Under the Sedition Act, some twenty-five persons were arrested; fifteen were indicted, most of them Republican editors; and ten were convicted and punished, the longest term being four years.

With his Federalist colleagues, both extremist and moderate, Bingham held certain strong convictions about the world situation. In 1798, these men looked on Revolutionary France and Napoleon with much the same revulsion and anger that men of good will in the fourth and fifth decades of the twentieth century looked on Germany and Hitler, or Soviet Russia and Stalin, and for many of the same reasons. They regarded England, the sole remaining power fighting France, as the last shield against an expansionist, aggressive and demoniacal tyranny. The Revolutionary French soldiers, "wiping their bloody hands on their horses' manes," were overrunning and plundering Europe, setting up puppet states, and encouraging revolt in neutral and unfriendly countries, all in the name of a new order.

The Federalists, indeed, spoke in phrases that were echoed in a later crisis. "The fate of England," William Bingham said, "will have a great influence on the political situation of this country. I cannot but entertain very serious apprehensions for the result when I see the preponderance that France is daily acquiring on the Continent, and no union of force or consort of governments to oppose her ambitious projects. . . . She has impressed a terror which operates like a stroke of a torpedo, and has benumbed all the faculties of the European powers. If she continues a little longer in her career, she will have Europe at her feet."

Fisher Ames: "One nation alone resists these new Romans and prevents the establishment of a universal domination and a despotism over the whole civilized world."

Harrison Gray Otis: "Great Britain . . . is the only barrier to the dreadful deluge, and when that is broken down, it will be time for us to prepare to be good and dutiful subjects to the French."

Senator George Cabot: "If England will persevere, she will save Europe and save us; if she yields, all will be lost. . . . She is now the only barrier between us and the deathly embraces of universal irreligion, immorality and plunder."

These were the words of men genuinely concerned for the safety of their country, though they are now seldom credited with sincerity in their views.* In the context of these convictions, it is understand-

* For example, Claude G. Bowers in *Jefferson and Hamilton:* "It was the fashion in those days to conceal a hatred of democracy under the cloak of a simulated horror over the crimes of the [French] terrorists." Or Joseph Charles, *The Origins of the American*

able, if not defensible, that the Federalists considered the American "French party" a threat to the national security. The country was young, the instruments of government were new, and "party faction" abroad had led to revolution. The French Directory was boasting of its control over American Republicans. The major Republican newspapers had nothing but praise for the French and blame for the British, and they were printing the most indecent personal invective and lies against the President and Federalist members of Congress. The party constantly boasted of irresistible French power and, almost as if on command, opposed every move to arm the country — even the fortifying of American ports and harbors.

The country, moreover, was in a state of open if undeclared hostility with France, and few Federalists doubted in 1798 that this would become full-scale war. If that happened, the possibility of French invasion seemed very real. The Federalists correctly suspected that Bonaparte, having upset the balance of power in Europe, planned to reestablish the French empire in North America by taking over Canada, Florida, and the American West. Rufus King sent a grave warning to Bingham from London in the fall of 1798:

> We deceive ourselves if we believe that the Directory believe us; they and their agents perfectly understand their business, and by our divisions are encouraged to persevere in their fixed purpose to overthrow our government and break up our Union. I respect your good sense and character too highly to express to you this opinion, did I not most religiously entertain it; and unless the Senators and Representatives, with a majority of our people likewise believe and act with vigor upon this opinion, the Government and the country are lost. No man is more deeply concerned than you are in the security and prosperity of the country; no one is more able to form a correct estimate of the dangers to which it is liable; I therefore hope that the crisis has drawn your attention to the subject.

A declaration of war was to have been the last major measure of the Congress before it retired. President Adams wanted a declaration; he

---

Party System: "We cannot, however, go so far as to say that war with France was to be merely a blind, an excuse of the High-Federalists for proceeding against their opponents at home. Rather, they regarded the principles of liberty and equality as infections which must be stamped out wherever they were to be found."

wrote a hot message to Congress virtually declaring war on France, there being "no alternative between actual hostilities on our part and national ruin." For good measure, he also declared war on the American Republicans, who had encouraged the French government, "by professions . . . of unqualified devotion to the French Republic," to believe that a majority of Americans preferred the French government to their own. He then put the message away and did not send it.

Some Federalists wanted a declaration of war on principle; some wanted it as retaliation against the mounting French attacks on American ships; a few hoped for war as a means of consolidating political power and crushing the "French party." Senator Theodore Sedgwick of Massachusetts was practical and frank. To Rufus King he wrote on July 1 that if Congress did not declare war, "the people . . . will be induced to believe that the friends of peace [i.e., Republicans] may save them from the calamity of war. But . . . if war be inevitable, it may reasonably be hoped that the people, in their selection of characters, will choose those who are best qualified to conduct it [i.e., Federalists]." If the motion was put, he said, it would pass the Senate with the vote of every Federalist Senator save one: William Bingham was opposed to a declaration of war.

The goal for the date of the declaration was set for July 4, Independence Day. Dependable party men from both houses of Congress met to caucus in Bingham's home on the evening of July 1. The leaders called for war. Senator Bingham and a number of Representatives refused. The motion was rejected by a majority of five votes; and thus was defeated what one historian has called "the most serious attempt in American history to declare war without a recommendation by the President." * Secretary of State Pickering, organizer of the drive for war, was enraged. To him, Bingham was thenceforth an undependable man.

The Senate adjourned its legislative duties on July 16 but at the President's request remained in executive session to approve the appointment of general officers of the new army. Hamilton and the cabinet members, without consulting Adams, had persuaded General Washington (now sixty-six) to come out of retirement as commander of the army. Washington did so with the understanding that Hamil-

* Manning J. Dauer, *The Adams Federalists,* 1953, p. 170.

ton (Adams' rival and enemy) would be his second in command and that the other "principal officers in the line and staff shall be such as I can place confidence in." He named Charles Cotesworth Pinckney and Henry Knox as third and fourth in line of command. Knox, who had outranked both Hamilton and Pinckney, besides having been Secretary of War, rejected the appointment with a hurt and reproachful letter.

To the list of nine brigadiers Washington sent from Mount Vernon, Adams added the name of William Stephens Smith, his daughter Nabby's husband, as adjutant general. Colonel Smith was extravagant and improvident and was addicted to what Mrs. Adams called "vissions, ideal schemes, etc." He had recently failed for a large sum in shady land speculations, causing heavy losses to his creditors. Some doubts had been cast on his honesty, but Adams was satisfied that he had simply been made a fool of by a Frenchman, "a swindler and a mountebank." The Colonel was given to long, silent absences, leaving Nabby and the children with his family in remote Lebanon Valley in New York state. Nabby wrote to her mother that existence had become a burden to her and that she was little short of distraction. Said Mrs. Adams to her sister, "Every heart knows its own bitterness."

The bitterness must have been compounded by the career of Royall Tyler, the Harvard law student whom Nabby, at the urging of her mother, had rejected as unstable and frivolous. Tyler was a successful lawyer on the way to becoming a popular and respected chief justice of the Supreme Court of Vermont and professor of jurisprudence at the University of Vermont. He had written several successful works for the stage, including *The Contrast* — the first important American play and the first American comedy produced by a professional company.* His picaresque novel, *The Algerine Captive,* was being widely read in 1798.

When Secretary Pickering saw Smith's name on the list of officers, he went at once to a group of Federalist Senators to complain of the impropriety of appointing a man who was a bankrupt and, besides, was suspected of having Republican sympathies. Three Senators called on Adams and advised him to withdraw the name. He refused. The next day, William Bingham and John Laurance of New York

* In it appeared "Jonathan," the first of a long line of stage Yankees.

waited on the President in his residence as a committee of two. The Senate, they reported, was ready to adjourn, having consented to all appointments except that of Colonel Smith. It was one of the most humiliating moments of John Adams' long life — an insult, "designed by a damned faction purposely to wound my feelings and character."

Bingham returned to inform the Senate that the President would have a further communication to make. A few minutes later, a two-line message was received nominating a William North as a substitute for Colonel Smith in the post of Adjutant General of the United States.

"All the actions of my life," Adams lamented to Abigail, "and all the conduct of my children have not disgraced me so much as this man. His pay will not feed his dogs; and his dogs must be fed if his children starve. What a folly!" And to Colonel Smith:

> Upon this occasion I must be plain with you. Your pride and ostentation, which I myself have seen with inexpressible grief for many years, have excited among your neighbors . . . envy and resentment. . . . It is a great misfortune to the public that the office I hold should be disgraced by a nomination of my son-in-law, which the Senate of the United States think themselves obliged to negative." *

John Adams left in mid-July for Braintree, where Abigail became seriously ill, and remained there for almost four months, some 400 miles from the capital, leaving his cabinet to run the government. The Federalists won the fall elections of 1798, partly through defections of Republican voters. Bingham was dubious about these political proselytes. "I am confident," he said, "that many of them possess a disorganizing mind, and that in their hearts there is still lurking a secret attachment to the French cause."

Indeed, the Republicans were recovering from their dismay over the XYZ Papers and were using the Alien and Sedition Acts to rally their forces. They expressed their organized opposition in resolutions written by Jefferson and Madison and passed by the Kentucky

---

* Adams later nominated Smith to command a regiment of the provisional army with the rank of lieutenant colonel — a lower rank than he had held fifteen years earlier. Adams hoped Smith would have the pride to refuse; he did not. Pickering again opposed the appointment, but the Senate passed it by a narrow margin.

and Virginia legislatures, declaring that the federal government had been consistently violating states' rights, charging that the new acts were unconstitutional, and hinting at resistance and secession. Finding little support for their position, they turned to a more rewarding issue. The Federalist Congress had imposed a tax on slaves (fifty cents a head on those between twelve and fifty years of age) and on real estate ("the window tax") to pay for its defense measures. Citizens who were indifferent to the Sedition Act were stirred to anger by their share of $2,000,000 in direct taxes and by a budget that had soared to nearly $8,000,000.

General Hamilton moved to Philadelphia and devoted his driving energy to recruiting, equipping, and training the new army. In choosing officers of the higher ranks, he was careful to name only those with demonstrable Federalist sympathies and connections. He recommended, however, that some of the appointments in the lower grades might be made without regard to political affiliation, observing that a Republican, if caught young enough, might be converted into a true American. General Washington did not agree. "You could as soon scrub a blackamoor white," he said, "as to change the principles of a profest democrat. . . . He will leave nothing uninterrupted to overturn the government of this country."

One of the Republicans to whom Hamilton refused a brigadier's commission, though Adams spoke in his behalf, was Aaron Burr. Colonel Burr, he felt, was a brave man, but he was an intriguer.

CHAPTER 26

The Confrontation

Mr. President, we have not the most distant idea of interfering with your official duties or powers. It is out of pure regard and respect for them that we have requested this interview.

William Bingham to President John Adams
February 23, 1799

PHILADELPHIA suffered another yellow fever epidemic in the summer of 1798, one almost as devastating as that of five years earlier. The Binghams fled at the end of July to Bellevue, their summer home. From there on the Jersey Coast Bingham wrote to his friend and fellow Senator, Colonel Jacob Read of South Carolina (he who had given the two fawns for the Mansion House lawn):

If some means cannot be adopted to prevent the introduction of these destructive fevers into our cities, they will be in a great measure depopulated, for independent of the risk of life, the inconveniences and loss resulting from the frequent and sudden removals of the inhabitants, are more oppressive than the tradesmen and lower class of people can continue to submit to. They will seek a more tranquil and less exposed situation. . . .

I see no prospect of its progress being arrested, but by an entire change in the atmosphere, by means of a severe frost, which cannot be looked for before the middle of October, until which time I expect my return will be retarded.

Your ideas are very just with respect to the salubrity of the air of Bellevue. We have enjoyed a perfect state of health, a cool summer, a great deal of exercise and luxurious living. We have had many visits from our friends, which has occasioned a diversity in our scenes of amusement.

In short, if my pleasure had not been checked by contemplating the sufferings of our devoted city, I might truly say that I never should have passed a more agreeable summer.

The wedding of Ann Louisa Bingham, seventeen, and Alexander Baring, just short of twenty-five, had been scheduled to take place at Lansdown in October, but since the epidemic precluded a return to the city or its outskirts, the wedding was held at Bellevue. On August 23, the commercial alliance between Bingham and the Barings became a family connection. Bingham wrote to accept the "friendly congratulations" of Colonel and Mrs. Read:

> It is an event the most anxious and interesting to the feelings of a parent, by fixing the future fortunes and influencing the happiness of his child. In the present instance, I experienced the greatest satisfaction, from the consideration of the unexceptionable character and amiable qualities of the gentleman with whom she is connected. When in the progress of time and the course of events you shall witness so solemn a scene in your own family, I hope, my friend, you may have cause to view it with the same cheerful composure that I witnessed this ceremony.

To General Knox, Bingham expressed a similar satisfaction at the match, though he observed cautiously that Mr. Baring had "more worth than property."

Bingham gave his daughter a marriage settlement of £500 a year. Back in Philadelphia, he bought and gave to the newly married couple the house in his block on Third Street that had belonged to Anne Bingham's Aunt Elizabeth Powel. This was the thirty-three-year-old, four-story Powel House, an elegant town residence with a symmetrical garden in the rear. Its broad doorway set between semi-engaged columns led to a spacious hall and a stairway paneled with solid Santo Domingo mahogany. The rooms had mahogany doors, fine woodwork and chimney pieces, decorative plaster ceilings, chandeliers of Irish cut glass, and Chinese wallpaper of painted scenes.*

*

When Bingham answered to the opening roll call of the third session of the Fifth Congress on December 3, 1798, there was a sense of impending crisis in the air. The High-Federalists were calling for a

---

* The Powel House, a property of the Philadelphia Society for the Preservation of Landmarks, today is open to the public. Rooms from the house are in the Metropolitan Museum and the Philadelphia Museum of Art.

declaration of war, with the implication that the full force of the Alien and Sedition laws would then be unleashed. John Fenno, editor of the leading Federal paper, the Philadelphia *Gazette of the United States,* greeted the lawmakers with a fiery editorial. The government, he said, was under a moral obligation to declare open and honorable war against France. To be sure, this formality would not much alter the country's relations with France, but it would very materially alter the internal situation.

> Until that is done, France will not abandon her hopes here; and divisions will be constantly excited and fomented by them. But that act would . . . at once . . . crush the French party in this country. At the same time, it would not create an enemy, but only put us in a situation to act with more energy against the enemy that has already attacked us.

As the basis for his address to Congress, Adams used a paper given him by Oliver Wolcott but largely dictated by Alexander Hamilton in New York. Nothing had been revealed in the conduct of the French, he told a crowded session, to justify relaxing the preparations for defense voted at the last session. French menaces and aggression were continuing. Americans wanted peace, but only vigorous preparations for war would strengthen America's hand in any settlement with France.

In June, Adams had declared to Congress, "I will never send another minister to France without assurances that he will be received, respected, and honored, as the representative of a great, free, powerful and independent nation." Now he changed the Hamilton-Wolcott material that had been given him in a slight but significant way. He said, "To send another minister *without more determinate assurances* that he would be received would be an act of humiliation." The message made a favorable impression; no one commented on Adams' signal to the French.

Preparations for war proceeded. The Senate drew up tighter restrictions on commercial intercourse with France; Bingham was one of three Senators appointed to align the bill with the House version. Both houses passed an act to authorize calling forth the militia "to execute the laws of the Union, suppress insurrection, and repel invasion." It passed another to increase the army to 30,000 men in the event of war. Bingham supported these bills. In the intervals between warlike measures, he voted for a bill to raise salaries in the executive department (passed); and he bolted his party in voting to permit aliens to buy, hold, and bequeath land in the Northwest Territory (defeated).

During this time, Alexander Baring added a new activity to his trading pursuits. The House of Baring bought 11,000 muskets from the British government and 330 cannon from the Woolwich Arsenal, and with government permission sent them to America. They were received by a consortium of buyers in Boston, New York, Baltimore, and Philadelphia, Tench Francis being the Philadelphia representative.

On Monday, February 18, 1799, an incredulous Thomas Jefferson, as presiding officer of the Senate, opened and read a message from the President that shocked and horrified the Federalist members. Without having consulted or informed Congress, his cabinet or his party, Adams announced that he would send still another peace envoy and minister to the French Republic. He requested the Senate to confirm William Vans Murray, now minister at The Hague, in that post. With the message he enclosed a letter to Murray from Louis Pichon, French *chargé d'affaires* at The Hague, containing an assurance from Talleyrand that if the United States would send another minister to Paris he would be received (Adams' exact words of the previous June were here used) "with the respect due to the representative of a great, free, powerful and independent nation." Since the letter came indirectly from the French government, Adams said, Murray would not go to Paris until a direct and explicit assurance had been received.

The message caused a sensation in the Senate chamber, in Philadelphia and, within a few days, throughout the country.* The Republicans were suspicious of Adams' motives but overjoyed at his action. The Federalists felt themselves betrayed; they had known nothing of the President's action before it happened; Talleyrand was the most perfidious double-dealer in Europe and his overture was a French trick; the country would lose its martial spirit and relax in its effort to arm itself; the French party and its editors would be strengthened,

---

* "It was one of the most stunning surprises in the history of American foreign policy." John C. Miller in *Alexander Hamilton: Portrait in Paradox*, 1959, p. 493.

and they would appear to be confirmed in their contention that the French were true friends of the United States; the country might be drawn into the European war on the side of France.

In their confusion and dismay, the Federalists maintained a decent if pained silence in public, but in their conversation and correspondence they attacked Adams with varying mixtures of rage, disappointment, and contempt. Some thought him mad; some thought he had gone over to the Republicans; others believed he was already angling for votes for a second term. Senator Theodore Sedgwick of Boston, a close family friend of the Adamses in earlier days, declared, "Had the foulest heart and ablest head in the world have been permitted to select the most embarrassing and ruinous measure, perhaps it would have been precisely the one which has been adopted." It was, he said, one of "the wild and irregular starts of a vain, jealous, and half frantic mind." * Hamilton decided that vanity, jealousy, and spite must have led Adams astray. "Passion," he observed, "wrests the helm from reason."

John Fenno was so shocked that he resigned his editorship of the *Gazette of the United States.* Sir Robert Liston, the British minister, reported to his foreign office that the rumor about Adams' being in his dotage was apparently untrue, but that the American government was tottering. "Rivalries have been irritated to madness," John Adams wrote to Abigail; and Abigail replied from Braintree that the appointment of Murray had stirred "the whole community . . . like a flock of frightened pigions." Both were amused — perhaps Abigail more than her husband — when a Federalist editor declared that if Mrs. Adams had only been in Philadelphia she never would have permitted the President to do such a thing.

Adams, in cold fact, had good reason to conclude that the French were reversing their policy and wanted peace with the United States; and, having begun to realize that his cabinet members were under Hamilton's control rather than his own, he had reason to act without consulting them.

Talleyrand had been surprised at the vehemence of the American response to the XYZ disclosures and at the extent of American rearm-

---

* Sedgwick had written an unctuous letter to Adams the previous September proposing himself for the vacancy on the United States Supreme Court caused by the death of James Wilson. There is no record of how Adams refused the proposal.

ament. He had no desire to face an army commanded by George Washington, the demigod of the age. The Americans now had four-teen warships and scores of armed merchant ships prowling the Car-ibbean sea. Jefferson had talked privately with Victor Constant du Pont de Nemours, French consul at Charleston, and told him that France's policies were certain to drive the United States into an alli-ance with Britain; du Pont's report of the conversation had impressed Talleyrand. Finally, Talleyrand was engaged in delicate negotiations to take back the Louisiana Territory from Spain and so outflank the United States, and to do this he needed time. Having concluded that he had overreached himself in his simple desire to bend the United States to French will and to make himself a little personal cash, he sent the letter to Pichon at The Hague with orders to pass it on to Murray.

On the evening of the same day the President's message was re-ceived, the Federalist Senators, almost in a state of shock, met in Bingham's house to determine a course of policy. There was nearly unanimous sentiment for rejecting the President's nomination of Murray and thereby to head off a third peace mission to France; but the moderates, of whom Bingham was one, realized the consequences of such an action. If Adams carried the fight for a settlement with France to the American people, he would win, for rank-and-file Fed-eralists respected the President and would follow his lead. If thwarted, he was even capable of resigning and turning the government over to Jefferson, the head of the French party.

The Senators drew up a plan. A committee of five would call on the President and ask him to withdraw his request. If he refused, he would be asked to add two other Federalists to serve as envoys with Murray. If he refused that, he would be told that the Senate would "negative" his nomination of Murray as a single envoy, regardless of the consequences. The Senators chosen to call on the President were Sedgwick, Bingham, James Ross, senior Pennsylvania Senator, Jacob Read of South Carolina, and Richard Stockton of New Jersey. "You would suppose," Pickering wrote sourly to George Cabot, "that all these might be depended on in every Federal question except Bing-ham." Bingham, Pickering felt, was undependable because of his vote against war the previous summer. He must be against war, Pickering decided, because he hoped to profit financially from certain commercial enterprises that the war crisis had interrupted.

These five men met, probably at Bingham's, on Thursday of that week, after the day's Senate session had ended. There was considerable debate and even some dissension. A majority of the members insisted that the Senate had the right to decide not only on the personal fitness of the envoy, which was relatively unimportant, but also on the main issue: the impropriety of the mission itself and the terms of the negotiations. The moderates prevailed again, citing the President's constitutional powers. The members agreed unanimously to limit themselves solely to the qualifications of Murray as an envoy. Sedgwick lamented that Adams had obliged them "to practice an infraction of correct principles, a direct communication between the President and the Senate."

There was discussion of Sedgwick's intemperate anger at Adams' heinous deed, and he was cautioned not to stir up trouble by mentioning Elbridge Gerry, Adams' pro-French Republican friend, or "Gerryism," in talking to the President.* As the oldest man present, at fifty-three, Sedgwick was named chairman of the committee; Bingham was named to speak for the committee during the actual confrontation with the President.

The committee then wrote a respectful letter to the President requesting permission to wait upon and discuss with him the subject of the nomination. An answer was returned immediately. Mr. Adams would be happy to see the group at his house at seven o'clock on Saturday evening. He would see them, however, *as gentlemen*, not as a committee. The meeting was to set no precedent in the handling of foreign affairs.

At the appointed hour on February 23, the group walked to the President's house at 190 Market Street, at Sixth, a block north of Congress Hall. A servant opened the door and led them to the drawing room. President Adams rose from his seat, advanced on the com-

---

* Gerry, the minority (Republican) member of the "XYZ" mission, had stayed in Paris against the indignant protests of his colleagues, Marshall and Pinckney. Wooed, coerced and threatened by Talleyrand, he hoped that he might yet save the United States from two terrible disasters: war with France and alliance with England. Pickering expressed the wish that Gerry might be guillotined but feared that he would return and, in the manner of James Monroe, write a book defending his conduct.

mittee, and at once made a statement. "His manner," Stockton recalled years later, "was that of a gentleman not well pleased addressing gentlemen whom he meant to rebuke; and there was something of passion and of conscious superiority, as I thought, in all that he said."

"Gentlemen," he began, "I am glad to see you as friends and members of the Senate. But, as a committee, interfering, as I think you are, with my executive duties, I cannot consent to receive you, and I protest against all such interference. I have a duty to execute, and so have you. I know and shall do mine, and want neither your opinion nor aid in its execution." Having made his position clear, he asked the five Senators to be seated.

Bingham answered for the group. They had not the most distant idea of interfering with the President's official duties or powers. It was out of pure regard and respect for those prerogatives that they had requested the interview. "A difference of opinion between the President and the Senate on such a matter as Mr. Murray's nomination," he said, "would be lamented by all the friends of your administration. It is only to avoid this that this committee has requested the interview."

President Adams read in this an intimation that the Senate might reject his nomination, and he became (in Stockton's words) "somewhat warm." "Well, then, gentlemen," he said, "if you are determined to interfere in diplomatic affairs, reject Mr. Murray. You have the power to do this, and you may do it, but it is upon your own responsibility."

One of the committeemen said, "Sending a minister to France, so soon after your resolution communicated to both houses that you would send none until you had received satisfaction for the insults already received, will be considered an act of humiliation. If France is sincere, she will send a minister to us."

The President replied, "Here you are all wrong, gentlemen. I know more of diplomatic forms than all of you. It was in France that we received the insult, and in France I am determined that we shall receive the reparation."

The Senators observed that Mr. Murray was not of sufficient stature for the mission. He had been absent from the country for two years, moreover, and could not know the state of public feeling. To send him to Paris "after three of our first men have been sent home appears to be abandoning our ground."

"I must defend the executive against oligarchic influence," Adams said. "It is absolutely necessary that I insist on the nomination." He emphasized that under no circumstances would Mr. Murray be permitted to leave Holland until positive assurance had been received from the French that he would be treated in a manner suitable to the minister of the United States. "Mr. Murray," the President said, "is a gentleman of talents, address, and literature, as well as of great worth and honor, and fully adequate to all that I should require of him, which would be a strict compliance with his instruction."

He was asked why he had not nominated Rufus King to the post. The President answered in words that indicate a display of exaggerated patience. "If Mr. King had been in Holland, I certainly should not have thought of any other character. But he is our ambassador to England, and England is at war with France, and France would consider it an insult if we sent them our ambassador to England, who, as soon as he had accomplished his business would return to England and carry with him all the information he might have collected in Paris. The French government would suspect me of sending them a spy from the Court of St. James's. I presume that Mr. King would not be pleased to be removed from England to France permanently."

One of the Senators asked why he had not nominated a commission of three or five instead of a single person. President Adams replied, "I have had a long experience of ten years in this kind of business and have often acted in commissions with various other gentlemen. I have three times been commissioned alone. I have found in general that business can be better done by one than by many, in much less time and with much less perplexity and expense."

Sedgwick then asked if the President would consider modifying the nomination by adding two more names to it. "Who would you have me send?" Adams demanded. "Shall I send Toph Parsons, or some other of your Essex rulers? * No, I will send none of them."

At this point Sedgwick's smoldering anger got the better of his good sense and his promise to restrain himself. He insinuated that

* Theophilus Parsons (1750–1813), a lawyer and later chief justice of the Massachusetts supreme court, was a leading member of the Essex Junto, an ultra-conservative Federalist clique in Massachusetts. He had greatly influenced John Adams' state constitution adopted in 1780.

Adams' Republican friend Elbridge Gerry had had some agency in producing the nomination (which, indeed, was true). This, said James Ross twenty-four years later, "roused the President into an excessive passion and rendered the remaining portion of our interview painful and altogether useless."

Seeing that no more was to be accomplished, the Senators rose and prepared to take their leave. There was much reason, they said, to apprehend that the Senate would reject the nomination unless it was altered so as to embrace more of the confidence of the country. "You are utterly mistaken in this anticipation," the President said. "I have known the Senate longer and better than any of you, and I am very certain of its support in my measures."

When the committeemen said flatly that the nomination would be rejected, Adams replied, "I will neither withdraw nor modify the nomination." And at the door, in some agitation: "I find that there is a party that is determined to rule me, but I will disappoint them. No one has done more to support General Washington than my family and I. Yes, have you already, so soon, forgotten what it was that roused the people to support General Washington against Genêt? I will tell you if you have. It was the publication of my son, John Quincy Adams,* which caused the people to rally around the government."

The Senators bowed and departed. On the street outside the house, Sedgwick swore angrily that he would defeat the nomination, and Read expressed his resentment at the President's manner; both were much offended. Ross and Stockton "laughed, being much diverted at the passion the old gentleman had put himself in for our attempting to help him out of the scrape." Bingham's feelings are not known.

The five went at once to Bingham's house and there met with the other Federalist Senators. The events of the confrontation were related in detail. There was a unanimous opinion that the nomination be rejected. After the vote, two or three Senators wished to wait a few days and give the President time to reflect, but they were overruled. Early the next morning, the five met and drafted a report recommending that the Senate, though it wished to restore tranquility, "do

* *Letters of Publicola,* an attack on Thomas Paine's *The Rights of Man,* on Jefferson for endorsing it, and on the so-called Jacobin spirit.

not advise and consent that said William Vans Murray be sole minister plenipotentiary to the French Republic."

When Adams heard the result of the Saturday-night caucus, he decided, again without any consultation with his cabinet members or party leaders, to accept the proffered compromise. He sent a message to the Sedgwick committee requesting it to withhold the report, as he was preparing a new recommendation on the mission.

The Senate received his message on Monday afternoon. "Much conversation," the President said, "and many manifestations of the public opinion" had led him to the belief that "a new modification of the embassy will give more general satisfaction to the legislature and to the nation." He nominated a commission of three: Murray; Federalist Oliver Ellsworth of Connecticut, Chief Justice of the United States Supreme Court; and Patrick Henry, late governor of Virginia, a fire-eating Republican who had recently become a conservative and a Federalist, largely because of his hatred of Thomas Jefferson.

The Senate — including the five members of the committee — voted to approve all three nominations. The Sedgwick committee was discharged, its report never officially delivered. Patrick Henry declined the nomination because of the state of his health and his advanced age (sixty-three); William Richardson Davie, Federalist governor of North Carolina, accepted the nomination in Henry's place.

The famous Fifth Congress adjourned for the last time on March 4, 1799. A few days later, word was received of a splendid American naval victory over the French. Benjamin Stoddert, a Baltimore merchant and shipowner, now an energetic and farsighted Secretary of the Navy, had sent four squadrons into the West Indies to convoy American merchant ships and to blockade the French privateers in their harbors. Three of these squadrons were under the command of the navy's senior naval officer, Commodore John Barry — he who twenty-three years earlier had blown up the *Nancy* in Delaware Bay. The fourth squadron, comprising the new frigate *Constellation* and four light vessels, sailed under Commodore Thomas Truxtun, the Willing and Morris master who had carried "his favorite" Anne Bingham to England in the spring of 1783 and a year later had taken the *Canton* to China. On February 19, off St. Kitts, Truxtun pursued and engaged the French frigate *L'Insurgente*. His ship had 38 cannon to the Frenchman's 40 and 309 men to his 409; but by superior gunnery Truxtun made the enemy strike and surrender. One American was killed and three were wounded; the French suffered twenty-nine killed, forty-one wounded. The Republican newspaper *Aurora*, embarrassed by this uncalled-for evidence of French weakness, called the defeat an "effect of British intrigue."

Word had been received a few days earlier of Admiral Horatio Nelson's decisive victory over the French fleet on the Nile on January 1. The prospect of a French invasion of North America now seemed remote. The country relaxed and prepared to wait out the result of Mr. Adams' new peace mission to France.

Having challenged the Hamilton wing of his party, Adams was in a strong position to assume real control and capitalize on his move for peace. He hastened to Braintree after Congress adjourned, however, and remained there for the next seven months, leaving control of the government in the hands of his three worst enemies: Hamilton, Pickering, and Wolcott. His friends begged him to remain in Philadelphia, but he explained calmly, "The Secretaries of State, Treasury, War, Navy and the Attorney General transmit me daily by the post all the business of consequence, and nothing is done without my advice and direction. . . . The post goes very rapidly, and I answer by the return of it, so that nothing suffers or is lost." *

Timothy Pickering was angered but not despondent at the decision to send a peace mission to France. It was a grievous mistake, he felt, and real damage had been done in the very act of making the nomination. Adams was "that old fool who mars everything." His character now could never be retrieved; he could not recover the confidence of the Federalists. But he, Pickering, could remedy the disaster in some degree by seeing that the envoys never sailed. If he delayed persistently enough, perhaps the Revolutionary government and Napoleon would be overthrown and the monarchy restored.

In May, 1799, formal assurance arrived from Talleyrand that the American peace mission would be courteously received and negotiated with on the highest level. The President ordered Pickering to prepare the envoys for their departure. Pickering ignored the order.

---

* An exchange of letters between Philadelphia and Braintree normally took nine days. In his four years in office, Adams was away from the seat of government a total of 385 days.

CHAPTER 27

The Golden Voyage: Meridian

And I may add that, notwithstanding the heat of party feelings, I was always treated with personal kindness and consideration by . . . the Willing, Bingham, and Powell families.

Albert Gallatin to Samuel Breck
June 20, 1843

MRS. BENJAMIN STODDERT, wife of the first Secretary of the Navy, daughter of one of Maryland's leading families, moved from Georgetown to Philadelphia with her husband and children in November, 1798. They stayed for a week at Mrs. White's boardinghouse, dining there once with General Washington, resplendent in his buff and blue uniform. They then moved into a partly furnished house owned by Major William Jackson. Mrs. Stoddert found Philadelphia quieter at night even than Georgetown ("nothing to be heard but the watchman"); had her ears pierced; admired the organ, the singing and the polite behavior of the congregation at St. Peter's Church; found the shops good but dear and the markets "a thing of no little consequence"; and entered into the round of social activities required of the wife of a cabinet officer. She described what she saw in shrewd, witty, and somewhat malicious letters to her relatives back in Maryland.

For some reason, Anne Bingham delayed calling on Mrs. Stoddert and so drew a tart comment:

Mrs. Bingham has at last thought proper to show her painted face here, and her two daughters — they were without paint. You must not suppose from my manner of speaking about Mrs. B. that I am offended with her for not coming before. I should have been better pleased if she had, to tell the truth; but if she had not come at all I should not have cared; though she is of great consequence, in some people's opinion, in the city. As she has put it in my power to go to her house, I shall certainly see all that I can by asking for. I am determined to see her garden, her greenhouse, and everything else that is worth seeing. Their house and all the outside look very pretty, and I daresay the inside corresponds with the external.

Mrs. Stoddert went at least once to Mrs. Bingham's for a tea party, but as she reported to Maryland, these were out of fashion in Philadelphia and "when company meets it is generally to dance and then to have supper. These are called balls." She was under promise to her sister to describe one of Mrs. Bingham's balls fully and without confusion. The opportunity soon arose, and Mrs. Stoddert sent off an extraordinary piece of social reporting.

To begin with the beginning, and relate just as it really was, or as it appeared to me, I believe will be best.

About half-past seven I called for Mrs. Harrison, and we made our appearance at Mrs. Bingham's. But instead of her being in a little room, as you have been told, till all her company arrived, she was seated at the head of the drawing-room, I should call it, or, in other words, on one side of the chimney, with three ladies only. There were some young ladies in another room, where her two daughters were also, who, upon my inquiring after their health, were sent for by their mamma.

I should suppose that it was near nine o'clock before the dancing commenced. At the end of the first dance, or near it, punch and lemonade were brought in. That was the first refreshment. Some time after, I think, it was brought in again, and soon after the best ice-cream, as well as the prettiest, that ever I saw was carried around in beautiful china cups and gilt spoons. The latter I had seen there before.

Except punch and lemonade, nothing more to eat till supper, which we were summoned to at eleven, when the most superb thing of the kind which I ever saw was presented to our view, — though those who have been there before say that the supper was not as elegant as they had seen there. In the middle was an orange-tree with ripe fruit; and where a common spectator might imagine the root was, it was covered with evergreens, some natural and some artificial flowers. Nothing scarcely appeared on the table without evergreens to decorate it. The girondole, which hangs immediately over the table, was let down just to reach the top of the tree. You can't think how beautiful it looked. I imagine there were thirty at the table, besides a table full in another room, and I believe every soul said, "How pretty!" as soon as they were seated; all in my hearing, as with one consent, uttered the same thing.

The only meats I saw or heard of were a turkey, fowls, pheasants, and tongues, the latter the best that ever I tasted, which was the only meat I ate. The dessert (all was on the table) consisted of every thing that one could conceive of except jelly; though I daresay there was jelly, too, but to my mortification, I could not get any. I never ate better than at Mrs. Bingham's. Plenty of blanc mange, and excellent. Near me were three different sorts of cake; I tasted all, but could eat of only one; the others were indifferent. Besides a quantity to eat, there was a vast deal for ornament, and some of them I thought would have delighted my little girl for her baby-house.

In short, take it altogether, it was an agreeable entertainment to me. Notwithstanding the crowd — or numbers, rather, for the house is so large that it was not crowded — there was no noise or the least confusion.

At twelve o'clock or a little after Mrs. Harrison and I left the ball. We were among the first to come away. Never did I see such a number of carriages, except on a race-ground.

No breath of scandal had touched Anne Bingham, but at the peak of her social power there was an undercurrent of criticism of the inner Bingham circle for being, by the definition of that time and place, sometimes indelicate in its language and indecorous in its manner. One of Anne's few surviving letters is perhaps a kind of evidence of a frivolous life. To one of the Mrs. Livingstons she wrote: Mrs. Bingham "is extremely sorry to be prevented the pleasure of waiting on Mrs. Livingston this evening — but a bad cold and pain in the head are her present companions in consequence of her last night's raking. . . . Mr. B. will wait on Mr. L. at nine o'clock."

In his memoirs, Joshua Francis Fisher spoke of his cousin Anne's kindness and courtesy to all, and in the next sentence:

There were then fashions prevalent in England which she had adopted, and had better not imitated . . . — too much freedom of speech and an interlarding of oaths, a most detestable custom adopted by Mrs. B. and her sisters, but not by my Aunt Harrison, who was disgusted by it.

Congressman Harrison Gray Otis gave an example of the naughty talk of the Willing sisters and their friends:

> Yesterday I dined at the Clymers, with the Bingham and Willing Party. . . . It was the first day of the Bingham's return from the country. . . . Dolly* then began to rally [Henry] Clymer on the subject of his *Stomacher* . . . and mentioned that one of the British princes (I think the Duke of York) who had lately married the Princess Wirtemburg [Würtemberg] has so protuberant a corporation that he was compelled to order a semicircular piece cut out of his dining table, to give him access to his plate. Mrs. Bingham expressed a hint of sympathy for the *Dutchess,* and Clymer told his sister Francis that he should soon be able to retort this *excellent jest* upon her. All this, and much facetious matter of the same kind was received with bursts of applause that would have done credit to the national convention especially by Miss Abby [Willing] and Miss Ann, who did not disguise their delight nor their bosoms.

If there is any known instance in which Anne Bingham used her wealth and power with a touch of petulance, it is in her quarrel with Thomas Wignell. Wignell was an actor — the best and best-liked comedian of his day — and a talented theater director and manager. While managing the Southwark Theater, he had drawn up plans for a new and grander house on Chestnut Street — one with 2000 seats, 900 of them in boxes, and with an entrance through a marble colonnade of eight Corinthian columns. He formed a joint stock company of sixty gentlemen, each subscribing $300. While the theater was building, he went to England and recruited top-flight talent.

The theater was a center of Republicanism, but the Binghams were on terms of friendship with Wignell and some of his company.† Bingham was one of the sixty subscribers, and Anne Bingham agreed to take a box at the new theater. She wanted to buy and own it, however, "at any price to be fixed by the manager," in the European

---

* Dorothy Willing Francis, sister of Mrs. Bingham, who had married her cousin, Thomas Willing Francis. Of Anne Bingham's three other sisters, Elizabeth had married Major William Jackson; Mary had married Henry Clymer, son of George Clymer, signer of the Declaration of Independence; and Abigail ("Miss Abby" above) would marry Richard Peters.

† The Frenchman Moreau de St. Mèry: "The actors are of a bearable mediocrity from the English point of view. The performance is boisterous. . . . It is not unusual to hear such words as Goddamn, bastard, rascal, son of a bitch."

manner. She would furnish and decorate the box, keep the key, and allow admission to no one except by her permission.

Wignell was tempted to accede to the request. He felt, however, that he should "act on the principles of his country's government, and on the recognition of feelings deeply pervading the structure of its society." All men should be free to come into his theater and be equal in it as long as they behaved themselves. On the basis of this democratic view, Wignell, politely and with expressions of gratitude for past favors, refused Mrs. Bingham's offer, and thus forfeited the patronage of the most powerful woman in Philadelphia. William Burke Wood (1779–1861), actor and theatrical manager, source of this story, reported, "The lady, though not capable of resentment, and expressing her acquiescence in his view as a sound one, scarcely ever visited the theater again."

An attempt was made to heal the breach — if there was one — between Wignell and Mrs. Bingham. The agent was Susanna Haswell Rowson, a remarkable woman Wignell had brought from England as one of his actresses, her husband joining the company as a member of the orchestra. Mrs. Rowson played, among other parts, the Nurse and Lady Capulet in *Romeo and Juliet,* Audrey in *As You Like It,* Mistress Quickly in *The Merry Wives of Windsor,* and Lady Sneerwell, in *The School for Scandal.* She was even more famous, however, as a playwright (*An American in England, Slaves in Algiers*), poetess, novelist, and composer of hymns, anthems, songs and sacred dirges. Her novel, *Charlotte Temple: A Tale of the Truth* (London, 1790, Philadelphia, 1794) was extravagantly successful and eventually had 161 printings in the eighteenth and nineteenth centuries.* An early feminist, Mrs. Rowson maintained in her writings that women were the intellectual equals of men. The view offended William Cobbett ("Peter Porcupine"), and he observed that he had found Mrs. Rowson's works "an excellent emetic."

A year or so after the disagreement between Wignell and Mrs. Bingham, Mrs. Rowson published, by subscription, a four-volume novel entitled *Trials of the Human Heart* — a story told, in the man-

---

* A posthumously published sequel, *Charlotte's Daughter* (1828), went through thirty-one printings, mostly under the title of *Lucy Temple.* These two Rowson works were the most popular novels in America before *Uncle Tom's Cabin.*

ner of the day, in letter form. Though still a member of Wignell's New Theater Company, she dedicated this to Mrs. Bingham, and she did so with Mrs. Bingham's permission:

> MADAM,
>
> . . . I am sensible were I to address a person of your understanding in the language of adulation, I should only excite your contempt. Nor is it necessary for me to set forth the many amiable traits in a character so well known, so universally esteemed and respected as Mrs. Bingham's. . . .
>
> Such as it is, [this work] may perhaps innocently amuse a leisure hour; and under the protecting sanction of your name, I do not fear its meeting a favourable reception from the public in general. For however trifling its own merits, your patronage will stamp a value on it, and raise it into that consequence it otherwise could never attain.

In the preface that followed, Mrs. Rowson took her revenge on William Cobbett by identifying him, though not by name, as "a kind of loathesome reptile" whose only aim "is to prevent the success of any work of genius." *Trials of the Human Heart,* unfortunately, despite Mrs. Bingham's protecting sanction, was the least successful of Mrs. Rowson's works.

In April, 1798, Abigail Adams met the Binghams again after many months. To her daughter, Abigail Smith, she wrote:

> I can say with truth that I think her a very fine woman, and vastly superior in manners and understanding to her husband; she has a fine person, affable manners, and a ladylike deportment. Money, money is his sole object, and he feels the weight of it; he is not without some talents, but they are all turned to gain; for that he would make sacrifices which a man who considers the honour and independence of his country at stake, would sooner sacrifice his life than submit to. I am warranted in saying this from his public conduct. Yet in company he is a social pleasant man, and always seemed good humored.

It is regrettable that Mrs. Adams was not more specific in her criticism of Bingham's actions. One may wonder to what extent her dislike of his political power led to dislike of his public conduct.

William Bingham was at the height of his power, affluence and well-being in those last several years of the century. He was, according to young Robert Gilmor, "a man of elegant manners and handsome appearance." He had managed to survive a panic that had ruined many of his colleagues, and he was now the richest man and largest landowner in the United States. He was married to a beautiful, fascinating and much-admired woman. His older daughter had made an excellent marriage, uniting his family with one of the most powerful houses in Europe; on June 9, 1799, she made him a grandfather when William Bingham Baring was born. (Anne Bingham thus became a grandmother at thirty-five.) The young Barings were close at hand and amiable company.

Apparently the Barings intended to remain in Philadelphia, for Bingham was thinking of building them a house at Lansdown. They spent the first summer of their marriage there in a house known as "The Hut." When Samuel Breck, Bingham's neighbor (and fellow-director of the Bank of the United States), proposed to buy or lease a small piece of the Lansdown property in order to remove some trees that impeded his view, Bingham declined politely for the reason that he would probably improve the estate "for one of my family." Breck replied five days later with a complaint that the absence of a fence was causing his cattle and horses to stray into Bingham's meadow. Bingham countered good-naturedly that it really was not his responsibility to build a fence to keep Breck's livestock out, but rather Breck's responsibility to build a fence to keep his own livestock in.

Under Thomas Willing's presidency, the Bank of the United States had become a powerful and productive institution, and Bingham was a dominant figure in shaping its policies.* The bank had moved in 1797 from Carpenters' Hall into a splendid new building of its own on Third Street — designed in the style of a Greek temple, built of soft white Pennsylvania marble, with a portico of Corinthian columns thirty feet high.†

Bingham's trade with Europe, Asia, and the West Indies was flourishing, for his ships were now able to sail under convoy of British men-

---

* Of the first Bank of the United States, Economist James O. Wettereau said in 1937, "One may well question whether the fundamental standards of banking honor, wisdom and integrity have ever risen above the high plane on which the first Bank of the United States was conducted."

† The building, though much eroded, still stands.

of-war, and French privateers had been reduced in numbers and effectiveness. With Gilmor and Willing and Francis, he opened up a profitable trade with the River La Plata region on the east coast of South America, though, as Bingham observed to his partners, "we have suffered so much by the perfidy of the Spaniards that I have lost all confidence in them."

On May 25, 1799, "by the greatest exertion and with difficulties almost insuperable," Bingham sent $32,800 to the State of Massachusetts, the last payment due on the Maine Lands. The development there was not prospering; the proprietors had invested almost $1.5 million in these lands and had received back less than $148,000. General Cobb, angry at "the great man in Philadelphia" for complaining about certain bills, had not written for eight months, withholding his letters, as he finally said to Bingham, "for reasons that in my mind are satisfactory." Nevertheless, despite these difficulties, the original obligation was at last discharged, and Bingham was spared the burden of recurrent payments.

He was more fortunate in his other lands. He sold 297,000 acres of not especially desirable land in Pennsylvania (now Lycoming County) to the French agent Omer Talon for $240,000; Talon, to Bingham's dismay, promptly resold to a Dutch company for $450,-000. In New York, at the confluence of the Susquehanna and Chenango rivers, he turned over his 15,040 acres to Joshua Whitney, a land agent, who laid out a town later named Binghamton. Town lots sold at $10 to $15 each. Bingham gave five acres for a town square at a reduced rate and donated land for a courthouse and other public buildings. He instructed Whitney to sell at the highest price possible but at the same time to "give a preference to quiet, industrious farmers who will give reputation to the neighborhood, as well as from their skill in the management of their farms as their orderly conduct." When Whitney proposed to build a public library, Bingham wrote him:

> I much approve of the institution of a library in your projected town, not only as a rational resource to the mind and furnishing agreeable occupation, but as inducing an attention to the literary information and instruction which is usually attended with an attachment to good principles of government. I shall either subscribe to the library or make it a present of a number of valuable books.

As a political figure, Bingham was conspicuously powerful in the Senate and in the party caucuses held in his home. John Adams gave some measure of that power when, in 1813, he recalled his position as President. "Washington and Adams," he said, "with all their under-strappers, tools, satilites and puppets, were . . . all governed by Willings, and Chews, and Bingham."

There was no abatement of party rancor with Adams' overture to France. The attacks of the Republican press were as biting and abusive as before, despite the curbs of the Sedition Law; Federalist editors responded in kind. Jefferson and Gallatin were ostracized by Philadelphia society; many people would turn away from both in the street, passing to the other side that they might not have to speak or touch their hats. The Vice President, Sedgwick reported to Rufus King, was "becoming more and more an object of abhorrence and detestation."

The Binghams, of course, were powerful enough to ignore, if they chose, the social cleavage between the political parties and the exclusion of Republican leaders from the city's social affairs. There is some evidence that they did so choose. Gallatin testified movingly in later life that the Binghams and their family connections had treated him with "personal kindness and consideration" during this period of hatred and aversion. Bingham worked constantly with Jefferson in the Senate; they met socially at the sessions of the American Philosophical Society; and Jefferson apparently continued to dine at the Mansion House, even in the years of bad feeling. In June, 1800, a rumor swept the country that the Vice President was dead at Monticello after a sudden illness of forty-eight hours. The Federalist newspapers printed the news with a marked absence of regret; but Dr. Rush informed Jefferson himself that "Mr. Bingham reported your supposed death in the most liberal and pathetic terms."

With his family and financial affairs in order, at a time when his fortunes were at the full, two distressing developments were preying on Bingham's mind.

The first concerned the suit brought against him twenty years earlier by the Cabots of Massachusetts, owners of the privateer *Pilgrim*, which had brought the Danish brig *Hope* into Martinique as a prize. Congress had adopted resolutions upholding Bingham's action in returning the *Hope* to its owner, promised to defray his expenses in this and in future suits in the *Pilgrim* affair, and requested the General Court of Massachusetts to discharge the liens entered against his property. Bingham assumed that the affair was settled and that he, merely a technical defendant, would have no further connection with the business.

He was wrong. In 1793 he found that the case was still active and that new demands were being made on him. He asked Alexander Hamilton to determine whether the matter could be settled through the Treasury or should be brought before the Congress again. President Washington referred the suit to the Attorney General and ordered him to defend it. Bingham was now thoroughly entangled in legal maneuvering and bureaucratic red tape. He had to put up $30,000 as security. The Circuit Court of the United States reversed two lower court decisions and ordered Bingham to pay damages of $30,000 and costs. This judgment was reversed in 1795, but three years later the Cabots again obtained a decision against him by default, this time for $37,000. John Davis, the U. S. District Attorney in Massachusetts, had failed to defend the suit — perhaps, General Knox suggested, because he had expected a fee from the defendant. Bingham explained that he had thought it not proper to pay a government official, adding, "I shall take your hint and remit Mr. Davis a handsome fee — *entre nous.*" He also retained Fisher Ames and Harrison Gray Otis to defend him in the Massachusetts courts. When the matter was reopened in 1799, Secretary Pickering wrote to Davis:

> This case has been so often adjudicated, it was hoped that Mr. Bingham and the U. States might have escaped further trouble. You have heretofore been informed that the U. States are ultimately responsible, by virtue of resolution of the Congress under the Confederation.

Bingham was to learn that the Cabots had obtained indubitable evidence in 1793 that the brig *Hope* and its cargo were indeed British property sailing under false papers and that both were therefore subject to legal seizure as prizes. If they had produced this evidence in 1793, the case would have been settled and their claim paid by the United States. "They had their reasons," Bingham said, "for concealing the information"; they hoped to drag out the case in the local

ANNE BINGHAM

Sketch by Gilbert Stuart

"Mrs. Bingham's portrait in my possession is a chef d'oeuvre of
Stuart, and exhibits great intelligence and sprightliness." — Joshua
Francis Fisher, Anne Bingham's first cousin once removed, in 1864.
The portrait is now owned by **Dr. Francis Fisher Hart** of Ambler,
Pennsylvania.

LADY WASHINGTON'S RECEPTION
Daniel P. Huntington

This romanticized painting by Huntington, widely distributed
as an engraving and sometimes called "The Republican Court,"
shows Anne Bingham as a dominant figure at center.

1. Mrs. John Adams
2. Mrs. Alexander Hamilton
3. John Jay
4. John Adams
5. Alexander Hamilton
6. John Dickinson
7. Mrs. George Washington
8. Mrs. Robert Morris

9. Thomas Jefferson
10. George Washington
11. Mrs. William Bingham
12. Mrs. William Stephens Smith
    (Abigail Adams Smith)
13. Mrs. Theodore Sedgwick
14. Robert Morris
15. Mrs. John Jay

16. Gouverneur Morris
17. Louis Philippe
18. Dr. Benjamin Rush
19. Bishop William White
20. Mrs. Harrison Gray Otis
21. John Hancock
22. Rev. Dr. Ashbel Green
23. General Henry Knox

BENJAMIN FRANKLIN
François Lazzarini

GEORGE WASHINGTON:
THE "LANSDOWNE" PORTRAIT
Gilbert Stuart

William Bingham made gifts of two famous art works that have been widely displayed. The Lazzarini statute of Franklin "with a Roman head," in Carrara marble, was presented to the Library Company, Philadelphia, in 1792 and now stands in its entry hall. The "Lansdowne" portrait of Washington by Gilbert Stuart, sometimes called "The Teapot Portrait" because of the President's pose, was commissioned by Bingham and given to the Marquess of Lansdowne in 1796 as a present from Mrs. Bingham.

HIGH STREET FROM THE COUNTRY MARKET PLACE
William Russell Birch

The view from the Philadelphia Market House shows General
Washington's "sham funeral" of December 26, 1799 — an empty
casket being ceremoniously drawn through the streets of Philadelphia, the capital city.

LOUIS-MARIE,
VICOMTE DE NOAILLES
*Albert Rosenthal, 1906, after
an engraving*

One of Bingham's closest friends
was General Noailles, hero of the
American Revolution, leader of the
early French Revolution, refugee
from the French Terror. He lived
in one of the out-buildings of
the Binghams' Mansion House.

CONSTANTINE CHASSEBOEUF,
COMTE DE VOLNEY
*Charles Willson Peale, 1807,
after Gilbert Stuart*

Count Volney, *savant* and ideologue,
was determined to find perfection
and the "new man" in America, but
after three years returned disillu-
sioned to France. He dined often
at the Binghams' Mansion House.

SCHUYLKILL BRIDGE, *John James Barralet*

Bingham was a dominant director of the first national bank, Alexander Hamilton's Bank of the United States, founded 1791, and a director of the private company that in 1801–1804 built the famous 1300-foot Permanent Bridge across the Schuylkill at Chestnut Street.

BANK OF THE UNITED STATES, THIRD STREET
William Russell Birch

GENERAL DAVID COBB
*Chester Harding, after
Gilbert Stuart*

Generals Cobb and Knox were
deeply involved in William Bingham's purchase of three million
acres of Maine lands, Cobb as his
agent, Knox as his high-living,
debt-ridden partner.

GENERAL HENRY KNOX
Charles Willson Peale

THE CAPITOL IN 1800 — NORTH WING
William Russell Birch, watercolor

Washington City and the unfinished Capitol Building as they looked in
1801 when Senator William Bingham traveled there to attend the first
session of Congress in the new capital.

GEORGETOWN AND FEDERAL CITY
Aquatint by T. Cartwright, 1801, after G. Beck painting

ALEXANDER BARING
Sir Thomas Lawrence

Alexander Baring traveled to the
United States in 1796 to buy one-
third of Bingham's land holdings
in Maine. As head of the House of
Baring, he became Lord Ashburton
and a mighty power in English
social and political affairs.

ANN BINGHAM BARING
*From a miniature owned by her
great-great granddaughter*

Ann, William and Anne Bingham's
elder daughter, married Alexander
Baring and subsequently became
Lady Ashburton.

MARIA MATILDA BINGHAM DE TILLY BARING

Sir Thomas Lawrence

Maria, the Binghams' second daughter, caused a sensation when she eloped at fifteen with a penniless French count twenty-one years her senior. Divorced at a heavy price, she later married Henry Baring, brother of her sister Ann's husband. Here she is shown with the two oldest of her five Baring children.

WILLIAM BINGHAM
Gilbert Stuart

Senator Bingham stands here in his palatial Mansion House in
1797 at the height of his power. President Adams wrote of "nocturnal caucuses at the pompous Mansion House" and charged in
1813 that he, Washington, and the country had really been
governed by Bingham and his family connections.

courts, make him personally responsible, and attach his Maine lands at a valuation set ridiculously low by their associates in the state offices. In view of the way the case had been mishandled, they seemed in a fair way to realize their aims.

The other distressing development concerned a claim against him for £1500 sterling made by his former agent in Europe, his brother-in-law, Major William Jackson. On December 8, 1797, eighteen months after his return from Europe, Jackson signed a complete release from all claims on Bingham for his services to that time, including his two trips to Boston and his two-year stay in Europe. He received in return the promised deed for the residuary profit on 100,-000 acres of Maine land — this in addition to £1500 for his expenses in Europe. A year later, in December, 1798, Jackson belatedly submitted an account for purchases he had made in Europe, totaling £327. He apparently had spoken slightingly of Bingham for not paying a bill never submitted, for Bingham wrote:

> I must confess myself exceedingly hurt, that such an account should have existed, unknown to me for so long a period, while others, I find, have been informed of it, under circumstances by no means flattering to my feelings.

He of course paid the money.

Jackson had hoped to receive the residuary profits on a second 100,000 acres for his services in England, and when this was not forthcoming he decided he was also entitled to a considerably larger sum — a commission on the sale to the Barings. Within a few hours of receiving his £327 for expenses, he sent Bingham a bill for another £1500 "to my commission of agency while employed to negotiate a sale of your Maine lands."

Bingham rejected the claim. The £1500 expense money and the profit on the 100,000 acres given Jackson, he said, were ample compensation and all that had been promised. Jackson had signed a deed recognizing this and releasing Bingham of further claim. Moreover,

> These sales were made subsequent to your departure from England. . . . They originated in overtures I made to gentlemen in England, under circumstances of a reduced price and more favorable situation, and were made through my agency alone.

Under these considerations, you may well imagine how much I was surprized at your new claim . . . which my duty to the Concern compels me to view as unfounded and inadmissable.

Jackson replied that the profit from the 100,000 acres was payment only for his earlier services in Boston; Bingham's promise of the profits on a second 100,000 acres was express and unequivocal. He wrote "with grateful pleasure" of Bingham's past acts of friendship, but insisted

My right . . . was absolute and unqualified. No renunciation of any other right was necessary to obtain an unconditioned deed for those profits. Nor could such a deed have been refused to me on any ground of law, equity, honor or conscience.

To have worded the deed, therefore, with a design of setting aside other rights suggests an idea so repugnant to a man of character that I must reject the belief of it as utterly unworthy of you, and as conveying an opinion which I am confident you cannot wish any man to entertain. . . .

After a "dispassionate perusal" of Jackson's letter, Bingham found no reason to change the opinion he had previously expressed. At the value he had placed on the lands in 1793, he said, he would have been promising Jackson a benefit of nearly $30,000 for his services, which was out of the question.

It is . . . curious that you should sign an instrument (which you retained in your possession some time previous to your signature) without any objections on your part, if you had reason to suppose that it barred any of your just claims.

In May, 1799, Bingham, "to accommodate you," offered to pay Jackson $2700 as the profits on the second 100,000 acres; he declined absolutely to recognize the claim for a £1500 commission. Jackson refused the offer. Bingham was faced with the possibility of a suit brought against him by a member of the family.

The *Pilgrim* suit and the quarrel with Jackson plagued Bingham during these years and corroded the pleasure he felt in happier events. In the spring of 1799, however, William and Anne Bingham were struck by a blow that made those troubles pale to insignificance.

CHAPTER 28

Scandal at the Republican Court

*Mrs. Bingham is very ill, I understand, and I have heard that Mr. Bing-
ham has lost his senses. I really feel for them, as I should for anybody
in their situation.*

Mrs. Benjamin Stoddert to her niece
April 15, 1799

THERE IS much evidence that Jacques Alexandre, Comte de Tilly —
"le beau Tilly" — was one of the handsomest men of his time. Although no portrait is known to exist, he was described as 5 feet, 5
inches tall, which was then considered of middle height; his hair was
dark, his face oval and rather pale, his nose regular, his eyes large and
black. He was known throughout Europe as an accomplished seducer, in an age known for its accomplished seducers. He had served
some time in prison for debt, and he paid a sizable sum to be smuggled from revolutionary France to England, where he lived for several years as a refugee. Arriving in New York in 1796, he wrote at
once to his friend Noailles, who replied:

> Madame de Lartigues told me of your plan to come to us. I took
> it for a fable, as there is nothing *romantic* here. . . . I shall be
> pleased to see you again, but I must confess to you that there could
> not be a more unfavorable moment for undertaking any affairs here.
> [Because of rising anti-French sentiment.]

Tilly proceeded to Philadelphia, and Noailles introduced him into
the Bingham household. At thirty-six, Tilly was a man of charm and
talent — a count,* a poet, an artist, a witty and amusing raconteur of
life at the French court, of his services as a page boy to Marie Antoinette, of his escape from the Revolutionaries disguised as a coachman.

---

* The validity of Tilly's title was doubtful, two branches of the family claiming the
hereditary rights.

The Binghams became fond of him — Anne because he was good company and amused her friends; William, possibly, because he pleased Anne. They must have known of his reputation for profligacy, and they must have found reason to disregard it. Perhaps they felt he was maligned, since Tilly, for his own reasons, was always on his best behavior with the Binghams. Only one fragment of their conversation has survived the centuries. After hearing him lament the perfidy of the mistresses he had known, Anne Bingham chided him with, "Believe me, you have made bad choices!" "One cannot do anything else, madame," Tilly replied, "among the women who allow themselves to be chosen."

Maria was especially attracted to this man almost two and a half times her age. She was only fifteen in 1799, but she was accomplished and mature beyond her years, and she had the French "gift of intimacy." She spent much time with her mother and in adult company; both parents were exceptionally fond of her. George Harrison, Mrs. Bingham's cousin, described as "the leading man of fashion in Philadelphia, remarkable for his elegant dress, his graceful dancing, his courteous manners . . . his great personal beauty," once spent an evening in the Bingham household with Harrison Gray Otis. He observed Maria intently. On leaving, he remarked to Otis that she would not "keep" long.

None of her young friends, none of the many cousins in the large family relationship, pleased Maria so much as the handsome, experienced, attentive French count. She sometimes extended him the family's invitations to dine, writing notes on gilt-edge satin paper that Tilly saved. A formal invitation in correct French: "Mr. and Mrs. Bingham beg Monsieur le Comte de Tilly to do them the honour of dining with them *en famille* [underlined] next Sunday." Two informal notes in English: "Miss Bingham presents her compliments to Count Tilly. She takes the liberty of sending him some chocolate, having remarked yesterday that he approved of it." "Miss Maria Matilda Bingham takes the liberty of offering Count Tilly some fruit just taken from the trees. She hopes it may prove acceptable to Count Tilly in his indisposition."

Something in this relationship must have disturbed the trusting parents, for it is known that on April 9, in some manner that is not clear, Bingham cautioned his daughter to be on her guard against Comte de Tilly.

Two days later, shortly after midnight, Maria Bingham stole from her parents' house, met Tilly, and went with him to the home of a French woman, where they were married by a minister of the Universalist Church. From there, as man and wife, they proceeded to Tilly's lodgings in the house of a milliner.

A servant in the Bingham household, an accomplice in the elopement, had for some reason been instructed to wake Maria's mother at an early hour and tell her what had happened. Anne Bingham was so upset that a doctor had to be summoned; he gave her laudanum. William Bingham, beside himself with rage, sent out search parties to rescue his daughter. The one headed by Alexander Baring went to Tilly's lodgings and there, at five o'clock in the morning, found the couple in bed together. Baring struck Tilly, and a tumult followed that must have wakened the household, the neighbors, and possibly that end of Philadelphia. Maria was gathered up and brought back to her sorrowing parents, where she remained against her will. There is an unproved and unprovable report that Commodore John Barry either then or later gave Tilly a sound thrashing.

Tilly was outraged by the removal and detention of his bride. He placed advertisements in the papers announcing her abduction, in the language usually reserved for runaway bond servants and unfaithful wives; and he retained a lawyer named Samson Levy* to force the parents to give back their child.

The elopement caused a sensation throughout the country second only to that produced by the XYZ disclosures. It gave rise to prodigious anger at the dissolute French nation, some genuine sympathy for the distracted parents, and much appropriate moralizing at the downfall of the proud, rich and mighty.

"Thus you see, my dear," Robert Morris wrote to his nineteen-year-old daughter from the Walnut Street prison, "that large fortunes do not always bring happiness, on the contrary misery to the possessor is

---

* Samson Levy, thirty-eight, was a member of one of Philadelphia's respected, upper-class Jewish families of long residence. His father was a member of the exclusive Dancing Assembly when it was founded in 1748 and signed the merchants' Non-Importation Oath in 1765. Samson Levy became a member of the Protestant Episcopal Church. He was one of the incorporators of the Pennsylvania Academy of the Fine Arts.

frequently the result, and this unfortunate young lady is one instance of it."

"What a deplorable event!" Chief Justice James Iredell wrote to his wife; "but the too natural consequence of unbounded prosperity and dissipation."

"The whole family are sunk in the deepest affliction and seem to admit of no consolation," Elias Boudinot, Director of the Mint, informed Mrs. Boudinot. "Thus you see that extravagant riches do not necessarily constitute the ingredient for exclusive happiness."

Mrs. Benjamin Stoddert wrote to her niece in Georgetown:

> Count Tilly, I think he is called, married Miss Bingham last week clandestinely. Neither Mr. nor Mrs. Bingham suspected any such thing. Between the hours of twelve and one in the night she eloped from her father's house and was carried by him to some French woman's, where they were married by a Mr. Jones, a Universalist (all of a piece, you see!) . . . The count is a man of horrid character in every sense of the word, besides not being worth a farthing; but that is nothing, for the lady's father is so rich that if a deficiency of money had been the only objection it could, and I daresay would, have been removed. What a misfortune it is to have only two children, with hundreds of thousands to give them, and for one to have acted as she has!

Her letter, written four days after the elopement, reported that Mrs. Bingham was very ill and that Mr. Bingham had lost his senses.

Bingham dispatched to his attorney, William Lewis, a letter containing a list of questions on his legal position and on the rules of divorce, and apparently told him to spare no expense in reaching a quick settlement. Lewis' answer was sympathetic:

> If, my dear sir, I shall be so fortunate as to succeed in my expectations of rendering essential services to a very dear friend and highly respectable family, from whom I with gratitude acknowledge that I have received every polite and friendly attention, my compensation will be real indeed. In a case which has occasioned so much affliction to those whom I both love and esteem, and which so much involves the future happiness or misery of a young lady whose heart and mind are equal if not superior to those of any other person that I know

of any age or sex, I can receive no pecuniary compensation, nor would anything of that kind be of estimation (however large) in my mind compared with the pleasure itself which I shall feel if my endeavors to serve you shall be equal to my wishes. . . .

On April 17, Bingham received the following letter from Samson Levy:

I have been applied to in a professional way by James Alexander Count de Tilly upon a subject highly important and interesting — The fact is, the intermarriage with Maria Matilda Bingham and himself took place on the 11th Inst. (inclosed you have a copy from the original Certificate of Marriage). The next day after his marriage his Lady was solicited to visit her Mama, who was represented as being very ill and in great distress, and from a sense of propriety and delicacy the Count was induced to agree.

There is strong reason now to believe that her not returning is only to be accounted for that the Lady his wife is restrained and deprived of her liberty — a circumstance of great misfortune to the Count and contrary to the union, the nature of the contract contemplated.

Levy, therefore, as counsel of Comte de Tilly, requested "that the lady be liberated and permitted to return or act as she may think proper." The proceedings of *habeas corpus,* he said, would be extremely painful to him.

The Law upon this occasion is well defined and settled. I therefore flatter myself that a deliberate and dispassionate consideration of the request contained will be granted — and am, Sir, without any intention whatever to injure either the feelings or happiness of yourself or family.

Maria, at first recalcitrant, then contrite, agreed to follow her parents' advice and to submit to any steps to undo what had been done. On April 25, in an effort to reclaim his young wife, Tilly caused a writ of habeas corpus to be delivered to Bingham. At a hearing before a state judge, Bingham replied that his daughter was not in his custody and that she was acting on her own volition; William Lewis satisfied the judge that the writ had not been issued in the proper manner.

Maria agreed to Lewis' proposal that she go before a magistrate and make "a solemn renunciation under oath of the Comte de Tilly forever, together with such reasons and statement of facts as her own prudence and good sense might dictate." The plan was changed because there was reason to fear that Tilly might attempt a forcible abduction. Maria (as Lewis told it) was averse both to seeing him and to any violent action that would cause more public talk and might have serious consequences.

On May 24, Samson Levy appealed to Lewis. He had been asked by Tilly to seek another writ of habeas corpus. Before troubling Mr. Bingham, Mr. Lewis or himself, he wished to ask as a gentleman: Was it true that Maria de Tilly would appear and answer for herself by giving a preference to her family? "If she shall so appear," Levy declared, "depend on it there will be such an end and conclusion put to the business as will ease the minds and anxiety of Maria de Tilly's friends. Your candid answer will much oblige one who wishes to act in no other character than as a gentleman."

Lewis replied:

> Maria de Tilly is left to herself, and whatever contact she may think proper to pursue will be the result of her own reflection and will . . . be her own office and voluntary act; but I am sure that her father will not wound her feelings by disturbing her voluntary repose and forcing her into the presence of a person [Tilly] who may now talk of "easing the mind and anxiety of her friends" but who thank God, has it *no longer* in his power to "give them much trouble" in this or any other respect.
>
> Maria knows her father's determinations to be irrevocably fixed, and he has the pleasure to know that hers are not only so, but that they are perfectly correspondent with his own. No overtures or proposals of any kind from the Count de Tilly will ever be listened to, and . . . all correspondence on the subject must now close.

Alexander Baring sent word of these events verbally to his family in London through a General Maitland, traveling on the April packet ship; but he wrote his father on May 7 of the anguish caused in Philadelphia:

The family remain in nearly the same state of suspense and uncertainty as the first day, though I have strong hopes a very disagreeable business will be patched up better than we have had reason to expect. There are circumstances of character which render any reconciliation out of the question. The man can not possibly be received into the family: this I believe is perfectly believed on all sides, and I am happy to say that not only an almost perfect change has been *operated* in the disposition of the poor girl, but I think I see symptoms of some effect being produced on the villain by the only means of effectually getting rid of him — giving him a small part of the temptation that seduced him, and to try this it must ultimately come. This circumstance . . . has been productive of more affliction and misery than I can express to you.

Tilly was indeed amenable to the suggestion that his wounded feelings might be assuaged by a cash settlement. A committee of three persons was chosen to represent each side: for Tilly, the Vicomte de Noailles, Guillaume de Boisclairaux (a Tilly relative) and Pierre Aupois, apparently a businessman of New York; for the Binghams, Thomas Willing, Alexander Baring, and either Tench Francis or Thomas Willing Francis, his son. Flanked by attorneys, the committees set to work. By Monday morning, June 10, they had drawn up a document acceptable to both sides.

Tilly made four demands:

He was to receive £5000 pounds sterling to pay his debts. He was to have an annuity of £500 sterling, to be paid wherever he wished, in any country save the United States. He was not to be disturbed in any manner whatsoever in connection with the circumstances of his marriage. He was to receive from Alexander Baring a letter, or a statement made through Noailles, that Alexander Baring "struck me in a moment of agitation, owing to the critical situation of Mrs. Baring and the harm she experienced." (There is no explanation for this mystifying provision.)

In return for the satisfaction of these demands, Tilly promised to leave Philadelphia and the United States; to return the Comtesse de Tilly's letters to her mother; to grant a divorce if that was desired; and never to cause trouble for the Bingham family. The compact concluded:

I desire the signature of Mr. Bingham to these articles before two o'clock this afternoon, and before ten o'clock tomorrow morning the absolute fulfilment of these conditions, so that I may leave instantly a country where I have been too unfortunate.

This document, in Noailles' handwriting, was delivered to Bingham, who carefully translated it into English in his own hand. He then wrote:

Mr. Bingham has received the paper concerning certain conditions offered on the part of Monsieur de Tilly — which under certain modifications, not substantially affecting the terms, he will agree to. The necessary paper, to carry the same into operation, shall be prepared immediately, so that Monsieur de Tilly may leave town tomorrow morning.

The "necessary paper" was delivered the same day, complete with signatures and tax stamp. Tilly was to leave Philadelphia and Pennsylvania within two days and the United States within twenty days. If he ever returned to the United States, if he wrote any letters of any kind to Maria, or if he gave any trouble whatever to Maria Matilda, her father, or any other member of the family, the annuity and the agreement would immediately cease and become null and void. Baring made the required statement to Noailles that he had struck the Comte de Tilly in a moment of agitation, owing to the critical situation of Mrs. Baring; and he ordered William Lewis to drop legal proceedings he had started against Tilly.

The £5000 was paid. Tilly left Philadelphia the next morning and sailed from New York to London in July, leaving his contract in the custody of Pierre Aupois. Before his departure, he wrote to Noailles the gay suggestion that he marry off one of his sons or a nephew to Maria after the divorce. Noailles, whose role as the sponsor and representative for Tilly must have caused him intense embarrassment and pain, answered with a restrained but cold rebuke:

I have the most tender regard for Maria and the most profound veneration for Mr. Bingham, but I would never consent, under any pretext whatever, that one of my children become the son-in-law of Mr. Bingham. I would not wish to reduce him to the necessity of receiving his charity. My nephew, Just de Noailles, who, they say, has married Mlle. de Durfort, is altogether a stranger to me. You may make whatever use you wish of this definite answer; it should put you at your ease as to the conduct you wish to follow.

Noailles wrote to Tilly again from Philadelphia on November 16:

You ask me to be frank with you, and you know that I have always been so, even to rudeness. Two different procedures have been considered by Maria's family: a legal separation and a divorce. Mr. Bingham and his daughter have preferred a divorce. The form it will take will not be painful to you, since the divorce will be blamed on the difference in ages and on seduction. No Frenchman has ever felt offended at being suspected of having irresistible charms.

Maria has been very much sought after all summer; her flight has been considered as nothing more than a rash escapade. She has made much progress in acquiring spirit and instruction, and she has perfected herself in the agreeable arts. The experience she has had in the marriage has been so terrible that it will not be easy for her to try it a second time. She has a singular talent for captivating hearts, but if she forms a new tie, it will be only as the result of a violent passion that she has long struggled against, and one approved by her parents, whose idol she is. . . .

Since your departure I have not heard your name mentioned once either in the family of Mr. Willing or of Mr. Bingham. Having communicated part of your letter to Mr. Bingham, I am sure that you are free to choose the place where you wish to live, and I can add that Mr. Bingham desires that you recover your health and happiness.

Tilly left London to live in Berlin, where he caught the fancy of the King of Prussia and was made court chamberlain. Anne Bingham made a resolute show of continuing life as it had been before, giving parties, entertaining friends, and making her social rounds with her daughters. The extreme French styles had begun to appear in America, and Maria and Ann Baring, both of them very young women, took them up a little ahead of their contemporaries. When Abigail Adams returned to Philadelphia in November, Mrs. Bingham and her daughters called. Mrs. Adams described the visit to her sister:

Amongst the ladies presented to me the Countess de Tilly has been of the number, by the appelation of Madame de Tilly. She has all the appearance and dress of a real French woman, rouged up to the ears: Mrs. Bingham did not appear to feel any embarresment at introducing her, tho I cannot say she did not creat one in me; for I really felt a reluctance at addressing her. So I talked to her mother and sister, and as there was much other company present I easily past her over.

And again a few months later:

The stile of dress . . . is really an outrage upon all decency. I will describe it as it has appeared even at the drawing room. A sattin peticoat of certainly not more than three breadths gored at the top, nothing beneath but a chemise. Over this a thin coat, a muslin sometimes, sometimes a crape made so strait before as perfectly to show the whole form. The arm naked almost to the shoulder and without stays or bodice. A tight girdle round the waist, and the "rich luxurience of naturs charms" without a hankerchief fully displayed.

The face, a la mode de Paris, red as a brick hearth. When this lady [Maria] has been led up to make her curtzey, which she does most gracefully, it is true, every eye in the room has been fixed upon her her [sic], and you might litterally see through her. But in this stile of dress, she has danced nor regarded the splitting out of her scanty coat upon the occasion. . . . To do justice to the other ladies, I cannot accuse them of such departures from female decorum, but they most of them wear their cloaths too scant upon the body and too full upon the bosom for my fancy. Not content with the *show which* nature bestows, they borrow from art, and litterally look like nursing mothers. To disguise the strait appearance of the gowns before, those aprons, which you say look like fig leaves, were adopted. The mother of the lady described and sister, being fine women and in the first rank, are leaders of the fashion, but they show more of the [bosom] than the decent matron, or the modest woman.

Divorces could be obtained only by an act of the state legislature, and Bingham spent much time at the turn of the year in Lancaster working to get the measure passed. The divorce was granted on January 17, 1800. The bill of particulars declared that Alexander de Tilly, who called himself a count, had bribed the servants of William

Bingham to deliver letters to Maria Bingham "of the tender age of fifteen or thereabouts." Tilly, in the course of the correspondence, "by acts the most seductive, fraudulent and iniquitous," had "ensnared" Maria "into a midnight elopement from the house of her parents." His object was said to be the extortion of money from her father. He offered "to sell and surrender and did actually sell and surrender all his marital rights for a pecuniary consideration," and then left the country. In order that "the innocent victims of his baseness may find comfort, that an example may be made to deter others from offending in a manner so fatal to the order of society and the happiness of individuals, and that the solemn contract of marriage may be vindicated from practices so immoral, irreligious, fraudulent and corrupt," the said contract was declared "to be void and annulled to all intents, constructions, and purposes whatsoever."

Harrison Gray Otis wrote to his wife the next day:

> First, then, I just learn that a bill for divorcing Maria Bingham has passed both houses at Lancaster, where Mr. Bingham now is. She was however every day walking with her mother while this business was pending and in a dress which you will hardly believe it possible for a lady to wear at least at this season. A muslin robe and her chemise, and no other article of cloathing upon her body. I have been regaled with the sight of her whole legs for five minutes together, and do not know "to what height" the fashion will be carried. The particulars of her dress I have from old Mrs. F——— who assures me that her chemise is fringed to look like a petticoat.
>
> However she and the whole family are evidently dejected.

Shortly after the divorce, Maria had a love-sick suitor, a young man named Erving, whom Otis considered "conceited, democratical and niggardly." Otis to his wife:

> Thursday evening Miss Peters gave a ball, to which by Erving's special request I procured his admission. Doubtless his principal view was to meet Maria, to whom his attentions were perfectly ridiculous. He scarcely spake to any other lady, first he danced with her, then sat by her, then followed her up and down when she danced with other persons like a shadow, and in short was so absolutely inattentive to the ladies of the family that I was mortified. It was

hinted to me that he has no chance of success, and that Mam'selle is not smitten.

Erving shortly thereafter received his dismissal.

A friend who saw Bingham in Lancaster during the divorce proceedings reported that he looked "careworn and aged." He was forty-eight.

CHAPTER 29

The End of an Era

I am apprehensive of the Result of the Contest which is about taking place for the election of a President. . . . There can be no well grounded hope, whilst one Party is disorganized, and the other acts as a firm and united Phalanx.

William Bingham to Rufus King
August 6, 1800

NEAR THE END of seven restful months in Braintree, John Adams received a confidential letter from Benjamin Stoddert, his Secretary of the Navy. The Hamilton faction of the party, Stoddert suggested, was conspiring to prevent Ellsworth and Davie, the envoys to France, from sailing. "Artful, designing men," moreover, were plotting to deny Mr. Adams reelection to the Presidency next fall. His presence was needed at the seat of government.

Reluctantly Adams left for Trenton (where the government had been moved because of another outbreak of yellow fever in Philadelphia), arriving in mid-October, 1799. Hamilton called on him there and in a strained interview tried to persuade him that the mission to France should be suspended, since a Bourbon king probably would soon be restored to the French throne. Adams called the notion preposterous and ordered Stoddert to have a government vessel ready to depart with the envoys on November 1. The breach in the Federalist ranks was now complete. Pickering declared that nothing could reunite the party but the withdrawal of John Adams from the Presidency and retirement to private life.

The envoys sailed from Newport, Rhode Island, on November 3. Their mission, Bingham advised Rufus King in London, was not very popular among "the best friends of the Administration." The country had gone to the expense of building up a navy and now could defend its commerce from the French. Little reliance could be placed on any French agreement.

Besides, if this attempt should eventuate in a renewal of the treaties with France, there will doubtless be found a strong party in Congress in favor of disarming; by which, if they should succeed, we shall again expose our commerce to insult and depredation, and lose the opportunity of establishing a naval force, which is so essential to the interests as well as conducive to the respectability of any country.

Six days after the envoys sailed, Napoleon Bonaparte, having returned unannounced to Paris from Egypt, staged a coup d'etat that overthrew the Directory and gave him absolute power for a term of ten years. A few weeks later he held a popular election in which his coup was "ratified." The Republic was dead, and with it the last bright dreams of the French Revolution and hopes for peace in Europe. France was ruled by a dictator more powerful, more ambitious, and more ruthless than the Bourbons who had preceded him.

The first session of the Sixth Congress assembled on December 2, 1799 — the last time it would ever meet in Philadelphia. The Federalists had been returned in full strength in the Senate and with a larger majority in the House than they had enjoyed for years. Despite their surprising victory, they were depressed, for they had lost the governorship of Pennsylvania to the state's chief justice, Thomas McKean, Jeffersonian. William Cobbett, as "Peter Porcupine," had done his acerbic best to elect Federalist Senator James Ross of Pittsburgh. He explained to the electorate that McKean was a "vile old wretch" who as chief justice was "not only canvassing as he goes his circuit . . . not only soliciting votes of the *present citizens*, but he is absolutely making new ones."

McKean . . . was guilty of the legal murder of two Quakers. . . . His private character is infamous; he beats his wife, and she beats him. He ordered a wig to be imported for him . . . refused to pay for it, was sued before the Mayor's Court. . . . He is a notorious drunkard. . . . He has been horse-whipped in the city tavern, and kicked in the street for his insolence to particular persons, and yet this degraded wretch is Chief Justice of the State.

But McKean campaigned on sensitive national issues: against the excise tax, the tax on land, a standing army, war measures, and the

Alien and Sedition laws. He won by an easy 6600 votes.* Installed as governor, he promptly introduced the spoils system to American political life, replacing some hundreds of state office holders with deserving Republicans, including twelve of his own relatives and connections.

Bingham and his colleague Jacob Read waited on President Adams to notify him that a quorum of the two houses was assembled. Adams' speech to a joint session at noon the following day (December 3) was brief. The country was prosperous, despite the state of war in much of the world. He had the painful duty to report that some of the people in certain counties of Pennsylvania, seduced by the arts and misrepresentations of designing men, had openly resisted the federal tax on houses and land.† The result of the mission to France was uncertain, but however it turned out, wisdom dictated a steady perseverance in a system of national defense.

On Thursday afternoon, December 12, 1799, General Washington returned to Mount Vernon after some hours spent riding over his 4000-acre estate in sleet and rain. The story is told that word awaited him there of the election of James Monroe, a man he disliked, as governor of Virginia, and that the news so stunned him that he sat for several hours in his wet clothes and then dined without changing. His throat became infected, apparently with a strain of virulent streptococcus. Two days later, having been bled four times and repeatedly blistered, purged, and made to vomit, he died.

The news reached Philadelphia three days later, on Tuesday evening, and was announced to the Congress the following morning. The country began a months-long period of mourning. Said Benjamin Rush: "The whole nation mourned for him as a father." Bingham was appointed to a joint Congressional committee to take "meas-

---

* Cobbett had sworn that he would leave the country if McKean was elected, and indeed he did migrate to New York and thence, in the spring of 1800, back to England and to a new career. He was speeded on his way by a $5000 judgment against him awarded to Dr. Benjamin Rush, whom he had long been attacking for his blood-letting. ("Dr. Rush is the Samson of Medicine, slaying his thousands and tens of thousands.") Pennsylvanians, he said on departing, were "the most malicious and cowardly race in existence," and he hoped that Dr. Rush would bleed them all to death.

† This was the rebellion of Pennsylvania Germans in Bucks and Northampton counties. The men shot the tax collectors in the legs and the women poured scalding water on them from the windows. Their leader, Militia Captain John Fries, was arrested, tried for treason in Philadelphia, and twice sentenced to death. Against the advice of Secretaries Pickering, Wolcott, and McHenry, President Adams pardoned and freed him.

ures suitable to the occasion and expressive of the profound sorrow with which Congress is penetrated on the loss of a citizen first in war, first in peace, and first in the hearts of his countrymen." Public business was suspended. The chairs in the Senate chamber were covered, the room was draped in black, and each member was to wear a crepe band around his left arm for thirty days. The Senators marched in a body to extend their condolences to President Adams. They resolved with the Representatives that the government should erect a marble monument in the city of Washington.

General Washington was buried at Mount Vernon, but the committee decided that it would be appropriate to hold a Congressional funeral service in Philadelphia. A draped empty coffin rested for several days before the Speaker's chair in the House. On December 26, in a procession lasting one and a quarter hours, this was carried through the streets by six sergeants, accompanied by a caparisoned and plumed white horse, with boots reversed in the stirrups. The Senators followed, two by two, marching to muffled drums, each member wearing his arm band and a white scarf. Then came the Representatives, thirty-four clergymen of all the different sects, twenty-four companies of militia, and all the dignitaries of the city. Sixteen cannon fired at half-hour intervals.

Four evenings later, in the New Theater, Thomas Wignell declaimed a "monody" written by Mrs. Rowson, to the accompaniment of solemn dirges. He stood before a large catafalque on which rested a portrait of the great man encircled by a wreath of oak leaves. An eagle dropped tears of blood; an inscription explained that these were the nation's tears. The mourning became competitive. Some three hundred orations and "eulogiums" were delivered throughout the country.* Fisher Ames spoke in Boston, Gouverneur Morris at a seven-hour ceremony in New York. In Europe, the entire British fleet lowered its flags to half mast. The French army wore mourning for ten days, and the Marquis de Fontannes delivered an official *éloge* that somehow turned into a panegyric of First Consul Bonaparte.

At noon on February 22, 1800, which would have been Washington's sixty-eighth birthday, Bingham walked with his colleagues to

---

* Two-thirds of these were delivered in New England. At a barbecue held by Jeffersonians in Fayette County, Kentucky, "in order to celebrate the recent successes of our allies the French," a toast was drunk to the memory of George Washington for his illustrious actions and services "down to the year 1787, but no farther."

the German Reformed Church on Race Street, there to listen to a "eulogium Pronounced on the Character of General Washington." It was written and delivered by Major William Jackson, the late President's aide-de-camp, protégé and friend. President and Mrs. Adams were in the audience, and Vice President Jefferson, and Sir Robert Liston, the British minister. For this solemn occasion, Major Jackson suspended his previously expressed views of General Washington as the automaton, the marble fountain of honor and office, the man of stone, the man of proud ignorance and base ingratitude, for whose views he had equal indifference and contempt.

> Who shall delineate a faithful portrait of that character which was perfect in all its relations — or in what language shall the story of that life be told, whose every action was above all praise? . . . Were mine the powers of description to produce a perfect image, I would present him to your raptured imagination — as he was seen in battle, calm and collected — as he appeared in council, dignified and serene — as he adorned society, gracious and condescending. . . .
>
> The dark night of the tomb shall not obscure the lustre of his fame — and, when brass and marble shall have fallen to decay, the sweet remembrance of his virtues, passing in proud transmission to remotest ages, shall endure forever.

Mrs. Stoddert observed that Major Jackson's oration "gave general satisfaction." Thomas Willing wrote his congratulations. Mrs. Adams found it "a very handsome one, and much better delivered than I had any idea he could perform," and hoped that "the good mans spirit" might now rest in quiet. Bingham sent a printed version, with all the other addresses he could collect, to Rufus King with the noncommittal observation, "Some . . . have a great share of merit, and others are below mediocrity."

Intense political feelings that had been held in check during the memorial services now flared up again with renewed vigor. The Federalists and the Jeffersonians prepared themselves for the fall Presidential election — the nation's first election between two fully formed parties, and one that would set the direction of the country for years to come.

The Sixth Congress passed no major legislation during its first session, but an action of the Senate became a major campaign issue, drew down popular wrath on the Federalists, and became, in the words of one historian, "one of the most notably dramatic conflicts between the Senate and press in our history."

William Duane, a thirty-nine-year-old printer on his way to becoming political boss of Philadelphia, had succeeded the late Benjamin Franklin Bache in the affections of Mrs. Bache and as editor of the *Aurora,* the country's most powerful Jeffersonian newspaper. Duane, carrying on a spirited castigation of the Federalists, suggested that John Adams was taking British gold to betray his country. Arrested for seditious libel of the President and the government, he defended himself in court with such boisterous skill that both President and government were beginning to regret that they had taken him on. When the United States Senate charged him with a breach of its privileges in the spring of 1800, it soon came to the same conclusion.

The Senate's troubles began with a bill introduced by Pennsylvania Senator James Ross through which the Federalists hoped to save the country for truth, righteousness, and Federalism in the Presidential election of 1800. The bill concerned the count of electoral votes in case of a disputed Presidential election. It would have given a Grand Committee of the House and Senate (both Federalist controlled) absolute power to decide in secret session the validity of any objections to any of the electoral votes, with no appeal from its decision. Duane obtained a copy of the bill, printed it, and pointed out in somewhat rude language that this was a brazen attempt to change the constitutional system of counting the Presidential vote, and to change it by statute rather than by constitutional amendment. The plan, he said, had been prepared at a Federalist caucus of United States Senators. In explaining the evils of caucuses ("or secret consultations"), he revealed the story of the first caucus.

> In the summer session of 1798 — when federal thunder and violence were belched from the pestiferous lungs of more than one despotic minion, a caucus was held at the house of Mr. William Bingham in this City. . . .
>
> Upon a division of the caucus it was found that [the Senators] were divided nine against eight. This majority . . . held the minority to their engagement, and the whole seventeen voted in Senate upon all the measures discussed at the caucus.
>
> Thus, it is seen that a secret self-appointed meeting of seventeen

persons dictated laws to the United States. . . . In other words, a *majority* of nine members of the Senate *rule* the other twenty three members.

The Senate had no Committee of Privileges, but it appointed five men to form one. The new committee then charged that Duane, in printing "false, defamatory, scandalous and malicious" statements "tending to defame the Senate . . . and to bring it into contempt and disrepute," had committed a high breach of privilege of the Senate. Bingham advised his colleagues that they would do better to send Duane to the courts, which would effectively punish him, "as the Sedition Law contemplated this offense and attaches a penalty to it"; but the Senate elected to try Duane and Bingham voted with his party. John Marshall was the only dissenting Federalist.* Duane, in the meantime, was blasting the Senate for its "monstrous attempt" as "enemies of our liberties" to coerce him and violate the freedom of the press.

When Duane appeared before the Senate to defend his conduct, he demanded to be represented by counsel. The Senate ruled that his two attorneys might appear but that they could not inquire into the jurisdiction of the Senate over such cases. The attorneys refused to appear under such restrictions. Duane, thus denied professional assistance, felt himself bound "by the most sacred duties, to decline any further voluntary attendance" before the Senate, and the Senate thereupon cited him for contempt.

Several weeks later, with Duane still at large and the Ross bill defeated in the House, Bingham presented a petition of the citizens of Philadelphia requesting the Senate to reconsider and drop its action against Duane. The Federalist Senators, still smarting under the attacks of the *Aurora*, attempted to keep the petition from being read on the floor. Bingham voted with his party against honoring the petition he had presented.† The vote was even. Jefferson cast one of his rare votes as presiding officer, broke the tie, and then read the peti-

---

* In a vote that does him more credit, Bingham a few weeks later voted with the majority against permitting slaves to be taken into the Mississippi Territory. Marshall, who braved the wrath of his fellow-Federalists for his Duane vote, cast his ballot in favor of the extension of slavery.

† Historian John Bach McMaster suggests that the choice of Bingham to present the petition was a senatorial "mark of especial derision" toward the Republicans, since Duane had denounced him as host to the "secret self-appointed meeting." It seems more likely that Bingham was simply serving a group of his constituents.

tion aloud. The signers "dreaded the introduction of rights unlimited and power unbounded." The Senate's action allowed neither trial by jury, nor confrontation of witnesses. Accusers should not be the judge, jury and punisher of the accused. "The surest safeguard of the rights and liberties of the people is the freedom of the press."

The Senate ignored the petition, found Duane guilty *in absentia,* and requested the President to instruct the attorney general to begin legal proceedings — a request Adams was most happy to comply with. But "very little exertion," Bingham wrote to Rufus King, "was made to discover and arrest him. He appeared publicly . . . and assumed great consequence from his sufferings as a persecuted patriot and martyr to the Liberty of the Press. He elevated himself into such notice as to be repeatedly toasted at the democratic feasts." Duane was indicted in October, 1800, but he was never brought to trial and never apprehended, even though he continued to publish the *Aurora* in Philadelphia. Apparently the sergeant at arms was secretly ordered not to find him. The Duane case dragged on and in a friendlier administration was dropped.

On May 14, 1800, Bingham reported to the Senate that President Adams had no further communication to make other than his best wishes for their safe return to their homes. The Senate adjourned, committed to meet again in the fall in Washington City.

Bingham was pessimistic about a Federalist victory in the coming election. He saw and lamented a "want of energy in the Administration." Jacobin principles were gaining ground in many states, he told Oliver Wolcott, and the party that supported them, "from a congeniality of sentiment, make a greater impression on the lower class of people." The Republicans, moreover, had "a better system and more industry than their opponents."

The Federalists felt that by every rule of justice and logic they deserved another four years in power. They had created a respectable government, giving it a strong central direction, and had passed the important measures that had made the government work, when many people were sure that it would fail. They had set up an admirable administrative organization.* They had guided the nation safely

* "Probably never in the history of the United States has the standard of integrity of the federal civil service been at a higher level." Leonard D. White, *The Federalists: A Study in Administrative History,* 1959, p. 514.

through eleven dangerous years, avoiding entangling alliances and outright war.

The national treasury was overflowing with gold and silver. The country that fifteen years earlier could not even pay the interest on its debt was now collecting, without strain or effort, $10.5 million annually. There were twenty-nine banks to provide the lifeblood of capital and credit. Those in Philadelphia alone had $10 million in reserves.

The strength of an industrial and commercial economy was beginning to assert itself. No fewer than fifteen factories in New England were now, in 1800, producing cloth by the Arkwright water frame method, and the nation was making its own window glass. The tonnage of the American merchant fleet in foreign trade was equal to that of the British dominions of six years earlier. The country was exporting nearly twice as much wheat and flour as it had in 1790. Thanks to Eli Whitney's invention, the southern states were exporting 25,000 bales of cotton annually. This trade and commerce were protected by a navy of nine frigates and twenty-five smaller vessels. In the summer of 1800, even while negotiations were progressing with Napoleon and Talleyrand, that navy captured some fifty French privateers in waters off the U.S. coast.

There were now no fewer than five cities with more than 20,000 population, and six others with more than 5000. Wages had risen to one dollar a day for a workman hired by the day, besides his board. Public works were going forward in the cities. Great new advances in science, medicine and the mechanical arts gave promise of a land where there would be no poverty and no ailment but old age. Smallpox inoculation, always dangerous, was giving way to the new vaccination treatment, in which the patient was infected, not with a mild case of smallpox, but with a milder cowpox. There was talk that someday the streets would be lighted with "inflammable air" made from soft coal. A tobacco merchant named Thomas Leiper was conducting experiments at Philadelphia's Bull's Head Tavern in which wheels of a carriage were made to fit "railways" of oak plank laid along a road; in this way, Leiper claimed, a horse could move three times the weight he could manage on a common road. The inventor Oliver Evans declared, "The time will come when people will travel in stages moved by steam engines at fifteen to twenty miles an hour."

Of all the American cities, none was making better use of the new developments than Philadelphia. A system of municipal cleaning of the streets had been set up, and fire protection was now a public service. A "watering system" designed by Benjamin Henry Latrobe, architect and engineer, was being installed. It was to take the pure, fresh water of the Schuylkill, carry it through a canal and tunnel to Center Square,* pump it by steam engines to an elevated 16,000-gallon tank, and thence, by gravity flow, through underground hollowed logs to hydrants in all the neighborhoods.

William Bingham was a moving spirit behind one of the grandest undertakings: a Permanent Bridge designed to cross the Schuylkill at Market Street, replacing the old floating bridge and connecting with the Lancaster Turnpike. With its approaches, the structure was 1300 feet long; its wooden center span, resting on two piers, soared an imposing 260 feet across the river. As a director of the Bridge Company, Bingham favored retaining the services of the famous English engineer, William Weston, despite his high fees, and he supported Weston's proposal to use a deep coffer dam — the first ever seen in America — in building the piers. The cornerstone of the Permanent Bridge was laid on October 18, 1800, in the presence of the mayor, members of the city council, directors of the Bridge Company, and a large assemblage of citizens. It would surmount great engineering obstacles and become known on both sides of the Atlantic as one of the noblest bridges of its day.

The country was prosperous; the Federalist record was good; the Congressional election of 1799 had been a great victory; but in 1800 one disaster after another struck down Federalist hopes.

The worst catastrophe came first, early in May, while Congress was still in session, and it brought others in its train. The Republicans swept the state of New York, thus assuring a solid slate of Republican electors in the fall Presidential election.† It was a tremendous personal victory for Aaron Burr, leader of a tireless, well-planned Re-

---

* Center Square, at Market and Broad, was used for fairs, Quaker meetings, a tavern, a bowling green, and a gallows tree. It is now occupied by City Hall.

† The Presidential election was not then a national campaign, but a series of local contests. In these, the relatively limited number of people who could vote chose Presidential and Vice Presidential electors or the legislators who would name the electors. The electors were to cast their votes in their states on December 4, 1800.

publican campaign, and it won him the nomination as Jefferson's
Vice Presidential candidate. The election was as great a personal defeat for Hamilton.

A few days after the New York defeat, Federalist leaders met in
secret caucus (that day's equivalent of the nominating convention)
and agreed to support John Adams for reelection. Few party leaders
wanted or admired Adams, but he had public support and he could
not be dropped. They named Charles Cotesworth Pinckney of
South Carolina, a hero of the XYZ Affair, as their Vice Presidential
candidate.

John Adams, angered by the New York defeat, now decided that
the time had come to rid himself of the Hamilton men in his cabinet.
He abruptly demanded the resignations of James McHenry and
Timothy Pickering, secretaries of War and State. Pickering replied,
"I do not feel it to be my duty to resign." He had "several matters of
importance to attend to"; he needed the money; and he intended
to stay at his post, he said, until March, when the President would
be replaced. Within an hour he received a curt note of dismissal.
He had to leave his office on such short notice that he had no
time (as he ruefully explained to Hamilton) to gather documents
that could be used to denote the unfitness of the President.

Senator John Marshall took Pickering's post; Congressman Samuel
Dexter of Massachusetts took McHenry's. Adams did not dismiss
Oliver Wolcott, his Secretary of the Treasury. He was unaware that
Wolcott had been Hamilton's chief supporter and informant in the
cabinet.

The dismissals produced elation in Republican ranks and conster-
nation among the Federalists. Now there were two Federalists caucuses. Those who supported Adams and opposed Hamilton's leadership met in Bingham's residence; those who supported Hamilton
and Pickering met in Senator Jacob Read's. "I will never more be
responsible for him [Adams] by my direct support," Hamilton declared on May 10, "even though the consequences should be the election of Jefferson. If we must have an enemy at the head of government, let it be one whom we can oppose, and for whom we are not
responsible, who will not involve our party in the disgrace of his foolish and bad measures." Hamilton began to lay plans by which Pinck-

ney might be elected President by withholding an electoral vote or two from Adams.*

It was a bitter campaign — perhaps the bitterest in United States history. The abuse and scandal, Abigail Adams said, were "enough to ruin and corrupt the minds and morals of the best people in the world"; and she added, "The Jacobins are a very wicked unprincipeld set of beings." But the "Jacobins" were united, determined and efficient, with young lieutenants and active printing presses in every state; the Federalists were divided and dispirited. Washington's protection and leadership were gone. The threat of war with France was almost gone, and with it the national unity that the threat had produced. Cobbett had been driven out of the country, young John Fenno of the *Gazette* had died of the yellow fever, and Duane and the *Aurora* made their charges without effective reply or counterattack. The Irish and the Germans, the farmers and the frontiersmen, were outraged variously by high taxes, an idle army, the sedition law, and the rich aristocrats who were running the government from the cities. There was talk among New England High-Federalists of secession from the Union if Jefferson was elected.

"Every effort must be made to exclude Mr. Jefferson," Bingham wrote to Oliver Wolcott in July. Considering the present state of European politics, he said, Jefferson's election would increase the hostility of England and "prove fatal to our tranquillity, so far as relative to our foreign relationships." † It might mean "an overthrow of the principles which have guided the administration since the establishment of our government." But the recent accounts he had received from various parts of the country convinced him that "no system" pervaded the Federalist conduct.

> Without this, it is impossible to ensure success. I shall use my best exertions to strengthen and support our tottering cause, and shall animate others to do the same; and flatter myself, notwithstanding our dreary prospects, we shall at length succeed.

A few weeks before the election, Hamilton lost his head and, in one

---

* Each elector voted for two persons of his choice without designating which he intended to make President. The method was changed in 1802 by the Twelfth Amendment.
† Bingham's prediction of conflict with England was borne out over the next twelve years.

of the strangest episodes in United States political annals, destroyed the last hopes of the Federalists. In a frantic struggle to retain control of his party, he printed an attack of some fifty pages on "the public conduct and character of John Adams." He told of "the disgusting egotism, the distempered jealousy, and the ungovernable indiscretion" of the President's temper. Adams was a man of undoubted integrity, but he did "not possess the talents adapted to the administration of government." He was a man driven by "a vanity without bounds and a jealousy capable of discoloring every object." He was "often liable to paroxysms of anger, which deprive him of self-command and produce very outrageous behavior to those who approach him." As examples of the wrong conduct produced by the President's "intrinsic defects" of character, Hamilton cited the pardoning of John Fries, sending the second mission to France, dismissing McHenry and Pickering, and refusing to appoint Hamilton as commander in chief to succeed Washington. Despite these weaknesses and sins, however, Hamilton advised his Federalist colleagues to support and vote for John Adams in the forthcoming election as the only Federalist who could win.

Hamilton intended this document to be sent only to Federalist leaders around the country, but Burr almost immediately obtained a copy and gave it to the Republican *Aurora* and the New London *Bee*. These, falling upon the document with incredulous delight, printed generous extracts.

Many Federalist leaders, including Bingham, were appalled. They refused to abandon Adams for Pinckney, and they indicated that they henceforth would no longer follow Hamilton's leadership. Noah Webster, editor of the New York *Spectator,* had admired and supported Hamilton. Now he spoke for these Federalists when he wrote and published an open letter to Hamilton in defense of Adams. "Your ambition, pride and overbearing temper," he concluded, "have destined you to be the evil genius of the country. . . . Your conduct on this occasion will be deemed little short of insanity." Thomas Cooper, a Republican editor who had just served six months in jail for libeling President Adams, called for prosecution of Hamilton under the Sedition Act.

Some Federalists found a wry satisfaction at this time in an attempted insurrection of slaves in Virginia, the stronghold of the party dedicated to the Jacobin principles of liberty and equality. The plot was uncovered as it was about to erupt. Forty-one slaves, including their leader, "General" Gabriel, were hanged in Richmond with the concurrence of Governor James Monroe; but the event had no discernible effect on the election.

In the summer of 1800, the government moved to Washington. Bingham arranged to attend the coming session of Congress there, but he would not stand for reelection. His decision to withdraw, he told Rufus King, had been determined some months before and was not caused by the move from Philadelphia.

There was good reason for his decision. Sixteen years after the birth of Maria, at thirty-seven years of age, Anne Bingham was again with child; she would be delivered in December. Anne had always been frail, and now, with another child, Bingham felt he should not leave home for the long periods required by continued service in the Senate. He decided to miss the first weeks of the session in Washington to stay with her until after the birth.

The child was born late in December — the son they both had hoped for. He was christened William.

CHAPTER 30

An Act of Man, An Act of God

As for the result of the election . . . neither party can decisively rely on the event, as it depends on the votes of some few persons who have not explicitly avowed their determination, even to such friends as had a right to expect from them this mark of confidence. . . . Tomorrow is the important day which will fix the fate of the two candidates.

William Bingham to Richard Peters
Washington City, February 10, 1801

HE LEFT Philadelphia by carriage on January 1, 1801. The road to Baltimore was one of the worst in the country, with its iron-hard ruts, its holes and ravines, but at least it was familiar. The post road south out of Baltimore was both bad and unknown. Through mile after mile of Maryland forest he rode without the sight of a person or a habitation — then perhaps a cabin in a clearing, perhaps a slave on a cart of whom to ask the distance to the next inn. He was nine days on the road.

He came at last to the Federal City. Along the near bank of the Potomac a large area had been cleared and some roads laid in the red mud. These led through tree stumps, brick kilns, piles of rock and rubble, gravel pits, and workmen's sheds and shanties. Standing on a hill between the woods and the river, a white sandstone building, the Capitol, dominated the whole scene. Its north wing was completed, the south wing only partly built, the long gap between them open to the elements. Some fifteen buildings clustered around it: seven or eight boardinghouses, a tavern, and a half-dozen small shops — a tailor, a shoemaker and a washerwoman, a grocery store, a dry goods store and an oyster market, a printer who sold stationery and pamphlets. For three-quarters of a mile there was no other human habitation of any kind.

A mile and a half to the west, toward the village of George Town, stood the President's Mansion, also of sandstone. It appeared from this distance to be completed, but it was said that the plastering was not finished and the main staircase not yet started. The floors, moreover, supported by green joists, had begun to sag, and the roof leaked. In this section were two or three hundred temporary wooden structures for workmen; a hundred substantial red-brick houses; and two public office buildings, one for Treasury, the other for War and Navy. Two others were blackened shells, gutted by fire before completion.

A roadway called Pennsylvania Avenue led from the Capitol through a mosquito-infested tidal marshland to the President's Mansion. Some of the tree stumps had not yet been removed from this road. Beside it for part of the distance ran a footpath, built up with stone chips and rubble from the buildings. Farther westward, on the Potomac hills, lay a small town of well-designed brick buildings. A mile to the south of the Capitol, beyond still another swamp, stood an empty warehouse, an unused wharf, and a block of twenty row houses. These were the unfinished dwellings started by Robert Morris before his bankruptcy and ruin. The only industry was a brewery, and there was no church.

Altogether, 3200 people lived in this place. Many of these were artisans who could be seen working languidly on the walls of the Capitol. About 600 slaves had been brought to labor in the gravel pits, on the roads, at the kilns and sawmills.

Such was Washington, the Federal City, as Bingham saw it on his arrival. The site had been the scene of an impressive ceremony ten years earlier when President Washington laid the cornerstone of the Capitol building in a Masonic ceremony. John Adams and a Federalist Congress would rule here for two more months. On March 4, 1801, Thomas Jefferson, Aaron Burr and the other Republicans would take over the administration, control the Congress, and run the country.

The second session of the Sixth Congress had convened on November 22, 1800, five days behind the appointed time. The six weeks that followed were marked by desultory attendance and indifferent attention to legislative business. Albert Gallatin, Republican floor leader of the House, was absent until January 12. Only token sessions were held through the second half of December, many of the members having fled to the comforts of Baltimore for the Christmas season.

Most of the members were living in the boardinghouses around the Capitol. The Republicans were at Conrad and McMunn's, the Federalists at Robert Peacock's. Almost none of the men had brought their families, since accommodations were known to be bad, expensive and scarce. They slept two to a bed and ate by the dozens at the long boardinghouse tables, the latest guests taking places nearest the door and farthest from the fireplace. They looked, Gallatin thought, like a refectory of monks. The charge was high: $15 a week for room, board, candles, wood, liquor, and service — $20 with a manservant.

Gallatin frankly called Washington "a hateful place." James Bayard, Delaware's sole Representative, declared, "There is a great want of society, especially female." Oliver Wolcott, who had been here since early summer, lamented that there was no industry or business; talking with the optimistic proprietors and entrepreneurs about the future of the city, he concluded that they were all crazy. "Their ignorance of the rest of the world," he said, "and their delusions with respect to their own prospects, are without parallel." Gouverneur Morris, recently returned from ten extraordinary years in the capitals of Europe, now in Washington to serve out an unfinished term in the Senate, was sardonic about the plentiful supply of building stone, the high quality of the bricks, the wide choice of sites for magnificent mansions.

The talk in Washington at the beginning of the new year was still of the election. Except for the loss of New York, President Adams had run stronger than in 1796, and for a time Federalist hopes had revived; but the unexpected loss of South Carolina's eight electoral votes was fatal. Adams received sixty-three votes. An excess of party loyalty had caused every Republican elector to vote for Jefferson and Burr, with the result that each had received seventy-three votes. The election would now be placed in the hands of the House of Representatives, whose members, on the second Tuesday of February — Constitution Day — would choose one of them as President, the other as Vice President.

The Senate chamber was smaller than that in Philadelphia, but it was magnificent with its high arched roof, large public gallery, and arcaded back wall of paneled piers with gilded capitals. The red chairs had been fashioned of mahogany brought specially from the West Indies, of morocco leather imported from London. Bingham answered his first roll call there on Monday, January 10, and spent the day listening to a debate on whether the grateful nation should erect a marble mausoleum or an equestrian statue to honor George Washington.* He soon became involved with the two important measures of this session: the treaty with France and reorganization of the federal judiciary system.

Governor William Davie had arrived from France in mid-December with a treaty, or "convention," signed at Morefontaine on September 30. The French, he reported, would pay indemnity for their seizures of American shipping only on one condition: the United States would have to reaffirm the Franco-American treaties of 1778 under which it guaranteed French possessions in the Western Hemisphere and permitted French privateers to bring English prizes into American ports. The American envoys refused to consider this: it would mean war with England. After seven months of negotiations, they signed a commercial treaty only — a convention that called upon both sides to treat each other's citizens and commerce fairly in perpetuity, and to return all captured private vessels not yet condemned in the courts. The main issues — continuation of the treaties and payment of French indemnity — were postponed to some possible future date. Davie defended the agreement on the ground that an accommodation had to be made at almost any cost, since the French and English were about to sign a peace treaty and the United States would be fighting France alone.

The Senate debated the convention for several weeks and then, in a last Federalist expression of hostility to France and to the Jeffersonians, defeated it by two votes. Bingham was distressed:

> An immense property is laying in the ports of France, subject to pillage and plunder, cargoes perishing, vessels diverted from their destined course, the premiums of insurance on the immense trade of this country continuing, during this uncertain state of things, at an advanced price.

He joined with Republicans and with those Federalists who still sup-

---

* Congress debated the cost and form of the monument for several years and then let it drop. The Washington Monument was built some fifty years later by public subscription.

ported Adams to bring the treaty to another vote. He moved from the floor that the life of the treaty be changed from perpetuity to eight years, and that the paragraph calling for future discussion of indemnities and treaties be struck out — changes, he said, that the French government would accept without a moment's hesitation. The Senate accepted the motion and on February 3, 1801, approved the Convention by a vote of 22 to 9. Thus was the half-war with France brought to an end.

The Judiciary Bill completely reorganized the second level of the federal courts. The overloaded circuit courts were increased in number from three to six, their judges from thirteen to thirty-three. The Supreme Court justices were freed of riding the district circuits. The reform was necessary, but the Federalists gave it an added dimension. They had lost control of the executive and legislative branches of government; now they would use the courts to save the country from the blunders and "mischievous designs" of the Jacobins. As an afterthought, they reduced the number of Supreme Court justices from five to four, to become effective with the next vacancy. Thus the Republicans would not be able to make an appointment when that vacancy occurred.

There was a rush to fill the judicial posts with deserving Federalists — twenty-three judgeships at $2000 a year for life and collateral offices: marshals, justices of the peace, district attorneys, and clerks. It was expected, Bingham wrote to Richard Peters, federal district judge for Pennsylvania, that "the President will give due weight to the recommendations of the members of the Senate, and the importance of filling the seats with Federal characters must be obvious." He called at the President's Mansion and came away with John Adams' concurrence in the nomination of William Tilghman of Philadelphia as chief justice of that district court.

Adams gave one of the judgeships in the Second Circuit to Oliver Wolcott, and Wolcott, after some deliberation, accepted, having decided that the offer was a sincere expression of atonement for past injury. To the vacant post of Chief Justice of the United States he appointed John Marshall of Virginia — a man whom Jefferson believed to be a timeserver and a weakling.* He appointed his improv-

---

* Congressman Elias Boudinot of New Jersey urged John Adams to appoint John Adams as Chief Justice.

ident son-in-law, Colonel Smith, as surveyor and collector of revenues of the District of New York; Congress, after avoiding the issue for seventy-three days, grudgingly confirmed him.

During the weeks following the election, Federalist leaders gradually began to realize the position of power they still held in the choice of a President. They had a majority of four votes in the House and controlled enough state delegations to keep Jefferson from getting the nine states he needed for election. They began to cast about for a best means to use their leverage. "Jefferson and Burr have equal votes," Oliver Wolcott wrote to his wife on December 31, "and the Federalists are doubting which to prefer. There will be intriguing here through the winter upon the high scale."

The Federalists met in secret session in mid-January to determine their course. Some of the New Englanders proposed that every effort be made to prevent the election of either man. If the deadlock continued until Inauguration Day, March 4, the Federalists in the Senate would appoint an acting President — John Marshall's name was mentioned — to serve until another general election could be held. The majority rejected this proposal as dangerous and extreme. The moderates proposed that Jefferson be required to make certain promises in return for the votes that would give him the Presidency. He should be pledged to uphold the financial structure of the country, retain government office holders below cabinet rank, maintain an adequate navy, and continue the policy of neutrality established by Washington and Adams — no alliance with France, no war with England.

The members then turned to still another plan — one that had been winning strong and growing support. Why not elect Aaron Burr President? If possible, work out an arrangement with Burr that would divide the Republicans, make him a grateful dependent, and retain at least some power in Federalist hands. If that was not possible, accept him as a better, safer choice than Jefferson.

No record of the January caucus exists, but the Federalist leaders were expressing their views freely in correspondence, and presumably they presented and debated their views at this meeting. Ex-Senator Theodore Sedgwick, now Speaker of the House, weighed the relative merits of the two men.

He [Burr] is ambitious — selfish — profligate. His ambition is of
the worst kind; it is a mere love of power, regardless of fame. . . .
His selfishness excludes all social affections; and his profligacy un-
restrained by any moral sentiment and defying all decency.

This is agreed, but then it is known that his manners are plausible — that he is dexterous in the acquisition and the use of the
means necessary to effect his wishes. . . . He holds to no pernicious
theories, but is a mere matter-of-fact man. His very selfishness prevents his entertaining any mischievous predilection for foreign
nations. . . . We have [in Jefferson] . . . a feeble and false, enthusiastic theorist and [in Burr] a profligate without character and
without property, bankrupt in both.

Between these choices, Sedgwick supported Burr.

John Marshall of Virginia, a moderate, could never forgive Jefferson's attacks on Washington. Jefferson's "foreign prejudices" in
favor of France made him "totally unfit" to be President. "I cannot
bring myself to aid Mr. Jefferson."

James Bayard of Delaware, a much-troubled man: "There would
be really cause to fear that the government would not survive the
course of moral and political experiments to which it would be sub-
jected in the hands of Mr. Jefferson."

George Cabot of Massachusetts: Burr was "less likely to look to
France for support than Jefferson, provided he could be supported at
home." Burr was "actuated by ordinary ambition, Jefferson by that
and the pride of Jacobinical philosophy. The former may be satisfied
by power and property, the latter must see the roots of our society
pulled up, and a new course of cultivation substituted."

Charles Carroll of Carrollton, Maryland: Burr would "act with
more decision than Jefferson, and go better with his party." But with
either nominee, the country was headed toward ruin. The choice
eventually would be between Bonapartean usurpation or Jacobinical
chaos.

Harrison Gray Otis of Massachusetts: "It is palpable that to elect
[Burr] would be to cover the opposition with *chagrin,* and to sow
among them the seeds of a morbid division."

Hamilton had come to his own painful decision and for weeks had
been sending a stream of letters to his friends in Washington, with

permission to use and show them discreetly. Jefferson's "politics are tinctured with fanaticism . . . he is too much in earnest in his democracy . . . he has been a mischievous enemy to the principal measures of our past administration. . . . He is crafty . . . not scrupulous about the means of success, nor very mindful of truth, and . . . he is a contemptible hypocrite." Still, there was "no fair reason to suppose him capable of being corrupted." He had "pretensions to character." One might expect of him "a temporizing rather than a violent system." Burr, on the other hand, was "as unprincipled and dangerous a man as any country can boast — as true a Cataline as ever met in a midnight conclave." He was a man "without probity . . . a voluptuary by system." His "elevation can only promote the purposes of the desperate and profligate." He "cares only for himself and nothing for his country."

And so Hamilton, "for the public good," pleaded with his colleagues to support Jefferson — the one man in the world, he said, he had the most reason to hate. His colleagues refused to take his advice and ignored his threat to leave the party if they did not. Under Sedgwick's leadership, they voted to support Burr — and to attempt to elect him to the Presidency.

Four Federalist Representatives opposed the vote and apparently refused to be bound by it. Three other leaders of the party were outspoken in their opposition to the Federalist plan. One was John Jay. Another was Gouverneur Morris, who emphasized a simple point that everyone else seemed to ignore: "Since it was evidently the intention of our fellow-citizens to make Mr. Jefferson their President, it seems proper to fulfil that intention." The third was William Bingham. "The Willing and Bingham connection," Albert Gallatin wrote to his wife in January, "have openly declared against the [Federalist] project and recommended an acquiescence in Mr. Jefferson's election."

While waiting for the day of the electoral count, and in intervals of his duties in the Senate, Bingham conducted various personal, business and governmental affairs. He sat on committees for choosing a health officer for Maryland; for drawing up a system of estimating foreign coins and currency; and for providing a "Naval Peace Establishment." He corresponded with General Cobb (who, with Bingham's approval, had taken on a second job as a member of the Massachusetts state legislature) on the sad lack of progress in selling the Maine lands. He advised the directors of the Bridge Company on matters pertaining to the Permanent Bridge. He notified Judge Peters, "Your salary has been raised to $2,000 and placed on the same footing as that of the district judges." He searched for a representative to serve the Bank of the United States in Washington. He corresponded with the trustees of Dickinson College about bonds he had given but which had somehow become lost. He exchanged letters with Cadell and Davis, London booksellers, concerning a list of 151 titles he and a colleague had ordered as a first consignment "for the intended library at Washington." * He wrote an angry letter to an unidentified correspondent on the "exceeding indifference" of his fellow merchants in not complaining to the Department of State about the depredations of the British cruisers on American shipping and the actions of

> their profligate judges of their lower courts of admiralty, their un-righteous sentences, with impunity. . . . The American government cannot remonstrate, for they are furnished with no cases on which to establish their remonstrances. . . .
>
> It is certainly not desirable that the first official act of the new Government towards Great Britain should exhibit a volume of complaints and should be cloathed in the language of invective and remonstrances.

He seems to have accepted with equanimity, or at least with resignation, the fact that his Senate seat was to be filled by the notorious Dr. George Logan, strict Quaker, pacifist, and devoted follower of Thomas Jefferson. Dr. Logan had attempted three years earlier, as a self-appointed emissary to Paris, to end the half-war with France.† He had led the opposition in 1793 to Bingham's Lancaster turnpike, calling its right of eminent domain a dangerous infringement of property rights and another evidence of "the late unjust and arbi-

---

* Bingham's list included Jefferson's *Notes on Virginia;* Gibbon's *Decline and Fall;* Hume's *History of England;* Voltaire's *Charles XII;* Bougainville's *Voyages;* Boswell's *Journal of a Tour to the Hebrides;* Morse's *American Geography;* Blackstone's *Commentaries; Irish Debates;* Smith's *Wealth of Nations;* Sheffield's *Commerce;* John Adams' *The American Constitution;* and Locke's *Works.*

† Because of him, Congress passed the "Logan Act," which forbade private citizens to undertake diplomatic negotiations without official sanction. It is still the law of the land.

trary laws by which a few wealthy men are incorporated and empowered to violate the rights of their fellow citizens."

*

There was a chill swirling snowstorm on the second Wednesday in February, the day on which the two houses were to meet to count the electoral vote. Washington was crowded with hundreds of visitors and every lodging house was filled, men sleeping three to a bed and on dining room tables. In one place, some fifty men spent the nights on blankets on the floor, covered by their greatcoats. Hamilton, still writing letters on behalf of Jefferson, remained in New York. Burr was in Albany, attending a meeting of the New York Assembly. He had refused Federalist pleas to present himself in Washington and work for his election. Historians cannot agree as to whether he was playing an honorable or a devious game.

Congress met in joint session at noon in the new Senate chamber, Thomas Jefferson presiding. He broke the seals on the electoral certificates and gave them to the tellers. The clerk read the totals that were expected: Jefferson 73, Burr 73, Adams 65, Pinckney 64, Jay 1. Jefferson announced that no election had taken place and that the House of Representatives must now decide whether Thomas Jefferson or Aaron Burr should be the next President.

The Representatives immediately retired to their temporary meeting place in a room behind the Senate chamber. The area was too small for its purpose, but space was still made available, as a courtesy, for the thirty-two Senators and President Adams. (The President did not attend; he was mourning "the greatest grief of my life," the death of his son Charles, an alcoholic, some weeks earlier in New York.) Bingham was present as a spectator with every other member of the Senate. Representative William Craik of Maryland was present under orders from his wife to vote for Jefferson or prepare for a divorce action. His Maryland colleague, Representative Joseph Nicholson, burning with a high fever, was helped to a cot that had been set up in an adjoining committee room, where he lay, attended by his wife. The meeting room itself was unheated and drafty.

By rules of procedure agreed on two days earlier, the doors were to be kept locked and no outsiders admitted. The session would continue without adjournment or consideration of other business until a

decision was reached. The vote would be limited to the two nominees. Each state delegation would vote among itself and then cast one
ballot for *Jefferson* or *Burr* in its state box; if the delegation was
evenly split, it would write the word *Divided*. The nominee receiving the votes of nine or more of the sixteen states would become President.

The sergeant at arms made the rounds with his boxes, collecting
the ballots under the watchful eye of Albert Gallatin, floor leader of
the Republicans and teller of the Pennsylvania delegation. The vote
was counted and checked. Speaker Sedgwick announced the result:
eight states for Jefferson, six states for Burr, two divided. Nicholson's
faltering vote for Jefferson, given from his sick bed, had divided his
delegation and kept Maryland's vote from going to Burr. William
Craik, on mature consideration, had decided to vote for Jefferson.*
Sedgwick at once called for a second vote. Many of the Representatives felt that on this round enough Republicans would change their
vote to give Burr the election; several Federalist newspapers had predicted that this would happen. But Sedgwick again announced:
"The tellers report, and the boxes agree, that eight states have voted
for Thomas Jefferson, six states for Aaron Burr, and two states are
divided." Five more ballots were taken in rapid succession without a
change in the result. Four Federalists in Virginia and North Carolina switched to Burr, giving him a numerical lead of 53 Representatives to 51, but the change made no difference in the state totals. It
was agreed to resume the voting at the end of one hour.

It had now darkened with the late winter afternoon and candles
were brought in. The snow continued to fall, visible through the
windows high up on the walls. There was tension and suspense, but no
passion. Delaware's James Bayard observed that the utmost harmony
and good humor prevailed throughout the first day's proceedings.
Bayard, a Federalist, could have given the election to Jefferson by
switching Delaware's single vote, but he declined to follow the advice
given in a cogent and persuasive letter from Hamilton.

The balloting continued until morning. Some members had sent
out for blankets, pillows and nightcaps and now lay sleeping about
the floors of the committee rooms; others sat wrapped in shawls or
greatcoats. The teller roused the members at one, at two, at two-

* The actual count of Representatives was 55 for Jefferson, 49 for Burr.

thirty, and at four. "It is ludicrous," said the *New York Commercial Advertiser,* "to see some of them running with anxiety from the committee rooms with their nightcaps on."

The twenty-seventh ballot was taken at eight Thursday morning, and when it brought no change, the next was set for noon. The weary-eyed, unshaven Representatives staggered out of the chamber and separated for breakfast and a few hours of rest. Senator Uriah Tracy of Connecticut thought "they looked banged badly." When the twenty-eighth ballot at noon brought no change, the House recessed until eleven o'clock the next day.

The Senate remained in session during these days, with Jefferson outwardly unperturbed in the chair. The members spent much of their time watching the proceedings in the House, discussing the deadlocked election, and meeting in party caucuses; but it was at this time that they passed the judiciary bill. To the rage of the Republicans, they began to confirm appointments to the bench.

One ballot was taken on Friday without either side breaking, and three more on Saturday, after which the House recessed until noon on Monday. Inauguration Day was now only a little more than two weeks away, with no prospect that the deadlock would be ended. The Republicans declared publicly that any Federalist move to place the administration of the government under an appointed official would be considered an attempt at usurpation and one to be resisted by force of arms. Governor Monroe let it be known that in such an event he would call a special session of the legislature, mobilize the Virginia militia, and march on Washington; he set up an around-the-clock relay of express riders to bring him news from the capital. Governor McKean announced that Pennsylvania militia would join the march. The editor of the *Boston Centinel* expressed his scorn of southern soldiers and threatened to send an army of New Englanders to put them down.

A grave constitutional crisis was at hand, and with it the threat of anarchy, or civil war, or both. James Madison proposed that Jefferson and Burr ignore the lame-duck Sixth Congress, call the new Seventh Congress immediately into session, and have it choose a President. The move was not "regular," he admitted, but the circumstances warranted such action. Gallatin vetoed the proposal; it was unconstitutional, and he would gamble that it would not be necessary. Not more than eighteen extreme Federalists, he felt, would follow their leaders, Representatives Henry Lee of Virginia and Roger Griswold of Connecticut, in an outright attempt to usurp power; if New England refused to join with the other states to resolve this crisis, then the Union must dissolve. Jefferson informed Madison and Monroe (but not Gallatin) of a plan to call a convention, reorganize the government, and amend the Constitution. "The very word *convention,*" he said, "gives them [the Federalists] the horrors, as in the present democratical spirit of America they fear they should lose some of the favorite morsels of the Constitution."

At the session on Saturday, the crowd about the Capitol was large, "democratical" in spirit, and impatient in its manner. There was a rumor that 1500 Virginians and Marylanders were poised outside the city, ready to move in and assassinate any acting President appointed by the Federalists.

At this point, Delaware's Bayard moved to break the deadlock. He was disgusted with Burr for not making the slightest effort to win an office that, Bayard felt, he could have had almost for the asking. The only purpose in continuing to support Burr now, he felt, was "to exclude Jefferson at the expense of the Constitution," and this would risk a civil war. And so he sent an emissary to Jefferson asking once again that he agree to the minimum demands of the Federalists: an untouched financial system, a strong navy, and retention of "meritorious" subordinate employees in their positions. Jefferson had declared to John Adams and Gouverneur Morris that he would make no terms and would never take office with his hands tied by any conditions. Bayard's emissary, however, returned with good news. He had seen Mr. Jefferson "and stated to him the points mentioned, and was authorized by him to say that they corresponded with his views and intentions, and that we might confide in him accordingly." * Thus armed, Bayard called a general meeting of Federalists on Sunday and there announced his intention to vote for Jefferson on the Monday ballot. "The clamor was prodigious," he said. "The violent spirits of the Party denounced me as a traitor to the Party." There was

---

* Both Bayard and his emissary, General Samuel Smith, Congressman from Baltimore, testified to these events under oath a few years later. Jefferson denied vehemently that he had made any promises. Many historians believe that the weight of the evidence is against him.

"great agitation and much heat. . . . Some were appeased; others furious; and we broke up in confusion."

The House reconvened at noon on Monday. To Margaret Smith, wife of the editor of Washington's *National Intelligencer,* "the mob gathered on the hillside hung like a thunder cloud over the Capitol, their indignation ready to burst." The latest rumor was that the citizens of Philadelphia had seized the public arms and would not put them down until Jefferson had been named President. Since the method of capitulation had not been worked out, Bayard continued to vote for Burr through two more ballots, the thirty-fourth and thirty-fifth. The House recessed once again. Joseph Nicholson had recovered from his fever; William Craik was still voting for Jefferson.

When the members reconvened at noon on Tuesday, February 17, the seventh day of the deadlock, it was generally known that the Federalists would concede. On the thirty-sixth ballot, Speaker Sedgwick, his visage drawn with anguish, announced the result: ten states for Jefferson, four for Burr, two not voting.

The crowd thronged to the Senate chamber to congratulate Thomas Jefferson, President-Elect. A three-man delegation headed for the Presidential Mansion to inform Mr. Adams of his successor. That night, many windows were illuminated in Washington and the celebration lasted until the early hours. In the room he shared at McMunn's, Gallatin wrote to his wife Hannah: "Thus has ended the most wicked and absurd attempt ever made by the Federalists."

Abigail Adams was in Philadelphia on February 19, on her way to Braintree, when the news of Jefferson's victory arrived. The artillery at the arsenal fired a salute of sixteen guns; the ships in the harbor hung out their banners; the editor of the *Aurora* cried, "The Revolution of 1776 now, and for the *first* time arrived at its completion." In his Orders of the Day, Colonel John Barker, commander of the Eighty-fourth Regiment of militia, hailed the election as a greater victory than that won over Cornwallis; it was "a triumph of reason and justice over folly and intrigue and a phalanx of domestic tyrants and sycophants." *The Gazette of the United States* reported that gin and whiskey had "risen in price 50 per cent since nine o'clock this morning. The bells have been ringing, guns firing, dogs barking, cats mewling, children crying, and Jacobins getting drunk ever since the news of Mr. Jefferson's election arrived in this city." Mrs. Adams, hearing the pealing of the bells of Christ Church, wondered that they should ring so wildly to celebrate the election of "an infidel."

Jefferson announced that James Madison would be the new Secretary of State; Levi Lincoln, Massachusetts Congressman, would be Attorney General; and Henry Dearborn of Maine, Secretary of War. He had trouble finding a Secretary of the Navy and lamented that Robert Morris, still in the Walnut Street prison, was not available for the position. He chose Bayard's emissary, General Samuel Smith, for the post. Gallatin was Jefferson's choice for Secretary of the Treasury, but the announcement was withheld as long as possible to avoid Federalist wrath. Robert Troup, Congressman from New York, called it "an appointment by all virtuous and enlightened men amongst us considered as a violent outrage on the virtue and respectability of our country." Bingham, however, knew Gallatin better than his colleagues, and he favored the appointment. He was, Gallatin told his wife on February 26, "quite sincere in his exertions in support of the intended nomination."

On the morning of March 4, Jefferson was honored by a parade of artillery and riflemen before his lodging at McMunn's, accompanied by salvos of guns and cannon. At noon he walked through an admiring throng to the Capitol, accompanied by Benjamin Stoddert, Adams' Secretary of the Navy, Samuel Dexter, his Secretary of the Treasury, and a group of Republican members of Congress. John Adams was not present. He had spent part of the previous evening signing some judges' commissions sent him by the Senate* and writing a curt note to Jefferson concerning the horses he would find in the government stables. At four-thirty that morning he had taken the northbound stagecoach. On the same stage, fleeing a ceremony that he considered the prelude to a Jacobinical reign of terror, was Speaker of the House Theodore Sedgwick.

Did anyone send an invitation to John Adams to attend the inauguration? If one was sent, did John Adams reject it? Did he write a note of congratulation to his successor? The facts are unrecorded. There was no precedent for the conduct of President or President-Elect, for no transfer of government from one opposing party to an-

* The appointments were forever remembered as "Adams' Midnight Judges."

other had ever taken place. Gallatin said of Adams: "You have no idea
of the meanness, indecency, almost insanity of his conduct, especially
of late. But he is fallen and not dangerous. Let him be forgotten."

Aaron Burr, recently arrived from New York, was in the Vice President's chair when Jefferson entered the Senate chamber. The members rose and Burr, with a gesture, indicted that Jefferson should take
the seat he had vacated. Jefferson sat down, Burr on his right, Chief
Justice John Marshall on his left — three men whose conflicts with
each other would make history in the years to come.

After a few minutes of silence, Jefferson rose and in a low, inaudi-
ble voice read his inaugural address.

> Let us, then, fellow-citizens, unite with one heart and one mind.
> Let us restore to social intercourse that harmony and affection with-
> out which liberty and even life itself are but dreary things. And let us
> reflect that, having banished from our land that religious intolerance
> under which mankind so long bled and suffered, we have yet gained
> little if we countenance a political intolerance as despotic, as wicked,
> and capable of as bitter and bloody persecutions. . . .
>
> Every difference of opinion is not a difference of principle. We
> have called by different name brethren of the same principle. We
> are all Republicans, we are all Federalists. If there be any among
> us who would wish to dissolve this Union or to change its republican
> form, let them stand undisturbed as monuments of the safety with
> which error of opinion may be tolerated where reason is left free to
> combat it. . . .

Alexander Baring, in his report on these events to his father, was
reassuring:

> The accession of Mr. Jefferson may have excited apprehension,
> but you may depend on it that they are unfounded. The personal
> dispositions of the man are strongly in favor of France, but the party
> that brought him in is too feeble to admit of his risking a measure
> which would inevitably ruin him. . . . He is watched with a very
> jealous eye and I am convinced, myself, that he has too much knowl-
> edge of the ground he stands on to risk any bold measure. . . .
>
> You may rely on it that there is no danger from this side at present
> unless goaded by increasing aggressions of the British cruizers. . . .
> If this country is forced into the war against us it will be our own

fault and I think we have enemies enough without uselessly provoking others. You might enjoy the satisfaction of completely prostrating the commerce of America, but you would ruin your best customer to create from an insignificant a very formidable power. . . .

I recommend your reading [Jefferson's speech] as it is the manifesto of the party and a declaration (I believe a just one) of his political creed. It is here much admired though I confess it confirms my invariable opinion of the man, that he is a visionary theorist. The expressions of moderation have conciliated many of the Federalists and he appears disposed to act conformably to them.

*

Bingham apparently was not present at Jefferson's inauguration on March 4. He was in Washington at least until Friday, February 27, for on that date, in his last known action as a Senator, he presented a petition by Philip Sloan, late a captive in Algiers, "praying to be reimbursed a sum of money stated to have been paid for his ransom from the Algerines." He was not present and did not vote three days later, when the Federalists, considering the Senate's farewell to Jefferson, tried (unsuccessfully) to eliminate the words, "a confidence derived from past events." At some unknown moment about this time he received alarming news: his wife was desperately ill.

Too soon after her confinement, against the instructions of her physician and the advice of her family and friends, Anne had gone on one of the gay sleighing parties she loved so much — possibly an all-night party with a fiddler beside the coachman, warm bricks for the feet, frequent stops at taverns for hot punch and oyster stew, and travel over the snow with incredible speed and smoothness.

She caught cold on this party; the cold settled in her chest; and she went into a rapid decline. The family, Alexander Baring said, was "in continued anxiety and alarm." He devoted much time and attention to Anne's care (though his wife was in the last months of pregnancy) before Bingham's return from Washington. Bingham found Anne in a serious condition. "Though her situation is by no means desperate," Baring wrote to his father on March 29, "it is highly critical, so much so as to leave the hopes and fears of those about her who understand her complaint nearly balanced."

The doctors diagnosed her illness as galloping consumption — a rapid form of tuberculosis, usually fatal — and ordered a sea voyage to a warmer climate. Bingham had a suite of cabins fitted out with great care on the *America*, one of the merchant ships in which he had an interest. To General Cobb he wrote on April 9:

> Her disorder has been gaining ground on her and the physicians have therefore recommended an immediate change of climate, and I shall embark with her tomorrow or the next day for the Island of Madeira, where I have great hopes that she will be restored to health, after experiencing the good effects of a sea voyage.

On Monday, April 13, Anne was carried slowly on a palanquin from the Mansion House to the Willing dock and there on board the *America*. A silent throng lined the streets to watch her departure. In the procession were Bingham, his daughter Maria, Anne's youngest sister, Abigail (doubly unhappy because of a broken engagement to a Mr. Cooper), and some family servants, all of whom were to make the voyage, and other members of the family and friends. Everyone was outwardly cheerful, but Baring wrote his father:

> Her case is considered perfectly hopeless here, and indeed she lost so much in the last few days before she was carried on a litter on board of the ship that our hopes were very faint of her recovering anywhere. The accounts we have received by the pilot who took the ship out have revived our expectations as she was considerably benefitted by the motion and the air of the sea, and we are now in the most anxious impatience to hear from her.

Thomas Willing wrote in his notebook:

> My daughter Bingham left . . . on board the Ship America Capt. Wills . . . reduced by a defluction on her breast to the lowest state of debility. My daughter is induced to try this voyage as the last hope for relief. May God grant success to the attempt and restore to health and to her family this amiable, deserving and beloved woman, justly esteemed an ornament to society and an honor to her sex.

In the ship's hold, someone — Captain Wills, or Thomas Willing, or William Bingham — had placed a lead-lined coffin.

Out at sea, with Anne sinking fast, Bingham changed the destination of the *America* from Madeira to Bermuda. It reached the islands on Thursday, May 7. Anne Bingham died at St. George four days later. She was buried in the main parishioners' section of old St. Peter's churchyard, on a hill overlooking St. George's Harbour, in a grave covered by an inscribed slab of Bermuda stone. She was thirty-seven.

In his notebook on May 26, Thomas Willing wrote:

> This day Mr. Bingham return'd from Bermuda where my dear daughter died on the 11th of May 1801.

CHAPTER 31

The Golden Voyage: Extremis

Some time since . . . I requested Mr. Smith that the lamps before Mr.
Bingham's door might no longer be lighted by the public. I find how-
ever that the watchman continues to do so. . . . I beg the favor of you
Sir to cause them to desist.

> Charles Willing Hare
> to George H. Baker,
> Philadelphia City Treasurer
> July 12, 1802

ALEXANDER BARING, writing to his father at the time of Maria's elopement with the Comte de Tilly, had declared that he and his wife Ann
were thinking of moving to England and that the elopement "has
perfectly determined . . . that we should completely renounce this
country.

I am persuaded that by remaining I could very considerably increase my fortune, but when what I have is collected and properly
employed, it will be as much as I covet to place me in a situation
which, in my opinion, no increase of wealth would much ameliorate.
. . . I confess I am ambitious of living in a society more worth
living for and living with than what America generally affords,
which is with a few exceptions very poor.

Baring thereupon began to make arrangements for the management of his American interests "that I may never be obliged by my
affairs to return." Thomas Willing Francis made overtures to Baring. He was doing all the work of Willing, Francis and Company, he
said, and receiving only one-third of the profits, and he would withdraw if he could make the Baring connection. He was, Baring
thought, the most eligible in point of intelligence, "but much too
dashing for a partner in general business." Thomas Willing was entirely occupied with the bank, and his son Thomas Mayne Willing

was "a very good young man but idle." Old Robert Gilmor was "by far the best merchant in the United States and the family looks likely to last." He advised his father to cultivate Gilmor, but he decided to curtail his own affairs "for want of a house here to which I could confide them."

Now with the death of Anne Bingham, the Barings saw no reason to linger in America. They prepared to sail for England in August of that summer of 1801.

On his return from Bermuda, William Bingham found life in Philadelphia a heavy burden. To General Cobb he wrote:

> The frame of mind in which my recent domestic affliction has left me, and the continued renewal of my grief from all the scenes which surround me, have induced me, by the advice of my friends, to make an excursion, and I have at length determined to accompany my daughter and Mr. Baring. . . .
>
> Many of my affairs will be deranged by this temporary absence. But there are few considerations that can be put into competition with tranquillity of mind.

His infant son he gave to the care of Thomas Willing. He placed certain of his business affairs in the hands of Willing and Francis, and he made his wife's nephew, Charles Willing Hare, his agent and legal representative. He gave Robert Gilmor charge of the investment of his surplus funds, including the $50,000 held as the Bingham share of their dissolved partnership. In August, he and Maria sailed for England with the Barings.

The passage was an uneventful one with good winds, the ship docking at Cowes, main port of the Isle of Wight. The party remained there a few days "to be relieved from the fatigue of our voyage" before proceeding to London. Sir Francis Baring and all his family, Bingham wrote to Noailles in Philadelphia, were extremely attentive and friendly. He and Maria spent some days at Stratton Park, one of the Baring estates near London, and then passed the rest of the year at Bath, in lodgings on Pultney Street. "We find the more tranquil scenes of this place," he said, "much more congenial [than London] to the present state of our feelings and dispositions."

In January, 1802, he returned with Maria to London, there again to enjoy the Baring hospitality at the house on Devonshire Square, to visit his daughter Ann, and to renew associations with Rufus King and the English friends he had known twenty years earlier. The kindness of the Barings, he said, "has been of so endearing a nature, as to create in my mind the strongest impression of gratitude." He saw much of his old friend, the Marquess of Lansdowne, now no longer active in public affairs.* Through Noailles he received a proposal from the Comte de Tilly that his £500 annuity be compounded by a lump sum payment of £5000. Bingham refused.

One year after Anne's death, Bingham wrote to her brother, Thomas Mayne Willing, to answer a question on how soon he intended to return:

> For a long time previous to my departure from America, I enjoyed no peace of mind under the afflicting association of ideas which continually presented itself, and I do not think that a revisit to the same objects would tend to restore my tranquillity.
>
> My plan of life must essentially vary as the scenes which constituted my domestic happiness have vanished and thereby compelled me to seek for other resources than those which have for so long a time engaged my attention.

He was much pleased, he said, to hear that his son William was in good health.

> I cannot express to you the degree of tenderness and anxiety I feel on his subject. He has claims upon me of a different and more endearing nature than are usually attached to the situation of children. He will never know the extent of the irreparable loss he has sustained, nor feel that poignancy of grief with which the remembrance of their misfortune afflicts his sisters.
>
> The warm and affectionate attachment which they experience from a number of their friends, particularly amongst the branches of Mr. Baring's family, only tends to bring to their recollection the still fonder endearments they were, under happier circumstances, in the constant habit of receiving.

* Lansdowne had publicly and vehemently opposed the war with France. In 1798, the French Directory apparently had chosen him (without his knowledge) as one of the Directory that would rule England when it was invaded and conquered, along with Thomas Paine and three others. Most of the English nobility and rich proprietors were to have been deported. His son, Lord Wycombe, went to Ireland in 1798 to support the rebels who had persuaded the French to land an invasion force there.

Bingham continued to invest in and profit from "adventures," but with somewhat less of his former drive and decisiveness. He had an interest with Willing and Francis, with Baring and with Gilmor in a number of ships and cargoes: among them the *Canton, Roebuck, Criterion,* and *America,* the last of which he bought outright. He commissioned his agents to sell some of the extensive properties he owned in and about Philadelphia. He corresponded at length with General Cobb, but with a mellow patience not found in the earlier letters. "Your account of the tide of population flowing so very rapidly toward you is very encouraging," he wrote to Cobb from London, but one feels that he was making a courteous answer to what he knew was an attempt to give an encouraging aspect to a hopeless cause. John Richards, the Barings' agent in Maine, was now writing, "The advance of this country will be slow and gradual. . . . It is more than ever my fix'd opinion that this will ultimately prove an advantageous speculation, but that the period of winding it up will not arrive for a great many years."

Cobb was now president of the Massachusetts Senate, and he became chief justice of the Court of Common Pleas. In both positions he worked effectively to protect Bingham's Maine interests. Massachusetts was becoming a Republican state, and part of the Republican program was directed against landed proprietors on behalf of squatter sovereignty in Maine. Only 425 of the 2500 settlers called for under the terms of sale had been placed on the Penobscot and Kennebec tracts. This deficiency, if not made up, would subject Bingham to a fine of $30 for each settler lacking, or a total of $62,250.

Bingham carried with him in Europe the weight and worry of the *Pilgrim* affair, now, after more than twenty years of litigation, in its culminating stages. Before leaving Philadelphia, tired of telling and retelling his story in endless manuscript copies, he had set forth "a fair and candid statement" of the whole matter in a printed pamphlet. He left for England with a judgment of almost $40,000 against him and the threat of having his Maine lands attached. He continued to fight, even when Fisher Ames told him he now had no recourse other than to pay. Charles Willing Hare, charging the Massachusetts courts with practicing "as much flagrant injustice . . . as has been ever known in this country," sought to arrest the proceedings of the plaintiffs, with a writ of error from the United States Supreme Court.

Bingham now had an additional worry. He had always been sure that Congress, having officially accepted responsibility for his actions in Martinique, would reimburse him for a lost judgment; but now he had reason to fear that a Republican Congress would refuse to honor the claim of a Federalist.

In October, 1801, the coalition of British leaders who had succeeded William Pitt signed a preliminary peace treaty with Bonaparte. "There perhaps never was an event," Bingham wrote to Thomas Willing from London, "which occasioned more sincere and heartfelt joy amongst all classes of people, for with the exception of but few persons, every part of the community suffered extremely from this very expensive war." To Noailles, still in Philadelphia: "The disposition to visit the Continent from motives of economy or curiosity is so prevalent amongst the English of a certain class that if passports could be procured, the number would be inconceivably great — and this desire, so strongly evinced, has sincerely alarmed the Government."

The peace was formalized by the Treaty of Amiens in March, 1802, and the English flocked to France to see the scenes of the Revolution and the panoply of the new ruler. But a month before the treaty was signed, Bingham predicted that the peace would be a short one. From London on February 5, 1802:

> The aggrandizing views of France begin to appear the subjection of all the southern powers of Europe to her dominating control [and have] excited the most alarming apprehensions. I hope our policy will be to cultivate the usefull arts, pursue our commerce, and remain at peace.

Indeed, First Consul Bonaparte was taking the Treaty of Amiens to mean that Britain had agreed to withdraw behind the protection of her fleet and permit him to invade, crush, loot, and annex any state that he coveted.

In America, the country was prosperous, and none of the calamities that had been predicted by the Federalists had happened. Jefferson, in fact, had moved to the political right, appropriating a considerable portion of the Federalist program and leaving the Federalists very little platform on which to stand or run. He did this partly as strategy, partly because he found he could not alter the economic system created by Washington and Hamilton, Robert and Gouverneur Morris, Bingham and Willing, and the other Federalist leaders. The country's economic course had been set and was beyond any change of direction. Jefferson lamented in 1802:

> When this government was first established, it was possible to have kept it going on true principles, but the contracted, English, half-lettered ideas of Hamilton destroyed that hope in the bud. We can pay off his debt in 15 years; but we can never get rid of his financial system. It mortifies me to be strengthening principles which I deem radically vicious, but this vice is entailed on us by the first error.

And the visionary philosopher then added most pragmatically:

> What is practicable must often controul what is pure theory; and the habits of the governed determine in a great degree what is practicable.*

At some time during the winter of 1801–02, Henry Baring, Alexander's younger brother, began to show more than fraternal interest in Bingham's daughter Maria, now almost nineteen. On April 10, 1802, he and Maria were quietly married in London. Bingham reported the event to General Cobb as "a connection in every respect highly gratifying. The interest you have always kindly taken in what regards my family induces me to mention the circumstance to you." Alexander Baring was in Philadelphia when he heard the news, having returned to America on family business. It was, he told Gilmor, "an event which though it did not much surprise me was unexpected."

---

* The Federalists never recovered from their defeat of 1800. Jefferson and George Clinton of New York were reelected over Charles Cotesworth Pinckney and Rufus King in 1804 by 162 electoral votes to 14, sweeping all states except Connecticut and Delaware. The Republican "Virginia Dynasty" ruled for twenty-four years. It ruled through Jefferson's disastrous second term, when he imposed an embargo on trade with Great Britain and hurt his own country far more than Britain. It ruled through "Mr. Madison's War" of 1812–1814, when the Republicans took the United States into the European war against England and on the side of Napoleon (as the Federalists had so insistently warned that they would) and saw Washington burned by an invading British army. It ruled through the "Era of Good Feelings," when James Monroe defeated Rufus King, the last Federalist candidate for President and even John Adams voted for Republican candidates and principles. One of the ultimata of the New England secessionists, the Essex Junto, was that no state should be allowed to send two men in succession to the Presidency.

Later that year, Bingham took his daughter Ann on a tour of the Continent following her confinement with a fourth child.* In France, he paid his respects to the several branches of Noailles' family and gave them "information about . . . your situation, your health and happiness." Under other circumstances, he had told Noailles, "with a small addition to the circle which surrounds me, these varied excursions would be delightful." He did find amusement in the splendor of the new court of Bonaparte, "which is rapidly making strides in establishing a parade and introducing a magnificence not surpassed in the most sumptuous days of the old regime."

He called on Robert Livingston, Minister to France, who was maintaining an elegant establishment and entertaining lavishly in Paris. The two men discussed the worsening crisis in Franco-American relations. The Spaniards, under French domination, had closed the port of New Orleans to American ships. Tennessee and Kentucky were threatening to invade and seize the port. Livingston gave Talleyrand a report of a speech in which Senator Ross of Pittsburgh demanded that President Jefferson send a 50,000-man army to take New Orleans.

Even more shocking was the delayed realization that Bonaparte, one day after signing the Morefontaine Convention with the United States in the fall of 1800, had made a secret treaty with Spain by which he forced that country to return to France the Louisiana Territory, comprising the entire Mississippi Valley. He was now taking steps to occupy the Territory with an army, restore the French colonial empire in America, and undo the results of the Seven Years War concluded in 1763. Bingham wrote anxiously to Rufus King:

> A rumor prevails that Spain has ceded Louisiana to France. . . .
> I most sincerely deprecate the consequences as affecting the United
> States, by creating seperate interests betwixt the eastern and western
> divisions of the Union, by affording an opportunity of exercizing
> an influence over the inhabitants of our Western country, who will
> be dependent on France for an outlet to their produce.
> This country [England] is not aware of the advantages this posses-
> sion will give to France as a maritime nation, by the employment of

---

* It cannot be determined who else accompanied them. Alexander Baring apparently was still in the United States.

such a quantity of commercial tonnage in transporting the bulky produce of the Mississippi. . . .

[General] Victor's troops [assembled in Holland] are certainly destined for Louisiana.

Despite his loyalty to France, Jefferson was horrified by Bonaparte's actions. He ordered Livingston to attempt to buy New Orleans outright from France, authorizing him to pay up to $10 million for New Orleans and the Floridas or $7.5 million for the Island of New Orleans alone. In March he sent James Monroe as a special envoy to help Livingston, with authority to make an advance payment of several million dollars as a guarantee of American good faith. Livingston and Monroe were to tell Bonaparte clearly that French occupation of New Orleans would cause the United States to "marry" the British fleet and nation. If Bonaparte refused to sell or to give a guaranteed "right of deposit" at the port, they were to proceed to London and "open a confidential communication with ministers of the British government" leading to "candid understanding and a closer connection with Great Britain."

The news that Monroe had landed was sent from Le Havre to Paris by heliograph.* Livingston frantically increased his efforts with Talleyrand to persuade the French to sell New Orleans before Monroe arrived to share the credit. He succeeded beyond his wildest expectations. One day after Monroe arrived, but before he had entered into the negotiations, Livingston committed the United States to buy the entire Mississippi Valley — about one million square miles. He and Monroe agreed on the price: 60 million francs ($11,250,000) for the land and 20 million francs ($3,750,000) to American citizens in settlement of all claims against France. "You may congratulate me," Livingston wrote to Rufus King.

At some point during the early negotiations, William Bingham somehow, somewhere, met with Talleyrand and, apparently on his own initiative, innocently proposed that France sell the entire Louisiana Territory to the United States. When the bargain was struck a few days or weeks later, Bingham not unnaturally concluded that the action had been taken on his suggestion. Christopher Gore, Ameri-

* A device for signaling in which the rays of the sun were received on a mirror and thence cast on a distant station.

can claims agent in London, wrote sardonically to Rufus King, "Bingham (who, by the way, thinks his conversations with Talleyrand effected the Convention) does not suppose that conveyances of land were made to any individuals prior to the cession [of the Louisiana Territory to the United States], but you know he gives himself credit for full as much knowledge as the world thinks him entitled to."

Bonaparte had made the decision himself, and he acted against Talleyrand's advice. He had good reasons to sell. He was about to reopen the war against Britain, and he needed money to mount an invasion. He had no navy, having lost some 350 vessels to British sea power, and he knew that Britain would immediately take over the Louisiana Territory when war broke out. Rufus King, in fact, had told Livingston, and Livingston had told Talleyrand, that this was the British intention. General Victor's troop transports had been icebound in Holland; and General Leclerc's army in Santo Domingo, which was to have occupied New Orleans, was being destroyed by yellow fever and rebellious blacks under Toussaint L'Ouverture. Louisiana was now clearly beyond Bonaparte's power to occupy, defend or even administer. And so he decided to raise money and spite the British by selling Louisiana to the Americans.

His treaty with Spain denied Bonaparte the right to sell the Louisiana Territory to a third nation. The French constitution denied him the right to sell French territory. The French legislature had not approved the sale — indeed, had not been consulted. These were mere technicalities to Bonaparte, if he thought of them at all. With a signature on a piece of paper, he sold an area more than five times the size of Continental France. The United States more than doubled its size and acquired all or major parts of what were to become thirteen states.* The Spaniards, in losing the Louisiana Territory, had consoled themselves with the thought that at least they had a stanch French ally between their colonial possessions and the Americans. Now they found the Americans on the border of Mexico and a thousand miles closer to California.

---

* All of Arkansas, Missouri, Iowa, Oklahoma, Kansas, Nebraska, and South Dakota; parts of Louisiana, Minnesota, North Dakota, Colorado, Montana, and Wyoming. "In taking Louisiana, we were the accomplices of the greatest highwayman of modern history, and the goods which we received were those which he compelled his unwilling victims to disgorge." Edward Channing, American historian, 1856–1931.

Jefferson lamented that the Constitution gave him no authority to spend $15 million to double the size of the country, but the lament was brief. He borrowed Hamilton's doctrine that the right to act in the public interest was an implied power of the Constitution, and he urged Congress to put "metaphysical subtleties" behind them in approving his action. "The Democrats have as I expected done more to strengthen the Executive," Gouverneur Morris wrote to Roger Griswold, "than Federalists dared think of even in Washington's day."

The Barings and the Hopes, acting as bankers for the United States, with Bingham as a participant, arranged to finance three-fourths of the payment to the French. Gallatin, drawing on the resources of the sound financial structure the Federalists had created, would pay the $3,750,000 American claims at home in cash. The Baring-Hope-Bingham combine would sell $11,250,000 in 6 per cent U. S. Government bonds redeemable in fifteen years. Alexander Baring, with his government's permission, went to Paris and concluded the negotiations. He then sailed for Washington in July, 1803, and there waited for Congress to ratify the treaty and the Treasury to issue the bonds. He carried with him Monroe's letter to Madison giving details of the transaction. Baring, while working more than five months in Washington, came to form a warm, lasting and productive friendship with Secretary of the Treasury Gallatin.

On receiving one-third of the bonds, Baring called on Robert Gilmor in Baltimore and left a set of duplicate papers in an iron chest, with permission to buy $200,000 worth of the bonds and instructions to complete the entire transaction if he met with any mishap. He sailed for England early in February, 1804. The other two-thirds of the bonds were sent by a special messenger to the American minister in Paris, who there delivered them to Hope and Company.

In the meantime, the Baring-Hope-Bingham combine had advanced $2,000,000 to the French Treasury prior to the arrival and sale of the bonds; and it advanced $6,500,000 more against the remaining two-thirds. Technically, the Barings, the Hopes, and William Bingham bought the Louisiana Territory from France and resold it to the United States. Gallatin estimated their profit on the transaction at $3,000,000.

Bingham had intended to make an "excursion" into Switzerland and from there sail leisurely down the Rhine River to Holland. He changed those plans and returned immediately to London when war broke out in May between France and England.* To Willing and Francis he wrote on July 1, 1803:

> Russia has offered her mediation — but whether the terms she proposes will be acceptable to England, on the basis of which may be founded a permanent peace, is not as yet ascertained.
>
> If the war should continue, it will be attended with more powerful exertions, and will be followed by more serious consequences, than has been known to exist in any contest for ages past.
>
> Every effort is making to rouse the people of this country and to impress on them a sense of the impending danger.

In a letter sent to General Cobb from Tunbridge Wells in August, Bingham conjectured optimistically (and mistakenly) that the purchase of the Louisiana Territory would not "occasion any extraordinary emigration from the New England states to the westward.

> In the scale of national policy and individual advantage, the District of Maine presents very superior advantages for settlement. The Atlantic states have now a distinct and seperate system to pursue, and every effort should be made to render their population more compact, and to prevent their inhabitants from being scattered over that immense western wilderness, thereby weakening the aggregate strength of the country, from their labor turning to so little account.

He wrote again to Cobb from London on October 15. He was sending some pamphlets he had gathered on "the present political state of the country." A military spirit pervaded all ranks of people in England, he said, and the most active and energetic measures had been adopted to repel an invasion if it should be attempted. He announced his intention to go home again.

> The time which I limited for my excursion to Europe being nearly expired, I contemplate returning the next season, except some unforeseen circumstances should occasion a further detention. I shall

---

* One of Bonaparte's professed reasons for breaking with England was that the exiled Count d'Artois wore the decorations of the old monarchy at a dress parade in England.

then be able to fulfill your views, on many points, which cannot be so well effected whilst we are at such a distance. Indeed my affairs essentially require my presence.

These were the last known letters but one that Bingham was to write.

What is apparently Bingham's last letter, undated, was written from Stevens Hotel, London, to his friend Sir Charles Blagden, physician, of Upper Berkeley Street, Portman Square, London. Sir Charles, fifty-six, was secretary and a fellow of the Royal Society, an author of medical papers, an antiquarian, and a pioneer in physical research (quicksilver, fiery meteors, the Gulf Stream, the tides of Naples, the properties of heat). Dr. Samuel Johnson called him "a delightful fellow" and the celebrated bluestocking Hannah More thought him "so modest, so sensible, and so knowing." Bingham wrote:

> I left Bath rather abruptly, the day after I had the pleasure of seeing you, having received an invitation to town for the purpose of viewing a library of books and tasting some wine, and which a gentleman detained in France has ordered to be sold and desired I might have the preference in purchasing.
>
> I still persevere in my intention of visiting South Wales, and shall be happy in availing myself of the letters which your brother in law had the goodness to offer me.
>
> I hope to have the pleasure of again meeting you at Bath in a few days.
>
> The recent accounts from France have impressed additional conviction with respect to the Consul's intention of immediate invasion — however notwithstanding appearances I still continue incredulous on this point.

Bingham became ill around this time and consulted Sir Charles in London. Indeed, he was suffering from a fatal illness. The clinical basis of his sickness cannot be determined, though the symptoms resemble those of a stroke. It has been suggested that he had never recovered from the shock of Anne's death and had lost his will to live. His letters give some evidence of this. To Noailles, perhaps his closest friend, he had written in the fall of 1801:

The irreparable loss I have sustained casts a gloom over all my pursuits and blunts the edge of every enjoyment of life. Whether time will moderate my feelings is an experiment yet to be tried. It may habituate me to a state of desperation, but it can never obliterate from my mind the recollection of those virtues . . . nor the reflection that they can never be restored.

The first evidence of serious illness appears in an undated note written by his daughter Ann to Sir Charles in London. It was sent from Wimbledon, a town on the southern edge of London, where Bingham was staying with Ann:

Having been for some days in London with my sister I have but just received your kind inquiries about Papa — he desires me to tell you how much obliged he is to you for your attention and hopes to thank you soon in person as we think of going to town in a very little time — he appears perfectly well eats and sleeps well and has the use of his hands — as to his pulse I have not felt them since Brighton — adieu Sir Charles

Sincerely yours
ANN BINGHAM

Another letter to Sir Charles, undated:

Papa is becoming very uncomfortable, tho not with more pain. Might he take ten drops of laudenum to quiet his fidgets — dont think of coming yourself, only write yes or no.

Sir Charles' answer is unknown, but about this time he favored "Miss Bingham" with a copy of a novel (title undecipherable) of which "the tender sensibilities of the heroine which is admirably portrayed by a thousand little circumstances, as well as the warm attachment of Duthmerta, his noble sentiments and final proof of constancy, never fail to interest."

Bingham, realizing the seriousness of his illness, had been working on his will. He signed it in Bath on January 30, 1804, "being of sound and disposing mind and memory but low in health." In a document that was to make legal history, he named five executors: Alexander Baring, Henry Baring, Robert Gilmor, Thomas Mayne

Willing, and Charles Willing Hare. He created a trust, appointed the executors as trustees, and, in the most detailed language, empowered them to continue the trust indefinitely by electing new trustees within six months when any vacancy occurred.

He left £10,000 sterling to Maria Matilda Baring, "being the marriage portion she has had reason to expect of me." He left £2000 to each of the executors. To his wife's sister, Abigail Willing, Spinster, he left £2000, and to her brother, Richard Willing, and her niece, Maria Clymer, £1000 each, all "as a proof of my affection." The income from his fortune went to his children. He instructed the trustees to pay his just debts and funeral expenses, to place a valuation on the real and personal estate, and to divide it into five equal parts. They were to hold two such parts in trust for his son William and the other three parts in trust for the daughters, Ann and Maria Baring, as tenants in common, not as joint tenants (thus keeping the Estate intact). He further instructed the trustees to sell any of the real estate they thought advisable and to invest the proceeds in the childrens' names in American stocks or funds. His son William was to join his sisters in England when he was eight years old, "for the purpose of receiving his education there."

Late in January, Bingham's relatives assembled in Bath — his two daughters, their children, Henry Baring (Alexander Baring was in America). William Bingham was on his deathbed. Sir Francis Baring was summoned, and the Marquess of Lansdowne. The London *Sun* for February 10 carried the notice:

Died — On Monday (6th) last, at Bath, in the 52nd year of his age, the Hon. William Bingham of Philadelphia, lately a Senator of the United States of America.

The funeral was held at Bath Abbey, and burial in the Abbey itself. Sir Francis Baring ordered a monument to be erected in the south aisle, near the west end of the church, executed by the renowned sculptor John Flaxman, R. A. — a bas-relief with two angels, their wings upright, holding wreaths in each hand, standing on either side of an inscription reading:

SACRED
TO THE HONOURABLE WILLIAM BINGHAM
A NATIVE AND SENATOR OF
THE UNITED STATES OF AMERICA.
WHERE
THE KNOWLEDGE OF THE INTERESTS OF HIS COUNTRY
AND HIS ZEAL FOR THEIR ADVANCEMENT
THE MARKS OF PATRIOTISM
EQUALLY ACTIVE AND ENLIGHTENED,
WILL BE LONG AND GRATEFULLY
REMEMBERED.
HE DIED IN THIS PLACE ON THE 7TH OF FEB^Y 1804
AGED 49 [52] YEARS
CUI PUDOR, ET JUSTITIAE SOROR
INCORRUPTA FIDES, NUDAQUE VERITAS*

On March 1, Sir Francis sent the news to Rufus King in America.

I am just returned from Bath and from paying my last respects
and duty to our friend Bingham; a melancholy task and still more
melancholy reflexion that such a man should be cut off in the
prime of life.

I never saw a more firm manly mind, nor (if I may use the word)
more stern integrity; solely occupied with the consideration of
what was correctly right, without suffering the slightest bias of partiality to operate upon his mind.

Sir Francis then referred to the terms of Bingham's unusual will.

And though my sons do not enjoy some advantages which the
customs both of America and of England sanction, yet I can say
most sincerely that they as well as myself are perfectly satisfied and
that we shall ever hold his memory in the highest respect and
reverence.

He was surrounded by the families of his two daughters and
Lord Lansdowne, whose attentions to him were incessant; indeed
nothing was omitted that could have been supplied.

---

* From Horace, Odes 1, Canto 24, verse 6, translated by John Conington (1825–1869):
"Piety, twin sister dear of justice! Naked truth, unsullied faith!" The next line, not on
the inscription, reads, "When will ye find his peer?"

England's prospects were so gloomy, Sir Francis told King in this letter, that he wrote of them "with reluctance." England was fighting Bonaparte "for the safety of the world." She was the bulwark to America, and the downfall of one would be followed by the destruction of the other. But "when I urged the safety of the world to Bingham, he never would admit that America under any circumstances could possibly be in danger."

In Philadelphia, Dr. Benjamin Rush wrote in his commonplace book:

Died at Bath, Wm. Bingham of this city. He left an estate valued at three million of dollars, half a million of which was in stock of different kinds. He was pleasant in his manners, amiable in his temper, liberal but said not [to] be charitable. . . . He acquired his immense estate by his own ingenuity. . . . In all his money speculations he was fortunate.

Epilogue

HEIRS OF 1804 TRUST TO DIVIDE $840,000
By the Associated Press

NORRISTOWN, Pa., Nov. *14 — The estate of a man reputed to be the richest American when the 13 colonies won independence has been ordered liquidated. Its present assets of $838,000 — all in cash — will be distributed to 315 heirs, some of them English. . . .*

Judge Taxis explained that under the terms of the trust it had no termination date and could therefore run indefinitely. He said that the rule of law against perpetuity did not apply in this instance. . . .

The estate at the time of Mr. Bingham's death was worth much more than it was today, because much of it has been sold in the intervening years. . . .

The New York Times
Page one, with Bingham portrait,
Sunday, November 15, 1964

RICH MEN dream of maintaining a kind of continuing control over their wealth after they are dead. William Bingham came as close as any man might to succeeding. His trust lasted for almost fifty years. The "Bingham Estate" that grew out of the trust lasted for another century as a phenomenon unique in American business and legal history. Until 1964 it continued to function, to renew itself, to pay out enormous sums to an ever-widening circle of heirs. Bankers studied the famous Bingham Estate with respect and lawyers regarded it with envy.

Charles Willing Hare, twenty-six in 1804, a shrewd and aggressive man, served as agent for the testamentary trustees until 1820. He first settled the suit over the ship *Pilgrim,* paying the Cabots $37,000 in damages. He arranged for action to be taken by the Pennsylvania, New York and Massachusetts legislatures to recognize the provisions of the Bingham Trust. He settled Major William Jackson's claims with a payment of $25,500. He collected General Knox's large debt to the Bingham Estate and the Barings by canceling Knox's claim to the residuary profits on 530,000 acres of Maine land. Then Hare attacked the problem of the penalty for failure to produce the required number of settlers on the Bingham Purchase.

The problem was an ominous one, and it grew more so each day. Maine went Democratic — Jeffersonian — in 1807, and there was angry talk of the evils and injustices of an absentee trust. Hare's solution was admirably simple. He made the leading Jeffersonians — including William King, who would become Maine's first governor — part owners of the Bingham Purchase. He sold them 65,000 choice acres of the Kennebec Million in return for the token payment of $5,000. For his investment Hare got a legislative resolve canceling the settlers' fee, a clear title to all the Maine lands, and possession of the deeds that had been held in escrow.

General Cobb, as a political power in Massachusetts, assisted in bringing about this arrangement. It was the last service of any consequence he was to perform. He continued as titular agent of the estate in Maine until 1820, when Hare's successor, reasoning that seventy-two was an age for earned retirement, paid him off.

The testamentary trustees wisely abandoned all attempts to develop the Maine lands for farming; they concentrated instead on lumbering. With the rise of this activity, there were some land sales beginning in 1820. Ironically, the settlements came not in the Penobscot Tract, on which so much development money had been poured under Baring's program, but rather in the mountainous and barren Kennebec Million, on which nothing had been spent. Lumbermen chopped away for decades at Bingham's white pine forests with scarcely appreciable inroads. By the middle of the century, the trustees had realized that none of the Bingham-Baring plans could be realized, and they had disposed of most of the Maine lands.

Maine became the twenty-third state in 1820. Ever since, it has been trying to do what William Bingham and Alexander Baring tried and failed to do in the last decade of the eighteenth century — attract settlers. In the seventh decade of the twentieth, the inhabitants number fewer than one million (1960 census). Portland, the largest city and commercial center, has 72,566. Gouldsborough has a population of 280; most of its city lots are pasture and its harbor is still undeveloped. Bingham (incorporated in 1812) is the site of a veneer factory and has 1260 inhabitants. There is a Hope (100), South Hope (170), Knox (30), South Knox (170), and a Baring (population not given). General Cobb's "great road," now commonly known as the "air line," still runs from Eddington to Calais through the Penobscot Tract; its blacktop paving was completed only in the last few years. On it there is no town with a population of more than 200.

The Pennsylvania and New York properties were another story altogether. The farm lands sold readily at good prices. An agent appointed by the successor trustees, vested with a power of attorney, administered the lands from an office in Wellsboro in Pennsylvania's Tioga County. There was some resistance from squatters. William Bingham Clymer, Anne Bingham's nephew, who took over as agent in 1844, was attacked in his bed and his papers burned, but the law upheld the Bingham rights and the estate prospered.

Then, in 1878 — though no one realized it at the time — the estate became enormously wealthy. Oil and gas were discovered near Bradford in Pennsylvania's McKean County. The Bingham lands, and those Bingham had bought in partnership with Thomas Willing and Thomas Mayne Willing, held one of the country's richest mineral veins. Beginning about 1914, with improved roads and the mass-produced automobile, oil royalties flowed in. In 1964, the successor trustees decided to liquidate. They sold the last real property, mainly oil rights in Western Pennsylvania, for $800,000 in July, 1964. In November, they went to the Montgomery County Orphans Court and arranged to terminate the estate.

On Sunday, November 15, 1964, one of the Stuart portraits of William Bingham appeared on the front page of the New York *Times*, with the story of his famous trust. R. Sturgis Ingersoll, Philadelphia attorney, one of two trustees in 1964, was quoted: "The oil properties were producing less and less income. With the multiplication of beneficiaries and with the expenses of handling the estate running up, we thought it wise to sell and terminate the trust."

The Bingham property, of course, went to his direct descendants, an extraordinarily large percentage of whom were and are members of British and French titled families. The trustees of the estate had also been administering the Willing share of the Pennsylvania lands bought in the Bingham-Willing partnership. Some $838,000 was distributed to 315 Bingham and Willing heirs in shares ranging from $25 to $55,000. Those in the United States were collateral descendants — the heirs of William and Anne Bingham's brothers and sisters. One of these, descended from Henry and Mary Willing Clymer, with rights to one-sixth of one-sixth of one-ninth of one share of the Bingham estate, had been receiving about $400 a year.*

*

Alexander Baring became a powerful and forceful figure in English life throughout the first half of the nineteenth century. He was appointed in 1805 to the Court of the Bank of England. From 1806 to 1835, he served in the House of Commons. He opposed restrictions on trade with the United States in the crucial years 1810–1812, writing a pamphlet on the subject, and fought the Reform measures of the 1830s. He was named Chancellor of the Exchequer in the Duke of Wellington's projected ministry of 1832, but, becoming alarmed at the antagonisms aroused in Parliament, he withdrew. He would, he said, "face a thousand devils rather than such a House of Commons."

Baring was made Alexander, First Baron Ashburton, in 1835. On the death of his father in 1810, he became head of Baring Brothers and Company, and over the next twenty years he made his firm the leading banking house in England, retiring with a personal fortune of £3 million sterling. The Duc de Richelieu, who succeeded Talleyrand as prime minister under the Restoration in France, declared, "There are six great powers in Europe: England, France, Russia, Austria, Prussia, and the Baring Brothers." In 1823, in one of the cantos of *Don Juan*, Byron asked,

> Who hold the balance of the world? Who reign
> O'er Congress, whether royalist or liberal?

His answer: Rothschild and Baring.

The firm continued to serve as bankers for the United States in England and to channel English private capital into American investments; throughout the century it always had an American on its board. In 1808, Sir Francis Baring was hissed at a public dinner

* For more information about the Bingham Estate see Appendix 5, page 474.

when he proposed a toast to the President of the United States. Throughout the War of 1812, his firm, though without instructions or remittances from Washington, regularly paid the interest on the United States debt owing to Britain. In 1839–1842, when a half-dozen American states, including Maryland and Pennsylvania, defaulted on their bonds, the Barings were criticized in the public press for their American connections. The papers named Alexander Baring and other international bankers as those "who own no country but the Bourse."

On two occasions, Alexander Baring played a large role in American affairs. When Albert Gallatin traveled to London as a commissioner seeking peace terms in the War of 1812, Baring served effectively as an intermediary between him and the British government. And in 1842, when another war threatened over Maine lands Britain had reannexed in the War of 1812, Sir Robert Peel sent Baring, now Lord Ashburton, to the United States on a mission of peace and friendship. From Washington on that visit, Baring wrote to his friend Gallatin in New York of his regret that his ship had been blown off its course and that he had been unable "to draw a little wisdom from the best well.

> You will probably be surprised at my undertaking this task at my period of life, and when I am left to my own thoughts, I am sometimes surprised myself at my rashness. People here stare when I tell them that I listened to the debates in Congress on Mr. Jay's treaty in 1795, and seem to think that some antediluvian has come among them out of his grave.

Lord Ashburton met with Daniel Webster, American Secretary of State, in talks to redefine and settle the American boundary between Maine and Canada. Because of ill health, and domestic duties, Ann Baring, Lady Ashburton, did not accompany her husband. To Daniel Webster she wrote:

> These honors were thrust upon him as the person most zealous in the cause of America, and the most sanguine as to the possibility of settling the long pending differences between the two countries. God grant that his best hopes may be realized, and that I may see him return with a treaty of peace in his pocket.

The Webster-Ashburton Treaty, considered a classic of diplomatic negotiation, fixed the Maine-Canada boundary on the St. Croix (Schoodic) River. The British opposition, led by Lord Palmerston, called it "The Ashburton Capitulation"; the Americans declared that Webster had been hoodwinked. Ashburton was offered and declined an earldom for his services.

Lord Ashburton died on a visit to his daughter Harriet's country house, the famous Longleat in Wilts, in 1848, in his seventy-third year. Joshua Francis Fisher, his American cousin-by-marriage, thought Baring "one of the most sensible persons I ever listened to." Sylvester Douglas, Lord Glenbervie, a diarist with a sardonic eye, called him "in his manners the best model of a natural, unaffected, plain, sensible, well-informed liberal merchant." "He was," Disraeli said, "the greatest merchant banker England perhaps ever had."

*

Alexander and Ann Baring had five sons and four daughters. Anne Eugenia, the oldest daughter, married Humphrey St. John Mildmay, descendant of an ancient and honorable English family. As a member of the Baring firm, he became a member of the Court of the Bank of England. The second daughter, Harriet, married Henry Frederick Thynne, who succeeded his father as the third Marquess of Bath. Two Baring sons died as young men, one of them as a naval lieutenant in the Mediterranean. A third took holy orders and became the rector of Itching-Stoke in Hampshire.

The oldest son, William Bingham Baring — William Bingham's first grandson, born in the Powel House in 1799 — succeeded to the title on his father's death in 1848. He had graduated from Oxford and had represented his father's boroughs in the House of Commons; but he was a shy, self-effacing man, and on becoming the second Baron Ashburton he retired from politics to intellectual pursuits and patronage of the arts. He was appointed a trustee of the National Gallery and president of the Royal Asiatic Society, the Royal Agricultural Society, and the Royal Geographic Society. He became Thomas Carlyle's patron and closest friend, leaving him a tax-free gift of £2000 in his will. William Makepeace Thackeray dedicated *Henry Esmond* "To the Right Honorable William Bingham, Lord Ashburton . . . for the sake of the great kindness and friendship which I owe to you and yours."

William Bingham Baring had married, in 1823, Harriet Mary, the oldest daughter of the sixth Earl of Sandwich. Lady Harriet became the reigning hostess of London — witty, intelligent, energetic and arrogant. Over Thomas Carlyle she exercised (in Froude's words) "a strange influence . . . for good and evil," in a relationship that caused deep anguish to Jane Welsh Carlyle. Jane's dislike for Lady Harriet and for the kind of useless life she was forced to lead on long visits to the Ashburtons' country estates embittered Carlyle's life.

Alexander Baring's second son, Francis, William Bingham's second grandson, was described by Joshua Fisher as

> a man of more than ordinary intellect, but with a bad temper and very disagreeable manners. He married a very handsome French woman, daughter of [Hughes Bernard] Maret, Duke of Bassano, Bonaparte's Secretary of State, and has chiefly resided in Paris. . . . I knew Francis Baring slightly, and also his sister, Mrs. Mildmay, who seemed a most pleasing, amiable woman — the only one of the family who did not seem to avoid the subject of American kinfolk.

The Baring family, the oldest British banking dynasty, has five separate peerages today (1969): Ashburton, Northbrook, Revelstoke, Cromer, and Howick. No other bank in London, and probably no other family, has sent as many directors to the Bank of England. The present Lord Ashburton, the Sixth Baron, is Sir Alexander Francis St. Vincent Baring, K.C.V.O., of Ashburton, Devon, a director of Baring Brothers and Co., Limited. He is William and Anne Bingham's great-great-great grandson by direct descent through their daughter Ann Bingham Baring.

*

Ann Baring, William Bingham's daughter, became the progenitor of one of England's richest and most distinguished families, but she had a cross to bear — the same one borne by Jane Welsh Carlyle. The ubiquitous and observant Joshua Fisher discovered it when he called on the Barings in 1831–32. Ann Baring, he said, received me with politeness and even kindness, but she had the reputation of heartlessness. She was not yet a peeress, and was very ambitious of high social position. She met with many mortifications, and from nobody so great as from her son's wife, Lady Harriet and her proud family, that of Earl Sandwich. I am told that at her son's marriage she was not invited to the dejeuner. Certainly Lady Harriet, who was the most perfect example of insolent ill breeding I ever saw, treated the poor old lady in her own house at the Grange with great coolness if not impertinence.*

Perhaps at the time I was there there may have been a political feud. Alexander Baring had turned both his sons out of their seats in his borough for voting the Reform bill, and I was told was caricatured as Brutus sacrificing his two sons for the good of his country.

It was no doubt through her son's marriage into the Bassano family that Ann became a devoted Bonapartist. She was so described in Lord Glenbervie's diary in 1817, when he attended one of the balls Mrs. Baring gave in her Paris residence. It was

crowded . . . yet meant to be select to the exclusion of all but the supposed flower of society. . . . Mrs. Baring is, notwithstanding her ambitious ball, a very agreeable and I understand excellent woman, with young daughters and the general pretence and very laudable or at least plausible reason for those things.

Ann Bingham Baring died at Bay House, near Gosport, England, on December 5, 1848, six months after her husband, in her sixty-sixth year.

*

Maria Matilda de Tilly Baring gave Henry Baring three sons and two daughters. Their son Henry Bingham Baring, following the family's proclivity for marrying titles, wedded a daughter of the sixth Lord Cardigan.

Maria's second marriage, like her first, ended unhappily. Henry

---

* Lord Houghton (William Monckton Milnes), a contemporary, wrote in a character sketch of Lady Harriet, "Towards her husband's family she assumed a demeanor of superiority that at times gave just offence, and which later efforts and regrets never obliterated."

Baring appears to have been dissolute and excessively fond of gambling, and perhaps for those reasons he withdrew in 1823 as a partner in the Baring firm. He divorced Maria that same year in a scandalous public trial, charging her with having had an affair with a Captain Webster. Of his cousin's divorce, Joshua Fisher wrote in his memoirs:

> Henry Baring, who could have had no sense of honour or delicacy in marrying her, which he no doubt did for her fortune, threw her into the most dissipated company, was glaringly unfaithful himself, and it is said laid a plan for her divorce when he had fallen in love with a young lady who became his second wife. Whether Captain Webster knowingly lent himself to his friend's scheme I know not. . . . Henry Baring . . . managed to retain the greatest part of her fortune.

After her second divorce, Maria moved to France and there, on June 9, 1826, she married a Marquis de Blaizel, a Frenchman who was a chamberlain of the Austrian Emperor. She lived in a rather equivocal position in Paris. The Austrian ambassador received her, but the English ambassador did not. King Louis Philippe, who had proposed to Maria's Aunt Abigail and had taken advantage of the Bingham hospitality when in exile, seems to have refused to receive her.

The third marriage, like the other two, was unsuccessful. Blaizel, a heavy gambler, used up money as fast as Maria could supply it. Joshua Fisher, meeting Maria in Paris, described her as

> then an old woman but quite an amusing one. She had seen the world in many phases, and had plenty of anecdotes which she told pleasantly. She was a very amiable kind hearted woman.

Aunt Abigail, Mrs. Richard Peters, continued to correspond with Maria as long as they lived. "Maria," she said to family and friends, "might have been indiscreet, but she was never criminal."

*

William Bingham, the only son of William and Anne Bingham, spent his first ten years at his Grandfather Willing's and then, following the terms of his father's will, joined his sisters in London in 1810, having been held an additional two years because of the threat of war between the two countries. Alexander Baring wrote the Willings:

> I was very glad to receive a sign of life from you by our young charge little William who is now at my elbow laboring very hard at a French lesson. . . . His sisters were of course delighted to see him. I must say for myself that not only I am not disappointed but the more I see him (and he is easily seen through) the more I am pleased with his disposition, and as to the head, that will be the business of the masters to stock. Nothing can be more amiable and affectionate than his temper. . . . We have already forgot that he is not one of our own children.
>
> He wants to a greater degree than I hardly ever witnessed habits of application, but I am not yet disposed to draw any conclusions to the disparagement of his natural capacity. I do not hesitate in my opinion that one of our good public schools will be the best place for him but as he is backward and must be brought gradually and mildly to the proper pitch of discipline.
>
> I am preparing to send him with my two oldest boys to a clergyman in Dorsetshire and with one of them I shall in a year or two send him to a great school, probably Eton. . . . I can assure you that every motive of affection for those to whom he is related and indeed for himself will induce me to look to his education with all the care of which I am capable.

Years later Joshua Fisher told of the unhappy end of the younger William Bingham:

> I suppose there was not much to be made of his poor capacity, but it was thought he was neglected by his sisters, and when he returned to this country upon his majority, about 1820, he had contracted bad habits at school, and as few acquirements as possible. His great fortune was probably his greatest misfortune. He got into all sorts of scrapes in this country. . . .
>
> William Bingham went afterwards to Canada, where he married a beautiful girl of the provincial noblesse, a Mademoiselle —— —— [Marie Charlotte Louise, daughter of the Honorable M. G. A. C. de Lotbeniere, afterwards Baroness de Vaudreuil in her own right]. She was just out of a convent, and the marriage was arranged between them, for otherwise she could not have married so coarse a man as W. B.

He had sense enough to know he could not take care of his estate and was glad to have settlements made which put him under the control, in a measure, of his wife — who turned out a pretty shrewd manager. They lived for some years in the best style at Montreal, where their house was open to all gay people, especially the officers of the English regiments. The opportunities of intrigue were not lost, and W. B. admitted that he was only certain of the legitimacy of his eldest son.

They afterwards went to Paris, where Madame, still handsome in mature years, and after her hair had become grey, lived a most scandalous life, changing her lovers with the fashions or seasons, and he sank into drunkenness and imbecility, was scarcely sane, and certainly was not presentable in his own house. Their daughters, or *hers,* married Frenchmen with some pretensions to rank, who now enjoy their fortune.*

*

The Mansion House, the Binghams' town residence, was the scene of a great auction sale on November 22, 1805. The populace thronged the house to examine, bid on and buy the furniture, silver and objects of art so lovingly collected two decades earlier. For the occasion, Anne's seven-foot-square canopy bed was displayed in the first-floor ballroom.†

The Mansion House itself was sold to a group who planned to convert it into a "tontine" coffee house — a luxurious cooperative club for Philadelphia businessmen. Benjamin Latrobe was retained to alter it for that purpose, but the subscriptions fell short, and the structure became, instead, the well-kept and popular Mansion House Hotel. When an early-morning fire in 1847 ruined the roof and damaged the interior, the hotel was torn down. In 1850, a mahogany dealer and cabinet maker named Bouvier, great-great-grandfather to Jacqueline Bouvier Kennedy Onassis, built a row of brownstone front residences on the lot. Some of them are still standing.

Lansdown, Bingham's estate on the Schuylkill, continued in the possession of the Barings and was used from time to time by members of the family visiting America. Joseph Bonaparte, elder brother of

---

* The Comte du Bois Guilbert, the Comte Douhet de Romarge, the Marquis d'Epersnil.
† See Appendix 4, page 467.

Napoleon, ex-King of Naples and ex-King of Spain, leased it for several years during his exile after the fall of the Bonaparte dictatorship. Julia, daughter of Benjamin Rush, dined there and heard Joseph complain indignantly of the way he had been treated by his brother.

Lansdown remained vacant for a number of years, cared for by a tenant, a Mr. Bones, who lived in "The Hut." It was set on fire and damaged on the Fourth of July, 1854, by fireworks in the hands of small boys. Twelve years later, some gentlemen of Philadelphia bought the property from the Barings at a favorable price and gave it to the city to add to Fairmount Park. The building was standing and might have been restored for a modest sum, but the park commissioners elected to tear it down and later to build there Horticultural Hall, a public conservatory. The site is now vacant.

*

Judge Thomas Willing lived to an advanced age, honored with the respectful appellation "The Regulator" for twenty-seven years of work in guiding the finances of the country. He resigned the presidency of the Bank of the United States in 1807, four years before Jefferson killed it by refusing to renew its charter. He died in 1821, at age ninety, leaving his estate of $1,000,000, including 122,000 acres of Pennsylvania land he had bought with William Bingham, to his four sons and four daughters. In an autobiographical essay he wrote:

> I have been greatly successful in my endeavours to increase my fortune; I have enjoyed as much domestic happiness as most men, and have received many flattering marks of public esteem and confidence. I have through life, enjoyed great good health, and at this day am free from any of those complaints which often attend a life of less regularity and sobriety.
>
> My success in life has not been derived from superior abilities, or extensive knowledge, a very small and scanty share of either having fallen to my lot; therefore it can only be ascribed to a steady application to whatever I have undertaken, a civil and respectful deportment to all my fellow citizens, and an honest and upright conduct in every transaction of life.

Samuel Breck, Bingham's young neighbor at Sweetbriar on the Schuylkill, his colleague on the board of the Bank of the United

States, lived on and on, long after the friends and associates of his youth were gone. He served a term in the national Congress, drafted the bill that established a public school system in Pennsylvania, worked devotedly for many years to help blind children, and served for five years as vice president of the Historical Society of Pennsylvania.

On July 28, 1858, Breck recorded that he was entering his eighty-eighth year. He put down his address: 1418 Arch Street. He recorded the temperature as he was writing: 94 degrees. And on that day, as it so often did, his mind returned to events of sixty years earlier, and once again to Anne Bingham.

> Mrs. Bingham stood above competition in her day; nor has anyone of equal refinement in address, or social stateliness, and graceful superintendence of a splendid establishment, been produced since in any circle of our city.

At ninety-one, a few months before he died, Samuel Breck attended a concert in Philadelphia. Fort Sumter had just been fired on and captured by southern secessionists. At the close of the singing of the national anthem, Breck sprang to his feet and, waving his hat over his head, called for three cheers for the United States of America.

"I was a man when they were formed," he called out, "and God forbid that I should live to witness their downfall."

Acknowledgments

Acknowledgments

I WISH TO EXPRESS my special indebtedness to the authors of the only two works of substance written on William Bingham before the present volume.

Miss Margaret L. Brown of New York City "discovered" William Bingham in the mid-1930s and spent many months in the preparation of three articles that are models of seminal research and scholarly writing.* Although Miss Brown did not have access to the Bingham Papers now in the Historical Society of Pennsylvania, nor to the Baring Papers now in the Manuscript Division of the Library of Congress, anyone who writes of William and Anne Bingham must build on the foundation she laid down. I was happy that I was able to find, meet and know Margaret Brown thirty years after the publication of those articles and was delighted that she looked favorably on my undertaking. She has read this work in manuscript. I am deeply grateful for her encouragement, advice and admonishment.

Frederick S. Allis, Jr., of Phillips Academy at Andover, Massachusetts, produced in 1954 a monumental two-volume, 1325-page work, *William Bingham's Maine Lands, 1790–1820.* These volumes, published by the Colonial Society of Massachusetts, contain the correspondence of William Bingham, his associates, and his adversaries pertaining to the "Bingham Purchase." One must admire the diligence, perception and accuracy with which Mr. Allis transcribed and annotated some 450 letters and documents, many of them faded, scarcely legible letterpress copies. In corresponding with Mr. Allis I have said that without his *Maine Lands* my own work would have taken at least a year longer for a less satisfactory result.

* "William Bingham, Agent of the Continental Congress in Martinique"; "Mr. and Mrs. William Bingham of Philadelphia — Rulers of the Republican Court"; and "William Bingham, Eighteenth Century Magnate," *Pennsylvania Magazine of History and Biography,* January, July, October, 1937.

I also wish to thank William F. Allison of Houston, Texas, for first calling my attention to the Bingham story, and Edmund Cohen of Malibu, California, for suggesting the title and for editorial counsel based on a careful reading of the work in typescript.

I am grateful to six others who also read the complete manuscript and made many helpful editorial suggestions: George Ketchum, Oscar Shefler, Dr. Isaac Sissman, William W. Taylor, and Lawrence C. Woods, Jr., all of Pittsburgh; and Lois Given Bobb of Moorestown, New Jersey.

In the course of researching and writing this work, I have received many courtesies and much assistance from dozens of other persons — friends, librarians, archivists, scholars, and owners of manuscripts and paintings — to whom I owe a full measure of gratitude. I extend my thanks to the following:

R. Sturgis Ingersoll of Philadelphia, a last trustee of the Bingham Estate, for patiently answering my queries over several years' time.

Nicholas Baring of Baring Brothers and Co. Limited, London, and the Baring archivist, T. L. Ingram, for permission to quote from the Baring Papers and to reproduce the portraits so credited in this work.

Nicholas B. Wainwright, Director, Henry Cadwalader, Executive Director, and John D. Kilbourne, Curator, of the Historical Society of Pennsylvania, Philadelphia, and the staff, for making available the riches of the Society's manuscript collections and for handling what must have seemed an endless stream of correspondence.

Professor Stuart Bruchey and Mrs. James O. Wettereau of New York City, for giving me certain extracts from the unpublished minutes of the Bank of the United States.

Miss Elizabeth Macfarlane of Pittsburgh, descendant of Henry and Mary Willing Clymer, for opening her family records to me.

The late George W. Williams, agent for the Bingham Estate in Wellsboro, Pennsylvania, for giving me his personal recollections of the operations of the Estate.

Keith Doms, Director of Carnegie Library in Pittsburgh, and Mrs. George Cunningham and Mrs. Henry J. Palmieri of its Pennsylvania Room, for special help and consideration in use of the Library's resources.

Dr. Francis Fisher Hart of Ambler, Pennsylvania, Robert Malezieu-Dehon of Paris, and George C. Homans of Boston, for permission to reproduce portraits they own of William Bingham, Anne Bingham, and Colonel and Mrs. William Stephens Smith. Mrs. Richard John Bramble Mildmay-White of Mothecombe, Holbeton, Plymouth, England, for permission to reproduce the portrait of Ann Bingham Baring, Lady Ashburton.

Miss Virginia Carollo and Mr. and Mrs. William Doberneck, for carrying out research assignments for me in Philadelphia; Miss Sylvia England, of London, for research work performed in England; Mrs. George P. Paine of Chapel Hill, North Carolina, for a research chore done in Paris; and Frank van der Linden of Washington, author of *The Turning Point: Jefferson's Battle for the Presidency,* for help in finding a Jefferson letter.

Also for help given: Dr. David C. Mearns, John C. Broderick, L. Quincy Mumford, and Milton Kaplan, executives of the Library of Congress; Stephen T. Riley, Director, and Malcolm Freiberg, Editor, Massachusetts Historical Society, Boston; Dr. M. Graham Netting, Director, and Dr. J. Kenneth Doutt, Curator of Mammals, Carnegie Museum, Pittsburgh; P. William Filby, Librarian and Assistant Director, and Thomas S. Eader, Assistant Librarian, Maryland Historical Society, Baltimore; John Alden, Keeper of Rare Books, Boston Public Library; Miss Elizabeth Baer, Evergreen House, Baltimore; William P. Barber, Curator, Woodford Mansion, Fairmont Park, Philadelphia; Dr. Whitfield J. Bell, Jr., Librarian, American Philosophical Society; William S. Ewing, Manuscript Librarian, William L. Clements Library, Ann Arbor; William Gauer, Vice President, Fidelity Bank, Philadelphia; James J. Heslin, Director, New York Historical Society; Robert W. Hill, Keeper of the Manuscripts, New York Public Library; Richard E. Kuehne, Director, West Point Museum, United States Military Academy; James E. Mooney, Editor, American Antiquarian Society, Worcester, Massachusetts.

Also Mrs. Sarah Morrison, The Adams Papers, Massachusetts Historical Society, Boston; Clayton E. Rhodes, Acting Librarian, Peabody Institute, Baltimore; Dr. Charles Coleman Sellers, Librarian, Dickinson College; Dr. George B. Tatum, Associate Professor, University of Pennsylvania; Lawrence W. Towner, Director, Newberry Library, Chicago; Maud M. Tracy, Chief Clerk, Alumni Records, University of Pennsylvania; F. J. B. Watson, Director, Wallace Collection, London; Walter Muir Whitehill, Director and Librarian of the Boston Athenaeum and Editor of the Colonial Society of Massachusetts; Mrs. E. S. Willing, Jr., Bryn Mawr, Pennsylvania; Edwin Wolf, II, Librarian, The Library Company of Philadelphia; and Martin I. Yoelson, Supervisory Historian, Independence National Historical Park, Philadelphia.

Finally, I am under much obligation to those at Houghton Mifflin Company, in Boston and New York, who helped me to produce this book: Linda Glick, who copy-edited the work and saw it through the press; and Editors Joyce Hartman and Richard McAdoo, who worked with me painstakingly on the manuscript and, among other services, resolutely kept it from running to three volumes.

ROBERT C. ALBERTS

Appendices

APPENDIX 1

A Diary in Martinique

CAPTAIN JOSEPH HARDY, *in command of the marines on board the frigate* Confederacy, *filled forty-two pages of private journal during his stay in Martinique. They give an absorbing and possibly unique account of what life and work were like aboard a Continental ship of war and in a foreign port. These extracts tell some of the problems William Bingham, Continental Agent, faced over a three-month period in struggling to get the disabled ship repaired and outfitted.**

*

Wednesday 29 December [*1779*]. Dined and spent the afternoon [in St. Pierre] with Mr. Bingham the Continental Agent. — in the Evening at the Dancing School where the Young Ladies and Gentlemen of the Town practice twice or thrice a Week they Dance extraordinarily well. . . .

Saturday 1st. January 1780: The Gunners Crew employed carrying Shot ashore &c Mr. Bingham came to Town. . . .

Sunday 2d. Several Gentlemen on board this morning viewing the Ship, also Mr. B. our Agent, who informs us he cannot procure Spars to fit us immediately. . . .

Saturday 8th. Carpenters caulking the Ships sides. . . . Capta. Harding ashore all day endeavoring to procure Spars for the Ship but can get no satisfaction from the Intendant. . . . The inattention that we have been treated with here as a Vessel in distress and an Ally calls loudly to his Christian Majesty for Redress as it is most undoubtedly a breach of the Treaty of Alliance.

Thursday 27th January. . . . Yesterday application was made formally to the Intendant for (only) Canvas sufficient to make our

---

* Quoted by permission from James L. Howard's *Seth Harding, Mariner — A Naval Picture of the Revolution,* Yale University Press, 1930.

Courses but he preemptorily refused it at the same time we were certainly assured of their being a large Quantity of it in the Public Stores. Thus is our refitting wantonly retarded by this Man, until we can be redressed by the General, who is at present out of Town, and owing to nothing more than a difference in Public Party affairs subsisting between the General and Intendant.

Friday 28th. Late last Night the 1st Lieutent. returned in the Barge from St. Pierrs but without any Spars the Continental Agent there having not Money to purchase any more. . . . A ship arrd. from St. P. with public Stores.

Tuesday 1st February. . . . Spent the Evening at the American Coffe-House [in St. Pierre] with several Gentlemen from America.

Wednesday 2d. Set off this morning at 6 O'clock . . . in the Cutter with Capa. Harding and Mr. Bingham . . . and arrived about 3 O'clock.

Friday 4th. Went ashore this forenoon on business with Mr. Bingham. He has made a formal demand of Spars &c to fit us which at last is complied with thro' the assistance of the General. . . . Mr. B. returned in the Barge. This Evening got from the Kings Yard a number of Spars for Topmasts, Top-gallant Masts, Steering Sail Booms, &c. Carpenters finished the Mainmast this Evening all ready to take in tomorrow Morning so that we shall soon begin to appear a little formidable. It really Animates us the sudden change and prospect we have to day of getting Refitted, tho' we might now been much forwarder in fitting had it not been for the Intendant's ungenerous and Villianous conduct in denying us those Articles which he had in his power to serve us with.

Sunday 6th. The great necessity of getting the Ship fitted with all Expedition obliged us to keep the Ship Crew at work to Day tho' it is the Sabbath. Notwithstanding our Chaplain delivered us abt. 11 OClk an excellent well adapted Sermon on the abominable Practice of Swearing. . . .

Sunday 13th March. Break of Day this morning hove the Ship ahead to her Anchor. took a Pilot on board 8 AM Warped out of the Carnage [careenage] and made Sail with a Light Breeze of wind. passed under the Admirals stern and Saluted him with Thirteen Guns and returned from him with Nine. . . . Beat into St. Pierrs and at 3 P.M. came to Anchor off the South part of the Town.

Monday 14th. . . . Received on board One hundred and Eleven Barrels of Beef, a Quantity of Cheese Rice Butter &c. a Crew employed Scraping the Quarter deck. . . .

Tuesday 15th. Went ashore this Morning on Publick business with the Agent. . . . Received on Board a Quantity of Provisions of different kinds. . . .

Friday 17th March.* . . . At 11 A.M. went ashore and Dined with Mr. B — spent the remainder of the Day in Town, returned on board in the Evening. This being St. Patricks day the Ships Crew endeavored to Celebrate it in their way among others one of the Centinals was found drunk laying down on the Gangway he was immediately confined in Irons.

Monday 20th. . . . Dined with Capta. H — at Mr. Binghams who is gone to Fort Royal to make a final Settlement of his Publick business as he designs to leave the Island and go passenger with us to America.

Friday 24th March. This morning the Captain sent off orders to Unmoor Ship and get ready for sailing in order to join the French fleet at Royal going on an Expedition Against the Island of St. Lucee. at 11 A.M. the Captain came on board soon after the Ship was underway. standing under her Topsails alongshore at half past twelve boarded by a boat with an express from Mr. Bingham to return to St. Pierrs. . . . before we put about saw the french Fleet coming out of the Bay and standing over for St. Lucee. we are now to return to America as soon as possible. . . .

Tuesday 28 March. In the forenoon received on board a large quantity of Cocoa Ship'd by Mr. Bingham. . . .

Wednesday 29th March. Mr. Bingham sent on board the greatest part of his Baggage this Evening. . . .

Thursday 30th March 1780. Signal for Sailing displayed early this Morning, got under way at St. Pierrs at 10 A.M. with 3 Brigs 1 Schooner and Sloop under our Convoy bound to America. — stretched under easy Sail along the Town, past eleven Mr. Bingham came on board who is going Passenger with us to America. — at 12. Saluted the Ships and Town with 13 Guns the Commodore returned it with Eleven. bore away and set Top G. Sails. . . .

---

* Captain Hardy here corrected a one-day error in his dates.

"A Clear and Succinct Account of My Agency"

BEFORE LEAVING *Martinique, William Bingham felt obliged to report to Congress on his mission. He did so on June 29, 1779, with this remarkable, previously unpublished narrative.*

*

I did myself the honor of writing to the Committee for foreign affairs in the Month of August last, requesting Permission to return to the Continent; — As they have not signified to me that, they disapproved of my Intentions, I flatter myself that the Proposal has met with their Acquiescence. I think it a duty incumbent on me, previous to my Departure, to lay before Congress a clear and succinct Account of my Agency during my Residence in this place; Should I take up more of their Time than the Subject merits, in the Recapitulation of my Services in the course of an active & laborious Employment, I must solicit their kind Indulgence, of which, few that enter into their august Presence, has a greater Occasion.

I was employed in the various Duties of Secretary to the Committee of Secret Correspondence, (now denominated Committee for foreign Affairs) when I had the honor of being appointed their Agent, for the purpose of transacting the Affairs of Congress, as well political as commercial in the French West Indies. Attached to the Service of my Country from Principle as well as Affection, I readily accepted the important Trust; — the confidence that hon[ble] Body placed in me, was a flattering Circumstance, & impelled me by an unremitting Assiduity to merit the distinguished favor; — The Instructions I received from the Committee were short, & only had in View an attention to some immediate Objects; — I was to endeavor to procure ten thousand Musquets, & a Quantity of Ammunition, & to engage the Credit of the United States for the Payment; — I was directed to feel the Pulse of the French Government, to know, whether it beat towards American Independancy; I was to cultivate an intimate & friendly Connection with the General, & People of Distinction here, to be enabled thereby, to procure & impart the most usefull Intelligence; to maintain a regular, frequent, & well-serv'd Correspondence with Mr. Deane in France, in order that Congress & him, might be duly & reciprocally informed, of every interesting Event that might be passing on either Side of the Water; — to learn from the General, whether he would permit the Entry of Prizes made by our Cruizers into the French ports, & protect them untill Opportunity offered of bringing them away; — These were the Heads of my Instructions; — If any unforeseen Events should happen, connected with the Interests, or that might be improved to the Advantage of the United States, it was left to my Prudence & Discretion to turn them to Account.

The Reception I met with from the General was flattering, & such as the Stile of my Recommendation & the political State of America would naturally entitle me to.

An injured and high-spirited People, arming in defence of its Liberties, & imploring Assistance from a great & gallant Nation, to protect them from the Insults & Oppressions of an enterprizing lawless Power, is a strong pathetic Address, to the Weaknesses & Passions of human Nature; — the undaunted firmness of the Americans, in resisting the Efforts of so unequal a Force as was employed to enslave them, excited in the Minds of Foreigners, the most generous & sympathetic Sentiments in their favor; — The French were engaged from Compassion to our Sufferings, to wish well to our Cause, & from the influence of political Considerations, to encourage the Revolt, & increase the intestine Commotions, that prevailed in America.

But, when the View of entering too far into our Quarrel led to a Prospect of being involved in it themselves, by a Rupture with G Britain, there were few that did not recoil at the Idea of the impending Danger that would attend it; — However, the situation of America at this Time, demanded, that an early Declaration of Something more than feeble & unsteady Support, should be given; as well as animate the drooping Spirits of lukewarm Patriots, as to im-

press the Enemy with a fearfull Apprehension of our foreign Connections; — If this could not be obtained in *Reality,* the *Appearance*
of it was still necessary, as it would naturally precipitate G. Britain,
in any hostile intentions She might have, towards the Power that
afforded us assistance; — To accomplish so desirable a Purpose soon
engaged my Attention, which at this difficult Juncture, required
no small Share of Prudence & address.

The trading People of France have always trembled at the
thoughts of a War with Great Britain, as they are thereby exposed
in their Commerce, to the greatest Calamities & Losses; the happiest
Effect of Politics & Power, — the Art of uniting War & Commerce,
so as to make them both turn out to Account, France has not as yet
discovered; I had therefore to encounter many & various Difficulties,
arising from Opposition of Interest in so formidable a Class of Men,
when matters were ripening to a Crisis, & the Appearance of active
& open Hostilities with G Britain was more than probable; — Those,
who were inclined to wish for a Continuation of Peace, united in a
powerful Party to oppose any measures that might tend to interrupt
it;

Finding that I could not bring over their interests to second my
Designs, it became necessary to engage their Self Love (susceptible
of strong impressions) in the Quarrel, by provoking the two Powers
to mutual Depredations on each other, by sowing the Seeds of
Jealousy & Discord betwixt them, & by affording them matter for
present Resentment, & renewing in their Minds the objects of their
antient Animosity, I was the more inclined to avail myself of this
expedient, as the Negotiations of Disputes betwixt two Rival Nations
generally turns out very unsatisfactory, & is usually refer'd to the
last Appeal, the ultima Ratio Regnum.

Hence, I took an early & active part in the arming of Privateers
out of this Port, to annoy and cruize against British Property.

The Protection which I procured for them & their Prizes, occasioned the most spirited Letters betwixt the French & English Governors, which joined to the Circumstance of these Vessels being
generally manned with the Subjects of France, gave room for the
most inflamatory Accounts of the Conduct of the French Commanders, to be transmitted to the English Ministry.

My situation at this time was critical. Altho it was natural to think that France would not remain a tame & timid Spectator of the Conquest of America, yet She had not *then* taken any decisive part in our Favor. The dread of G Britain seemed to have become a political Habit, which infected her Councils, & occasioned them to be constantly fluctuating; — She therefore only gave us such Encouragement, & afforded us such Assistance, as would incline us to persist in the Quarrel, & waste each others Strength in mutual Hostilities; — but seem'd determined to adhere to the principles of political prudence, in avoiding every Step, that might lead to a Declaration of war. The Expostulations of the British Governor against my Conduct, became every day more & more importunate, but a political Maneuvre which I had recourse to, & which would not be prudent to commit to Paper, inclined the General not to regard them, altho I am confident he then acted in Violation of positive Orders received from his Court.

Petitions were sent to Parliament from many of the trading Cities of England, complaining of the active Part which the inhabitants of Martinico took in the American War, & of the Depredations committed on English Property, by the Subjects of France, & praying for Redress. — These occasioned severe & pointed memorials to the Court of Versailles, which with the answers given thereto, had a happy Effect in quickening the Resentments of each court, & in embittering that Spirit of national Emulation, which the Appearance of the Times, & a Sense of reciprocal Injuries, animated and called forth into Action; — the Scenes that had been transacted in these Seas, generally formed the most lively subject of the Complaints of the British Ambassador; — in Consequence of these Memorials, Ordonnances were often issued, requiring the French Governor to remedy & redress the Grievances complained of; but I always found some plausible pretext to prevent their taking Effect; — Sometimes, by acting in such a Manner as to save Appearances; — Sometimes by convincing the General that it was naturally to be expected that the Reins of Government would be relaxed, at a Distance from the Seat of Empire, & that these Ordonnances were only political Strokes, intended to appease the Minds of the English, untill France was prepared to assume a higher & more imposing Tone; — Indeed, I have carried my Efforts to embroil the two Nations, to such Lengths, that I have often been complained of to the General, as a very dangerous

Person; — my personal Intimacy, & the partial & distinguishing marks of favor with which he has always honoured me, have sometimes saved me from the Effects of his political Anger; & the ardent Desire with which military Men pant after war, may have frequently inclined him to wink at my Schemes, that would result to so desireable an Object.

Long before the Treaty of Commerce took place with the Court of Versailles, I had procured a Number of Privileges for the American Trade, which were not granted to the most favor'd foreign Powers; — By my Solicitations, I had Convoys appointed for our Vessels bound to the Continent, to protect them from the British Cruizers amongst the Islands.

My pen was not idle in the Service; — it was often employed in writing Treatises (for the perusal of the Intendant & which were forwarded to the Ministry) on the Subject of the capital Advantages which France would derive, from a political & commercial Connection with America.

The unexpected arrival of the Ship *Seine* here, afforded me an opportunity of rendering an essential Service to Congress; — She was too valuable a Vessel to trust to the dangerous Navigation amongst the Islands. I accordingly took from her above two thirds of her Cargo, & had so much interest with the General as to prevail on him to dispatch the Remainder, in the Name & on Account of his most Christian Majesty as a Storeship intended for the Garrison at Miquelon; — The Event justified in every Respect the propriety & prudent Precaution of the Measure; she unfortunately fell a Sacrifice to an English Frigate soon after her Departure.

That part of her Cargo which was taken out, was consequently saved to the United States, & the Capture of the Remainder was so happily disposed to occasion a Subject of reciprocal Complaint & Altercation betwixt the two Courts, that every one believed I had fixed the Matter accordingly, & gave me Credit for my Plan, as a deep Scheme of Machiavelian Policy.

With regard to that Part of my Instructions on the Subject of forwarding Advices, I soon foresaw that I could not place sufficient Reliance on the Punctuality of Mr. Deane, to answer the Intentions of Congress; — I therefore cultivated with peculiar Attention an extensive Correspondence with a Variety of Persons in Europe & the

West Indies, by which means, I procured the most interesting & authentic Intelligence, which I carefully forwarded to the Committee for foreign Affairs; I need only to refer to Letters wrote that hon^ble Body, & their answers thereto, (conveying the most flattering Marks of Approbation) for my Services in that Line of my official Duty; — I duly informed them of the various Changes that took place in the political System, & of the Succour & Assistance which France afforded us, increasing with our Successes, by regular & insensible Gradations, untill they terminated in an Acknowledgment of our Independency, a moral Certainty of which as early as the month of February 1778 I announced to the Committee, who had then been deprived of any authentic Accounts from Europe for a long time.

Various & important Objects in the Affairs of this Department that required a proper Attention (as well here as in the other french Islands) often times presented, which my Instructions hardly reached by Implication; These I took under my Cognizance, & arranged to the best of my Knowledge, in which the improving of favorable Occurrances to the Advantage of the Service, was always the Extension, by which my Line of Conduct was regulated.

The Commencement of the War in America displayed such surprizing Efforts of Wisdom & Firmness, of Fortitude & Self Denial, with all the Train of Patriot Virtues, as History will be proud to record. Our Successes against so formidable a Force astonished our most sanguine Friends, & palled our Enemies with fear; they occasioned the Sentiments of the most able Politicians in G Britain, most sensibly to change, & as they found they could not conquer, they were willing to relent; — a refractory & seditious Spirit of Opposition to ministerial Measures, gathered new strength, & formed a Stumbling Block in the Road to Conquest.

This occasioned a Schism in the established Mode of thinking, which prevented G Britain from acting with that collected force, which an Union of Sentiments & Councils would have enabled her to do.

It was not sufficient therefore that we should be successfull, — it was necessary that our Successes should be made known, as well in England, as throughout the different States of Europe. I was placed in a most happy Situation to facilitate this important Business. I was constantly and regularly furnished with the most recent American Transactions, which I industriously made public thro the Channel of the Martinico Gazette, which has obtained the Character in Europe of giving the most authentic Detail of the military Operations in America.

On the acknowledgment of American Independency by the Court of Versailles, the vindictive Acts of Parliament in regard to our Captive Seamen began to operate amongst the Islands in their full force, & our Prisoners were suffered to languish in all the Miseries of a tedious Confinement. Motives of Humanity, & a sense of Duty, urged me to make an application to the Governor of Antigua for settling a Cartel for a mutual Exchange, & I had no doubt but that the good Effects that would thereby reciprocally arise to each Party, would induce him to comply.

My first Letter not being replied to, I wrote a second, to which he returned an indecent & ungentlemanly Answer; — It gave me Pain to find that my Efforts to promote so desireable an Object, had proved unavailing; — I waited with the most anxious Expectation for a more favorable Opportunity for Success. On the arrival of Admiral Byron & General Grant in these Seas, I renewed my Application. I interested their humanity in favor of this unfortunate Class of Men, & pointed out in so forcible a Manner the bad Tendency of a Perseverance in a Refusal, that they at length acquiesced in the Proposal, & a regular Exchange of Prisoners has taken place, as far as the relative State of Numbers will admit. Many of these unhappy Sufferers have experienced the Benefit of this Arrangement, which would extend its salutory Effects to all the Americans in Captivity amongst the Islands, if I had but a sufficient Number of English Prisoners to offer as Objects of Exchange.

Perhaps it may be thought proper that this Intelligence should be made public, as I have heard that many of the American Seamen object to West India Voyages, from the Apprehensions they are under of being taken, & confined in loathesome Prisons, without the Prospect of a Release.

Thus Gentlemen have I given you as concise an Account as the Nature of the Subject would admit, of the capital Objects of my Agency in the political Line. My exertions for your Service in the Commercial Department, have been equally great, & not less usefull.

At a Time when the Inhabitants of America were animated with an enthusiastic Ardor in defence of their Liberties, & when a powerfull Force was sent out to subject them, there was nothing wanting, but Arms, Ammunition, & Cloathing, to make them feel a Confidence in their own Strength, & to put them in a Situation to resist the Efforts, & baffle the attempts of their Enemies; — at this critical time, big with momentous Consequences, I was charged with a Commission for obtaining these essential Articles; — the Importance of the Object claimed my peculiar Attention. Notwithstanding the Difficulties that arose, from the Risk that our Vessels were exposed to from the Enemy's Cruizers, that thereby made the prospect of receiving Remittances very precarious, upon my arrival in this place, I not only exerted myself in forwarding as many of these Articles as my Credit could procure, but gave the greatest Encouragement to the Speculations of private Adventurers in every Kind of European Merchandize, as well as West India Produce.

Not finding a sufficiency of Arms to complete the Number I was directed to purchase, I engaged with some French Merchants to import a Quantity, which Engagement, had an excellent Effect in encouraging others to make the same Importation.

By my Efforts, a very large & seasonable Supply was obtained; At the end of the year 1776, Congress was indebted to me Liv 211948.8.8 chiefly for the Amount of Arms, Powder, etc. furnished at different times — a very large Sum! — for the payment of which I had a Reliance on Remittances from America, & a Promise from the hon^ble Committee that as their Vessels were liable to capture, as soon as any should be taken, others should be dispatched in their Room, untill my Engagements were entirely fulfilled.

However, Payments becoming due, & Remittances failing me, I began to be persecuted from every Quarter. My credit was brought in Question, & the unfavorable Accounts at that time received of our military operations, previous to the Affair of Trenton, put a finishing Stroke to it. Writs were served upon me by many of my Creditors, & Executions taken out against me; — By paying the most importunate, & calming the Temper of the more moderate, I found a temporary Relief, & this deceitful Calm led me into new Engagements, by which my Credit & my Feelings were again sacrificed. — I appeal to the State of my second & third Accounts Current, transmitted to the hon^ble the Committee, by which the Ballances were increased to the enormous Sums of Liv 254316.8.8, & Liv 343105.1.1, to justify my Assertion. Notwithstanding my Disappointment I did not remit my usual Efforts for the public Welfare, & I went on as cheerfully in contracting new Engagements for the Service, as if I had received the most ample Remittances for the old ones.

By an Acct Current since Transmitted to the Committee, the Ballance in my favor was Liv 247068.7.3 — Soon after the Date of which, the Deane Frigate & the armed Brig General Gates arrived here, & required considerable Outfits, which consisted of Articles sold only for Cash; I then found myself in a critical Situation; their Disbursements, with the Engagements to be entered into for Hospital Accounts, Maintenance of Prisoners, Expenses of forwarding them, etc., would amount to a very considerable Sum; — I must either have declined furnishing these Vessels with the necessary supplies, & thereby have retained them in port, or have drawn on the Honble the Commissioners in France for the Amount; — I preferred the latter Alternative, as the most eligible & the most conducive to the Good of the Service, & hope that Congress will acquiesce in the propriety of my Choice. By this Opportunity I shall have the honor of transmitting my last Acct current, Ballance in my favor, Livs (blank).

Justice towards a Person who has been faithfully devoted to the public Service will doubtless incline Congress immediately to liquidate this Account that I may be enabled thereby to do Honor to the Engagements I have entered into, — more especially as the most urgent Reasons impel me to desire Permission to return to the Continent, & as the State of my Health absolutely requires it; — as the most important Objects of my appointment are happily compleated, & no longer demand an Attention, my feelings do not suffer in the Request. — I flatter myself with the hopes of returning in the Month of October or November; & if Congress Should not appoint some Person in my Stead, I shall previous thereto, leave the Transaction of the continental Affairs to the Care of a Gentleman of Known Integrity & Abilities, that they may not suffer by my Absence.

Whether my Agency has been interesting to America, by promoting the glorious Cause She is engaged in, is left to your august Body to determine; — for my own Part, I claim no Merit but from the Purity & Rectitude of my Intentions, my Activity, & my Zeal for your service; — The public Interest alone has always been my Guide — but if I have undertaken a Task beyond my Abilities to accomplish I cannot expect to be honoured with the public Approbation, which invariable in its Decisions, never consults any thing but its own Advantage; — in that Case, I shall be more afflicted, than surprized.

If my services had been more conspicuous, I might perhaps have had much to fear from the Voice of Calumny — their Mediocrity then may have protected me from the pursuits of the envious, which however could never have deprived me of the Consolation to think, — that for the good of my Country

> Quod potui, feci; — faciant meliora potentes!
> I've done my best — let abler men do more

I have the honor to be with great Respect

Honble Gentlemen
Your obedient and very
humble servant
Wm Bingham

Anne Bingham to Thomas Jefferson

WHEN ANNE WILLING BINGHAM *left Europe in the spring of 1786, she had promised to tell her friend Thomas Jefferson, within one year, "truly and honestly whether you do not find the tranquil pleasures of America preferable to the empty bustle of Paris." Jefferson wrote her from Paris on February 7, 1787, to remind her of the promise. Her reply, written from Philadelphia about June 1, 1787, is the only known letter of substance by Anne Bingham — and one that reveals something of her character and mind.*

*

I am too much flattered by the Honor of your letter from Paris, not to acknowledge it by the earliest opportunity, and to assure you that I am very sensible of your attentions. The Candor with which you express your sentiments, merits a sincere declaration of mine.

I agree with you that many of the fashionable pursuits of the Parisian Ladies are rather frivolous, and become uninteresting to a reflective Mind; but the Picture you have exhibited, is rather overcharged. You have thrown a strong light upon all that is ridiculous in their Characters, and you have buried their good Qualities in the Shade. It shall be my Task to bring them forward, or at least to attempt it. The state of Society in different Countries requires corresponding Manners and Qualifications; those of the french Women are by no means calculated for the Meridian of America, neither are they adapted to render the Sex so amiable or agreable in the English acceptation, of those words. But you must confess, that they are more accomplished, and understand the Intercourse of society better than in any other Country. We are irresistibly pleased with them, because they possess the happy Art of making us pleased with ourselves; their education is of a higher Cast, and by great cultivation they procure a happy variety of Genius, which forms their Conversation, to please either the Fop, or the Philosopher.

In what other Country can be found a Marquise de Coigny, who, young and handsome, takes a lead in all the fashionable Dissipation of Life, and at more serious moments collects at her House an assembly of the Literati, whom she charms with her Knowledge and her bel Esprit. The Women of France interfere in the politics of the Country, and often give a decided Turn to the Fate of Empires. Either by the gentle Arts of persuasion, or by the commanding force of superior Attractions and Address, they have obtained that Rank and Consideration in society, which the Sex are intitled to, and which they in vain contend for in other Countries. We are therefore bound in Gratitude to admire and revere them, for asserting our Privileges, as much as the Friends of the Liberties of Mankind reverence the successfull Struggles of the American Patriots.

The agreable resources of Paris must certainly please and instruct every Class of Characters. The Arts of Elegance are there considered essential, and are carried to a state of Perfection; the Mind is continually gratified with the admiration of Works of Taste. I have the pleasure of knowing you too well, to doubt of your subscribing to this opinion. With respect to my native Country, I assure you that I am fervently attached to it, as well as to my Friends and Connections in it; there is possibly more sincerity in Professions and a stronger desire of rendering real services, and when the Mouth expresses, the Heart speaks.

I am sensible that I shall tire you to Death from the length of this Letter, and had almost forgot that you are in Paris, and that every instant of your Time is valuable, and might be much better employed than I can possibly do it. However, I shall reserve a further examination of this subject to the Period, when I can have the happiness of meeting you, when we will again resume it. I feel myself under many obligations for your kind present of les Modes de Paris; they have furnished our Ladies with many Hints, for the decoration of their Persons, and I have informed them to whom they are indebted. I shall benefit by your obliging offer of service, whenever I shall have occasion for a fresh Importation of Fashions; at present I am well stocked having lately received a variety of Articles from Paris.

Be so kind as to remember me with affection to Miss Jefferson — tell her she is the envy of all the young Ladies in America, and that I should wish nothing so much as to place my little Girl, under her inspection and protection, should she not leave Paris before I re-visit it. I shall hope for the pleasure of hearing from you, and if you accompany another book of fashions, with any new Opera's or Comedies, you will infinitely oblige me. It is quite time I bad you adieu, but remember that this first of June I am constant to my former opinion, nor can I believe that any length of time will change it. I am determined to have some merit in your eyes, if not for taste and judgment, at least for consistency.

Allow me my dear Sir to assure you that I am sincerely & respectfully yours &c.,

A BINGHAM

An Auction in Philadelphia

THE "PUBLIC VENDUE" *of personal property of William Bingham, Esquire, deceased, held at the Mansion House on Third Street in November, 1805, was the greatest auction sale the country had seen up to that time. An advertisement in the* United States Gazette *for November 16 listed a "Catalogue of the principal articles of furniture and plate":*

HALL

1 Large Lamp
12 Windsor Chairs
3 Composition Pedestals
2 Marble ditto with busts of Voltaire and Rosseau
4 Bronze Figures

1 Female figure composition stone
    A Dial on Composition pedestal
2 Marble medallions in gilt frames
3 Busts of Franklin

FRONT ROOM SOUTH

1 Looking-glass, 5 f. 9 i. by 3 f. 9 i.
1 ditto 7 f. 3 i. by 5 f.
1 ditto 4 f. 6 i. by 1 f. 10 i.
3 Chintz window curtains
    A lot, various pieces gilt china
1 small bureau
12 Mahogany arm chairs with dimity covers
2 Settees with ditto

2 Mahogany dining tables
3 Ditto breakfast ditto
1 Music stand and stool
1 Night ditto with marble top
2 Japanned dove cages
2 Small bird ditto
1 Pair cut glass lamps
1 Pair armed brass ditto
1 Derbyshire spar urn and 2 figures
5 Pair brass andirons
1 Polished steel shovel and tongs

Bellows shovel and tongs
1 Tea urn
2 Mahogany writing desks and box with telescope
1 Large china churn

10 China milch pans
4 Mahogany knife cases
1 Plate warmer
6 lamps and a cat [*sic*]
1 Piano forte

FRONT PARLOUR NORTH

1 Looking-glass 8 f. 4 i. by 4 f. 3 i.
1 Ditto 7 f. 10 i. by 5 f. 11 i.
2 Ditto 5 f. 6 i. by 3 f. 10 i.
2 Ditto 5 f. 3 i. by 2 f. 10 i.
4 Oval ditto
2 Rush bottom settees
10 Ditto arm chairs
10 Ditto single ditto

1 Mahogany breakfast table
1 Secretary
1 Range of dining tables containing 7 pieces
5 Mantle ornaments
2 Venetian blinds
1 Harpsichord

DINING ROOM

2 Looking-glasses 7 f. 8 i. by 4 f. 3 i.
4 Sets dimity curtains
1 Pair glass chandeliers
1 Pair girandoles
2 Large mahogany urn knife cases
3 Smaller ditto
2 Large japanned ditto
2 Marble water vases
1 Large mahogany side board
1 Mahogany wine cooler
24 Mahogany chairs morocco bottom
1 Pair brass andirons
1 Shovel and tongs
1 Brass fender and bellows
1 Large dining set white French china, gilt edges — 350 pieces
Blue dinner set of china, gilt edges
Lot blue china — 8 dozen pieces

Desert set china blue and gold
1 Dining set French china about 100 pieces
1 Tea set of blue and gold china on waiter — 43 pieces
1 Tea set save [Sèvres] china — 47 pieces
19 Glass goblets
20 Plain
6 gilt tumblers
6 Cut glass ditto
25 Plain wine glasses
1 Pair salts
20 Lemonade glasses
32 Figured wine ditto
37 Ditto claret ditto
19 Champainge ditto
2 Cut glass quart decanters
11 Ditto pint ditto
12 Ditto water goblets

10 Decanters and goblets plain, cut
20 Cut glass dishes and
3 small cups
3 Baskets
2 butter
3 sugar tureens with gilt edges
2 Save [Sèvres] china bowls and
plates
Tea set French china about 30
pieces
3 Fruit dishes
8 plates ditto

Desert set pink and gold china
1 Large plateau with 17 marble
figures
1 Large range of dining tables
6 Patent brass lamps
3 Ditto ditto with reflectors
5 Glass ditto
1 Moon light shade
2 Japanned paper trays
Knives and forks silver mounted
Desert ditto ditto

LIBRARY

1 Secretary
1 Copying machine
3 mahogany Book Cases
4 Bronze Figures ⎤
2 Urns │
2 Busts ⎬ on ditto
1 Centre piece ⎦

A collection of paintings, prints,
&c.

DRAWING ROOM

1 Looking glass 7 f. 6 i. by 5 f.
1 glass Chandelier
4 Girandoles
4 gilt Candlesticks
6 large Arm Chairs ⎤
9 small ditto │
1 Sopha ⎬ to match
1 Sopha │
4 gilt Figures ⎦
8 sets blue sattin Window Curtains with gilt cornices

2 fire Screens
Shovel, Tongs and Fender
2 gilt branch Candlesticks
3 china and gold vases
2 Pots of artificial flowers with
glass covers
2 small Busts on Pedestals
1 elegant Carpet 33 f. 6 i. by 23 f.

BALL ROOM

1 mahogany Bedstead 7 feet square with canopy, curtains; mattress &c complete
1 carpet 22 feet square
6 Marseilles Bed Quilts worked
1 Ditto do. plain
4 pieces Sattin
1 piece do. worked with Gold
2 Mandarin Figures
15 chairs, stuffed Bottoms
1 range of Dining Tables

1 large mahogany writing Desk
1 Clock and Orrery
2 Settees stuffed
3 sets muslin Window Curtains
2 ditto Chintz do.
1 do. pink silk do.
8 counterpanes Marseilles Quilting
21 table Cloths
35 Napkins

BED ROOM

1 State bedstead with damask sattin curtains
1 Looking glass 5 f. 7 i. by 3 f. 11 i.
1 Toilet ditto
1 Dressing ditto
8 Arm chairs, damask stuffed bottoms

1 Set of drawers
1 Cane cradle
1 Dressing table
1 Work stand, mahogany

DRESSING ROOM

2 Mahogany bureaus

1 Closet for papers

FRONT ROOM UP STAIRS S. W. CORNER

A full length portrait of Mrs. Siddons in the Grecian Daughter
2 Girandoles with mirrors
3 Sets yellow and scarlet window curtains
12 Yellow and pink chairs with silk bottoms

1 Sopha to match ditto
1 Japanned and gold bureau
1 Elegant clock
3 Card tables
1 Lottery table
2 Mahogany corner cupboards
1 Gold-fish bottle
1 Pair of large andirons

Shovel, tongs, fender, and bellows

1 Carpet 16 feet 8 inches by 24 feet 6 inches

2 Boxes of counters

THIRD STORY

1 Mahogany high post bedstead with curtains

8 Mahogany chairs

1 Clothes press

1 Chest of drawers

Bedsteads, beds and bedding

12 Mahogany chairs stuffed bottoms

1 Sopha to match

1 Table linen press with drawers

1 Mangle

A variety of kitchen utensils

Window cornices

5 Boxes of candles

4 Bags of coffee

2 Cases fowling pieces

1 Ditto pistols

Marble vases

Marble jambs, and head pieces for chimney

Ditto slabs

Composition stone ornaments, from the manufactory of Coade, London, consisting of Fascia Medallions Entablatures Mouldings, and Key stones

PLATE
Weighed by Mr. Joseph Lownes

	oz.	dwt.
1 Soup tureen	111	10
1 ditto do.	111	15
1 punch Vase	96	5
4 sauce Tureens		
4 ladles for do.	114	
4 plated stands for ditto		
6 Salts and 6 ladles	31	12
1 Dutch kettle with Lamp	49	10
1 soup Ladle	5	5
3 Coasters	6	10
4 Vegetable dishes	154	14
4 Covers for ditto	80	7

1 pair Candlesticks	26	0
2 round waiters, beaded edges	22	8
6 Plates	96	5
6 wine labels	2	6
1 fish Knife	3	13
1 small round Shaving Box	3	18
1 tea Urn	113	5
1 coffee Urn	43	
1 tea Caddy	18	5
1 sugar Dish	13	15
1 cream Ewer	9	15
1 cake Basket	48	15
3 doz. Tea Spoons, gilt, 9 oz. 16 dwt. each doz.	29	8
1 sugar Tongs to match	1	14
2 silver Goblets gilt inside	15	15
2 Salts without Glasses	3	0
1 soup Ladle	5	12
1 Strainer	5	18
1 bread Basket old fashion	39	10
1 large Tray	78	10
11 Forks	33	
4 do. small	8	8
12 desert Spoons	13	
6 do. do. French	11	12
6 do. do. English	6	10
17 Table do.	38	5
6 do. French	18	17
1 large oval Dish	30	17
1 smaller do.	22	10
4 smaller do.	75	15
2 smaller do.	32	5
2 small round waiters old fashion	28	13
1 pair Coasters	4	6
2 Skewers	3	18
3 gravy Spoons	16	8
1 punch Ladle	1	10
19 French Forks	55	8
16 do. do.	39	3

5 desert Spoons	5	14
4 tea Spoons	2	
1 mustard Ladle	0	12
6 table Spoons	13	5
1 sugar Tongs	0	18

PLATED WARE

1 large Oval Dish gadroon edges	1 pair Coasters
1 smaller do. do.	1 dish Cross
1 smaller do. do.	1 coffee Ewer
1 round plate do.	1 egg Frame with Ladles complete
1 Snuffers and Tray	4 oval Stands for Salts with silver edges

The plate may be seen at Mr. Lownes's, Front street near the Draw-bridge, any day previous to the sale.

A. PETTIT & CO. AUC'RS.

The Bingham Estate

WHEN THE "BINGHAM TRUST" was liquidated in November, 1964, more than 160 years after William Bingham's death (see pages 430–433), there was surprise that the estate should have remained operative through so many decades and curiosity as to how it overcame the rule of law against perpetuity. In addition, a puzzling question arose: if William Bingham left the income of his fortune to his three children, why was the estate paying income to 315 heirs, many of whom were not direct descendants of William and Anne Bingham?

I am indebted to R. Sturgis Ingersoll, one of the last two trustees of the Bingham Estate, for kindly providing the following explanation. He set the record straight in letters written on August 13, 1968, and February 21, 1969:

> William Bingham by his last will left his estate in trust to named trustees with income to be paid to his [children], with principal on their death to their issue. . . .
>
> Mr. Bingham's control of the property by will ended when his daughters died, and the property vested in their descendants. . . . They found difficulty in managing the American properties and by Deed in 1853 and by Deed in 1862 transferred all their American properties to my uncle, Joseph Reed Ingersoll, then Minister to the Court of St. James, and John Craig Miller, with authority to manage and sell all their American properties with proceeds paid to the grantors or their heirs and assigns. A surviving trustee named in the Deeds had power to appoint a successor trustee in substitution of a deceased trustee. Although these trustees were always referred to as trustees, they were in fact agents. At any time any party in interest might have brought suit to partition the property. This never occurred. You will recognize, therefore, that the rule against perpetuities had no bearing. . . .

On Mr. Bingham's death in 1804 his executors noted that there were entries in his books that the acquisition of the lands in north-western Pennsylvania was a joint venture as between himself, with an interest of .486884; his father-in-law, Thomas Willing, with an interest of .383353; and his brother-in-law, Thomas Mayne Willing, with an interest of .129763.

Mr. Bingham's testamentary executors, his testamentary trustees, his heirs and eventually the trustees under the two Deeds by the English owners of 1853 and 1862 honored these entries. On all sales of the northwestern Pennsylvania properties and on royalties the division was made in the appropriate fractions as between Mr. Bingham's heirs and assigns and the heirs and assigns of the two Willings.

*

A parchment indenture in the author's possession shows that on January 26, 1826, in Philadelphia, certain real and personal property was divided into five approximately equal parts for division among the three children. The property included 1076 acres of open land, much of it on Boon's, Tinicum, Province and Carpenter's islands; 2 houses, 9 city lots; 5 shares of Lancaster Turnpike stock; 17 shares of Union Canal stock; and one share of the Philadelphia Library. Those conducting the division "proceeded . . . to allot two of the shares or divisions . . . to William Bingham [Jr.] Esquire in the following manner.

> First, three papers of equal size were marked respectively with the letters ABC and being placed in a hat Abraham Shoemaker Esquire drew one of them for William Bingham which on being opened was found to be marked with the letter C.
> Then two papers of equal size were marked respectively with the letters D and E and were placed in another hat when Abraham Shoemaker drew one of them for William Bingham which on being opened was found to be marked with the letter D.
> The allotments or divisions in the annexed Schedule C and D were thereupon declared to belong to William Bingham Esquire.

Notes and Sources
Bibliography

Notes and Sources

REFERENCES to sources are keyed to the Bibliography by the last name of the author or editor, and in some instances by the name of the volume, publication or manuscript collection. Where two or more works by the same author are cited, the title is identified by its name or initials. The following initials identify other sources.

APS	American Philosophical Society
BaP	Baring Papers, Baring Brothers & Co., Limited
CFA	Committee for Foreign Affairs
CSC	Committee of Secret Correspondence
DAB	Dictionary of American Biography
HSP	Historical Society of Pennsylvania
LC	Library of Congress
MHS	Massachusetts Historical Society
NA	National Archives
NYHS	New York Historical Society
NYPL	New York Public Library
PMHB	Pennsylvania Magazine of History and Biography
PRO, CO	British Public Record Office, Colonial Office
SC	Secret Committee (of Commerce)
WBP, LC	William Bingham Papers, Library of Congress
WBLB	William Bingham Letter Books, at the Historical Society of Pennsylvania

PREFACE

Page

ix Mark A. DeWolfe Howe. The quoted phrases are from his review of James Morton Smith's *Freedom's Fetters* in the *William and Mary Quarterly*, Vol. 13, 1956, p. 573.

xi Wilmarth S. Lewis. Quoted by Allis, Foreword, vii.

CHAPTER 1.   A CERTAIN ACTION AT DELAWARE BAY

3 Resolve by Congress. Force, VI, 1674.

3 *Reprisal.* Clark, 10. I wish to acknowledge my indebtedness in Chapters 1 and 2 to William Bell Clark's excellent *Lambert Wickes — Sea Raider and Diplomat*, Yale University Press, 1932.

480 : Notes and Sources

3 Grand Union. PRO, CO, 5/125, 192, Chapman to Admiral Young.

4 Wickes and crew. Clark, 14.

5 Commons. Philadelphia did not have a "Commons" in the conventional sense. An area so referred to was apparently at the end of Chestnut Street.

6 Wickes to CSC. Force, VI, 919.

7 Action at Delaware Bay. Force, VII, 14; Allen, I, 142–45; PRO, Admiralty, 51/4279, *Orpheus* Log; Clark, 46–51; Footner, 26–29; Barney, 39–40.

8 WB confined to *Reprisal.* This is an assumption.

CHAPTER 2.   BACKGROUND FOR A MISSION

10 Morris to Deane. Deane, NYHS, 1886, 137.

10 Bingham forebears. Sawtelle, 212.

10 Epitaph. *PMHB,* V, 1881, "Notes and Queries," 237.

11 "Billy Bingham." Burd, 182; Balch, *Assemblies,* 23.

11 Stamper. Scharf-Westcott, II, 883.

11 Molly Stamper. Sawtelle, 213.

11 Bingham family. Brown, "Bingham in Martinique," 55–56; Sawtelle, 213. James and John, of whom little is known, were registered for the College of Philadelphia in 1756, two years before William. Montgomery, 532.

12 Pine Street purchase. Scharf-Westcott, II, 883; H. W. Smith, II, 487.

12 Carriage. Oberholzer, I, *Phila.,* 229; Scharf-Westcott, II, 883.

12 William matriculated. Letter to the author from the chief clerk of Alumni Records, University of Pennsylvania, Feb. 9, 1967.

12 College life. Cheyney, 94–95. One of the Latin tutors WB came in contact with was the Scot immigrant, James Wilson, later his business partner and a justice of the U. S. Supreme Court. While teaching at the College, Wilson was studying law with John Dickinson.

12 Graduated with honors. *Pennsylvania Gazette,* Dec. 1, 1768. It was the year of the first commencement of the College's medical school. In a separate ceremony, ten young men were given the degree of Bachelor of Physics — the first medical degrees given in America.

12 Father died. *Ibid.,* Feb. 23, 1769.

13 Master of Arts. *Ibid.,* July 11, 1771.

13 Gilmor on WB. Gilmor, *Memoir,* notes facing 17.

13 Two ships. *PMHB,* XXVIII, 1904, 359, 501, "Ships Register for the Port of Philadelphia." WB also owned in 1775 the schooner *Fair Lady,* 60 tons, built in New England.

13 Galloways. Eberlein, *Portrait,* 74. Betsey's suitor later became a judge. Betsey succeeded in eloping with a British officer, though he too had been threatened with shooting. The marriage turned out unhappily. Joseph Galloway's estates were confiscated during the Revolution when he joined the Loyalist cause.

13 Grand Tour. "Letters and Papers of John Singleton Copley and Henry Pelham," M.H.S., Colls., Vol. 71, 1914, pp. 206, 209; Bridenbaugh, 171, 193.

17 WB secretary. NA Micro 90, WB to Congress, June 29, 1779.

17 Rousseau-Voltaire agreed. Hale, 67.

17 Bonvouloir. Wharton, I, 333; Durand, 5. Bonvouloir communicated with the CSC through another Frenchman, Daymons, a librarian. It may be assumed that WB, as secretary of the committee, attended this secret meeting.

19 Choice of WB as agent. The statement is made in the *DAB* and elsewhere that WB had spent several years in Martinique before the Revolution as British consul. The statement is incorrect.

19 Conference with Morris. WBP, LC, June 3, 1776.

20 WB's orders. HSP, June 3, 1776.

20 Willing committee. Ford, III, 453.

24 Condition of Hornet. Clark, 44.

24 CSC to WB. Force, VI, 783.

24 SC to Wickes. Force, VI, 783.

CHAPTER 3.   FIRST DAYS IN MARTINIQUE

25 Morris to Deane. Deane, NYHS, 1886, 235.

25 Wickes sailed. Force, VII, 180, Wickes to CSC, July 11, 1776; Clark, 52.

25 Franklin on *Reprisal*. Van Doren, *BF*, 564; Clark, 96; Hale, I, 243.

25 Friends with Wickes. Clark, 65.

26 Capture of *Friendship*. Force, VII, 180, Wickes to CSC, July 11, 1776; Clark, 54.

26 Prize money. Paullin, 36, 41.

26 Crew volunteered. Several years later, after having served dutifully on the *Reprisal*, Second Officer Thomas Norwood was captured by the British and courtmartialed. He explained that he, like the other officers, had entered American service "through the advice and repeated solicitations of Captain Wickes," but only in order to escape, when an occasion offered, "from such dangerous and unprecedented employ." Clark, 54.

26 Two more prizes. They were the 80-ton schooner *Peter*, of Liverpool, loaded with sugar, coffee, cocoa, cotton, and 100 hogsheads of rum, and the 80-ton brigantine *Neptune*, carrying a cargo of rum from Antigua to Cork. Wickes sent off both vessels as prizes and enlisted numbers of their crews in the American service. The third ship was an Irish ship, *Duchess of Leinster*, bound for Dublin. Unable to man her with a prize crew and unwilling to sink her, Wickes told the captain, "I will not distress you, because I am sure the Irish would not distress us. I wish you a safe passage." Force, VII, 249, Wickes to CSC, July 13, 1776; Clark, 55–56.

27 First battle in foreign waters. Augur, 108.

27 WB sent ashore. Deane, Conn., 32, WB to Deane, Aug. 5, 1776. Wickes probably also sent his three captive merchant masters ashore at the same time, since his newly recruited English crewmen would fight better away from a master's inhibiting gaze.

28 Battle with the *Shark*. PRO, Admiralty, 51/895, 13; PRO, 5/125, Chapman to Admiral Young; Force, VII, 609, 706, VIII, 323; Clark, 56–60. The English captain did not hear Wickes' response to his challenge.

28 "Without much damage." Force, VII, 609, Letter from St. Eustacia, July 27, 1776.

28 WB's account. Deane, Conn., 32, WB to Deane, Aug. 5, 1776.

28 "Precipitate flight." Force, VII, 706, Letter from St. Pierre, Aug. 1, 1776. This letter is not attributed to WB, but use of the word *caress* in this and a following letter by WB (below) indicate that he was the author.

28 "Caressed beyond measure." Deane, Conn., 32, WB to Deane, Aug. 5, 1776.

29 Courcey's account. Force, VII, 1179, Bartlett to Whipple, Aug. 27, 1779; Clark, 61–62.

29 Chapman's account, footnote. PRO, CO, 5/125, 192–93, Chapman to Admiral Young, July 29, 1776.

29 First visit by a naval officer. Clark, 60.

29 *Shark* returned. Force, VIII, 323, Bartlett to Whipple, Sept. 14, 1776; Clark, 61.

29 Chapman guarded. Deane, Conn., 32, WB to Deane, Aug. 5, 1776.

30 Argout cordial. *Ibid.;* Force, VII, 1179, VIII, 323.

31 British protest. The British captain was under secret orders to anchor close to the *Reprisal,* follow her out, and take her to Antigua, but he arrived too late. Clark, 63.

31 Argout withdrew convoy offer. Deane, Conn., 25, WB to Deane, undated.

31 Called on Harrison. APS, Microframe 13, CSC to Harrison, June 3, 1776.

31 French *negociant,* or merchant. His name was Peter Begorrat; he owned an armed sloop that he wanted to run to America and sell. WB gave him a cargo and a letter to Morris. Deane, Conn., 32; WBP, LC, Willing and Morris to WB, Sept. 14, 1776.

31 Bought sabers. WBP, LC, Morris to WB, Sept. 27, No. 8, 1776, June 20, 1777.

31 Three letters to CSC. Force, VIII, 425.

32 First letter to Deane. Deane, Conn., 27–31, Aug. 4, 1776.

32 Independence declared. Deane, Conn., 33, WB to Deane, Aug. 5, 1776.

32 Lectured Morris. WBP, LC, Sept. 14, 1776.

33 French officers. They were the Marquis de Malmady, Jean Louis Imbert, Christian de Colerus, and Jean Louis de Virnejout. Clark, 64.

33 Wickes' return voyage. WBP, LC, Morris to WB, Sept. 14, 1776; Clark, 66, 67, 373.

33 Turned over Frenchmen. Congress appointed Malmady and Colerus majors in the Continental army by brevet and Virnejout a brevet captain, giving each an advance of two months' pay. Imbert, reputedly "an accomplished engineer," was sent to General Washington with one month's pay. Clark, 68; Force, VIII, 323.

34 WB's share. HSP, Morris to WB, June 20, 1777.

34 "Too many members to keep secrets." Burnett, *Letters,* II, 110–11.

34 Sent French papers. WBP, LC, Willing and Morris to WB, Nov. 8, 1776.

34 Preferred more powder. HSP, SC to WB, Oct. 21, 1776.

34 Franklin to WB. Force, VIII, 425–27, Sept. 21, 1776. On the subject of French officers, Franklin wrote WB, "Your remarks have been very proper. . . . Give general discouragement to those that apply, and recommend none but such as the General will pledge his word for, and you may even intimate to him that if too many come over, the Congress will not know what to do with them." (*Ibid.*) Morris wrote him, "I must . . . request you to spare me all you can in the introduction of French officers to me. . . . Really they are flocking over in such numbers from every port and by every ship that I don't know what we shall do with them." WBP, LC, Feb. 16, 1777.

35 Received arms and powder. Force, VIII, 425. The Committee sent a list of medicines it needed and asked for "good blankets and other woolen goods suitable for soldiers, with some more muskets, powder, gun flints, salt petre,

sulphur, etc. . . . observing that we now want clothing for our troops beyond any other articles."

35 First private letter from Morris. WBP, LC, Sept. 14, 1776. WB was authorized to make a bargain with a French merchant "on the best terms in your power . . . to the value of £2000." If he wished, he might take in some more partners "so as to reduce the risque to thirds or fourths just as you like."

35 Propriety of mixing business. *Ibid.* Morris justified his practice of including shipments of his own in government vessels on the ground that, having deprived himself of the profits of his regular business through government service, he should be allowed to compensate his loss somewhat by this means. Ver Steeg has an interesting analysis of the morality of Robert Morris' public conduct. Wallace, 334; ver Steeg, 11, 23–27.

35 "A pleasing account sales." WBP, LC, Sept. 14, 1776.

35 Stamper offered money. WBP, LC, Nov. 8, 1776.

35 Vendue on the Wharf. WBP, LC, Morris to WB and Harrison, Nov. 7, 1776.

36 Morris' advice. WBP, LC, Oct. 20, 1776.

CHAPTER 4.   SOME EVENTS OF A PUBLIC NATURE

37 Morris to WB. WBP, LC, Oct. 20, 1776.

37 I have drawn heavily on two works in describing St. Pierre and life in Martinique: Lafcadio Hearn's beautifully written *Two Years in the French West Indies,* 1890; and the diary of Marine Captain Joseph Hardy, printed entire in James L. Howard's *Seth Harding, Mariner,* Yale University, 1930 (see Appendix 1).

38 Martiniquaise. An ordinance passed in 1724 prohibited marriage and concubinage between the races, but this was a country where legal European-style marriages were rare and concubinage was common. The women were the carriers of burdens on the island. A *porteuse,* carrying 100 or even 150 pounds on her head, would walk for miles with a smooth, fast stride over the mountain roads, under a sun that was intolerable to others. Hearn, 97–106, 338.

39 Theater and dancing school. Howard, 214, 217.

39 General Lee. Deane, Conn., 68, WB to Deane, Feb. 2, 1777.

40 Harrison to Morris, footnote. Lorenz, 102; John Work Garrett Library, Baltimore, Jan. 8, 1777.

40 Matters favorable for America. Deane, Conn., 61, WB to Deane, Dec. 24, 1776.

40 Urgent, pleading letter. HSP, SC to WB, Oct. 21, 1776.

41 250,000 livres debt. WBP, LC, WB to Morris, Aug. 7, 1781.

41 Morris in despair. WBP, LC, Sept. 27, 1776. Morris advised WB to become friends "with a man of known integrity and honor with whose trust you can safely commit any property that may be in your hands should such unhappy news come to you. This friend should receive and cover it as his own until you order otherwise, for if America proves unfortunate in this contest, we doubt much if the [French] government will protect [our] agents. . . . But all this is mere apprehension, you'll keep it closely to yourself . . . without imparting your design to any person living."

41 Hodge. Force, VIII, 427, 1198–99; Augur, 169, 192.

42 Franklin-Jefferson. Burnett, *Letters*, II, 110–11.

42 Double-distilled bastard. Fisher, *Recollections*, 212.

43 Arthur Lee. His character and actions are described in Augur; Van Doren, *BF;* Monaghan; and Miller, *TF,* among others.

43 WB and Hortalez. Force, VIII, 425–27, CSC to WB, Sept. 21, 1776.

45 Deane shipments. Deane, NYHS, 1886, 247, Deane to Morris, Sept. 17, 1776.

45 Largest shipments. F. Wharton, II, 182–83, Deane to WB, Oct. 25, 1776.

46 WB to Commissioners on route of shipments. Deane, Conn., 88, April 6, 1777.

46 Congress complained. HSP, SC to WB, Oct. 21, 1776.

46 *Cornelia & Molly.* WBP, LC, WB to CSC, Jan. 17, 1777.

46 Morris apologetic. WBP, LC, Feb. 16, 1777.

47 Cheerfully contracted. NA Micro 90, WB to Congress, June 29, 1779.

47 WB too young. Force, IX, 1481, CSC to Commissioners, Dec. 30, 1776.

47 Morris to WB, a better aspect. WBP, LC, Oct. 20, 1776.

48 Countrymen roused. Deane, Conn., 75, WB to Deane, Feb. 28, 1777.

48 *Seine.* The full story of the *Seine,* whose loss was a kind of triumph for the American cause, can be pieced together from Deane, Conn., 81, 84, 87, 97, 98; and NA Micro 90, WB to Congress, Oct. 13, 1777, and June 29, 1779. The *Seine* sailed on March 30 and was taken by a British frigate the same evening, possibly because Captain Morin took a course into a dangerous area in the channel between Martinique and Dominica and left a light burning in his caboose that revealed his position. Bingham wrote to Deane of his dark suspicions of some "sinister motive" in Captain Morin.

On board the *Seine* was a Mr. Nick Davis, a passenger from France. He had arrived in Martinique with a warm letter of recommendation from William Carmichael, Silas Deane's secretary, requesting that "all civility and assistance" be shown him. Davis had had an unlucky run of play on the voyage; he told Bingham a plausible story of funds due him from Deane; and Bingham lent him a considerable sum of money. When the *Seine* was captured on the way to Boston, Davis defected to the enemy. Salt was rubbed into this wound when the Commissioners in Paris objected to repaying Bingham his loan. With the eloquence of a man who has lost money and has been made to look foolish, Bingham stormed to Deane: "Such perfidious and treacherous conduct cannot even be approved by our enemies, altho they may love the treason, they will detest the traitor, and the name of such a man, if not too insignificant to blot the page of history, will be handed down to posterity with distinguished infamy and with the curses and execrations of all honest men."

CHAPTER 5. THE FIRE IS LIGHTED AT THE EXTREMITIES

49 Stormont to Vergennes. Stevens, June 11, 1777, No. 1548.

49 Carmichael and Catherine. Einstein, 422. As liaison man between Deane and Beaumarchais and charged with recruiting and outfitting privateers to prey on English shipping, Carmichael recruited into American service a nineteen-year-old marquis, Marie Joseph Paul Yves Roch Gilbert du Motier Lafayette.

49 Carmichael to WB. F. Wharton, II, 346.

49 WB and privateers. NA Micro 90, June 29, 1779. Americans devoted more

concentrated attention to privateering during the Revolution than to any other military activity, and in some months, more men were patrolling the seas in privately owned warships than were serving in Washington's armies.

50 WB's partners. Brown, "Martinique," 66; HSP, Welsh to Franklin, Oct. 20, 1777.

50 Fleet of 60, 14 prize vessels. Augur, 94.

51 Morris, Ord, and *Retaliation*. HSP, Dec. 4, 1776, Feb. 12, 1777; Lincoln, *Naval Records*, 438.

51 Morris on privateering. WBP, LC, Apr. 25, 1777.

51 Two Guinea men. The two captured slavers, the *Gascoyne* and the *Fox*, carried 284 male slaves, 45 women, 105 boys, and 41 girls. They were sold at auction, the men bringing around 800 livres Martinique each, women 660 to 725, the boys 660, and girls 600. A pregnant woman brought 800 livres; a "meagre" woman 200; a sick boy 230. An old man and woman, "almost dead and good for nothing," were given away. The auction netted 326,988 livres after deduction of expenses and WB's 5 per cent commission. Expenses included soldiers to guard the ships in port, bread and bananas for the slaves, the King's physician and surgeon for visiting the slaves, and payment to a Negro to come and preach Christianity to them. The proceeds, including receipts for the guns, the ivory and sale of one of the ships, was divided: one-half to the crews; one-third of the other half to Robert Morris, one-third to Coctiny de Prejent, and one-third to WB. (Library Company, *Adventures of Ships Owned by William Bingham, 1777–1779* — WB's account book of his cargoes shipped and prizes taken.)

51 £13,780 prize. HSP, Morris statement of accounts, Nov. 21, Dec. 14, 1778.

52 Losses by capture. One Bingham captain, John Welsh, wrote Dr. Franklin from Fortune Gaol in Portsmouth, England, "of my misfortune of being taken prisoner and brought here from the West Indies where I commanded a privateer fitted out by William Bingham, Esq. . . . [am] in a distressed situation. . . . Any favor I may receive will be greatly thankful, as William Bingham or Rich Harrison of Martinico would be answerable. . . . I draw [on you] for 20 guineas." HSP, Welsh to Franklin, Oct. 20, 1777. WB complained to Morris on Aug. 10, 1777, that he had met "with very considerable losses in privateers." WBP, LC.

52 Prejent. WBP, LC, Morris to WB, Dec. 3, 1776; HSP, Morris to WB, June 20, 1777, May 7, 1778.

52 "Ministerial fortune." WBP, LC, Feb. 12, 1777.

52 "A fine ship sold." *Ibid.*, Apr. 25, 1777.

52 WB to Morris on Prejent. WBP, LC, Aug. 10, 1777.

53 Stormont and Vergennes. Stevens, June 11, July 9, Dec. 10, 1777, Nos. 1548, 1568, 1766.

54 Morris scolded. WBP, LC, Morris to WB, Oct. 20, 1776.

54 Morris on blankets. *Ibid.*, Nov. 21, 1778. In the matter of WB's unfortunate loan to Davis (see note, p. 48.) Morris wrote: "That same Nick Davis is a rascall of the first stamp and I wonder you could run the risque of trusting him or any other person with so much money. It is not approved of. I will take care to have this passed in your account but advise you to be extremely cautious how you part with public money in future or you may suffer loss of the money and be charged with want of discretion."

55 77,596 livre debt. HSP, Morris to WB, Jan. 12, 1778.

55 Morris on Prejent. WBP, LC, Oct. 1, 1778.

56 Morris regret. HSP, Feb. 10, 1779. Morris was upset by the misconduct of his half-brother Tom Morris, whom he had attempted to reform by making him his commercial representative in France. Tom misapplied funds (including money received for prizes brought in by Captain Wickes), gambled and drank away large sums entrusted to him, and quarreled with the other American agents in Europe. He caused Robert Morris to be humiliated and "vastly hurt" before he died of alcoholism in France in 1778. HSP, Morris to WB, Jan. 12, 1778.

56 Present for Mrs. Morris. HSP, Morris to WB, Mar. 5, 1779.

56 WB to Committee of Commerce on Prejent. WBP, LC, Jan. 27, 1779. Congress received the 50 cases of arms safely. Neeser, 154.

56 Charles Willing. WBP, LC, Willing and Morris to WB, Apr. 25, 1777.

56 Captain Biddle. NA. 332. Roll 6, Marine Letter Book, No. 0135, Feb. 15, 1777.

57 Medicines sold. WBP, LC, Oct. 1, 1778.

57 WB's mother. *Ibid.*, May 5, Oct. 1, 1778.

57 Bouillé. Library Company, du Simitière Papers, Congress to WB, June 26, 1777.

57 WB to Commissioners. Deane, Conn., 103–4.

57 Franklin to Grand. Stevens, July 5, 1777, No. 2064.

58 Bouillé reversal. NA Micro 90, WB to Congress, Dec. 3, 1777.

58 "My situation was critical." *Ibid.*, June 29, 1779.

59 French sloop on secret mission. *Ibid.*, Aug. 1, 1777; Stevens, Wentworth to Suffolk, No. 306, Nov. 16, 1777.

59 Bancroft. R. B. Morris, xii, 10. His duplicity was first revealed with publication of the Auckland Papers in 1891.

60 Bancroft on WB. Stevens, Bancroft to Wentworth, May 27, 1777. No. 254.

CHAPTER 6. THE FIRE REACHES THE CENTER

61 Secret Committee (of Commerce) to WB. Library Company, du Simitière Papers. This rude admonition is contained in very rough draft form, unsigned and undated, on a blank fourth page of a three-page letter dated Sept. 13, 1777, from Henry Livingston, with Washington's army at Philadelphia, to his father, Philip Livingston, austere member of the Secret Committee (of Commerce). Someone of the Committee had composed an almost identical paragraph in the rough draft of a letter addressed to WB on June 26, 1777. It appears that neither version was sent, and certainly that neither was received, since WB received no letters from the Committee in these months. It is worth noting that WB's letters to the Secret Committee (of Commerce) and the Marine Committee were factual, informative and tightly written, quite unlike those sent to the Committee of Secret Correspondence and Foreign Affairs.

62 Galloway and Willing. Westcott, 340.

62 Morris dissolved partnership. HSP, Jan. 12, 1778. Willing got himself and his former partner into trouble when he innocently sent a messenger to Congress, by way of Robert Morris, carrying a verbal offer of peace terms that General Howe had given him. The Congress had just passed a resolution

declaring it a traitorous action to discuss terms with the enemy. The Council of Safety threw the messenger into jail and sharply censured both Morris and Willing. Fitzpatrick, X, 98.

63 WB shocked. APS, Franklin Papers, Vol. 7, 2, No. 105–6, WB to Commissioners, Nov. 14, 1777.

63 "Glorious success." *Ibid.,* Nov. 28, 1777.

63 WB on Bouillé's reversal. NA Micro 90, WB to Congress, Dec. 28, 1777.

63 Military goods shipped. Stevens, Wentworth intelligence report, Nov. 16, 1777, No. 306.

63 Reason for French change. NA Micro 90, WB to Congress, Dec. 28, 1777.

64 Paid import duty. *Ibid.*

64 Morris on French alliance. WBP, LC, May 5, 1778, Morris to WB.

65 Adams on Franklin. Warren-Adams, 209.

65 Vergennes on Adams. Brant, II, 136.

65 Radical Pennsylvania constitution. Of the state constitution, Dr. Rush wrote to Anthony Wayne, "It has substituted mob government for one of the happiest governments in the world. . . . A single legislature is big with tyranny. . . . All governments are dangerous as they approach to simplicity." Said John Adams, "No country ever will be long happy, or even entirely safe and free, which is thus governed. . . . Pennsylvania will be divided and weakened, and rendered much less vigorous in the cause by the wretched ideas of government which prevail in the minds of many people in it." Eberlein-Hubbard, *Diary,* 200; Smith, *JA,* 279–80.

66 French consul his partner. HSP, Holker to WB, Aug. 25, 1779.

66 Jenifer and Hooe. Brown, "Martinique," 65.

66 Harrison to WB. HSP, Nov. 1, 1778, Feb. 27, 1779.

66 Peters to Morris on Privateer Circle. Henkels, 96–97.

67 *Retaliation* cargo. HSP, Morris Papers, Apr. 24, 1780.

67 Exchange of prisoners. NA Micro 90, Apr. 13, June 29, July 2, 1779. See Appendix 2.

67 Andrew Nihell. NA Micro 90, WB to Congress, Feb. 10, 1779.

67 Conyngham, NA Micro 90, WB to Marine Committee, Mar. 27, 1779; Neeser, 150, WB to Conyngham, Nov. 29, 1778; Allen, I, 356–61; WBP, LC, WB to Congress, Jan. 27, 1779; *PMHB,* XXII, 1898, 485, "Narrative of Captain Gustavus Conyngham, USN."

68 Asked to resign. NA Micro 90, June 29, 1779.

68 Martinique *Gazette. Ibid.*

68 WB's health. *Ibid.,* WB to Congress, Mar. 27, June 29, 1779.

69 No word for one year. HSP, WB to Congress, Feb. 8, 1778.

69 Bouillé raised eyebrows. APS, No. 38, WB to Congress, Mar. 5, June 16, 1778.

69 CFA wrote WB on treaty, footnote. F. Wharton, II, 581.

69 WB pleaded for news. NA Micro 90, WB to Congress, Mar. 27, 1779.

69 Morris' plea for an executive. Burnett, II, 178; Sumner, I, 7.

69 Committee sitting in judgment. Sumner, I, 7.

69 WB to Commissioners. APS Franklin Papers, Vol. 8, 2, No. 150, Mar. 5, 1778. WB added, "I hope you will do me the justice to believe that this request does not arise from a vain and idle curiosity, but from a sincere desire of taking advantage of the variety of circumstances that may offer, and of

improving them to the support and service of the general cause. The con-
texture of the body politic is formed so curiously that the smallest change in
the minutest member will sometimes have a very sensible effect upon the
whole system."

70 "My sinking credit." NA Micro 90, Jan. 26, 1778.

70 "Racked with persecution." *Ibid.*, Feb. 17, 1779.

70 WB on Bouillé, impropriety. HSP, Feb. 8, 1778.

71 WB proposal. WBP, LC, Sept. 28, 1778.

71 Navy Board reply. NA 332, Roll 6, Marine Letter Book, No. 0242, John
Brown to WB, Feb. 28, 1780.

71 Lovell to Abigail Adams, footnote. Smith, *JA*, 336, 353, 407, 470.

72 Lovell to WB. F. Wharton, II, 512, 553, 554, 581, Mar. 2, Apr. 16, May 14,
1778.

72 *General Gates and Deane.* NA Micro 90, WB to Congress, Feb. *17*, Mar. *20*,
Mar. *27*, June *29*, 1779; APS, No. 160, Mar. *3*, 1779. Nicholson told Bingham
that Congress had recently adopted a resolution that the officers of the navy,
when in foreign ports where there was an American agent, should be paid
"in solid coin in the amount of their pay, within a month of the time of their
demand." The ships took on tar, cordage, vegetables, oil, nails, beef, green
tea, sugar, chocolate, nutmeg, pork, candles, wine, and limes. Back in Philadelphia some weeks later, the Marine Committee considered their disbursements "very extravagant"; it ordered the Navy Board in Boston to examine
them and to charge whatever it thought excessive to Captains Waters and
Nicholson, to be deducted from their pay. NA 332, Roll 6, Marine Letter
Book, No. 0242, Apr. 19, 1779.

French Admiral d'Estaing complicated matters at Martinique by desiring
Captain Nicholson to join the French fleet with his new frigate. Bingham
refused to issue the order. Estaing, "much offended," threatened to send a
copy of his refusal to the American Congress. NA Micro 90, WB to Congress,
Apr. 13, 1779.

73 WB to Franklin. NA Micro 90, WB to CFA, April 13, 1779; APS, Franklin
Papers, No. 160, Mar. 3, 1779.

CHAPTER 7. LAST DAYS IN MARTINIQUE

74 Jay to Congress. F. Wharton, III, 449.

74 Cruise of the *Confederacy.* Johnston, I, 251; R. B. Morris, 1–6; Howard,
105–16; Allen, I, 406; Monaghan, 125, 130.

75 "Commodiously settled." MHS, H. B. Livingston to mother, Oct. 25, 1779.

76 Six feet of water. Middlebrook, I, 50.

76 Mrs. Jay charmed. Monaghan, 130.

76 WB called Jay "Jack." Swiggett, *GM*, 144. The author gives no source for
the statement.

76 Bouillé obliging. F. Wharton, III, 448.

76 Mrs. Jay's activities. Monaghan, 130; R. B. Morris, 5–6.

76 Liqueurs for Washington. Fitzpatrick, XX, 119.

76 Jay bought Negro boy. He freed him in 1787. Sparks, *Dip. Corr.*, III, 185,
Jay to father, May 23, 1780.

77 Carmichael. Monaghan, 127, 158.

77 Farce, duel. Howard, 214.

77 Jay to Congress. F. Wharton, III, 446, Dec. 25, 1779.
77 WB advanced money. *Ibid.,* 510, Jay to Congress, Feb. 20, 1780.
77 Jay on WB. F. Wharton, III, 436, *et seq.*
78 Franklin refused draft. NA Micro 90, WB to Congress, Nov. 3, 1779; F. Wharton, III, 743, Franklin to Congress, May 31, 1780.
78 WB and Intendant. NA Micro 90, WB to Congress, Nov. 3, 1779; WBP, LC, Oct. 9, 1779.
78 *Pilgrim* affair. Brown, "Martinique," 83–87; Allis, 1125, 1127, 1128–38; NA Micro 90, WB to Congress, Feb. 2, Aug. 22, 1779.
79 Jay on WB. F. Wharton, III, 449.
79 Congress spent £100,000 Jay was to borrow. Burnett, *Letters,* IV, xxxiii. Jay, at the cost of many months of scalding humiliation, was able to borrow only $174,011 at the Spanish court.
80 Board of Admiralty. NA, 332, Roll 6, Marine Letter Book, No. 0242, John Brown to WB, Feb. 28, 1780.
80 Captain Hardy, footnote. Howard, 213–46.
80 WB recapitulation. NA Micro 90, June 29, 1779. See Appendix 2.
81 WB to successors, WBP, LC, Mar. 26, 1780.
81 WB and cocoa. Howard, 246.
81 Mulatto boy. Watson, I, 194.
82 Bouillé on WB. NA Micro 90, Bouillé to Congress, Mar. 13, 1780.
82 *Confederacy* salute. Howard, 247.

CHAPTER 8. ENTER ANNE WILLING

85 WB to Jay. Johnston, I, 364.
85 Coldest winter. Watson, II, 357.
86 Settled in Pine Street House. On No. 11, 1782, Charles Wilson Peale sent a letter addressed to WB "to the House in Pine Street." APS.
86 Presented Bouillé's letter. Burnett, *Letters,* V, 173.
86 Memorial on *Pilgrim.* NA Micro 90, Record Group 360, June 6, 1780.
86 Claim for salary. Ford, XVII, 490.
86 Enlisted as private. Dorland, 57.
86 WB and umbrella. Watson, I, 194.
86 Permission to return home. Ford, XVI, 241.
86 Special committee. Ford, XX, 645.
86 Lovell to Morris. NA Micro 90, July 5, 1780.
86 £7000. Burnett, *Letters,* IV, xxxii; Ford XVIII, 849, 890.
87 507,641 livres. Ford, XX, 645.
88 "Education in patriotic hands." Eberlein, *Diary,* 271; Nevins, 265–66.
88 WB to Jay. Johnston, I, 365, July 1, 1780.
88 Gouverneur Morris, footnote. Morris' friend and physician, a Dr. Jones, who was not in Philadelphia when the accident happened, maintained that the leg should not have been removed. Morris became the subject of a notable case history among surgical lecturers of the day. Sparks, *GM,* I, 223.
89 Luzerne, stop begging. Sumner, I, 299.
89 George III, Washington to Congress. Sumner, I, 258. In Feb., 1781, the French government advised Congress to accept mediation of the war, on the basis that each side would retain the territory it then held.
89 WB to Jay. Johnston, I, 364.

89 Bank of Pennsylvania, East, 208; Sumner, II, 21–24; Lewis, 17–23; Konkle, 90–97.

90 WB to Jay. Johnston, I, 365.

91 Poem to Bank. Hammond, 42.

91 Met Anne Willing. They would not have met at the Dancing Assembly. WB was a member, but Anne was too young to attend.

92 Willing background. Balch, WP, *L&P;* Brown, "Mr. and Mrs. William Bingham," 287; Eberlein, *Port.,* 32; Griswold, 13–16, 255; Jordan; Konkle; Macfarlane; Scharf-Westcott, I, 276, II, 1694; Watson, I, 208; Westcott, 339–41. Anne's great grandmother was a Harrison, the granddaughter of two members of the court that condemned and executed Charles I.

92 Willing and Morris. Ver Steeg, 4; Oberholzer, *RM,* 8.

93 Assembly episode. Balch, *Assemblies,* 48.

93 Willing and Declaration. Balch, *WP,* xxxv.

94 Willing to Morris, shock. Henkels, 98, Oct. 1, 1777.

94 Adams dined. Butterfield, II, 132. Adams wrote: "He [Willing] told us of a law of this place, that whereas oysters, between the months of May and Septr. were found to be unwholesome food, if any were brought to markett they should be forfeited and given to the poor."

94 Education of women. Bridenbaugh, 48–52; Brooks, 43.

95 One European visitor. Bridenbaugh, 96.

95 Aunt Anne and Col. Bouquet. Balch, *WP,* 28; *PMHB,* III, 1879, 130–31.

95 "Willing Molly" Byrd. Wecter, 27.

96 Aunt Elizabeth Powel. Fisher, *Recollections,* 208–9. Fisher declared of the Powel marriage, "It was said love had not much part in the affair, on her part at least. . . . When he died [in the plague of 1793] it was perhaps a great relief to his wife, who wrote a monumental epitaph that would fill a folio page and never wearied herself with praising him. Perhaps she felt she had neglected her duties in his last illness, leaving him to die alone in an outhouse at Powelton, where there was no danger of infection; though perhaps she did not know it, for she was panic-stricken at the very idea of epidemic disease."

96 Fragonard beauty. The phrase is Dixon Wecter's.

96 "Manners a gift." Griswold, 254.

96 Rawle on WBs. *PMHB,* XXXV, 1911, 398, Anna Rawle to Mrs. Samuel Shoemaker, Nov. 4, 1780.

CHAPTER 9.   OF DEATH, A BANK, AND MARCHING ARMIES

98 WB to Willing. HSP.

98 Chastellux in Philadelphia. Chastellux, I, 143, 147, 164.

98 Chastellux at ball. He said, "On passing into the dining room, the Chevalier de la Luzerne offered his hand to Mrs. [Robert] Morris, and gave her the precedence, an honor rather generally bestowed on her, as she is the richest woman in the city, and all ranks here being equal, men follow their natural bent by giving the preference to wealth."

99 Mrs. Jay to Mrs. Morris. Young, 166, Apr. 22, 1781.

100 Jay congratulations. Jay, II, 88–91, Jay to WB, Sept. 8, 1781.

100 Jay code. *Ibid.,* 90. Jay said, "Whenever you write me, which I hope will be often, recollect that your letters will, in nine instances out of ten, be in-

spected before they reach me." British intelligence had little difficulty in breaking such codes as Jay's. See Augur, 76.

100 Livingston to G. Morris. Swiggett, *GM*, 81.

100 Death of Mrs. Willing. *PMHB*, V, 1881, 455. The Willing family, Dr. Benjamin Rush observed, "always dress the dead bodies of each other, or in other words, lay each other out." Rush, *Auto.*, 227.

101 Deaths of Benezet, Stamper. Brown, "Mr. and Mrs. William Bingham," 288.

102 WB sought appointment. Burnett, *Letters*, V, 555, Thomas Burke to WB, Jan. 30; 563, Feb. 6(?), 1781.

103 Livingston not invited. Dangerfield, 144.

103 Expected 5 per cent commission. Swiggett, *GM*, 100.

103 Morris as Financier. Ferguson, 118, 120; Sumner, I, 265–67; II, 22; ver Steeg, 22–27. In his diary, Morris wrote, "This appointment was unsought, unsolicited, and dangerous to accept, as it was evidently contrary to my private interests and . . . must inevitably expose me to the resentment of disappointed and designing men, and to the calumny and detraction of the envious and malicious." He announced that he would himself do no business with the government, or if it became necessary to do so from time to time, he would appoint a special board to review his accounts.

104 WB to Morris. WBP, LC, Aug. 7, 1781. WB recapitulated for Morris "the leading points on which the nature of my claim is founded." His expenses, "necessarily and indispensably incurred," totaled 161,000 livres Martinique. Bingham presented a claim for 110,000 to cover both his salary and expenses, absorbing 51,000 himself. "A scrupulous attention to motives of delicacy would not permit me to charge the whole of my expences to the account of the Public, when some profitable private business that I was engaged in enabled me to support a part of them. But the right of doing it was still unquestioned."

There had been hints, he said, that deductions should be made from his accounts because of private advantages from his commercial transactions as an agent. If the public benefits resulting from them were taken into consideration, however, he should rather be entitled to *compensation* for extra and important services.

"Immediately on my arrival in the West Indies, I risked my personal credit to the amount of Liv. 250,000 for arms, ammunition & cloathing, which by arriving at a critical time, assisted in enabling our army to keep the field & give a check to the encroachments of the enemy. Ever since that time, Congress has generally been indebted to me a much larger sum, which, if I had had the use of, I might have efficiently converted to my own private purposes, so as to have derived ten times the advantage that the advances to Congress will procure me."

104 Morris to Lovell. NA Micro 90, Sept. 7, 1781. Morris felt that the total of WB's expenses, commissions and salary amounted to more than anyone expected it to be. He accepted WB's explanation, however, that living costs on the island were "much higher than we could then suppose, that his commissions was absorbed in losses, and the salary far short of what has been allowed other gentlemen who had much less trouble and were not more useful."

104 WB one-page memorial. NA Micro 90, no date (probably Nov., 1781).

105 Morris to Franklin. F. Wharton, V, 35, Morris to Grand, Dec. 3, 1781; V, 227, Franklin to Morris, Mar. 7, 1782.

105 Final settlement of account. Sumner, II, 17; "Martinique," Brown, 82–83.

105 Lee on WB. Harvard Papers, fMS, Am 811, vol. 8, Documents 162–63. Observations on Mr. Bingham's Accounts by J. Pennell, no date. Cited by Ferguson, p. 199.

106 WB wrote bylaws. HSP, WB to Willing, Dec. 29, 1783.

106 "Ablest banker," footnote. Wettereau, "New Light," 277.

106 Subscription of $400,000. Subscribers to the Bank of Pennsylvania had not been repaid for their loans for military supplies; they were entitled, by permission of Congress, to convert their shares in the old bank into shares in the new one.

106 Bank of North America. Balch, *WP*, xlix; Dorfman, I, 225; East, 288; Ferguson, 123; Hammond, 48; Konkle, 98–107; Lewis, 32–6; Studenski, 29; Sumner, II, 22; ver Steeg, 67; *PMHB*, LXVI, 1942, 9–12.

106 WB invested $42,800. Lewis, 133.

110 WB at Luzerne banquet. There is no record that Bingham was present at this affair, but as a leading merchant and a friend of Luzerne, he would not have been absent.

CHAPTER 10. A VICTORY AND A VOYAGE

111 Wilson to WB. HSP.

112 Flags and banners. Only four of the flags surrendered at Yorktown appear to have survived. The West Point Museum has two of the colors carried by the Ansbach-Bayreuth Regiments; two others have been transferred, one on permanent loan to the museum at Yorktown and one to the Smithsonian Institution. (Letter to the author from Richard E. Kuehne, Director of the West Point Museum, January 15, 1968.)

112 Tench Francis. Oberholzer, *Phila.*, I, 295; Hammond, 50. Morris also obtained funds for the Bank through sale of goods captured at Yorktown.

112 Bank of N. A. East, 288; Konkle, 98–104; Studenski, 29; Dorfman, I, 225; Hammond, 50; ver Steeg, 66; Ferguson, 123; Lewis. Among the other directors were James Wilson; Thomas Fitzsimmons, Irish-born merchant and liberal member of the Continental Congress; Samuel Inglis, merchant of Philadelphia, close business associate of Robert Morris, later of WB; John Maxwell Nesbitt, Irish-born merchant, treasurer of the Pennsylvania Board of Navy; General Samuel Meredith, brother-in-law of George Clymer and one of three men who had given £10,000 to the Bank of Pennsylvania; Samuel Osgood, Congressman from Massachusetts, member of various finance committees of the Congress, one of the Samuel Adams anti-Federalist faction; and Timothy Matlack, merchant, assistant secretary of Congress, a dedicated supporter of the Pennsylvania Constitution, one of the founders of the new dissident Society of Free (or "fighting") Quakers. The election of Osgood and Matlack was an attempt to pacify political opposition to the Bank by including political opponents on the board. Fitzsimmons became one of the founders, and Nesbitt the first president, of the Insurance Company of North America. Meredith became the first Treasurer of the United States. Osgood became the first Postmaster General of the United States.

113 Willing to Massachusetts bank. Hammond, 66; Dorfman, I, 260.

114 Boxes marked silver. Lewis, 42.

114 Willing on Bank's success. Ver Steeg, 116.

114 Assembly objection. Hammond, 53. Feeling some doubt as to the validity of the charter granted by Congress, the directors elected to seek a charter from the State of Pennsylvania. The memorial presented to the Assembly met strong political opposition. Sixteen Whig members refused their approval unless Thomas Willing was dismissed as president. "We consider it highly impolitic and unjust," they resolved, "to establish by an act of the Legislature in so eminent and honorable a station the man who not only abandoned the cause of our country in the hour of our deepest distress and calamity, but whilst the British army was in Philadelphia actually suffered himself to be employed by them as an instrument and agent of their insidious attempts to debauch the minds of the people, and even to reduce our public councils into submission. We think that loading with honors a man who so lately did what he could to enslave this country is a discouragement to the Whigs, is a wound to the cause of patriotism, and is trampling on the blood of those heroes and martyrs who have fallen in defence of our liberty." Despite this partisan attack, the Pennsylvania charter was approved by a vote of 27 to 24.

114 Bingham, Inglis and Gilmor. Gilmor, *Memoir*, 17.

115 Partnership with Wilson. Smith, *Wilson*, 162.

116 Biddle, inland money. Biddle, 238.

116 Gilmor on WB. Gilmor, *Memoir*, notes facing 17.

116 Battle of the Saints. Chastellux, 308.

117 Southern refugees. Ford, XXI, 786; HSP, McKean Papers, I, 64, McKean to WB, July 25, 1781.

117 Quakers declined to help refugees, opposed War of Independence. Oberholzer, *Phila.*, 301; Eberlein, *Portrait*, 197.

117 Islands. Oberholzer, I, *Phila.*, 312; HSP, Act of Agreement, May 27, 1783. New Jersey annexed Petty's, Biddle's, Burlington, Chester, Shiverses, Harmanus Helms, and Red Bank Islands; Pennsylvania annexed Windmill, League, Hog, Little Tinicum, and Mud (or Fort) Islands. Several of the islands had been used in the fortification and river barricades erected during the Revolution.

117 College in Carlisle. Morgan; E. W. Biddle; Dickinson College; Rush, *Letters*, 46, 294–97; Goodman, 322.

118 WB subscribed £400. Morgan, 33; Rush, *Letters*, 296.

119 French exuberance. Merlant, 137.

119 Luzerne party for Dauphin. Oberholzer, *Phila.*, I, 298–99. When Luzerne told of the death at the French court of the King's aunt, Congress wrote to its "Great, Faithful and Beloved Friend and Ally, Louis the Sixteenth of France and Navarre," to express its "extreme grief" and "to offer a tribute of sorrow to the memory of your most dear and beloved aunt, the Princess Sophie Philippina Elizabeth Justina," of whom probably not one Congressman had ever heard. Sparks, *Dip. Corr.*, XI, 99–100.

120 WB lent government $20,000. Swiggett, *GM*, 101.

120 Anne's Uncle James. Jordan, 125.

120 Lee on WB. *Warren-Adams*, II, 184.

120 End of war. Robert Gilmor, landing in Europe as WB's partner, met Captain Joshua Barney (See Chapter 1) as he was embarking for America with the peace treaty. In Amsterdam, Gilmor, unable to speak French or Dutch, found his classical Latin a useful substitute. Gilmor, *Memoir*, 18.

CHAPTER 11.   MR. AND MRS. WILLIAM BINGHAM OF CAVENDISH SQUARE

121 Much of the content of Chapter 11 and 12 is derived from letters exchanged between WB and Thomas Willing. WB's unpublished letters, all in the HSP Society Collection, are dated Jun. 5, Jul. 30, Aug. 27, Oct. 14, Nov. 3, Dec. 29, 1783; Jan. 18, Jan. 26, Feb. 19, Apr. 18, Apr. 27, Jun. 1, Jun. 16, Jun. 17, Dec. 10, 1784. Willing's are Balch, *WP*, Jun. 22, Oct. 20, Nov. 29, 1783, Aug. 29, 1785; HSP, Sep. 12, 1783, Mar. 12, 1785; Konkle, Sep. 18, 1783, August, 1785.

121 Bingham quotation. Work cited, p. 13.

121 Truxtun. Washington called him "worth a regiment." Miller, *FE*, 217.

122 Wilson on money. Dickinson College Coll., Wilson to WB, May 15, 1784.

123 Jay in London. Monaghan, 225; Butterfield, III, 149.

123 Adams in London. Adams and Jay had worked together in opposing Franklin's pro-French policy and in asserting the American right to negotiate for peace with England independent of French knowledge and concurrence, despite the pledge of Congress not to do so.

123 Dr. Price. Monaghan, 224; Dickinson College Coll., WB to Rush, Jan. 1, 1784.

124 Jay and Deane. Jay, II, 144.

125 Deane's reputed authorship. J. Q. Adams, I, 108.

126 WB "in a hurry." Dickinson College Coll., WB to Rush, Jan. 1, 1784.

127 WB to Rush. WBP, LC, Nov. 6, 1783.

127 WB to Fitzsimmons. HSP, Nov. 29, 1783.

129 Rush to WB. Library Company, Miscellaneous Correspondence of Dr. Rush, 1783, no day or month.

129 WB to Dickinson. Dickinson College Coll., WB to Montgomery, Aug. 10, 1783; WB to trustees, Dec. 29, 1783. WB attributed his lack of success to the effects of the American war "so visible in the marks of public and private distress." A contributory cause must have been the competition. An official of Dartmouth, Dr. Witherspoon of the College of New Jersey at Princeton, and representatives of several other "seminaries" had come to Europe seeking "benefactions." All went straight to Dr. Franklin, who advised them to desist, declined to become concerned, and embarrassed the solicitors by asking how much had been subscribed to the institutions by well-to-do persons at home. The very request, he said, was disgraceful to the United States in revealing it as a nation too poor to provide for the education of its own children. Franklin, *Writing*, 600–601.

130 WB on balloon. Dickinson College Coll., WB to Rush, Jan. 1, Feb. 6, 1784.

130 Tobacco at Nantes. HSP, Jonathan Williams to WB, Feb. 1, 1784.

130 Inglis death. WB had lent his name to a sizable personal note for Inglis, in a routine transaction witnessed by Willing, in order that Inglis might get it discounted at the Bank. Now he found that he was responsible for making the note good. "This," he said, "is smarting with a vengeance for an act of friendship and will read me a lesson of caution."

133 Increase in Bank shares. The directors enlarged its issue of shares from $400,000 to $2 million in order to keep the Assembly from chartering a rival institution. The projectors of the new institution became stockholders in the old and withdrew their petition. Brunhouse, 150–51; Bolles, 345.

133 Vaughan introduced WBs to Lansdowne. APS, Benjamin Vaughan Papers, BVp46, Lansdowne to Mrs. Vaughan, no date.

134 Bentham and Shelburne. Fitzmaurice, II, 316, 322; *London Quarterly Review*, Oct., 1855, 279.

134 Committee of Gentlemen. Clements Library, WB to Lansdowne, Feb. 15, 1794.

134 Lansdowne's civilities. *Ibid.*, Mar. 4, 1787, Oct. 22, 1791.

135 Bowood. Fitzmaurice, II, 310 *ff;* R. B. Morris, 260, 329; Atkinson, 45–7.

CHAPTER 12. THE GRAND TOUR

137 Mrs. Adams on Mrs. WB. American Antiquarian Society, Sept. 30, 1785.

137 Binghams called on Adams. Adams Papers Microfilm, Reel 363, WB to Adams, June 26, 1784.

138 Adams at court at The Hague. Butterfield, III, 167. The errors in French grammar and accents are John Adams'.

138 "Polite attentions." Adams Papers Microfilm, Reel 363, WB to Adams, June 26, 1784.

138 Entertained by Henry Hope. WBLB, 480, WB to Gilmor, Feb. 4, 1793.

138 Hotel Muscovy, servants. DeWindt, I, 29.

138 WB to Willing. The WB-Willing information is taken from letters they exchanged in 1784–85. See note to p. 121.

139 Diplomatic post. Jefferson, *Papers*, IX, 563; XI, 245, 247.

139 Visited Franklin. *Ibid.*, VII, 310.

140 Visited Chastellux. Chastellux, 18. He was soon to marry a young Irishwoman named Marie Brigitte Plunkett, who was lady-in-waiting to the Duchess d'Orleans; he died in 1788, shortly before the birth of their child.

140 Twenty-three powers. Among them were Saxony, Hamburg, Naples, Sardinia, Venice, Genoa, Tuscany, Tunis, and Tripoli.

140 Jefferson disliked WB. See p. 152.

140 Mrs. WB on society. Jefferson, *Papers*, XI, 392.

141 Mrs. WB to Jefferson. *Ibid.* See Appendix 3.

142 Dined with Madame Helvetius. Mrs. Adams' description of this dinner is one of the most amusing and quoted passages in American letters.

142 Mrs. Adams to Mrs. Warren on Anne Bingham. C. F. Adams, II, 203, Sept. 5, 1784.

142 Mrs. Adams to niece. *Ibid.*, II, 208, Dec. 3, 1784.

142 Miss Adams. All material by Miss Adams, except as otherwise noted, is from her *Journal and Correspondence,* De Windt, pages 16, 17, 19, 20, 27–29, 33–36, 41, 44, 47–49, 52, 56, 70, 71. The original manuscript of this work, unfortunately, is now lost.

144 William Jackson. Dorland, 161–64; Balch, *L&P,* cix–cxviii.

144 Laurens-Jackson mission. Hale, 455; Aldridge, 316; Bolles, 241. Col. Laurens, the son of Peace Commissioner Henry Laurens, was killed in a minor skirmish with British partisans in one of the last engagements of the war.

144 Morris to WB. HSP, Nov. 5, 1783.

145 Moved to Palais Royal. DeWindt, I, 44.

146 Nabby moralizing. On March 20 she wrote: "I have heard (the Marquise de la Fayette) express her disapprobation of gaming, or indeed of play; even Mrs. B. is not so pleased with it as when she first arrived. As an American lady, she might always have excused herself from playing, if she had wished it, 'but,' said Mrs. ——, 'I became fond of it, before the winter was over, and have won sometimes twenty guineas of an evening.' Of all practices, this is to me the most detestable." (DeWindt, I, 59.)

146 Jeffries. He was an American Loyalist who had seen service on the British side in the Revolution.

147 Mlle. Bertin, footnote. Roof, 77; Jefferson, *Papers,* XI, 124, Jefferson to Anne Bingham, Feb. 7, 1787.

149 Gilbert Stuart. Flexner; Park; Mount. "The Skater" hangs in the National Gallery of Art in Washington.

150 Divided Stuart painting, footnote. The works are now in the possession of M. Robert Malézieux-Dehon of Paris, descendant of Henry and Mary Willing Clymer, by whose permission two are here reproduced. See Wharton, *Salons,* 141.

150 Malicious gossip, footnote. Tanselle, 16–18.

150 Mrs. Adams to sister comparing English and American women. American Antiquarian Society, Sept. 30, 1785.

151 WB to Jefferson. Jefferson, *Papers,* VIII, 328.

151 WB and Jay. Jay, II, 164, 166.

151 Jefferson's packages. Jefferson, *Papers,* IX, 146, 153, 228.

152 Jefferson on WB. *Ibid.,* VII, 94, Jefferson to Madison, Jan. 30, 1784.

152 WB to Rush from Paris. Dickinson College Coll., Nov. 10, 1784.

153 Mrs. Bingham's picture sold. Gilmor, *Memoir,* facing 18.

153 Mrs. Adams to son on Binghams. Adams Papers Microfilm, Reel 167, Feb. 16, 1786.

153 Miss Adams to brother on Mrs. B. Adams Papers Microfilm, Reel 367, Feb. 13, 1786.

154 Presentation at Court. *Ibid.,* Feb. 13 and 16, 1786; American Antiquarian Society, Miss Adams to Lucy Cranch, Feb. 20, 1786.

154 Looked like Bacchus. American Antiquarian Society, Mrs. Adams to sister, Sept. 30, 1785.

154 Court ball. Same as for Court presentation, above.

155 Miss Adams on WB. Adams Papers Microfilm, Reel 367, Feb. 26, 1786.

156 Dey of Algiers. Wharton, *Salons,* 142.

CHAPTER 13. "REST FOR THE SOLE OF MY FOOT"

157 WB to Willing. HSP, Dec. 10, 1784.

157 Land. WB commissioned Willing from London to buy from Richard Peters an adjoining lot on which he had an oral option in return for some favor he had rendered Peters.

157 Manchester House. Fisher, *Recollections,* 189. Manchester House became known as Hertford House when it passed into the possession of the third Marquess of Hertford (1777–1842) — the model for Lord Steyne in Thackeray's *Vanity Fair.* Sir Richard Wallace, illegitimate half brother of the fourth marquess, inherited the house and its collection of art and furnishings.

158 European purchases. See Appendix 4.
158 First silver pronged forks. Fisher, *Recollections*, 201.
159 Ann Warder. Warder, 52.
159 Rented Logan's house. Tolles, *PMHB*, 400.
160 Mordecai Lewis. Eberlein, *Portrait*, 455. The partnership ended in 1794.
160 China trade. Brown, "Eighteenth Century Magnate," 399; Eberlein, *Portrait*, 455.
161 Sleighing. Priest, 47, Mar. 18, 1794.
161 Tilghman. Pleasants, 145–46, Molly Tilghman to Polly Pearce, Feb. 18, 1787.
162 The Mansion House is described in Scharf-Westcott, II, 911; Watson, I, 223, 414; Halsey, 168; Westcott, 344; Griswold, 260–62.
162 Two fawns. WBLB, 155, WB to Read, Oct. 10, 1791. Jacob Read, a general in the War of Independence, was a Senator from South Carolina and later a judge of the supreme court of his state.
163 WB's servants. Fisher, *Recollections*, 202; Oberholzer, *Phila.*, I, 398.
163 Bulfinch. Halsey, 168.
163 Wansey at the Mansion House. Wansey, 136.
163 Cousin of Mrs. Bingham. He was Joshua Francis Fisher, grand nephew of Thomas Willing by way of the Powels and Francises.
163 Breck on Binghams. Breck, *Recollections*, 201–3.
164 Monroe, footnote. Bowers, *J and H*, 130.
164 Canaan Company. Smith, *Wilson*, 162–63; Brown "Eighteenth Century Magnate," 432; Seward, I, 27.
164 Member of the Cincinnati. Dorland, 61.
165 American Philosophical Society. Lingelbach, 47–49; Jackson, *Encyclopedia*, I, 66–71. Robert Morris contributed £23.5, his pay as a member of the State Assembly. Dr. Franklin contributed the largest sum, £100.
165 Society for Political Enquiries. Scharf-Westcott, I, 445; Charles Biddle, 223; Smith, *Wilson*, 204. The first meeting was held May 11, 1787, when the members heard and discussed a paper by Tench Coxe, merchant and political economist, on the industrial and commercial development of the United States. The Society was not outstandingly successful and did not meet after Franklin's death.
166 Fire protection. Wainwright, 247–52; H. W. Smith, I, 465; Smith, *Wilson*, 203; Lippincott, 244–49; Krout-Fox, 25; McMaster, *History*, II, 539–42. Each member bound himself to provide four leather water buckets, one basket, one bag marked with the name of the owner and of the company, an axe, and a wrench for unscrewing rope bedsteads for removal. On hearing of a fire, the member was obliged to "immediately repair to the scene . . . and there employ his best endeavors to preserve the goods and effects of such members of the company as should be in danger." At night, the neighbors customarily placed candles in the windows to provide light for the fire-fighters. To prevent looting, two members constantly attended the doors of the burning house, and all goods removed in the bags and baskets were placed under guard.
166 Second Troop. Dorland; J. L. Wilson, 49; Baker, 190; "Articles or By-Laws for the Government of the Second Philadelphia City Troop of Horse," Henry Tuckniss, printer, Philadelphia, 1799. The Troop customarily met at Epples Tavern near the Middle Ferry. The uniforms were splendid, as

befitted a corps of dragoons. The cap was leather with a bearskin crest, a band of leopard's skin, a cockade of black leather, and the tail of a buck worn with the white side out. The neck-stock was black leather. The jacket: blue cloth roundabout, edged with buff, with a buff collar, with three rows of buttons. The under waistcoat: buff twilled wool with four rows of buttons. Breeches: black buckskin. Boots: long with flaring tops. Also a pair of silver or plated spurs; buff leather gloves; a brass or gilt-mounted sword of a uniform design, carried in a buff belt across the shoulder; a "substantial pair" of horseman's pistols; and a cartouche box on a belt of black leather worn around the waist. Also a saddle with buff pad, with crupper and a black leather breastplate, and with blue and buff girths. Any member found wanting any of the enumerated articles on parade inspection was fined twenty-five cents.

166 College of Philadelphia. Montgomery, 89; H. W. Smith, II, 27, 310; Dorfman, I, 267. Dr. Rush, then in one of his conservative phases, called the defeat of the radicals "an important revolution in favor of the wisdom, virtue and property of Pennsylvania." He was restored to his position as professor of chemistry.

166 Trustees. Among them were Franklin, Thomas Willing, Samuel Powel, the Right Reverend William White, Robert Morris, and James Wilson.

166 Rush dined at Binghams'. Rush, *Letters,* 395.

167 Franklin and Marshall. *Ibid.,* 364, 412, 420–29. The opening prayer was delivered in German. The Reverend Gotthilf Henry Ernest Muhlenberg, youngest son of the patriarch of the family, brother of the hero of the Revolution, was elected principal.

168 Dickinson-Rush-Nisbet. *Ibid.,* 315 *ff; Morgan, 28–66; *Dickinson College,* 50.

168 WB to Rush on America. Dickinson College Coll., Nov. 10, 1784; HSP, Sept. 28, 1785.

CHAPTER 14. IN THE SERVICE OF STATE AND COUNTRY

170 WB to Lansdowne. Shelburne Papers, Clements Library.

170 Presented credentials. Burnett, *Letters,* VIII, 508.

170 Congress of the Confederation. See Burnett, *CC;* Fiske; King, I, 199. William Blount of North Carolina went to Congress early in 1787 only because he thought he might be chosen president, having explained to his brother that if he was not so elected he would return home as soon as possible. "Congress," wrote John Adams in 1786, "is not a legislative, but a diplomatic assembly." Carl Van Doren has likened the position of the Congress of the Confederation after the Revolution to that of the United Nations after World War II. Burnett, *CC,* 673; McMaster, *History,* I, 391; Van Doren, *Rehearsal,* viii.

170 Abigail Adams Smith on Congress. DeWindt, 95, Aug. 13, 1788.

171 Madison on WB. Ford, XXIII, "Notes of Debate by James Madison," 724.

172 Madison accused in 1808, footnote. Rossiter, *Convention,* 330.

172 WB's instructions. Brunhouse, 194. They read further that if the interests of Pennsylvania should come into competition with the national interests, then Pennsylvania should recede only so far and in proportion as the other states submitted.

172 "Energetic government." APS, Richard Price Papers, BP 93, WB to Price, Dec. 1, 1786.

172 WB to Price. *Ibid.*

172 Shays' Rebellion. The Rebellion caused a sharp reversal in the secessionist trend among the New England states. It brought Washington to a belief in a strong centralized government.

173 "Our resources are great." APS, Richard Price Papers, BP 93, WB to Price, Dec. 1, 1786.

174 WB on committees. Ford, XXXII, 57, 80; XXXIII, 725.

175 WB to Lansdowne. Clements Library, Shelburne Papers, 110, Mar. 4, 1787.

175 Washington in Philadelphia. Baker, 176 *ff;* Joseph Jackson, 140–46.

176 Pennsylvania delegation. Clinton Rossiter in *The Grand Convention* (p. 149) conjectures that if the original framers of the Constitution had been "dead, dying, abroad, or otherwise occupied, Pennsylvania could have sent these other well-wishers of a stronger national government": Thomas Mc-Kean, Arthur St. Clair, William Bingham, Benjamin Rush, Tench Coxe, Timothy Pickering, F. A. Muhlenberg, and any one of a dozen respectable merchants.

177 Plea to WB to return. Burnett, *Letters,* VIII, 614, 617, Thomson to WB, June 25, July 8, 1787.

178 Contribution to political thought. John Truslow Adams, 106.

178 Ohio Company. Burnett, *Letters,* VIII, xli; Smith, *St. Clair,* xlii; McMaster, *History,* I, 505–14; Cutler, I, 292–305.

179 Value of certificates. Ferguson, 252–53.

CHAPTER 15. LAST CHANCE FOR UNION

181 WB motion. Burnett, *Letters,* VIII, xlvii.

181 WB in Congress. Ford, XXXIII, 391, 758.

182 Plan of action. Burnett, *Letters,* VIII, xlvi, xlvii, 646–47; McMaster-Stone, 3, 4.

184 WB to Fitzsimmons. Burnett, *Letters,* VIII, xlvi, 646.

185 WB motion. *Ibid.,* xlvii.

185 Proceedings Penna. Assembly. McMaster-Stone, 3–5, 28–39, 60–63.

187 WB's messenger. Jefferson, *Papers,* XII, 230.

187 Seizure of McCalmont-Miley. The crowd was reputedly led by Commodore John Barry. Eberlein, *Diary,* 310.

189 Anti-Federalist attacks. Fiske, 330; Van Doren, *Rehearsal,* 180. The Pennsylvania anti-Federalists could not support the proposed Federal Constitution because in so doing they would condemn their own radical Pennsylvania state constitution.

189 Wilson assaulted. Bowen, 277. He had a law practice in Carlisle.

190 WB a prospect. Brunhouse, 124.

CHAPTER 16. THE MASTER BUILDERS

193 WB to Hamilton. Wettereau, *Letters,* 679.

193 Shippen dinner. Griswold, 153.

194 Maclay owned land. Maclay, *Sketches,* xii. Maclay owned some 180 acres, on part of which stands the present state capitol building. He was the son-in-law of John Harris of Harrisburg. In his introduction to Maclay's

Journal, Charles Beard says wittily: "Maclay was unacquainted with that great law of political science according to which the bee fertilizes the flower that it despoils, working wonders in destiny beyond the purposes of the hour."

194 Maclay and titles. Maclay, *Journal,* 2, 7, 25, 26, 29.

195 WB escorted Washington. Jos. Jackson, "Washington," 147; Hiltzheimer, 412–13.

197 WB in New York. Ford, XXXIV, 359, 399, 400; HSP, Willing to WB, June 29, Aug. 7, Aug. 29, 1788.

198 Quakers harried Southerners. Griswold, 232.

198 WB on Rhode Island. Burnett, *Letters,* VIII, 773, WB to Willing, Aug. 7, 1788. During this absence from Philadelphia, letters were exchanged that throw additional light on the pleasant family relationship of the Binghams and Willings. In June, 1788, when she was sixteen, Dorothy (Dolly) Willing wrote her brother-in-law: "I am greatly flattered by my dear Mr. Bingham's affectionate attention to me. The sash is beautiful and the handsomest I have ever seen and the only plaid.

"I was extremely diverted with your idea of the manner in which I should dispose of it. Although I do not at present possess any of those attractions that you mention, yet I will strive to attain them, and if I should be so unfortunate as not to succeed, I will then follow your advice and have recourse to my girdle." (HSP, June 25, 1788.)

Thomas Willing sent word to WB: "When you write next to my Daughter D—— I desire you will treat her as a child, and not put it into her head, poor babe, that she is now, or soon ought to be a fine lady — such language is enough to turn the head of any brat in town — the Scotch sash is very pretty." (Balch, *WL,* 135.)

198 WBs in New York. Among their guests were President and Mrs. Washington, as indicated by a letter written on June 8, 1789, from Tobias Lear, Washington's secretary, to Colonel Clement Biddle in Philadelphia: "The President is desirous of getting a sett of those waiters, salvers, or whatever they are called, which are set in the middle of a dining table to ornament it. . . . Mr. Morris and Mr. Bingham have them. . . ." *PMHB,* XLIII, 1919, 67.

198 Northwest Penna. lands. Burnett, *Letters,* VIII, 760; Maclay, *Journal,* 122; HSP, WB to Governor on Lake Erie Lands, no date; Ford, XXXIII, 391.

198 WB and widows. HSP, Report of Oct. 10, 1789. (Gratz Coll, Box 3.)

198 Aid for Dickinson College. Dickinson College Coll., WB to William Irvine, Feb. 26, 1789.

199 Value of Treasury certificates. Ferguson, 252–53.

199 Harvard owned certificates. *Ibid.,* 274.

200 WB and certificates. WBP, LC, Morris to WB, Mar. 10, May 5, 1778; Watson, I, 414. WB had also asked Joseph Warren of Boston, who was serving as his commercial agent there, to buy up certificates for him. Warren was able to buy only $1500 worth. HSP, Warren to WB, June 9, July 8, 1778.

200 WB borrowed £60,000. Davis, I, 197; Rush, *Auto.,* 269.

200 "Bloodhound certificate man." Watson, I, 414.

200 Hamilton asked WB. Wettereau, *Letters,* 672; Hamilton, *Papers,* V, 432–33, VI, 656.

200 Hamilton-Morris-Bingham philosophy. Among others, ver Steeg, 68; Kirkland, 284; Mitchell, *AH*, 147; Ferguson, 120–24.

202 Wettereau's discovery. Wettereau, *Letters;* B. Mitchell, 37–38.

205 WB's postscript. His request for such information was improper and Hamilton certainly ignored it. See his letter refusing similar information to Henry Lee. Wettereau, *Letters,* 670–71.

206 Ruin to land speculators, footnote. Nathaniel Gorham, Massachusetts merchant, president of Congress in 1786, had contracted to buy immense tracts of land in western New York with certain depreciated securities that he was assembling. He was ruined when they suddenly quadrupled in value. Rossiter, *Convention,* 319.

207 Rush to Fitzsimmons. Rush, *Letters,* 569, Aug. 5, 1790.

207 State constitution. Rush, *Auto.,* 130, 178.

207 Franklin's funeral. Oberholzer, *Phila.,* I, 345; H. W. Smith, II, 324–25.

208 Adams' distaste. Aldridge, 413.

208 Lazzarini statue. WBLB, 37, WB to Nicholas Low, June 3, 1791; 57, WB to Thomas Buckholm, Sept. 30, 1791, and May 9, 1792; Oberholzer, *Phila.,* I, 410; Scharf-Westcott, II, 1180; Peterson, 136; Library Company, WB to Company, Apr. 4, 1792. The Library Company was then at Fifth and Chestnut.

209 Legend about statue, footnote. Burt, *PP,* 245.

209 WB considered for governor. Maclay, *Journal,* 206; Tinkom, 34.

209 WB elected speaker. Brown, "Eighteenth Century Magnate," 391; Tinkom, 38, 46.

209 Maclay on WB. Maclay, *Journal,* 355.

CHAPTER 17. THE EAGLE RISING FROM A ROCK

211 WB to Lansdowne. Clements Library, Shelburne Papers.

211 Mrs. Adams on Anne Bingham. C. F. Adams, 349, Mrs. Adams to her daughter, Nov. 21, 1790.

212 Philadelphia exports. Lippincott, 275; Powell, 226.

212 Mrs. Adams on "constellation of beauties." C. F. Adams, 351, Dec. 26, 1790.

212 Frenzy of inhabitants. Griswold, 272. Theodore Sedgwick, Federalist Congressman from Massachusetts, wrote his wife that he had paid one hundred calls in three months and was still fifty in arrears. Welch, 137.

212 Rochefoucauld. *Travels,* IV, 106.

213 WB to Penn. WBLB, 219, Jan. 19, 1792.

213 Breck on Mrs. WB. Breck, APS, W9453, pp. 25–27.

213 Fisher on Mrs. WB. Fisher, *Recollections,* 200, 202. The best-known description of Anne Bingham appears in *The Republican Court* (1855), pp. 253–54, by Rufus Wilmot Griswold (1815–1857), journalist, editor and literary executor of Edgar Allan Poe. Griswold, who undoubtedly talked with people who had known her, wrote, "Her style, her beauty, her influence, the elegance of her house, the taste and aristocratic distinction of the assemblages which frequently adorned it, have become as household words in the city which was the scene of them, and indeed are historical in the annals of the higher social life of America. . . . Sprightly, easy, winning, are terms which describe the manners of many women, but while truly describing hers, they would describe them imperfectly, unless they gave the

idea that they won from all who knew her a special measure of personal interest and relation. Receiving neither service nor the promise of it, every one who left her yet felt personally flattered and obliged; really exclusive in her associates, she gave to none the slightest offence; with great social ambition at the basis of her character, no aspirant for the eminence of fashion felt that she was thwarting her aims; and with advantages, personal, social, and external, such as hardly ever fail to excite envy from her sex, such was her easy and happy turn of feeling, and such the fortunate cast of her natural manners, that she seemed never to excite the sting of unkindness nor so much as awaken its slumber or repose."

214 Adams bemused by Anne Bingham. When John Adams arrived in Philadelphia in November, 1794, for the new session of Congress, he found that a friend had hired lodgings for him across from the Mansion House. To Adams' complaint that the lodgings were drab and stuffy, the friend replied that Adams could look out of his upstairs window and see the beautiful Mrs. Bingham walking in her garden. Adams moved to the Francis Tavern on Fourth Street. Smith, *JA,* 864, 911.

214 Anne Bingham and Judge Chase. Ellet, *Queens,* 146.

214 Purchases in Europe. WBLB, 25, WB to Pierre Richard, June 18, 1791; 73, Sept. 11, 1791; and 99, Nov. 20, 1791; 130, WB to Etienne Cathalan, Oct. 18, 1791; 164, WB to Boyer, Mozler and Zimmerman, Oct. 5, 1791; 212, WB to Robert Gilmor, Mar. 10, 1792; 237, Dec. 11, 1791; and 240, Dec. 6, 1791. See also Brown, "Mr. and Mrs. William Bingham," 309, 316.

215 WB sent £500 to Vaughan. WBLB, 103, WB to Vaughn, Nov. 13, 1791.

216 WB's congratulations to French Assembly. HSP, WB to Lafayette, Apr. 9, 1791.

217 Brissot-Warville. The "frank and tender hearts" of young American girls, Brissot said, had nothing to fear from the perfidy of men, for "examples of this perfidy are rare; the vows of love are believed, and love always respects them, or shame follows the guilty." Philadelphians, having a government truly fraternal and living together as brothers, had no need of soldiers, forts or police. He was surprised that the death penalty for crimes had not been abolished, for Americans were so pure, the means of living so abundant, and misery so rare, that there was no need for such punishment. He was pained to see New England children bow to adults, for it looked slavish. In all seriousness he eulogized the potato: "The potato! There is the food for the man who wants to be, and is capable of being, free!" Warville, 46, 75, 95, 313, 318, 334, 374; Ellery, 74–84; Fay 285.

218 Callender. Among other things, he called Washington "a traitor, a perjuror and a robber." He turned on Thomas Jefferson ten years later and circulated the charge that Jefferson fathered a number of children with Sally Hemings, his wife's half-sister, one of his slaves at Monticello.

218 "Count Bingham." Welch, 137.

218 Fisher on WB's wealth. Fisher, *Recollections,* 193.

218 *The Times, a Poem.* The additional lines on "Rapax" read:

> But shall the hardened knave deride my rhymes?
> *Repax!* the Muse has slightly touched thy crimes.
> She dares to wake thee from the golden dream,
> In peculation's various arts supreme,

To rouse the worm that slumbers in thy breast,
And tell thee, Rapax! thou must never rest! . . .
Tho' *Luxury* attract the worldly wise,
Who, when they most caress thee, most despise. . . .
But when *misfortune's* thunders fiercely roll,
And *conscience,* long insulted, stings thy soul;
When pining sickness lowers thy tow'ring pride,
And *hope,* the good man's comfort, is denied,
Deserted by the sneaking, fawning train,
Truth will allow thou hast not lived in vain.

219 Maclay charge. Maclay, *Journal,* 395–96.
220 Biddle to Gilchrist. HSP, Clement Biddle Letter Book, 284–85.
220 Maclay animadversions. Maclay, *Journal,* 120, 122, 128, 140, 260, 306, 361.
220 WB to Montgomery on retirement. WBLB, 148, Oct. 17, 1791.
220 Wilson's digest. HSP, Wilson to WB, Jan. 14, 1791; Smith, *Wilson,* 343.
221 Peale's museum. APS, Peale to WB, Apr. 5, 1792, letter book copy. "I am very much obliged to you," Peale wrote on April 5, 1792, "for your friendship in your endeavors to have this bill passed, and which will be ever gratefully remembered." Ten years earlier, in his much-interlined and scarcely legible Letter Book, Peale composed three letters pleading for four guineas as payment of one-half the price of a miniature he was then painting of Mrs. Bingham and child. "My feelings are hurt by my being obliged to be so importunate, and why you have not deigned to answer my letters I know not. The charge I made is much lower than usual [this sentence crossed out]. I began the picture in the time the enclosed card specifies, although I had but one sitting then, and the charge is lower than common for having action in which hands are introduced is generally an additional charge. I should not have called on you if the building which I have just finished had not brought me into some difficulties for want of cash." There is no record of the Peale miniature, though there is a C. W. Peale miniature catalogued as a portrait of William Bingham in Carnegie Museum, Pittsburgh.
221 Bunch of Grapes Tavern. United States *Gazette,* 1805 auction notice (see Appendix 5); S. T. Freeman Catalog, May 31, 1966, 10. WB's other activities as revealed in his letters of this time: He refused Thomas Forman a loan of £500. ("It would give me particular pleasure to oblige you, but I could not do it without very great inconvenience, which must plead to you my excuse.") He declined to make a loan to James Campbell, tried to get him a loan elsewhere, failed, and advanced him $500 on a co-signature. ("I entertain the highest opinion of the qualities of your heart.") He dunned Mr. Izard for taxes owed on a house occupied in 1783 and 1784. He demanded £200 from his friend Cadwalader Morris on a long overdue loan. He refused a loan to Walter Roe, as well as his offer to buy certain Bingham lots. He was unable to lend Major McPherson $600 but offered to endorse his note at the Bank.

In the spring of 1793, when he had to meet a note for $30,000 and "must command all the resources within my power," WB sent out polite but firm requests for payments of notes signed by Benjamin Rush (£150 dating back to 1782, £101 interest at 6 per cent); Charles Thomson (£433 dating to 1788,

£40 interest); James Wilson (£1617 dating to 1783, £841 interest); and his attorney William Lewis (£4214). WBLB, 51, 60, 140, 142, 325, 355, 395, 475, 476, 477, 565.

221 Captain Barry, footnote. HSP, WB to Barry, June 17, 1791.

221 WB to Gilmor on candidacy. WBLB, 258, WB to Gilmor, Sept. 17, 1792.

221 WB one of most active board members. James Wettereau, banking historian, wrote in *Two Letters:* "Some recently discovered minutes of the board of directors of the first Bank of the United States reveal that he [Bingham] was one of the most active, astute, and influential directors of that powerful quasi-public corporation, helping to shape its policy along soundly conservative lines." Dr. Wettereau died before his planned publication of these minutes. They will be published by Dr. Stuart Bruchey, Professor in the Department of History at Columbia University, author of works on American economic history. I am indebted to Dr. Bruchey and Mrs. Wettereau for kind permission to cite from the minutes several examples of Bingham's work on the board.

The Bank Minutes for Dec. 26, 1794, record that he was one of a committee of three to negotiate a loan of $2 million with the Secretary of the Treasury. On April 1, 1800, he and Jacob Read drew up recommendations (approved) for dealings with the Office of Discount and Deposit at Charleston. The Minutes of April 18, 1800, in WB's handwriting, show him the head of a committee "to whom was referred the consideration of the propriety of discontinuing the receipt and transmission of the dividends on Public Debt on Account of Foreigners." On April 22, 1800, he was one of a committee (with Samuel Breck, Isaac Wharton, and two others) "to whom it was referred to prepare instructions for the Government of the Office of Discount and Deposit at Norfolk." WB, Dr. Bruchey says, "appears to have himself drawn up the detailed instructions to that new office, for his name alone is endorsed at the bottom of the instructions."

221 "Friendly compliments." WBLB, 121, 137, WB to Gilmor, Oct. 15 and 22, 1791.

221 WB withdrew £5000. Brown, "Eighteenth Century Magnate," 404.

222 PSPIRIN. Dorfman, I, 284–85; Oberholzer, *Phila.,* I, 347; Scharf-Westcott, I, 445, 465.

222 PSEMUA. Oberholzer, *Phila.,* 319; Davis, I, 429; Hutcheson, 151–59; Scharf-Westcott, I, 461. On Oct. 5, 1791, WB wrote to the Society, "I approve exceedingly of the Plan, both as indicative of Public Spirit and as affording a well grounded hope of private emolument. I will therefore give it every support in my power, and, influenced by these considerations, do subscribe 5,000 dollars." WBLB, 48.

222 Stone coal. Upham, II, 416, Apr. 9, 1789.

222 Cotton gin. Davis I, 473. Nothing came of the Pearce-Marshall machine or of WB's rumored offer to invest in it. Eli Whitney invented his gin one year later.

222 Collection of pamphlets. *PMHB*, XXV, 1901, "Notes and Queries," 138.

222 Town garden. APS, BV46p, WB to Benjamin (?) Vaughan, Nov. 9, 1789.

222 Leased Lansdown. Hearing that John Penn intended to return to Philadelphia in the spring of 1792 and wanted to occupy Lansdown, WB wrote a

courteous letter on January 12: "It is natural to believe that you would be desirous of repossessing yourself of a country seat to which Mrs. Penn and yourself must be particularly attached. . . . I never viewed myself as a tenant on any other conditions than an entire subservience to your interest and convenience. The moderate terms on which the lease was granted could imply no other species of arrangement. I therefore cheerfully resign the same, with my best wishes for your long enjoyment of Lansdown." WBLB, 219, Jan. 19, 1792; *PMHB*, LXXXI, 1957, 246–47.

222 WB to Knox on Lansdown. Brown, "Mr. and Mrs. William Bingham," 306; MHS, Knox Papers, WB to Knox, Apr. 23, 1797.

222 Adams on Lansdown, footnote. Westcott, 347.

223 "Bellevue" at Black Point. The reader is referred to Margaret Brown's "Mr. and Mrs. William Bingham," 301–5, for a four-page description of the Binghams' pioneering venture to the northern New Jersey shore.

223 Windsor chairs. WBLB, 280, June 23, 1792, WB to Nicholas Low.

223 WB to Vaughan for equipment. WBLB, 101, 103, Nov. 20, Nov. 13, 1791.

224 Resigned from Troop. WBLB, 167, WB to the Gentlemen of the City Troop of Light Horse, May 5, 1792.

224 Newspapers. WBLB, 276, WB to Nicholas Low, July 5 1792.

224 WB to Gilmor on foreign trade. WBLB, 43, 352, Jan. 24, 1791, Dec. 5, 1792.

224 *Harmony*. WBLB, 184, 190, WB to Gilmor, Mar. 11, Apr. 7, 1792.

224 *Louisa*. WBLB, 121 and 332, WB to Gilmor, Oct. 23, 1791, May 16, 1792; 130, WB to Etienne Cathalan, Oct. 18, 1791; Brown, "Eighteenth Century Magnate," 399–400.

225 WB to Gilmor on panic. Bingham, "having a number of engagements falling due," did not borrow from the banks. They were, he said, "rather inclined to assist those who it was supposed were more critically circumstanced, than it was conjectured I could possibly be. I did not, from delicacy, urge my pretensions, and therefore failed in procuring that facility I was entitled to." WBLB, 184, WB to Gilmor, April 11, 1792.

225 Duer. Duer had been Hamilton's assistant in the Treasury Department. Hamilton tried to get financial help for him through Thomas Willing, but Willing said he could do nothing. Duer died in debtors' prison.

226 Help for Mordecai Lewis. WBLB, 177, WB to Robert Gilmor, Apr. 24, 1792.

CHAPTER 18. THE LANDS IN THE EAST

227 Knox to WB on Maine purchase. Allis, 85.

227 WB's land investment. Wansey, 137.

227 Land in Baltimore. WBLB, 253, WB to Gilmor, Sept. 26, 1792.

227 Land in Federal City. WBLB, 366, WB to George Walker, Nov. 28, 1792.

227 Pennsylvania lands. Brown, "Eighteenth Century Magnate," 411–12. WB owned some 200,000 acres in partnership with Thomas and Thomas Mayne Willing. See p. 475.

228 Exempt taxes, aliens could own. WBLB, 176, WB to Wilhelm and Jan Willink, Apr. 25, 1792.

228 WB felt land values would rise. East, 299. Land purchases were greatly stimulated at this time by the "Pultney Purchase." Sir William Pultney

bought 1.2 million acres of Robert Morris' New York lands — Morris owned nearly one-half of western New York — and quickly resold them to European investors at a profit of $2.5 million.

228 Adlum. Kent-Deardorff; WBLB, 319, WB to Adlum, May 18 (?), 1792. The datelines are taken from HSP, Bingham Estate Papers.

228 Knox description. Breck, *Recollections*, 209; Callaghan, 23–26. Knox had lost the two smaller fingers of his left hand in a hunting accident and kept the hand wrapped in a black silk handkerchief.

229 "Mr. Bingham . . . solid." Allis, 82.

229 Description of Maine. Allis, 13.

230 Jackson. Allis, 93–95; WBLB, 512, 518, WB to Jackson, Dec. 21, 1792, Knox to Duer, Dec. 21, 1792; HSP, WB to George Read, Mar. 5, 1789; Littell, 366, Jackson to Washington, Dec. 5, 1792.

231 WB in Boston. Allis, 95–103, 245, 378–79; MHS, Knox Papers, WB to Knox, Jan. 13, 1793.

232 Penalty of $30. Allis, 674.

232 WB Maine pamphlet. Jackson saw this through the press. Allis, 278.

234 Jackson reluctant to go. Allis, 381, WB to Jackson, June 3, 1793.

234 WB to Jackson on compensation. *Ibid.*

234 Appeal for Irish settlers. Allis, 238.

235 Jackson's outpouring to WB. HSP, May 26, 1793.

236 Paper mills, steel, iron, nails, wool, steam power. Warville, 466–67; Kirkland, 307; Brooks, 145.

236 Carding machines. WB had sought the help of Jefferson in obtaining machines or models from France. Jefferson wrote to him on Sept. 25, 1789, the day before he left Paris to return to the United States, to report that a complete set of machines for carding and spinning cotton could be delivered in Paris within five weeks of receipt of the order, at a cost of 12,000 livres tournois. "To work by hand a compleat set of machines requires five men three women and five children, but if the machines are worked by water there will be no occasion for the men." University of Virginia Library.

236 Canal. WB was on the board of managers of several canal companies. He favored the use of lotteries for financing such public works and in January, 1792, delivered one of his rare speeches in the Pennsylvania Assembly in their support. His theme: "Interest is the mainspring in the dealings of men of business." Oberholzer, *Phila.*, I, 347; Dorfman, I, 285; Davis, I, 429.

236 Lancaster Pike. Landis; Scharf-Westcott, I, 466, 487; Davis, II, 218–20; Kirkland, 229; McMaster, II, 553–56; Hulbert, 106–7. Oberholzer, *Phila.*, 404; Hiltzheimer, 419.

236 Bad roads. William Hamilton, whose family business in Lancaster required him to make frequent use of the old Lancaster Road, said he could compare it to nothing "but being chin deep in hasty pudding." Senator William Giles, en route from the south over a wretched road, was thrown from his carriage and crippled for life. Upham, IV, 96, Oberholzer, *Phila.*, I, 348.

237 WB tour of road. WBLB, 262, WB to Mordecai Lewis, Aug. 10, 1792.

237 WB Turnpike work. He wrote to General Cobb on Nov. 7, 1795: "I would recommend on all occasions that will admit of it, the work that is undertaken to be done by contract. I have been a manager for several years of

the canal and turnpike companies and was always urging their work to be done by contract." Allis, 553.

237 New England laborers. WBLB, 358, WB to General Hand, Dec. 5, 1792.

237 WB to Mifflin. *Ibid.*, 359, Dec. 1, 1792. The Turnpike started on the west side of the Schuylkill opposite Philadelphia at the Middle Ferry. It crossed the Brandywine near Downington, crossed Conestoga Creek, and came into Lancaster at the east end of King Street. By law, the width was twenty-one feet in a maximum right of way of sixty-eight feet, with ditching and drainage on each side. Gates were seven miles apart.

238 Gallatin's forty committees. Walters, 39.

239 WB impressed. *Ibid.*, 40.

239 Farmer opposition. The Pennsylvania German farmers looked upon toll roads as "injurious to the rights of free men." Bingham conducted what today would be called a vigorous public relations program to counteract this opposition. In 1906, the historian John Bach McMaster wrote, "To this day, in every town along the route, old men may be found who delight to recall the times when the pike was in its prime, when trade was brisk, when tavern-keepers grew rich, when the huge sheds were crowded with the finest of horses, and when thousands of Conestoga wagons went into Philadelphia each week, creaking under the yield of the dairy and the produce of the famous Pennsylvania farms." McMaster, *History*, II, 555, 556; Wansey, 155, 210.

239 Gallatin upheld board. H. Adams, 85; Walters, 47.

239 Gallatin chosen over WB. Tinkom, 149.

CHAPTER 19. IN THE YEAR OF PLAGUE AND TERROR

240 Jackson to WB. HSP, date given.

241 WB on war. WBLB, 479, WB to Gilmor, Feb. 15, 1793. WB was correct in his analysis. "Of all the strokes of good fortune [for the United States], the outbreak in 1792 of a world war, lasting almost unbroken for twenty-two years, was the most considerable." Kirkland, 195.

241 "The seeds of luxury." Hazen, 192.

242 Genêt and Louisiana. Genêt chose as his agent for "the Louisiana affair" the French naturalist and explorer André Michaux. The American Philosophical Society, at Jefferson's urging, had collected money to finance Michaux on a trip "to explore the Interior Country." Bingham made a subscription of $50. Michaux was to go "from the Mississippi River along the Missouri and westerly to the Pacific Ocean . . . and on his return to communicate to the said Society the information he shall have acquired of the geography of the said country, it's inhabitants, soil, climate, animals, vegetables, minerals and other circumstances of note." Genêt ordered Michaux to use this mission as a pretext to go to Kentucky. There he was to arrange with General George Rogers Clark for the invasion of Louisiana, giving him up to 3000 livres and a commission as a major general in the French army. Jefferson modified his support when Genêt revealed these plans to him, and the expedition was reduced in scope. Jefferson was to try again ten years later with Meriwether Lewis and William Clark. Fay, 328; Parton, *Jefferson*, 495; DAB; APS Subscription Contract, 1793.

242 Meeting of merchants. Griswold, 293.

243 *L'Ambuscade* dinner. Fay, 321–28; Minnigerode, 216; Griswold, 292; Hazen, 182.

244 Jefferson's admonition to Short. Jefferson, *Works*, VII, 201–6, Jan. 3, 1793.

246 Refugees. To his daughter Martha, Jefferson wrote that he had heard the news "that the patriotic party [i.e., the Santo Domingo revolutionists] had taken possession of 600 aristocrats and monocrats, had sent 200 of them to France, and were sending 400 here. . . . I would wish we could distribute our 400 among the Indians, who would teach them lessons of liberty and equality." *Ibid.*, VII, 345, May 26, 1793.

246 Yellow fever. Rush, *Letters*, 638–734, 827; Powell. Oliver Wolcott, Alexander Hamilton's comptroller of the treasury, observed that whenever the wind blew up from the swamps and meadows south of the city, the number of fever cases increased, and that when the cool wind blew from the north, the cases diminished. From this he concluded that the number of sick increased with warm air and decreased with cold. Gibbs, I, 112, Wolcott to Washington, Oct. 20, 1793.

247 Lewis to Rush. Powell, 69.

247 Noailles warning. Breck, *Recollections*, 193–94.

247 Jefferson on Hamilton's cowardice. Jefferson, *Works*, VIII, 33, Jefferson to Madison, Sept. 8, 1793.

249 Jackson's European mission. He was accompanied on the trip by Thomas Willing Francis, son of Tench Francis and nephew of Thomas Willing, "a very agreeable and interesting young man" with whom he lived in London "on terms of the most friendly intimacy." Unless otherwise noted, Jackson's letters and activities will be found in Allis, 280–385.

249 Jackson and Priestly. HSP, Jackson to WB, Aug. 8, 1793. Jackson found the French royalist emigrés in England to be "miserably poor," including even their princes, and unable to obtain enough of their assets even to pay their passage to America. "They are indeed the most wretched of mankind and . . . with the exception of perhaps five or six persons, in extreme indigence."

249 Jackson and G. Morris. Morris wrote to Washington on Mar. 12, 1794: "Major Jackson, who has been here for some time, gave me two successors [as U. S. minister to France], first Mr. Bingham and then Mr. [Thomas] Pinckney; giving in the latter case Mr. Pinckney's place [as minister to England] to Mr. Bingham. So it is easy, you see, to fill up vacancies." A. C. Morris, II, 59.

250 Jackson an extreme enthusiast. It seems possible that he may have absorbed the ideas of Dr. Priestley, who was being driven out of England because of his pro-French sympathies, or of Lord Lansdowne, who at this time was publicly opposing war with the French Republic and William Pitt's repressive security measures. On his return to England, Jackson for a time was involved in a cloak-and-dagger negotiation with "a gentleman whose name I must not, at present commit to paper." This concerned a possible sale of 1,000,000 acres to the French government for about £500,000 to be paid for with the crown jewels of France "at a fair valuation (that is to say as much as they could be resold for)." "Rely on my prudence and

zeal," Jackson exhorted Bingham. Nothing came of the negotiations. Allis, 361, Nov. 18, 1794.

CHAPTER 20. THE SENATOR FROM PENNSYLVANIA

253 Wolcott on riots. Gibbs, I, 218.

253 Jackson to WB on war. Allis, 300, Aug. 22, 1793.

253 WB to Lansdowne, merchants angry. Clements Library, Shelburne Papers, no date.

255 Two-thirds of U. S. revenues from trade with Britain. Miller, *AH*, 292.

255 Meeting of merchants. Madison, *Letters*, II, 5, Madison to Jefferson, Mar. 9, 1794; *PMHB*, LXIII, 1939, 125.

255 WB to become U. S. Senator. Madison, *Letters*, II, 29, Madison to Jefferson, Dec. 21, 1794.

256 WB to Lansdowne. Clements Library, Shelburne Papers, no date.

256 Whiskey Rebellion. As Speaker of the House, Bingham signed the thanks the Pennsylvania Assembly voted to the officers and men of the militia of the Commonwealth.

257 WB elected Senator. Timkom, 152.

257 Jay Treaty. Lord Sheffield, author of the trade policy WB attacked in 1784, expressed the view in 1812 that the English had been "perfectly duped" into signing the Jay Treaty. Decades later, American Admiral Alfred T. Mahan, author of *Seapower,* declared that England's signature on any treaty with the United States at that time was an event of "epochal significance," constituting a recognition of American nationality that was even more important than the technical recognition of independence forced from the British in 1783. Bemis, *Jay's Treaty,* 270.

258 WB favored Jay Treaty. Marshall, V, 627.

259 Wolcott on mob. Gibbs, I, 218.

259 Scene at WB's house. *Ibid.; Gazette of the United States,* July 27, 1795.

260 Jackson welcomed. Allis, 383, Statement by Jackson in 1807.

260 Jackson wedding. Joseph Jackson, "Washington," 152.

260 Baring on wedding, footnote. Allis, 613, Baring to J. W. Hope, Dec. 8, 1795.

262 Deportment of Senators. Scharf-Westcott, I, 489; S. Mitchell, 83; Bernhard, 163; Swanstrom, 178, 197, 244.

262 WB in Senate. *Annals,* V, 54, 103, 113, 114, 119, VI, 1519.

263 Did not speak often in debate. The Manuscript Division, Library of Congress, has Bingham's handwritten notes for several speeches he delivered in the Pennsylvania Assembly and the United States Senate. One is a defense of the federal tax on whiskey. Another, dated Jan. 18, 1791, gives three cogent "Reasons why it is not incumbent on the Legislature to enforce a Declaration on the part of the members of their religious belief." A subject heading for another speech reads, "The great object is to find the men best calculated to serve the State in the Legislature and the Federal Government, and whether they are taken from the banks of the Delaware, or the Susquehanna, or of the Monongahela is a point of no consequence." His notes for a speech on a "Resolution in favor of appointing a person to revise the Laws" reads, in part: "Large Districts prevent corruption. Carthage, Greece and Rome. In small Districts the Representative may receive instructions

from his constituents which are opposed to the general views and wishes of the people. A Representative is deemed dependent on his Constituents and accountable to them — the monied interest is an important one. Suppose they instructed him to vote against taxing to support public credit because they possessed no public funds — to the men of the State who had a greater portion than its share. On his vote might depend the fate of the day. Monopoly of the carrying trade by the City. . . ."

263 Rumor, WB minister to France. Madison, *Letters,* II, 84, Madison to Monroe, Feb. 26, 1796.

264 Hired Cobb as agent. By the terms of the ten-year contract signed in March, 1795, Cobb was to live on the lands and devote his full-time services to enhancing their value. He was to oversee the surveyors, supervise the building of roads and sawmills, interview prospective settlers, take care of the registration of deeds, discourage squatters, stop the spoliation of the timber, and lay out a town at a suitable spot on or near the seacoast. For these services he was to receive an annual salary of $1500, a lot in the town of Gouldsborough, $1000 toward the building of a house there, 2000 acres of land "of the average quality," and the residuary profit on the sale of 2000 acres. Said Alexander Baring, "Bingham made a hard bargain with him." Allis, 465, 501–3, 655, Baring to Hope and Co., May 26, 1796.

264 Cobb on Philadelphia, footnote. Allis, 465.

264 Knox's notes discounted. Allis, 571, WB to Knox, Aug. 15, 1795.

264 WB to Knox, "novel thing." MHS, Knox Papers, Aug. 20, 1795.

264 Would endorse no more notes. *Ibid.,* WB to Knox, Apr. 10, 1797.

265 "Immense sales in west." *Ibid.,* Sept. 12, 1795.

265 Would try Europe again. Allis, 580, WB to Knox, Sept. 12, 1795.

265 "Cruel and embarassed." Allis, 570, WB to Knox, Aug. 15, 1795.

265 Francis Baring to WB. Allis, 592–94, Aug. 31, 1795.

266 WB instructions to Cobb, Knox, H. Jackson. Allis, 595–605, 628.

CHAPTER 21. THE BARINGS STRIKE A BARGAIN

The material on Bingham, Baring, Knox and Cobb in this chapter, except as otherwise indicated, is found in the exchanges of letters and their annotations in *William Bingham's Maine Lands,* edited by Frederick S. Allis, Jr., Chapter Ten, "The Sale to Baring."

268 Not to marry an American. Nolte, 159.

268 House of Baring. Hidy; Wechsburg, 99–103.

269 Alexander Baring. Hidy, 29, 46; Gilmor, *Memoir,* facing 40.

270 Coach overturned. Cobb, slightly bruised on the arm, did not get back in the coach but rather "tediously walked through the mud" until daybreak.

271 "Loves long letters." Callaghan, 342. Cobb spoke critically to WB of Knox's "anxiety for seeing his Madam [in Boston]. . . . He should attend to this business, at this time, above all other concerns." Allis, 538, Knox to Cobb, Sept. 29, 1795; 632, Cobb to WB, Jan. 11, 1796.

272 Negotiations were stalemated. During this period, Baring took to attending the House debates on the Jay Treaty, in which, to Bingham's distress, Republican hatred of England was being voiced often and eloquently. Order and decorum, he reported to London, were much better observed than in the House of Commons. "You hear no personalities, no abuse, and during

the whole course of the most interesting discussion on a subject on which all national prejudices and passions were excited to the highest, there was not a single sound from the galleries, which are very extensive and very crowded. I confess I had no idea of the possibility of so popular a government being so well organized." Allis, 660, May 26, 1796.

275 Baring ultimatum. HSP, Baring to WB, Feb. 7, 1796.

277 WB's difficulties. These were further heightened by the circulation of two inaccurate rumors. Word spread that WB owned one million more acres than he actually did. And Philadelphians heard that Baring paid WB 100,000 guineas in his purchase, about twice the true amount. WB wrote to Knox, "Some of my most particular friends, at this moment of general distress . . . have applied to me for temporary loans. I have been forced to lend some smaller sums, where I could not enter into a detailed explanation, but I have been under the disagreeable necessity of refusing many." Brown, "Eighteen Century Magnate," 424; Allis, 746, WB to Knox, Apr. 23, 1796.

277 Baring on future of America. He expressed what was then a radical view in writing: "There can be no doubt of anybody who has been in this country that the republican government is the only suited to it and that it is morally impossible that any other should supersede it. . . . The people from long and gradual habits are riper for a greater degree of liberty or rather for a freer constitution than any other. . . . The dangers that you might apprehend from the principles of this government on making comparison with the countries known to you would probably be exaggerated when applied to this." Allis, 658. Baring to Hope and Co., May 26, 1796.

281 Adams and Iredell. Adams Papers Microfilm, Reel 381, Adams to Mrs. Adams, Apr. 30, 1796.

281 Baring sent speech to London. Allis, 660, May 26, 1796.

282 Girls conversed well. Gilmor, *Tour,* 74.

282 Baring on WB. BaP, Baring to Hope and Co., Feb. 26, 1796; Allis, 667, 797, 889.

284 Expedition to Maine. BaP, Baring to Hope and Co., Feb. 26, 1796; Allis, 654, May 26, 1796.

CHAPTER 22.   MR. BINGHAM ADMINISTERS AN OATH

285 Washington to Knox. Fitzpatrick, XXXV, 85.

285 Expedition to Maine. The story of the expedition is told in the letters and notes in Allis' *Maine Lands,* 754–801.

285 John Richards. NYHS, WB to Rufus King, Nov. 29, 1796. The material relating Richards to WB is dropped from the letter as printed in King, II, 112. The omission perhaps offers a moral to those engaged in historical research in this period. Bingham found Richards "an English gentleman of very amiable manners and great merit."

285 Noailles. Sherrill, 34; Breck, *Recollections,* 165–66, 199–200.

287 Washington to WB. Fitzpatrick, XXXV, 87.

287 The *Mercury.* She had "an excellent spacious and high cabin exclusively of four separate staterooms, about 93 tons burthen."

287 The Bingham party's visit to Montpelier is described briefly in "Lady Knox" by Diana Forbes-Robertson, *American Heritage,* April 1966, 77–78. The

present "Montpelier," a faithful reconstruction, stands about one mile from its original site.

288 Reverend Coffin. Maine Historical Society, "Missionary Tour in Maine," 326–27.

288 Baring to Labouchère. BaP, Aug. 12, 1796. Allis calls this letter "the only really informal one in the Baring Papers."

290 Landsdowne Portrait. Flexnor, 128–36; Park, II, 854; Fitzpatrick, XXXV, 21. Stuart used the actor-comedian Moreton to stand as model for the figure of Washington, because of the actor's "natural grace." The result was unfortunate, for Stuart achieved the improbable result of making the giantlike President look like a pygmy. Wood, 244.

290 WB to Ceracchi on art. WBLB, 370, Nov. 13, 1792. Ceracchi was later guillotined by Napoleon.

291 Washington to Stuart. Fitzpatrick, XXXV, 31.

291 WB to King on portrait. King, II, 112, Nov. 29, 1796.

291 Bingham's replica. Some critics have claimed that the painting in the Pennsylvania Academy, given by Bingham's heirs, is the original. Internal evidence would seem to bear them out, since Washington's figure in this version is stunted and it is somewhat lengthened and improved in the version sent to Lansdowne in England. These critics have discounted a letter written and signed by Stuart in 1823 in which he said the version in England was the original.

The testimony of young Gilmor, written on July 27, 1797, on visiting Stuart's painting room (see p. 310), seems conclusive: "Stewart (*sic*) came in, received us in the most welcome manner, offered us refreshments and conducting us to his painting room which he had fitted up in his stable. The picture he had there of the President was the first copy he had made of the celebrated full length which he had painted for Mr. Bingham intended as a present to the Marquis of Lansdowne. It was supposed one of the finest portraits that ever was painted. This copy was for Mr. Binghams own use and from which Stewart told us he had engaged to finish copies to amount of 70 or 80,000 dollars at the rate of 600 dollars a copy. . . . He has the appearance of a man who is attached to drinking, as his face is bloated and red." I personally feel that since Bingham specifically commissioned the painting for Lord Lansdowne, he could not possibly have sent him any version but the original. Hart; Gilmor, *Tour*, 75.

292 Lansdowne to Jackson. Balch, *L&P*, 306, Mar. 5, 1797.

292 WB to King on engraving rights. King, II, 199, July 10, 1797.

292 WB and Stuart confrontation. Longacre, 139–40.

294 WB drew up response. *Annals*, VI, 1519. "We cannot look forward to your retirement without our warmest affections and most anxious regards accompanying you, and without mingling with our fellow-citizens at large in the sincerest wishes for your personal happiness that sensibility and attachment can express."

294 WB's votes in Senate. *Annals*, V, 50, 71, 79, 110; VI, 1519.

294 Elected president of Senate. *Annals*, VI, 1551.

295 Bingham's guests at Washington dinner. Griswold, 362. The person who wept most copiously was Mrs. Robert Liston, wife of the British minister.

295 Jefferson inauguration. *Annals*, VI, 1580–81.

296 Adams inauguration. Among others, Scharf-Westcott, I, 488, Rochefoucauld, IV, 363–65. The oath was unquestionably administered after Adams' address. He later told Abigail, "I was very unwell, had no sleep the night before, and really did not know but I should have fainted. I was in great doubt whether to say anything or not beside repeating the oath. . . . I did not know whether I should get through or not."

297 Farewell Washington dinner. There is no specific mention that Bingham attended this dinner, but he would have been present both as a merchant and a member of Congress.

298 Pickering to WB on invitation. Upham, III, 171.

300 Jefferson on Bonaparte. LC, Jefferson Papers, Jefferson to Madison, June 15, 1797; Jefferson to Thomas Randolph, Jan. 11, 1798; Miller, *AH*, 453. In 1814, Jefferson changed his mind; he called Bonaparte "the Attila of the age . . . the ruthless destroyer of 10 millions of the human race, whose thirst for blood appeared unquenchable, the great oppressor of the rights and liberties of the world. . . . I had supposed him a great man." Cappon, 431, Jefferson to Adams, July 5, 1814.

CHAPTER 23. THE DOOMBAH AND OTHER VISITORS

303 Twining. Twining, 34.

303 French in Philadelphia. Sherrill, Childs. Among the foods introduced by the French were pastries, chicken croquettes, bread raised with yeast, *blanc mange, ice cream meringue glacé*, and several vegetables.

304 70 books published. Brooks, 13.

304 G. Morris on Talleyrand. Talleyrand, I, xxxiv.

304 Phineas Bruce story. *Ibid.*, I, 180; Allis, 54.

304 Mansion House closed to Talleyrand. Twing, 160. "It is essential," Talleyrand wrote back to France, "to have a good reputation in this country."

305 Rochefoucauld on WB. Rochefoucauld, III, 356, IV, 103.

306 WB to King on Rochefoucauld. King, II, 331, June 5, 1798.

306 Breck on Volney. Scharf-Westcott, II, 921.

306 Volney on Americans and terrain. Fay, 442; Brooks, 6. Volney was the first European scholar to visit the Middle East beyond Greece, spending four years in Egypt and Syria.

306 Lafayette on American women, footnote. Sherrill, 130.

307 Philippe portrait of Abigail. HSP, Breck to John McAllister, July 29, 1858.

307 Philippe's courtship of Abigail. Fisher, *Recollections;* 155–56; Wharton, *Salons*, 155–56. A number of social historians (among them, Griswold, Scharf, Westcott, Oberholzer, Wecter) have mistakenly reported that Louis-Philippe courted one of Bingham's daughters and that it was Bingham who gave the refusal in the words quoted. In his life of Gilbert Stuart (1964) Charles Merrill Mount attributes the refusal to Bingham and uses it as evidence that he had a cold character (p. 198).

307 "Old Square Toes." Morison, II, 130, Otis to wife, Nov. 20, 1797.

308 "A welcome to come." Balch, *WP*, lviii.

308 Louis-Philippe's journey. Gilmor, *Tour*, 76; Morris Bishop, "Louis Philippe in America," *American Heritage*, April, 1969. The two younger princes died of consumption in exile in 1807 and 1808. Louis-Philippe recovered most of his enormous estates and became king of France in 1830.

308 Birch. Library Company, Birch, typescript of autobiography, 33, 34.

309 Gilmor. Gilmor, *Tour.*

311 Lord Henry Stuart. In June, 1798, Lord Henry saved the life of Mrs. Benjamin Rush when a collision with a large Lancaster wagon on the floating bridge across the Schuylkill threw the carriage in which she was riding into the water. Rush, *Letters,* 806.

311-17 Twining adventures. Twining, *Travels.* He was the great-grandson of the founder of Twinings, the oldest firm of tea merchants in England, established in 1706 and still in business.

312 Ashmead. *PMHB,* LXXXII, 1958, William Bell Clark, "The John Ashmead Story" 42–45. The *India* was a new 401-ton ship, the upper deck without a cabin and flush from head to stern, carrying a crew of twenty-two men and armed with six four-pound cannon for protection against pirates. On board was one of the younger sons of Robert Gilmor senior, sent to India "with the view of learning the business of an India voyage under Mr. Pringle," the purser.

313 Alexander Baring. When Alexander and Henry Baring called on Twining at his hotel, Twining wrote, "I thought the former a clever, well-informed young man. He was, I understand, come to America on account of Messrs. Hope's house, of Amsterdam, to purchase a large tract of land in the province of Maine, belonging to Mr. Bingham. I knew his brother in Bengal, the eldest son of Sir Francis Baring." When Twining returned the call a few days later, he found the two brothers fencing.

315 Priestley sermon. Priestley's radical views excluded him from all but the Universal Church. At the height of his popularity, he offended many Philadelphians with some extremely frank discourse in describing the vice and debauchery of the heathen world. Said Judge Iredell indignantly. "He spoke in plain terms of priests castrated and men and women put to death in the very act of fornication — the altars being scenes of lust, etc." McRee, II, 461, 463; Rush, *Letters,* 773.

CHAPTER 24.   PANIC AND PASSION IN PHILADELPHIA

318 WB to King. King, II, 199. Minor corrections have been made in the text as printed in King, as a result of checking against the originals in the New York Historical Society.

318 150 companies failed. Rush, *Autobiography,* 236.

318 WB loan to Wilson. Smith, *Wilson,* 361.

318 Harrison debt to WB. Fisher, *Recollections,* 228; MHS, Knox Papers, WB to Knox, Dec. 12, 1797.

319 Willing withdrew. Young, 203; Oberholzer, *RM,* 321.

319 Morris, fraudulent payment. Fisher, *Recollections,* 229.

320 WB on sale of Morris house. Channing, IV, 112.

320 WB to Knox on "calamitous period." In answer to still another plea from Knox for still another loan, WB wrote: "With every disposition to oblige you that friendship or my best wishes can induce, I find it entirely out of my power to take up your two notes of 2,500 dollars each. . . . I cannot even pay the debts that I owe, not having the means of liquidating a bond which I gave the insurance company for $20,000, except that I have recourse to

bank negotiations." But rather than borrow money at excessive interest rates, as others were doing, with the risk of starting rumors about his solvency, he "would sacrifice any property I have, at any price." His credit on the Barings in London "was abandoned as soon as the bargain was made with Mr. Baring as it was with his father and was conditional as to the purchase."

Knox was unable to pay when his $17,500 debt to Baring fell due. He asked WB to persuade Baring to give him a postponement; WB declined "as I am very delicately situated in relation thereto." Knox then asked Baring directly for an extension and Baring refused, drawing on him for the amount due. Knox simply returned the draft unpaid. WB thereupon paid Baring the money and revealed to Knox that he had guaranteed payment — a fact he had not previously disclosed because, "knowing that your mind, which is delicate on such subjects, might be oppressed with my appearance of additional obligations." "God knows," Knox wrote, "I feel the humiliation sufficiently." Allis, 731, Apr. 8, 1796; 826–27, Dec. 22, 1796; 912; MHS, Knox Papers, Knox to WB, June 4, Nov. 20, 1797; WB to Knox, June 10, Nov. 2, Dec. 7 and 12, 1797; Brown, "Eighteenth Century Magnate," 426.

320 WB bought Lansdown. MHS, Knox Papers, WB to Knox, June 10, Dec. 12, 1797; Knox to WB, Nov. 20, 1797; Allis, 1195, Cobb to C. W. Hare, Mar. 2, 1806. Greenleaf had become owner of Lansdown through his marriage to Ann Penn, niece of John Penn.

320–22 WB, Baring, Cobb references. Allis, 830, 847, 889, 897, 911, 915, 916, 924, 933, 934.

322 Baring program. Allis, 919–35, Feb. 1798. Cobb and Richards were to cut a straight road from Gouldsborough to the upper townships; cut a road to the Penobscot River; erect gristmills and sawmills to secure the water heads; start a village north of Gouldsborough, establish a land office; hire a resident surveyor and chainman; clear up the status of the squatters ("It is natural for large proprietors to be unpopular, but you will experience very much the reverse when the people become aware of the general benefits the country at large derives from your efforts"); lay out a series of farms of exactly 160 acres each; procure a packet boat, label it conspicuously *Gouldsboro Packet,* and speedily establish a service between Gouldsborough and Boston; procure a sailing boat of ten or twenty tons for inland navigation; erect comfortable taverns at the new communities as they were formed ("Care must be taken that those who are induced to come on your lands are not disappointed and for this purpose some little show should be attended to in your improvements. Being in a good or bad tavern to a visitor has often a great effect on opinion"); and start a newspaper.

322 Cobb quarreled with WB. See note, p. 364.

322 Baring to father. BaP, May 31, June 1, 1797.

323 Baring to WB from Boston. Allis, 935.

323 Sir Francis comment. *Ibid.,* 914, June 1, 1797.

323 WB led delegation. *Annals,* VII, 471.

324 French took 340 ships. Beveridge, II, 224. By an order of March, 1797, any American captured on an English ship was considered a pirate and subject to immediate hanging, even though he had been impressed into service by

the British against his will. Because of Republican opposition in the Congress, U. S. merchant ships could not legally arm themselves. (Jefferson and Madison felt that steps to rearm would irritate the French still further.) In two months in 1798, Philadelphia merchants lost a half-million dollars in shipping to French vessels based in the West Indies. One of Thomas Willing's ships was taken in waters behind one of the American capes. Insurance rates soared and American merchants began to transport their goods on British vessels, which were convoyed by warships. Miller, *FE,* 213; McMaster, *History,* II, 319.

324 WB's lament on ships. Allis, 842, WB to Cobb, Mar. 7, 1797.

324 WB to King on dread of war. King, II, 199, July 10, 1797.

324 Invasion of South, footnote. This was the common Federalist analysis of the time. Gibbs, II, 60.

326 Hamilton as President. Article II of the Constitution specified, "No person except a natural born citizen, or a citizen of the United States at the time of the adoption of this Constitution, shall be eligible to the office of President." Some Republicans felt the qualifying provision was adopted out of deference to Hamilton.

329 Hamilton letter to Monroe. Hamilton Papers, Library of Congress, July 24, 1797.

330 Jackson advice. Hamilton Papers, Library of Congress, Jackson to Hamilton, July 24, 1797. Mrs. Hamilton remained loyal to her husband and blamed all the difficulties on Monroe. Hamilton rewarded her with the words, "You are all that is charming in my estimation, and the more I see of your sex the more I become convinced of the judiciousness of my choice." Miller, *AH,* 462.

330 Knox on Hamilton's confession. Allis, 865, Sept. 16, 1797.

330 Cobb on Hamilton. Allis, 867, Oct. 1, 1797. Hamilton's friend Noah Webster, editor of the powerful and respected New York *Minerva,* wrote with distaste, "What shall we say . . . of a man who has borne some of the highest civil and military employments, who could deliberately . . . publish a history of his private intrigues, degrade himself in the estimation of all good men, and scandalize a family, to clear himself of charges which no man believed?"

331 WB and Hamilton papers. Mitchell, *AH,* 421; Hamilton Papers, Library of Congress, WB to McHenry, Nov. 18, 1799; WB to Hamilton, July 21, 1801.

CHAPTER 25. HALF-WAR WITH FRANCE

333 Sedgwick to King. King, II, 352.

333 Jefferson, "insane message." LC, Jefferson Papers, Jefferson to Madison, Mar. 21, 1798.

333 Federalists "war hawks." Smith, *JA,* 1035. Jefferson apparently introduced the phrase; it was much used by James Callender.

334 Leaders knew contents. Welch, 170; S. Mitchell, 151.

334 Talleyrand, $625,000 in bribes, footnote. Miller, *FE,* 211.

334 Beaumarchais. He died in poverty. In 1835, after long and complicated negotiations on the several million francs owed Beaumarchais, Congress offered

his heirs a choice of getting nothing or of accepting 800,000 francs as payment in full. They accepted.

336 Jefferson on XYZ dispatches. Smith, *JA*, 960.

336 Young Hare, footnote. Robert Hare (1781–1858) became an outstanding American chemist and teacher, conducting pioneer research in the constitution of salts and inventing the oxyhydrogen blowpipe (1801), a galvanic instrument called a "calorimotor," the use of the mercury cathode in electrolysis, and an electric furnace. S. Mitchell, 171; Jordan, 130.

336 Baring on Adams. Allis, 919, to J. W. Hope, Apr. 31, 1798.

336 WB met Marshall. Boudinot, I, 141, Boudinot to wife, June 21, 1798.

337 WB to King. King, II, 331, June 5, 1798.

337 Caucus in WB's house. *Annals,* X, 114; Dauer, 170; Morison, 97. In a letter to Harrison Gray Otis of Apr. 4, 1823, Adams wrote of "nocturnal caucuses at the pompous Mansion House." Morison, 97.

337 WB's votes. *Annals,* VII, 535, 537, 539, 541, 544, 546, 563, 582, 584, 587, 606, 610, 611; VIII, 2214, 2230.

338 WB's vote on Alien and Sedition laws. *Annals,* VII, 575, 578, 590–91, 597, 599.

338 "Reign of Terror," footnote. Miller, *C in F; FE,* 234; Childs, 188. The laws were less severe than the Republican Sedition Act of 1812, the Smith Act of 1940, and the Executive Order of February, 1942. Page Smith writes in *John Adams* (p. 978), "We can leave the Alien and Sedition Acts to the periodic indignation of righteous historians who will be happy if their own nation and their own times show no grosser offenses against human freedom."

339 "Bloody hands." Swiggett, 391.

339 WB on England. King, II, 425, WB to King, Sept. 30, 1798.

339 Ames, Otis, Cabot. Ames, II, 125; Morison, I, 51, 349.

339 Bowers, Charles, on Federalists, footnote. Bowers, *J and H,* 82; Charles, 138.

340 King's warning. King, II, 479–80, King to WB, Dec. 8, 1798.

341 Adams and war. Smith, *JA*, 954.

341 Sedgwick and war. King, II, 352, Sedgwick to King, July 1, 1798.

341 Caucus. WB against war. *Annals,* X, 114; King, II, 352–53; Dauer, 169. Liston, the British minister, reported to his government that the caucus showed it was not possible to carry the motion for a declaration of war against France.

343 WB waited on President. *Annals,* VII, 624.

342–43 John Adams and Colonel Smith. Smith, *JA,* 890, 979, 992; S. Mitchell, 131, 252; King, II, 593, Goodhue to Pickering, June 2, 1800; Tanselle. In 1806, the federal government prosecuted Colonel Smith for complicity in fitting out a revolutionary expedition to drive the Spaniards out of South America and claim the land for the United States and Great Britain. He was acquitted, but his career, once again, was blighted. He recovered sufficiently to be elected in 1812 a Federalist member of Congress. Abigail Smith, fatally ill with cancer, resolved to die in her parents' home. She had a bed placed in a carriage and started out on a 300-mile journey from Lebanon Valley, New York, to Boston, attended by her children and an affectionate sister-in-law. She arrived fifteen days later, haggard, drawn with pain, but tearfully happy to embrace her father and her mother. She died three weeks later, on August 30, 1813. Colonel Smith hurried from Washington to Braintree and arrived just before Abigail's death.

343 WB on proselytes. King, II, 425, WB to King, Sept. 30, 1798.

CHAPTER 26. THE CONFRONTATION

345 WB to Adams. Upham, III, 440.

345 WB to Read on yellow fever. NYPL, Sept. 22, 1798.

346 WB to Read on daughter's marriage. *Ibid.*

346 WB to Knox on Baring's worth. MHS, Sept. 30, 1798.

346 £500 settlement on Ann. McRee, 572.

346 Gave Powel House. Eberlein, *Portrait,* 373.

347 WB to align bill. *Annals,* VIII, 2207.

348 WB supported defense measures. *Ibid.,* 2216, 2222, 2224, 2230.

348 Barings and 11,000 muskets. Hidy, 32.

349 Sedgwick on Adams. Hamilton, *Works* (J. C. Hamilton, ed.), VI, 396, Sedgwick to Hamilton, Feb. 19, 1799.

349 Sedgwick proposed self for court, footnote. Welch, 190.

349 Liston report. Dauer, 240.

350–54 Confrontation between Senators and Adams. The episode is covered in Upham, III, 439–44; Welch, 186–91; Gibbs, II, 204–12; John Adams *Works,* IX, 248–50. The dialogue is taken from the later accounts of the participants.

351 Pickering on Gerry, footnote. King, II, 374, June 13, 1798.

356 Pickering on "that old fool." Ingersoll, I, 271.

356 Pickering ignored order. Gibbs, II, 269–70; Morison, 167.

CHAPTER 27. THE GOLDEN VOYAGE: MERIDIAN

357 Gallatin on Bingham kindness. Henry Adams, 203.

357 Mrs. Stoddert. Rowland, 808, Jan. 23, 1799; 805, 809–18.

359 Anne Bingham to Mrs. Livingston. HSP, Dreer Collection, no date.

359 Fisher on Anne Bingham. Fisher, *Recollections,* 202.

360 Moreau on theater, footnote. St. Méry, 347.

360 Otis at Clymers'. Morison, 135.

360 Anne Bingham and Wignell. Wood, 340–42.

361 Mrs. Rowson. Vail; DAB; Charles Evans, *American Bibliography,* X, 1795–96, Columbia Press, Chicago, 1929, p. 188.

362 Mrs. Rowson's dedication. Rowson, vii-x. I am indebted to Dr. Charles Coleman Sellers of Dickinson College for calling my attention to this long-forgotten fact.

362 Mrs. Adams on Binghams. DeWindt, II, 153–54.

363 Gilmor on W. B. Gilmor, *Memoir,* notes facing 18.

363 Birth of William Bingham Baring. Brown, "Mr. and Mrs. William Bingham," 321.

363 WB to Breck. Library Company, July 20, 1799. The letter is unique in that it reveals in Bingham a sense of wry humor. ". . . If a few pannels of fence will effectually prevent the exit, they shall be furnished — but on this point I believe you are mistaken — for if your cattle and horses have the habit of swimming, they will make their intrusions in whatever part of the meadow

is left unguarded. If you keep a fence all round your own meadow to prevent your neighbor's cattle getting in, would not that effectually prevent your own cattle getting out? And in case I used my meadow for pasturing (instead of reserving it for mowing) might not my cattle, if they preferred your grass, make the same intrusion on your premises as yours have on mine? —for the same road would be equally open to both parties if they had the same propensities. In which case I should have the similar complaints to make of the inattention of your farmer in keeping up his fences and should tell him 'to remove the beam from his own eye before he attempted to take away the mote from his neighbors.' . . . However, in order to prevent any further difficulty, I have desired the exit to be remedied, as far as lays in my power."

363 WB a dominant figure on Bank board. See note, page 221.

363 Banking honor, footnote. Wettereau, "New Light," 285.

364 Trade with La Plata. HSP, Orders to Captain Wills, May 3, 1800, Nov. 30, 1801; to James Baxter and William Blodget, supercargoes, Dec. 1, 1801; WB to Willing and Francis, Nov. 22, 1801; Brown, "Eighteenth Century Magnate," 402. The partners sent Captain Thomas Wills and the *Canton,* lately arrived from Bengal, to La Plata with a cargo valued at $162,652 and already sold by contract at a profit of about 30 per cent. The *Canton* was to be joined by the *America,* also loaded with merchandise. The major portion of the funds they received in Montevideo was to be invested in 40,000 to 50,000 ox hides for each ship, bought at $2.50 apiece. Care was to be taken that the hides were of the first quality, free from worms, damage, and the horn roots commonly left in the hides to increase their weight. "No ship is better calculated for the proposed voyage than the *Canton,* and if she is loaded with judgment and every crevice filled that is not absolutely necessary for the accommodation of yourself and crew, she will no doubt bring back 50,000 hides at least." For this voyage, Capt. Wills received $50 a month, plus $1 a day while in port, his table at sea, and the privilege of shipping six tons of merchandise out and back.

364 WB sent last payment. Allis, 963; Boston Public Library, WB to State Treasurer, May 25, 1799.

364 Invested almost $1.5 million. Allis, 901.

364 Cobb angry. Cobb did not write WB from May 18, 1798, to Jan. 31, 1799; WB complained to Knox, "The General seems to have a most insuperable aversion to writing." Cobb then charged WB with sending him remarks "dictated by a spirit of unfriendliness sufficient to dampen the ardor of the most faithful servant." In a kind of apology, WB wrote that Cobb had "essentially misconceived" his intentions. Cobb was egged on by General Henry Jackson of Boston, Knox's agent. He told Cobb, "It most certainly . . . discovers in him [Bingham] a little, mean, and unworthy conduct, very far from what you had a right to expect from him, and I think you ought most certainly to take a proper stand in this busines." Again: "I think its trifling with abilities, time, and property, to *crawl* and to continue *crawling* as you have done for a year or two past. . . . As to Mr. Bingham I have that same opinion of him you have." Again: "Nothing but a steady and determined conduct in you will keep (the great man in Philadelphia) within the bounds of decincy and order." Allis, 911, 941, 945, 949, 956, 1050–51, 1053,

H. Jackson to Cobb, Aug. 30, Dec. 2, 1798, Mar. 7, 1799; Cobb to WB, June 9, 1800; WB to Cobb, June 26, 1800.

364 Sale to Talon. Allis, 893, 894, 906, Baring to Henry Hope, Dec. 12, 1797; to J. W. Hope, Dec. 31, 1797. "Bingham is mad," Baring wrote, "not that they [the Dutch company] have been cheated but that he did not share the spoil."

364 Binghamton. Seward, Chapters II, III.

365 Adams on WB's power. *PMHB*, LX, 1936, 453, "Some Unpublished Letters of John Adams and Richard Rush," Adams to Richard Rush, Oct. 8, 1813.

365 Jefferson ostracized. Fisher, *Recollections*, 242.

365 Sedgwick on Jefferson. King, II, 353, Sedgwick to King, July 1, 1798.

365 Gallatin on WB. Henry Adams, 203, Gallatin to Samuel Breck, June 20, 1843.

365 Jefferson apparently dined with WBs. The relationship between Jefferson and the Binghams is not clear. John Dos Passos declares that the Binghams were leaders in the movement to freeze Jefferson out of Philadelphia society (*The Men Who Made the Nation*, p. 334), but he gives no source for the statement and I have been able to find none. Paul Leicester Ford, in his edition of Jefferson's writings (VI, 116), said that it was a tradition to his day (1895) that only three of Jefferson's equals (George Logan, Charles Thomson, David Rittenhouse) would have him at their houses. Claude Bowers, on the other hand, wrote in *Young Jefferson* (p. 433) that the mutual admiration and liking between Jefferson and Anne Bingham continued during Anne's lifetime; in *Jefferson and Hamilton* (p. 130) he wrote that Jefferson could always count on a gracious reception from Mrs. Bingham, though he was not comfortable among the other guests. Bowers gave no source for either statement.

365 WB liberal on Jefferson. Rush, *Letters*, 820, Rush to Jefferson, Aug. 22, 1800.

365 *Pilgrim* affair. President Washington referred the suit to Charles Lee, attorney general, and ordered him to defend it. WBLB, 468, WB to Alexander Hamilton, Feb. 26, 1793; 412, WB to Judge Sullivan, Nov. 8, 1793.

366 WB on fee to Davis. Allis, 1125, 1150.

366 Pickering order to Davis. MHS, Mar. 5, 1799.

366 WB charge of concealed information. Brown, "William Bingham in Martinique," 87.

367–68 WB and Jackson. HSP, Jackson to WB, Dec. 12, 1798, February 19, 1799; WB to Jackson, Dec. 12 and 13, 1798, Feb. 27, May 13, 1799. Jackson wrote, "I could almost wish there were no claims to interfere with the sentiments (your act of friendship) has impressed, or any cause to abate the sensations which a remembrance of it must always excite."

CHAPTER 28. SCANDAL AT THE REPUBLICAN COURT

369 Mrs. Stoddert on Binghams. Rowland, 810.

369 Tilly background. Tilly, *Memoirs*, 6–7, 15, 24, 32–33; Fisher, *Recollections*, 194; McRee, II, 571–72.

369 Noailles to Tilly. Tilly, *Memoirs*, 24.

370 Tilly exchange with Anne Bingham. *Ibid.*, 372.

370 George Harrison. Fisher, *Recollections*, 185.

370 Harrison on Maria. Morison, I, 137.

370 Maria's notes to Tilly. Tilly, *Memoirs*, 25.

371 WB cautioned Maria. McRee, II, 572.

371 Elopement. McRee, II, 571–72. It is not entirely certain that Baring's search party discovered Tilly and Maria. Baring may have struck Tilly on a later occasion rather than on the night of the elopement.

371 John Barry struck Tilly. The statement is made in an article clipped from the Boston *Journal*, not dated, in the possession of Miss Elizabeth Macfarlane of Pittsburgh.

371 Levy. Morais, 38–42.

371 Elopement a sensation. Fay, 455–57.

371 Morris to daughter. HSP, June 26, 1799.

372 Iredell to wife. McRee, II, 571–73.

372 Boudinot to wife. Boudinot, II, 151.

372 Mrs. Stoddert to niece. Rowland, 810.

372 Lewis to WB offering services. HSP, Lot 6520, no date.

373 Levy to WB on Maria. *Ibid.*, April 17, 1799.

373 Writ of habeas corpus. McRee, II, 573.

374 Levy to Lewis, as a gentleman. HSP, Lot 6520, May 24, 1799.

374 Lewis to Levy on Maria's independence. *Ibid.*, May 25, 1799.

375 Baring to father on anguish. BaP, May 7, 1799. General Maitland, by whom this letter was sent, appears to have come to America in connection with the Barings' shipment of arms to the U. S. (page 348). BaP, Sir Francis Baring to Alexander Baring, Jan. 20, 1799.

375 Tilly's demands. HSP, Lot 6520, no date; Tilly, *Memoirs*, 28–29; *Mémoires*, 245–50. The documents in the Ellis edition of the *Memoirs* were translated back into English from the French rather than being quoted from the original documents in English; they leave something to be desired in accuracy. Tilly's sentence on Baring is mistranslated to read, "I demand that Mr. Baring shall write to me . . . that he pushed me in a moment of agitation, on account of the condition of his wife."

376 WB's contract with Tilly. HSP, Lot 6520, June 11, 1799; Tilly, *Memoirs*, 29.

376–77 Noailles to Tilly. Tilly, *Memoirs*, 30–31; no date. The French edition reads (p. 253) *"Ayant communiqué partie de votre lettre à M. Bingham, je suis certain que vous pouvez choisir le lieu qu'il vous conviendra d'habiter, et puis ajouter que M. Bingham désire que vous recouvriez votre santé, et que vous soyez heureux."* The Ellis edition mistranslates this, "I have communicated your letter to me in part to Mr. Bingham. He leaves you completely free to stay where you please. I should add that Mrs. (*sic*) Bingham cherishes sincere feelings towards you, and good wishes for your health and happiness." The French editor, of course, assumed that Noailles was Anne Bingham's lover. He was the only person known to say so.

378 Mrs. Adams to sister. S. Mitchell, *New Letters*, 214–15, Nov. 15, 1799.

378 Mrs. Adams on modern dress. *Ibid.*, 241–42, Mar. 18, 1800.

379 Divorce charges. Oberholzer, I, 388–89. In 1806, Tilly persuaded the executors of Bingham's estate to pay off his annuity with a single lump sum. He left Germany, where he had become court chamberlain to the King of Prussia, spent some time in Paris, and then settled in Brussels. There, in poor health and bad circumstances, he took to gambling and ran up debts of

honor he could not pay. On the day after Christmas, in 1816, he killed himself. He left behind the manuscript of his memoirs — the adventures of a lesser Casanova. The work was published in three volumes in Berlin in 1825–27, in Paris in 1828, and, under the editorship of Havelock Ellis, in New York in 1932. Joshua Fisher declared it "not fit for any library." It touched only briefly on his American experiences, but his German editor recreated the Bingham-Tilly relationship from Tilly's papers and told it in his preface.

379 Otis to wife. Morison, I, 137.
380 "Careworn and aged." Sawtelle, 225.

CHAPTER 29. THE END OF AN ERA

381 WB to King. King, III, 284.
381 WB to King on mission to France. King, III, 92, Sept. 2, 1799.
382 Cobbett on McKean. Peeling, 322; Melville, 110.
383 Cobbett on Rush, footnote. Rush, *Letters*, 1213–18; Struthers Burt, 243. Cobbett became an English agitator, a member of Parliament, and the author of the English classic, *Rural Rides*.
383 McKean, spoils system. Peeling, 323–25.
383 WB waited on Adams. *Annals*, X, 10.
383 Washington and Monroe. Swiggett, *GM*, 341.
383 WB on funeral committee. *Annals*, X, 17, 403; Morison, I, 141. According to J. F. Fisher, *Recollections* (p. 192), many Democrats rejoiced at Washington's death.
384 Kentucky toast, footnote. S. Mitchell, 238.
385 Jackson's eulogium. Jackson, work cited; Rowland, 817; Balch, *L&P*, cxvii; S. Mitchell, 235; King, III, 206, WB to King, Mar. 5, 1800.
385 Willing congratulations. Balch, *L&P*, cxvii.
385 Mrs. Adams on Jackson. S. Mitchell, 235.
385 WB sent to King. King, III, 206, Mar. 5, 1799.
386–88 Duane affair. It is described in *DAB;* Swanstrom, 217–22, 304–8; *Annals*, X, 67–184; Malone, 464–66; Payne, 175; J. M. Smith, *FF*, 278–306; Hildreth, V, 352–53; McMaster, *History* II, 462–65, among others. Beveridge called it dramatic conflict. II, 454.
387 WB advised to send Duane to court. King, III, 285, WB to King, Aug. 6, 1800.
387 WB vote on slavery, footnote. *Annals*, X, 183.
388 WB to King on Duane. King, III, 284, Aug. 6, 1800.
388 WB reported to Senate. *Annals*, X, 184.
388 WB on Jacobin gains. King, III, 285, WB to King, Aug. 6, 1800.
389 National growth and prosperity. A. C. Morris, II, 390, 391; Hammond, 144; Carman, II, 11; Hicks, 152; W. Wilson, III, 173; Dauer, 197; Rochefoucauld, III, 101.
389 Nine frigates, 50 French vessels. Hildreth, V, 358, 399.
389 Large cities. Philadelphia (69,403), New York, Baltimore, Boston, Charleston, Salem, Providence, Richmond, Portsmouth, Albany, and Savannah. The population of the U. S. in 1800 was 5,308,000, double that at the start of the Revolution, one-third greater than in 1790.
389 "Inflammable air." Scharf-Westcott, I, 486, 514.

389 Thomas Leiper. Information taken from a caption on an engraving hanging in the Pennsylvania State Museum, Harrisburg.

390 Street cleaning, fire protection. Krout-Fox, 23, 25.

390 Watering System. Scharf-Westcott, I, 500–501, 510; Hamlin, 157–65. The system cost $200,000. The water was pumped by two of Nicholas Roosevelt's large steam engines. Latrobe designed a landscaped pumping station — a white marble temple in the Greek style — to conceal the tank and the engines. Stockholders received their water free for three years; others paid $5 a year. The first water poured out of the city's hydrants in January, 1801.

390 Permanent Bridge. Scharf-Westcott, I, 503; Oberholzer, *Phila.*, I, 405; HSP, WB to Richard Peters, Feb. 1, 1801. The Bridge — the first covered bridge in America — was completed in 1804 at a cost of $300,000.

391 Pickering's dismissal. Upham, III, 486–88. Pickering was the first cabinet officer discharged by a President. He prepared to retire to some wild forest lands he owned in Pennsylvania, there to live, as he told President Adams, reproachfully, *"on bare creation."* His Federalist friends intervened and paid him a charitable $25,000 for his lands, and Pickering settled in Massachusetts. He was elected a U. S. Senator in 1803 and a member of the House in 1813–17. In both positions he fought the Republicans at every turn and corresponded diligently in gathering evidence of what he considered the crimes and follies of President John Adams. Pickering was among the leaders of an unsuccessful secessionist movement that planned to draw New England, New York and New Jersey out of the Union if a list of demands was not met. Among the others who participated with him were Harrison Gray Otis, George Cabot, Roger Griswold, and Uriah Tracy. In one of the last political acts of his life, Alexander Hamilton strongly condemned the movement.

391 Two Federal caucuses. Kurtz, 395.

392 WB to Wolcott on excluding Jefferson. Gibbs, II, 388, 398, July 23, Aug. 6, 1800.

393 Webster on Hamilton. Smith, *JA,* 1045. William Duane declared that Hamilton's pamphlet did more harm to the Federalists than all the labors of his *Aurora.*

394 WB to King on retirement. King, III, 285, Aug. 16, 1800.

CHAPTER 30. AN ACT OF MEN, AN ACT OF GOD

395 WB to Peters. HSP, WBP.

395–96 Washington in 1801. A. C. Morris, II, 393–96; Morison, I, 144; Bayard, 119; Hildreth, V, 392–95; Channing, IV, 245–47; Beveridge, III, 1–2; Gibbs, II, 377–78; S. Mitchell, 256–59. It is probable that WB traveled to Washington with Senator James Ross, since they both first reported on the same day.

396 Working languidly. Smith, *JA,* 1050, Mrs. Adams' observations.

397 Senate chamber. The floor of the room, 86 by 49 feet in size, rested on ground level; its gallery rested on the same level as the main floor of the building. In 1809, Benjamin Latrobe remodeled the chamber into two rooms by raising the floor to the level of the gallery. The Senators took over this chamber the following year and met there until new quarters were built in the new wing in 1859. The room below the Senate chamber was used by the Supreme Court until it moved into the vacated Senate chamber above, remaining there until the 1930s. The lower chamber, used for a time for

meetings of the Atomic Energy Commission, now serves as a storehouse for furniture; the upper chamber is used for Senate committee meetings.

398 WB present Jan. 10, 1801. *Annals*, X, 733.

398 WB on need for treaty. Library Company, 7469F126, WB to ?, Feb. 23, 1801.

399 WB on treaty with France. BaP, Alexander Baring to father, Jan. 21, 1801; Ingersoll, I, 296.

399 WB and judgeships. HSP, WB to Richard Peters, Feb. 1, 1801; WB to ?, Feb. 27, 1801.

399 Adams appointed Wolcott. After a fifteen-year career as a judge, farmer, manufacturer and banker (president of the Bank of America), Wolcott changed his politics, became a Republican, and, in 1817, was elected governor of Connecticut. He caused an ultra-liberal new state constitution to be drafted and presided over the convention at which it was adopted. He served outstandingly as governor until his voluntary retirement in 1827. Ironically, his early papers, edited in two volumes in 1846 by a member of his family, make up an impassioned attack on Republicans and a self-righteous defense of extreme Federalism. Wolcott was at Hamilton's death-bed following his duel with Burr in 1804.

399 Boudinot proposal to Adams, footnote. Smith, *JA*, 1064.

400 Wolcott on intriguing. Gibbs, II, 462, Dec. 31, 1800.

401 Opinions on Burr and Jefferson. Welch, 226; Beveridge, II, 537–38; Parton, Burr, I, 270, 273; Morison, I, 205; Mitchell, *AH*, 492.

402 WB supported Jefferson. H. Adams, 254.

402–3 WB committee work. *Annals*, X, 748, 753.

403 WB and bridge company. HSP, WB to Judge Richard Peters, Feb. 1, 1801; Powers, 288–91.

403 WB to Peters on salary. HSP, Feb. 27, 1801.

403 Washington representative of Bank. Gibbs, 387, 397, WB to Wolcott, July 23, Aug. 6, 1800.

403 Lost bonds. Dr. J. H. Morgan (*Dickinson College,* 33) says that Bingham did not pay his original subscription of £400 despite efforts of the trustees in 1789 to collect it. On Sept. 28, 1785, however, writing from The Hague, Bingham told Dr. Rush, "I have wrote to Mr. Willing and desired him to pay the amount of my subscription in loan office certificates to the college." (HSP) The minutes of the trustees for 1789 conceivably may have referred to a later Bingham subscription, since no amount is mentioned. It is not likely that Dr. Rush would have remained a friend of Bingham, as he did, if Bingham had reneged on his subscription. See Rush, *Letters,* 456, Apr. 9, 1788, where Rush advised John Montgomery, "We now have 1000 dollars of unfunded certificates and may have 1000 more as soon as we call on Mr. Bingham for his subscription. . . . If we delay . . . these certificates may rise to 5/- or 7/6 in the pound." The following year (Feb. 26) Bingham tried to get state aid for the college. (Dickinson College Coll., WB to William Irvine.)

On Jan. 12, and Feb. 2, 1801, John Montgomery corresponded with the College about Bingham's "missing certificates"; the College appears to have been collecting dividends on these and the inquiry a routine one. (Dickinson College Coll.)

403 List of books. *Annals*, X, 168; Library of Congress, Cadell & Davis, London, to WB and Robert Waln, Dec. 11, 1800. The volumes were sent in eleven "hair trunks." These volumes, with all the others in the Congressional Library, were burned to ashes when the British took Washington on August 24, 1814, and set fire to public building in retaliation for the raid on York in Upper Canada (now Toronto), in which the Americans burned the Parliament buildings with the library and archives and carried off the plate from the church. See David C. Mearns, *The Story Up to Now: The Library of Congress, 1800–1946*, Washington, 1947, p. 15.

403 WB's angry letter on merchants. Library Company, 7469F126, Feb. 23, 1801.

403 Logan as Senator. John Peter Gabriel Muhlenberg had defeated Logan for Bingham's seat but resigned after a few weeks to become supervisor of revenue for Philadelphia. Logan was then appointed.

407 Jefferson's promise to Smith. See Lodge, *Cabot*, 423; Hildreth, II, 407.

408 Mrs. Adams on election. Smith, *JA*, 1062. Stephen Girard supplied the gunpowder to celebrate Jefferson's victory in Philadelphia. McMaster, *Girard*, I, 397.

408 Col. Barker's Orders of the Day. Scharf-Westcott, I, 508. A group of Philadelphia's young Republicans, on the other hand, meeting to draw up plans for Inaugural Day festivities, declared that they hoped to avoid "any marks of insult or defiance" to the defeated Federalists.

409 Robert Morris not available. Morris remained in the Walnut Street prison until August, 1801, when he was freed under a liberalized bankruptcy law passed earlier by the Federalists. Gouverneur Morris took his old associate in to his home at Morrisiana, New York, for a long recuperative visit. In his diary the younger Morris wrote, "He came to me lean, low-spirited, and as poor as a commission of bankrupters can make a man whose effects will, it is said, not pay a shilling in the pound. . . . I sent him home fat, sleek, in good spirits and possessed of the means of living comfortably the rest of his days. So much for the air of Morrisiana." Robert Morris lived five more years on a $1500 annuity provided by Gouverneur Morris. When his holdings were released in 1880, after years of phenomenal litigation, the heirs received $9692.49.

409 Troup on Gallatin appointment. King, IV, 454, Troup to King, May 22, 1801.

409 WB supported Gallatin. H. Adams, 265.

409 Adams and Sedgwick on same coach. Welch, 230. Some accounts hold that Sedgwick left Washington alone in a private carriage. Adams' feelings at the time were expressed some years later in his words, "I have been disgraced and degraded and I have a right to complain."

Adams and Jefferson were reconciled through the tireless efforts of Dr. Rush, who in 1812 persuaded them to begin a correspondence with each other. Until their deaths on the same day (July 4, 1826), the two exchanged letters — 109 from Adams, fifty-two from Jefferson. "Whether you or I were right," Adams wrote, "posterity must judge." Hamilton and Adams were never reconciled.

410 Baring to father on inauguration. BaP, Mar. 29, 1801.

411 Philip Sloan. *Annals*, X, 753, 760.

411 Baring on Anne's illness. BaP, Mar. 29, May 12, 1801.

411 Doctors diagnosed galloping consumption. Gilmor, *Memoir,* notes facing 18.

412 WB to Cobb on Anne's illness. WBLB, April 9, 1801.

412 Abigail's broken engagement. *PMHB,* XLII, 1918, "Notes and Queries," Benjamin Latrobe to James Eakin, Apr. 13, 1801, 183. Miss Abigail, now 24, married Richard Peters, three years her junior, on Mar. 1, 1804. Records of Christ Episcopal Church.

412 Baring to father on Anne Bingham. BaP, May 12, 1801.

412 Willing on daughter. HSP, Apr. 14, May 26, 1801.

412 Lead-lined coffin. *PMHB,* LXII, 1938, Latrobe to Eakin, Apr. 13, 1801, 183.

413 Burial in Bermuda. The inscription on the slab of Bermuda stone covering the grave has been worn away. At the east end is a Celtic cross inscribed with Tudor roses and IHS. At the other end stands a marble slab about five feet high on a pediment of granite. It was erected in 1883 by Edward Shippen Willing and Mary Willing Clymer and maintained thereafter with funds supplied by them to the church. It reads: "In memory of Anne Willing, daughter to Thomas Willing of Philadelphia and wife of William Bingham, U. S. Senator. Born Aug., 1764 at Philadelphia. Died May 11, 1801 at Bermuda. This tomb is restored by her relatives Edwd. S. Willing and Mary W. Clymer 1883."

CHAPTER 31. THE GOLDEN VOYAGE: EXTREMIS

414 Hare to Baker. Library Company, Y12 7326 F65. The city was lighted by 662 lamps consisting of three branches each, enclosed in square glass lanterns, on posts along the sidewalks. They consumed 8,606 gallons of whale oil annually. St. Méry, 260.

414 Baring to father on renouncing America. BaP, May 7, 1799.

415 WB to Cobb, life a heavy burden. Allis, 1124, June 30, 1801. WB ended a letter to Cobb on Aug. 1, one day before sailing, with unaccustomed emotion, with the words, "God bless you." (WBLB.)

415 Gilmor, $50,000. HSP, WB to Gilmor, Jan. 1, 1802.

415 Voyage to England. WB to Noailles, Oct. 24, 1801.

416 Kindness of the Barings. HSP, WB to Noailles, Nov. 27, 1801.

416 Lansdowne and war, footnote. To Major Jackson he had written in 1797, "State of health, and many other circumstances, would make me consider it as a great calamity to return to my public situation. I know but *one* circumstance which could reconcile me to it, which is next to impossible: that I could have it in my power to introduce a little more civilization among nations, and to put war at a greater distance." Fitzmaurice, II, 418; Swiggett, 330; Balch, *L&P,* 306.

416 WB to T. M. Willing on his return. HSP, May 22, 1802.

417 WB's interest in ships. HSP, WB to Willing and Francis, Oct. 7, 1801, Mar. 28, July 1, 1803.

417 Sale of Philadelphia land. HSP, WB to Gilmor, Jan. 1, 1802.

417 WB to Cobb on flow of population. Allis, 1170.

417 Richards on Maine. Allis, 1115, Richards to Hope and Co., June 7, 1801. In 1815, Richards advised the Barings to sell their Maine holdings at less than first cost. Allis, 1246, Oct. 15, 1815.

417 *Pilgrim* affair. Allis, 1126, 1148–50, 1160, WB to Knox, July 20, 1801; WB to Cobb, Oct. 6, 1802; Hare to Cobb, June 13, 1803.

418 WB to Willing, joy at peace. HSP, Oct. 11, 1801.

418 WB to Noailles, English visiting France. HSP, Oct. 24, 1801.

418 Peace would be short. NYHS, WB to ?, Feb. 5, 1802.

419 WB to Cobb on Maria's marriage. Allis, 1152, Oct. 6, 1802.

419 Baring to Gilmor on brother's marriage. HSP, June 16, 1802.

420 Tour of continent. HSP, WB to Thomas Mayne Willing, Sept. 6, 1802.

420 Noailles' family. HSP, WB to Noailles, Nov. 27, 1801. Noailles had remained in Philadelphia to settle a law suit. He succeeded in having his name erased from the list of *emigrés* and in winning back his French properties. He did not return to France, however, even though he had not seen his sons there for more than a decade. On a visit to Santo Domingo in 1804, he accepted a commission in the French army under General Rochambeau, son of his former commander. He held the Mole St. Nicholas there for five months against a besieging force of natives and a blockading squadron of British vessels. He ran the blockade, escaping with his men to a Cuban port, and proceeded with a small force to Havana, sailing in the schooner *Courier*. En route he met the *Hazard*, an English corvette of seven guns. Using his excellent English to deceive her commander, he drew close enough to board and capture her in what has been called "one of the most romantic struggles in French naval history." He took the *Hazard* to Havana as a prize, but died there of his wounds.

420 Court of the First Consul. NYHS, WB to Rufus King, Jan. 3, 1803.

420 Bonaparte's plans. NYHS, Nov. 24, 1801, WB to King, Jan. 3, 1803. Bonaparte had written in 1801, "My intention is to take possession of Louisiana with shortest delay, and that this expedition be made in the utmost secrecy."

422 Gore to King on WB. King, IV, 315.

422 Channing on Louisiana Purchase, footnote. Quoted without reference by Muzzey, *Jefferson*, 231. I have not found the passage in Channing's works; I would welcome information on the exact source.

423 Baring-Hope-Bingham combine. Hidy, 34; Gilmor, *Memoir*, notes facing p. 40.

424 WB returned to England. HSP, WB to Willing and Francis, Mar, 28, July 1, 1803.

424 WB to Cobb. Allis, 1169, 1172, Aug. 28, Oct. 15, 1803. On Bonaparte's projected invasion of England, Bingham wrote to Cobb, "I never believed that it was the system of Bonaparte to pursue this course, except urged to the adoption of it by imperious circumstances. He risks everything by attempting such a coup de main. But, by protracting the war, he forces this country to an immense expenditure, diminishes its resources by curtailing its commerce, deranges its finances by increasing its debt, and will eventually create great discontents in consequence of such an adverse state of things, whilst his additional armaments are maintained at comparatively very little additional expense, having quartered them upon the dependent states which surround him."

425 WB to Dr. Blagden. APS, 3740–42, no date.

426 WB to Noailles, his "irreparable loss." HSP, Nov. 27, 1801.

426 Ann Baring to Dr. Blagden. APS, 2736–38, no date.

426 Dr. Blagden to Ann Baring. APS, 2739, no date.

427 Flaxman monument. Sir Francis Baring wrote out the inscription in his own hand. (BaP, Sept. 3, 1808.) The monument still stands, though it is somewhat in need of repairs.

428 Baring to King on WB's death. King, IV, 384, Mar. 1, 1804.

429 Rush on WB. Rush, *Autobiography*, 268–69.

EPILOGUE

430 Hare settled Pilgrim suit. Allis, 1174.

431 Settled Jackson's claim. Allis, 384. Major Jackson was removed from his post as Surveyor of Customs in an 1801 sweep of Federalists from government service. He was, President Jefferson said, influencing the votes of his subordinates at the Custom House. From 1801 to 1815, Jackson edited the *Political and Commercial Register* in Philadelphia, a Federalist paper. In August, 1814, he was chairman of a meeting of citizens organized to defend the city against possible British attack during "Mr. Madison's War." In 1816, his brother officers of the Revolutionary army appointed him their lobbyist in an unsuccessful attempt to persuade Congress to make an equitable settlement of their promised half pay for life. His last public act was to tender the welcome of the City of Philadelphia to the Marquis de Lafayette in 1824.

431 Settled Maine penalty. Allis, 1176, 1212.

431 Disposed of Maine lands. Two million acres were put on public sale, much of it in 1828 at the minimum price of 75 cents an acre. The Estate continued to own substantial acreage on Mount Desert Island into the middle of this century. Allis, 1253–54; HSP, Bingham Estate Memo, June 1, 1935; William Allen, "Bingham Land," MHS Collection, vol. 7, 1876, p. 359.

431 Maine communities today. Allis, 1254. Mr. Allis has a moving description of his visit to these communities. His conclusions are just: the Bingham speculation failed because the very assumptions on which it was based were unsound. Settlers seldom had the ready money with which to purchase lands. "Had the state governments during this period abandoned their attempt to make wild lands a source of revenue, had they adopted a policy similar to that of the Homestead Act [of 1862], much human misery and financial loss might have been avoided. As it was, few if any of the speculators in wild lands did better than break even." (1252.)

433 Alexander Baring. Hidy, 39, 45–47; Wechsburg, 99–100, 111, 122–27; Henry Adams, 318, 323, 552, 668–69; Gilmor, *Memoir*, notes facing 40, 41; Walters, 268, 271–73, 286, 374; Bickley, II, 287; Scharf-Westcott, II, 920; Fisher, *Recollections*, 197–98; Burke's *Peerage*; Cockayne's *Complete Peerage*.

434 Ann Baring to Daniel Webster. Van Tyne, 254, Jan. 12, 1842. Webster-Ashburton Treaty. The British had invaded Maine in the War of 1812 and reannexed the Maine Coast from the Penobscot to Passamaquoddy Bay.

435 Anne Eugenia Baring, Ann's oldest child, born in the Powel House, died in a fire in Nice in 1839. (Letter to the author from Mrs. Richard John Bramble Mildmay-White of Mothecombe, Holbeton, Plymouth, England, July 31, 1968.)

435–36 William Bingham Baring and the Carlyles. Froude, I, 423 *ff*, II, 295.

436 Fisher on Francis Baring. Fisher, *Recollections*, 198.

436 Baring wealth. In 1883, at the height of the Baring power, the family estates in England totaled 70,000 acres, with annual rents of £53,000. Cockayne, 278.

436 Present-day Barings. Lord Cromer, recent head of the Bank of England, is not a Bingham descendant; he is descended from Henry Baring by his second wife.

436 Fisher on Ann Baring. Fisher, *Recollections*, 197–98.

437 Houghton on Ann Baring. Houghton, 220. In this obscure but remarkable character study, Houghton declared that Lady Harriet's manner, even when apparently cruel, was rather "the outburst of judicial severity." Of the Barings she said, "They are everywhere, they get everything. The only check upon them is that they are all members of the Church of England; otherwise, there is no saying what they would do." Houghton found "something offensive . . . in the constant enjoyment he (William Bingham Baring) took in the display of her genius and effervescence of her gaiety." Among two pages of her "thoughts and expressions" were: "I forget everything, except injuries," and "When one sees what marriage generally is, I quite wonder that women do not give up the profession."

437 Ann Baring in Paris. Bickley, II, 287. Though a Bonapartist, Ann Baring told Lord Glenbervie this anecdote in 1817. At a meeting of Napoleon's Council, the Emperor being absent, some of the members expressed their surprise at the severity of a Napoleonic edict. Joseph Bonaparte said, "Gentlemen, do not be surprised. This man is no tyrant, as Homer was no poet." (Bickley, II, 251.)

437 Maria and Henry Baring. Hidy, 45, Fisher, *Recollections*, 195–96. At the time of the divorce and of Thomas Willing's death, Alexander Baring wrote cryptically to Thomas Cadwalader, who had asked to be made the Bingham Estate agent in Philadelphia, "We have had difficulties and delicacies to meet, difficulties more of feeling than of interest, but at last the trust agency has been new modelled and as [two words undecipherable] trustees appear satisfied we are equally so. All that has passed on this subject I need not nor of course could not explain. I must however my dear sir say in my brothers name as well as my own . . . that there is no person living to whom we should, if circumstances had permitted it, have confided with more confidence any business of importance. . . ." HSP, July 20, 1823.

438 Mrs. Peters on Maria. Undated note by Mary Willing Clymer in possession of Miss Elizabeth Macfarlane of Pittsburgh.

439 Baring on young William Bingham. BaP, Baring to T. M. Willing, Aug. 10, 1810.

439 Fisher on young Bingham. Fisher, *Recollections*, 197–98. Baring's comments to Willing on young William Bingham's lack of natural capacity (above) discount Fisher's conclusion that his poor capacity was the result of neglect by his sisters.

439 Marriage into French families. Westcott, 348.

440 Mansion House. Dorland, 190; Hamlin, 191.

440 Lansdown House. Breck, *Recollections*, 249; Westcott, 349–50.

441 Thomas Willing. Balch, *WP*, 127, 173.

442 Breck on Anne Bingham. HSP, July 29, 1858.

442 Breck at 91. DAB; Fisher, *Memoir*, 36.

Bibliography

MANUSCRIPT SOURCES

THIS WORK, as the first biography of William Bingham, has drawn heavily on unpublished manuscript material. The following collections were consulted and used.

Historical Society of Pennsylvania, Philadelphia

The mother lode of William Bingham manuscript material is found here, beginning with the dozens of letters Robert Morris wrote during the Revolution to his young agent in Martinique. None of Bingham's letters to Morris have survived, and, unfortunately, no collection of the letters of Morris has ever been published.

Other important Bingham material is found on the Society's shelves in collections bearing the names Clement Biddle, Dreer (built on the business correspondence of Robert Gilmor), Etting, Franklin, Gratz, Irvine, Meredith, Richard Peters, Wallace, and Society Collection. In addition to the Morris letters, these contain a large amount of correspondence to and from Alexander Baring, Samuel Breck, Thomas Burke, Thomas Fitzsimmons, Benjamin Franklin, Robert Gilmor, Richard Harrison, William Jackson, Lafayette, James Lovell, Viscount Noailles, Benjamin Rush, Charles Thomson, Thomas Willing, James Wilson, the Committee of Secret Correspondence (Foreign Affairs) and the Secret Committee (of Commerce). Since the manuscripts are admirably indexed and identified, I have not named each individual collection in citing my sources.

Of special interest are the seventeen letters Bingham wrote from Europe to Thomas Willing, his wife's father. These are the only "personal" letters of Bingham that have survived. Not previously available to those who have written on Bingham, the letters reveal for the first time something of his true character and the depth of his devotion to Anne Bingham. No letters between Anne and William Bingham, and none of Anne's letters from Europe, praised by her father for their wit and liveliness, are known to exist.

The most important single Bingham item is the William Bingham Letter Book — two volumes of hand-pressed copies of the letters written in 1791–93 on matters of business. This Letter Book, totaling 618 pages, has recently been made available on microfilm. The letter books for all other years have disappeared.

The Society is the repository for the Bingham Estate Papers, placed there in 1949 by the Estate's trustees: 40,000 items in 200 boxes covering the period 1777–1911.

National Archives of the United States, Washington

Archives has included in its *Papers of the Continental Congress* (Microcopy No. 257, totaling 204 microfilm reels) a single reel (Item 90, Roll 118) known as *The William Bingham Papers*. This contains a body of letters from Robert Morris to Bingham, from Bingham to the Secret Committee and the Committee of Secret Correspondence, and related letters for the period 1776–1783.

Miscellaneous Papers of the Continental Congress (Microcopy No. 332, totaling nine reels) contains on Roll 6, *Papers Relating to Naval Affairs,* a number of letters from Robert Morris to Bingham and to ships' captains ordered to Martinique. The Marine Letter Book on this reel includes a letter from the Marine Committee to Bingham.

Library of Congress, Manuscript Division, Washington

The Library's *William Bingham Papers* comprise some fifty letters from Bingham to the Congressional committees and to Bingham from Robert Morris, all during the Revolutionary period.

A few letters to, from, and about Bingham can be found in the Manuscript Division's various collections, including the Personal Manuscript folders filed under "William Bingham" and other individual names (example: Benjamin Rush).

Baring Brothers & Co., Limited, London

The Baring Archives, DEP 3, contains a wealth of correspondence relating to Alexander Baring's first trip to America and his purchase of the lands in Maine. The Library of Congress, Manuscript Division, has seventy-eight reels of Baring Papers microfilm, obtained in 1959 from the Public Archives of Canada, Ottawa. The originals, pertaining to Canada, the United States, and Latin America, were transferred from the Public Record Office, London, to Ottawa in 1926.

American Philosophical Society, Philadelphia

The Society has, in its Franklin Papers, nine letters from Bingham to Dr. Franklin and his fellow Commissioners in Paris (1777–79) and two letters to or relating to Bingham on his departure in 1776 for Martinique. Its other collections contain letters to or from Samuel Breck, James Lovell, Richard Price, and Benjamin Vaughan; the Charles Willson Peale Letter Book, which contains some half-dozen references or letters to Bingham; and Samuel Breck's "Recollections of the Members of the American Philosophical Society."

The Library Company, Philadelphia

The Library Company has a dozen-odd letters to or from Samuel Breck, Charles Willing Hare, Benjamin Rush, and an unnamed correspondent (February 23, 1801); the manuscript of William Birch's autobiography; the papers relating to Bingham's gift of the Franklin statue to the Library; and the account book of Bingham's shipping "Adventures" for 1777–79.

Dickinson College Library, Carlisle, Pennsylvania

The Library Collection contains about twenty letters exchanged between Bingham and Fisher Ames, William Irvine, John Jay, Benjamin Rush, James Wilson, and the Trustees of the College.

Houghton Library, Harvard University, Cambridge, Massachusetts

The Arthur Lee Papers contain a critical memorandum on the settlement of Bingham's Martinique accounts.

Massachusetts Historical Society, Boston

The Society has, in the Knox Papers, a large body of letters exchanged between Bingham and General Henry Knox; and, in the Cobb Papers, the letters between Bingham and General David Cobb. (The Knox Papers belong to the New England Historic Genealogical Society.) It also has a letter from Bingham to Lord Lansdowne (February 15, 1784) and, in the Pickering Papers, several letters on Bingham affairs.

In the Adams Manuscript Trust Collection (608 microfilm reels now in the long, early process of being published entire) are found many of the Adams letters quoted in Chapter 12 of this work.

American Antiquarian Society, Worcester, Massachusetts

The Society has thirty-one letters written (1784–86) to the Cranch family from Europe, one by John Quincy Adams, six by Miss Abigail Adams, and twenty-four by Mrs. John (Abigail) Adams. Four of these refer to or contain passages on William and Anne Bingham.

New York Public Library, New York

NYPL has a letter from Bingham to Colonel Jacob Read (September 22, 1798); several Bingham letters on business matters; and, from the Emmet Collection, a 1785 letter from Bingham to Thomas Willing.

New York Historical Society

The Society has the originals of the letters exchanged between Rufus King and Bingham. These were published in the invaluable six-volume King correspondence (1894), but excisions, faulty wording, and a deficient index make it advisable to check the printed letters against the originals. The Society also has a letter to Bingham from Robert Morris (April 25, 1777) and one from Bingham to an unknown correspondent (February 5, 1802).

Royal Society, London

The Society has the originals of the letters exchanged in 1803 between Sir Charles Blagden and William and Anne Bingham. Copies of these are obtainable from the American Philosophical Society, Philadelphia.

Boston Public Library, Boston

The Library has several unpublished Bingham letters relating to the Maine purchase and a letter to Bingham from James Lovell (June 12, 1779).

William L. Clements Library, University of Michigan, Ann Arbor

In its La Caita-Shelburne Collection, the Library has three letters from Bingham to Lord Shelburne, Marquess of Lansdowne (March 4, 1787, October 22, 1791, and one undated, probably 1794).

J. Pierpont Morgan Library, New York

A letter from James Wilson to Bingham dated June 16, 1786.

John Work Garrett Library, Johns Hopkins University, Baltimore

A letter from Robert Morris to Bingham dated February 25, 1777; and a letter (quoted) to Morris from Benjamin Harrison, January 8, 1777.

Library of the University of Virginia, Charlottesville

In the Thomas Jefferson Collection, a letter from Jefferson in Paris to Bingham dated September 25, 1789.

Public Record Office, London

Logs of the *Shark, Kingfisher* and *Orpheus;* and a report from Captain Chapman to Admiral Young, June and July, 1776.

PRINTED SOURCES

Adams, Charles Francis, ed. *Letters of Mrs. Adams, The Wife of John Adams,* 2 vols., enlarged fourth edition, Boston: Little and Brown, 1848.

Adams, James Truslow. *The Epic of America.* New York: Blue Ribbon, 1941.

Adams, John. *The Works of,* 10 vols., Charles Francis Adams, ed. Boston: Little, Brown, 1850–56.

Adams, John Quincy. *Memoirs,* C. F. Adams, ed., vol. I. Philadelphia: Lippincott, 1874.

Adams, Henry. *The Life of Albert Gallatin.* Philadelphia: Lippincott, 1879.

Aldridge, Alfred Owen. *Benjamin Franklin, Philosopher and Man.* Philadelphia: Lippincott, 1965.

Allen, Gardner W. *A Naval History of the American Revolution,* 2 vols. New York: Russell and Russell, 1962 (1913).

Allis, Frederick S., Jr. *William Bingham's Maine Lands, 1790–1820,* 2 vols. Boston: Publication of the Colonial Society of Massachusetts, 1954.

Ames, Fisher. *Works,* 2 vols., Seth Ames, ed. Boston: Little, Brown, 1854.

Annals of Congress: The Debates and Proceedings of the Congress of the United States, 42 vols., Joseph Gales and W. W. Seaton, eds. Washington, 1834–56.

Atkinson, Charles Milner. *Jeremy Bentham: His Life and Work.* London: Methuen, 1905.

Augur, Helen. *The Secret War of Independence.* New York: Duell, Sloan and Pearce, 1955.

Baker, William S. "Washington After the Revolution, 1787." *Pennsylvania Magazine of History and Biography,* XIX, 1895.

Balch, Thomas Willing, ed. *Letters and Papers Relating Chiefly to the Provincial History of Pennsylvania.* Philadelphia: Crissy and Markley, 1855.

————. *The Philadelphia Assemblies.* Philadelphia: Allen, Lane and Scott, 1916.
————. ed. *Willing Letters and Papers.* Philadelphia: Allen, Lane and Scott, 1922.
Ballagh, James Curtis, ed. *The Letters of Richard Henry Lee,* 2 vols. New York: Macmillan, 1912.
Barney, Joshua. *A Biographical Memoir,* Mary Barney, ed. Boston: Gray and Bowen, 1832.
Bayard, James A. *Papers, 1796–1815.* Washington: Annual Report of the American Historical Association for the Year 1913, vol. II, 1915.
Bemis, Samuel Flagg. *The Diplomacy of the American Revolution.* New York: Appleton-Century, 1935.
————. *Jay's Treaty: A Study in Commerce and Diplomacy.* New York: Macmillan, 1924.
Bernhard, Winfred E. A. *Fisher Ames: Federalist and Statesman, 1758–1808.* Chapel Hill, N. C.: Institute of Early American History and Culture, University of North Carolina Press, 1965.
Beveridge, Albert J. *The Life of John Marshall,* 4 vols. Boston: Houghton Mifflin, 1916–19.
Bickley, Francis, ed. *The Diaries of Sylvester Douglas, Lord Glenbervie.* Boston: Houghton Mifflin, 1928.
Biddle, Charles. *Autobiography.* Philadelphia: E. Claxton, 1883.
Biddle, Edward W. *The Founding and Founders of Dickinson College.* Carlisle: privately printed, 1920.
Bingham, William. *Letter from an American Now Resident in London, to a Member of Parliament . . . on the Commerce of the United States.* Philadelphia, 1784.
————. *A Description of the Situation, Climate, Soil and Productions of Certain Tracts of Land in the District of Maine and Commonwealth of Massachusetts.* Philadelphia, 1793.
Birch, William. *Historic Views of Philadelphia* (28 plates). Philadelphia, 1800.
Bolles, Albert S. *The Financial History of the United States from 1774 to 1789.* New York: Appleton, 1896 (1879).
Borden, Morton. *The Federalism of James A. Bayard.* New York: Columbia University Press, 1955.
Boudinot, J. J., ed. *The Life, Public Services, Addresses and Letters of Elias Boudinot,* 2 vols. Boston: Houghton Mifflin, 1896.
Bowen, Catherine Drinker. *Miracle at Philadelphia: The Story of the Constitutional Convention.* Boston: Little, Brown, 1966.
Bowers, Claude G. *Jefferson and Hamilton: The Struggle for Democracy in America.* Boston: Houghton Mifflin, 1925.
————. *Jefferson in Power: The Death Struggle of the Federalists.* Boston: Houghton Mifflin, 1936.
————. *The Young Jefferson, 1743–1789.* Boston: Houghton Mifflin, 1945.
Brant, Irving. *James Madison, The Nationalist, 1780–1787.* Indianapolis: Bobbs-Merrill, 1948.
Breck, Samuel. *Recollections.* Horace Elisha Scudder, ed. Philadelphia: Porter and Coates, 1877.
————. *Sketch of Improvements already made in Pennsylvania.* Philadelphia, 1818.

Bridenbaugh, Carl and Jessica. *Rebels and Gentlemen: Philadelphia in the Age of Franklin*. New York: Oxford University Press, 1962 (1942).

Brooks, Van Wyck. *The World of Washington Irving*. Philadelphia: Blakiston, 1944.

Brown, Margaret L. "William Bingham, Agent of the Continental Congress in Martinique"; "Mr. and Mrs. William Bingham of Philadelphia, Rulers of the Republican Court"; "William Bingham, Eighteenth Century Magnate." *Pennsylvania Magazine of History and Biography*, LXI, January, July, October, 1937.

Brunhouse, Robert L. *The Counter-Revolution in Pennsylvania, 1776–1790*. Harrisburg: Pennsylvania Historical Commission, 1942.

Bulwark of Liberty: Early Years at Dickinson, 2 vols. Essays by W. J. Bell, Jr., L. H. Butterfield, Boyd Lee Spahr, and others. New York: Revell, 1950.

Burd, Edward. *The Burd Papers, 1763–1828*, Lewis Burd Walker, ed. Pottsville: privately printed, 1899.

Burke's Genealogical and Heraldic History of the Peerage, 104th edition, London, 1967.

Burnett, Edmund Cody. *The Continental Congress*. New York: Macmillan, 1941.

———, ed. *Letters of Members of the Continental Congress*, 8 vols. Washington: Carnegie Institution, 1921–36.

Burt, Nathaniel. *The Perennial Philadelphians*. Boston: Little, Brown, 1963.

Burt, Struthers. *Philadelphia: Mr. Penn's Holy Experiment*. London: Rich and Cowan, 1945.

Butterfield, Lyman H., ed. *The Adams Papers: Diary and Autobiography of John Adams*, 4 vols. New York: Atheneum, 1964.

Callaghan, North. *Henry Knox, General Washington's General*. New York: Rinehart, 1958.

Cappon, Lester J., ed. *The Adams-Jefferson Letters*, 2 vols. Chapel Hill, N. C.: Institute of Early American History and Culture, University of North Carolina Press, 1959.

Carman, Harry J. *Social and Economic History of the United States*, vol. I, 1500–1820. Boston: Heath, 1930.

Channing, Edward. *A History of the United States*, 6 vols. New York: Macmillan, 1905–30.

Charles, Joseph. *The Origins of the American Party System*. New York: Harpers, 1961 (1956).

Chastellux, Marquis de. *Travels in North America in the Years 1780, 1781, and 1782*, 2 vols. Howard C. Rice, ed. Chapel Hill, N. C.: Institute of Early American History and Culture, University of North Carolina Press, 1963.

Cheyney, Edward Potts. *History of the University of Pennsylvania*. Philadelphia: University of Pennsylvania Press, 1940.

Childs, Frances Sergeant. *French Refugee Life in the United States, 1790–1800*. Baltimore: *Institut Français de Washington*, Johns Hopkins Press, 1940.

Clark, William Bell. *Lambert Wickes: Sea Raider and Diplomat*. New Haven: Yale University Press, 1932.

Cobbett, William. *Porcupine's Works*, 12 vols. London, 1801.

Cokayne's Complete Peerage, Vicary Gibbs, ed. London: St. Catherine's Press, 1910.

Colonial Records of Pennsylvania, 16 vols. Harrisburg, 1851–53.

Coolidge, Philip T. *History of the Maine Woods.* Bangor, Maine: privately printed, 1963.

Coxe, Tench. *A View of the United States of America.* Philadelphia, 1794.

Cunningham, Noble E., Jr. *The Jeffersonian Republicans: The Formation of Party Organization, 1789–1801.* Chapel Hill, N. C.: Institute of Early American History and Culture, University of North Carolina Press, 1963 (1957).

Cutler, William Parker and Cutler, Julia Perkins. *Life, Journals and Correspondence of Rev. Manasseh Cutler,* 2 vols. Cincinnati: Robert Clarke, 1888.

Dangerfield, George. *Chancellor Robert R. Livingston of New York.* New York: Harcourt, Brace, 1960.

Dauer, Manning J. *The Adams Federalists.* Baltimore: Johns Hopkins Press, 1953.

Davis, Joseph Stancliffe. *Essays in the Earlier History of American Corporations,* 2 vols. New York: Russell and Russell, 1965 (1917).

(Deane, Silas.) *The Deane Papers,* 5 vols. *Collections of the New York Historical Society for the Years 1886, 1887, 1888, 1889, 1890.* New York: Printed for the Society, 1887–91.

(———.) *The Deane Papers.* Hartford: Connecticut Historical Society, XXIII, 1930.

DeWindt, Caroline Amelia Smith, ed. *Journal and Correspondence of Miss Adams, Daughter of John Adams, Second President of the United States — Written in France and England in 1785,* 2 vols. Boston: Wiley and Putnam, 1841.

Dictionary of American Biography, 20 vols. Allen Johnson and Dumas Malone, eds. New York: Scribner, 1928–1936.

Dorfman, Joseph. *The Economic Mind in American Civilization,* 5 vols. New York: Viking, 1946–49.

Dorland, W. A. Newman. "The Second Troop Philadelphia City Cavalry." *Pennsylvania Magazine of History and Biography,* XLV, 1921 and succeeding numbers.

Dos Passos, John. *The Men Who Made the Nation.* New York: Doubleday, 1957.

Du Fourge, William. *Madinina, "Reine des Antilles."* Paris: *Étude de Moeurs Martiniquaises,* 1929.

Durand, John. *New Materials for the History of the American Revolution.* New York: Henry Holt, 1889.

East, Robert A. *Business Enterprise in the American Revolutionary Era.* Gloucester, Mass.: Peter Smith, 1964 (1938).

Eberlein, Harold Donaldson and Hubbard, Cortlandt Van Dyke. *Diary of Independence Hall.* Philadelphia: Lippincott, 1948.

———. *Portrait of a Colonial City.* Philadelphia: Lippincott, 1939.

Einstein, Lewis. *Divided Loyalties: Americans in England During the War of Independence.* Boston: Houghton Mifflin, 1933.

Ellery, Eloise. *Brissot de Warville.* Boston: Houghton Mifflin, 1915.

Ellet, Elizabeth F. L. *Court Circles of the Republic, or the Beauties and Celebrities of the Nation.* Philadelphia: Philadelphia Publishing Co., 1869(?).

———. *The Queens of American Society.* New York: Scribner, 1867.

Fay, Bernard. *The Revolutionary Spirit in France and America,* trans. Ramon Guthrie. New York: Harcourt Brace, 1927.

Ferguson, E. James. *The Power of the Purse: A History of American Public Finance.* Chapel Hill, N. C.: Institute of Early American History and Culture, University of North Carolina Press, 1961.

Fisher, Joshua Francis. *Memoir of Samuel Breck.* Philadelphia, 1863.

———. *Recollections.* Sophia Cadwalader, ed. Boston: privately printed, 1929.

Fiske, John. *The Critical Period of American History, 1783–1789.* Boston: Houghton Mifflin, 1916 (1888).

Fitzmaurice, Lord Edmund George. *Life of William, Earl of Shelburne, afterwards First Marquess of Lansdowne,* 2 vols. London: Macmillan, 1912.

Fitzpatrick, John C., ed. *The Writings of George Washington,* 39 vols. Washington: Government Printing Office, 1931–1944.

Flexner, James Thomas. *Gilbert Stuart: A Great Life in Brief.* New York: Knopf, 1955.

Footner, Hulbert. *Sailor of Fortune: The Life and Adventures of Commodore Barney, U. S. N.* New York: Harper, 1940.

Force, Peter, ed. *American Archives,* Fourth Series, 6 vols., Fifth Series, 3 vols. Washington: 1833–1851.

Ford, Worthington Chauncey, ed., *et alia. Journals of the Continental Congress,* 34 vols. Washington, 1904–1937.

Franklin, Benjamin. *Autobiographical Writings,* Carl Van Doren, ed. New York: Viking, 1945.

Gibbs, George, ed. *Memoirs of the Administrations of Washington and John Adams, Edited from the Papers of Oliver Wolcott,* 2 vols. New York: printed by subscription, 1846.

Gilmor, Robert. *Memoir or Sketch of the History of Robert Gilmor of Baltimore as Derived from his Books and Papers in Possession of His Eldest Son, and from Conversations with his Father and Mother on the Subject, at Various Times.* Baltimore: privately printed, 1840.

———. "Memorandums Made in a Tour to the Eastern States in the Year 1797." *Bulletins of the Boston Public Library,* vol. II, New Series, vol. 3, Nos. 88–91, April 1892 — January 1893. Boston: 1893.

Goodman, Nathan G. *Benjamin Rush, Physician and Citizen.* Philadelphia: University of Pennsylvania Press, 1934.

Graydon, Alexander. *Memoirs of a Life Chiefly Passed in Pennsylvania.* Edinburgh: William Blackwood, 1822 (1811).

Griswold, Rufus Wilmot. *The Republican Court, or American Society in the Days of Washington.* New York: Appleton, 1856.

Hacker, Louis M. *The Shaping of American Tradition.* New York: Columbia University Press, 1947.

Hale, Edward E., *Franklin in France.* Boston: Roberts Brothers, 1888.

Halsey, R. T. H. and Towner, Elizabeth. *The Homes of Our Ancestors as Shown in the American Wing of the Metropolitan Museum of Art of New York.* New York: Garden City Press, 1937.

Hamilton, Alexander. *Works,* 12 vols. Henry Cabot Lodge, ed. New York: Putnam, 1904.

———. *Papers,* 13 vols. to date, 14 and 15 to appear in 1969. Harold Coffin

Syrett and Jacob E. Cooke, eds. New York: Columbia University Press, 1961–1969.

Hamlin, Talbot. *Benjamin Henry Latrobe.* New York: Oxford University Press, 1955.

Hammond, Bray. *Banks and Politics in Early America.* Princeton: Princeton University Press, 1957.

Hart, Charles Henry. "Stuart's Lansdowne Portrait of Washington." *Harper's Magazine.* August, 1896.

Hawke, David. *In the Midst of a Revolution.* Philadelphia: University of Pennsylvania Press, 1961.

Hazelton, George C., Jr. *The National Capitol, Its Architecture, Art and History.* New York: Taylor, 1902.

Hazen, Charles Downer. *Contemporary American Opinion of the French Revolution.* Gloucester, Mass.: Peter Smith, 1964 (1897).

Hearn, Lafcadio. *Two Years in the French West Indies.* New York: Harper, 1923 (1890).

Henkels, Stan V., ed. *The Confidential Correspondence of Robert Morris,* Catalogue No. 1183. Philadelphia, 1917.

Hicks, John D. *A Short History of American Democracy.* Boston: Houghton Mifflin, 1946.

Hidy, Ralph W. *The House of Baring in American Trade and Finance.* Cambridge, Mass.: Wheaton College, 1942.

Hildreth, Richard. *The History of the United States of America,* 6 vols. New York: Harper, 1854–55.

Hiltzheimer, Jacob. "Extracts from the Diary of." *Pennsylvania Magazine of History and Biography,* XVI, 1892.

Holdsworth, John Thom and Dewey, Davis R. *The First and Second Banks of the United States.* Washington: Government Printing Office, 1910.

Houghton, Lord (Richard Monckton Milnes). *Monographs Personal and Social.* New York: Holt and Williams, 1873.

Howard, James L. *Seth Harding, Mariner: A Naval Picture of the Revolution.* New Haven: Yale University Press, 1930.

Hulbert, A. B. *Historic Highways,* vol. 2. Cleveland: Arthur H. Clark, 1904.

Hutcheson, Harold. *Tench Coxe: A Study in American Economic Development.* Baltimore: Johns Hopkins Press, 1938.

Ingersoll, Charles J. *Recollections, Historical, Political, Biographical, and Social,* 2 vols. Philadelphia: Lippincott, 1861.

Jackson, Joseph. *Encyclopedia of Philadelphia,* 4 vols. Harrisburg: National Historical Association, 1931–33.

———. "George Washington in Philadelphia." *Pennsylvania Magazine of History and Biography,* LVI, 1932.

Jackson, William. *Eulogium on the Character of General Washington. . . .* Philadelphia: Printed by John Ormrod, 1800.

Jay, William. *The Life of John Jay,* 2 vols. New York, 1833.

Jefferson, Thomas. *Papers,* 17 vols. to date, Julian Boyd, ed. Princeton: Princeton University Press, 1950.

———. *Works,* Paul Leicester Ford, ed., 10 vols. New York: Putnam, 1892–99.

Jenkins, Howard Malcolm. *Pennsylvania, Colonial and Federal,* 4 vols. Philadelphia: Pennsylvania Historical Publishing Co., 1903–04.

Johnston, Henry P., ed. *The Correspondence and Public Papers of John Jay,* 4 vols. New York: Putnam, 1890–1893.

Jordan, John W. *Colonial and Revolutionary Families of Pennsylvania,* 3 vols. New York: Lewis, 1911.

Journal of the Senate of the United States of America, Fourth, Fifth and Sixth Congresses. Philadelphia, 1796–1801.

Kent, Donald H. and Deardorff, Merle H. "John Adlum on the Allegheny." *Pennsylvania Magazine of History and Biography,* LXXXIV, 1960.

King, Charles R., ed. *The Life and Correspondence of Rufus King,* 6 vols. New York: Putnam, 1894–1900.

Kirkland, Edward C. *A History of American Economic Life.* New York: Appleton-Century-Crofts, 1933.

Konkle, Burton Alva. *Thomas Willing and the First American Financial System.* Philadelphia: University of Pennsylvania Press, 1937.

Krout, John Allen and Fox, Dixon Ryan. *The Completion of Independence.* New York: Macmillan, 1944.

Kurtz, Stephen G. *The Presidency of John Adams: The Collapse of Federalism.* Philadelphia: University of Pennsylvania Press, 1957.

Landis, C. I. "The First Long Turnpike in the United States." *Papers of the Lancaster Historical Society,* Vol. XX, No. 8. Lancaster, 1916.

Lewis, Lawrence, Jr. *A History of the Bank of North America.* Philadelphia: Lippincott, 1882.

Lincoln, Charles H. *The Revolutionary Movement in Pennsylvania, 1760–1776.* Philadelphia: University of Pennsylvania Press, 1901.

———. ed. *Naval Records of the American Revolution, 1775–1778.* Washington: Government Printing Office, 1906.

Lingelbach, William E. "Philosophical Hall." *Transactions of the American Philosophical Society,* New Series, Vol. 43. Philadelphia, 1953.

Lippincott, Horace Mather. *Early Philadelphia: Its People, Life and Progress.* Philadelphia: Lippincott, 1917.

Littell, Charles Willing. "Major William Jackson, Secretary of the Federal Convention." *Pennsylvania Magazine of History and Biography,* II, 1878.

Lodge, Henry Cabot. *Life and Letters of George Cabot.* Boston: Little, Brown, 1877.

———. *Alexander Hamilton.* Boston: Houghton Mifflin, 1899.

Longacre, James B. "Extracts from the Diary of." *Pennsylvania Magazine of History and Biography,* XXIX, 1905.

Loomis, Stanley. *Paris in the Terror: June 1793–July 1794.* Philadelphia: Lippincott, 1964.

Lorenz, Lincoln. *John Paul Jones.* Annapolis: U. S. Naval Institution, 1943.

Macfarlane, James R. *George Clymer.* Pittsburgh: privately printed, 1927.

Maclay, William. *Journal,* Edgar Maclay, ed. New York: Boni, 1927 (1890).

———. *Sketches of Debate in the First Senate of the United States.* Harrisburg: Lane S. Hart, 1880.

Madison, James. *Writings,* 9 vols., Gaillard Hunt, ed. New York: Putnam, 1900–10.

———. *Letters and Other Writings,* 4 vols., H. D. Gilpin, ed. Philadelphia: Lippincott, 1865.

Main, Jackson Turner. *The Antifederalists: Critics of the Constitution, 1781–1788.* Chapel Hill, N.C.: University of North Carolina Press, 1961.

Malone, Dumas. *Jefferson and the Ordeal of Liberty.* Boston: Little, Brown, 1962.

Markoe, Peter. *The Times, a Poem.* Philadelphia, 1788.

Marshall, Christopher. *Passages from the Rembrancer,* William Duane, ed. Philadelphia: James Crissy, 1839.

Marshall, John. *The Life of George Washington,* 5 vols. Philadelphia, 1804–07.

McMaster, John Bach. *A History of the United States from the Revolution to the Civil War,* 7 vols. New York: Appleton, 1904.

———. *The Life and Times of Stephen Girard, Mariner and Merchant,* 2 vols. Philadelphia: Lippincott, 1918.

——— and Stone, Frederick D. *Pennsylvania and the Federal Constitution.* Philadelphia: Historical Society of Pennsylvania, 1888.

McRee, Griffith J. *Life and Correspondence of James Iredell,* 2 vols. New York: Peter Smith, 1949 (1857).

Melville, Lewis. *The Life and Letters of William Cobbett,* 2 vols. London: John Lane, 1913.

Merlant, Joachim. *Soldiers and Sailors of France in the American War for Independence,* trans. Mary Bushnell Coleman. New York: Scribner, 1920.

Middlebrook, Louis F. *History of Maritime Connecticut During the American Revolution,* 2 vols. Salem, Mass.: Essex Institute, 1925.

Miller, John C. *Triumph of Freedom.* Boston: Little, Brown, 1948.

———. *Crisis in Freedom: The Alien and Sedition Acts.* Boston: Little Brown, 1951.

———. *Alexander Hamilton, Portrait in Paradox.* New York: Harper and Row, 1959.

———. *The Federalist Era, 1789–1801.* New York: Harper and Row, 1960.

Minnigerode, Meade. *Jefferson, Friend of France, 1793: The Career of Edmond Charles Genêt.* New York: Putnam, 1928.

Mitchell, Broadus. *Alexander Hamilton: The National Adventure.* New York: Macmillan, 1962.

Mitchell, Stuart, ed. *New Letters of Abigail Adams, 1788–1801.* Boston: Houghton Mifflin, 1947.

Monaghan, Frank. *John Jay, Defender of Liberty.* New York: Bobbs-Merrill, 1935.

Montgomery, Thomas Harrison. *A History of the University of Pennsylvania.* Philadelphia: George W. Jacobs, 1900.

Morais, Henry Samuel. *The Jews of Philadelphia.* Philadelphia: LevyType, 1894.

Morgan, James Henry. *Dickinson College.* Carlisle: Dickinson College, 1933.

Morison, Samuel Eliot. *The Life and Letters of Harrison Gray Otis, Federalist,* 2 vols. Boston: Houghton Mifflin, 1913.

Morris, Anne Cary, ed. *Diary and Letters of Gouverneur Morris,* 2 vols. London: Keegan Paul, Trench, 1889.

Morris, Richard B. *The Peacemakers: The Great Powers and American Independence.* New York: Harper and Row, 1965.

Mount, Charles Merrill. *Gilbert Stuart: A Biography.* New York: W. W. Norton, 1964.

Neeser, Robert Wilder. *Letters and Papers Relating to the Cruises of Gustavus Conyngham.* New York: Naval Historical Society, 1915.

Nevins, Allan. *The American States During and After the Revolution.* New York: Macmillan, 1924.

Nolte, Vincent. *Memoirs,* Burton Rascoe, ed. New York: Watt, 1934 (1854).

Oberholzer, Ellis Paxton. *Philadelphia: A History of the City and its People,* 4 vols. Philadelphia: Clark, 1912.

———. *Robert Morris: Patriot and Financier.* New York: Macmillan, 1903.

Park, Lawrence. *Gilbert Stuart: An Illustrated Descriptive List of His Works,* 4 vols. New York: Rudge, 1926.

Parton, James. *The Life and Times of Aaron Burr,* 2 vols. Boston: Fields and Osgood, 1870 (1864).

———. *Life of Thomas Jefferson.* Boston: Houghton Mifflin, 1899 (1874).

Paullin, Charles Oscar. *The Navy of the American Revolution.* Cleveland: Burrows, 1906.

Payne, George Henry. *History of Journalism in the United States.* New York: Appleton, 1920.

Peeling, James Hedley. "Governor McKean and the Pennsylvania Jacobins." *Pennsylvania Magazine of History and Biography.* LIV, 1930.

Pennsylvania Archives, First Series. Samuel Hazard, ed., 12 vols. Harrisburg, 1852–1856.

Peterson, Charles E. "Carpenters' Hall." *Transactions of the American Philosophical Society,* New Series, Vol. 43. Philadelphia, 1953.

Pleasants, J. Hall, ed. "Letters of Molly and Hetty Tilghman." *Maryland Historical Magazine,* Vol. xxi, No. 2, June, 1926.

Powell, John Harvey. *Bring Out Your Dead: The Great Plague of Yellow Fever in Philadelphia in 1793.* Philadelphia: University of Pennsylvania Press, 1949.

Powers, Fred Perry. *The Historic Bridges of Philadelphia.* Publication No. 11 of the City History Society of Philadelphia. Philadelphia, 1914.

Priest, William. *Travels in the United States of America.* London, 1802.

Repplier, Agnes. *Philadelphia: The Place and the People.* New York: Macmillan, 1925 (1898).

Robin, Abbe. *New Travels Through North America.* Philadelphia, 1783.

Rochefoucauld-Liancourt, François, Duc de la. *Travels Through the United States of North America,* 4 vols. London, 1800.

Roof, Katherine Metcalf. *Colonel William Smith and Lady.* Boston: Houghton Mifflin, 1929.

Rossiter, Clinton. *Alexander Hamilton and the Constitution.* New York: Harcourt, Brace and World, 1964.

———. *The Grand Convention.* New York: Macmillan, 1966.

Rowland, Kate Mason. "Philadelphia a Century Ago." *Lippincott's Monthly Magazine,* Vol. 62, 1898.

Rowson, Susanna. *Trials of the Human Heart.* Philadelphia, 1795.

Rush, Benjamin. *Autobiography,* George W. Corner, ed. Philadelphia: published for the American Philosophical Society, Princeton University Press, 1948.

———. *Letters,* 2 vols., Lyman H. Butterfield, ed. Published for the American Philosophical Society. Princeton: Princeton University Press, 1951.

St. Méry, Moreau de. *American Journey,* Kenneth and Anna M. Roberts, eds. and trans. New York: Doubleday, 1947.

Sawtelle, William Otis. "William Bingham of Philadelphia and His Maine Lands." *Publications of the Genealogical Society of Pennsylvania,* Vol. IX, No. 3, March, 1926.

Schachner, Nathan. *Aaron Burr, A Biography.* New York: Stokes, 1937.

——. *Alexander Hamilton.* New York: Appleton-Century, 1946.

——. *The Founding Fathers.* New York: Capricorn, 1954.

——. *Thomas Jefferson, A Biography.* New York: Yoseloff, 1957.

Scharf, J. Thomas and Westcott, Thompson. *History of Philadelphia,* 3 vols. Philadelphia: L. H. Evarts, 1884.

Seward, William Foote. *Binghamton and Broome County, New York — A History.* New York, 1924.

Sheffield, John Baker Halroyd, Lord. *Observations on the Commerce of the United States.* London, 1784.

Sherrill, Charles H. *French Memories of Eighteenth Century America.* New York: Scribner, 1915.

Skeel, Emily E. F., ed. *Notes on the Life of Noah Webster,* 2 vols. New York: privately printed, 1912.

Smith, Charles Page. *James Wilson, Founding Father.* Chapel Hill, N. C.: University of North Carolina Press, 1956.

——. *John Adams,* 2 vols. New York: Doubleday, 1962.

Smith, Horace Wemyss. *Life and Correspondence of the Rev. William Smith, D.D.,* 2 vols. Philadelphia, 1879.

Smith, James Morton. *Freedom's Fetters: The Alien and Sedition Laws and American Civil Liberties.* Ithaca, N. Y.: Cornell University Press, 1956.

Smith, Margaret Bayard. *The First Forty Years of Washington Society,* Gaillard Hunt, ed. New York: Scribner, 1906.

Smith, William Henry. *The St. Clair Papers,* 2 vols. Cincinnati: Robert Clarke, 1882.

Sparks, Jared, ed. *Diplomatic Correspondence of the American Revolution,* 12 vols. Boston: Nathan Hale and Gray and Bowen, 1830.

——. *Life of Gouverneur Morris,* 3 vols. Boston: Gray and Bowen, 1832.

Stevens, Benjamin Franklin, ed. *Facsimiles of Manuscripts in European Archives Relating to America, 1773–1783,* 25 vols. London, 1889–1895.

Stevens, John Austin. *Albert Gallatin.* Boston: Houghton Mifflin, 1884.

Studenski, Paul and Krooss, Herman E. *Financial History of the United States.* New York: McGraw Hill, 1952.

Sumner, William Graham. *The Financier and the Finances of the American Revolution,* 2 vols. New York: Dodd, Mead, 1891.

Swanstrom, Roy. *The United States Senate, 1787–1801.* Document No. 64 of the 87th Congress. Washington: Government Printing Office, 1962.

Swiggett, Howard. *The Extraordinary Mr. Morris.* Garden City, N. Y.: Doubleday, 1952.

Talleyrand, Prince de. *Memoirs,* le duc de Broglie, ed., 2 vols. London: Griffith Farren Okedon and Welsh, 1891.

Tanselle, G. Thomas. *Royall Tyler.* Cambridge, Mass.: Harvard University Press, 1967.

Thomas, Early Bruce. *Political Tendencies in Pennsylvania, 1783–1794.* Philadelphia: Temple University Press, 1938.

Tilly, Alexandre, Comte de. *Mémoires.* Paris, 1828.

———. *Memoirs,* Havelock Ellis, ed. New York: Farrar and Rinehart, 1932.

Tinkcom, Harry Marlin. *The Republicans and Federalists in Pennsylvania, 1790–1801.* Harrisburg: Pennsylvania Historical and Museum Commission, 1950.

Tolles, Frederick B. *George Logan of Philadelphia.* New York: Oxford University Press, 1953.

———. "Town House and Country House, Inventories from the Estate of William Logan, 1776." *Pennsylvania Magazine of History and Biography,* LXXXII, 1958.

Twining, Thomas. *Travels in America.* New York: Harper, 1894.

Upham, Charles W. *The Life of Timothy Pickering,* 4 vols. Boston: Little, Brown, 1873.

Vail, R. W. G. *Susannah H. Rowson: The Author of Charlotte Temple.* Worcester, Mass.: American Antiquarian Society, 1933.

Van der Linden, Frank. *The Turning Point: Jefferson's Battle for the Presidency.* Washington, D.C.: Luce, 1962.

Van Doren, Carl. *Benjamin Franklin.* New York: Garden City Publishing Co., 1941.

———. *Secret History of the American Revolution.* New York: Viking, 1941.

———. *The Great Rehearsal.* New York: Viking, 1948.

Van Tyne, C. H., ed. *The Letters of Daniel Webster, from Documents Owned Principally by the New Hampshire Historical Society.* New York, 1902.

Ver Steeg, Clarence L. *Robert Morris: Revolutionary Financier.* Philadelphia: University of Pennsylvania Press, 1954.

Wainwright, Nicholas B. "Philadelphia's Eighteenth-Century Fire Insurance Companies." *Transactions of the American Philosophical Society,* New Series, Vol. 43. Philadelphia, 1953.

Wallace, David Duncan. *The Life of Henry Laurens.* New York: Putnam, 1915.

Walters, Raymond, Jr. *Albert Gallatin: Jeffersonian Financier and Diplomat.* New York: Macmillan, 1957.

Wansey, Henry. *The Journals of an Excursion to the United States in the Summer of 1794.* London, 1796.

Warder, Ann. "Extracts from the Diary of." *Pennsylvania Magazine of History and Biography,* XVIII, 1894.

Warren-Adams Letters, Being Chiefly a Correspondence Among John Adams, Samuel Adams and James Warren, 2 vols. Boston: Massachusetts Historical Society, 1917.

Warville, J. P. Brissot de. *New Travels in the United States of America.* London, 1792.

Watson, John Fanning. *Annals of Philadelphia and Pennsylvania in Ye Olden Times,* 2 vols. Philadelphia: Lippincott, 1870 (1857).

Wechsburg, Joseph. *The Merchant Bankers.* Boston: Little, Brown, 1966.

Wecter, Dixon. *The Saga of American Society.* New York: Scribner, 1927.

Welch, Richard E., Jr. *Theodore Sedgwick, Federalist: A Political Portrait.* Middletown, Conn.: Wesleyan University Press, 1965.

Westcott, Thompson. *Historic Mansions and Buildings of Philadelphia.* Philadelphia: Porter and Coates, 1877.

Wettereau, James O. "Letters from Two Business Men to Alexander Hamilton on Federal Fiscal Policy, November, 1789." *Journal of Economic and Business History,* Vol. 3 (1930–1931).

——. "New Light on the First Bank of the United States." *Pennsylvania Magazine of History and Biography,* LXI, 1937.

——. "The Oldest Bank Building in the United States." *Transactions of the American Philosophical Society,* New Series, Vol. 43. Philadelphia, 1953.

Wharton, Anne Hollingsworth. *Salons, Colonial and Republican.* Philadelphia: Lippincott, 1900.

——. *Through Colonial Doorways.* Philadelphia: Lippincott, 1893.

Wharton, Francis, ed. *The Revolutionary Diplomatic Correspondence of the United States,* 6 vols. Washington: Government Printing Office, 1889.

White, Leonard D. *The Federalists: A Study in Administrative History.* New York: Macmillan, 1959 (1948).

——. *The Jeffersonians: A Study in Administrative History.* New York: Macmillan, 1954.

Whitney, Janet. *Abigail Adams.* Boston: Little, Brown, 1947.

Wilson, Joseph Lapsey, ed. *Book of the First Troop Philadelphia City Cavalry.* Philadelphia, 1915.

Wilson, Woodrow. *A History of the American People,* 6 vols. New York: Harper, 1902.

Young, Eleanor. *Forgotten Patriot: Robert Morris.* New York: Macmillan, 1950.

Index

Index

566 : *Index*

Rittenhouse, David, scientist, 208, 242, 325, 520
Robespierre, Maximilien, 240, 244, 250, 300
Robin, Abbé, French army chaplain, 109, 110
Robinson, Captain James, 40
Rochambeau, General Jean Baptiste, Comte de, 98, 108, 109, 110
Rochefoucauld-Liancourt, Duc de la, 212; tours the U.S., 305; deplores WB's ownership of Maine lands, 305
Rodney, Admiral George Brydges, Baron, 116
Roe, Walter, 503
Romney, George, artist, 149
Roosevelt, Nicholas, engineer, 523
Ross, Dr., 314
Ross, Senator James, 120, 260; on Senate committee challenging Adams, 350–55; 382, 386–87; demands that U.S. seize New Orleans, 420; 523
Rousseau, Jean-Jacques, 17, 159, 467
Rowson, Susanna Haswell: described, 361; dedicates novel to Anne Bingham, 362; 384
Rush, Dr. Benjamin, 87, 90; described, 117; founds Dickinson College, 117–18, 168; 123, 127, 129, 130, 152, 165, 166; founds Franklin and Marshall College, 167; brings Dr. Nisbet to Dickinson College, 168; 177; outraged at Hamilton's fiscal policy, 207; 208; his work during yellow fever epidemic, 246–48; 298, 318, 365, 383; on WB's death, 429; 441; on the Pennsylvania constitution, 487; 491, 498, 499, 503, 524; reconciles Alams and Jefferson, 525
Rush, Julia, Benjamin Rush's daughter, 441
Rush, Julia Stockton (Mrs. Benjamin), 514

St. Clair, General Arthur, 174, 177, 180
St. Just, Louise Antoine de, 240
St. Méry, Moreau de, 160; described, 303; 305; on Philadelphia theater, 360

St. Pierre, Martinique, 27, 28, 32, 34; described, 37–39; 42, 46, 51, 69, 72; John Jay arrives at, 76; 78, 80; WB leaves, 82
Schuyler, General Philip, 16, 326
Scioto Company, 178–80
Second Philadelphia City Troop of Horse, WB forms and captains, 166; 195; resigns captaincy, 224; 257, 497
Secret Committee, later Committee of Commerce, 4, 17, 19; orders Captain Wickes to take WB to Martinique, 24; 34, 35, 40, 56, 61, 486
Sedgwick, Senator Theodore, 218; charges that WB opposes war with France, 333, 341; 334, 349; heads Senate committee challenging Adams, 350–55; 365; supports Burr over Jefferson, 400–401; 405; announces Jefferson victory, 408; 409, 501, 525
Shays, Captain Daniel, 172, 173, 174, 499
Sheffield, John Baker Holroyd, Lord, his attack on U.S. trade policy, 125; 509
Shelburne, Earl of. *See* Lansdowne, Marquess of
Shelburne, Lady Louisa, 133, 135
Sherlock, Mr., 309–11
Shippen, Nancy, 99
Shippen, Dr. William, 193, 259
Short, William, Jefferson's secretary in France, 244–45
Siddons, Mrs. Sarah, actress, 124, 159, 470
Sloan, Philip, Algerine captive, 411
Smith, Abigail Adams (Mrs. William Stephens), described, 141; views on various persons, 142–48; on the William Binghams, 142–48, 496; breaks engagement to Royall Tyler, 150; at Court of St. James's, 154–55; 171, 211; unhappy in marriage to Colonel Smith, 342; 362; later career, 517–18
Smith, Adam, economist, 125, 269
Smith, Margaret, 408
Smith, General Samuel, 407, 409